Austria

Catherine Le Nevez,
Marc Di Duca, Anthony Haywood, Kerry Walker

PLAN YOUR TRIP

HELEN CATHCART/LONELY PLANET

COFFEE AND CAKE IN VIENNA, P376

ROBERT NIEDRING/GETTY IMAGES ©

THE ZILLERTAL, P303

ON THE ROAD

Contents

UNDERSTAND

SURVIVAL GUIDE

COVID-19

We have re-checked every business in this book before publication to ensure that it is still open after the COVID-19 outbreak. However, the economic and social impacts of COVID-19 will continue to be felt long after the outbreak has been contained, and many businesses, services and events referenced in this guide may experience ongoing restrictions. Some businesses may be temporarily closed, change opening hours, or require bookings; some unfortunately may have closed permanently. We suggest you check with venues before visiting for the latest information.

Right: Traunkirchen (p219) on the shore of the Traunsee

DIETERMEYRL/GETTY IMAGES ©

WELCOME TO

Austria

Austria looks small on the map, but most of it is vertical, so there's always another mountain pass, alpine view or hamlet to discover. I'm never happier than when nearing a 2000m precipice on a trail in Tyrol or Salzburgerland, as the last light makes the summits blush. Alpenglühen, they call it. Then there are Vienna's coffee houses and phenomenal art, romantic, vine-laced Wachau, the crystal-clear lakes of Salzkammergut and Carinthia's medieval villages, plus the castles, abbeys and cakes everywhere. What's not to love?

By Kerry Walker, Writer
@kerrywalker
For more about our writers, see p416.

Austria

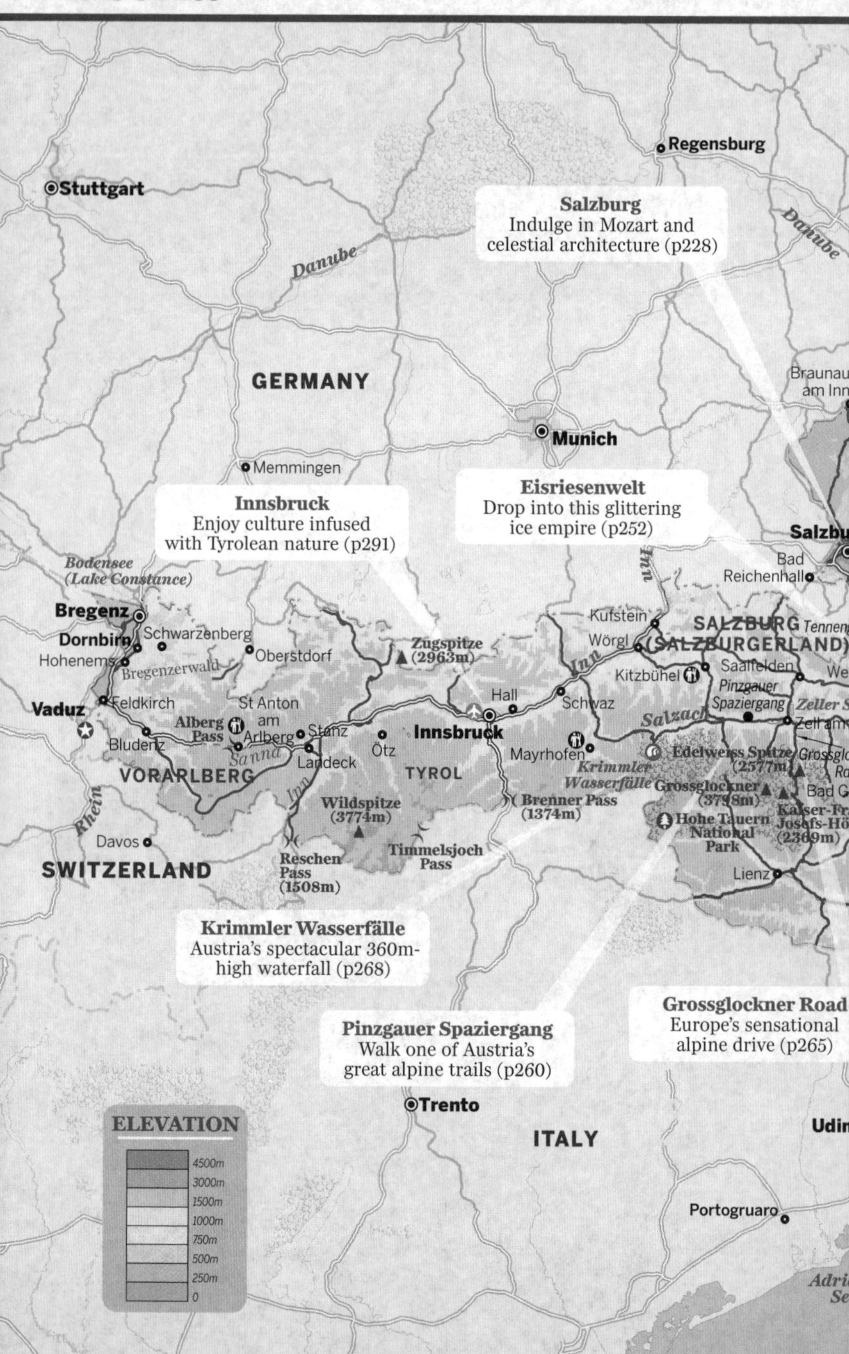

Salzburg
Indulge in Mozart and celestial architecture (p228)
Eisriesenwelt
Drop into this glittering ice empire (p252)
Innsbruck
Enjoy culture infused with Tyrolean nature (p291)
Krimmler Wasserfälle
Austria's spectacular 360m-high waterfall (p268)
Pinzgauer Spaziergang
Walk one of Austria's great alpine trails (p260)
Grossglockner Road
Europe's sensational alpine drive (p265)
Regensburg
Stuttgart
Danube
GERMANY
Braunau am Inn
Munich
Memmingen
Bodensee (Lake Constance)
Bregenz
Dornbirn
Hohenems
Schwarzenberg
Oberstdorf
Bregenzerwald
Vaduz
Feldkirch
Bludenz
Alberg Pass
St Anton am Arlberg
Stanz
Landeck
Sanna
VORARLBERG
Rhein
Inn
Davos
SWITZERLAND
Zugspitze (2963m)
Ötz
Innsbruck
Hall
Schwaz
TYROL
Wildspitze (3774m)
Reschen Pass (1508m)
Timmelsjoch Pass
Brenner Pass (1374m)
Kufstein
Wörgl
Kitzbühel
SALZBURG (SALZBURGERLAND)
Salzach
Mayrhofen
Krimmler Wasserfälle
Saalfelden
Pinzgauer Spaziergang
Zell am See
Edelweiss Spitze (2577m)
Grossglockner (3798m)
Hohe Tauern National Park
Lienz
Bad Reichenhall
Trento
ITALY
Portogruaro
ELEVATION
4500m
3000m
1500m
1000m
750m
500m
250m
0

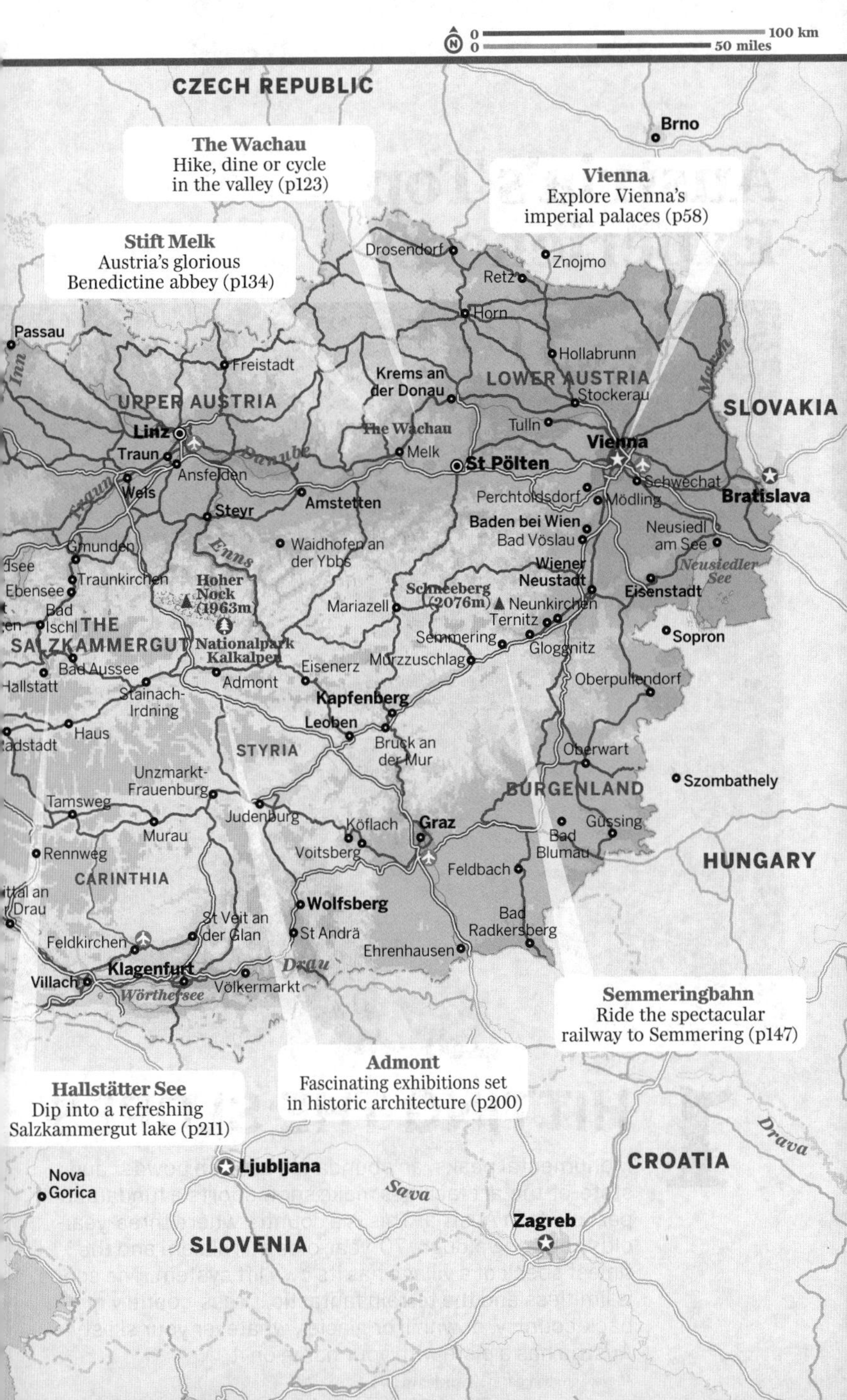

0 100 km
0 50 miles
CZECH REPUBLIC
The Wachau
Hike, dine or cycle in the valley (p123)
Vienna
Explore Vienna's imperial palaces (p58)
Stift Melk
Austria's glorious Benedictine abbey (p134)
Brno
Drosendorf
Znojmo
Retz
Horn
Hollabrunn
Passau
Inn
Freistadt
Krems an der Donau
LOWER AUSTRIA
Stockerau
Morava
SLOVAKIA
UPPER AUSTRIA
Linz
The Wachau
Tulln
Vienna
Traun
Danube
Melk
St Pölten
Ansfelden
Schwechat
Bratislava
Wels
Traun
Amstetten
Perchtoldsdorf
Mödling
Steyr
Baden bei Wien
Neusiedl am See
Gmunden
Enns
Waidhofen an der Ybbs
Bad Vöslau
Traunkirchen
Hoher Nock (1963m)
Wiener Neustadt
Neusiedler See
Ebensee
Schneeberg (2076m)
Neunkirchen
Eisenstadt
Bad Ischl
THE SALZKAMMERGUT
Mariazell
Ternitz
Sopron
Nationalpark Kalkalpen
Semmering
Gloggnitz
Bad Aussee
Eisenerz
Mürzzuschlag
Hallstatt
Stainach-Irdning
Admont
Kapfenberg
Oberpullendorf
Leoben
Haus
Radstadt
Bruck an der Mur
STYRIA
Oberwart
Unzmarkt-Frauenburg
BURGENLAND
Szombathely
Tamsweg
Judenburg
Köflach
Graz
Güssing
Murau
Bad Blumau
Rennweg
Voitsberg
HUNGARY
CARINTHIA
Feldbach
Spittal an der Drau
Wolfsberg
St Veit an der Glan
Bad Radkersberg
Feldkirchen
St Andrä
Ehrenhausen
Klagenfurt
Drau
Villach
Wörthersee
Völkermarkt
Semmeringbahn
Ride the spectacular railway to Semmering (p147)
Admont
Fascinating exhibitions set in historic architecture (p200)
Hallstätter See
Dip into a refreshing Salzkammergut lake (p211)
Drava
Nova Gorica
Ljubljana
CROATIA
Sava
Zagreb
SLOVENIA

Austria's Top Experiences

1 HITTING THE SLOPES

Monumental peaks, an abundance of fresh powder and state-of-the-art facilities make snow sports a fundamental part of life in Austria. This is a country where three-year-olds can snowplough, 70-year-olds still slalom and the tiniest speck of a village has its own lift system. The scope is limitless and the terrain fantastic. Cross-country or back-country, downhill or glacier, whatever your ski style, Austria has a piste with your name on it.

Above: Snowboarder in Mayrhofen (p307)

VADIM PETRAKOV/SHUTTERSTOCK ©

Mayrhofen

Invigorating cross-country trails, exhilarating toboggan rides and enchanting snowshoe hikes are all on offer at Mayrhofen, while serious thrill seekers can tackle heart-pounding downhill runs including Austria's steepest piste, the Harakiri, with a 78% gradient. p307

Right: Paragliders in Mayrhofen

BORIS-B/SHUTTERSTOCK ©

FRANZ FALTERMAIER/GETTY IMAGES ©

St Anton am Arlberg

St Anton am Arlberg is legendary for the longest ski circuit in the Alps – the 85-km Run of Fame, crossing the Arlberg, Flexen and Hochtannberg mountain passes, with a dizzying 18,000m difference in altitude – as well as its sizzling-hot après-ski scene. p324

Above: Skiers and snowboarders in St Anton am Arlberg

Kitzbühel

Austrian skiing was born in Kitzbühel in 1893, when pioneer Franz Reisch hurtled down Kitzbüheler Horn on the first alpine run. With its charming preserved medieval centre, it retains a sense of tradition that makes it one of the country's most storied places for downhill skiing and snowboarding today. p310

Above: Downhill skiing in Kitzbühel

2 INSPIRING DAY HIKES

Austria's cloud-piercing mountains, plunging glacier-chiselled valleys, swirling rivers and sparkling lakes will have you itching to lace up your hiking boots and set off to explore tantalisingly off-the-radar corners of the country. Locals delight in telling you that the best – in fact, the only – way to see these majestic landscapes is on foot. And they're right. Here a peerless network of walking trails brings you that much closer to nature.

JIMMYR/GETTY IMAGES ©

IMAGEBROKER/MORITZ WOLF/GETTY IMAGES ©

TRABANTOS/SHUTTERSTOCK ©

Zillertal Circuit

Starting at a turquoise-coloured reservoir, the Schlegeisspeicher, the Zillertal Circuit is a classic alpine hike that rewards walkers with magnificent vistas of the icy peaks of the Zillertal Alps. p304

Top: Hikers on the Berliner Höhenweg, part of the Zittertal Circuit

Pinzgauer Spaziergang

Traversing tarn forest, wildflower-flecked meadows and rugged limestone cliffs, the astonishingly beautiful high-alpine route Pinzgauer Spaziergang affords mesmerising views of the Hohe Tauern National Park and Kitzbühel Alps. p260

Avove: Pinzgauer Spaziergang

3 WATER, WATER EVERYWHERE

Along with mighty rivers made for adventure activities, land-locked Austria is blessed with hundreds of glittering lakes. When the weather warms up, these watery oases burst into life as playgrounds for strolling, sunbathing and swimming, and water sports galore.

Below: Fun on Wörthersee (p282)

MARTIN STEINTHALER/GETTY IMAGES ©

DAITOZEN/GETTY IMAGES ©

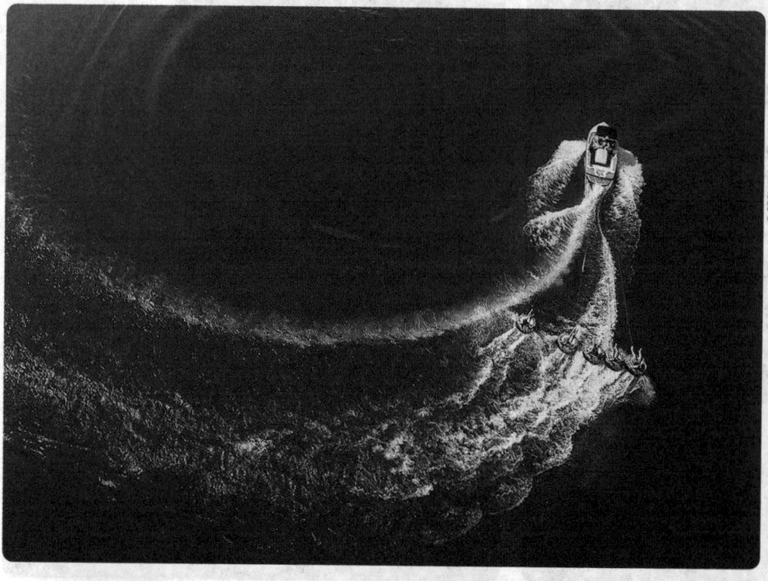

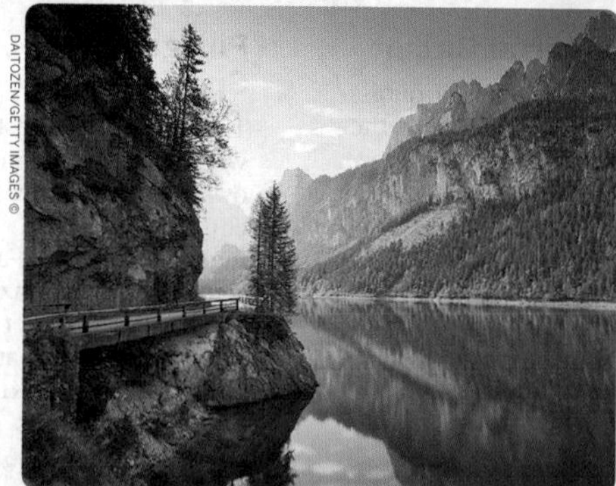

Salzkammergut Lakes

With its jewel-coloured alpine lakes, the Salzkammergut is one of Austria's most picturesque regions for dipping into crystal-clear waters, such as those of the Wolfgangsee, Mondsee, and Hallstätter See, spectacularly set at the foot of the precipitous Dachstein mountains. p207

Left: Gosausee (p212)

Carinthian Lakes

The pure waters of Carinthia's glacier-formed lakes, such as the region's largest, the Wörthersee, and most voluminous, the Millstätter See, can reach Celsius temperatures in the high 20s in summer, making them prime for water sports such as waterskiing, wakeboarding and scuba diving with far-reaching visibility. p269

Left: Millstätter See (p283)

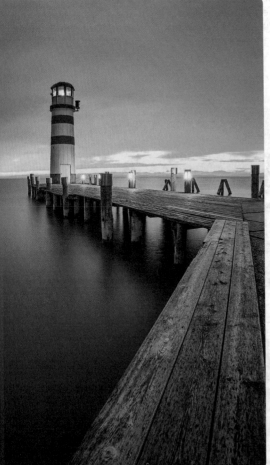

Neusiedler See

In Burgenland, Europe's second-largest steppe lake, the Neusiedler See, is also warm thanks to its shallow depths and benevolent winds. Kite-surfing and sailing are popular here. The main activity base is Podersdorf am See, on the lake's eastern shore. p153

Left: The lighthouse in Podersdorf am See (p156)

4 BAROQUE MONASTERIES

Austria's greatest works of art are those wrought for God, some say. Gazing up at the glory of the country's colossal monasteries, you may well agree. As well as their sheer scale, what causes visitors' jaws to drop is the exuberant beauty of baroque architecture with all the trimmings – gilt glistening with ethereal golden hues, gleaming marble, a profusion of stuccowork such as plump cherubs and vibrantly coloured frescoes.

Stift Melk

Strikingly lit up at night, the twin-spired monastery church of Benedictine abbey-fortress Stift Melk is a baroque tour de force, replete with prancing angels and ceiling paintings. Such opulence continues in the library and marble hall, both embellished with illusionary trompe l'oeil tiers. p134

Below: Stift Melk

Admont's Benedictine Abbey

Situated deep in the rifts of Styria's Gesäuse mountains, Admont's Benedictine abbey is a remarkable fusion of landscape, architecture and museum space. The baroque library is adorned with frescoes, while the abbey's museums bring together the region's natural history and contemporary art. p200

Top left: Benedictine Abbey in Admont

Augustiner Chorherrenstift

Although St Florian's Augustinian monastery, the Augustiner Chorherrenstift, dates from at least 819, it is an exemplar of baroque style. Its basilica is a wonder with a gilded 18th-century organ and an altar carved from pink Salzburg marble. p168

Top right: The library in the Augustiner Chorherrenstift

5 LAVISH PALACES

Austria's extravagant palaces open the doors to an understanding of the history that shaped the nation. Within these immense complexes, the grandiose architecture, furnishings and troves of treasures are testament to centuries of power plays and the unlimited riches that secured the work of the finest craftspeople of their time. Nowadays visitors can tour the palaces' hallowed halls and discover illuminating museums, unique attractions and graceful grounds and gardens.

Hofburg, Vienna

The mighty Habsburg monarchy ruled for over six centuries. In Vienna's city centre, their HQ, the Hofburg, whisks you back to the age of empires: marvel at the treasury's imperial crowns, the Spanish Riding School's equine ballet and the chandelier-lit apartments fit for Empress Elisabeth. p59

Below: Hofburg, Vienna

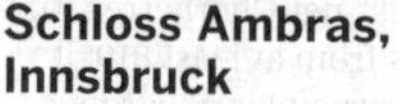

Schloss Ambras, Innsbruck

Tyrol ruler Archduke Ferdinand II transformed Innsbruck's Schloss Ambras from a castle to this sumptuous pile. Art, armour and curiosities are among its extensive collections. p294

Above: Schloss Ambras

Schloss Eggenberg, Graz

Built at the behest of Johann Ulrich for the Eggenberg dynasty, Graz' grand palace contains intruiging museums within its walls and grounds. p181

Right: One of the rooms in Schloss Eggenberg

6 SOUNDS OF MUSIC

TICHR/SHUTTERSTOCK ©

No other nation on earth can outshine Austria when it comes to classical music. In the 18th and 19th centuries, the country was a veritable production line of great composers, Mozart, Strauss, Mahler, Haydn and Schubert among them. Their stirring works reverberate as loudly as ever at magnificent concert halls, and renowned music festivals like the Bregenzer Festspiele and century-old Salzburg Festival are staged against uplifting lakeside or mountain backdrops.

Mozart's Geburtshaus, Salzburg

Mozart was born in Salzburg's baroque Altstadt at what is now Mozart's Geburtshaus, which features instruments and memorabilia. p234

Staatsoper, Vienna

Guided tours go behind the scenes of Vienna's resplendent gold-and-crystal-adorned Staatsoper but nothing beats attending an opera or ballet at one of the finest concert halls in the world. p114

Above: Staatsoper, Vienna

Opernhaus, Graz

The opera house in Austria's second-largest city is a confection of neobaroque and neorococo styles. p189

7 GROUND-BREAKING GALLERIES

While Austria's cache of venerable museums showcase priceless masterpieces from throughout the ages, in recent years, a fresh breath of air has been sweeping through the cities, bringing with it a dynamic blend of historic and contemporary venues. Some of the most eye-catching galleries are actually the newest, and make fitting backdrops for the modern and contemporary artworks and installations on display. Prepare to see Austria in a different light.

ALIZADA STUDIOS/SHUTTERSTOCK ©

ARON M/SHUTTERSTOCK ©

MuseumsQuartier, Vienna

The MuseumsQuartier encompasses 60 cultural institutions such as the white-limestone Leopold Museum and the dark-basalt MUMOK. p73

Top left: Museumsplatz with MUMOK

Kunsthaus Graz

Contemporary exhibitions rotate at Kunsthaus Graz – a bulbous building with a BIX ('big' and 'pixels') media facade consisting of 930 adjustable fluorescent lamps. p181

Above left: Kunsthaus Graz

Lentos, Linz

Linz' striking glass-and-steel gallery Lentos shelters one of Austria's foremost modern art collections. p161

Above right: Lentos, Linz

8 FLAVOURS OF AUSTRIA

SINA ETTMER PHOTOGRAPHY/SHUTTERSTOCK ©

KEMTER/GETTY IMAGES ©

Organic, foraged, artisan, farm-to-fork: these concepts aren't buzzwords in Austria but have long been second nature. Asparagus in spring, *Marille* (apricots) in summer, mushrooms and game in autumn – ingredients at the country's markets and restaurants swings with the seasons. You can also taste right at the source: cheeses at alpine dairies, schnapps at distilleries, and beer and wine (even at monasteries where they're still made by monks), just for starters.

Wachau Wine Tasting

Wine tasting is widespread across Austria's 16 prestigious viticulture areas. A lovely place to start sampling is the Domäne Wachau, in a glorious vine-ribboned stretch of Lower Austria's Danube Valley granted Unesco World Heritage status. p130

Top left: Domäne Wachau

Bregenzerwald Käsestrasse

Driving through the beautiful dairy country of Bregenzerwald along the Käsestrasse ('cheese road') presents numerous opportunities to visit local *Sennereien* (dairy farms) and taste their wares. p338

Bottom left: A cheese maker in Bregenzerwald

Stanz Schnapps Tasting

Amid apple and plum orchards, the tiny Tyrol village of Stanz has scores of schnapps distilleries and rustic huts for tastings. p321

Need to Know

For more information, see Survival Guide (p383)

Currency
Euro (€)

Language
German

Visas
Generally not required for stays of up to 90 days; as of 2021 non-EU nationals need prior authorisation under the new European Travel Information and Authorisation System (ETIAS) process for Schengen Area travel.

Money
ATMs widely available. Maestro direct debit and Visa and MasterCard credit cards accepted in most hotels and midrange restaurants.

Mobile Phones
Travellers from outside Europe will need a tri- or quad-band (world) mobile phone for roaming. Local SIM cards (about €15) are easily purchased for 'unlocked' phones. Visitors from the EU can roam freely.

Time
Central European Time

When to Go

Mild to hot summers, cold winters
Warm to hot summers, mild winters
Mild year-round
Cold climate

High Season
(Jun–Sep)

- High season peaks from July to August.
- In lake areas, the peak is June to September.
- Prices rise over Christmas and Easter.
- Salzburg is busiest in July and August for the Salzburg Festival.

Shoulder
(Apr–May & late Sep–Oct)

- The weather's changeable, the lakes are chilly and the hiking's excellent.
- Sights are open and less crowded.

Low Season
(Nov–Mar)

- Many sights are closed at this time of year.
- There's a cultural focus in Vienna and the regional capitals.
- Ski resorts open from mid-December.
- High season for skiing is mid-December to March.

Useful Websites

Embassy of Austria (www.austria.org) US-based website with current affairs and information.

Lonely Planet (www.lonelyplanet.com/austria) Destination information, hotel reviews and more.

Österreich Werbung (www.austria.info) National tourism authority.

Tiscover (www.tiscover.com) Information and accommodation booking.

Important Numbers

To dial from outside Austria, dial the international access code, country code, city code, then number.

Austria's country code	☎43
International access code	☎00
International operator & information	☎11 88 77 (inland, EU & neighbouring countries); 0900 11 88 77 (other countries)
Mountain rescue	☎140
Emergency (police, fire, ambulance)	☎112

Exchange Rates

Australia	A$1	€0.63
Canada	C$1	€0.70
Japan	¥100	€0.78
New Zealand	NZ$1	€0.60
Russia	RUB1	€0.012
UK	UK£1	€1.17
USA	US$1	€0.88

For current exchange rates, see www.xe.com.

Daily Costs

Budget: Less than €100

- Dorm beds or cheap doubles: about €25 per person
- Self-catering or lunch specials: €8–12
- Cheap museums: €4

Midrange: €100–200

- Doubles: €80–200
- Two-course meal with glass of wine: €30
- High-profile museums: €12

Top end: More than €200

- Plush suites and doubles in major cities: from €200
- Pampering at spa facilities: €40–100
- Fine dining and wine pairing: €70

Opening Hours

Banks 8am or 9am–3pm Monday to Friday (to 5.30pm Thursday)

Cafes 7am or 8am–11pm or midnight; traditional cafes close at 7pm or 8pm

Offices and government departments 8am–3.30pm, 4pm or 5pm Monday to Friday

Post offices 8am–noon and 2–6pm Monday to Friday; some open Saturday morning

Pubs and bars 5.30pm–between midnight and 4am

Restaurants Generally 11am–2.30pm or 3pm and 6–11pm or midnight

Shops 9am–6.30pm Monday to Friday (often to 9pm Thursday or Friday in cities), 9am–5pm Saturday

Arriving in Austria

Vienna International Airport The City Airport Train (CAT; €11, 16 minutes) leaves the airport every 30 minutes from 6.09am to 11.39pm. Vienna Airport Lines buses run every 30 minutes 24/7; it's 20 minutes to Schwedenplatz (central Vienna). A single costs €8. Expect to pay €25 to €50 for a taxi.

Graz Airport Trains leave the airport from 4.31am to 11.45pm Monday to Saturday, and from 5.10am Sunday, at least hourly. An hour's ticket costs €2.40. Expect to pay about €25 for a taxi.

Innsbruck Airport Bus F serves the airport. Buses depart every 15 or 20 minutes from Maria-Theresien-Strasse (€2.30, 16 minutes); taxis charge about €10 for the same trip.

Salzburg Airport Buses 2, 10 and 27 (€2, 19 minutes) depart from outside the terminal every 15 minutes from 5.30am to 11pm. A taxi between the airport and the city centre costs €15 to €20.

Getting Around

Public transport is excellent for reaching even remote regions, but it takes longer. Most provinces have an integrated transport system offering day passes covering regional zones for both bus and train travel.

Car Small towns and even small cities often have limited or no car-hire services, so reserve ahead from major cities.

Train & Bus Austria's national railway system is integrated with the Postbus bus services. Plan your route using the ÖBB (www.oebb.at) or Postbus (www.postbus.at) websites.

For much more on **getting around**, see p396

First Time Austria

For more information, see Survival Guide (p383)

Checklist

➡ Make sure your passport is valid for at least six months from your arrival date

➡ Get a visa if you need one

➡ Arrange travel and medical insurance if needed

➡ Check that your credit/debit card can be used with ATMs internationally

➡ Make copies of all important documents and cards

➡ Turn off data roaming on mobile (cell) phone

What to Pack

➡ Hiking boots (with profile for snow), plus flat, comfortable shoes for city cobbles

➡ Waterproof jacket (summer) or padded, thermal jacket (winter)

➡ Dressy clothes for a night at the theatre or smart restaurants

➡ Daypack

➡ Sunscreen for high alpine elevations

➡ Electrical adapter if needed

Top Tips for Your Trip

➡ Explore towns and cities at night when they are beautifully illuminated. Or consider an easy night hike for a different perspective.

➡ Choose a convenient city, small town or village as a regional hub and explore on day trips – public transport is efficient and inexpensive.

➡ Austria isn't just about randomly ticking off sights – factor in ample lazy time for simply lingering in coffee houses or *Beisln* (small taverns/restaurants) in Vienna and Salzburg between sights.

➡ Book train tickets in advance online to save time and look out for discounted *Sparschiene* tickets, which can slash the cost of travel.

What to Wear

Winter can be cold and the ground icy, so several layers of warm clothing and good shoes are essential, along with gloves, scarf and a hat. In summer, wear layers you can peel off and make sure you have something for occasional rain. Especially in larger cities, Austrians tend to dress up well in the evening or for good restaurants, but jeans are fine even for upmarket clubs and restaurants if combined with a good shirt or blouse and a men's sports coat *(Sakko)* or women's summer jacket.

Sleeping

Tourist offices invariably keep lists and details of accommodation; some arrange bookings (free, or for a small fee).

Hotels From budget picks to five-star luxury in palatial surrounds.

B&Bs Also called pensions and *Gasthöfe*; range from simple city digs to rustic mountain chalets.

Private Rooms *Privat Zimmer* usually represent great value (doubles go for as little as €50).

Farmstays Geared towards families. Some only operate during summer.

Alpine Huts These go with the snow, opening from roughly late June to mid-September. Advance bookings are essential.

Camping Most resorts and cities have camp sites, usually in pretty, natural settings.

Taxes

Mehrwertsteuer (MWST; value-added tax) is 20% for most goods. Non-EU visitors can claim a MWST refund on purchases over €75.01; see www.globalblue.com for details.

Bargaining

Bargaining in shops is not really a part of Austrian culture. Flea markets are the exception; or when negotiating a longer than usual period of rental for, say, a kayak or a bicycle, you can ask whether there's a cheaper rate they can offer.

Tipping

Bars About 5% at the bar and 10% at a table.

Hotels One or two euros per suitcase for porters and for valet parking in top-end hotels. Leaving loose change for cleaners is appreciated.

Restaurants Tip about 10% (unless service is abominable). Round up the bill, state the amount as you hand the bill back or leave the tip in the bill folder when you leave.

Taxis About 10%.

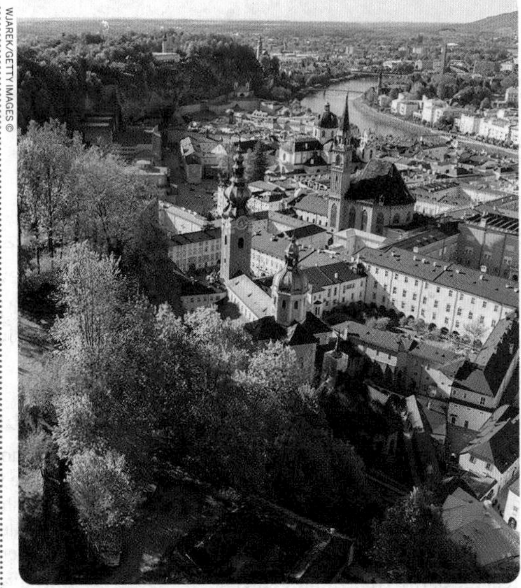

A view of Salzburg from Festung Hohensalzburg (p228)

Etiquette

Austrians are fairly formal and use irony to alleviate social rules and constraints rather than debunk or break them overtly.

Telephone Always give your name at the start of a telephone call, especially when making reservations. When completing the call, say *auf Wiederhören* ('goodbye'), the customary telephone form.

Greetings Use the *Sie* (formal 'you') form unless you're young-ish (in your 20s) and among peers, or your counterpart starts using *du* (informal 'you'). Acknowledge fellow hikers on trails with a *Servus*, *Grüss di* (or the informal *Grüss dich*) or *Grüss Gott* (all ways of saying 'hello!').

Eating & Drinking Bring chocolate or flowers as a gift if invited into a home. Before starting to eat, say *Guten Appetit*. To toast say *Zum Wohl* (if drinking wine) or *Prost!* (beer), and look your counterpart in the eye – not to do so is impolite and reputedly brings seven years of bad sex.

Language

In Vienna, the regional capitals and tourist areas (such as around lakes or in resorts), you'll find that many people speak English, especially in restaurants and hotels. In much of the countryside, however, it's a slightly different picture, and you should equip yourself with a few necessary phrases.

Conductors on trains and many bus drivers know enough English to help with necessities.

What's New

Green energy initiatives, innovative solutions to encourage slower, more responsible and more rewarding travel, and a slew of socially minded initiatives, along with recent and revamped openings across the cities and magnificent landscapes, are fuelling inspiration for visitors to discover or rediscover Austria.

Sound of Music World Museum

Hum 'Do-Re-Mi' quietly to yourself as you explore this engaging Salzburg museum (p234), which goes behind the scenes to look at the making of the movie and the real life of the Trapp family singers.

Sigmund Freud Museum

Devoted to the father of psychoanalysis, this compelling museum (p81) in Vienna's Alsergrund neighbourhood is where Freud developed his most groundbreaking theories. It is fresh from a multimillion euro makeover and expansion.

Unhashtag Vienna

'See Klimt, not #Klimt' is the slogan of the Viennese initiative Unhashtag Vienna (www.unhashtag.vienna.info), aimed at luring travellers away from their smartphones and encouraging digital detox. The city's gardens, markets and coffee houses are just perfect for this. A related campaign, Unrating Vienna (www.unrating.wien.info) sets out to counter online rating obsessions, asking visitors 'who decides what you like?' Both campaigns aim to make travel in the capital more rewarding.

Ski + City Pass

Reaching the cream of the slopes from Innsbruck just got that much easier, with

LOCAL KNOWLEDGE

WHAT'S HAPPENING IN AUSTRIA

By Catherine Le Nevez, Lonely Planet writer

Austrians take any and every opportunity to get out into the glorious outdoors, and it's not surprising that the country is a European role model for climate protection. As well as revising an already-ambitious target to use 100% renewable energy by 2030 (originally set for 2050), it also plans to be carbon neutral by 2040 and to put a price on CO_2 emissions.

Austria has seen tumultuous times lately, though, with resurgent extreme-right politics, hardening immigration policies, multiple waves of the COVID-19 pandemic, and the country's youngest-ever chancellor, Sebastian Kurz, ousted twice in corruption scandals – first following the 'Ibiza-gate' revelations in 2019, leading to the government's collapse, and then, following his re-election, again in 2021, during investigations regarding manipulated opinion polls, with his foreign minister Alexander Schallenberg taking the chancellorship reins.

Yet some really heartening social tourism initiatives are thriving, such as a refugee-run hotel and tours by the homeless, giving visitors a unique and meaningful perspective. And years of campaigning by gay rights groups paid off in 2019 when a Constitutional Court ruling saw the country achieve marriage equality.

this new combined culture-and-ski pass, covering 13 different areas, including the Stubai Glacier.

The Glass Garden

See Salzburg's baroque-dome-encrusted skyline from on high at the Glass Garden (p246) at Schloss Mönchstein, serving ingredient-driven dishes in glass-canopied surrounds.

Haus der Geschichte Österreich

A newcomer to the Hofburg in Vienna, Austria's first museum (p64) of contemporary history takes a romp through the period from the mid-19th century to the present.

Haus der Musik

Opened to much acclaim, Innsbruck's Haus der Musik (p67) has given the city a cutting-edge architectural icon, with a bronze ceramic-tiled façade. Its roster of plays, concerts and workshops is top-drawer stuff.

Museum der Illusionen

It's all an illusion at this hands-on museum (p65) in Vienna, where star exhibits include tilted rooms, mirages, an infinity room and a giant kaleidoscope. Sounds fun? It is!

Schlossberg Slide

Brace yourself for a rip-roaring ride on Graz' Schlossberg Slide (p184). The 175m slide bills itself as the highest underground slide in the world. It's over in 40 seconds but what a buzz...

Hotel Taggenbrunn

Immerse yourself in the vines at this design-minded winery hotel (p281) in Carinthia. Set in picturesque countryside, it has grape-themed rooms, vineyard views and wine-tasting sessions.

LISTEN, WATCH AND FOLLOW

For inspiration and up-to-date news, visit www.lonelyplanet.com/Austria/travel-tips-and-articles.

Travel Tyrol (www.traveltyrol.com) Austria-wide travel blog by a Tyrol-based writer with a focus on family travel.

Vienna Würstelstand (www.viennawurstelstand.com) English-language info on Vienna's bars, restaurants and events.

Vienna Unwrapped (www.vienna-unwrapped.com) Vienna planning advice in English.

Austrian Adaptation (www.austrianadaptation.com) Slow travel and expat life.

Insta @naikon_ Inspirational images.

iAustria (www.iaustria.info) Handy app for outdoor activities and accommodation.

FAST FACTS

Food trend Vegetarian and vegan dining

Percentage of renewable energy used in Austria 80

Percentage of Austrians who drink coffee 92

Pop 8.9 million

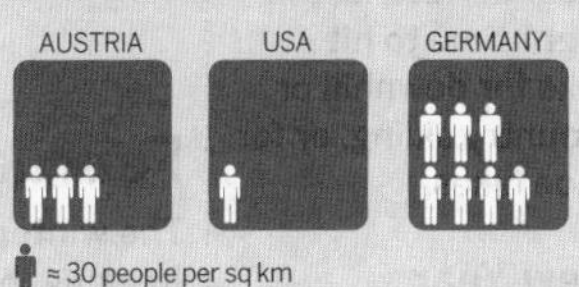

Social Tourism

Vienna shows its social side in a growing raft of enterprises putting people first and making travel matter: cue the likes of Shades Tours (p94; guided tours with the homeless), refugee-run boutique hotel Magdas (p100) and generation-spanning cafe Vollpension (p104), run by *Omas* (grandmas) and *Opas* (grandpas) along with their families.

Month by Month

TOP EVENTS

Salzburg Festival, July

Styriarte, June

Christmas markets, December

Bregenzer Festspiele, August

Donauinselfest, June

January

One of the coldest months of the year in Austria, this is the right time to hit the peaks for downhill or cross-country skiing, or for snowshoe hikes.

New Year Concerts

Vienna rings in the new year on 1 January with classical concerts. The Vienna Philharmonic's performance in Vienna's Staatsoper is a glittering affair. (p114)

Hanneshof Hot Air Balloon Week

Hot air balloons take to the night skies in Filzmoos in late January as the ski resort hosts the spectacular Hanneshof Hot Air Balloon Trophy. (p254)

Mozartwoche

An ode to the city's most famous son, Mozart Week stages concerts in Salzburg in late January. (p238)

Perchtenlaufen

Locals dress as *Perchten* (spirits crowned with elaborate headdresses) and parade through the streets across much of western Austria in a celebration to bring good fortune and bountiful harvests for the year.

February

The winter months are freezing, but in Vienna the museums and cultural scene are in full swing. Crowds are down. On the slopes the skiing is usually still excellent.

Opernball

Of the 300 or so balls held in Vienna in January and February, the Opernball (www.wiener-staatsoper.at) is the most lavish.

March

The sun is thawing the public squares. Hiking and cycling are becoming possible from late March, but many sights outside Vienna are still dormant.

Osterfestspiele

Salzburg celebrates Easter in grand musical style with this festival of orchestral highlights at the Festpielhaus, as well as choral concerts and opera. (p238)

Ostermärkte

Vienna leaps into spring at a series of Easter markets, where eggs, floral decorations and food and drink celebrate the start of a new season. (p95)

April

Spring has properly sprung and city gardens are at their blooming best. Room rates and crowds remain low. Snow still polishes the highest peaks of the Alps.

May

Cities are a delight on spring days: uncrowded and often warm. A hike to a mountain *Alm* (meadow) becomes a romp through flowers, and from April

onwards all sights and activities flick to summer schedules.

✩ Wiener Festwochen

In Vienna, arts from around the world, from dance performances to theatre productions and concerts, hit stages across the city until mid-June. (p97)

✩ Musikwochen Millstatt

In Millstatt in Carinthia, a string of concerts are held between May and September, mostly in the medieval abbey church. (p284)

June

The snow finally melts and hiking and kayaking are excellent, with near-empty trails and warm but not overly hot weather. Mountain lakes are warming up. Big-hitting sights in Vienna and Salzburg start to get crowded.

✩ SommerSzene

Salzburg's cutting-edge dance, theatre, film, visual arts and music bash brings a true burst of summer to the city from mid- to late June. (p238)

✩ Donauinselfest

Vienna gets down for a free three-day festival of rock, pop, hardcore, folk and country music on the Donauinsel in late June. (p97)

✩ Styriarte

Graz' most important cultural festival offers almost continuous classical concerts in June and July, some of which are held in Renaissance courtyards. (p186)

July

School holidays begin in July, the time when families enjoy the warm weather on lakes and in the mountains. Cities can be sweltering and crowded, but restaurant dining is at its alfresco best.

✩ ImPulsTanz

Vienna's premier avant-garde dance festival takes place from mid-July to mid-August, with the participation of dancers, choreographers and teachers in this five-week event. (p97)

✩ Salzburg Festival

World-class opera, classical music and drama take the stage by storm in Salzburg from late July to August, when the whole city is swept up by festival fever. (p238)

Spectaculum

On the last Saturday in July, electric lights are extinguished and the town of Friesach returns to the Middle Ages. (p280)

August

School holidays continue to propel families into the resorts, making things a bit crowded. Hit some isolated spots in the fine weather – seek out a *Heuriger* (wine tavern) or an alpine peak.

✩ La Strada Graz

This upbeat summer arts festival brings street theatre, dance, puppet theatre and 'nouveau cirque' to the streets of Graz. (p186)

✩ Bregenzer Festspiele

Beginning in late July and continuing until late August, this is Vorarlberg's top-class cultural event, with classical music and performances on a floating, open-air stage. (p333)

September

The temperatures are beginning a gradual descent and crowds are tailing off. Museums and most of the activities are still in season, however, and a couple of top-class festivals are revving into action.

Mountain Yoga Festival

St Anton practises tree pose for its Mountain Yoga Festival, giving the resort an added dose of Zen in early September. (p327)

✩ Herbstgold

International and Austrian performers take the audience through the range of works by Josef Haydn throughout much of September in his home town of Eisenstadt. (p150)

✩ Brucknerfest

Linz stages its most celebrated festival, a tremendous six-week series of high-calibre classical concerts based on Austrian composer Anton Bruckner. (p164)

October

Goldener Oktober – the light picks out the golds and russets of autumn, the mountains are growing chilly at night, the wine harvest is in and some museums are preparing to close for winter.

Steirischer Herbst

Held in Graz each autumn, this avant-garde festival has a bold line-up of new music, theatre, film, art installations and more. (p186)

Viennale Film Festival

For two weeks from mid-October, city cinemas host screenings from fringe films through documentaries to short and feature films. (p97)

November

Many museums outside the capital have gone into winter hibernation, the days are getting short and the weather can be poor. Cafes, pubs and restaurants become the focal point.

St Martin's Day

Around 11 November the new wine is released and St Martin's Day is marked with feasts of goose washed down by the nectar of the gods.

Wien Modern Festival

Contemporary music and pop culture take to the fore at this three-week festival, held at two dozen venues across Vienna. (p97)

December

Snow! Ski resorts are gathering momentum and in Vienna and other cities the theatres and classical-music venues are in full swing – often the best performances are during the coldest months.

Christmas Markets

Christkindlmärkte (Christmas markets) bring festive sparkle, handicrafts, mulled wine and good cheer to Vienna and the rest of Austria from early December until the 24th. (p95)

Silvester

Book early for the night of 31 December, celebrated with fireworks and a blaze of crackers and rockets on Vienna's crowded streets. (p97)

Itineraries

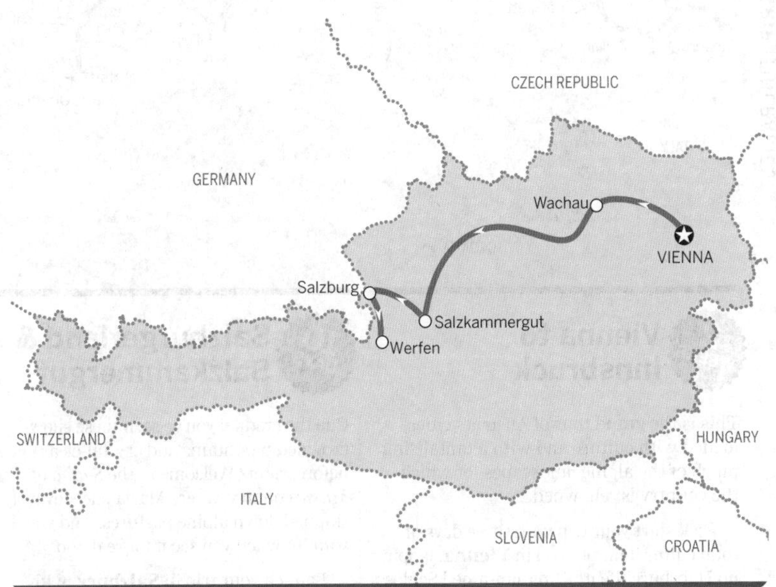

2 WEEKS Vienna to Salzburg

This itinerary is Austria in a nutshell, winging you from Vienna's opulent palaces and coffee houses to the vine-stitched Wachau Valley, and west to the Alps in Salzburgerland. Mozart, Maria and landscapes no well-orchestrated symphony or yodelling nun could ever quite capture – this one has the lot.

Devote a couple of cultural days to swanning around Habsburg palaces, world-class galleries hung with Klimts and sumptuous coffee houses in **Vienna**. A breezy hour's train ride west and you're in the heart of wine country and on the Danube in the picture-book **Wachau**. Linger for a day or two to lap up the castles, abbeys and local rieslings.

Swing west now for two days to the **Salzkammergut**, where cinematic mountain backdrops rim lakes of bluest blue. Base yourself in ludicrously pretty Hallstatt for peak-gazing swims and a visit to Dachstein's astonishing ice caves.

From here, head west to **Salzburg** for a feast of baroque art, prince-archbishop palaces, Mozart and more. After a couple of days, tag on a day in **Werfen** with its high-on-a-hill castle and extraordinary Eisriesenwelt – all backdropped by the Tennengebirge's jagged limestone peaks.

Vienna to Innsbruck

This is the grand tour of Austria's cities, loaded with culture and with a tantalising pinch of the alpine landscapes for which the country is renowned.

Kick-start your trip with three days of total cultural immersion in **Vienna**, lapping up Habsburg life in Klimt-crammed Schloss Belvedere or opulent Schloss Schönbrunn, before heading west along the Danube Valley to **Krems an der Donau**. Pause here for cutting-edge galleries and wine tastings, factoring in a trip to the spirit-lifting Benedictine abbey-fortress in **Melk**.

On day seven (a day or two earlier in winter), head to **Linz**, an industrial city that has rediscovered its creative mojo with edgy galleries like Lentos and Ars Electronica. The trail to mountain-rimmed **Hallstatt** and the lakes of the Salzkammergut are soothingly beautiful on day eight.

From Hallstatt, either venture to **Salzburg**, a pristine, castle-topped baroque city, or stop off in lakeside **Zell am See**, where hiking trails thread among some of Austria's highest peaks, before continuing to **Innsbruck** for a dose of culture, hiking, skiing – whatever takes your fancy.

Salzburgerland & Salzkammergut

Cue the credits: you've seen these snow-crowned mountains and crystal-clear lakes before, right? Welcome to the *Sound of Music* country, where Maria once joyously skipped down alpine pastures. And you'll want to when you see it for real, too.

Launch your trip in **Salzburg**, with three days combing the back alleys and clambering up to the high-on-a-hill castle in Mozart's hometown. You can hook onto a *Sound of Music* tour or zoom up to the Alps from here. Or detour to Italianate Schloss Hellbrunn or **Hallein**'s salt works.

From Salzburg, the road dips to the most picturesque of the lakes in the Salzkammergut, the **Wolfgangsee**, where summertime swimming, walking and cycling are splendid. Tick off lesser-known towns on hikes or rides over a few days.

From St Wolfgang or St Gilgen, it's a short bus hop to **Bad Ischl**, a base for exploring other Salzkammergut lakes over the next three days. The most dramatic is Hallstätter See, with **Hallstatt** or laid-back **Obertraun** perfect for overnighting. Near Obertraun, take a cable car to Dachstein's surreal ice caves, and tack on a hike.

Top: Dom St Jakob (p295), Innsbruck

Bottom: Murinsel (p185), Graz

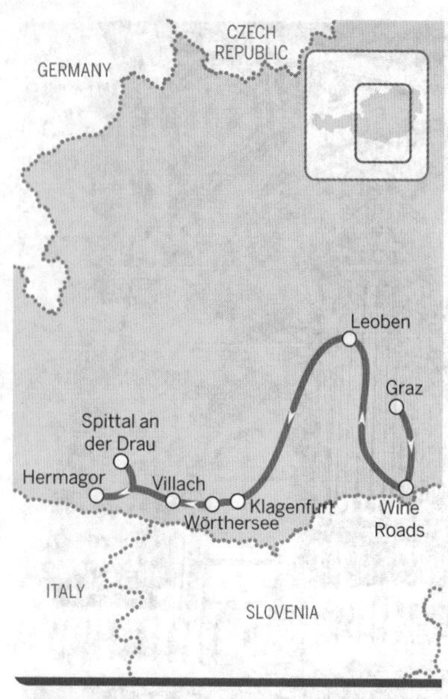

Styria & Carinthia

Austria beyond the obvious? This spin of the south takes you to chilled-out, culture-packed Graz, the vineyards of Styria, the turquoise Wörthersee and many other lakes, villages and little-known trails besides.

Factor in three or four days to slip under the surface of **Graz**, Austria's easygoing second city, where space-age galleries, Renaissance courtyards and a spirited food and nightlife scene rival for your attention. On the third day, venture out along the south Styrian **wine roads**, a Tuscan-like landscape with vineyards at every bend.

A train takes you to Klagenfurt via **Leoben** where you can break the journey for a few hours and check out its MuseumsCenter Leoben. The remaining five days can be divided between **Klagenfurt** and **Wörthersee**, **Villach** or **Spittal an der Drau**, towns with a sprinkling of sights and plenty of outdoor activities. Towns such as **Hermagor** in the Gail Valley have great cycling, hiking and (in winter) skiing possibilities.

For a food, wine and culture focus, plan more time around Graz in Styria. For swimming and other activities, plan more time in Carinthia.

Tyrol

One word: mountains. Wherever you go in Tyrol you'll be confronted by big, in-your-face, often snow-dusted mountains. Grab your hiking boots or skis and dive into these incredible alpine valleys.

Start with a few days in **Innsbruck**. Stroll the historic *Altstadt* (old town), taking in galleries, Habsburg treasures and upbeat nightlife. On the third day, take the futuristic funicular to the Nordkette, or eyeball Olympic ski jump, Bergisel. From Innsbruck, go south for skiing at the **Stubai Glacier** or west to the baroque abbey in **Stams**.

Then head west to the **Ötztal**, where you can dip into prehistory at Ötzi Dorf and thermal waters at Aqua Dome. Spend the next few days rafting near **Landeck**, exploring the Rosengartenschlucht gorge, or hiking and skiing in **St Anton am Arlberg**.

In week two, retrace your steps to Innsbruck and swing east. Factor in a day for the medieval town of **Hall in Tirol** and Swarovski Kristallwelten in **Wattens**. The alpine **Zillertal** will have you itching to head out hiking, canyoning, rafting or skiing. Round out at fortress-topped **Kufstein** and the legendary mountains of **Kitzbühel**.

Skiing in Mayrhofen (p307)

Plan Your Trip

Skiing & Snowboarding

No matter whether you're a slalom expert, a fearless freerider or a beginner, there's a slope for you in Austria. The Swiss and French Alps may have the height edge, but this is Europe's best all-rounder. It's the origin of modern skiing (thanks to Schneider's Arlberg technique), birthplace of Olympic legends and spiritual home of après-ski. Here you'll find cruising, knee-trembling black runs and summer glacier skiing – perfection for every taste and ability.

Top Slopes

Cruise, carve, party and quake in your boots at some of these top spots:

Top descents The Streif, part of the epic Hahnenkamm, is Kitzbühel's king of scary skiing. Mayrhofen's Harakiri is Austria's steepest run, with a gradient of 78%. It's pitch black and *there's no turning back...*

Top family skiing Filzmoos for its uncrowded nursery slopes, chocolate-box charm and jagged Dachstein mountains. Heiligenblut is refreshingly low-key and has a ski kindergarten.

Top snowboarding Mayrhofen is a mecca to freeriders, and some say it has Austria's most *awesome* terrain park, Vans Penken.

Top après-ski Join the singing, swinging, Jägermeister-fuelled fun in St Anton am Arlberg, Austria's après-ski king. Wild inebriation and all-night clubbing are the winter norm in raucous rival Ischgl.

Top glacier skiing The Stubai Glacier has snow-sure pistes within easy reach of Innsbruck. Head to the Kitzsteinhorn Glacier for pre- and postseason skiing at 3203m, with arresting views of the snowy Hohe Tauern range.

Best Skiing Regions

Ski Amadé (p263) Austria's biggest ski area, covering is Salzburgerland's Ski Amadé. It extends over 760km of pistes in 25 resorts divided into five snow-sure regions. The resorts include low-key Radstadt and family-friendly Filzmoos, and every level is catered for, from quiet tree-lined runs to off-piste touring.

Ski Arlberg (p325) This is one of Austria's most famous ski regions with good reason featuring 306km of slopes to explore. Its centrepiece is St Anton am Arlberg, where expert skiers and boarders rave about its great snow record, challenging terrain and terrific off-piste. Ski Arlberg is also home to the most happening après-ski in Austria, if not Europe. Across the valley lie the resorts of Lech and Zürs in Vorarlberg.

Kitzbühel (p310) The legendary Hahnenkamm, 185km of groomed slopes, a car-free medieval town centre and upbeat nightlife all make Kitzbühel one of Austria's most popular resorts. Critics may grumble about unreliable snow – with a base elevation of 762m, Kitzbühel is fairly low by alpine standards – but that doesn't stop skiers who come for the varied downhill, snowboarding and off-piste.

Zillertal 3000 (p307) Mayrhofen is the showpiece of Zillertal 3000, which covers 199km of slopes and 66 lifts in the stunning Zillertal. As well as being heaven for intermediate skiers, Mayrhofen has Austria's steepest black run, 78% gradient of the Harakiri, and appeals to freestylers for its fantastic terrain park. Even if snow lies thin in the valley, it's guaranteed at the nearby Hintertux Glacier.

Zell am See–Kaprun (p257) Following expansion and the arrival of two new cable cars, Zell am See–Kaprun now has a staggering 408km of pistes, which are covered by a single ski pass. Even if the snow coverage is thin on the lower slopes, there's fresh powder and a terrain park at the Kitzsteinhorn Glacier to play in. The après-ski in Zell am See's car-free old town is lively but not rowdy. The entire region affords gorgeous views of the glacier-capped Hohe Tauern range.

Silvretta-Montafon (p344) The iconic arrow-shaped peak of Piz Buin (3312m) looms over the Silvretta-Montafon ski area. Situated in the south-east corner of Vorarlberg, this calm and beautiful valley's quiet resorts appeal to families, cruisers and ski tourers. As well as 246km of slopes, there is lenty to do away from the pistes, from sledding to winter hiking.

Silvretta Arena (p323) Ischgl is the centrepiece of the Silvretta Arena, comprising 239km of prepared slopes. High slopes above 2000m mean guaranteed snow, mostly geared towards confident intermediates, off-piste fans and boarders. The resort has carved a name for itself as a party hotspot, with big-name season opening and closing concerts, and pumping (borderline sleazy) après-ski. For those seeking a quieter vibe, Galtür, Kappl and Samnaun (Switzerland) are nearby.

Sölden (p319) The Ötztal is defined by some of the wildest and highest mountains in Austria. Its main ski resort is snow-sure Sölden, with 145km of slopes between 1350m and 3340m, a state-of-the-art lift network and a crazy après-ski scene. The terrain is intermediate heaven, but presents more of a challenge on long runs such as the 50km Big 3 Rally and off-piste. A bonus to skiing here is the snow reliability on two glaciers – Rettenbach and Tiefenbach – making this a great pre- or late-season choice.

Lift Passes

Costing around €300 or thereabouts for a week, lift passes are a big chunk out of your budget. The passes give access to one or more ski sectors and nearly always include ski buses between the different areas. Lift passes for lesser-known places may be as little as half that charged in the jet-set resorts. Count on around €35 to €50 for a one-day ski pass, with substantial reductions for longer-term passes. Children usually pay half-price, while under-fives ski for free (bring a passport as proof of age).

Most lift passes are now 'hands-free', with a built-in chip that barriers detect automatically, and many can be prebooked online.

Safety

- Avalanches are a serious danger in snowbound areas and can be fatal.
- If you're skiing off-piste, never go alone and always take an avalanche pole (a collapsible pole used to determine the location of an avalanche victim), a transceiver, a shovel and – most importantly – a professional guide.
- See www.lawine.at (in German) for the avalanche risk and snow coverage by region.
- UV rays are stronger at high altitudes and intensified by snow glare; wear ski goggles and sunscreen.
- Get in good shape before hitting the slopes and build up gradually.
- Wear layers to adapt to the constant change in body temperature; make sure your head, wrists and knees are protected (preferably padded).
- Before you hurtle down that black run, make sure you're properly insured and read the small print: mountain-rescue costs, medical treatment and repatriation can soon amount to triple figures.

Websites

Bergfex (www.bergfex.com) A great website with piste maps, snow forecasts for the Alps and details of every ski resort in Austria.

If You Ski (www.ifyouski.com) Resort guides, ski deals and info on ski hire and schools.

Skiing in St Anton am Arlberg (p324)

SUMMER SNOW

If the thought of pounding the powder in summer appeals, hightail it to glaciers such as the Stubai Glacier, Hintertux Glacier and Kitzsteinhorn Glacier, where, weather permitting, there's fine downhill skiing year-round.

MadDog Ski (www.maddogski.com) Entertaining ski guides and insider tips on everything from accommodation to après-ski.

On the Snow (www.onthesnow.co.uk) Reviews of Austria's ski resorts, plus snow reports, webcams and lift pass details.

Where to Ski & Snowboard (www.wheretoskiandsnowboard.com) Key facts on resorts, ranked according to their upsides and downsides, plus user reviews.

World Snowboard Guide (www.worldsnowboardguide.com) Snowboarder central, with comprehensive information on most Austrian resorts.

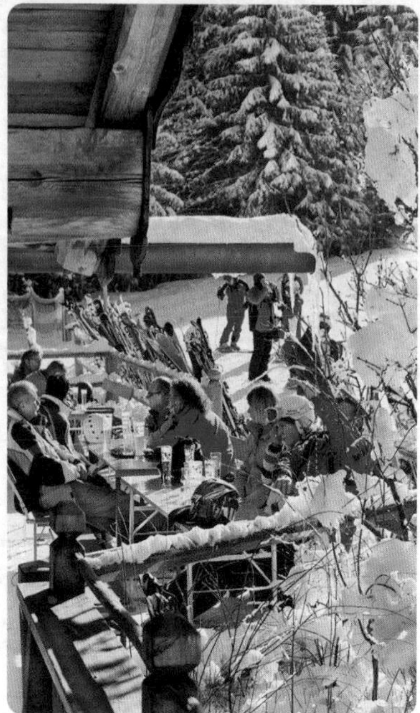
BORIS-B/SHUTTERSTOCK ©

Après-ski

Equipment Hire & Tuition

Skis (downhill, cross-country, telemark), snowboards, boots, poles and helmets can be rented at sport shops like Intersport (www.intersport.at) in every resort. Ski, snowboard or cross-country ski rental costs around €25/125 per day/week, or €50/200 for top-of-the-range gear. Boot hire is around €17/64 per day/week. With Intersport, children 14 and under pay half-price, under-10s get free ski hire when both parents rent equipment, and you can ski seven days for the price of six.

Most ski resorts have one or more ski schools; for a list of regional ski schools, visit Snowsport Austria (www.snowsportaustria.at). Group lessons for both adults and children typically cost €65 per day (two hours in the morning, two hours in the afternoon), €215 for four days and €265 for six days. The more days you take, the cheaper the per-day rate gets. Private instruction is available on request. Kids can start learning from the age of four.

Cross-Country Skiing

Cross-country skiing *(Langlauf)* in Austria is considerably greener and cheaper than downhill skiing – a day pass costs as little as €3 with a guest card. The two main techniques are the classic lift-and-glide method on prepared cross-country tracks *(Loipen)* and the more energetic 'skating' technique. The basics are easy to master at a cross-country school and tracks are graded from blue to black according to difficulty.

Seefeld features among Austria's top cross-country skiing destinations, with 256km of *Loipen* criss-crossing the region including a floodlit track. Zell am See is another hotspot, with 40km of groomed trails providing panoramic views of the Hohe Tauern mountains. Other great resorts to test your stamina and stride include the Bad Gastein region, with 90km of well-marked cross-country trails. To search for cross-country regions and packages, see www.langlauf-urlaub.at (in German).

SLOPE SAVERS

It's worth checking websites such as www.igluski.com, www.skiingaustria.co.uk, www.ifyouski.com and www.j2ski.com for last-minute ski deals and packages. Local tourist offices and www.austria.info might also have offers.

You can save time and euros by prebooking ski and snowboard hire online at Snowbrainer (www.snowbrainer.com), which gives a discount of up to 50% on shop rental prices.

The Zillertal (p303)

Plan Your Trip

Hiking in Austria

Der Berg ruft (the mountain calls) is what Austrians say as they gallivant off to the hills, and what shopkeepers post on closed doors in summer. For Austrians, Wandern (walking) is not a sport, it's second nature. Kids frolic in alpine pastures, nuns Nordic-walk in the hills, super-fi t 70-somethings trek over windswept 2000m passes – such wanderlust is bound to rub off on you. With towering peaks, forestcloaked slopes and luxuriantly green valleys, the landscapes are perfect and walking opportunities are endless. Strike into Austria's backyard, listen closely and you too will hear mountains calling...

Walk Designations

Austria is criss-crossed with well-maintained *Wanderwege* (walking trails), which are waymarked with red-white-red stripes (often on a handy rock or tree) and yellow signposts. Bear in mind, though, that these are no substitute for a decent map and/or compass in the Alps. Like ski runs, trails are colour-coded according to difficulty:

Blue The blue routes (alternatively with no colour) are suitable for everyone; paths are well marked, mostly flat and easy to follow.

Red The red routes require a good level of fitness, sure-footedness and basic mountain experience. They are sometimes steep and narrow, and may involve scrambling and/or short fixed-rope sections.

Black For experienced mountain hikers with a head for heights, black routes are mostly steep, require proper equipment and can be dangerous in bad weather.

Walking Light

If you love long-distance hiking but find carrying a rucksack a drag, you might want to consider *Wandern ohne Gepäck* (literally 'walking without luggage'). Many regions in Austria now offer this clever scheme, where hotels transport your luggage to the next hotel for a small extra charge. Visit www.austria.info or www.wanderhotels.com for more details.

If you would prefer your Sherpa to be of the cute and woolly kind, llama trekking could be just the thing. Many towns now offer this family favourite. Nothing motivates kids to walk quite like these hikes, which reach from two-hour forest strolls to two-week treks on pilgrimage routes. The llamas carry your luggage and leave you free to enjoy the scenery. Contact local tourist offices for more options.

ÖAV Membership

Before you hit the trail in the Austrian Alps, you might want to consider becoming a member of the Österreichischer Alpenverein (ÖAV, Austrian Alpine Club; www.alpenverein.at). Adult membership costs €57 per year and there are significant discounts for students and people aged under 25 or over 61. Membership gets you discounts of up to 50% at Austrian (ÖAV) and German (DAV) alpine huts, plus other benefits including insurance, workshops, access to climbing walls countrywide and discounts on maps. The club also organises walks. There is an arm of the club in England, the Austrian Alpine Club (www.aacuk.org.uk). You should allow at least two months for your application to be processed.

Of the 1000-odd huts in the Austrian Alps, 241 are maintained by the ÖAV.

Weather

If there's one rule of thumb in the Austrian Alps, it's to never take the weather for granted. It may *look* sunny but conditions can change at the drop of a hat – hail, lightning, fog, torrential rain, you name it. Check the forecast before embarking on long hikes at high altitudes. Tourist offices also display and/or provide mountain-weather forecasts.

Österreichischer Alpenverein (www.alpenverein.at) A reliable web source for forecasts for the alpine regions.

Snow Forecast (www.snow-forecast.com) Up-to-date snow forecasts for major Austrian ski resorts.

Wetter Österreich (www.wetter.at) One- to nine-day weather forecasts, plus up-to-date weather warnings.

Safety

Most walker injuries are directly attributable to fatigue, heat exhaustion and inadequate clothing or footwear. Falling as a result of sliding on grass, scree or iced-over paths is a common hazard; watch out for

Top: The Ötztal (p318), Tyrol

Bottom: The Stubaital (p302), Tyrol

TOP FIVE LONG-DISTANCE HIKES

NAME	START	FINISH	DISTANCE	DURATION
Adlerweg	St Johann in Tyrol near Kitzbühel	St Anton am Arlberg	300km	3-4 weeks
Berliner Höhenweg	Finkenberg near Mayrhofen	Mayrhofen	70km	8 days
Arnoweg	Salzburg	Salzburg	1200km	2 months
Stubai Höhenweg	Neustift im Stubaital	Neustift im Stubaital	120km	8 days
Salzburger Almenweg	Pfarrwerfen near Werfen	Pfarrwerfen	350km	1 month

black ice. On high-alpine routes, avalanches and rock falls can be a problem. A few common-sense rules will help you stay safe when walking:

➡ Always stick to the marked and/or signposted route, particularly in foggy conditions. With some care, most walking routes can be followed in fog, but otherwise wait by the path until visibility is clear enough to proceed.

➡ Study the weather forecast before you go and remember that weather patterns change suddenly in the mountains.

➡ Increase the length and elevation of your walks gradually, until you are acclimatised to the vast alpine scale; this will help prevent altitude sickness and fatigue.

➡ Where possible, don't walk in the mountains alone. Two is considered the minimum number for safe walking, and having at least one additional person in the party will mean someone can stay with an injured walker while the other seeks help.

➡ Inform a responsible person, such as a family member, hut warden or hotel receptionist, of your plans, and let them know when you return.

SOS SIX

The standard alpine distress signal is six whistles, six calls, six smoke puffs, six yodels – that is, six of whatever sign or sound you can make – repeated every 10 seconds for one minute. If you have a mobile phone, make sure you take it with you. Mountain rescue (reached by calling 140) in the Alps is very efficient but extremely expensive, so make sure you have adequate insurance – read the fine print.

Resources

Websites

Get planning with the routes, maps and GPS downloads on the following websites:

Bergfex (www.bergfex.com) Plan your dream hike with detailed route descriptions (many are in German) and maps, searchable by region, fitness level and length. Free GPS downloads.

Austria Info (www.austria.info) Excellent information on walking in Austria, from themed day hikes to long-distance treks. Also has details on national parks and nature reserves, hiking villages and special walking packages. Region-specific brochures are available for downloading.

Naturfreunde Österreich (NFÖ, Friends of Nature Austria; www.naturfreunde.at) Hundreds of walking routes, walk descriptions, maps and GPS downloads, including Nordic walking and snowshoeing routes. Also information on NFÖ huts, tips on mountain safety and up-to-date weather reports.

LEVEL	HIGHLIGHTS	RESOURCES
moderate	Classic alpine landscapes from the Kaisergebirge's limestone peaks to the Arlberg region's rugged mountainscapes	See www.tirol.at for maps, brochures and route descriptions
demanding	High-alpine, hut-to-hut route taking in the beautiful lakes, glaciers and mountains of the Zillertal Alps	See www.naturpark-zillertal.at for a detailed route description in German; Alpenvereinskarte 1:25,000 map No 35 *Zillertaler Alpen* covers the route
demanding	Epic circular tour of the Austrian Alps, taking in gorges, valleys and Hohe Tauern National Park's glacial landscapes	Rother's walking guide to Arnoweg covers the trail in detail.
moderate-demanding	A classic circular hut-to-hut route passing glaciers, rocky peaks and wild alpine lakes	Download maps and route descriptions at www.stubaier-hoehenweg.at; Cicerone's *Trekking in the Stubai Alps* is a reliable guide
moderate	A hut-to-hut route taking in Salzburgerland's fertile *Almen* (alpine pastures), karst scenery and the eternally ice-capped peaks of Hohe Tauern	See www.salzburger-almenweg.at for detailed route descriptions, maps and a virtual tour

Österreichischer Alpenverein (www.alpenverein.at) Search for alpine huts and find information on events, tours, hiking villages and conservation. There's a section on the country's 10 *Weitwanderwege* (long-distance trails), which stretch from 430km to 1400km and showcase different areas of Austria's stunning landscape.

Maps

The best place to stock up on maps is a *Tabak* (tobacconist), newsagent or bookshop. Usually they only have local maps, although bookshops in the major cities offer a wider selection. Outdoor-activities shops usually sell a limited variety of walking maps. Many local tourist offices hand out basic maps that may be sufficient for short, easy walks.

A great overview map of Austria is Michelin's 1:400,000 national map No 730 *Austria*. Alternatively, the ANTO (Österreich Werbung, Austrian National Tourist Office; www.austria.info) can send you a free copy of its 1:800,000 country map. Visit www.austrianmap.at for a zoomable topographic country map. The following high-quality walking maps can be purchased online:

Freytag & Berndt (www.freytagberndt.com) Publishes a wide selection of reliable 1:50,000-scale walking maps.

Kompass (www.kompass.de) Has a good series of 1:50,000 walking maps and includes a small booklet with contact details for mountain huts and background information on trails.

ÖAV (www.alpenverein.at) Produces large-scale (1:25,000) walking maps that are clear, detailed and accurate.

Accommodation

Hiking Hotels

Gone are the days when hiking meant a clammy tent and week-old socks. Austria has seriously upped the ante in comfort with its so-called *Wanderhotels* (hiking

WALK DESCRIPTIONS IN THIS GUIDE

➡ The times and distances for walks are provided only as a guide.

➡ Times are based on the actual walking time and do not include stops for snacks, taking photos, rests or side trips. Be sure to factor these in when planning your walk.

➡ Distances should be read in conjunction with altitudes – significant elevation can make a greater difference to your walking time than lateral distance.

HIKING EQUIPMENT CHECKLIST

Clothing
- windproof and waterproof jacket
- breathable fleece
- loose-fitting walking trousers, preferably with zip-off legs
- hiking shorts
- T-shirts or long-sleeved shirts
- socks (polypropylene)
- sun hat
- sunglasses
- swimwear (optional)

Footwear
- walking boots with a good grip
- trekking sandals or thongs
- socks

Other Equipment
- backpack or daypack
- sleeping bag
- water bottle
- map
- compass
- Swiss Army knife

For Emergencies
- emergency food rations
- first-aid kit
- torch (flashlight) with batteries and bulbs
- whistle
- mobile (cell) phone
- transceiver
- shovel
- avalanche pole

Miscellaneous Items
- camera and lenses
- umbrella
- insect repellent
- high-energy food (eg nuts, dried fruit, bread, cured meat)
- at least 1L of water per person, per day
- sunscreen (SPF30+)
- toiletries, toilet paper and towel
- stuff sacks

For Hikes above 2000m
- thermal underwear
- extra clothing
- gaiters
- gloves
- warm hat
- walking sticks

hotels). These hotels are run by walking specialists who offer guided walks from leisurely strolls to high-alpine hikes, help you map out your route and have equipment (eg poles, flasks and rucksacks) available for hire. Most establishments are family-run, serve up regional cuisine and have a sauna or whirlpool where you can rest your weary feet. See www.wanderhotels.com for something to suit every taste and pocket, from farmstays to plush spa hotels.

Going a step further are Austria's Wanderdörfe (www.wanderdoerfer.at), a countrywide network of 43 hiker-friendly villages in 47 regions. Here, you can expect well-marked short- and long-distance walks, beautiful scenery and alpine huts, good infrastructure (eg trains and/or hiking buses) and hosts geared up for walkers. You can order a free brochure online.

Hut-to-Hut Hiking

One of the joys of hiking in Austria is spending the night in a mountain hut. These trailside refuges give you the freedom to tackle multiday treks in the Alps with no more than a daypack. The highly evolved system means you're hardly ever further than a five- to six-hour walk from the next hut, so there's no need to lug a tent, camping stove and other gear that weighs hikers down. Huts generally open from mid-June to mid-September, when the trails are free of snow; the busiest months are July and August, when advance bookings are highly recommended. Consult the ÖAV for hut contact details and opening times.

Accommodation is in multibed dorms called *Matratzenlager*, or in the *Notlager* (emergency shelter – wherever there's space) if all beds have been taken. Blankets and pillows are provided but you might need to bring your own sleeping sheet. In popular areas, huts are more like mountain inns, with drying rooms and even hot showers (normally at an extra charge).

Most huts have a convivial *Gaststube* (common room), where you can socialise and compare trekking tales over drinks and a bite to eat. ÖAV members can order the *Bergsteigeressen* – literally 'mountaineer's meal' – which is low in price but high in calories, though not necessarily a gastronomic treat! It's worth bringing your own tea or coffee, as *Teewasser* (boiled water) can be purchased from the hut warden.

Silvretta Hochalpenstrasse (p344)

Plan Your Trip

Cycling & Adventure Sports

Austria is one of Europe's most bike-friendly lands. It is interlaced with well-marked cycling trails that showcase the mountains, valleys and cities from their best angles. Whether you want to test your stamina on hairpin bends and leg-aching mountain passes, blaze downhill on a mountain bike in the Alps or freewheel leisurely around the country's glorious lakes, Austria has routes that will take your breath away.

Transporting Bikes

Look for the bike symbol at the top of timetables or on the ÖBB (Österreiche Bundesbahn, Austrian Federal Railway; www.oebb.at) website to find trains where you can take your bike. Bike tickets within Austria cost 10% of the full ticket price, while for international routes they cost €12.

Many of Austria's leading resorts have cottoned onto the popularity of downhill mountain biking and now allow cyclists to take their bikes on the cable cars for free or for a nominal charge in summer, allowing you to enjoy the downhill rush without the uphill slog!

Accommodation

Throughout Austria you'll find hotels and pensions (B&Bs) geared up for cyclists, particularly in the Alps. So-called *Radhotels* go a step further with everything from storage facilities to bike repairs and staff well informed on local routes. You can browse for bike-friendly hotels by region on www.bike-holidays.com and www.radtouren.at. Local tourist offices can also point you in the right direction and sometimes offer special packages.

When to Go

Warmer temperatures from May to October beckon cyclists, while downhill mountain bikers head to the Alps from late June to mid-September. Snow rules out cycling at higher elevations in winter, but this can be a quiet time to explore Austria's valleys. Pedalling up alpine passes in July and August can be a hot, thirsty business; take sunscreen and water, and factor in breaks.

Cycling & Mountain Biking

Websites

Radtouren (www.radtouren.at) An excellent site listing Austria's major cycling routes and hotels.

Radfahren (www.radfahren.at) Easy-to-navigate website with descriptions on cycling trails (including long-distance routes), bike-friendly hotels, bike rental and transport throughout Austria. Has interactive maps.

Bike Holidays (www.bike-holidays.at) Search by region for mountain-bike (MTB) trails, cycling routes, freeride parks and bike hotels in Austria.

Maps & Guides

Local tourist offices usually stock brochures and maps on cycling and mountain biking. Cycle clubs are another good source of information. For more detailed maps and guides:

Kompass (www.kompass.at) For cycle tour maps at scales between 1:125,000 and 1:50,000. Covers long-distance routes well, including those along the Bodensee, Danube and Inntal.

Esterbauer (www.esterbauer.com) Produces the Bikeline series of cycling and mountain-biking maps and guides, which give comprehensive coverage of Austria's major trails.

Freytag & Berndt (www.freytagberndt.at) Stocks a good selection of cycling maps and produces the *Austria Cycling Atlas* detailing 160 day tours.

Rentals

City and mountain bikes are available for hire in most Austrian towns and resorts. Intersport (www.intersport.at) has a near monopoly on rental equipment, offering a selection of quality bikes in 260 stores throughout Austria. Day rates range from around €18 for standard bikes to €25 for e-bikes (electric bikes). All prices include bicycle helmets and there's a 50% reduction on children's bikes. Those who want to plan their route ahead can search by region and reserve a bike online.

Cycling Routes

There's more to cycling in Austria than the exhilarating extremes of the Alps, as you'll discover pedalling through little-explored countryside with the breeze in your hair and the chain singing. There are plenty of silky-smooth cycling trails that avoid the slog without sacrificing the grandeur; many of them circumnavigate lakes or shadow rivers.

Danube Cycle Path Shadowing the mighty Danube for 380km from Passau to Bratislava, this cycle route takes in some lyrical landscapes. Wending its way through woodlands, deep valleys and orchards, the trail is marked by green-and-white signs on both sides of the river. Esterbauer's Bikeline *Danube Bike Trail* is useful for maps and route descriptions. See www.donauregion.at for details on the route and an interactive map, and www.donau-radweg.info for tours.

Inn Trail Starting in Innsbruck and travelling 302km through Austria to Schärding, the Inn Trail (www.innregionen.com) sticks close to the turquoise Inn River. It's basically downhill all the way, passing through fertile farmland, alpine valleys and castle-topped towns in Tyrol, Bavaria and Upper Austria. The final stretch zips through bucolic villages and countryside to Schärding. The route is well marked, but signage varies between regions.

Bodensee Cycle Path Touching base with Bregenz in Vorarlberg, this 270km cycleway encircles the Bodensee (Lake Constance), Europe's third-largest lake. Marked with red-and-white signs, the mostly easygoing trail zips through Austria, Germany and Switzerland, passing woodlands, marshes, orchards, vineyards and historic towns. Come in early autumn for fewer crowds, new wine and views of the Alps on clear days. Visit www.bodensee-radweg.com for details.

Salzkammergut Trail This 345km circular trail explores the pristine alpine lakes of the Salzkammergut, including Hallstätter See, Attersee and Wolfgangsee. Though not exactly flat, the trail is well signposted (R2) and only moderate fitness is required. To explore in greater depth, pick up Esterbauer's Bikeline *Radatlas Salzkammergut*.

Tauern Trail Rolling through some of Austria's most spectacular alpine scenery on the fringes of the Hohe Tauern National Park, the 310km Tauern Trail is not technically difficult, but cycling at high altitude requires stamina. It begins at Krimml, then snakes along the Salzach River to Salzburg, then further onto the Saalach Valley and Passau. The trail is marked with green-and-white signs in both directions. For maps and GPS tracks, see www.tauernradweg.com.

Mountain Biking

The Austrian Alps are an MTB (mountain biking) hotspot, with hairpin bends, backbreaking inclines and heart-pumping descents. The country is criss-crossed by mountain-bike routes, with the most challenging terrain in Tyrol, Salzburgerland, Vorarlberg and Carinthia. Following is a sample of the tours and regions that attract two-wheeled speed demons.

Dachstein Tour Hailed as one of the country's top mountain-bike routes, this three-day tour circles the rugged limestone pinnacles of the Dachstein massif and blazes through three provinces: Salzburgerland, Upper Austria and Styria. You'll need a good level of fitness to tackle the 182km trail that starts and finishes in Bad Goisern, pausing en route near Filzmoos. For details, see www.dachsteinrunde.at.

Salzburger Almentour On this 146km trail, bikers pedal through 30 *Almen* (mountain pastures) in three days. While the name conjures up visions of gentle meadows, the route involves some strenuous climbs up to tremendous viewpoints like Zwölferhorn peak. Green-and-white signs indicate the trail from Annaberg to Edtalm via Wolfgangsee. Route details and highlights are given online (www.almentour.com, in German).

Silvretta Mountain Bike Arena Sidling up to Switzerland, the Silvretta Mountain Bike Arena in the Patznauntal is among the biggest in the Alps, with 1000km of trails, some climbing to almost 3000m. Ischgl makes an excellent base, with a technique park and plenty of trail information available at the tourist office. The 15 freeride trails for speed freaks include the Velill Trail, involving 1300m of descent. Tour details are available at www.silvretta-bikeacademy.at (in German).

Kitzbühel Covering 800km of mountain-bike trails, the Kitzbühel region ranks as one of Austria's top freewheeling spots. Routes range from 700m to 2300m in elevation and encompass trial circuits, downhill runs and bike parks. The must-experience rides include the Hahnenkamm Bike Safari from Kitzbühel to Pass Thurn, affording far-reaching views of Grossglockner and Wilder Kaiser.

Stubaital & Zillertal These two broad valleys running south from the Inn River in Tyrol are flanked by high peaks criss-crossed with 800km of mountain-bike trails. The terrain is varied and the landscape splendid, with gorges, waterfalls and glaciers constantly drifting into view. Highlights include the alpine route from Mayrhofen to Hintertux Glacier and the dizzying roads that twist up from Ginzling to the Schlegeisspeicher.

GPS FREEWHEELING

It's easier to navigate Austria's backcountry and find little-known bike trails with a GPS tour. Check www.bike-gps.com for downloadable cycling and mountain-biking tours. Alternatively, head to www.gps-tour.info for hundreds of tours in Austria.

Grossglockner (p256), Hohe Tauern National Pa

Adventure Sports

Rock Climbing & Vie Ferrate

Synonymous with mountaineering legends like Peter Habeler and South Tyrolean Reinhold Messner, Austria is a summertime paradise for ardent *Kletterer* (rock climbers). In the Alps there's a multitude of climbs ranking all grades of difficulty. Equipment rental (around €10) and guided tours are widely available.

If you're not quite ready to tackle the three-thousanders yet, nearly every major resort in the Austrian Alps now has a *Klettersteig* (via ferrata). These fixed-rope routes, often involving vertical ladders, ziplines and bridges, are great for getting a feel for climbing; all you'll need is a harness, helmet and a head for heights.

Resources

ÖAV (www.alpenverein.at) Official website of the Austrian Alpine Club, with a dedicated page on climbing (in German).

Bergsteigen (www.bergsteigen.com) Search by region or difficulty for climbing routes, vie ferrate and ice-climbing walls.

Rock Climbing (www.rockclimbing.com) Gives details on more than 1000 climbing tours in Austria, many with climbing grades and photos.

Regions

For serious mountaineers, the ascent of Grossglockner (3798m), Austria's highest peak, is the climb of a lifetime. Professional guides can take you up into the wild heights of the Hohe Tauern National Park, a veritable climbing nirvana.

Sheer granite cliffs, bizarre rock formations and boulders make the Zillertal Alps another hotspot, particularly Ginzling and Mayrhofen.

Other climbing magnets include Pelstein in Lower Austria, the limestone peaks of the Dachstein and the Tennengebirge in Salzburgerland.

Canyoning

For a buzz, little beats scrambling down a ravine and abseiling down a waterfall while canyoning. This wet, wild sport has

Paragliding near Innsbruck (p291)

become one of the most popular activities in the Austrian Alps. Guided tours costing between €50 and €80 for half a day abound. Most companies provide all the gear you need, but you should bring swimwear, sturdy shoes, a towel and a head for heights. A good level of fitness is also recommended.

Top locations for canyoning include Mayrhofen in the Zillertal, the Ötztal and Lienz.

Paragliding

Wherever there's a mountain and a steady breeze, you'll find paragliding and hang-gliding. On a bright day in the Alps, look up to see the sky dotted with people catching thermals to soar above peaks and forests. In many resorts, you can hire the gear, get a lesson or go as a passenger on a tandem flight; prices for the latter start at around €100. Most people fly in summer, but a winter's day can be equally beautiful.

Tyrol is traditionally a centre for paragliding, with narrow valleys and plenty of cable cars. A good place to head is Zell am Ziller. Another scenic paragliding base is Zell am See in the rugged Hohe Tauern National Park.

Find the best place to spread your wings at www.flugschulen.at, which gives a regional rundown of flight schools offering paragliding and hang-gliding.

Water Sports

Rafting & Canoeing

Rafting, canoeing or kayaking the swirling white waters of Austria's alpine rivers are much-loved summertime escapades. Big rivers that support these fast-paced sports include the Enns and Salza in Styria; the Inn, Sanna and Ötztaler Ache in Tyrol; and the Isel in East Tyrol. Tours start from around €40 and usually include transport and equipment.

Well-known rafting centres include Landeck, Innsbruck for adventures on the Inn, Zell am Ziller and St Anton am Arlberg.

Swimming & Diving

Bath-warm or invigoratingly cold? Alpine or palm-fringed? Much of Austria is pristine lake country and there are scores to choose from. Carinthia is famed for its pure waters, which can heat up to a pleasantly warm 28°C in summer; Millstätter See and Wörthersee offer open-water swimming and scuba diving with great visibility. You can also make a splash in lakes such as Hallstätter See and Attersee in Salzkammergut, and Bodensee in Vorarlberg.

On the Beach

There's no sea for miles, but nearly all of Austria's major lakes are fringed with *Strandbäder* (lidos) for an invigorating dip, many of which have beaches, outdoor pools and barbecue areas. Some are free, while others charge a nominal fee of around €4 per day. If you dare to bare all, *Freikörperkultur* (FKK; nudist) beaches, including those at **Hard** (www.hard-sport-freizeit.at; Hard; adult/child €4.90/2.50; ⏲9am-8pm mid-May–early Sep) on Bodensee, Hallstätter See, Milstätter See and even the Donauinsel (p89) in Vienna, welcome skinny-dippers.

Plan Your Trip

Eat & Drink Like a Local

Schnitzel with noodles may have been Maria's favourite, but there's way more to Austrian food nowadays thanks to a generation of new-wave chefs adding a pinch of imagination to seasonal, locally grown ingredients in farm-to-fork menus. Worldly markets, well-stocked wineries and a rising taste for organic, foraged flavours are all making Austria a culinary destination to watch like never before.

The Year in Food

Spring (Mar–May)

Chefs add springtime oomph to dishes with *Spargel* (asparagus) and *Bärlauch* (wild garlic). *Maibock* (strong beer) is rolled out for beer festivals in May.

Summer (Jun–Aug)

It's time for *Marille* (apricot) madness in the Wachau, touring dairies in Tyrol and the Bregenzerwald, and eating freshwater fish by lake shores. Bludenz reaches melting point in July with its Milka Chocolate Festival. Every village gets into the summer groove with beer festivals and thigh-slapping folk music.

Autumn (Sep–Nov)

Misty autumn days dish up a forest feast of mushrooms and game, and *Sturm* (young wine) brings fizz to *Heuriger* (wine tavern) tables. Sip new *Most* (perry and cider) in the Mostviertel's orchards. Goose lands on tables for St Martin's Day (11 November).

Winter (Dec–Feb)

Try *Vanillekipferl* (crescent-shaped biscuits) and mulled wine at lit-up Christmas markets. Vienna's coffee houses are the perfect winter warmer.

Food Experiences

Though Austria can't be put on the same culinary pedestal as France or Italy, food is still likely to be integral to your travels here: whether you're sipping tangy cider in the apple orchards of the Mostviertel, sampling creamy alpine cheeses in the Bregenzerwald or eating local fish on the shores of the Salzkammergut's looking-glass lakes.

Meals of a Lifetime

Esszimmer (p246) Andreas Kaiblinger works culinary magic with market-fresh ingredients at this Michelin-starred number in Salzburg.

Obauer (p253) The Obauer brothers believe in careful sourcing at this address of foodist rigour in the Alps.

Mayer's (p261) Michelin-starred dining with a dash of romance at this lakefront palace in Zell am See.

Die Wilderin (p299) A welcome addition to Innsbruck with foraged flavours, occasional live jazz and a bistro buzz.

Waldgasthaus Triendlsäge (p317) Hop in a horse-drawn sleigh to reach this woody winter wonderland of a restaurant, hidden in the forest above Seefeld.

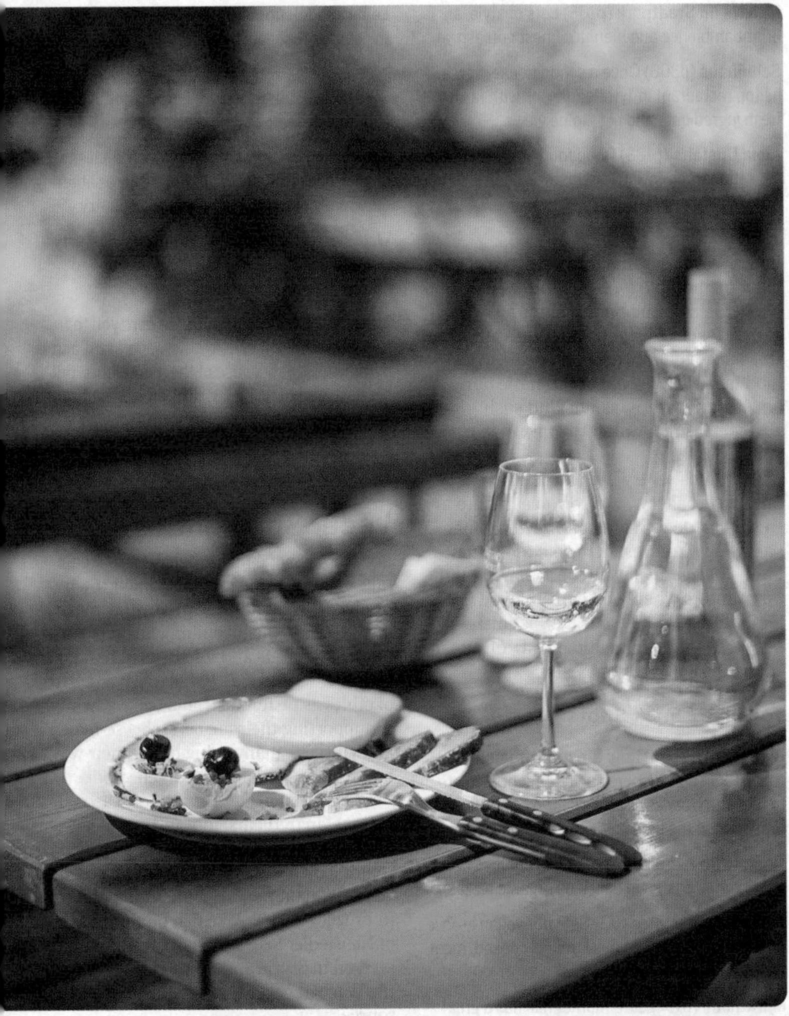

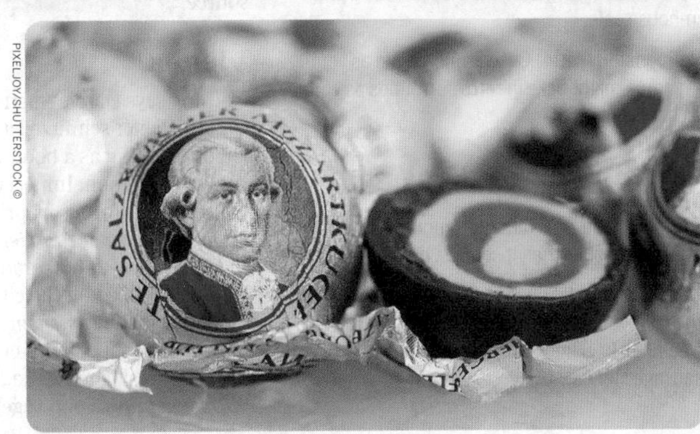

Top: A meat and cheese platter seved with wine

Bottom: Mozartkugeln (p51)

PIXELJOY/SHUTTERSTOCK ©

Meierei im Stadtpark (p106) Lots of style, a bright ambience and Vienna's finest goulash.

Schulhaus (p306) Once a schoolhouse, now a hilltop restaurant in Tyrol's Zillertal, with farm-fresh ingredients and big Alpine views.

Aiola Upstairs (p188) Good food enjoyed with a sensational view over Graz' historic centre.

Cheap Eats

It's not all about fine dining: some of your most memorable food experiences are likely to be on the hoof. Vienna's *Würstelstände* (sausage stands) are the stuff of snack legend, but there's more to street food here. Falafel, bagels, organic burgers, healthy wraps, salads and sushi to go – you'll find it all in the mix in Austria's worldly cities.

On almost every high street there is a *Bäckerei* (bakery), where you can grab a freshly made roll, and a *Konditorei* for a pastry or oven-fresh *Krapfen* (doughnut). Many *Metzgereien* (butchers) have stand-up counters where you can sink your teeth into a *Wurst* (sausage), schnitzel or *Leberkässemmel* (meatloaf roll), often with change from €5.

Top Five Snack Spots

Bitzinger Würstelstand am Albertinaplatz (p100) Join opera-goers and late-night nibblers to bite into a cheesy *Käsekrainer* or spicy *Bosna* bratwurst at the king of Vienna's sausage stands.

Organic Pizza Salzburg (p242) What it says on the tin: thin, crisp and delicious organic pizzas.

Swing Kitchen (Map p72) Get your vegan groove on with some of the tastiest, home-cooked, meat-free burgers in Vienna.

Markthalle (p167) Linz' market hall has a great in-house cafe.

Vollpension (p104) Cake as incredible as your grandma might bake in retro surrounds as comfy as her living room.

Dare to Try

Graukäse The Zillertal's grey, mouldy, sour-milk cheese is tastier than it sounds, honest!

Käsekrainer A fat cheese-filled sausage, way off the calorie-counting Richter scale. It's a popular wee-hour, beer-mopping snack at Vienna's sausage stands.

Leberknödelsuppe Dig into liver dumpling soup, the starter that gets meals off to a hearty kick all over Austria.

Rindfleischsulz Jellied beef brawn, often drizzled in pumpkin-seed-oil vinaigrette.

Schnecken *Escargots* to the French, snails to English speakers, these gastropods are slithering onto many of the top menus in the country.

Waldviertel Mohn Poppy dumplings, desserts, strudels and noodles add a floral addition to menus in the Waldviertel.

Zillertaler Bauernschmaus We dare you to try this farmer's feast of cold cuts, sauerkraut and dumplings. Not because of the ingredients, but because pronouncing it will surely get your tongue in a twist!

Local Specialities

Locavore is huge in Austria, where locals take genuine pride in their home-grown produce. Bright and early Saturday morning, you'll see them combing farmers markets, baskets and jute bags in hand, for whatever is seasonal. It's as much a matter of ethics as taste: Austrians believe firmly in supporting their farmers, cheese-makers and vintners, many going out of their way to buy organic, regionally sourced goods.

Chefs often make the most of seasonal, regional ingredients, too, and many have been quick to piggyback on the Slow Food trend (look for the snail symbol) in recent years. Piquant *Bergkäse* mountain cheese in Bregenzerwald, lake fish on the shores of Neusiedler See, dark, nutty pumpkin-seed oil in Styria and tangy rieslings from the Wachau never taste better than at the source.

Vienna

Nothing says classic Austrian grub like the classic Wiener schnitzel, a breaded veal cutlet, often as big as a boot, which is fried to golden perfection. Imperial favourites with a Hungarian flavour – paprika-spiced *Fiakergulasch* and *Tafelspitz mit Kren* (boiled beef with horseradish) – are big. Wines produced on the city's fringes are served at rustic *Heurigen* with hunks of dark bread topped with creamy, spicy Liptauer fresh cheese. Regionally grown *Suppengemüse* (soup vegetables such as carrots, celery, radish and root vegetables) pop up at markets and on menus.

Vienna is naturally also king of Austria's *Kaffeehaus* (coffee house) scene.

Lower Austria

If one fruit could sum up this region, the Wachau's tiny, juicy *Marille* (apricot), made into jam, schnapps and desserts, would rise to the challenge. Spreading north of the Danube Valley, the rural Waldviertel peps up everything from pasta to desserts with poppy seeds, while the orchard-wealthy Mostviertel to the south is cider and perry country. Some of Austria's finest wines are produced in the vines that march up the hillsides here, including tangy Grüner Veltiner and riesling whites, fruity Zweigelt and medium-bodied *Blauburgunder* (pinot noir) reds. Trout, carp and asparagus are also fished and grown locally.

Salzburg & Salzburgerland

Salzburg's *Mozartkugel* is a chocolate-coated pistachio marzipan and nougat confection that ungraciously translates as 'Mozart's Ball'. Like Upper Austrians, Salzburgers lean heavily towards noodle and dumpling dishes like cheese and onion-topped *Pinzgauer Kasnocken*, but this gives way to fish in the lakeside Salzkammergut. *Salzburger Nockerln*, the town's favourite desserts, are massive soufflé-like baked concoctions (don't even ask how many egg whites are in them!) sprinkled with icing sugar.

Burgenland

Like Lower Austria, Burgenland is one of Austria's premier wine regions, but it is also famous for its Neusiedler See fish – species like perch-pike, pike, carp and catfish. Toss in nuts, orchard produce and ham from a species of woolly pig called the Mangalitza, and the region makes for a mouth-watering trip.

Carinthia

Cheese, hams and salamis, game, lamb and beef count among the regional produce in mountainous Carinthia. Wherever there are lakes, you'll also find trout and other freshwater fish on menus. On meat-free Fridays, some Carinthians dig into local pasta known as *Kärntner Nudel*, filled with potato, cheese, mint, wild parsley-like chervil, mushrooms and any number of combinations of these.

Styria

Styria is also a producer of Mangalitza ham, as well as beef locally produced from Almochsen cattle, raised in mountain meadows in the region about 30km northeast of Graz. What the visitor to Styria, however, will immediately notice is that pumpkin oil is used to dress everything from salads to meats. This healthy, dark oil has a nutty flavour and here it often stands on tables alongside the salt and pepper.

Tyrol & Vorarlberg

These two regions have one thing in common: cheese, most notably what is called locally *Heumilchkäse* (hay-milk cheese), which aficionados claim is the purest form of milk you can find. *Gröstl*, or *Gröstel* in some other regions, is a fry-up from leftovers, usually potato, pork and onions, topped with a fried egg, but there are sausage varieties and the *Innsbrucker Gröstl* or *Gröstl Kalb* has veal.

Upper Austria

With Bavaria in Germany and Bohemia in the Czech Republic just over the border, it's unsurprising that Upper Austria is one of the country's *Knödel* (dumpling) strongholds. Sweet tooth? Well, you won't want to miss *Linzer Torte*, a crumbly tart with a lattice pastry top, filled with almonds, spices and redcurrant jam.

How to Eat & Drink

When to Eat

Frühstuck (breakfast) Austrians are the first to reel off the old adage about breakfast being the most important meal of the day. During the week, the locals may just grab a jam-spread *Semmel* (roll) and a coffee or a bowl of muesli, but at the weekend breakfast is often a leisurely, all-morning affair. A rising number of coffee houses and cafes have Sunday brunch buffets for around €15 to €20, with everything from sunny-side-up eggs to salmon, antipasti, cereals, fresh-pressed juices and *Sekt* (sparkling wine). You won't need to eat again until dinner.

MAGONE/GETTY IMAGES ©

Top: A sign outside a Heurigen

Bottom: Schnitzel (p50)

Mittagessen (lunch) Another meal locals rarely skip, lunch is often a soup or salad followed by a main course. Standard hours are 11.30am to 2.30pm.

Kaffee und Kuchen (coffee and cake) The exception to not snacking between mealtimes is this three o'clock ritual. Indulge at a local *Konditorei* (cake shop) or coffee house.

Apéritif The trend for predinner drinks is on the rise. The pavement terrace tipple of choice? Aperol spritz.

Abendessen (dinner) Late-night city dining aside, Austrians tend to eat somewhat earlier than their European counterparts, with kitchens open from 7pm to 9pm or 9.30pm. Many places have a *Kleine Karte* (snack menu) outside of these hours.

Where to Eat

Beisln/Gasthäuser Rural inns often with wood-panelled, homely interiors and menus packed with *gutbürgerliche Küche* (home cooking) – *Tafelspitz*, schnitzel, goulash and the like.

Brauereien Many microbreweries and brewpubs serve meaty grub, too. Their beer gardens are popular gathering spots in summer.

Cafes These can range from bakery-cafes for a quick coffee and sandwich to all-organic delis and *Eiscafés*, or ice-cream parlours.

Heurigen Going strong since medieval times, Austria's cosy wine taverns are often identified by a *Busch'n* (green wreath or branch) hanging over the door.

Imbiss Any kind of snack or takeaway joint, the most famous being the *Würstelstand* (sausage stand).

Kaffeehäuser Vienna's 'living rooms' are not only famous for their delectable tortes, cakes and arm-long coffee menus. Many also serve inexpensive breakfasts, lunches and snacks around the clock.

Konditoreien Traditional cake shop cafes; many do a sideline in confectionery.

Neo-Beisln New-wave *Beisln* often with retro-cool decor and a creative, market-fresh take on Austrian classics. Typically found in the cities (especially Vienna).

Restaurants Cover a broad spectrum, from pizzeria bites to Michelin-starred finery.

Menu Decoder

Degustationsmenü Gourmet tasting menu

Hauptspeise Main course – fish, meat or *vegetarisch* (vegetarian)

Kindermenü Two- or three-course kids' menu; sometimes includes a soft drink

Laktosefrei/Glutenfrei Lactose-/gluten-free

Mittagstisch/Mittagsmenü Fixed lunch menu; usually two courses, with a soup or salad followed by a main

Nachtisch Dessert, sometimes followed by coffee or a glass of schnapps

Speisekarte À la carte menu

Tagesteller Good-value dish of the day; generally only served at lunchtime

Vorspeise Starter, appetiser

Weinkarte Wine list

Etiquette

Table reservations Booking is highly advisable to snag a table at popular and top-end restaurants, especially in peak season. Call around a week in advance.

Menus English menus are not a given, though you'll often find them in city hotspots like Salzburg and Vienna and in ski resorts. If in doubt, there's usually a waiter/waitress who can translate.

Bon appétit Dining with a group of Austrians? It's polite to wish them *guten Appetit* or *Mahlzeit* before digging in.

Water You can try your luck by asking for complimentary tap water *(Leitungswasser)*, but it's not really the done thing, especially in upmarket places. Go local and order *stilles* (still) or *prickelndes* (sparkling) *Mineralwasser* (mineral water).

Dress Smart casual is the way to go in fancier establishments, where the locals dress up for dinner. In more relaxed places, jeans, trainers (sneakers) and T-shirts are fine.

Paying *Zahlen, bitte* or *die Rechnung, bitte* are the magic words if you want to pay.

Tipping Around 10% is customary if you were satisfied with the service. Add the bill and tip together and hand it over to the waiter/waitress by saying *stimmt so* (keep the change).

Regions at a Glance

Vienna

Art & Architecture
Music
Drinking in Style

Imperial Palaces & Galleries

Palaces, churches and art spaces such as the Hofburg, Schloss Schönbrunn, Schloss Belvedere, Stephansdom, the MuseumsQuartier and Albertina make it literally impossible to turn a corner in Austria's capital without bumping into an architectural or artistic masterpiece.

Classical Music Highs

Listen to the music of Mozart at palatial venues across town, visit Mozart's former home, embrace decadence and operatic greats at the Staatsoper or head to the Klangforum where the up-and-coming composers perform.

Coffee Houses & Characterful Bars

Viennese coffee houses are legendary: sip, read, pause in palatial surrounds like Café Gloriette or at hip modern renditions such as Vollpension. Grab a cocktail in Secessionist architect Adolf Loos' minuscule bar or visit a *Heuriger* (wine tavern).

p58

Lower Austria & Burgenland

Food
Culture
Outdoor Activities

Local Produce

The Wachau region of the Danube Valley has top-class restaurants and local produce such as beef, cheeses and Waldviertel poppy seed, whereas Burgenland around the Neusiedler See is famous for its increasingly impressive wines, and *Heurigen*, where nothing beats a glass of Austria's finest to wash down a cold platter.

Cultural Highs

Stift Melk in the Wachau region is the monarch among abbeys, Schloss Grafenegg is a top-class venue for outdoor music and opera, Krems and Schloss Schallaburg host great exhibitions, and Eisenstadt has its splendid Schloss Esterházy.

Cycling & Water Sports

The most popular cycling path in Lower Austria is along the Danube River in the beautiful Wachau region. For lakeside cycling and watersports, don't miss the Neusiedler See in Burgenland.

p122

Upper Austria

Culture
Architecture
Great Outdoors

Avant-Garde Arts

Linz' strikingly lit Ars Electronica Center propels visitors into the future with robotic wizardry and virtual voyages, while the rectangular Lentos gallery hosts cutting-edge art exhibitions. Modern art and sculpture also hang out in the Landesgalerie.

Historic Abbeys & Churches

Kremsmünster's Benedictine abbey and St Florian's baroque Augustinian abbey hide a rich stash of ecclesiastical treasures. Linz has the neo-Gothic Neuer Dom and opulent Alter Dom, while Kefermarkt is known for the Gothic altar in its church.

Country Escapes

Rolling countryside is scattered with storybook towns like Steyr and spa retreats like Bad Hall. Off-the-grid farmstays in the Mühlviertel and Traunviertel offer total peace. Hike in the little-known limestone wilderness of the Nationalpark Kalkalpen.

p159

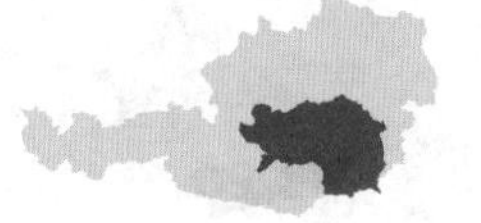

Styria

Culture
Outdoor Pursuits
Wine

Cultural Graz

Famous for its festivals throughout the year, the capital, Graz, makes up for its small size with some big cultural hits and an ensemble of top-rated museums, including Schloss Eggenberg.

Hiking, Biking & Skiing

Hiking trails abound in Styria – some easy, others challenging – and good hikes and mountain-bike rides can be had in the cleaved valleys of the remote Nationalpark Gesäuse, or in the more popular Schladming area. Here, the mountains soar to dizzying heights and the pistes rev to life in winter.

Vineyards & Wine Roads

The wine at restaurant tables often hails from the vineyards hugging the slopes on the nearby Slovenian border. Tangy riesling whites and full-bodied pinot reds are complemented by some cracking restaurants on the south Styrian wine roads.

p179

The Salzkammergut

Lakes
Outdoor Pursuits
Natural Highs

Lake Swimming

With its contrast of soaring mountains and deep lakes nestled in steeply walled valleys, the Salzkammergut is the best place to slip into lake waters. Some of these are cold – very cold – but others such as the Hallstätter See, the Wolfgangsee or Mondsee are perfect for challenging open-water swimming or quick dips.

Hiking, Cycling & Skiing

Hallstatt and Obertraun are terrific bases for lakeside hiking, forays into the heights of the Dachstein mountains – don't miss the 5 Fingers – and winter ski rambles. The cycling is superb in the Salzkammergut, too – both the mountain variety and easier touring.

Salt Mines & Ice Caves

Go in search of the 'white gold' that gives the region its name at Hallstatt's showcase salt mines. Or delve into a subzero world of glittering ice at the Dachstein caves.

p207

Salzburg & Salzburgerland

High Culture
Natural Wonders
Drinking in History

Palaces & Spas

Salzburg's regal Residenz, the magnificent baroque *Altstadt* and the Festung Hohensalzburg are cultural highlights. The city hosts the renowned Salzburg Festival, whereas Bad Gastein is famous for its radon-laced springs.

Ice Caves & Waterfalls

Hikers are captivated by the Tennengebirge's landscapes. Underground lies Eisriesenwelt, the world's largest accessible ice caves, near the Liechtensteinklamm gorge. Hohe Tauern National Park is a 'greatest hits' of alpine scenery, with glaciers, 3000m peaks and 380m-high Krimmler Wasserfälle.

Coffee Houses & Brewpubs

Cake comes with a dollop of history at grand coffee houses like Bazar and Sacher. Swing over to monastery-run brewery Augustiner Bräustübl or the cavernous StieglKeller for a 365-day taste of Oktoberfest.

p226

Carinthia

Lakes
Winter Sports
Cycling

Lake Swimming

The Wörthersee is a summer playground for the rich, the famous and the rest of us. This is warm in summer and convenient to Klagenfurt, but those who like their waters cooler can head for Weissensee, Austria's highest alpine swimming lake.

Top Slopes

At the far-flung but popular Nassfeld ski field near Hermagor, skiers take the 6km-long Millennium-Express cable car up to the slopes for some top skiing. Nordic skiing, ski hikes and ice skating are also excellent, especially in some of the province's rugged and remote regions.

Mountain Biking

Eleven kilometres downhill on one mighty run – mountain biking is a favourite pastime in Carinthia, but so too is touring on the trails and routes around Hermagor, Weissensee or outside Villach.

p269

Tyrol & Vorarlberg

Skiing
Outdoor Activities
History & Heritage

Star Slopes

Tyrol has Austria's finest slopes – quite some feat in this starkly mountainous country. Alpine resorts like St Anton am Arlberg, Kitzbühel, Mayrhofen and Ischgl excel in downhill, off-piste and upbeat après-ski. Seefeld has cross-country runs of Olympic fame.

High-Level Hiking & Cycling

Tyrol has some of the most scenic alpine hiking and cycling in Austria. Summer calls high-altitude walkers and mountain bikers to the valleys and peaks of the ruggedly beautiful Zillertal, Ötztal and Patznauntal. In Vorarlberg, cyclists and beach-goers descend on glittering Bodensee.

Palaces & Dairies

Palatial Hofburg, Renaissance Schloss Ambras and galleries of Old Masters beckon in Innsbruck. In Vorarlberg, soak up the back-to-nature feel in the rolling dairy country of the Bregenzerwald, sprinkled with farmstays and chocolate-box villages like Schwarzenberg.

p290

On the Road

Vienna

01 / POP 1,888,776

Includes ➡

Best Places to Eat

➡ Steirereck im Stadtpark (p106)

➡ Lingenhel (p106)

➡ Plachutta (p104)

➡ Griechenbeisl (p103)

Best Places to Stay

➡ Grand Ferdinand Hotel (p98)

➡ Magdas (p100)

➡ Grätzlhotel (p100)

➡ DO & CO (p98)

Why Go?

With its baroque streetscapes, rambling imperial palaces, winding cobbled lanes, extraordinary art-filled museums, grand *Kaffeehäuser* (coffee houses) and cosy wood-panelled *Beisln* (bistro pubs) dishing up hearty portions of *Wiener Schnitzel* (breaded veal cutlet), *Tafelspitz* (prime boiled beef) and goulash – as well as a musical heritage that includes Mozart, Haydn, Beethoven, Schubert, Strauss, Brahms and Mahler – the Austrian capital is steeped in history. Yet it's also at the cutting edge of design, architecture, contemporary art, and new directions in drinking and dining.

Not only is this a city that holds on to its traditions, it also incorporates them in everything from high-fashion *Dirndls* (women's traditional dress) through to sweets made from resurrected recipes, third-wave coffee served at inspired neo-retro cafes, and a thriving contemporary music scene. Vienna's past is alive in its present, and, by extension, its future.

When to Go

➡ Vienna has such a strong range of sights and activities that any time – summer or winter – is a good time to go.

➡ July, August and holidays such as Easter, Christmas and New Year are the most crowded – be sure to book accommodation well ahead if you're travelling at these times.

➡ Easter markets in the two weeks or so leading up to Easter herald the arrival of spring.

➡ While crowds are down in spring and autumn, weather can be changeable.

➡ In summer catch some rays on the Danube at summer beach bars.

➡ In December go ice skating in front of the *Rathaus* (town hall) or sip *Glühwein* (mulled wine) at one of the capital's atmospheric Christmas markets.

History

A key Roman outpost, then the hub of the Holy Roman Empire and the last bastion of the Occident against Ottoman Turks, Vienna experienced a creative explosion of high culture from the 18th century. Wars, the abolition of the monarchy, uprising and Austro-fascism followed before the city reemerged in the mid-20th century as the capital of a modern Austrian state.

Sights

Vienna's magnificent series of boulevards, the Ringstrasse, encircles the Innere Stadt (city centre), with many of the city's most famous sights situated on or within it, including the monumental Hofburg palace complex. The soaring Stephansdom (p67) cathedral marks the Innere Stadt's heart. Just outside the Ringstrasse are exceptional museums including the Kunsthistorisches Museum Vienna (p74) and the ensemble making up the MuseumsQuartier (p73), while attractions further afield include the sumptuous palaces Schloss Schönbrunn (p90) and Schloss Belvedere (p84), and the woodlands and meadows of the Prater (p89), topped by Vienna's iconic Ferris wheel, the Riesenrad (p89).

The Hofburg & Around

★Hofburg — PALACE

(Imperial Palace; Map p68; ☎01-533 75 70; www.hofburg-wien.at; 01, Michaelerkuppel; D, 1, 2, 71 Burgring, U Herrengasse) Nothing symbolises Austria's resplendent cultural heritage more than its Hofburg, home base of the Habsburgs from 1273 to 1918. The oldest section is the 13th-century **Schweizerhof** (Swiss Courtyard), named after the Swiss guards who protected its precincts. The Renaissance **Swiss Gate** dates from 1553. The courtyard adjoins a larger courtyard, **In der Burg**, with a monument to Emperor Franz II adorning its centre. The palace now houses the Austrian president's offices, the preserved Kaiserappartements and a raft of museums.

The Hofburg owes its size and architectural diversity to plain old one-upmanship; new sections were added by the new rulers, including the early baroque **Leopold Wing**, the 16th-century **Amalia Wing**, the 18th-century **Imperial Chancery Wing** and the Gothic **Burgkapelle** (Royal Chapel).

See also palace tour on p66.

★Kaiserappartements — PALACE

(Imperial Apartments; Map p68; ☎01-533 7570; www.hofburg-wien.at; 01, Michaelerplatz; adult/child €15/9, incl admission to the Sisi Museum and the Silberkammer; incl guided tour €18/10.50; 9am-6pm Jul & Aug, to 5.30pm Sep-Jun; D, 1, 2, 71 Burgring, U Herrengasse) The Kaiserappartements, once the official living quarters of Franz Joseph I and Empress Elisabeth, are dazzling in their chandelier-lit opulence. The **Sisi Museum** is devoted to Austria's most beloved empress, with a strong focus on the clothing and jewellery of Austria's monarch. Multilingual audio guides are included in the admission price. Guided tours (English available) take in the Kaiserappartements, the Sisi Museum and the **Silberkammer** (Imperial Silver Collection), whose largest silver service caters for 140 dinner guests.

★Kaiserliche Schatzkammer — MUSEUM

(Imperial Treasury; Map p68; ☎01-525 24-0; www.kaiserliche-schatzkammer.at; 01, Schweizerhof; adult/child €12/free; 9am-5.30pm Wed-Mon; U Herrengasse) The Hofburg's Kaiserliche Schatzkammer contains secular and ecclesiastical treasures (including devotional images and altars, particularly from the baroque era) of priceless value and splendour – the sheer wealth of this collection of crown jewels is staggering. As you walk through the rooms you'll see magnificent treasures such as a golden rose, diamond-studded Turkish sabres, a 2680-carat Colombian emerald and, the highlight of the treasury, the imperial crown.

★Neue Burg Museums — MUSEUM

(Map p68; ☎01-525 24-0; www.khm.at; 01, Heldenplatz, Hofburg; adult/child €16/free; 10am-6pm Fri-Wed, to 9pm Thu Jun-Aug, closed Wed Sep-May; D, 1, 2, 71 Burgring, U Herrengasse, Museumsquartier) Three Neue Burg museums can be visited on one ticket. The **Sammlung Alter Musik Instrumente** (Collection of Ancient Musical Instruments) contains a wonderfully diverse array of instruments. The **Ephesos Museum** features artefacts unearthed during Austrian archaeologists' excavations at Ephesus in Turkey between 1895 and 1906. The **Hofjägd und Rüstkammer** (Arms and Armour) museum contains armour dating mainly from the 15th and 16th centuries. Admission includes the Kunsthistorisches Museum Vienna (p74) and all three Neue Burg museums. Audio guides cost €5.

Vienna Highlights

1 Schloss Schönbrunn (p90) Savouring the bombastic pomp and the views from its gardens.

2 Kunsthistorisches Museum Vienna (p74) Plunging into the artistic vortex of the Museum of Art History, a whirl of Habsburg treasures from Egyptian tombs to priceless paintings.

3 Schloss Belvedere (p84) Drawing breath as you ramble through lavishly frescoed apartments, sculpture-strewn gardens and a gallery home to Klimt's masterworks.

4 Stephansdom (p67) Scaling Vienna's glorious Gothic cathedral and beloved icon.

5 MuseumsQuartier (p73) Hanging out in this art space spiked with bars and alive with urban energy.

6 Riesenrad (p89) Spinning around in the giant rectangles dangling off Vienna's oversized Ferris wheel, in the Prater outdoor area.

7 Café Sperl (p109) Slowing down and indulging in cake and coffee at one of Vienna's legendary coffee houses.

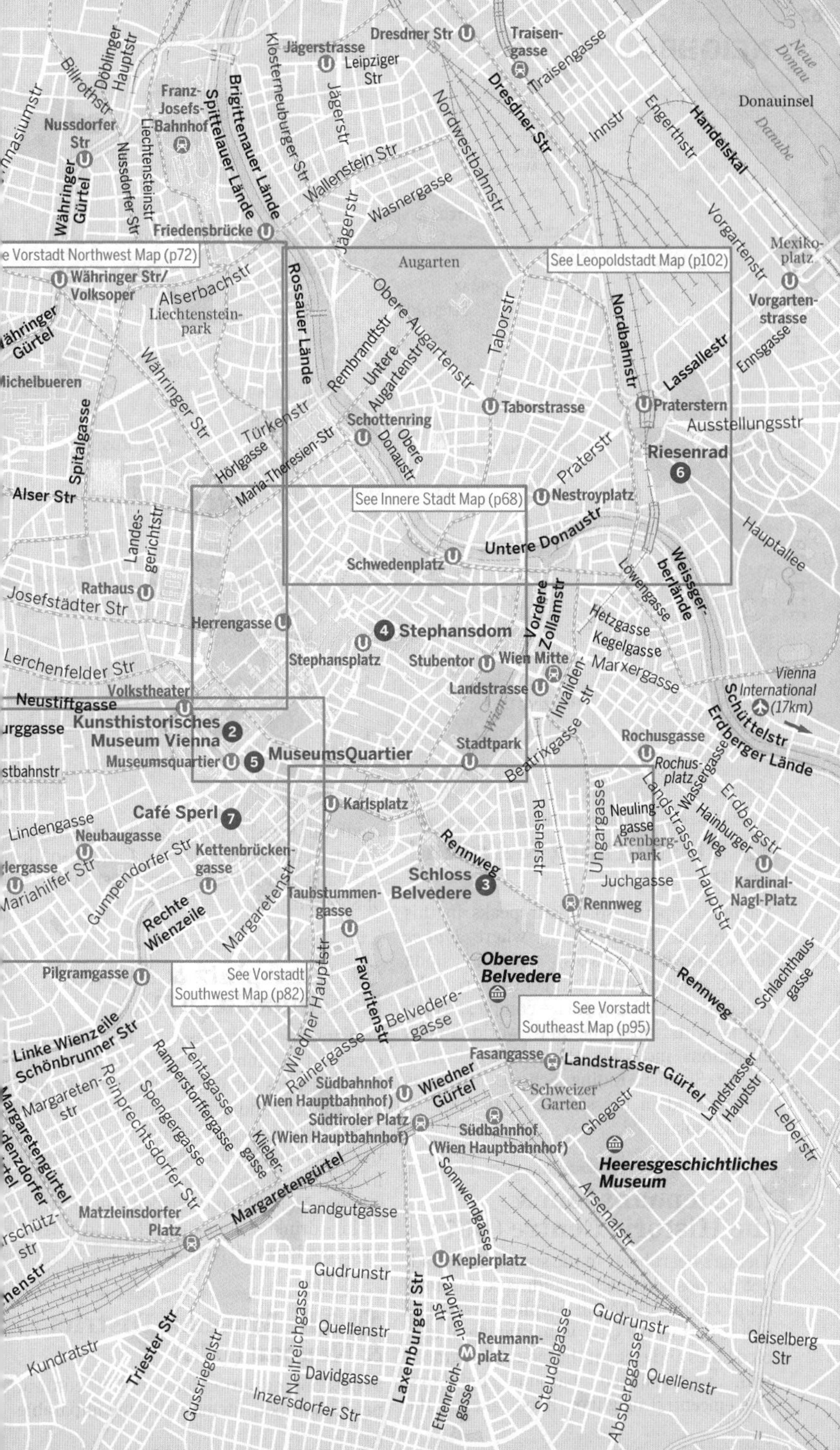

Dresdner Str
Jägerstrasse
Leipziger Str
Traisengasse
Neue Donau
Donauinsel
Danube
Döblinger Hauptstr
Billrothstr
Franz-Josefs-Bahnhof
Nussdorfer Str
Währinger Gürtel
Spittelauer Lände
Brigittenauer Lände
Klosterneuburger Str
Jägerstr
Nordwestbahnstr
Dresdner Str
Traisengasse
Innstr
Engerthstr
Handelskai
Liechtensteinstr
Nussdorfer Str
Wallenstein Str
Wasnergasse
Friedensbrücke
Vorgartenstr
Mexikoplatz
See Vorstadt Northwest Map (p72)
Augarten
See Leopoldstadt Map (p102)
Währinger Str/ Volksoper
Alserbachstr
Liechtensteinpark
Rossauer Lände
Obere Augartenstr
Taborstr
Nordbahnstr
Vorgartenstrasse
Ennsgasse
Währinger Gürtel
Rembrandtstr
Untere Augartenstr
Lassallestr
Michelbueren
Währinger Str
Taborstrasse
Praterstern
Ausstellungsstr
Spitalgasse
Türkenstr
Schottenring
Obere Donaustr
Hörlgasse
Maria-Theresien-Str
Riesenrad
6
Praterstr
Alser Str
See Innere Stadt Map (p68)
Nestroyplatz
Landesgerichtstr
Untere Donaustr
Hauptallee
Schwedenplatz
Weissgerberlände
Löwengasse
Rathaus
Josefstädter Str
Herrengasse
4 Stephansdom
Vordere Zollamstr
Hetzgasse
Kegelgasse
Stephansplatz
Stubentor
Wien Mitte
Marxergasse
Lerchenfelder Str
Landstrasse
Invalidenstr
Vienna International (17km)
Volkstheater
Neustiftgasse
Schüttelstr
Kunsthistorisches Museum Vienna
2
Wien
Erdberger Lände
Burggasse
Rochusgasse
Beatrixgasse
MuseumsQuartier
Museumsquartier
5
Stadtpark
Rochusplatz
Westbahnstr
Wassergasse
Ungargasse
Landstrasser Hauptstr
Karlsplatz
Reisnerstr
Neulinggasse
Arenbergpark
Hainburger Weg
Erdbergstr
Café Sperl
7
Lindengasse
Neubaugasse
Rennweg
Kettenbrückengasse
Gumpendorfer Str
Mariahilfer Str
Schloss Belvedere
3
Juchgasse
Kardinal-Nagl-Platz
Taubstummengasse
Rennweg
Rechte Wienzeile
Margaretenstr
Oberes Belvedere
Schlachthausgasse
Pilgramgasse
See Vorstadt Southwest Map (p82)
Wiedner Hauptstr
Favoritenstr
Belvederegasse
See Vorstadt Southeast Map (p95)
Rennweg
Linke Wienzeile
Schönbrunner Str
Rampersdorffergasse
Zentagasse
Rainergasse
Fasangasse
Landstrasser Gürtel
Margaretenstr
Reinprechtsdorfer Str
Spengergasse
Südbahnhof (Wien Hauptbahnhof)
Wiedner Gürtel
Schweizer Garten
Landstrasser Hauptstr
Leberstr
Margaretengürtel
Kliebergasse
Südtiroler Platz (Wien Hauptbahnhof)
Südbahnhof (Wien Hauptbahnhof)
Ghegastr
Heeresgeschichtliches Museum
Margaretengürtel
Landgutgasse
Sonnwendgasse
Arsenalstr
Matzleinsdorfer Platz
Keplerplatz
Gudrunstr
Neilreichgasse
Laxenburger Str
Favoritenstr
Quellenstr
Reumannplatz
Steudelgasse
Gudrunstr
Absberggasse
Quellenstr
Geiselberg Str
Kundratstr
Triester Str
Gussriegelstr
Davidgasse
Inzersdorfer Str
Ettenreichgasse

NEIGHBOURHOODS AT A GLANCE

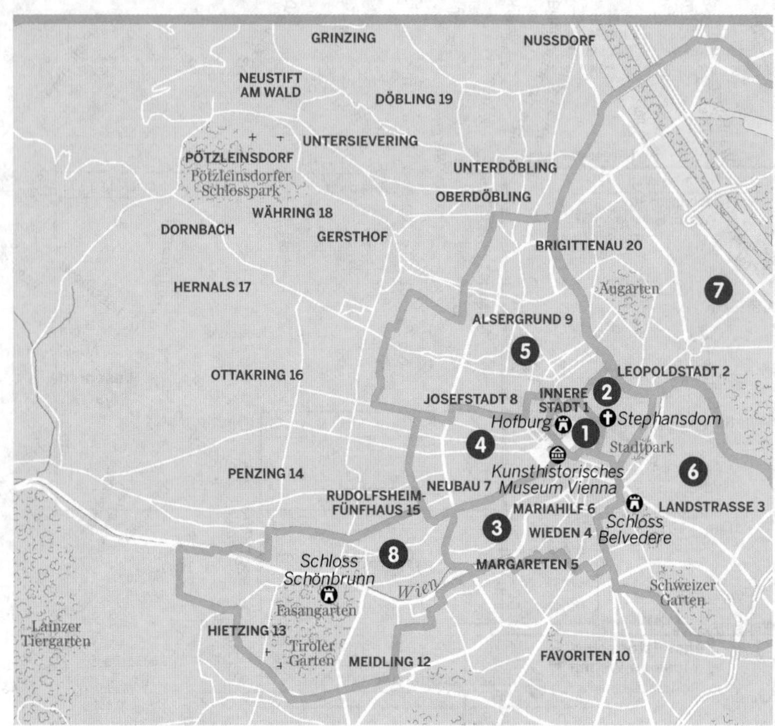

❶ The Hofburg & Around (p59)

Vienna's imperial splendour peaks in this part of the Innere Stadt, where *Fiaker* (horse-drawn carriages) rumble along curved, cobbled streets. Its centrepiece is the magnificent Hofburg palace complex, which brims with museums and world-famous attractions including the waltzing horses of the Spanish Riding School. Museums also abound in the streets north towards Stephansplatz.

❷ Stephansdom & the Historic Centre (p67)

Vienna's heart beats in the streets surrounding its most distinctive landmark, the towering Gothic cathedral Stephansdom. The oldest part of the city, with a tangle of cobbled lanes and elegant thoroughfares graced with pastel-shaded baroque buildings, this epicentral neighbourhood takes in the medieval Jewish quarter in the northwest, the stretch down to Danube Canal's southern bank and the areas northeast and east of Stephansplatz.

❸ Karlsplatz & Around Naschmarkt (p71)

Fringing the Ringstrasse in the southeast corner of the Innere Stadt, this neighbourhood includes the city's sublime Staatsoper opera house, and extends south beyond Vienna's enormous market and food paradise, the Naschmarkt, into some of the city's most interesting *Vorstädte* (inner suburbs): Margareten, Mariahilf and Wieden. There's great eating, drinking and nightlife, and a truly Viennese *Vorstadt* character.

❹ The Museum District & Neubau (p73)

Showstopping attractions in this cultural neighbourhood include the incomparable

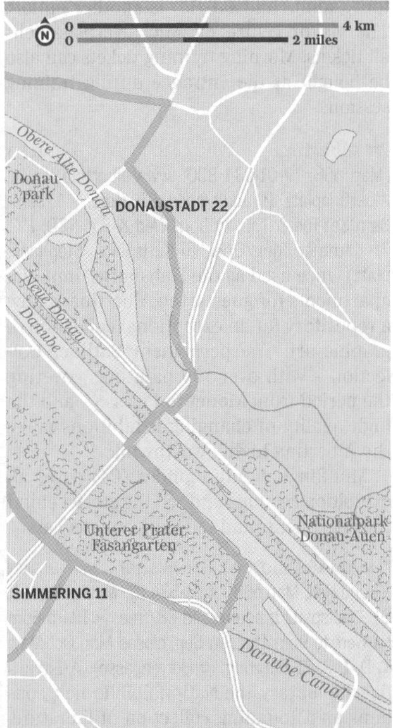

Kunsthistorisches Museum Vienna (Museum of Art History), packed with old masters; the former imperial stables comprising the MuseumsQuartier's cache of museums, cafes, restaurants, bars and performance spaces; and the Renaissance-style Burgtheater, where premieres have included works by Mozart and Beethoven. To the west, hip Neubau is an incubator for Vienna's vibrant fashion, art and design scenes.

5 Alsergrund & the University District (p81)

Bookended by one of Europe's biggest universities, Alsergrund (9th district) counts Gustav Mahler and Karl Kraus among its former residents. In this cultured neighbourhood of churches and leafy squares, Franz Schubert notated and Sigmund Freud navigated the unconscious. The gravitas of such history seeps through its cavern-like cafes and bars.

Alsergrund spills south into Josefstadt (8th district), which moves to a similar groove and is scattered with low-key restaurants, cafes and shops. Further west lies the ethnically diverse Ottakring (16th district) and a new Viennese generation bestowing a gentrifying glow on Yppenplatz.

6 Schloss Belvedere to the Canal (p83)

The crowning glory of this art-rammed neighbourhood is Schloss Belvedere and its gardens, which can easily absorb an entire day of your time. Spread out across the neighbourhood, other crowd-pullers include the kaleidoscopic KunstHausWien, as well as museums homing in on everything from military history to art fakes. Some cracking cafes, delis and restaurants have popped up recently, making breaks between sightseeing all the more pleasurable.

7 Prater & East of the Danube (p89)

Welcome to one of Vienna's hippest and most happening districts – Leopoldstadt, the city's Jewish quarter. The neighbourhood has discovered newfound cool of late, with graffiti art, beach bars by the Danube Canal (Donaukanal), and a raft of enticing new boutiques, restaurants, galleries and edgy cafes hiding down its still-sleepy backstreets. Its centrepiece is the Prater where the Riesenrad (Ferris wheel) of *The Third Man* fame spins amid all the fun of the fair. Further east is the Danube River and Danube Island recreation area.

8 Schloss Schönbrunn & Around (p89)

The sun-yellow Schloss Schönbrunn dominates this well-to-do residential neighbourhood and the tight original village streets outside the palace's walls give way to a relatively suburban feel. The ensemble of suburbs adjoining the neighbourhood to the north – Fünfhaus, Rudolfsheim and Ottakring – also make for an interesting taste of everyday Viennese life.

Haus der Geschichte Österreich MUSEUM
(hdgö; House of Austrian History; Map p68; ☎01-534 10-805; www.hdgoe.at; 01, Heldenplatz, Neue Burg, Hofburg; adult/child €8/free; ⏰10am-6pm Tue, Wed & Fri-Sun, to 9pm Thu; 🚊D, 1, 2, 71 Burgring) Opened within the Hofburg in 2018, Austria's first museum of contemporary history spans the period from the mid-19th century to the present. Exhibits, documents, photos and films cover political, cultural, economic and social history, including the First Republic's 1918 founding, Nazi occupation, migrations, protest culture, democracy and science. The evolving collection includes, for example, a football used in a 2018 friendly match against Germany, which Austria won. English-language guided tours lasting 1½ hours depart at 3pm on Saturdays (adult/child €4/free).

★ **Spanish Riding School** PERFORMING ARTS
(Spanische Hofreitschule; Map p68; ☎01-533 90 31-0; www.srs.at; 01, Michaelerplatz 1; tickets €27-225, standing room €13; ⏰hours vary; UHerrengasse) Vienna's world-famous Spanish Riding School is truly reminiscent of the imperial Habsburg era. This equestrian show is performed by Lipizzaner stallions formerly kept at an imperial stud established at Lipizza (hence the name). The graceful stallions perform an equine ballet to a classical-music program while the audience watches from pillared balconies – or the cheaper standing area – and chandeliers shimmer above.

There are many different ways to see the Lipizzaner. Performances are the top-shelf variant, and for seats at these you will need to book several months in advance. The website lists performance dates and you can order tickets online. As a rule of thumb, performances are at 11am on Sunday from mid-February to June and mid-August to December, with frequent additional performances on Saturday and occasionally other days of the week.

For standing-room tickets, book at least one month in advance. During the summer break, it hosts special 'Piber meets Vienna' performances (€13 to €48). Visitors to the *Morgenarbeit* (morning training sessions; adult/child €15/7.50, 10am to noon Tuesday to Friday mid-August to June) can drop in for part of a session.

One-hour guided tours (adult/child €18/9; 2pm, 3pm and 4pm Tuesday to Sunday), held in English and German, take you into the performance hall, stables and other facilities. A combined morning training and tour (adult/child €31/15) is another option. The visitor centre on Michaelerplatz sells all tickets. Morning training tickets can also be bought at the entrance during training sessions.

★ **Albertina** GALLERY
(Map p68; ☎01-534 830; www.albertina.at; 01, Albertinaplatz 1; adult/child €16/free; ⏰10am-6pm Sat-Tue & Thu, to 9pm Wed & Fri; 🚊D, 1, 2, 71 Kärntner Ring/Oper, UKarlsplatz, Stephansplatz) Once used as the Habsburgs' imperial apartments for guests, the Albertina is now a repository for an exceptional collection of graphic art. The permanent Batliner Collection – with over 100 paintings covering the period from Monet to Picasso – and the high quality of changing exhibitions make the Albertina highly worthwhile.

Multilingual audio guides (€4) cover all exhibition sections and tell the story behind the apartments and the works on display.

Nationalbibliothek Prunksaal LIBRARY
(Grand Hall; Map p68; ☎01-534 10; www.onb.ac.at; 01, Josefsplatz 1; adult/child €8/free; ⏰10am-6pm Fri-Wed, to 9pm Thu Jun-Sep, closed Mon Oct-May; 🚊D, 1, 2, 71 Burgring, UHerrengasse) Austria's flagship library, the Nationalbibliothek, contains an astounding collection of literature, maps, globes of the world and other cultural relics; its highlight, though, is the **Prunksaal** (Grand Hall), a majestic baroque hall built between 1723 and 1726, with a fresco by Daniel Gran. Commissioned by Karl VI (whose statue is under the central dome), the library holds some 200,000 leather-bound scholarly tomes. Audio guides cost €3.

Rare volumes, mostly from the 15th century, are stored within glass cabinets, opened to beautifully illustrated pages of text. The exquisite fresco by Gran depicts the emperor's apotheosis.

A combined ticket that includes the **Esperantomuseum** (Map p68; ☎01-534 10-425; www.onb.ac.at; 01, Herrengasse 9, ground fl; adult/child €5/free; ⏰10am-6pm Tue, Wed & Fri-Sun, to 9pm Thu; 🚊D, 1, 2, 71 Burgring, UHerrengasse), **Globenmuseum** (Map p68; ☎01-534 10-425; www.onb.ac.at; 01, Herrengasse 9, 1st fl; adult/child €5/free; ⏰10am-6pm Tue, Wed & Fri-Sun, to 9pm Thu; 🚊D, 1, 2, 71 Burgring, UHerrengasse) and **Papyrusmuseum** (Map p68; ☎01-534 10-425; www.onb.ac.at; 01, Heldenplatz; adult/child €5/free; ⏰10am-6pm Tue, Wed & Fri-Sun, to 9pm Thu; 🚊D, 1, 2, 71 Burgring,

VIENNA IN...

Two Days

Jump on tram 1 at Schwedenplatz (platform B) and circle the **Ringstrasse** for a brief but rewarding informal tour of the boulevard's buildings. Get out at Kärntner Strasse and wander towards the heart of the city, where the glorious **Gothic Stephansdom** (p67) awaits. Make your way to the **Hofburg** (p59) before crossing the Ringstrasse to the **Kunsthistorisches Museum Vienna** (p74), home to a breathtaking art collection. Recharge your batteries at one of the many Innere Stadt restaurants before attending a performance at the **Staatsoper** (p114).

On day two visit imperial palace **Schönbrunn** (p90) before heading to the **MuseumsQuartier** (p73), a vast ensemble of museums, cafes, restaurants and bars inside former imperial stables. Take an early dinner at Vienna's celebrated **Naschmarkt** (p104), then cross the city for a ride on the **Riesenrad** (p89) Ferris wheel. Finish the day with local food and a drink in a traditional *Beisl*.

Four Days

Start the third day with an exploration of the **Schloss Belvedere** (p84), an unequalled baroque palace. See Klimt's sumptuous *Beethoven Frieze* in the **Secession** (p71), then end the night in one of the city's lively bars.

The fourth day is best dedicated to your special interests. You might focus on music, dropping into the Sammlung Alter Musik Instrumente in the **Neue Burg Museums** (p59), repose in a coffee house, then spend the afternoon visiting the **Haus der Musik** (p67) or **Mozarthaus** (p70). After that, cap off the visit with music in a club or in a classical venue like the **Musikverein** (p114) to experience the music of Beethoven or Mozart where it was originally played.

Ⓤ Herrengasse) as well as the Literaturmuseum (p70) costs €16.50.

Museum der Illusionen MUSEUM
(Museum of Illusions; Map p68; ☎01-532 22 55; www.museumderillusionen.at; Wallnerstrasse 4; adult/child €12/8; ⏲10am-8pm; Ⓤ Herrengasse) Vienna's mind-bending Museum of Illusions, opened in 2017, confounds your senses through its 40 interactive optical illusions and installations. They include stereograms (3D pictures with 'hidden' objects), tilted rooms, mirages, a giant kaleidoscope, an infinity room, and a tunnel with spinning images on the walls that make it impossible to keep your balance (despite the central walkway not moving). It's fascinating for kids and adults alike.

Burggarten GARDENS
(Castle Garden; Map p68; www.bundesgaerten.at; 01, Burgring; ⏲6am-10pm Apr-Oct, 7.30am-5.30pm Nov-Mar; 🚋D, 1, 2, 71 Burgring, Ⓤ Museumsquartier) FREE Tucked behind the Hofburg, the Burggarten is a leafy oasis amid the hustle and bustle of the Ringstrasse and Innere Stadt. The marble statue of Mozart is the park's most famous tenant, but there's also a statue of Franz Joseph in military garb. Lining the Innere Stadt side of the Burggarten is the **Schmetterlinghaus** (Butterfly House; Map p68; ☎01-533 85 70; www.schmetterlinghaus.at; 01, Burggarten; adult/child €7/4; ⏲10am-4.45pm Mon-Fri, to 6.15pm Sat & Sun Apr-Oct, to 3.45pm Nov-Mar; 🚋D, 1, 2, 71 Burgring, Ⓤ Karlsplatz) and the beautiful *Jugendstil* (art nouveau) **Palmenhaus** (Map p68; ☎01-533 10 33; www.palmenhaus.at; 01, Burggarten; ⏲10am-midnight Mon-Fri, from 9am Sat, 9am-11pm Sun; 🚋D, 1, 2, 71 Burgring, Ⓤ Karlsplatz, Museumsquartier) bar.

Kapuzinergruft MAUSOLEUM
(Kaisergruft; Map p68; www.kapuzinergruft.com; 01, Tegethoffstrasse 2; adult/child €7.50/4.50, incl guided tour €10.50/7.50; ⏲10am-6pm Fri-Wed, from 9am Thu; Ⓤ Stephansplatz) Beneath the **Kapuzinerkirche** (Church of the Capuchin Friars; Map p68; www.erzdioezese-wien.at; ⏲8am-6pm; Ⓤ Stephansplatz) The Kapuzinergruft is the final resting place of most of the Habsburg royal family, including Empress Elisabeth. Opened in 1633, it was instigated by Empress Anna (1585–1618). Her body and that of her husband, Emperor Matthias (1557–1619), were the first entombed in this impressive vault. A total of 149 Habsburgs are buried here, including 12 emperors and 19 empresses. Only three Habsburgs are

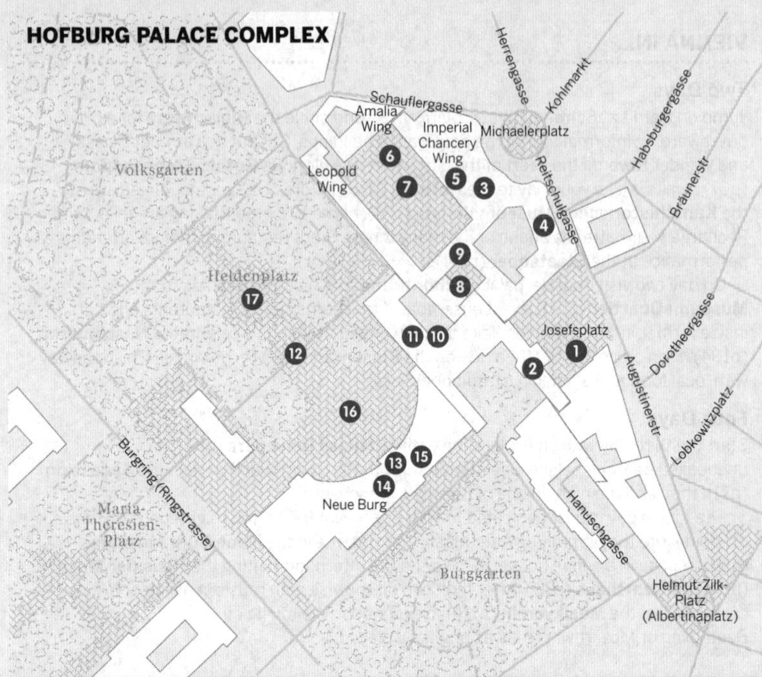

Palace Tour
The Hofburg

LENGTH ONE HOUR TO ONE DAY

The Hofburg is a jigsaw puzzle of monumental buildings. For the full effect, enter from Michaelerplatz, as the monarchs used to. First, though, admire the pretty square just to the south, 1 **Josefsplatz**, named after Joseph II and adorned with the equestrian monument to Emperor Josef II. Josefsplatz also serves as the entrance to the 2 **Nationalbibliothek Prunksaal** (p64).

Pass through the 3 **Michaelertor** and neobaroque Michaelertrakt. The Michaelerplatz side of the building is lined with statues of Hercules and evocative fountains depicting the Power of the Land and the Power of the Sea. On the left of the hall is the 4 **Spanish Riding School** (p64) and its visitor centre, on the right the 5 **Kaiserappartements** (p59).

Straight ahead, you reach the large courtyard 6 **In der Burg**, with a monument to 7 **Emperor Franz I**, the last in a long line of Holy Roman emperors after Napoleon brought about the collapse of the Reich in 1806.

The oldest part of the Hofburg is the 8 **Schweizerhof** (Swiss Courtyard), named after the Swiss guards who used to protect its precincts. This is reached via the Renaissance 9 **Swiss Gate**, which dates from 1553. The 13th-century courtyard gives access to the 10 **Burgkapelle** (p114) and the 11 **Schatzkammer** (p59).

Straight ahead is 12 **Heldenplatz** (Hero's Sq) and the 13 **Neue Burg**, built between the second half of the 19th century and WWI. The Neue Burg houses the three 14 **Neue Burg Museums** (p59) as well as the 15 **Haus der Geschichte Österreich** (p64). The balcony is where Hitler addressed a rally during his 1938 visit to Vienna after the *Anschluss*. Facing each other on Heldenplatz are monuments to 16 **Prince Eugene of Savoy** (closest to the Neue Burg) and 17 **Archduke Karl** (Charles of Austria). Pass through the Äusseres Burgtor (Outer Palace Gate) to the Ringstrasse.

notable through their absence here. The last emperor, Karl I, was buried in exile in Madeira, and Marie Antoinette (daughter of Maria Theresia) still lies in Paris. The third is Duc de Reichstadt, son of Napoleon's second wife, Marie Louise, who was transferred to Paris as a publicity stunt by the Nazis in 1940. Also on display are rows of urns containing the internal organs of the Habsburgs. One of the many privileges of being a Habsburg was to be dismembered and dispersed after death: their hearts are in the Augustinerkirche in the Hofburg and the rest of their bodies are in the Kapuzinergruft.

English-language, hour-long guided tours take place at 3.30pm Wednesday to Saturday.

Augustinerkirche CHURCH
(Augustinian Church; Map p68; ☎01-533 70 99; http://augustinerkirche.augustiner.at; 01, Augustinerstrasse 3; ⏰7.30am-5.30pm Mon, Wed & Fri, to 7.15pm Tue & Thu, 9am-7.30pm Sat & Sun; Ⓤ Stephansplatz, Herrengasse) The real highlight of the 14th-century Gothic Augustinerkirche is not its pale, vaulted interior but the Herzgruft, a crypt containing silver urns with the hearts of 54 Habsburg rulers. The crypt is open on Sunday after the 11am Mass (celebrated with a full choir and orchestra) – turn up around 12.30pm. The church hosts regular evening classical music concerts; check schedules at http://hochamt.augustiner.at. Sometimes on a visit you can catch the choir practising. Many Habsburg weddings took place here.

Michaelerplatz Roman Ruins ROMAN SITE
(Map p68; 01, Michaelerplatz; Ⓤ Herrengasse) FREE Ringed by gorgeous architecture, Michaelerplatz is centred on Roman ruins that are reputed to have been a brothel for soldiers. This cobblestoned circular 'square' is a major pick-up point for tours by *Fiaker* (horse-drawn carriages).

Stephansdom & the Historic Centre

★Stephansdom CATHEDRAL
(St Stephen's Cathedral; Map p68; www.stephanskirche.at; 01, Stephansplatz; adult/child incl audio guide or guided tour €6/2.50, all-inclusive ticket €14.90/3.90; ⏰9-11.30am & 1-4.30pm Mon-Sat, 1-4.30pm Sun, English tours 10.30am Mon-Sat; Ⓤ Stephansplatz) Vienna's Gothic masterpiece Stephansdom – or Steffl (Little Stephan), as it's ironically nicknamed – is Vienna's pride and joy. A church has stood here since the 12th century, and reminders of this are the Romanesque **Riesentor** (Giant Gate) and **Heidentürme** (Towers of the Heathens). From outside, the first thing that will strike you is the glorious tiled roof, with its dazzling row of chevrons and Austrian eagle. Inside, the magnificent Gothic stone pulpit presides over the main nave, fashioned in 1515 by Anton Pilgrim.

One often-overlooked detail is the pulpit's handrail, which has salamanders and toads fighting an eternal battle of good versus evil up and down its length. The baroque high altar, at the very far end of the main nave, shows the stoning of St Stephen. The chancel to its left has the winged **Wiener Neustadt altarpiece**, dating from 1447; the right chancel has the Renaissance red-marble **tomb of Friedrich III**. Under his guidance the city became a bishopric (and the church a cathedral) in 1469. Note that the main nave is closed during Mass (held up to eight times a day).

The all-inclusive ticket covers the audio-guided tour, a **catacomb tour** (Catacombs; Map p68; ☎01-515 523 054; 30min tour adult/child €6/2.50; ⏰tours 10-11.30am & 1.30-4.30pm Mon-Sat, 1.30-4.30pm Sun), the **south tower** (Südturm; Map p68; adult/child €5/2; ⏰9am-5.30pm) and the **north tower** (Boomer Bell; Map p68; adult/child €6/2.50; ⏰9am-5.30pm). Guided tours lasting 30 minutes include a visit to the nave.

★Haus der Musik MUSEUM
(Map p68; www.hausdermusik.com; 01, Seilerstätte 30; adult/child €13/6, incl Mozarthaus Vienna €18/8; ⏰10am-10pm; 👪; 🚋2, 71 Schwarzenbergplatz, Ⓤ Karlsplatz) The Haus der Musik explains the world of sound and music to adults and children alike (in English and German) in an amusing and interactive way. Exhibits are spread over four floors and cover everything about how sound is created, from Vienna's Philharmonic Orchestra to street noises. The staircase between floors acts as a piano; its glassed-in ground-floor courtyard hosts musical events. After 8pm, adult admission drops to €6.50.

Innere Stadt

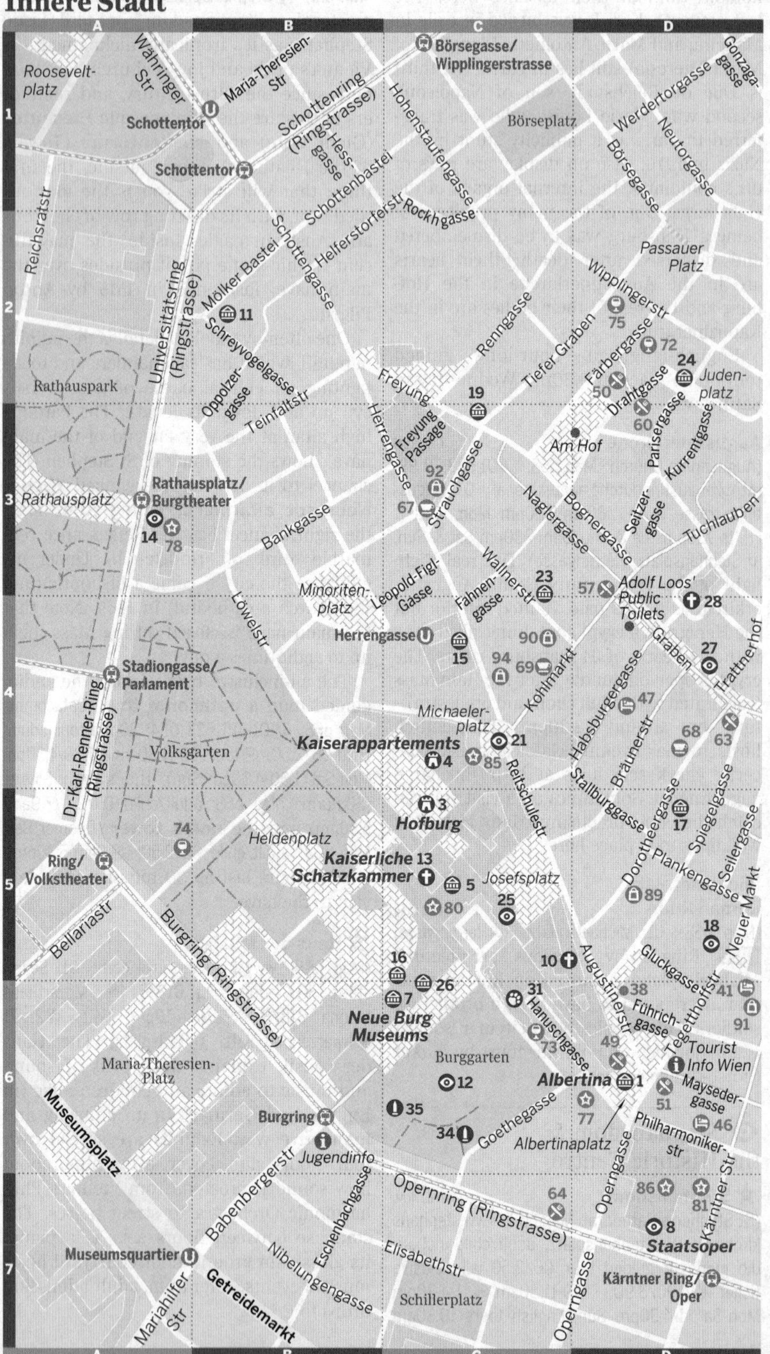

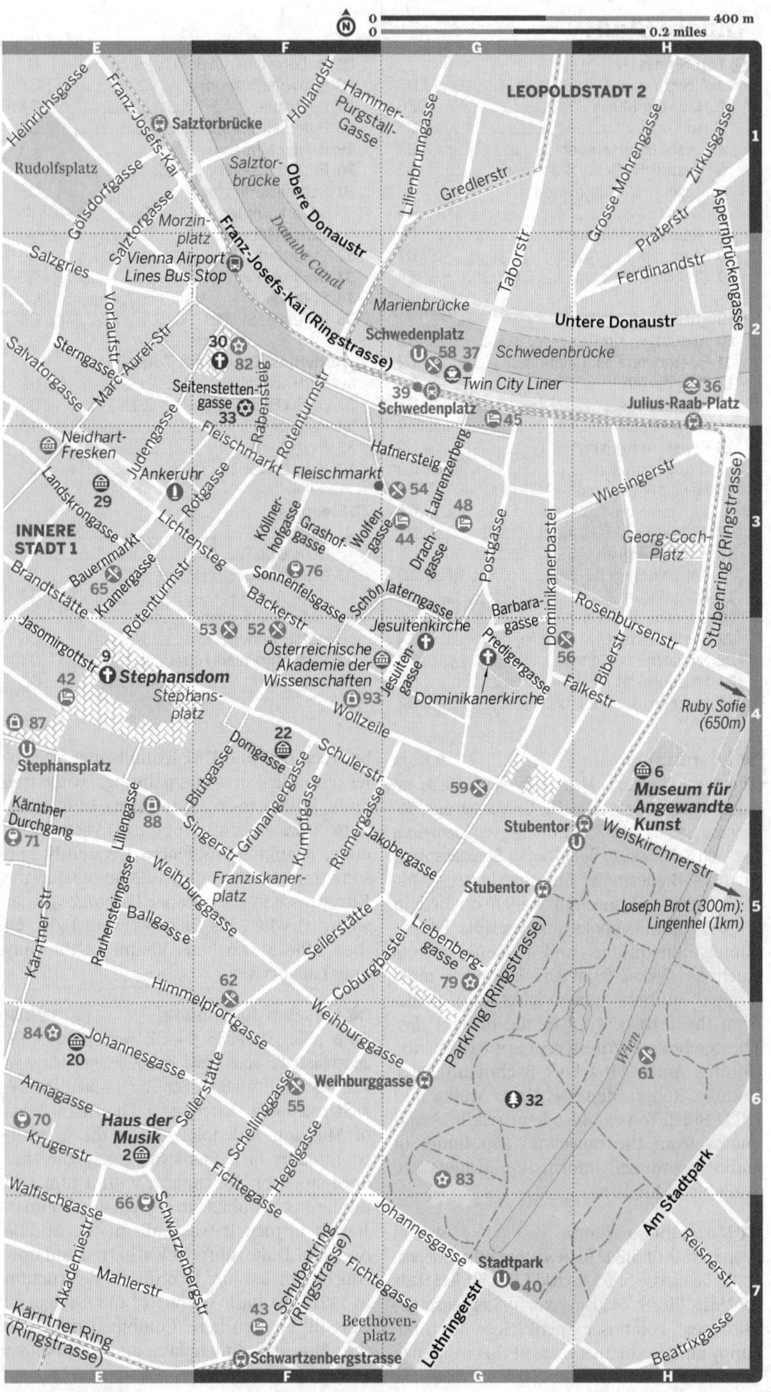

0 400 m
0 0.2 miles
LEOPOLDSTADT 2
Salztorbrücke
Heinrichsgasse
Franz-Josefs-Kai
Hollandstr
Hammer-Purgstall-Gasse
Lilienbrunngasse
Grosse Mohrengasse
Zirkusgasse
Rudolfsplatz
Salztorbrücke
Obere Donaustr
Gredlerstr
Gölsdorfgasse
Salztorgasse
Morzinplatz
Franz-Josefs-Kai (Ringstrasse)
Danube Canal
Taborstr
Praterstr
Asperbrückengasse
Salzgries
Vienna Airport Lines Bus Stop
Ferdinandstr
Marienbrücke
Untere Donaustr
Vorlaufstr
Schwedenplatz
Sterngasse
Marc-Aurel-Str
Salvatorgasse
Schwedenbrücke
Twin City Liner
Seitenstettengasse
Rabensteig
Schwedenplatz
Julius-Raab-Platz
Neidhart-Fresken
Judengasse
Fleischmarkt
Rotenturmstr
Hafnersteig
Laurenzerberg
Ankeruhr
Rotgasse
Fleischmarkt
Wiesingerstr
Landskrongasse
Köllnerhofgasse
Grashofgasse
Wolfengasse
Drachgasse
Postgasse
Dominikanerbastei
Stubenring (Ringstrasse)
INNERE STADT 1
Lichtensteg
Georg-Coch-Platz
Bauernmarkt
Kramergasse
Sonnenfelsgasse
Schönlaterngasse
Brandstätte
Rotenturmstr
Bäckerstr
Barbaragasse
Rosenbursenstr
Jesuitenkirche
Jasomirgottstr
Österreichische Akademie der Wissenschaften
Jesuitengasse
Predigergasse
Stephansdom
Biberstr
Stephansplatz
Dominikanerkirche
Falkestr
Ruby Sofie (650m)
Wollzeile
Stephansplatz
Domgasse
Schulerstr
Museum für Angewandte Kunst
Blutgasse
Grünangergasse
Kumpfgasse
Riemergasse
Liliengasse
Kärntner Durchgang
Stubentor
Weiskirchnerstr
Singerstr
Jakobergasse
Weihburggasse
Franziskanerplatz
Stubentor
Rauhensteingasse
Ballgasse
Seilerstätte
Joseph Brot (300m); Lingenhel (1km)
Kärntner Str
Liebenberggasse
Coburgbastei
Himmelpfortgasse
Parkring (Ringstrasse)
Johannesgasse
Weihburggasse
Wien
Annagasse
Seilerstätte
Weihburggasse
Schellinggasse
Haus der Musik
Krugerstr
Hegelgasse
Am Stadtpark
Fichtegasse
Walfischgasse
Schwarzenbergstr
Johannesgasse
Akademiestr
Reisnerstr
Mahlerstr
Schubertring (Ringstrasse)
Stadtpark
Fichtegasse
Kärntner Ring (Ringstrasse)
Beethovenplatz
Lothringerstr
Beatrixgasse
Schwartzenbergstrasse
VIENNA

Innere Stadt

Top Sights
1 Albertina D6
2 Haus der Musik E6
3 Hofburg C5
4 Kaiserappartements C4
5 Kaiserliche Schatzkammer C5
6 Museum für Angewandte Kunst H4
7 Neue Burg Museums C6
8 Staatsoper D7
9 Stephansdom E4

Sights
10 Augustinerkirche C5
11 Beethoven Pasqualatihaus B2
12 Burggarten C6
13 Burgkapelle C5
14 Burgtheater A3
15 Esperantomuseum C4
Globenmuseum (see 15)
16 Haus der Geschichte Österreich C5
17 Jüdisches Museum D5
18 Kapuzinergruft D5
Kapuzinerkirche (see 18)
19 Kunstforum C3
20 Literaturmuseum E6
21 Michaelerplatz Roman Ruins C4
22 Mozarthaus Vienna F4
23 Museum der Illusionen C3
24 Museum Judenplatz D2
25 Nationalbibliothek Prunksaal C5
26 Papyrusmuseum C6
27 Pestsäule D4
28 Peterskirche D4
29 Römer Museum E3
30 Ruprechtskirche F2
31 Schmetterlinghaus C6
Silberkammer (see 4)
Sisi Museum (see 4)
32 Stadtpark G6
33 Stadttempel F2
34 Statue of Franz Josef C6
35 Statue of Mozart C6

Activities, Courses & Tours
36 Badeschiff H2
37 DDSG Blue Danube G2
38 Redbus City Tours D6
39 Ring Tram G2
40 Vienna Walks & Talks G7

Sleeping
41 Aviano D6
42 DO & CO E4
43 Grand Ferdinand Hotel F7
44 Hotel Austria G3
45 Hotel Capricorno G2
46 Hotel Sacher D6
47 Pertschy Palais Hotel D4
48 Ruby Lissi G3

★**Literaturmuseum** MUSEUM
(Literature Museum; Map p68; www.onb.ac.at/museen/literaturmuseum; 01, Grillparzerhaus, Johannesgasse 6; adult/child €7/free; 10am-6pm Tue, Wed & Fri-Sun, to 9pm Thu; U Stephansplatz) An 1844 Biedermeier building houses Austria's literature museum, which opened in 2015. It contains books, manuscripts, letters, photos, illustrations and personal effects (such as desks) from the country's most seminal authors, playwrights and poets, from the 18th century to the present day. The celebrated writers represented include Günther Anders, Ingeborg Bachmann, Peter Handke, Robert Menasse, Herta Müller and Hilde Spiel. You can also hear readings and quotes from the museum's 550 hours of audio recordings. Information leaflets are available in English.

★**Mozarthaus Vienna** MUSEUM
(Map p68; 01-512 17 91; www.mozarthausvienna.at; 01, Domgasse 5; adult/child €11/4.50, incl Haus der Musik €18/8; 10am-7pm; U Stephansplatz) The great composer spent close to three happy and productive years at this residence between 1784 and 1787. Exhibits include copies of music scores and paintings, while free audio guides re-create the story of his time here. Mozart spent a total of 11 years in Vienna, changing residences frequently and sometimes setting up his home outside the Ringstrasse in the cheaper *Vorstädte* (inner suburbs) when his finances were tight. Of these, the Mozarthaus Vienna is the only one that survives.

★**Museum Judenplatz** MUSEUM
(Map p68; 01-535 04 31; www.jmw.at; 01, Judenplatz 8; adult/child incl Jüdisches Museum €12/free; 10am-6pm Sun-Thu, to 5pm Fri; ; U Stephansplatz, Herrengasse) The main focus of Museum Judenplatz is on the excavated remains of a medieval synagogue that once stood on Judenplatz, with a film and numerous exhibits to elucidate Vienna's Jewish history. It was built in the Middle Ages, but Duke Albrecht V's 'hatred and misconception' led him to order its destruction in 1421. The basic outline of the synagogue can still be seen here. Combined tickets to the Museum Judenplatz and **Jüdisches**

Museum (Jewish Museum; Map p68; ☎01-535 04 31; www.jmw.at; 01, Dorotheergasse 11; adult/child incl Museum Judenplatz €12/free; ⏰10am-6pm Sun-Fri; Ⓤ Stephansplatz) are valid for four days.

Stadttempel SYNAGOGUE

(Map p68; ☎01-531 04-0; www.ikg-wien.at; 01, Seitenstettengasse 4; tours adult/child €5/free; ⏰guided tours 11.30am & 2pm Mon-Thu Apr-Oct, 11.30am Mon-Thu Nov-Mar; 🚊1, 2 Schwedenplatz, Ⓤ Schwedenplatz) Vienna's main synagogue, seating 500 people, was completed in 1826, after *Toleranzpatent* reforms by Joseph II in the 1780s granted rights to Vienna's Jews to practise their religion. This paved the way for improved standing for Jews and brought a rise in fortunes. Built in an exquisite Biedermeier style, the main prayer room is flanked by 12 ionic columns and is capped by a cupola. Security is tight; you'll need your passport to gain entry.

When it was built, only Catholic places of worship were allowed to front major streets, so the Stadttempel was built inside an apartment complex – because of this, it was the sole survivor of 94 synagogues in Vienna following the November Pogroms of 1938.

Römer Museum MUSEUM

(Map p68; ☎01-535 56 06; www.wienmuseum.at; 01, Hoher Markt 3; adult/child €7/free; ⏰9am-6pm Tue-Sun; Ⓤ Stephansplatz) This small expanse of Roman ruins dating from the 1st to the 5th century CE is thought to be part of the officers' quarters of the Roman legion camp at Vindobona. You can see crumbled walls, tiled floors and a small exhibition of artefacts here, along with a 3D film with English subtitles.

Karlsplatz & Around Naschmarkt

★ Secession MUSEUM

(Map p82; www.secession.at; 01, Friedrichstrasse 12; adult/child €9.50/6; ⏰10am-6pm Tue-Sun; Ⓤ Karlsplatz) In 1897, 19 progressive artists swam away from the mainstream Künstlerhaus artistic establishment to form the *Wiener Secession* (Vienna Secession). Among their

Vorstadt Northwest

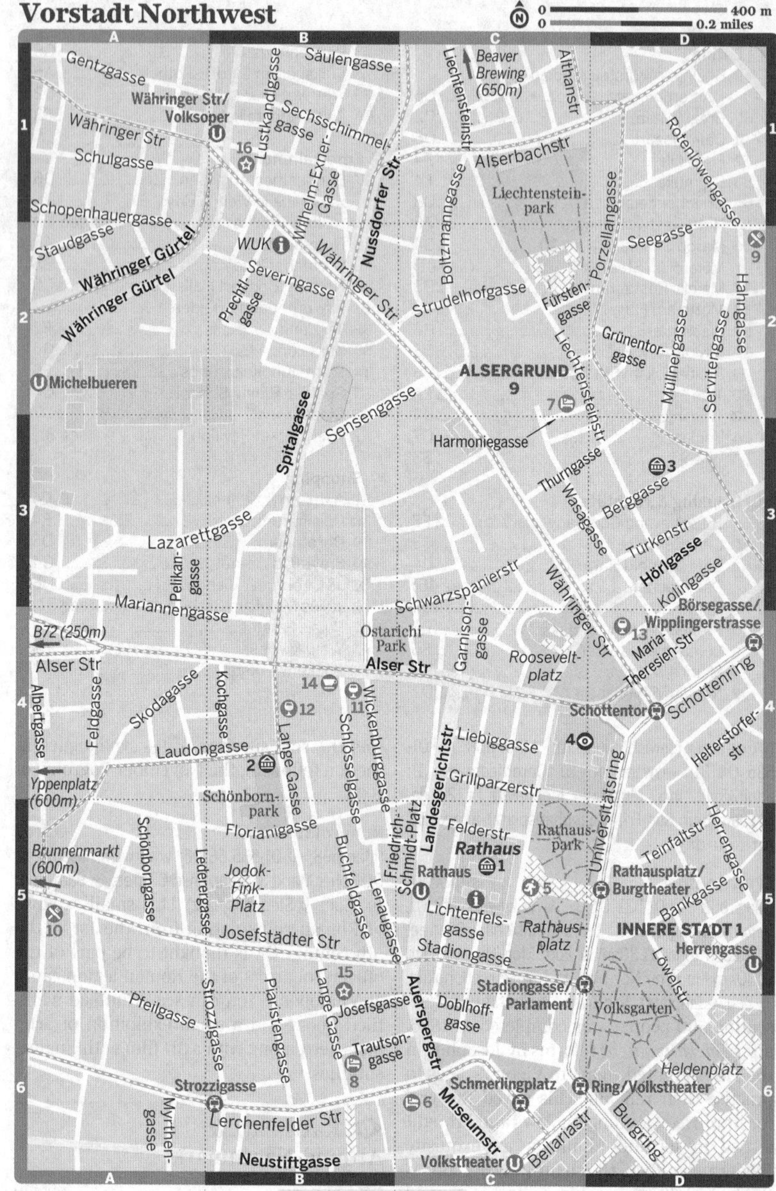

number were Gustav Klimt, Josef Hoffmann, Kolo Moser and Joseph Olbrich. Olbrich designed the new exhibition centre of the Secessionists, which combined sparse functionality with stylistic motifs. Its biggest draw is Klimt's exquisitely gilded *Beethoven Frieze*. One-hour guided tours in English (€3) take place at 11am Saturday. An audio guide costs €3.

★Karlskirche CHURCH

(St Charles Church; Map p95; www.karlskirche.at; 04, Karlsplatz; adult/child €8/4; ⏲9am-6pm

Vorstadt Northwest

Mon-Sat, noon-7pm Sun; U Karlsplatz) Built between 1716 and 1739, after a vow by Karl VI at the end of the 1713 plague, Vienna's finest baroque church rises at the southeast corner of Resselpark. It was designed and commenced by Johann Bernhard Fischer von Erlach and completed by his son Joseph. The huge elliptical copper **dome** reaches 72m; the highlight is the lift to the cupola (included in admission) for a close-up view of the intricate frescos by Johann Michael Rottmayr.

Akademie der Bildenden Künste MUSEUM
(Academy of Fine Arts; Map p82; www.akbild.ac.at; 01, Schillerplatz 3; adult/child €12/free; 10am-6pm Wed-Mon; D, 1, 2 Kärntner Ring/Oper, U Museumsquartier, Karlsplatz) Founded in 1692, the Akademie der Bildenden Künste is an often-underrated art space. Its gallery concentrates on Flemish, Dutch and German painters, including important figures such as Hieronymus Bosch, Rembrandt, Van Dyck, Rubens, Titian, Francesco Guardi and Lucas Cranach the Elder. The supreme highlight is Bosch's macabre triptych of *The Last Judgment* altarpiece (1504–08), depicting the banishment of Adam and Eve on the left panel, and the horror of Hell in the middle and right panels. Audio guides cost €2.

The Museum District & Neubau

Kunsthistorisches Museum Vienna MUSEUM
See p74.

★ **MuseumsQuartier** MUSEUM
(Museum Quarter; MQ; Map p82; 01-523 58 81; www.mqw.at; 07, Museumsplatz; 49 Volkstheater, U Museumsquartier, Volkstheater) The MuseumsQuartier is a remarkable ensemble of museums, cafes, restaurants and bars inside former imperial stables designed by Fischer von Erlach. This breeding ground of Viennese cultural life is the perfect place to hang out and watch or meet people on warm evenings. With over 90,000 sq metres of exhibition space – including the **Leopold Museum** (Map p82; www.leopoldmuseum.org; adult/child €14/10; 10am-6pm Fri-Wed, to 9pm Thu Jun-Aug, closed Mon Sep-May), **MUMOK** (Museum Moderner Kunst, Museum of Modern Art; Map p82; www.mumok.at; adult/child €12/free; 2-7pm Mon, 10am-7pm Tue, Wed & Fri-Sun, 10am-9pm Thu), **Kunsthalle Wien** (Arts Hall; Map p82; 01-521 890; www.kunsthallewien.at; adult/child €8/free; 11am-7pm Tue, Wed & Fri-Sun, to 9pm Thu), **Architekturzentrum** (Vienna Architecture Centre; Map p82; 01-522 31 15; www.azw.at; adult/child €9/2.50; architecture centre 10am-7pm, library 10am-5.30pm Mon, Wed & Fri, to 7pm Sat & Sun) and **Zoom** (Map p82; 01-524 79 08; www.kindermuseum.at; exhibition adult/child €6/free, activities child €5-7, accompanying adult €6; Tue-Sun) – the complex is one of the world's most ambitious cultural hubs.

If you're planning on visiting several museums, combined tickets are available from the **MQ Point** (01-523 58 81; www.mqw.at; 07, Museumsplatz 1; 10am-7pm; U Museumsquartier, Volkstheater). The **MQ Station Ticket** (€32) includes entry into every museum (Zoom only has a reduction) and a

(Continued on page 80)

TOP SIGHT
KUNSTHISTORISCHES MUSEUM VIENNA

The Habsburgs built many bombastic palaces but, artistically speaking, the Kunsthistorisches Museum Vienna is their magnum opus. Occupying a neoclassical building as sumptuous as the art it contains, the museum takes you on a time-travel treasure hunt – from classical Rome to Egypt and the Renaissance. If your time's limited, skip straight to the old master paintings in the Picture Gallery.

Picture Gallery

The Kunsthistorisches Museum Vienna's vast Gemäldegalerie (Picture Gallery) is by far and away the most impressive of its collections. Devote at least an hour or two to exploring its feast of old masters.

Dutch, Flemish & German Painting

First up is the **German Renaissance**, where Lucas Cranach the Elder stages an appearance with engaging Genesis tableaux like *Paradise* (1530) and *Fall of Man* (aka *Adam and Eve;* 1537). The key focus, though, is the prized Dürer collection. Dürer's powerful compositions, sophisticated use of light and deep feeling for his subjects shine through in masterful pieces like *Portrait of a Venetian Lady* (1505), the spirit-soaring *Adoration of the Trinity* (1511) and the macabre *Martyrdom of the Ten Thousand* (1508).

Rubens throws you in the deep end of **Flemish baroque** painting next, with paintings rich in Counter-Reformation themes and mythological symbolism. The monumental *Miracles of St Francis Xavier* (1617), which used to hang

DON'T MISS

- Dutch Golden Age paintings
- Italian, Spanish & French collection
- Kunstkammer
- Offering Chapel of Ka-ni-nisut

PRACTICALITIES

- KHM, Museum of Art History
- Map p82
- www.khm.at
- 01, Maria-Theresien-Platz
- adult/child incl Neue Burg museums €16/free
- ⏲10am-6pm Fri-Wed, to 9pm Thu Jun-Aug, closed Mon Sep-May
- U Museumsquartier, Volkstheater

in Antwerp's Jesuit church, the celestial *Annunciation* (1610), the *Miracles of St Ignatius* (1615–20) and the *Triptych of St Ildefonso* (1630) all reveal the iridescent quality and linear clarity that underscored Rubens' style. Mythological masterworks move from the gory, snake-riddled *Medusa* (1617) to the ecstatic celebration of love in *Feast of Venus* (1636).

In 16th- and 17th-century **Dutch Golden Age** paintings, the desire to faithfully represent reality through an attentive eye for detail and compositional chiaroscuro is captured effortlessly in works by Rembrandt, Ruisdael and Vermeer. Rembrandt's perspicuous *Self-Portrait* (1652), showing the artist in a humble painter's smock, Ruisdael's palpable vision of nature in *The Large Forest* (1655) and Vermeer's seductively allegorical *The Art of Painting* (1665), showing Clio, Greek muse of history, in the diffused light of an artist's studio, are all emblematic of the age.

Keenly felt devotional works by Flemish baroque master **Van Dyck** include *The Vision of the Blessed Hermann Joseph* (1630), in room XXIII, in which the Virgin and kneeling monk are bathed in radiant light, and *Virgin and Child with Saints Rosalie, Peter and Paul* (1629), in room XIV. An entire room (X) is given over to the vivid depictions of Flemish life and landscapes by Flemish Renaissance painter **Pieter Bruegel the Elder**, alongside his biblical star attraction, *The Tower of Babel* (1563).

Italian, Spanish & French Painting

The first three rooms here are given over to key exponents of the **16th-century Venetian** style: Titian, Veronese and Tintoretto. High on your artistic agenda here should be Titian's *Nymph and Shepherd* (1570), elevating the pastoral to the mythological in its portrayal of the futile desire of the flute-playing shepherd for the beautiful maiden out of his reach. Veronese's dramatic depiction of the suicidal Roman heroine *Lucretia* (1583), with a dagger drawn to her chest, and Tintoretto's *Susanna and the Elders* (1556), watched by two lustful power brokers, are other highlights.

Devotion is central to Raphael's *Madonna of the Meadow* (1506) in room III, one of the true masterpieces of the **High Renaissance**, as it is to the *Madonna of the Rosary* (1607), a stirring Counter-Reformation altarpiece by **Italian baroque** artist Caravaggio in room V. Room VII is also a delight, with compelling works like Giuseppe Arcimboldo's anthropomorphic paintings inspired by the seasons and elements, such as fruit-filled *Summer* (1563), *Winter* (1563) and *Fire* (1566). Look out, too, for

GUIDED TOURS

For more insight, pick up a multilingual audio guide (€5) near the entrance. The KHM runs 30-minute guided tours in English (€4); tours of the Picture Gallery and Kunstkammer take place at 4pm on Sunday, and the Egyptian, Near Eastern and Antiquities collections at noon on Sunday. There are also regular guided tours in German. See www.khm.at for details.

As you climb the ornate main staircase of the Kunsthistorisches Museum Vienna, your gaze is drawn to the ever-decreasing circles of the cupola, and marble columns guide the eye to delicately frescoed vaults, roaring lions and Antonio Canova's mighty statue of Theseus Defeats the Centaur (1805). Austrian legends Hans Makart and the brothers Klimt have left their hallmark between the columns and above the arcades – the former with lunette paintings, the latter with gold-kissed depictions of women inspired by Greco-Roman and Egyptian art.

Venetian landscape painter Canaletto's *Schönbrunn* (1761), meticulously capturing the palace back in its imperial heyday.

Of the artists represented in the rooms dedicated to **Spanish, French and English** painting, the undoubted star is Spanish court-painter Velázquez. Particularly entrancing is his almost 3D portrait of *Infanta Margarita Teresa in a Blue Dress* (1651–73), in room XII, a vision of voluminous silk and eight-year-old innocence. English painter Sir Joshua Reynolds' studied *Portrait of a Young Lady* (c 1760–5) and French painter Jean-Marc Nattier the Younger's *Princess Maria Isabella of Parma* (1758) are both in room XIII.

Kunstkammer

Imagine the treasures you could buy with brimming coffers and the world at your fingertips. The Habsburgs did just that, filling their *Kunstkammer* (cabinet of art and curiosities) with an encyclopaedic collection of the rare and the precious: from narwhal-tusk cups to table holders encrusted with fossilised shark teeth. Its 20 themed rooms containing 2200 artworks open a fascinating window on the obsession with collecting curios in royal circles in Renaissance and baroque times.

The biggest crowd-puller here is Benvenuto Cellini's allegorical *Saliera* (salt cellar), room XXIX, commissioned by Francis I of France in 1540, which is exquisitely hand-crafted from rolled gold, ivory and enamel. Among the Kunstkammer's other top-drawer attractions are the wildly expressive, early-17th-century ivory sculpture *Furie* (Master of the Furies), the serenely beautiful *Krumauer Madonna* (1400), a masterpiece of the Bohemian Gothic style, and Gasparo Miseroni's lapis lazuli *Dragon Cup* (1570), a fiery beast glittering with gemstones.

Egyptian & Near Eastern Collection

Decipher the mysteries of Egyptian civilisations with a chronological romp through this miniature Giza of a ground-floor collection, beginning with **predynastic** and **Old Kingdom** treasures. Here the exceptionally well preserved **Offering Chapel of Ka-ni-nisut** spells out the life of the high-ranking 5th-dynasty official in reliefs and hieroglyphs. The Egyptian fondness for adornment finds expression in artefacts such as a monkey-shaped kohl container and fish-shaped make-up palette.

Stele, sacrificial altar slabs, jewellery boxes, sphinx busts and pharaoh statues bring to life the **Middle Kingdom** and **New Kingdom**. The Egyptian talent for craftsmanship shines in pieces like a turquoise ceramic hippo (2000 BCE) and the gold seal ring of Ramses X (1120 BCE). The **Late Period** dips into the land of the pharaohs, at a time when rule swung from Egypt to Persia. Scout out the 3000-year-old *Book of the Dead of Khonsu-mes,* the polychrome mummy board of Nes-pauti-taui and Canopic jars with lids shaped like monkey, falcon and jackal heads.

Stone sarcophagi, gilded mummy masks and busts of priests and princes transport you back to the **Ptolemaic** and **Greco-Roman** period. In the **Near Eastern** collection, the representation of a prowling lion from Babylon's triumphal Ishtar Gate (604–562 BCE) is the big attraction.

Greek & Roman Antiquities

This rich Greek and Roman repository reveals the imperial scope for collecting classical antiquities, with 2500 objects traversing three millennia from the Cypriot Bronze Age to early medieval times.

Cypriot and Mycenaean Art catapults you back to the dawn of Western civilisation, 2500 years ago. The big draw here is the precisely carved votive statue of a man wearing a finely pleated tunic. Among the muses, torsos and mythological

statuettes in **Greek Art** is a fragment from the Parthenon's northern frieze showing two bearded men. The arts flourished in **Hellenistic** times, evident in exhibits like the *Amazonian Sarcophagus,* engraved with warriors so vivid you can almost hear their battle cries. In **pre-Roman Italy**, look for sculptures of Athena, funerary crowns intricately wrought from gold, and a repoussé showing the Titans doing battle with the gods.

The sizeable **Roman** stash includes the 4th-century CE *Theseus Mosaic* from Salzburg, a polychrome, geometric marvel recounting the legend of Theseus. You'll also want to take in the captivating 3rd-century CE *Lion Hunt* relief and the 1st-century CE *Gemma Augustea,* a sardonyx bas-relief cameo. Early medieval showstoppers include the shimmering golden vessels from the **Treasure of Nagyszentmiklós**, unearthed in 1799 in what is now Romania.

Kunsthistorisches Museum Vienna Cocktails

Sipping a cocktail under the Kunsthistorisches Museum Vienna's dome, illuminated with dazzling projections, is unforgettable. The museum organises monthly Kunstschatzi cocktail evenings (7pm to 11pm Tuesday; €16, not including museum admission), during which DJs work the decks and the Picture Gallery remains open all evening. Check schedules and prebook online.

COIN COLLECTION

A piggy bank of gigantic Habsburg proportions, this coin collection covers three halls and three millennia on the 2nd floor (rooms I, II and III). The 2000 notes, coins and medallions on display are just a tiny fraction of the Kunsthistorisches Museum Vienna's 700,000-piece collection.

The coin collection's first hall presents medals of honour, first used in Renaissance Italy around 1400, and showcases gold and silver House of Habsburg wonders. The second hall travels through monetary time, from the birth of the coin in Lydia in the 7th century BCE to the 20th century. Look out for classical coins, like the stater embellished with a lion head, in circulation under Alyattes, King of Lydia (610–560 BCE), and Athenian coins featuring the goddess Athena and her owl symbol. The third hall stages one-off exhibitions.

Kunsthistorisches Museum Vienna

HALF-DAY TOUR OF THE HIGHLIGHTS

The Kunsthistorisches Museum Vienna's scale can seem daunting; this half-day itinerary will help you make the most of your visit.

Ascend the grand marble staircase, marvelling at the impact of Antonio Canova's *Theseus Slaying the Centaur*. Turn right into the Egyptian and Near Eastern Collection, where you can decipher the reliefs of the ❶ **Offering Chapel of Ka-ni-nisut** in room II. Skip through millennia to Ancient Rome, where the intricacy of the ❷ **Gemma Augustea Cameo** in room XVI is captivating. The other wing of this floor is devoted to the Kunstkammer Wien, hiding rarities such as Benvenuto Cellini's golden ❸ **Saliera** in room XXIX.

Head up a level to the Picture Gallery, a veritable orgy of Renaissance and baroque art. Moving into the East Wing brings you to Dutch, Flemish and German Painting, which starts with Dürer's uplifting

Gemma Augustea Cameo
Greek & Roman Antiquities, Room XVI
Possibly the handiwork of imperial gem-cutter Dioscurides, this sardonyx cameo from the 1st century CE shows in exquisite bas-relief the deification of Augustus, in the guise of Jupiter, who sits next to Roma. The defeated barbarians occupy the lower tier.

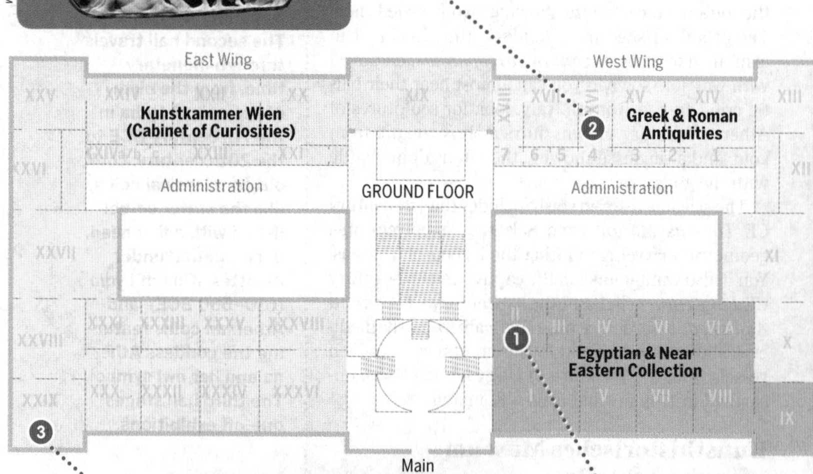

Saliera
Kunstkammer Wien, Room XXIX
Benvenuto Cellini's hand-wrought gold salt cellar (1543) is a dazzling allegorical portrayal of Sea and Earth, personified by Tellus and trident-bearing Neptune. They recline on a base showing the four winds, times of day and human activities.

Offering Chape of Ka-ni-nisu
Egyptian & Nea Eastern Collectior Room
Reliefs and hieroglyph depict the life of high ranking 5th-dynasty offici Ka-ni-nisut, together wit his wife, children an entourage of mortuar priests and servants This 4500-year-old tom chamber is a spectacul leap into the afterlif

❹ **Adoration of the Trinity** in room XV, takes in meaty Rubens and Rembrandt works en route, and climaxes with Pieter Bruegel the Elder's absorbingly detailed ❺ **The Tower of Babel** in room X. Allocate equal time to the Italian, Spanish and French masters in the halls opposite. Masterpieces including Raphael's ❻ **Madonna of the Meadow** in room 4, Caravaggio's merciful ❼ **Madonna of the Rosary** in room V and Giuseppe Arcimboldo's ❽ **Summer** in room 7 steal the show.

TOP TIPS

➡ Pick up an audio guide and a floor plan in the entrance hall to orient yourself.

➡ Skip to the front of the queue by booking your ticket online.

➡ Visit between 6pm and 9pm on Thursday for fewer crowds.

➡ Flash photography is not permitted.

The Tower of Babel
Dutch, Flemish & German Painting, Room X
The futile attempts of industrial souls to reach godly heights are magnified in the painstaking detail of Bruegel's *The Tower of Babel* (1563). Rome's Colosseum provided inspiration.

Madonna of the Meadow
Italian, Spanish & French Painting, Room 4
The Virgin Mary, pictured with infants Christ and St John the Baptist, has an almost iridescent quality in Raphael's seminal High Renaissance 1506 masterpiece, set against the backdrop of a Tuscan meadow.

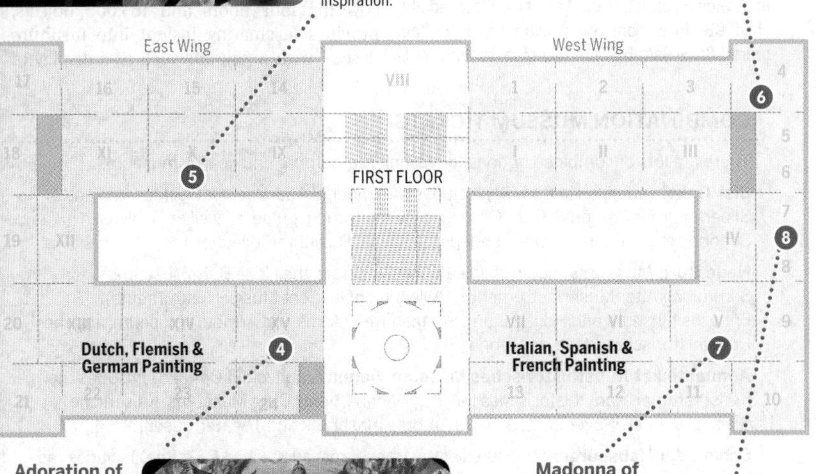

Adoration of the Trinity
Dutch, Flemish & German Painting, Room XV
Dürer's magnum-opus altarpiece was commissioned by Nuremberg merchant Matthäus Landauer in 1511. Angels, saints and earthly believers surround the Holy Trinity, while Dürer hides in the bottom right-hand corner.

Madonna of the Rosary
Italian, Spanish & French Painting, Room V
Caravaggio's trademark chiaroscuro style brings depth, richness and feeling to this 1607 masterpiece. Holding infant Jesus, the Madonna asks St Dominic to distribute rosaries to the barefooted poor who kneel before her.

Summer
Italian, Spanish & French Painting, Room 7
Italian court painter Giuseppe Arcimboldo's *Summer* (1563) was a hit with the Habsburgs. The most striking of his four seasons cycle, this masterwork celebrates seasonal abundance in the form of a portrait composed of fruit and vegetables.

30% discount on performances in the Tanzquartier Wien; the **MQ Type Ticket** (€26) gives admission into the Leopold Museum, MUMOK, Kunsthalle and reduced entry into Zoom, plus a 30% discount on the Tanzquartier Wien.

★Rathaus HISTORIC BUILDING

(City Hall; Map p72; ☎01-502 55; www.wien.gv.at; 01, Rathausplatz 1; ⏲tours 1pm Mon, Wed & Fri Sep-Jun, 1pm Mon-Fri Jul & Aug; 🚋D, 1, 2, 71 Rathausplatz/Burgtheater, Ⓤ Rathaus) FREE Vienna's neo-Gothic City Hall, completed in 1883 by Friedrich von Schmidt (who designed Cologne Cathedral) and modelled on Flemish city halls, with lacy stonework, pointed-arch windows and spindly turrets, is the highlight of the Ringstrasse boulevard's 19th-century architectural ensemble. Bronze statues of Joseph Lanner and Johann Strauss I stand in the fountain-filled **Rathauspark**. Free one-hour guided tours are in German; multilingual audio guides are also free.

★Naturhistorisches Museum MUSEUM

(Museum of Natural History; Map p82; www.nhm-wien.ac.at; 01, Maria-Theresien-Platz; adult/child €12/free, planetarium extra €5/3, rooftop tours €8; ⏲9am-6.30pm Thu-Mon, to 9pm Wed, rooftop tours in English 3pm Fri, Sat & Sun Apr-Dec, 3pm Sun Jan-Mar; Ⓤ Volkstheater) Four billion years of natural history are covered at Vienna's Naturhistorisches Museum. Among its minerals, fossils and dinosaur bones are exceptional finds like the teeny 25,000-year-old Venus of Willendorf and a meteorite collection of 1100 pieces. Audio guides cost €5.

The late-19th-century building, with its elaborately stuccoed, frescoed halls and cupola, is the mirror image of the Kunsthistorisches Museum Vienna (p74) opposite. Rooftop tours (children under 12 not allowed) take you up to view the ornate architecture.

Hofmobiliendepot MUSEUM

(Imperial Furniture Collection; Map p82; ☎01-524 33 57; www.hofmobiliendepot.at; 07, Andreasgasse 7; adult/child incl audio guide €10.50/6.50, incl 1hr guided tour €12.50/7.50; ⏲10am-6pm Tue-Sun; Ⓤ Zieglergasse) The Habsburgs stashed away the furniture not displayed in the Hofburg, Schönbrunn, Schloss Belvedere and their other palaces at the Hofmobiliendepot. A romp through this regal attic of a museum, covering four floors and 165,000 objects, provides fascinating insight into furniture design, with highlights such as a display of

COMBINATION MUSEUM TICKETS

There are lots of combined options for visiting the Hofburg and nearby museums.

Sisi Ticket (adult/child €34/21) Includes the Imperial Apartments, Sisi Museum and Silberkammer (Imperial Silver Collection) with an audio guide, as well as Schloss Schönbrunn and the Hofmobiliendepot (Imperial Furniture Collection).

Neue Burg Museums (adult/child €16/free) Includes the Neue Burg Museums' Sammlung Alter Musik Instrumente (Collection of Ancient Musical Instruments), Ephesos Museum and Hofjagd- und Rüstkammer (Arms and Armour) museum, and the Kunsthistorisches Museum Vienna.

Annual ticket Kunsthistorisches Museum Vienna (adult/child €44/25) Includes the Kunstkammer, Kunsthistorisches Museum Vienna, Neue Burg Museums, Kaiserliche Schatzkammer, Wagenburg, Schloss Ambras Innsbruck and Theatermuseum.

Schatz der Habsburger (Treasures of the Habsburgs; adult/child €22/free) Includes the Kunsthistorisches Museum Vienna, Neue Burg Museums and Kaiserliche Schatzkammer.

Masterticket (adult/child €24/free) Includes the Neue Burg Museums, Kunsthistorisches Museum Vienna and the Leopold Museum.

Die Kostbarkeiten des Kaisers (Treasures of the Emperors; adult/child €24/free) Includes the Kaiserliche Schatzkammer and Morgenarbeit (morning training sessions) at the Spanish Riding School.

Nationalbibliothek Universal-Wochenticket (€16.50) Includes entry to the Nationalbibliothek's Esperantomuseum, Globenmuseum and Papyrusmuseum, the Nationalbibliothek Prunksaal and the Literaturmuseum. Valid for seven days.

VIENNA'S DISTRICTS

The 23 Wiener *Bezirke* (Vienna districts) spiral out clockwise from the centre like a snail shell (although in some instances leapfrog position). The Innere Stadt (01) sits at the centre, encircled by the Ringstrasse. Roughly between the Ringstrasse and the Gürtel ring road are the Vorstädte (inner suburbs): 02 (Leopoldstadt), 03 (Landstrasse), 04 (Wieden), 05 (Margareten), 06 (Mariahilf), 07 (Neubau), 08 (Josefstadt) and 09 (Alsergrund). Outside the Gürtel are the Vororte (outer suburbs): 10 (Favoriten), 11 (Simmering), 12 (Meidling), 13 (Hietzing), 14 (Penzing), 15 (Rudolfsheim-Fünfhaus), 16 (Ottakring), 17 (Hernals), 18 (Währing), 19 (Döbling) and 20 (Brigittenau). Districts 21 (Floridsdorf) and 22 (Donaustadt) are on the city's northeastern flank, while 23 (Liesing) sits on the southwestern edge.

Every address in Vienna begins with the district number, starting with 01 for the Innere Stadt, with street numbers starting closest to the city. The district number is easily identifiable by the middle two digits of its four-digit post code; so, for example, 1010 is the 01 (Innere Stadt).

Each of the *Bezirke* has its own style and character. Within or straddling these districts, you'll often find smaller neighbourhoods, such as the romantic, cobblestoned Spittelberg, 07, behind the MuseumsQuartier, and the foodie favourite Freihausviertel on the edge of the 04 and 05 districts.

imperial travelling thrones, Emperor Maximilian's coffin and Empress Elisabeth's neo-Renaissance bed from Gödöllő Castle. One of the more underrated museums in the city, it's included in the Sisi Ticket.

Alsergrund & the University District

Sigmund Freud Museum MUSEUM
(Map p72; www.freud-museum.at; 09, Berggasse 19; adult/child €12/4; 10am-6pm; 1, D Schlickgasse, U Schottentor, Schottenring) Sigmund Freud is a bit like the telephone – once he happened, there was no going back. This is where Freud spent his most prolific years and developed the most significant of his groundbreaking theories; he moved here with his family in 1891 and stayed until forced into exile by the Nazis in 1938.

University Main Building UNIVERSITY
(Map p72; 01-427 70, tours 01-427 71 7675; https://events.univie.ac.at; 01, Dr-Karl-Lueger-Ring 1; guided tours adult/child €5/3; 7am-10pm Mon-Fri, to 7pm Sat; D, 1, 71 Schottentor, U Schottentor) FREE Founded in 1365, Vienna's venerable university was the first in the German-speaking countries. Today it enrols up to 95,000 students. Grand Duke Rudolf IV (1339–65) used Paris' Sorbonne as his inspiration, and it was just as well he wasn't around in 1520 during the Reformation, because in that year his 'Sorbonne' was shoehorned into the Church. There are guided tours in English on Saturdays at 11.30am.

Kunstforum GALLERY
(Map p68; www.bankaustria-kunstforum.at; 01, Freyung 8; adult/child €11/6; 10am-7pm Sat-Thu, to 9pm Fri; U Herrengasse) The private Kunstforum museum gets about 300,000 visitors each year, and for good reason – it stages an exciting program of changing exhibitions, usually highlighting crowd-pleasing modernist or big-name contemporary artists. The work of Miquel Barceló, Fernando Botero, Frida Kahlo, Balthus and Martin Kippenberger have all had their turn in recent years.

Beethoven Pasqualatihaus MUSEUM
(Map p68; www.wienmuseum.at; 01, Mölker Bastei 8; adult/child €5/free; 10am-1pm & 2-6pm Tue-Sun; D, 1, 2 Schottentor, U Schottentor) Beethoven resided on the 4th floor of this house from 1804 to 1814. (He apparently lived in around 80 places in his 35 years in Vienna, but thankfully not all of them are museums.) During that time he composed Symphonies 4, 5 and 7 and the opera *Fidelio*, among other works. His two rooms (plus another two from a neighbouring apartment) have been converted into this airy museum, which has a not-too-overwhelming collection of portraits, articles and personal belongings.

Vorstadt Southwest

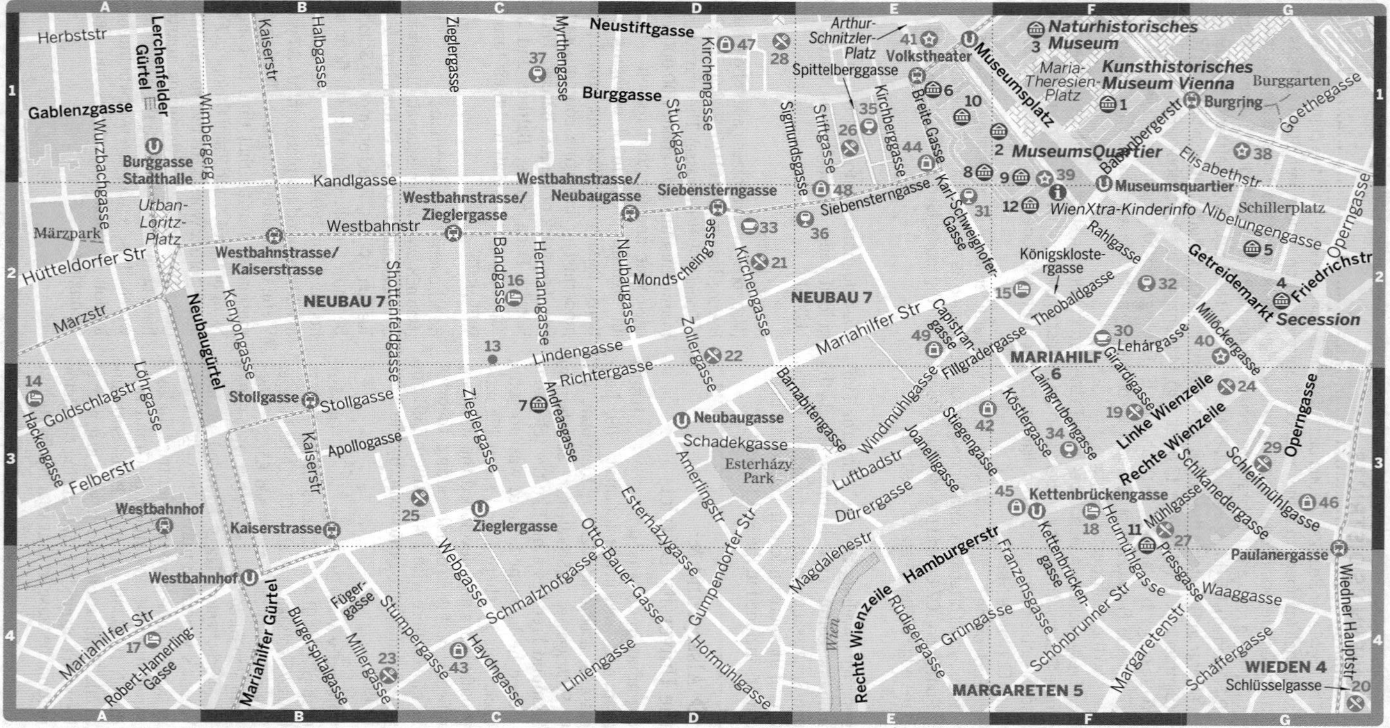

0 — 400 m
0 — 0.2 miles

Herbststr
Lerchenfelder Gürtel
Gablenzgasse
Wurzbachgasse
Burggasse Stadthalle
Urban-Loritz-Platz
Märzpark
Hütteldorfer Str
Märzstr
Goldschlagstr
Löhrgasse
Hackengasse
Felberstr
Westbahnhof
Mariahilfer Str
Robert-Hamerling-Gasse
Kaiserstr
Halbgasse
Wimbergerg
Kandlgasse
Westbahnstrasse/Kaiserstrasse
Neubaugürtel
Kenyongasse
Stollgasse
Kaiserstrasse
Mariahilfer Gürtel
Burgerspitalgasse
Fügergasse
Millergasse
Stumpergasse
NEUBAU 7
Shottenfeldgasse
Westbahnstr
Westbahnstrasse/Zieglergasse
Zieglergasse
Myrthengasse
Bandgasse
Hermanngasse
Lindengasse
Richtergasse
Andreasgasse
Apollogasse
Webgasse
Schmalzhofgasse
Haydngasse
Liniengasse
Neustiftgasse
Burggasse
Westbahnstrasse/Neubaugasse
Neubaugasse
Stuckgasse
Kirchengasse
Siebensterngasse
Mondscheingasse
Zollergasse
Neubaugasse
Schadekgasse
Esterházy Park
Amerlingstr
Esterházygasse
Otto-Bauer-Gasse
Gumpendorfer Str
Hofmühlgasse
Sigmundsgasse
Stiftgasse
Kirchberggasse
Spittelberggasse
Arthur-Schnitzler-Platz
Volkstheater
Breite Gasse
Karl-Schweighofer-Gasse
Mariahilfer Str
Capistrangasse
Barnabitengasse
Windmühlgasse
Luftbadstr
Dürergasse
Magdalenestr
Wien
Rechte Wienzeile
Rüdigergasse
Hamburgerstr
Museumsplatz
Naturhistorisches Museum
Maria-Theresien-Platz
Kunsthistorisches Museum Vienna
MuseumsQuartier
Museumsquartier
WienXtra-Kinderinfo
Babenbergerstr
Burgring
Burggarten
Goethegasse
Elisabethstr
Schillerplatz
Nibelungengasse
Operngasse
Friedrichstr
Getreidemarkt
Secession
Rahlgasse
Königsklostergasse
Theobaldgasse
Fillgradergasse
MARIAHILF 6
Lehárgasse
Girardigasse
Millöckergasse
Linke Wienzeile
Rechte Wienzeile
Laimgrubengasse
Köstlergasse
Stiegengasse
Joanelligasse
Kettenbrückengasse
Kettenbrückengasse
Franzensgasse
Grüngasse
Schönbrunner Str
Heumühlgasse
Mühlgasse
Pressgasse
Schikanedergasse
Schleifmühlgasse
Operngasse
Paulanergasse
Waaggasse
Margaretenstr
Schäffergasse
MARGARETEN 5
WIEDEN 4
Schlüsselgasse
Wiedner Hauptstr

Vorstadt Southwest

Top Sights
1 Kunsthistorisches Museum Vienna ... F1
2 MuseumsQuartier ... F1
3 Naturhistorisches Museum ... F1
4 Secession ... G2

Sights
5 Akademie der Bildenden Künste ... G2
6 Architekturzentrum Wien ... E1
7 Hofmobiliendepot ... C3
8 Kunsthalle Wien ... E1
9 Leopold Museum ... F1
10 MUMOK ... E1
Naschmarkt ... (see 24)
11 Third Man Museum ... F3
12 Zoom ... F2

Activities, Courses & Tours
13 Shades Tours ... C2

Sleeping
14 Boutiquehotel Stadthalle ... A3
15 Das Tyrol ... F2
16 Hotel am Brillantengrund ... C2
17 Wombat's City Hostel ... A4
18 Wombat's City Hostel Naschmarkt ... F3

Eating
19 Café Drechsler ... F3
20 Entler ... G4
21 Figar ... D2
22 Liebling ... D2
23 MiLL ... B4
24 Naschmarkt ... G3
25 Swing Kitchen ... C3
26 Tian Bistro ... E1
27 Ubl ... F3
28 Veganista ... D1
29 Vollpension ... G3

Drinking & Nightlife
30 Café Sperl ... F2
31 Donau ... E2
32 Felixx ... F2
33 J Hornig Kaffeebar ... D2
34 Mango Bar ... F3
35 Melete Art Design Cocktails ... E1
36 Siebensternbräu ... E2
37 Wirr ... C1

Entertainment
38 Burg Kino ... G1
39 Dschungel Wien ... F1
Tanzquartier Wien ... (see 12)
40 Theater an der Wien ... G2
41 Volkstheater ... E1

Shopping
42 Beer Lovers ... E3
43 Blühendes Konfekt ... C4
44 Die Werkbank ... E1
45 Flohmarkt ... F3
46 Gabarage Upcycling Design ... G3
47 Runway ... D1
48 Schokov ... E2
49 Teuchtler Records ... E2

The house is named after its longtime owner, Josef Benedikt Freiherr von Pasqualati.

Museum für Volkskunde MUSEUM
(Map p72; www.volkskundemuseum.at; 08, Laudongasse 15-19; adult/child €8/free; ⏲10am-5pm Tue, Wed & Fri-Sun, to 8pm Thu; 🚋5, 33 Laudongasse, Ⓤ Rathaus) Housed in turn-of-the-18th-century **Palais Schönborn**, this folklore museum gives a taste of 18th- and 19th-century rural dwellings, and is stocked with handcrafted sculptures, paintings and furniture from throughout Austria and its neighbouring countries. Many of the pieces have a religious or rural theme, and telltale floral motifs are everywhere. Temporary exhibitions are regularly featured.

Schloss Belvedere to the Canal

Schloss Belvedere PALACE
See p84.

★ Heeresgeschichtliches Museum MUSEUM
(Museum of Military History; www.hgm.at; 03, Arsenal; adult/under 19yr €7/free, 1st Sun of month free; ⏲9am-5pm; Ⓤ Südtiroler Platz) The superb Heeresgeschichtliches Museum is housed in the Arsenal, a large neo-Byzantine barracks and munitions depot. Spread over two floors, the museum works its way from the Thirty Years' War (1618–48) to WWII, taking in the Hungarian Uprising and the Austro-Prussian War (ending in 1866), the Napoleonic and Turkish Wars, and WWI. Highlights on the 1st floor include the Great Seal of Mustafa Pasha, which fell to Prince Eugene of Savoy in the Battle of Zenta in 1697.

★ Museum für Angewandte Kunst MUSEUM
(MAK; Museum of Applied Arts; Map p68; www.mak.at; 01, Stubenring 5; adult/under 19yr €12/free, 6-10pm Tue €5, tours €3.50; ⏲10am-6pm Wed-Sun, to 10pm Tue, English tours noon Sun;

(Continued on page 88)

TOP SIGHT
SCHLOSS BELVEDERE & GARDENS

A masterpiece of total art, Belvedere is one of the world's finest baroque palaces. Designed by Johann Lukas von Hildebrandt (1668–1745), it was built as a summer residence for the brilliant military strategist Prince Eugene of Savoy, conqueror of the Turks in 1718. Eugene had grown up around the court of Louis XIV and it shows – this is a chateau to rival Versailles.

Oberes Belvedere

Rising splendidly above the gardens and commanding sweeping views of Vienna's skyline, the Oberes Belvedere is one of Vienna's unmissable sights. Built between 1717 and 1723, its peerless art collection, showcased in rooms replete with marble, frescoes and stucco, attests to the unfathomable wealth and cultured tastes of the Habsburg empire.

Ground Floor: Medieval & Modern Art

The **Sala Terrena** is a grand prelude to the ground floor, with four colossal Atlas pillars supporting the weight of its delicately stuccoed vault. Spread across four beautifully frescoed rooms, **Medieval Art** leads you through the artistic development of the age, with an exceptional portfolio of Gothic sculpture and altarpieces, many from Austrian abbeys and monasteries. Top billing goes to the Master of Grosslobming's sculptural group, whose fluid, expressive works embodied the figurative ideal; among them is the faceless *St George with Dragon* (1395), with a rather tame-looking dragon at his feet. Other heavenly treasures include Joachim's polyptych *Albrechtsaltar* (1435), one of the foremost examples of

DON'T MISS

- The Klimt collection
- Sala Terrena
- The gardens
- The impressionist collection
- Marmorsaal

PRACTICALITIES

- Map p95
- www.belvedere.at
- 03, Prinz-Eugen-Strasse 27
- adult/child Oberes Belvedere €16/free, Unteres Belvedere €14/free, combined ticket €22/free
- 9am-6pm Sat-Thu, to 9pm Fri
- D, 71 Schwarzenbergplatz, U Taubstummengasse, Südtiroler Platz

Gothic realism, and the *Znaim Altar* (1445), a gilded glorification of faith showing the Passion of Christ.

Modern Art & Interwar Period is particularly strong on Austrian expressionism. Attention grabbers here include Oskar Kokoschka's richly animated portrait of art-nouveau painter *Carl Moll* (1913). Egon Schiele is represented by works both haunting and beguiling, such as *Death and the Maiden* (1915) and his portrait of six-year-old *Herbert Rainer* (1910). Other standouts include Oskar Laske's staggeringly detailed *Ship of Fools* (1923) and Max Oppenheimer's musical masterpiece *The Philharmonic* (1935), with a baton-swinging Gustav Mahler.

First Floor: From Klimt to Baroque

The 1st-floor **Vienna 1880–1914** collection is a holy grail for Klimt fans, with an entire room devoted to erotic golden wonders such as *Judith* (1901), *Salome* (1909), *Adam and Eve* (1917) and *The Kiss* (1908). Works by German symbolist painter Max Klinger (1857–1920), as well as portraits by secessionist Koloman Moser and Norwegian expressionist Edvard Munch, also feature. The centrepiece is the **Marmorsaal**, a chandelier-lit marble, stucco and trompe l'oeil confection, crowned by Carlo Innocenzo Carlone's ceiling fresco (1721–23) celebrating the glorification of Prince Eugene. **Baroque & Early-19th-Century Art** pays tribute to Austrian masters of the age, endowed with highlights such as Johann Michael Rottmayr's lucid *Susanna and the Elders* (1692) and Paul Troger's chiaroscuro *Christ on the Mount of Olives* (1750).

Second Floor: Impressionists & Romantics

In **Neoclassicism, Romanticism & Biedermeier Art**, you'll find outstanding works such as Georg Waldmüller's *Corpus Christi Morning* (1857), a joyous snapshot of impish lads and flower girls bathed in honeyed light. Representative of the neoclassical period are clearer, more emotionally restrained pieces such as Jacques-Louis David's gallant *Napoleon on Great St Bernard Pass* (1801) and François Gérard's portrait *Count Moritz Christian Fries and Family* (1804). The Romantic period is headlined by the wistful, brooding landscapes and seascapes of 19th-century German painter Caspar David Friedrich.

French masters share the limelight with their Austrian and German contemporaries in **Realism & Impressionism**, where you'll feel the artistic pull of Renoir's softly evocative *Woman after the Bath* (1876), Monet's sun-dappled *Garden at Giverny* (1902) and Van Gogh's *Plain at Auvers* (1890), where wheat fields ripple under a billowing sky. Lovis Corinth's tranquil *Woman Reading Near a*

COMBINED TICKETS

Buying printable tickets online saves time, but they can't be exchanged or refunded. Combined ticket options are available, including one covering the Oberes and Unteres Belvedere (adult/under 19 years €22/free) and one including Belvedere 21 (€25/free). Combined tickets are valid for two weeks after the first visit.

Prince Eugene was an avid hunter, a passionate collector of fossils and shells, and a keen gardener and zoologist. He brought a touch of the exotic to the Belvedere gardens, filling them with rare plants from across the globe. His pride and joy was his menagerie, which housed a lion, an Indian wolf and ostriches, among others.

GUIDED TOURS

Audio guides in various languages can be hired for €5 at the Oberes Belvedere and €4 at the Unteres Belvedere; you'll need to leave ID as a deposit. One-hour themed tours focusing on a specific period or artist cost €4 and are in German. Times vary, but generally there are tours at 3pm and/or 4pm on weekends, plus 10.30am on Sunday.

Goldfish Tank (1911) and Max Liebermann's *Hunter in the Dunes* (1913) epitomise the German impressionist style.

Gardens

Belvedere: 'beautiful view'. The reason for this name becomes apparent in the baroque garden linking the upper and lower palaces, which was laid out in around 1700 in classical French style by Dominique Girard, a pupil of André le Nôtre of Versailles fame. Set along a **central axis**, the gently sloping garden commands a broad view of Vienna's skyline, with the Stephansdom and the Hofburg punctuating the horizon.

The three-tiered garden is lined by clipped box hedges and flanked by ornamental parterres. As you stroll to the **Lower Cascade**, with its frolicking water nymphs, look out for Greco-Roman statues of the eight muses and cherubic putti embodying the 12 months of the year. Mythical beasts squirt water across the **Upper Cascade**, which spills down five steps into the basin below. Guarding the approach to the Oberes Belvedere are winged sphinxes, symbols of power and wisdom, which look as though they are about to take flight any minute.

South of the Oberes Belvedere is the **Alpengarten** (www.bundesgaerten.at; 03, Prinz-Eugen-Strasse 27; adult/child €3.50/2.50; 10am-6pm late Mar-early Aug; D, O Quartier Belvedere, U Hauptbahnhof), a Japanese-style garden nurturing alpine species, at its fragrant best from spring to summer, when clematis, rhododendrons, roses and peonies are in bloom. North from here is the larger Botanischer Garten (p89), belonging to the Vienna University, with tropical glasshouses and 11,500 botanical species, including Chinese dwarf bamboo and Japanese plum yews.

Unteres Belvedere

Built between 1712 and 1716, **Unteres Belvedere** (Lower Belvedere; Map p95; 03, Rennweg 6; adult/child €14/free, combined ticket with Oberes Belvedere €22/free; 10am-6pm Sat-Thu, to 9pm Fri; 71 Unteres Belvedere) is a baroque feast of state apartments and ceremonial rooms. Most lavish of all is the red marble **Marmorsaal**, an ode to Prince Eugene's military victories, with stucco trophies, medallions and Martino Altomonte's ceiling fresco showing the glorification of the prince and Apollo surrounded by muses. At eye level are sculptures taken from Georg Raphael Donner's mid-18th-century **fountain** on Neuer Markt. Snake-bearing Providentia (Prudence) rises above four putti grappling with fish, each of which symbolises a tributary of the Danube (Donau).

In the **Groteskensaal**, foliage intertwines with fruit, birds and mythological beasts in the fanciful grotesque style that was all the rage in baroque times. This leads through to the **Marmorgalerie**, a vision of frilly white stucco and marble, encrusted with cherubs and war trophies. Maria Theresia put her stamp on the palace in the adjacent **Goldkabinett**, a mirrored cabinet dripping in gold.

Temporary exhibitions are held in the **Orangery**, with a walkway gazing grandly over Prince Eugene's private garden. Attached to the Orangery is the **Prunkstall**, the former royal stables, where you can now trot through a 150-piece collection of Austrian medieval art, including religious scenes, altarpieces, sculpture and Gothic triptychs.

Belvedere 21

The modernist, glass-and-steel Austria Pavilion, designed by Karl Schwanzer for Expo 58 in Brussels, was reborn as **Belvedere 21** (www.belvedere21.at; 03, Arsenalstrasse 1; adult/under 18yr €8/free; 11am-6pm Wed-Sun, to 9pm Fri; O, 1, 18 Fasangasse, U Hauptbahnhof) in 2011, with exhibitions devoted to 20th- and 21st-century art, predominantly Austrian. Adolf Krischanitz left his clean aesthetic imprint on the open-plan gallery, which sits just south of the Oberes Belvedere in the Schweizergarten.

OBERES BELVEDERE

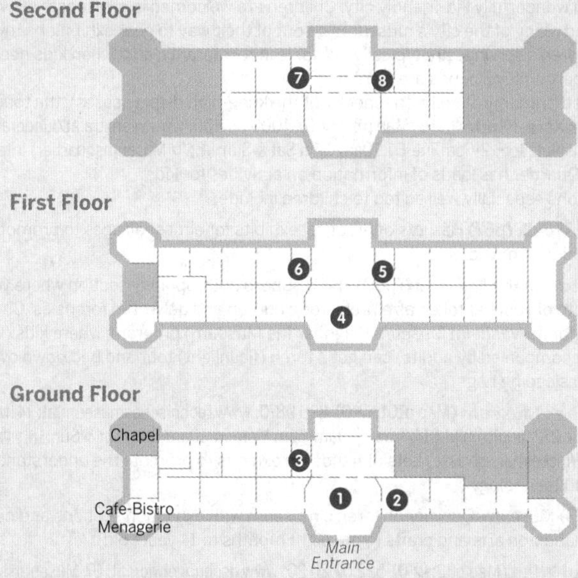

Museum Tour Oberes Belvedere

LENGTH FOUR HOURS

The scale of the Oberes Belvedere (Upper Belvedere) can be overwhelming. This half-day itinerary will help you pin down the highlights, though bear in mind that paintings are frequently shifted around for exhibitions.

Gaze up to the mighty Atlas pillars supporting the ❶ **Sala Terrena** and turn right into ❷ **Medieval Art**, displayed in exuberantly frescoed halls. You'll be drawn to the Gothic brilliance of the Master of Grosslobming's sculptures, such as *St George with Dragon* and *Kneeling Mary*. Note the soul-stirring *Albrechtsaltar* and the *Znaim Altar* depicting the Passion of Christ. Andreas Lackner created the *Abtenauer Altar* (1518), a gilded trio of bishops that once adorned the high altar of the parish church of Abtenau in Salzburg. Exit and turn left into ❸ **Modern Art & Interwar Period**, where Egon Schiele's expressionistic portrait of *Herbert Rainer* and Max Oppenheimer's evocative *Philharmonic* steal the show.

Saunter up the ornately stuccoed Prunkstiege staircase, marvelling at the opulence of the ❹ **Marmorsaal**. Turn right to reach ❺ **Vienna 1880–1914**, a peerless repository of fin-de-siècle and secessionist art. The Klimt collection is second to none, shimmering with golden-period stunners like *Judith* and *The Kiss*. Across the way in ❻ **Baroque & Early-19th-Century Art**, look out for light-fantastic works such as Johann Michael Rottmayr's *Susanna and the Elders* and Paul Troger's *Christ on the Mount of Olives*.

On the 2nd floor, turn left into ❼ **Neoclassicism, Romanticism & Biedermeier Art**. Notice neoclassical wonders such as François Gérard's portrait of *Count Moritz Christian Fries and Family*, then move past landscapes and still lifes to the Romantic era. Here, look out for Caspar David Friedrich's mist-enshrouded *Rocky Landscape of the Elbe Sandstone Heights*. Georg Waldmüller's mirthful *Corpus Christi Morning* takes pride of place in the Biedermeier collection. Round out with impressionist masterworks in ❽ **Realism & Impressionism**, where exceptional works include Max Liebermann's *Hunter in the Dunes*, Monet's *Woman after the Bath* and Van Gogh's *Plain at Auvers*.

VIENNA FOR CHILDREN

Vienna is a wonderfully kid-friendly city. Children are welcomed in all aspects of everyday life, and many of the city's museums go out of their way to gear exhibitions towards them. Children's servings are typically available in restaurants, and, when kids need to burn off energy, playgrounds are plentiful.

Marketed primarily at children (check out the knee-high display cases), the tourist office **WienXtra-Kinderinfo** (Map p82; ☎01-4000 84 400; www.wienxtra.at/kinderaktiv; 07, Museumsplatz 1; ⏲2-6pm Tue-Fri, 10am-5pm Sat & Sun; ; U Museumsquartier) in the MuseumsQuartier has loads of information on activities for kids.

Attractions especially well suited to children include:

Haus der Musik (p67) Has lots of practical exhibits for almost all ages to promote an understanding of music.

Naturhistorisches Museum (p80) Has a superb anthropology section where you can have a photo of yourself taken as a prehistoric human and delve into forensics. Check for schedules for its *Nacht im Museum* (Night at the Museum) program, where kids (who must be accompanied by adults) can get a torch (flashlight) tour and bed down overnight (BYO sleeping bags).

Technisches Museum (Map p101; ☎01-899 98-0; www.technischesmuseum.at; 14, Mariahilfer Strasse 212; adult/child €14/free; ⏲9am-6pm Mon-Fri, 10am-6pm Sat & Sun; ; 10, 46, 49, 52, 60 Winckelmannstrasse) Lots of hands-on exhibits to promote the understanding of science and technology.

Zoom (p73) MuseumsQuartier children's museum with exhibition sections and programs of hands-on arts and crafts (from eight months to 14 years old).

Dschungel Wien (Map p82; ☎01-522 07 20 20; www.dschungelwien.at; 07, Museumsplatz 1; tickets adult/child from €9/6; ⏲box office 4-6pm Mon-Fri; ; U Museumsquartier, Volkstheater) Children's theatre in the MuseumsQuartier with dance and occasional English performances.

Kindermuseum (p92) Schloss Schönbrunn children's museum.

Marionetten Theater (Map p101; ☎01-817 32 47; www.marionettentheater.at; 13, Schloss Schönbrunn; tickets adult €11-39, child €9-25; ⏲Mon, Wed & Fri-Sun; ; U Schönbrunn) Puppet shows at Schloss Schönbrunn.

2 Stubentor, U Stubentor) MAK is devoted to craftsmanship and art forms in everyday life. Each exhibition room showcases a different style, which includes Renaissance, baroque, orientalism, historicism, empire, art deco and the distinctive metalwork of the Wiener Werkstätte. Contemporary artists were invited to present the rooms in ways they felt were appropriate, resulting in eye-catching and unique displays. The 20th-century design and architecture room is one of the most fascinating, and Frank Gehry's cardboard chair is a gem.

Stadtpark PARK

(City Park; Map p68; 01, 03; 2 Weihburggasse, U Stadtpark) FREE Opened in 1862, the Stadtpark is a tranquil pocket of greenery, with winding paths and willow-tree-rimmed duck ponds. It's great for strolling or relaxing in the sun and a favourite lunchtime escape for Innere Stadt workers. The park spans the Wien River, which empties into the Danube Canal.

KunstHausWien MUSEUM

(Art House Vienna; Map p102; www.kunsthauswien.com; 03, Untere Weissgerberstrasse 13; adult/child €12/5; ⏲10am-6pm; 0, 1 Radetzkyplatz) The KunstHausWien, with its bulging ceramics, wonky surfaces, checkerboard facade, technicolor mosaic tilework and rooftop sprouting plants and trees, bears the inimitable hallmark of eccentric Viennese artist and ecowarrior Friedensreich Hundertwasser (1928–2000), who famously called the straight line 'godless'. It is an ode to his playful, boldly creative work, as well as to his green politics.

Hundertwasserhaus LANDMARK

(03, cnr Löwengasse & Kegelgasse; 1 Hetzgasse) This residential block of flats bears all the wackily creative hallmarks of Hundertwasser, Vienna's radical architect and lover of uneven surfaces, with its curvy lines, crayon-bright colours and mosaic detail.

It's not possible to see inside, but you can cross the road to visit the **Hundertwasser Village** (www.hundertwasser-village.com; 03, Kegelgasse 37-39; 9am-6pm) FREE, also the handiwork of Hundertwasser.

Botanischer Garten GARDENS
(www.botanik.univie.ac.at; 03, Mechelgasse/Praetoriusgasse; 10am-6pm; 0, 1, 71 Rennweg) FREE These botanic gardens, belonging to the Vienna University, have tropical glasshouses and 11,500 species from six continents, including wonders such as Chinese dwarf bamboo, ginkgo biloba, tulip trees and Japanese plum yews.

Prater & East of the Danube

★Prater PARK
(Map p102; www.wiener-prater.at; ; U Praterstern) FREE Spread across 60 sq km, central Vienna's biggest park comprises woodlands of poplar and chestnut, meadows and tree-lined boulevards, as well as children's playgrounds, a swimming pool, a golf course and a race track. Fringed by statuesque chestnut trees that are ablaze with russet and gold in autumn and frilly with white blossom in spring, the central Hauptallee avenue is the main vein, running straight as a die from the Praterstern to the Lusthaus (p107).

Twirling above the **Würstelprater** (Prater Vienna; Map p102; www.prater.at; Prater 7; rides €1.50-5; 10am-midnight;) amusement park is one of the city's most visible icons, the **Riesenrad** (Map p102; www.wienerriesenrad.com; 02, Prater 90; adult/child €12/5; 9am-midnight, shorter hours winter;). Built in 1897, this 65m-high Ferris wheel of *The Third Man* fame affords far-reaching views of Vienna.

Augarten PARK
(Map p102; www.kultur.park.augarten.org; 03, Obere Augartenstrasse; 6am-dusk; U Taborstrasse) FREE This landscaped park from 1775 is dotted with open meadows and criss-crossed by paths lined with elm, lime, chestnut and maple trees. You can kick a ball in one section, let the kids stage a riot in a playground in another, or visit the **porcelain museum** (Augarten Porcelain Museum; Map p102; www.augarten.at; 02, Obere Augartenstrasse 1; adult/child €7/5, incl guided tour €13/11; 10am-6pm Mon-Sat; U Taborstrasse). The park contains the city's oldest baroque garden. Among the park's most eye-catching features are the austere *Flaktürme* (flak towers) in its northern and western corners.

Schloss Schönbrunn & Around

Schloss Schönbrunn PALACE
See p90.

Activities

Swimming & Water Sports

★Donauinsel OUTDOORS
(Danube Island; U Donauinsel) The svelte Danube Island stretches some 21.5km from opposite Klosterneuburg in the north to the Nationalpark Donau-Auen in the south and splits the Danube in two, creating a separate arm known as the Neue Donau (New Danube). Created in 1970, it is Vienna's aquatic playground, with sections of beach (don't expect much sand) for swimming, boating and a little waterskiing.

Alte Donau WATER SPORTS
(22, Untere Alte Donau; U Alte Donau) The Alte Donau (Old Danube), a landlocked arm of the river, is separated from the Neue Donau by a sliver of land. It carried the main flow of the river until 1875. Now the 160-hectare water expanse is a favourite of Viennese sailing and boating enthusiasts, and also attracts swimmers, walkers, fisherfolk and, in winter (if it's cold enough), ice skaters.

Badeschiff SWIMMING
(Map p68; www.badeschiff.at; 01, Danube Canal; adult/child €6.50/2; 9am-8pm May-Sep; 1, 2 Schwedenplatz, U Schwedenplatz) Swim on (not in!) the Danube. Floating on the bank of the Danube, between Schwedenplatz and Urania, this 28m-long lap pool has multiple decks with umbrella-shaded sun loungers and an open-air football pitch on the platform suspended above. It doubles as a bar at night; in winter the pool closes and the ship is a bar and restaurant only. Both the bar and kitchen are open year round, with drinks available until 1am and food until 10pm.

Ice Skating

Wiener Eistraum ICE SKATING
(Map p72; www.wienereistraum.com; 01, Rathausplatz; adult/child from €8/5.50, preheated skate hire €7.50/5.50; 10am-10pm late Jan-early Mar;

(Continued on page 94)

TOP SIGHT
SCHLOSS SCHÖNBRUNN

The Habsburg empire is revealed in all its frescoed, gilded, chandelier-lit glory in the wondrously ornate apartments of Schloss Schönbrunn, which are among Europe's best-preserved baroque interiors. Stories about the first public performance of wunderkind Mozart or Empress Elisabeth's extreme beauty and fitness regimes bring Austrian history to life as you explore the 40 rooms open to the public.

State Apartments

The Imperial Tour (using a free audio guide or app) begins at the frescoed **Blue Staircase**, which makes a regal ascent to the palace's upper level. First up are the 19th-century apartments of Emperor Franz Joseph I and his beloved wife Elisabeth, a beauty praised for her tiny waist and cascading tresses. You then visit lavishly stuccoed, chandelier-lit apartments such as the **Billiard Room**, where army officials would pot a few balls while waiting to attend an audience, and Franz Joseph's **study**, where the emperor worked tirelessly from 5am. The iron bedstead and washstand for morning ablutions in his bedroom reveal his devout, highly disciplined nature.

Empress Elisabeth, or 'Sisi' as she is fondly nicknamed, whiled away many an hour penning poetry in the ruby-red **Stairs Cabinet**, and brushing up on various European languages while her ankle-length locks were tended in the privacy of her **dressing room**. Blue-and-white silk wall hangings adorn the **imperial bedroom** that Franz and Sisi sometimes shared. The neo-rococo **Empress' Salon** features portraits of some of Maria Theresia's 16 children, including Marie Antoinette in hunting garb, poignantly oblivious to her fate at the French guillotine in

DON'T MISS

- State Apartments
- Neptunbrunnen
- Gloriette
- Wagenburg

PRACTICALITIES

- Map p101
- ☎ 01-811 13-0
- www.schoenbrunn.at
- 13, Schönbrunner Schlossstrasse 47
- adult/child Imperial Tour €16/11.50, Grand Tour €20/13, Grand Tour with guide €24/15
- 8am-6.30pm Jul & Aug, to 5.30pm Apr-Jun, Sep & Oct, to 5pm Nov-Mar
- U Schönbrunn, Hietzing

1793. Laid with leaded crystal and fragile porcelain, the table in the **Marie Antoinette Room** is where Franz Joseph used to dig into hearty meals of goulash and schnitzel (health-conscious Sisi preferred beef broth and strawberries out of view).

More portraits of Maria Theresia's brood fill the **Children's Room** and the **Balcony Room**, graced with works by court painter Martin van Meytens. Keep an eye out for the one of ill-fated daughter **Maria Elisabeth**, considered a rare beauty before she contracted smallpox. The disease left her so disfigured that all hope of finding a husband vanished, and she entered convent life.

In the exquisite white-and-gold **Mirror Room**, a six-year-old Mozart performed for a rapturous Maria Theresia in 1762. Fairest of all is the 40m-long **Great Gallery**, where the Habsburgs threw balls and banquets, a frothy vision of stucco, mirrors and gilt chandeliers, topped with a fresco by Italian artist Gregorio Guglielmi showing the glorification of Maria Theresia's reign. Decor aside, this was where the historic meeting between John F Kennedy and Soviet leader Nikita Khrushchev took place in 1961.

Wandering through the porcelain-crammed **Chinese Cabinets** brings you to the equestrian fanfare of the **Carousel Room** and the **Hall of Ceremonies**, with five monumental paintings showing the marriage of Joseph, heir to the throne, to Isabella of Parma in 1760. Mozart, only four at the time of the wedding, was added as an afterthought by the artist, who took several years to complete the picture, by which time the virtuoso was a rising star.

If you have a Grand Tour ticket, you can continue through with a guide or audio guide to the palace's **east wing**. Franz Stephan's apartments begin in the sublime **Blue Chinese Salon**, where the intricate floral wall paintings are done on Chinese rice paper. The jewel-box pietra dura tables, inlaid with semiprecious stones, are stellar examples of Florentine craftsmanship. The negotiations that led to the collapse of the Austro-Hungarian Empire in 1918 were held here. A century before, Napoleon chose Schönbrunn as his HQ when he occupied Vienna in 1805 and 1809, and the **Napoleon Room** was where he may have dreamed about which country to conquer next. Look for the portrait of his only legitimate son, Napoleon II, Duke of Reichstadt, shown as a cherubic lad in the park at Schloss Laxenburg.

Passing through the exquisite rosewood **Millions Room**, the **Gobelin Salon**, filled with Flemish tapestries, and the **Red Salon** brimming with Habsburg portraits, you reach Maria Theresia's **bedroom**, with a throne-like four-poster bed covered in red velvet and gold embroidery. This is where Franz Joseph was

PALMENHAUS

Londoners may think they're experiencing déjà vu on sighting the **Palmenhaus** (Palm House; Map p101; 13, Maxingstrasse 13b; adult/child incl Wüstenhaus €6/4.50; ⌚9.30am-6pm May-Sep, to 5pm Oct-Apr; Ⓤ Hietzing). This was built in 1882 by Franz Segenschmid as a replica of the one in London's Kew Gardens. Inside is a veritable jungle of tropical plants from around the world.

The small Wüstenhaus (Desert House; Map p101; ☎01-877 92 94-500; www.zoovienna.at; 13, Maxingstrasse 13b; adult/child €6/4.50; ⌚9am-6pm May-Sep, to 5pm Oct-Apr; Ⓤ Hietzing) **near the Palmenhaus makes good use of the once-disused Sonnenuhrhaus (Sundial House) to recreate arid desert scenes. Its four sections – Africa, the Middle East, the Americas and Madagascar – are home to rare cacti and live desert animals, such as the naked mole rat from East Africa.**

born in 1830. Gilt-framed portraits of the Habsburgs hang on the red-damask walls of Archduke Franz Karl's **study**, and the tour concludes in the **Hunting Room**, with paintings noting Schönbrunn's origins as a hunting lodge.

Schloss Schönbrunn Gardens

Laid out in the formal French style, the beautifully tended palace **gardens** (Map p101; 6.30am-dusk) FREE, within the sprawling Schlosspark, are appealing whatever the season: a symphony of colour in the summer and a wash of greys and browns in winter. Opened to the public by Joseph II in 1779, the grounds contain a number of attractions in the tree-lined avenues that were arranged according to a grid and star-shaped system between 1750 and 1755. Between 1772 and 1780 Johann Ferdinand Hetzendorf added some of the final touches to the park under the instructions of Joseph II: fake **Roman ruins** (Map p101; 6.30am-dusk) in 1778; the **Neptunbrunnen** (Neptune Fountain; Map p101; 10am-4pm mid-Apr–Sep), an equally empire-boosting Greek-mythology-themed folly in 1781; and the crowning glory, the **Gloriette** (pictured p90; Map p101; 13, Schlosspark; adult/child €4.50/3.20; 9am-7pm Jul & Aug, to 6pm Apr-Jun & Sep, to 5pm Oct-early Nov; 8A, 63A Gassmannstrasse, U Schönbrunn), in 1775. The view from the Gloriette is, as the name suggests, glorious.

The palace gained its name from the **Schöner Brunnen** (Map p101; 10am-4pm mid-Apr–Sep). The original fountain now pours through the stone pitcher of a nymph near the Roman ruins. The garden's 630m-long **Irrgarten** (Maze; Map p101; adult/child €6/3.50, combination ticket with Kindermuseum €12/8, with Kindermusum & Tiergarten €28/16; 9am-6pm mid-Mar–early Nov;) is a classic hedge design based on the original maze that occupied its place from 1720 to 1892; adjoining this is the **Labyrinth**, a playground with games, climbing equipment and a giant mirror kaleidoscope.

East of the palace is the **Kronprinzengarten** (Privy Garden; Map p101; adult/child €3.80/3; 9am-6pm Apr-early Nov), a replica of the baroque garden that occupied the space around 1750.

Kindermuseum

Schönbrunn's **Kindermuseum** (Children's Museum; Map p101; www.kaiserkinder.at; adult/child €9.50/7.50, combination ticket with Irrgarten €12/8, with Irrgarten & Tiergarten €28/16; 10am-5pm;) does what it knows best: imperialism. Activities and displays help kids discover the day-to-day life of the Habsburg court, and then dress up in princely or princessly outfits and start ordering the serfs (parents) around. Other rooms devoted to toys, natural science and archaeology all help to keep them entertained. **Guided tours** in German are a regular feature, departing at 10.30am, 1.30pm and 3pm.

Wagenburg

The **Wagenburg** (Imperial Coach Collection; Map p101; www.kaiserliche-wagenburg.at; adult/child €9.50/free; 9am-5pm mid-Mar–Nov, 10am-4pm Dec–mid-Mar) is *Pimp My Ride,* imperial-style. On display is a vast array of carriages, including Emperor Franz Stephan's coronation carriage, with its ornate gold plating, Venetian glass panes and painted cherubs. The whole thing weighs an astonishing 4000kg. Also look for the dainty child's carriage built for Napoleon's son, with eagle-wing-shaped mudguards and bee motifs.

Tickets for Schloss Schönbrunn

The best way to get a ticket is to buy it in advance online. Print the ticket yourself or show it on your phone to be scanned on entry.

menhaus (p91)

An **Imperial Tour** ticket (adult/child €16/11.50) includes an audio-guided (or app-guided) tour of 22 rooms. A **Grand Tour** ticket (audio-guided adult/child €20/13, with guide €24/15) includes all rooms in the Imperial Tour and the additional 18 rooms of the palace that can be visited. The palace's Grand Tour accompanied by an English-speaking guide departs at 11am and 3pm daily year-round.

If you plan to see several sights at Schönbrunn, it's worth purchasing a combination ticket.

From April to October, the summer-season **Classic Pass** (adult/child €26.50/16.50) is valid for an audio-guided Grand Tour of Schloss Schönbrunn (including all 40 rooms open to the public) and visits to the Kronprinzengarten (Crown Prince Garden), Irrgarten (maze) and Labyrinth, and Gloriette with its panoramic viewing terrace. A Classic Pass that includes a guided Grand Tour per adult/child costs €30.50/18.50.

The summer-season **Classic Pass Plus** adds in the Tiergarten (zoo). With an audio-guided Grand Tour per adult/child it costs €40/23, with a guided Grand Tour it costs €44/25.

Year-round, the Sisi Ticket (p80) covers key Hofburg sites includes Schloss Schönbrunn.

ZOO

Established in 1752 as a menagerie, the Schönbrunn **Tiergarten** (Map p101; www.zoovienna.at; 13, Maxingstrasse 13b; adult/child €20/10, combination ticket with Irrgarten & Kindermuseum €28/16; ⌚9am-6.30pm Apr-Sep, to 5.30pm Mar & Oct, to 5pm Feb, to 4.30pm Nov-Jan; 🚌56A, 56B, 58A Tiroler Gasse, Ⓤ Hietzing) is the world's oldest continually operating zoo. Among its 8500 animals are giant pandas, giraffes and Siberian tigers. Feeding times are staggered throughout the day – check maps to find out who's dining when. The zoo is laid out like a bicycle wheel, with pathways as spokes and an octagonal pavilion at its centre.

During the summer season, a little tourist 'train' (on wheels), the Schönbrunner Panoramabahn (Map p101; www.zoovienna.at; day ticket adult/child €8/4; ⌚10am-5pm Apr-Oct), **loops around Schloss Schönbrunn's grounds, stopping at nine attractions including the palace, Tiergarten and Gloriette viewing point. A complete circuit takes 50 minutes; you can hop on and off all day. It's a handy option for resting tired feet and skipping the steep hills.**

D, 1, 2, 71 Rathausplatz/Burgtheater, U Rathaus) In the heart of winter, Vienna's Rathausplatz transforms into two connected ice rinks covering a total of 9000 sq metres. It's a magnet for the city's ice skaters, and the rinks are complemented by DJs, food stands, special events and *Glühwein* bars. The skating path zigzags through the nearby park and around the entire square.

There's a free skating area for beginners and children, open 9am to 4pm Monday to Friday, 8am to 10pm Saturday and Sunday (you still need to pay for skate hire). At 5pm Monday to Friday, eight curling lanes set up here.

Wiener Eislaufverein ICE SKATING

(Map p95; www.wev.or.at; 03, Lothringerstrasse 22; adult/child €7.30/6.30, boot hire €6.50; 9am-8pm Sat-Mon, to 9pm Tue-Fri; D Schwarzenbergplatz, U Stadtpark) Fancy a twirl? At 6000 sq metres, the Wiener Eislaufverein is the world's largest open-air ice-skating rink. It's close to the Ringstrasse and Stadtpark. Remember to bring mittens and a hat.

Tours

★ Space & Place WALKING

(0680 125 43 54; www.spaceandplace.at; tours €10) For the inside scoop on Vienna, join Eugene on one of his fun, quirky, English-language tours. The alternative line-up keeps evolving: from **Vienna Ugly Tours**, homing in on the capital's uglier architectural side, to **Midnight Tours**, showing you the city after dark. Tours typically last 2½ hours. See the website for dates and meeting points.

Fiaker Carriage Rides TOURS

(20min/40min/1hr tour €55/80/110; 10am-9pm) Drawn by a pair of horses, these traditional-style open carriages seating up to four passengers are an iconic way to see Vienna. In 2016 the city introduced measures to address animal welfare concerns, including reducing service hours, and stopping tours in 35°C-plus temperatures. Lines of horses, carriages and bowler-hatted drivers congregate at Stephansplatz, Albertinaplatz and Heldenplatz at the Hofburg.

Drivers generally speak English and will point out places of interest en route. Short tours take you through the old town, while long tours include the Ringstrasse.

To learn more about the horses and their care, take a Secrets of the Fiaker tour with **Riding Dinner** (0660 706 05 02; https://vienna.ridingdinner.com; Secrets of the Fiaker tour per person €25, dinner tours per carriage from €295), which includes a tour of the stables and a carriage ride.

Ring Tram TOURS

(Map p68; 01-712 46 83; www.wienerlinien.at; 01, Schwedenplatz, Platform C; adult/child €10/5; 10am-5.30pm; 1, 2 Schwedenplatz, U Schwedenplatz) You can do a DIY tour of the Ringstrasse by public tram, but if you prefer a seamless tour with video screens and multilingual commentary, hop on the Ring Tram tour, which operates an unbroken 30-minute loop around the Ringstrasse (no stops). Tour tickets are valid for one complete circuit.

DDSG Blue Danube CRUISE

(Map p68; 01-588 80; www.ddsg-blue-danube.at; 01, Schwedenbrücke; 1½hr tours adult/child €23/11.50; hours vary; 1, 2 Schwedenplatz, U Schwedenplatz) DDSG Blue Danube's boats cover a variety of cruise routes; some of the most popular include circumnavigating Leopoldstadt and Brigittenau districts using the Danube Canal and the Danube as their thoroughfare. Select tours include passing through the Nussdorf locks (built by Otto Wagner around 1900) or continuing on to the Wachau. Tours run year-round, weather permitting – check schedules online.

Redbus City Tours BUS

(Map p68; 01-512 40 30; www.redbuscitytours.at; 01, Kärntner Strasse 25; adult/child valid 24hr €25/17, 48hr €32/21; 9am-7pm; D, 1, 2, 71 Kärntner Ring/Oper, U Karlsplatz) These hop-on, hop-off tours include a 1½-hour route covering the main sights in and around the Innere Stadt and two-hour tours hitting all of the city's big sights. Buses leave from outside the Albertina.

Shades Tours WALKING

(Map p82; 01-997 19 83; www.shades-tours.com; 07, Impact Hub Vienna, Lindengasse 56; walking tours €18; U Zieglergasse) Shades reveals central Vienna from a unique perspective, with two-hour walks guided by formerly homeless residents. Offered in English and German, the tours are a real eye-opener. It also provides integration-aimed tours led by refugees. See the website for dates, bookings and meeting points. Participants must be aged 14 and above.

Vorstadt Southeast

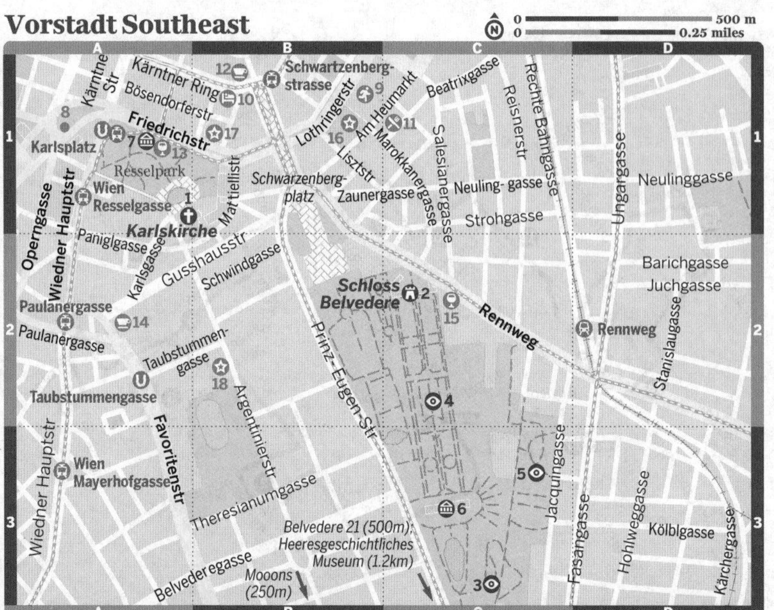

Vorstadt Southeast

Top Sights
1 Karlskirche ... A1
2 Schloss Belvedere ... C2

Sights
3 Alpengarten ... C3
4 Belvedere Gardens ... C2
5 Botanischer Garten ... C3
6 Oberes Belvedere ... C3
7 Stadtbahn Pavillons ... A1
Unteres Belvedere ... (see 2)

Activities, Courses & Tours
8 3.MannTour ... A1
9 Wiener Eislaufverein ... B1

Sleeping
10 Hotel Imperial ... B1

Eating
11 Gmoakeller ... C1

Drinking & Nightlife
12 Café Schwarzenberg ... B1
13 Club U ... A1
14 Kaffeefabrik ... A2
15 Salm Bräu ... C2

Entertainment
16 Konzerthaus ... B1
17 Musikverein ... B1
18 Radiokulturhaus ... B2

Festivals & Events

★Christkindlmärkte CHRISTMAS MARKET
(www.wien.info/en/shopping-wining-dining/markets/christmas-markets; mid-Nov–24 Dec) Vienna's much-loved Christmas market season runs from around mid-November to Christmas Eve. Magical *Christkindlmärkte* in streets and squares have stalls selling wooden toys, festive decorations and traditional food such as *Würstel* (sausages) and *Glühwein*. The centrepiece is the **Wiener Weihnachtstraum Christkindlmarkt** (www.wienerweihnachtstraum.at; 01, Rathausplatz; mid-Nov–26 Dec; D, 1, 71 Rathausplatz/Burgtheater, U Rathaus) on Rathausplatz but you'll find them across the city including at **Schloss Schönbrunn** (www.weihnachtsmarkt.co.at; 13, Schloss Schönbrunn; late Nov-early Jan; ; U Schönbrunn).

Ostermärkte FAIR
(Easter Markets; www.wien.info/en/shopping-wining-dining/markets/easter-markets; Mar/Apr) Easter markets at several locations throughout Vienna, including **Am Hof** (www.ostermarkt-hof.at; 01, Am Hof; Mar/Apr; U Herrengasse) in the centre and at **Schloss Schönbrunn**

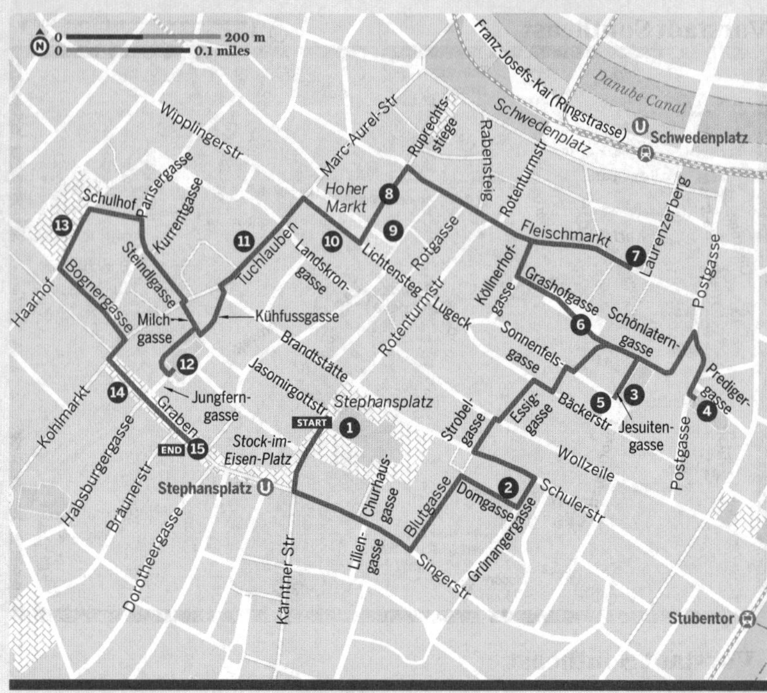

City Walk
The Historic Centre

START STEPHANSDOM
FINISH GRABEN
LENGTH 3KM; 90 MINUTES TO FIVE HOURS

Begin at Vienna's signature cathedral, **1 Stephansdom** (p67). After following a small section of Kärntner Strasse, you'll wind through the atmospheric backstreets to **2 Mozarthaus Vienna** (p70), where the great composer lived for almost three years.

A series of narrow lanes leads you down towards two fine baroque churches. The interior of the **3 Jesuitenkirche** is pure deception, with frescos creating the illusion of a dome, while the 1634 **4 Dominikanerkirche** is a fine example of early baroque church building. The Jesuitenkirche is opposite the **5 Österreichische Akademie der Wissenschaften** (Austrian Academy of Sciences; www.oeaw.ac.at) FREE, housed in a university building dating from 1755.

During daylight hours, you can enter **6 Heiligenkreuzerhof** from the eastern side (at night time, enter it from Grasshofgasse). During the Christmas period, this lovely, tranquil courtyard is filled with traditional decorations.

Busy **7 Fleischmarkt** is the heart of the traditional Greek quarter of Vienna, where the Greek merchants settled from the 18th century. Climb the stairs and enter the lively 'Bermuda Triangle' of bars on **8 Judengasse**, the centre of the traditional Jewish quarter. These days, Hoher Markt – Vienna's oldest square – is a busy commercial street. Highlights here include the art-nouveau **9 Ankeruhr**, a mechanical clock with historic figures marking the time as they pass over the clock face, and the **10 Römer Museum** (p71), Roman ruins dating from the 1st to the 5th century. You'll then pass the remarkable **11 Neidhart-Fresken** mural and reach the impressive **12 Peterskirche**, with a fresco on the dome painted by Johann Michael Rottmayr and a golden altar.

Northwest of here, **13 Am Hof** is spiked by an impressive Mariensäule column. As you make your way along Graben back towards Stephansplatz, pop into **14 Adolf Loos' Public Toilets**, with mahogany-panelled stalls, then admire the 1693 gilded baroque **15 Pestsäule memorial** to Vienna's 75,000 plague victims.

(www.ostermarkt.co.at; 13, Schloss Schönbrunn; Mar/Apr; ; U Schönbrunn, Hietzing), herald the arrival of spring with traditional Easter decorations, and floral and Easter egg displays. There are also food and drink stalls and handicrafts, along with activities for kids. Markets typically take place in the two weeks leading up to Easter.

Jazz Fest Wien MUSIC

(www.viennajazz.org; late Jun–mid-Jul) From late June to mid-July, Vienna swings to jazz, blues and soul flowing from the Staatsoper and a number of clubs across town, with many free concerts on outdoor stages.

Wien Modern MUSIC

(www.wienmodern.at; late Oct-late Nov) Modern classical and avant-garde music, including many world-first performances, feature at this month-long festival at over two dozen venues Vienna-wide.

Wiener Festwochen ART

(Vienna Festival; www.festwochen.at; mid-May–mid-Jun) A wide-ranging program of theatrical productions, concerts, dance performances and visual arts from around the world, the month-long Wiener Festwochen takes place at various venues city-wide.

Donauinselfest MUSIC

(https://donauinselfest.at; late Jun) FREE Held over three days on a weekend in late June, the Donauinselfest features a feast of rock, pop, folk and country performers, and attracts almost three million onlookers. Best of all, it's free!

Lange Nacht der Museen CULTURAL

(Long Night of Museums; http://langenacht.orf.at; ticket adult/child €15/12; 1st Sat Oct) On the first Saturday of October, around 700 museums nationwide open their doors to visitors between 6pm and 1am. One ticket (available at museums) allows entry to them all – including scores in Vienna alone. The ticket price also includes public transport around town.

ImPulsTanz DANCE

(www.impulstanz.com; mid-Jul–mid-Aug) Vienna's premier avant-garde dance festival attracts an array of internationally renowned troupes and newcomers over a month in summer. Performances are held in the MuseumsQuartier, Volkstheater and many other venues.

Viennale Film Festival FILM

(www.viennale.at; late Oct-early Nov) The country's best film festival features fringe and independent films from around the world, including international premieres. Screenings take place at numerous locations around the city over two weeks.

Silvester NEW YEAR

(New Year's Eve; www.wien.info/en/music-stage-shows/new-years-eve; 31 Dec) The Innere Stadt becomes one big party zone for Silvester, which features outdoor concerts, food and drink stalls, waltzing classes and fireworks.

Sleeping

Vienna's lodgings cover it all, from luxury establishments where chandeliers, antique furniture and original 19th-century oil paintings abound and cutting-edge, statement-making design hotels to inexpensive youth hostels. In between are homey, often family-run *Pensionen* (guesthouses), many traditional, and less ostentatious hotels, plus a smart range of apartments.

The Hofburg & Around

Pertschy Palais Hotel HOTEL €€

(Map p68; 01-534 49-9; www.pertschy.com; 01, Habsburgergasse 5; s/d/f from €142/157/233; ; U Herrengasse, Stephansplatz) The baroque, 18th-century-built Palais Cavriani's quiet yet central location, just off the Graben, is hard to beat. Staff are exceedingly friendly, and children are warmly welcomed (toys for toddlers and high chairs for tots are available). Decorated in creams, royal reds and golds, its 55 spacious, antique-furnished rooms have parquet floors. Family rooms have period fireplaces (alas, not in use).

Aviano PENSION €€

(Map p68; 01-512 83 30; www.avianoboutiquehotel.com; 01, Marco-d'Aviano-Gasse 1; s/d/ste from €89/119/135; ; U Stephansplatz) Aviano offers a supercentral position, high standards and all-round value for money. Rooms feature high ceilings and whitewashed antique furnishings; corner rooms have a charming alcove and bay window. Breakfast (€12) is served in a bright, sunny room and on a small balcony overlooking the courtyard in summer. Extra beds (per person €30 to €39) make it a good family option.

★Hotel Sacher HISTORIC HOTEL €€€
(Map p68; ☎01-514 561 555; www.sacher.com; 01, Philharmonikerstrasse 4; d/ste from €417/767; ; D, 1, 2, 71 Kärntner Ring/Oper, U Karlsplatz) Stepping into Hotel Sacher is like turning back the clocks 100 years. The lobby's dark-wood panelling, original oil paintings, deep-red shades and heavy gold chandelier are reminiscent of a fin-de-siècle bordello. The smallest rooms are surprisingly large and suites are truly palatial. Extras include a taste of the cafe's (p108) famous *Sacher Torte* on arrival.

Stephansdom & the Historic Centre

★Grand Ferdinand Hotel DESIGN HOTEL €€
(Map p68; ☎01-918 80; www.grandferdinand.com; 01, Schubertring 10-12; dm/d/ste from €30/176/470; ; 2, 71 Schwarzenbergplatz) An enormous taxidermied horse stands in the reception area of this ultra-hip hotel. The Grand Ferdinand is shaking up Vienna's accommodation scene by offering parquet-floored eight-bed dorms with mahogany bunks alongside richly coloured designer rooms with chaise longues and chandeliered suites with private champagne bars. Breakfast (€29) is served on the panoramic rooftop terrace, adjacent to the heated, open-air infinity pool.

Hotel Capricorno HOTEL €€
(Map p68; ☎01-533 31 04-0; www.schick-hotels.com/hotel-capricorno; 01, Schwedenplatz 3-4; s/d from €124/148; P; 1, 2 Schwedenplatz, U Schwedenplatz) Set behind an unpromising mid-20th-century facade, Hotel Capricorno has been stunningly made over in lustrous velveteens in zesty lime, orange, lemon and aubergine shades. Most of its 42 rooms have balconies (front rooms overlook the Danube Canal; rear rooms are quieter). It's 600m northeast from Stephansdom (around a 10-minute stroll).

Ruby Lissi BOUTIQUE HOTEL €€
(Map p68; ☎01-205 55 18-0; www.ruby-hotels.com; 01, Fleischmarkt 19; d from €119; @; 1, 2 Schwedenplatz, U Schwedenplatz) Guitars are available for loan at this rocking hotel, which has in-room Marshall amps (and soundproofing!). The hotel's own radio station plays in the bar and can be streamed on in-room tablets. Rooms have vintage and designer furniture; bathrooms are open-plan but can be screened by curtains. Breakfast (€16) is organic; bike hire per day costs €10.

Hotel Austria HOTEL €€
(Map p68; ☎01-515 23; www.hotelaustria-wien.at; 01, Fleischmarkt 20; s/d/tr/q from €88/120/174/192; @; 1, 2 Schwedenplatz, U Stephansplatz, Schwedenplatz) This elegant 46-room hotel offers some of the best value in the Innere Stadt. Cosy rooms come with minibars and kettles for tea and coffee. Cheaper singles (from €71) and doubles (from €103) have private showers but share toilets. Bike hire costs €8 per day. The 2nd-floor terrace stays open until 10pm. Cots and babysitting services are available.

★DO & CO DESIGN HOTEL €€€
(Map p68; ☎01-241 88; www.docohotel.com; 01, Stephansplatz 12; d/ste from €248/706; ; U Stephansplatz) Up-close views of Stephansdom extend from higher-priced rooms at this swanky hotel, and all 43 rooms and suites come with state-of-the-art entertainment systems and multi-country power sockets. Some have in-room Jacuzzis, but be aware that bathrooms (not toilets) have transparent glass walls. Cathedral views also unfold from the 6th-floor bar and 7th-floor rooftop restaurant and terrace.

Karlsplatz & Around Naschmarkt

Wombat's City Hostel Naschmarkt HOSTEL €€
(Map p82; ☎01-897 23 36; www.wombats-hostels.com; 04, Rechte Wienzeile 35; dm/s/d from €22/65/86.50; @; U Kettenbrückengasse) Bright and modern, Wombat's City Hostel Naschmarkt directly overlooks Vienna's biggest market, and is within easy walking distance of the city's main sights. Well-lit, airy dorms and private rooms come with en suite bathrooms and free lockers; great facilities include a self-catering kitchen, laundry and a lively bar. The all-you-can-eat breakfast costs €4.90.

The original Wombat's Vienna hostel is near Westbahnhof.

Das Tyrol DESIGN HOTEL €€
(Map p82; 01-587 54 15; www.das-tyrol.at; 06, Mariahilfer Strasse 15; d/studios from €175/215; P ❄ 📶; U Museumsquartier) Design is the watchword at Das Tyrol. Done out in taupes, creams and golds, the spacious rooms feature bold original artworks, marble bathrooms and amenities including Nespresso machines. Corner rooms have small balconies overlooking Mariahilfer Strasse. The gold-tiled spa has a sauna and a 'light therapy' shower where you can watch fish swim in the aquarium.

★ **Hotel Imperial** HISTORIC HOTEL €€€
(Map p95; 01-501 100; www.marriott.com; 01, Kärntner Ring 16; d/ste from €364/470; @ 📶; D, 1, 71 Karlsplatz, U Karlsplatz) This rambling former palace, with all the marble and majesty of the Habsburg era, has service as polished as its crystal. Suites are filled with 19th-century paintings and genuine antique furniture (and come with butler service), while 4th- and 5th-floor rooms in Biedermeier style are far cosier and may come with a balcony. A lavish breakfast buffet costs €41.

The Museum District & Neubau

Hotel am Brillantengrund HOTEL €
(Map p82; 01-523 36 62; www.brillantengrund.com; 07, Bandgasse 4; s/d/tr/q from €59/69/89/109; @ 📶; 49 Westbahnstrasse/Zieglergasse) In a lemon-yellow building set around a courtyard strewn with potted palms, this community linchpin works with local artists and hosts regular exhibitions, along with DJs, live music and other events such as pop-up markets and shops. Parquet-floored rooms are simple but decorated in '50s to '70s themes with vintage furniture, local artworks, and retro wallpapers and light fittings.

Pension Wild PENSION €
(Map p72; 01-406 51 74; www.pension-wild.com; 08, Lange Gasse 10; s/d/tr from €59/69/89, s/d without bathroom from €49/59; 📶; 2 Rathaus, U Rathaus) In a 1904 patrician house, Wild is one of the few openly gay-friendly *Pensionen* in Vienna, and the warm welcome extends to all walks of life. Simple top-floor 'luxury' rooms have light-wood furniture, private bathrooms and minibars. All are spotlessly clean and kitchens are there for guests to use. Bike storage is free; bike hire per day costs €15.

★ **Boutiquehotel Stadthalle** HOTEL €€
(Map p82; 01-982 42 72; www.hotelstadthalle.at; 15, Hackengasse 20; s/d/f from €78/128/181; P 📶; 9/49 Beingasse) Achieving a zero-energy balance, this hotel makes the most of solar power, rainwater collection and LED lighting, and has a roof planted with fragrant lavender. Vivid shades of purple, pink and peach enliven the 79 vintage-meets-modern rooms. They're split over two buildings divided by an ivy-draped courtyard where organic breakfasts (including honey from its rooftop hives) are served in fine weather.

25hours Hotel DESIGN HOTEL €€
(Map p72; 01-521 510; www.25hours-hotels.com; 07, Lerchenfelder Strasse 1-3; d/ste from €115/149; P 📶; 46 Auerspergstrasse, U Volkstheater) Decked out in bold colours, with big-top-style murals and pod-shaped rugs, the 217 Dreimeta-designed rooms here include 34 suites with kitchenettes. Suites have floor-to-ceiling windows with grandstand views of the Hofburg. The **Dachboden** (Map p72; www.dachbodenwien.at; 07, Lerchenfelder Strasse 1-3; 3pm-1am; 📶; 46 Auerspergstrasse, U Volkstheater) rooftop bar, Mermaid's Cave sauna area and free use of cool Schindelhauer bikes for whizzing about town make it a class act.

Alsergrund & the University District

Hotel Harmonie HOTEL €€
(Map p72; 01-317 66 04; www.harmonie-vienna.at; 09, Harmoniegasse 5-7; s €153-228, d €173-243, ste €218-258; @ 📶; U Rosauer Lände) Lodged in an original Otto Wagner building, this family-run, eco-conscious hotel is a cut above most hotels in Alsergrund. The bright, allergy-friendly rooms are jazzed up by the dynamic paintings of artist Luis Casanova Sorolla. There's also a fitness room and a library lounge area. Prosecco and honey from a Viennese beekeeper appear at breakfast, which emphasises regional and organic produce.

Schloss Belvedere to the Canal

Mooons BOUTIQUE HOTEL €€
(01-962 26; www.mooons.com; 04, Wiedner Gürtel 16; d €89-150; ; Hauptbahnhof) Boutique-chic Mooons brings a dash of contemporary cool to the neighbourhood surrounding Schloss Belvedere. A striking black facade dotted with circular windows gives way to a sexy, monochrome, gold-kissed interior that's very millennial glam. Rooms are minimalist, with smart TV, rain showers and a 'virtual concierge', and there's a fitness room and roof terrace with far-reaching city views.

Ruby Sofie BOUTIQUE HOTEL €€
(01-20 57 71 20; www.ruby-hotels.com; 03, Marxergasse 17; d €103-205; ; Wien Mitte) 'Lean luxury' is the ethos of this slick boutique hotel occupying the Sofiensäle, a grand former concert hall. Interiors are minimal-stylish, the vibe laid-back, and the pared-down rooms with oak floors have vintage furnishings, docking stations, in-room tablets and rain showers. There's also a library, a bar that loans out a guitar, a yoga terrace and bike rental (€10 per day).

Prater & East of the Danube

★Grätzlhotel BOUTIQUE HOTEL €€
(Map p102; 01-208 39 04; www.graetzlhotel.com; 02, Grosse Sperlgasse 6; d excl breakfast €93-125; Taborstrasse) Where electricians, lamp makers and bakers once plied a trade, the Grätzlhotel has injected new life into Leopoldstadt with ultracool interiors courtesy of some of Vienna's top architects. Just around the corner from Karmelitermarkt, the suites are minimalist and streamlined, with vintage lights and homey touches – kitchens with Nespresso makers, retro radios and Viennese Saint Charles Apotheke toiletries.

★Magdas BOUTIQUE HOTEL €€
(Map p102; 01-720 02 88; www.magdas-hotel.at; 02, Laufbergergasse 2; d €70-150; Praterstern) How clever: the Magdas is a hotel making a difference, as the staff who welcome guests are refugees. The former retirement home turned modestly priced boutique hotel is sustainable on all levels. The rooms are retro cool, with one-of-a-kind donated artworks, knitted lampshades courtesy of nimble-fingered volunteers, and upcycling. The pick have balconies overlooking the Prater, just around the corner.

Schloss Schönbrunn & Around

Angel's Place GUESTHOUSE €
(Map p101; 0660 773 05 35; www.angelsplacevienna.com; 15, Weiglgasse 1; d/apt from €55/133; ; Schönbrunn) A wine cellar has been converted into this cute guesthouse a 650m stroll northeast of Schloss Schönbrunn's gates. Its basement rooms are cosy, with wood floors, whitewashed walls and original brick vaulting, and guests can use a shared kitchen. The ground-floor, four-person apartment comes with its own kitchen and a private entrance.

Eating

Dining in Vienna gives you a taste of the city's history, at street stands sizzling up sausages, in candlelit vaulted-cellar wine bars and earthy, wood-panelled *Beisln* serving goulash and *Wiener Schnitzel*; its present, at hip cafes, multiethnic markets and international eateries; and its future, at innovative spaces with a wave of exciting chefs pushing in new directions.

The Hofburg & Around

★Bitzinger Würstelstand am Albertinaplatz STREET FOOD €
(Map p68; www.bitzinger-wien.at; 01, Albertinaplatz; sausages €3.50-4.70; 8am-4am; D, 1, 2, 71 Kärntner Ring/Oper, Karlsplatz, Stephansplatz) Behind the Staatsoper, Vienna's best sausage stand has cult status. Bitzinger offers the contrasting spectacle of ladies and gents dressed to the nines, sipping beer, wine or Joseph Perrier champagne while tucking into sausages at outdoor tables or the heated counter after performances. Mustard comes in *Süss* (sweet, ie mild) or *Scharf* (fiercely hot).

Trześniewski SANDWICHES €
(Map p68; www.trzesniewski.at; 01, Dorotheergasse 1; 1/8 sandwiches €1.40/8.40; 8.30am-7.30pm Mon-Fri, 9am-6pm Sat, 10am-5pm Sun; Stephansplatz) Trześniewski has

Schönbrunn

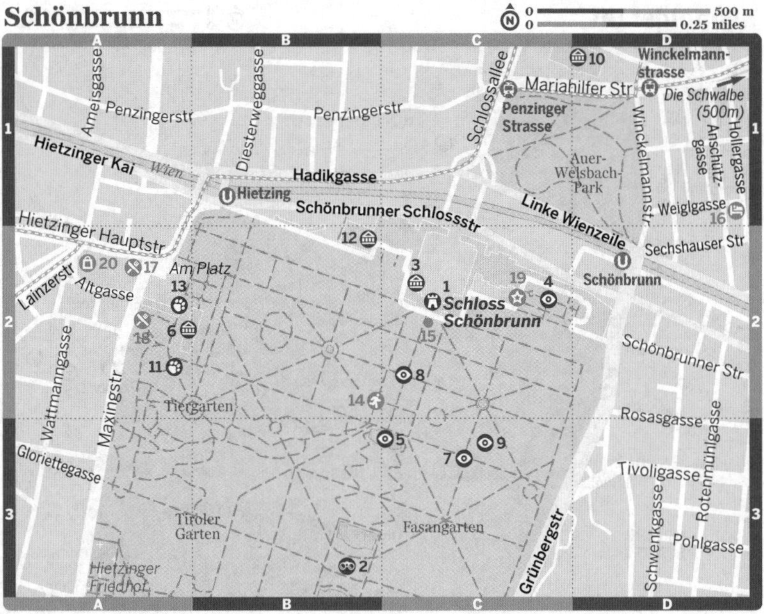

Schönbrunn

Top Sights
1 Schloss Schönbrunn C2

Sights
2 Gloriette B3
3 Kindermuseum C2
4 Kronprinzengarten C2
5 Neptunbrunnen C3
6 Palmenhaus A2
7 Roman Ruins C3
8 Schloss Schönbrunn Gardens C2
9 Schöner Brunnen C3
10 Technisches Museum D1
11 Tiergarten A2
12 Wagenburg B2
13 Wüstenhaus A2

Activities, Courses & Tours
14 Irrgarten B2
15 Schönbrunner Panoramabahn C2

Sleeping
16 Angel's Place D1

Eating
17 Brandauers Schlossbräu A2
18 Maxing Stüberl A2

Drinking & Nightlife
Café Gloriette .... (see 2)

Entertainment
19 Marionetten Theater C2

Shopping
20 1130Wein A2

been serving exquisite open-faced finger-style sandwiches since 1902. Choose from 22 delectable toppings incorporating primarily Austrian-sourced produce – chicken liver; smoked salmon and horseradish cream cheese; wild paprika and red pepper; egg and cucumber – on dark Viennese bread. This branch is the flagship of a now 11-strong chain in Vienna.

Café Mozart CAFE €€
(Map p68; 01-241 00-200; www.cafe-mozart.at; 01, Albertinaplatz 2; mains €14-32, cakes & pastries €4.50-8.50, mains €14-32; kitchen 8am-11.30pm, bar to midnight; ; U Karlsplatz) Opening to a covered terrace, 1794-established Café Mozart serves classic Viennese cakes including *Apfelstrudel* (apple strudel), *Esterhazy Torte* (layered almond cake), *Sacher Torte* (chocolate cake with apricot jam) and *Rehrücken* (chocolate-almond

Leopoldstadt

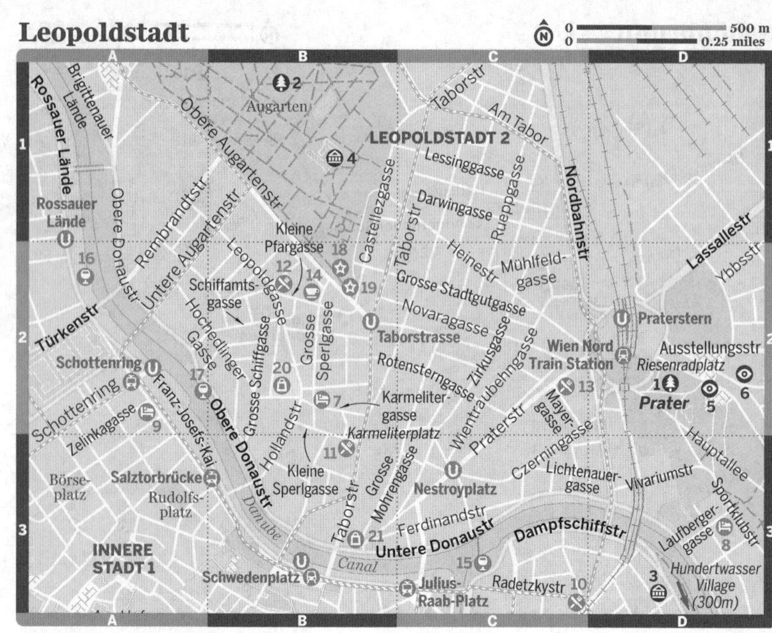

Leopoldstadt

Top Sights

1 Prater ... D2

Sights

2 Augarten ... B1
3 KunstHausWien ... D3
4 Porzellanmuseum im Augarten ... B1
5 Riesenrad ... D2
6 Würstelprater ... D2

Sleeping

7 Grätzlhotel ... B2
8 Magdas ... D3
9 Österreichischer Jugendherbergsverband ... A2

Eating

10 Garage 01 ... C3
11 Harvest ... B3
12 Skopik & Lohn ... B2
13 Supersense ... C2

Drinking & Nightlife

14 Sperlhof ... B2
15 Strandbar Herrmann ... C3
16 Summer Stage ... A2
17 Tel Aviv Beach ... A2

Entertainment

18 Kino wie noch nie ... B2
19 MuTh ... B2

Shopping

20 Karmelitermarkt ... B2
21 Stilwerk Wien ... B3

mousse dipped in dark chocolate). More substantial dishes span *Tafelspitz* (boiled beef) with creamed spinach potato salad to beef goulash with bread dumplings.

★ **Meinl's Restaurant** INTERNATIONAL €€€
(Map p68; ☎01-532 33 34 6000; www.meinlamgraben.at; 01, Graben 19; mains €27-39, 4-course menus €79; ⏲8am-11pm Mon-Fri, from 9am Sat; 📶; Ⓤ Stephansplatz) Meinl's combines cuisine of superlative quality with an unrivalled wine list and views of Graben. Creations at its high-end restaurant span calamari and white-truffle risotto, and apple-schnapps–marinated pork fillet with green beans and chanterelles. The providore, **Julius Meinl am Graben** (Map p68; www.meinlamgraben.at; 01, Graben 19; ⏲8am-7.30pm Mon-Fri, 9am-6pm Sat; Ⓤ Stephansplatz), has a cafe and a sushi bar, and the cellar wine bar serves great-value lunch menus.

Stephansdom & the Historic Centre

Simply Raw Bakery VEGAN €
(Map p68; www.simplyrawbakery.at; 01, Drahtgasse 2; dishes €7-12; 9am-6pm Mon-Sat; ; Herrengasse) At Simply Raw, superfoods, nuts, seeds, fruit, veggies and herbs are organic, everything is vegan, and nothing is cooked above 42°C to preserve the vitamin content. The vintage-style black-and-cream floor tiles, chandelier and striped feature wall form a charming backdrop for dishes like banana bread with homemade hazelnut-and-cocoa spread, avocado cake with vegan sour cream, and pumpkin and poppy-seed tart.

Marco Simonis Bastei 10 CAFE €
(Map p68; 01-512 20 10; www.marcosimonis.com; 01, Dominikanerbastei 10; dishes €7.50-16; 8.30am-9pm Mon-Fri; ; Stubentor) A hybrid interior-design shop, deli and cafe with wooden stools and high tables, this is a bright, stylish spot for breakfast (try the smoked salmon with poached eggs), gourmet brunch baguettes, soups and salads, tasting platters, smoothies and fresh juices. Afterwards browse for everything from cookbooks to candles, glassware and freshly cut flowers.

★ **Wrenkh** BISTRO €€
(Map p68; 01-533 15 26; www.wrenkh-wien.at; 01, Bauernmarkt 10; mains €11.50-30; 11am-10pm Mon-Sat; ; Stephansplatz) Wrenkh specialises in vegetables, like lentils in white-wine sauce with bread dumplings, roast sweet potato stuffed with goat's cheese, and pumpkin soufflé with pistachio pesto. It also creates some superb fish-based dishes (grilled mountain-stream trout with smoked-garlic potato salad) and meat options (dry-aged rib-eye with miso and aubergine crème). On weekdays, bargain-priced two-/three-course lunch menus cost €10.50/11.50.

Brezl Gwölb AUSTRIAN €€
(Map p68; 01-533 88 11; www.brezl.at; 01, Ledererhof 9; mains €11-21.50; 11.30am-midnight; Herrengasse) Hidden down an alley near Freyung, Brezl Gwölb has won a loyal following for its winningly fresh Austrian home cooking. Atmospherically lit by candles, with classical music playing in the background, the crypt-like cellar magics you back in time with its carvings, brick arches, wrought-iron lanterns and alcoves. No wonder the place overflows with regulars.

Figlmüller AUSTRIAN €€
(Map p68; 01-512 61 77; www.figlmueller.at; 01, Wollzeile 5; mains €13-20.50; 11am-9.30pm; ; Stephansplatz) Vienna would simply be at a loss without Figlmüller. This famous *Beisl* has a rural decor and some of the biggest (on average 30cm in diameter) and best schnitzels in the business. Wine is from the owner's vineyard, but no beer is served. Its popularity has spawned a second location nearby on **Bäckerstrasse** (Map p68; 01-512 17 60; www.figlmueller.at; 01, Bäckerstrasse 6; mains €13.50-22; 11am-9.30pm; Stephansplatz) with a wider menu (and drinks list).

Huth Gastwirtschaft AUSTRIAN €€
(Map p68; 01-513 56 44; www.zum-huth.at; 01, Schellinggasse 5; mains €12.90-18.90; noon-11pm; 2 Weihburggasse) One of several local neo-*Beisln* in this under-the-radar part of Innere Stadt, Huth serves superb Viennese classics such as *Wiener Schnitzel* with cranberry sauce and parsley potatoes, *Selchfleisch* (smoked pork with sauerkraut) and desserts including *Topfenstrudel* (quark-filled strudel) in a high-ceilinged main dining room, vaulted brick cellar and a summer terrace.

Motto am Fluss INTERNATIONAL €€
(Map p68; 01-252 55 10; www.mottoamfluss.at; 01, Franz-Josefs-Kai 2; restaurant mains €12.50-29, cafe dishes €5-12.50; restaurant 11.30am-2pm & 6-11.30pm Mon-Fri, 6-11.30pm Sat & Sun, cafe 8am-midnight daily, bar 6pm-4am daily; ; 1, 2 Schwedenplatz, Schwedenplatz) Located inside the Wien-City ferry terminal, with dazzling views of the Danube Canal, Motto am Fluss' restaurant serves Austro-international cuisine with quality organic meats, fish such as Donau trout, and vegetarian and vegan options. Its upstairs cafe does great all-day breakfasts, cakes and pastries, and its bar is a superbly relaxed hang-out for Austrian wines, beers and house-creation cocktails.

★ **Griechenbeisl** AUSTRIAN €€
(Map p68; 01-533 19 77; www.griechenbeisl.at; 01, Fleischmarkt 11; mains €17-29; 11.30am-11.30pm; ; 1, 2 Schwedenplatz, Schwedenplatz) Dating from 1447, and frequented by Beethoven, Brahms, Schubert and Strauss among other luminaries, Vienna's oldest restaurant has vaulted rooms, wood panelling

DON'T MISS

NASCHMARKT

Vienna's famous **market and eating strip** (Map p82; www.wien.gv.at; 06, Linke & Rechte Wienzeile; 6am-7.30pm Mon-Fri, to 5pm Sat; ; Karlsplatz, Kettenbrückengasse) began life as a farmers market in the 18th century, when the fruit market on Freyung was moved here. Interestingly, a law passed in 1793 said that fruit and vegetables arriving in town by cart had to be sold on Naschmarkt, while anything brought in by boat could be sold from the decks.

The fruits of the Orient poured in, the predecessors of the modern-day sausage stand were erected, and sections were set aside for coal, wood and farming tools and machines. Officially, it became known as Naschmarkt ('munch market') in 1905, a few years after Otto Wagner bedded the Wien River down in its open-topped stone and concrete sarcophagus. This Otto Wagnerian horror was a blessing for Naschmarkt, because it created space to expand. A close shave came in 1965 when there were plans to tear it down – it was saved, and today the Naschmarkt is not only the place to shop for food but has a **flea market** (Map p82; 05, Linke Wienzeile; 6.30am-2pm Sat; Kettenbrückengasse) each Saturday.

and a plant-fringed front garden that's lovely in summer. Every classic Viennese dish is on the menu, along with three daily vegetarian options.

★Plachutta — AUSTRIAN €€€

(Map p68; 01-512 15 77; www.plachutta-wollzeile.at; 01, Wollzeile 38; mains €19-27.20; 11.30am-11.15pm; Stubentor) If you're keen to taste *Tafelspitz*, you can't beat this specialist wood-panelled, white-tableclothed restaurant. It serves no fewer than 13 varieties from different cuts of Austrian-reared beef, such as *Mageres Meisel* (lean, juicy shoulder meat), *Beinfleisch* (larded rib meat) and *Lueger Topf* (shoulder meat with beef tongue and calf's head). Save room for the Austrian cheese plate.

Karlsplatz & Around Naschmarkt

★Vollpension — CAFE €

(Map p82; www.vollpension.wien; 04, Schleifmühlgasse 16; dishes €5-10; 7.30am-10pm Mon-Sat, 8am-8pm Sun; ; Karlsplatz) This white-painted brick space with mismatched vintage furniture, tasselled lampshades and portraits on the walls is run by 15 *Omas* (grandmas) and *Opas* (grandpas) along with their families, with over 200 cakes in their collective repertoire. Breakfast (eg avocado and feta on pumpernickel bread) is served until 4pm; lunch dishes include a vegan goulash with potato and tofu. Cash only.

Entler — AUSTRIAN €€

(Map p82; 01-504 35 85; www.entler.at; 04, Schlüsselgasse 2; mains €14-28.50; 5-10pm Tue-Sat; ; 1, 62 Mayerhofgasse) While the setting beneath a vaulted ceiling is traditional, the cuisine here is cutting edge. Reinventions of Austrian classics include *Bergkässe* (hard cow's cheese) and black-truffle soup, pork medallions stuffed with apricots and smoked ham, roast hare strudel, and, for dessert, a walnut mousse sphere with hazelnut ice cream and candied hazelnut shards.

Ubl — AUSTRIAN €€

(Map p82; 01-587 64 37; 04, Pressgasse 26; mains €12-24; noon-2pm & 6-10pm Wed-Sun; Kettenbrückengasse) The menu at this much-loved *Beisl* is loaded with Viennese staples, such as *Wiener Rindsgulasch* (Viennese beef goulash), *Schweinsbraten* (roast pork) and four types of schnitzel, and is enhanced with seasonal cuisine throughout the year. You could do worse than finish the hefty meal off with a stomach-settling plum schnapps. The tree-shaded garden is wonderful in summer.

Veggiezz — VEGAN €€

(Map p68; 01-890 00 32; www.veggiezz.at; 01, Opernring 6; dishes €8-14; 11am-10pm Mon-Fri, noon-11pm Sat, noon-10pm Sun; ; D, 1, 2, 71 Kärntner Ring, Karlsplatz) In a bright, white space with sage-green chairs, pinewood floors and herbs growing in wall-mounted planter boxes, Vegiezz offers an all-vegan menu. It spans burgers, fries, quinotto (quinoa-based risotto) bowls and desserts such as avocado mousse with seasonal fruit, accompanied by homemade lemonade served in mason jar glasses.

MiLL AUSTRIAN €€
(Map p82; 01-966 40 73; www.mill32.at; 06, Millergasse 32; mains €11-21; 4-11pm Mon & Fri, 11.30am-2.30pm & 4-11pm Tue-Thu, 11am-4pm Sun; U Westbahnhof) This bistro, with a hidden courtyard for summer days, feels like a local secret. Scarlet-painted brick walls and wooden floors create a warm backdrop for seasonal dishes such as sweet-potato goulash or Styrian chicken salad drizzled in pumpkin-seed oil. Sunday is an all-you-can-eat brunch buffet (€19).

Café Drechsler CAFE €€
(Map p82; www.cafedrechsler.at; 06, Linke Wienzeile 22; mains lunch €9.50-12.50, dinner €12.50-14.90; 8am-midnight Mon-Sat, 9am-midnight Sun; U Kettenbrückengasse) A giant decoupage of ripped posters covers one wall at lively Drechsler. It's especially popular at brunch for poached eggs (with truffle aioli or spicy avocado), pancakes and French toast. Beyond Austrian dishes, lunch and dinner menus make international forays, from Indian masala curry to Thai papaya salad. Cocktails include a Ho-gu (prosecco, limoncello, elderberry syrup, mint and soda).

The Museum District & Neubau

Liebling CAFE €
(Map p82; 01-990 58 77; www.facebook.com/liebling1070; 07, Zollergasse 6; dishes €3.50-11; kitchen 9am-10pm, bar 9am-2am Mon-Thu, to 4am Fri & Sat, to midnight Sun; U Neubaugasse) No sign hangs above the door at Liebling, whose distressed walls, stripped-back floorboards and mishmash of flea-market furniture create a cool, laid-back vibe. Settle in for breakfast (until 4pm), sip fresh-squeezed juices, and lunch on wholesome daily specials like spinach-feta strudel or pumpkin and pine-nut wraps, topped off with chocolate-lavender cake. By night the bar is rocking. Cash only.

Swing Kitchen VEGAN €
(Map p82; www.swingkitchen.com; 07, Schottenfeldgasse 3; dishes €5-9; 11am-10pm; U Zieglergasse) Eco-minded Swing Kitchen calculates that its all-organic vegan burgers use 93% less land, 85% less water, 96% less grain, 95% less energy and produce 92% less greenhouse emissions than meat-based burgers. Its four varieties include a vegan schnitzel Vienna burger and Swing Burger with smoky barbecue sauce. Fries and onion rings are cooked in vegetable oil; there are also salads.

Figar CAFE €
(Map p82; 01-890 99 47; http://1070.figar.net; 07, Kirchengasse 18; breakfast €4.50-9.50, mains €10-16; kitchen 8am-10.30pm Mon-Fri, 9am-10.30pm Sat & Sun, bar to midnight Sun-Wed, to 2am Thu-Sat; 49 Siebensterngasse, U Neubaugasse) Splashed with a street-art-style mural, this neighbourhood favourite serves mighty breakfasts until 4pm, from Working Class Hero (sausage, mushrooms, homemade baked beans, spinach and skewered roast cherry tomatoes) to Exquisite (Viennese Thum ham, chorizo, Emmental and scrambled eggs), plus yoghurt, muesli, porridge and pastries. At night it morphs into a craft cocktail bar with a soundtrack of house music.

Veganista ICE CREAM €
(Map p82; www.veganista.at; 07, Neustiftgasse 23; 1/2/3 scoops €1.80/3.60/4.80; noon-11pm Mon-Thu, 11am-11pm Fri-Sun; 49 Volkstheater) Set up by two vegan sisters, Veganista's nondairy ice cream is made with organic, regional ingredients. Each day sees 18 flavours available, with some unusual ones in the mix such as basil, green tea, blueberry-lavender or date.

★ **Tian Bistro** VEGETARIAN €€
(Map p82; 01-890 466 532; www.tian-bistro.com; 07, Schrankgasse 4; mains €9-18; 5.30-10pm Mon, noon-10pm Tue-Fri, 10am-10pm Sat & Sun; 49 Siebensterngasse) Colourful tables are set up on the cobbled laneway outside Tian Bistro in summer, while indoors, a glass roof floods the atrium-style, greenery-filled dining room in light. It's the cheaper, more relaxed offspring of Michelin-starred vegetarian restaurant **Tian** (Map p68; 01-890 46 65; www.tian-restaurant.com; 01, Himmelpfortgasse 23; 4-/6-/8-course lunch menus €89/109/127, 8-course dinner menu €127; 6-9pm Tue, noon-2pm & 6-9pm Wed-Sat; 2 Weihburggasse, U Stephansplatz) ,

and serves sensational vegetarian and vegan dishes, such as black-truffle risotto with Piedmont hazelnuts, as well as brunch until 1pm on weekends.

Alsergrund & the University District

Stomach AUSTRIAN €€

(Map p72; ☎01-310 20 99; 09, Seegasse 26; mains €15-30; ⊙4pm-midnight Wed-Sat, 10am-10pm Sun; Ⓤ Rossauer Lände) Stomach has been serving belly-rumblingly good food for years. The menu brims with carefully plated meat, fish and vegetable dishes, including Styrian roast beef, cream-of-pumpkin soup, and, when in season, wild boar and venison. The interior is authentically rural, and the overgrown garden pretty. 'Stomach', interestingly, comes from rearranging the word Tomaschek, the butcher's shop originally located here.

Schloss Belvedere to the Canal

Garage 01 INTERNATIONAL €

(Map p102; ☎01-308 45 03; www.garage01.at; 03, Viaduktbogen 5, Radetzkyplatz; lunch €8.90-9.80, mains €11-19; ⊙noon-midnight Tue & Wed, to 2am Thu-Sat; 🚊0, 1 Radetzkyplatz) One of the hippest kids on the block, this bar-restaurant under the railway viaduct arches goes for the stylishly distressed look, with raw brickwork, peeling plaster and bentwood chairs. Come for cocktails, the occasional gig and a bite to eat – there's everything from tapas to mains like wild garlic, asparagus and pea risotto, and short ribs with wasabi and king oyster mushrooms.

★**Lingenhel** EUROPEAN €€

(☎01-710 15 66; www.lingenhel.com; 03, Landstrasser Hauptstrasse 74; lunch €10-13, mains €17-26; ⊙8am-10pm Mon-Sat; Ⓤ Rochusgasse) Lingenhel is an ultraslick deli-shop-bar-restaurant, lodged in a 200-year-old house. Salamis, wines and own-dairy cheeses tempt in the shop, while the pared-back, whitewashed restaurant homes in on season-inflected modern European food. As simple as trout with peas, turnip and orange, and scallop and asparagus risotto, this is food that tastes profoundly of what it ought to.

Joseph Brot BISTRO €€

(www.joseph.co.at; 03, Landstrasser Hauptstrasse 4; breakfast €6.90-14.80, lunch mains €10-16.50; ⊙bakery 7.30am-9pm Mon-Fri, 8am-6pm Sat & Sun, bistro 8am-9pm Mon-Fri, to 6pm Sat & Sun; Ⓤ Wien Mitte) Purveyors of Vienna's finest bread, Joseph Brot's bakery, bistro and patisserie is a winner. Besides wonderfully fresh loaves – organic olive-tomato ciabatta and rye-honey-lavender, for instance – it does wholesome breakfasts, speciality teas, healthy smoothies and yummy pastries. Season-driven specials such as sourdough *Spätzle* (noodles) with mountain cheese, lemon shallots and hispi cabbage star on the lunch menu in the stripped-back bistro.

Meierei im Stadtpark AUSTRIAN €€

(Map p68; ☎01-713 31 68; www.steirereck.at; 03, Am Heumarkt 2a; mains €19-22, set breakfasts €21-25; ⊙8am-11pm Mon-Fri, 9am-7pm Sat & Sun; 🌶; Ⓤ Stadtpark) In the green surrounds of Stadtpark, the Meierei is most famous for its goulash served with lemon, capers and creamy dumplings, and its selection of 120 types of cheese. Served until noon, the bountiful breakfast features gastronomic showstoppers such as poached duck egg with forest mushrooms and pumpkin, and corn waffles with warm tomato salad and sheep's cheese.

Gmoakeller AUSTRIAN €€

(Map p95; ☎01-712 53 10; www.gmoakeller.at; 03, Am Heumarkt 25; lunch €8.20, mains €10-18; ⊙11am-midnight Mon-Sat; Ⓤ Stadtpark) Sizzling and stirring since 1858, this atmospheric cellar is as traditional as it gets, with parquet floors, brick vaults and warm wood panelling. The classic grub – *Zwiebelrostbraten* (onion-topped roast beef) or Carinthian *Kas'nudeln* (cheese noodles) – goes nicely with tangy Austrian wines. Tables spill out onto the pavement in summer.

★**Steirereck im Stadtpark** GASTRONOMY €€€

(Map p68; ☎01-713 31 68; http://steirereck.at; 03, Am Heumarkt 2a; mains €38-58, 6-/7-course menus €149/165; ⊙11.30am-2.30pm & 6.30pm-midnight Mon-Fri; Ⓤ Stadtpark) Heinz Reitbauer is at the culinary helm of this two-starred Michelin restaurant, beautifully lodged in a 20th-century former dairy building in the leafy Stadtpark. His tasting menus are an exuberant feast, fizzing with natural, integral flavours that speak of a chef with exacting standards. Wine pairing is an additional €79/89 (six/seven courses).

Prater & East of the Danube

★Supersense CAFE €
(Map p102; https://the.supersense.com; 02, Praterstrasse 70; 2-course lunch €10, breakfast €3.80-9.20; 9.30am-7pm Tue-Fri, 10am-5pm Sat; U Praterstern) Housed in an ornate Italianate mansion dating to 1898, this retro-grand cafe brings a breath of cool air to the Prater area. The cafe at the front, which rolls out locally roasted coffee, great breakfasts and day specials, gives way to a store that trades in everything from vinyl to cult Polaroid cameras, calligraphy sets and hand-bound notebooks.

Harvest VEGAN €
(Map p102; 0676 4927790; www.harvest-bistrot.at; 02, Karmeliterplatz 1; mains €4.50-11, brunch €16.60, lunch €8.80; 2pm-midnight Mon-Fri, from 10am Sat & Sun; ; 2 Karmeliterplatz, U Nestroyplatz) A bubble of bohemian warmth, Harvest swears by seasonality in its superhealthy vegetarian and vegan dishes, swinging from lentil, pear, walnut and smoked tofu salad to coconutty vegetable curries. Candles, soft lamplight and mismatched vintage furniture set the scene, and there's a terrace for summer dining. Alt Wien roasted coffee, homemade cakes and weekend brunches round out the picture.

★Skopik & Lohn EUROPEAN €€
(Map p102; 01-219 89 77; www.skopikundlohn.at; 02, Leopoldsgasse 17; mains €11-29; 6pm-1am Tue-Sat; U Taborstrasse) The spidery web of scrawl that creeps across the ceiling at Skopik & Lohn gives an avant-garde edge to an otherwise French-style brasserie – all wainscoting, globe lights, cheek-by-jowl tables and white-jacketed waiters. The menu is modern European, with a Mediterranean slant, delivering spot-on dishes like slow-braised lamb with mint-pea purée, almonds and polenta, and pasta with summer truffle and monkfish.

Lusthaus AUSTRIAN €€
(01-728 95 65; 02, Freudenau 254; mains €13-20; noon-10pm Mon-Tue & Thu-Fri, to 6pm Sat & Sun; ; 77A Lusthaus) A stroll along the Prater's chestnut-shaded avenues works up an appetite for all-Austrian grub at this former 16th-century Habsburg hunting lodge. The pavilion was rebuilt in 1783 to host imperial festivities and the like. Today it shelters a chandelier-lit cafe and restaurant serving classics like beef broth with sliced pancakes, *Wiener Schnitzel* and *Marillenknödel* (apricot dumplings).

Schloss Schönbrunn & Around

Maxing Stüberl AUSTRIAN €€
(Map p101; www.maxingstuberl.at; 13, Maxingstrasse 7; mains €9-18.50; 5pm-midnight Mon-Fri, 1pm-midnight Sat & Sun; U Hietzing) Johann Strauss' one-time favourite, this dark-wood-panelled restaurant serves fabulously traditional dishes using produce from the owner's home region of Pielachtal, Lower Austria. Start with boiled beef aspic with onions and pumpkin-seed oil; continue with mains like fried blood sausage with sauerkraut and roasted potatoes or chicken cooked on an iron griddle; and finish with curd dumplings and stewed berries.

Brandauers Schlossbräu AUSTRIAN €€
(Map p101; 01-879 59 70; www.bierig.at; 13, Am Platz 5; mains €10.50-25; 10am-midnight; ; U Hietzing) This microbrewery rolls out hoppy house brews, speciality beers (including an organic one) and above-average pub fare. Famous spare ribs feature alongside the usual hearty suspects such as goulash and schnitzel as well as vegetarian options including salads and cheese-laden dumplings. The €9.90 lunch buffet is great value. Sit in the leafy courtyard when the sun's out.

Drinking & Nightlife

In this city where history often waltzes with the cutting edge, the drinking scene spans vaulted wine cellars here since Mozart's day to boisterous beer gardens, boho student dives, and cocktail, retro and rooftop bars. And with over 700 hectares of vineyards within its city limits, a visit to a *Heuriger* (wine tavern) is a quintessential Viennese experience.

The Hofburg & Around

★Café Leopold Hawelka COFFEE
(Map p68; www.hawelka.at; 01, Dorotheergasse 6; 8am-midnight Mon-Thu, to 1am Fri & Sat, 10am-midnight Sun; U Stephansplatz) Opened in 1939 by Leopold and Josefine Hawelka, whose son Günter and grandsons Amir and Michael still bake the house-speciality *Buchteln* (jam-filled, sugar-dusted yeast rolls) to

the family's secret recipe, this low-lit, picture-plastered coffee house is a living slice of Viennese history. Artists and writers who have hung out here have included Friedensreich Hundertwasser, Elias Canetti, Arthur Miller and Andy Warhol.

★Loos American Bar COCKTAIL BAR

(Map p68; www.loosbar.at; 01, Kärntner Durchgang 10; ⏲noon-4am; Ⓤ Stephansplatz) Loos is *the* spot in the Innere Stadt for a classic cocktail such as its signature dry martini, expertly whipped up by talented mixologists. Designed by Austrian architect Adolf Loos in 1908, this tiny 27-sq-metre box (seating just 20 or so patrons) is bedecked from head to toe in onyx, marble, mahogany and polished brass, with space-enhancing mirrored walls.

★Volksgarten ClubDiskothek CLUB

(Map p68; www.volksgarten.at; 01, Burgring 1; ⏲9pm-6am Thu, from 11pm Fri & Sat Apr–mid-Sep; 🚊D, 1, 2, 71 Ring/Volkstheater, Ⓤ Museumsquartier, Volkstheater) Spilling onto the Volksgarten's lawns, these early-19th-century premises are split into three areas: the Wintergarten lounge bar with vintage 1950s furnishings and palms; Cortic Säulenhalle (column hall), hosting live music and theme nights; and the hugely popular ClubDiskothek. Check the agenda online.

Café Sacher COFFEE

(Map p68; www.sacher.com; 01, Philharmonikerstrasse 4; ⏲8am-midnight; 🚊D, 1, 2, 71 Kärntner Ring/Oper, Ⓤ Karlsplatz) With a battalion of waiters and an air of nobility, this grand cafe is celebrated for its *Sacher Torte,* a wonderfully rich iced-chocolate cake with apricot jam once favoured by Emperor Franz Joseph. For the full-blown experience, head to the opulent chandelier-lit interior. There's also a covered pavement terrace, and a 1920s-styled tearoom, Sacher Eck, next door serving the same menu.

★Demel CAFE

(Map p68; www.demel.at; 01, Kohlmarkt 14; ⏲8am-7pm; 🚌1A, 2A Michaelerplatz, Ⓤ Herrengasse, Stephansplatz) Within sight of the Hofburg, this elegant and regal cafe has a gorgeous rococo-period salon. Demel's specialities include the *Annatorte* (a calorie-bomb of cream and nougat) and the *Fächertorte* (with apples, walnuts, poppy seeds and plum jam). The window displays an ever-changing array of edible art pieces (ballerinas and manicured bonsai, for example).

CAKE WARS: THE SACHER TORTE

Eduard Sacher, the son of the *Sacher Torte* creator Franz Sacher, began working at Demel in 1934, bringing the original recipe and sole distribution rights with him. Between 1938 and 1963 legal battles raged between Demel and Café Sacher over the trademark and title. An out-of-court settlement gave Café Sacher the rights to the phrase 'Original Sacher Torte', and Demel the rights to decorate its torte with a triangular seal reading 'Eduard-Sacher-Torte'. Each cafe still claims to be a cut above the other; try both and decide.

Stephansdom & the Historic Centre

★Kruger's American Bar BAR

(Map p68; www.krugers.at; 01, Krugerstrasse 5; ⏲6pm-3am Mon-Thu, to 4am Fri & Sat, 7pm-2am Sun; 🚊D, 1, 2, 71 Kärntner Ring/Oper, Ⓤ Stephansplatz) Retaining original decor from the 1920s and '30s, this dimly lit, wood-panelled American-style bar is a legend in Vienna, furnished with leather Chesterfield sofas and playing a soundtrack of Frank Sinatra, Dean Martin et al along with contemporary jazz. Cocktails such as highballs, fizzes, daiquiris and Collinses come in classic versions and creative spin-offs (eg Pisco Collins and lychee daiquiri).

★Needle Vinyl Bar BAR

(Map p68; www.needlevinylbar.com; 01, Färbergasse 8; ⏲11am-1am Mon-Sat, 2pm-1am Sun; 📶; Ⓤ Herrengasse) Retro-styled Needle Vinyl Bar has bare-brick walls, mismatched furniture, light fittings made from vintage gramophones, and a vinyl library of jazz, blues and rock to browse before giving the bar staff your requests. Designed like a vinyl record, the drinks list covers classic cocktails, local wines and Vienna-brewed beers. The bar's retractable glass frontage slides wide open in warm weather.

Zwölf Apostelkeller PUB

(Twelve Apostle Cellar; Map p68; 01-512 67 77; www.zwoelf-apostelkeller.at; 01, Sonnenfelsgasse 3; 11am-midnight; U Stephansplatz) Occupying a vast, dimly lit tri-level cellar dating back to the Romanesque and Gothic period, Zwölf Apostelkeller has a spirited atmosphere bolstered by traditional *Heuriger* ballads from 7pm daily. In addition to outstanding local wines there's also a good choice of schnapps and beer, and a menu of traditional dishes (schnitzel, suckling pig, *Tafelspitz*) made from all-Austrian ingredients.

1516 Brewing Company MICROBREWERY

(Map p68; www.1516brewingcompany.com; 01, Schwarzenbergstrasse 2; 10am-2am; 2 Schwarzenbergstrasse, U Karlsplatz) Copper vats and bare-brick walls create an industrial backdrop at this locally loved venue, which brews beers from malted wheat, rye and rice, including unusual varieties such as Heidi's Blueberry Ale. The awning-shaded terrace gets packed in summer. Arrive early for a good seat when it screens international football (soccer) games.

Karlsplatz & Around Naschmarkt

★Café Sperl COFFEE

(Map p82; www.cafesperl.at; 06, Gumpendorfer Strasse 11; 7am-10pm Mon-Sat, 10am-8pm Sun, closed Sun Jul & Aug; ; U Museumsquartier, Kettenbrückengasse) With its gorgeous *Jugendstil* fittings, grand dimensions, cosy booths and unhurried air, 1880-opened Sperl is one of the finest coffee houses in Vienna. The must-try is *Sperl Torte,* an almond-and-chocolate-cream dream. Grab a slice and a newspaper, order a coffee (from some three dozen kinds) and join the people-watching patrons. A pianist plays from 3.30pm to 5.30pm on Sundays.

★Café Schwarzenberg CAFE

(Map p95; www.cafe-schwarzenberg.at; 01, Kärntner Ring 17; 7.30am-midnight Mon-Fri, 8.30am-midnight Sat & Sun; ; 2, 71 Schwarzenbergplatz) One of the last remaining grand Viennese coffee houses on the Ringstrasse, this 1861 beauty has chandelier-lit vaulted ceilings, wood-panelled walls, marble tables and studded leather seats. Secessionist architect and designer Josef Hoffmann was among its patrons and it still draws a local crowd for its coffee, international newspapers, flaky *Warmer Topfenstrudel* (warm cheese-curd strudel) and sublime *Sacher Torte*.

★Kaffeefabrik CAFE

(Map p95; www.kaffeefabrik.at; 04, Favoritenstrasse 4-6; 8am-6pm Mon-Fri, 11am-5pm Sat; U Taubstummengasse) It's all about the beans at this small, whitewashed cafe-shop. Its small-batch speciality coffee is roasted in Burgenland to bring out the individual aromas of fair-trade beans sourced from Sumatra, India, Ethiopia, Ecuador, Brazil and Nicaragua. A Dalla Corte Evolution – the crème de la crème of espresso makers – and two Fiorenzato F64 Evo grinders ensure each cup is expertly made.

Club U CLUB

(Map p95; www.club-u.at; 01, Künstlerhauspassage; 9pm-4am; ; U Karlsplatz) Club U occupies one of Otto Wagner's **Stadtbahn Pavillons** (Map p95; www.wienmuseum.at; adult/child €5/free; 10am-6pm Tue-Sun Apr-Oct) on Karlsplatz. It's a small, student-favourite bar-club with regular DJs and a wonderful outdoor seating area overlooking the pavilions and park. Happy hour runs from 9pm to 11pm.

The Museum District & Neubau

★Melete Art Design Cocktails COCKTAIL BAR

(Map p82; www.melete.at; 07, Spittelberggasse 18; 5-10pm Thu & Fri, 3-10pm Sat; ; 49 Volkstheater) Both an art gallery and a hopping bar, Melete ingeniously pairs changing art exhibitions with inventive drinks. Its 'Africa' exhibition, for instance, featured cocktails like Madagascan Sunrise (vanilla-infused rum, hibiscus syrup and mango juice), while 'Art of Light' inspired concoctions such as Solar (yellow Chartreuse, gin, sweet vermouth and yuzu). Artworks exhibited are for sale; check the program online.

LOCAL KNOWLEDGE

SCHANIGÄRTEN

When the weather warms up, Viennese life spills outdoors to the *Schanigärten*. Unlike *Gastgärten* (beer gardens), *Schanigärten* set up on public property such as pavements and sometimes parking areas and squares according to inexpensive permits issued by authorities, which are valid from 1 March to 15 November. Actual opening dates depend on the weather each season.

★J Hornig Kaffeebar COFFEE

(Map p82; www.jhornig.com; 07, Siebensterngasse 29; ⌚7.30am-7pm Mon-Fri, 9am-7pm Sat & Sun; 📶; 🚋Siebensterngasse) Farm-direct beans roasted on-site at this third-wave coffee specialist are utilised in espresso, pour-over, Aeropress, ice-drip and cold-brew techniques to create a perfect cup, which you can pair with locally baked cakes. The state-of-the-art space has a stainless-steel ceiling, industrial fixtures and designer plywood chairs, and plenty of power sockets to recharge your devices.

Donau CLUB

(Map p82; www.donautechno.com; 07, Karl-Schweighofer-Gasse 10; ⌚8pm-4am Mon-Thu, to 6am Fri & Sat, to 2am Sun; Ⓤ Museumsquartier) DJs spin techno to a pumped crowd at this underground club with soaring columns, striking digital projections on the walls, and its own on-site *Würstelstand* (sausage stand). It's easily missed – look for the grey metal door. Hours can vary.

Siebensternbräu MICROBREWERY

(Map p82; www.7stern.at; 07, Siebensterngasse 19; ⌚11am-midnight; 📶; 🚋49 Siebensterngasse) Sample some of Vienna's finest microbrews at this lively, no-nonsense brewpub. Besides hoppy lagers and malty ales, there are unusual varieties like chilli or wood-smoked beer. Try them with pretzels or pub grub like schnitzel, goulash and pork knuckles (lunch mains €6.90, dinner mains €7.90 to €18.90). The courtyard garden fills up quickly in the warmer months.

Wirr BAR, CLUB

(Map p82; www.wirr.at; 07, Burggasse 70; ⌚8am-2am Sun-Wed, to 4am Thu-Sat; 🚋46 Strozzigasse) On weekends it's often hard to find a seat on the time-worn sofas at this colourful, alternative bar with walls covered in local artists' works. Electro clubbing events take place in the cellar at **Dual** (www.clubdual.at).

🍷 Alsergrund & the University District

★POC Cafe COFFEE

(Map p72; www.facebook.com/pg/poccafe; 08, Schlösselgasse 21; ⌚8am-5pm Mon-Fri; 🚋5, 43, 44 Lange Gasse, Ⓤ Schottentor) Friendly Robert Gruber is one of Vienna's coffee legends and his infectious passion ripples through this beautifully rambling, lab-like space. POC stands for 'People on Caffeine'; while filter, espresso-style or a summertime iced-cold brew are definitely this place's raison d'etre, it's also known for moreish sweets like killer poppy-seed cake, cheesecake or seasonal fruit tarts.

Birdyard COCKTAIL BAR

(Map p72; www.thebirdyard.at; 08, Lange Gasse 74; ⌚5.30pm-2am Tue-Sat; Ⓤ Rathaus) *Willkommen* (welcome) to one of Vienna's hottest drinking dens, lavishly decked out with trippy exotic murals of tropical birds, flowers and ferns – some of them courtesy of Romanian street artist Saddo. The cocktails are just as weird and wondrous – for instance, Peanut Butter Jelly Time, with Angostura bitters, rum, cranberries and peanut butter.

Beaver Brewing CRAFT BEER

(www.beaverbrewing.at; 09, Liechtensteinstrasse 69; ⌚4pm-midnight Mon-Thu, noon-1am Fri & Sat, noon-10pm Sun; Ⓤ Wien Währinger Strasse) There's an urban beat to this white-walled, postindustrial, American-style microbrewery, which pairs great craft beer, such as Magog (a barrel-aged dark ale) and crisp, hoppy IPAs, with comfort food like pulled-pork nachos, burgers and smoky spare ribs. There are no hipsters here and staff are genuinely eager to please.

Botanical Gardens COCKTAIL BAR

(Map p72; www.botanicalgarden.at; 09, Kolingasse 1; ⌚6pm-2am Tue-Thu, to 3am Fri & Sat; Ⓤ Schottentor) A subterranean mirror of Cafe Stein's sunny spaces above, Botanical Gardens makes for a cosy, magical retreat once Vienna's weather turns chilly. A dark nautical theme ticks all the cocktail-revival-scene boxes, but with enough local eccentricity to keep things interesting.

Achtundzwanzig WINE BAR

(Map p72; www.achtundzwanzig.at; 08, Schlösselgasse 28; ⌚4pm-1am Mon-Thu, to 2am Fri, 7pm-2am Sat; 🚊1, 43, 44 Lange Gasse, Ⓤ Schottentor) Austrian wine fans with a rock-and-roll sensibility will feel like they've found heaven at this black-daubed *Vinothek* (wine bar) that vibes casual but takes its wines super seriously. Wines by the glass are all sourced from small producers – many of them are organic or minimal-intervention and friends of the owners – and are well priced at under €4 a glass.

Café CI CAFE

(www.ci.or.at; 16, Payergasse 14; ⌚8am-2am Mon-Sat, from 10am Sun; 🚊2 Neulerchenfelder Strasse, Brunnengasse, Ⓤ Josefstädter Strasse) Something's always happening at this cafe founded to support new immigrants 30 years ago, be it a reading, an exhibition, or language or dance classes. In summer, its terrace throngs with Ottakringer locals sipping organic beers; in winter they retreat inside to browse the daily papers and dig into heart-warming goulash or *ćevapčići* (spicy Serbian sausages; mains €7 to €11, snacks €4.50 to €7.50).

Summer Stage BEER GARDEN

(Map p102; ☎01-315 52 02; www.summerstage.at; 09, Rossauer Lände; ⌚5pm-1am May-Sep; Ⓤ Schottenring, Rossauer Lände) This Viennese summer favourite has sprawling, riverside terrace spaces for drinking, with food trucks and a glassed-in area for when the weather turns.

Schloss Belvedere to the Canal

Strandbar Herrmann BAR

(Map p102; www.strandbarherrmann.at; 03, Herrmannpark; ⌚10am-2am Apr-early Oct; 📶; 🚊O Hintere Zollamstrasse, Ⓤ Schwedenplatz) You'd swear you're by the sea at this hopping canal-side beach bar, with beach chairs, sand, DJ beats and hordes of Viennese livin' it up on summer evenings. Cocktail happy hour is from 5pm to 6pm. Cool trivia: it's located on Herrmannpark, named after picture-postcard inventor Emanuel Herrmann (1839–1902).

LGBTIQ+ VIENNA

Vienna's main point for gay and lesbian information, **Die Villa** (☎01-586 81 50; www.dievilla.at; 06, Linke Wienzeile 102; ⌚5-8pm Mon, Wed & Fri; Ⓤ Pilgramgasse), has advice and information on what's on offer in the city. The tourist office website www.wien.info/en/vienna-for/gay-lesbian has extensive information on the scene.

The headlining event on the gay and lesbian calendar is the **Regenbogen Parade** (Rainbow Parade; www.viennapride.at/regenbogenparade) in mid-June.

Mariahilf (6th district) and Margareten (5th district), fanning out around the Naschmarkt, have a higher than average concentration of gay and lesbian bars.

Popular hang-outs include the following:

Felixx (Map p82; www.felixx-bar.at; 06, Gumpendorfer Strasse 5; ⌚10am-2am Sun-Thu, to 3am Fri & Sat; Ⓤ Museumsquartier) Chandeliers, mini–disco balls, striped wallpaper and leather lounges make this one of Vienna's classiest gay bars. Themed events might include 'girl bands' or 'retro' with '70s and '80s music; check the online calendar for the week's agenda. Its on-site **cafe** is especially popular for Sunday's 'drag brunch'.

Why Not? (Map p68; www.why-not.at; 01, Tiefer Graben 22; ⌚10pm-4am Fri & Sat; 📶; Ⓤ Herrengasse) Why Not? is a fixture of Vienna's gay scene. The small club quickly fills up with mainly young guys; there are three bars and a dance floor. Cover charges vary depending on the event.

Mango Bar (Map p82; www.why-not.at; 06, Laimgrubengasse 3; ⌚10pm-6am Fri & Sat; Ⓤ Kettenbrückengasse) Mango attracts a young gay crowd with good music, friendly staff and plenty of mirrors to check out yourself and others. There are three bars, a dance floor and a darkroom. It's often the place where the party continues for those who don't want the night to end.

THE THIRD MAN

Sir Alexander Korda asked English author Graham Greene to write a film about the four-power occupation of postwar Vienna. Greene flew to Vienna in 1948 and met with a British intelligence officer who told him about the underground police who patrolled the huge network of sewers beneath the city, and the black-market trade in penicillin. Greene put the two ideas together and created his story.

Shot in Vienna in the same year, the film perfectly captures the atmosphere of postwar Vienna using an excellent play of shadow and light.

The Third Man won first prize at Cannes in 1949 and the Academy Award for Best Cinematography (Black-and-White) in 1951, and was selected by the British Film Institute as 'favourite British film of the 20th century' in 1999. For years, the **Burg Kino** (Map p82; 01-587 84 06; www.burgkino.at; 01, Opernring 19; tickets €8-9.50; D, 1, 2 Burgring, U Museumsquartier) has screened the film on a weekly basis.

The film's popularity has spawned the **Third Man Museum** (Map p82; www.3mpc.net; 04, Pressgasse 25; adult/child €8.90/4.50, guided tour incl admission €10; 2-6pm Sat, guided tours 2pm Wed; U Kettenbrückengasse). True aficionados may want to take the English-language **Third Man Tour** (Map p68; www.viennawalks.com; Third Man Tour adult/child €20/17.50), covering the main locations used in the film, or **3.MannTour** (Map p95; 01-4000 3033; www.drittemanntour.at; 01, Girardipark; tour adult/child €10/5; by reservation Thu-Sun May-Oct; U Karlsplatz) of Vienna's 19th-century former sewers as clips from the black-and-white film are projected on the walls.

Salm Bräu MICROBREWERY
(Map p95; www.salmbraeu.com; 03, Rennweg 8; 11am-midnight; 71 Unteres Belvedere, U Karlsplatz) Salm Bräu brews its own *Helles* (pale lager), *Pils* (pilsner), *Märzen* (red-coloured beer with a strong malt taste), *G'mischt* (half *Helles* and half *Dunkel* – dark) and *Weizen* (full-bodied wheat beer, slightly sweet in taste). It is smack next to Schloss Belvedere and hugely popular.

Prater & East of the Danube

★Sperlhof COFFEE
(Map p102; 02, Grosse Sperlgasse 41; 4pm-1.30am; ; U Taborstrasse) Every Viennese coffee house ought to be just like the wood-panelled, poster-plastered, fantastically eccentric Sperlhof, which opened in 1923. It still attracts a motley crowd of coffee sippers, daydreamers, billiard and ping-pong players, and chess whizzes today. If you're looking for a novel, check out the selection of secondhand books, many of which are propped up on the outside windowsills.

Tel Aviv Beach BAR
(Map p102; https://neni.at/restaurants/tel-aviv-beach-bar; 02, Obere Donaustrasse 65; noon-midnight Apr-Oct; U Schottenring) Providing land-locked Austria's capital with a dash of Mediterranean beach life, Tel Aviv started as a pop-up but is now a permanent summer fixture. When the sun's out, it's a fine spot to dig your toes into sand, listen to DJs spin mellow tunes and enjoy a cocktail with oriental-themed food.

Schloss Schönbrunn & Around

Café Gloriette COFFEE
(Map p101; www.gloriette-cafe.at; 13, Gloriette, Schloss Schönbrunn; 9am-dusk; U Schönbrunn, Hietzing) Café Gloriette occupies the neoclassical Gloriette, high on a hill behind Schloss Schönbrunn, built for the pleasure of Maria Theresia in 1775. With sweeping views of the Schloss, its magnificent gardens and the districts to the north, Gloriette has arguably one of the best vistas in all of Vienna. It's a welcome pit stop after the short climb up the hill.

☆ Entertainment

From opera, classical music and theatre to live rock or jazz, Vienna provides a wealth of entertainment opportunities. The capital is home to the German-speaking world's oldest theatre, the Burgtheater (p115), as well as the famous Wiener Sängerknaben (Vienna Boys' Choir) and the Vienna Philharmonic Orchestra, which performs in the acoustically superb Musikverein (p114).

☆ The Hofburg & Around

Hofburg Concert Halls CLASSICAL MUSIC
(Map p68; ☎01-587 25 52; www.hofburgorchester.at; 01, Heldenplatz; tickets €45-110; 🚋D, 1, 2, 71 Burgring, Ⓤ Herrengasse) The Neue Hofburg's concert halls, the sumptuous Festsaal and Redoutensaal, are regularly used for Strauss and Mozart concerts, featuring the Hofburg Orchestra and soloists from the Staatsoper and Volksoper. Performances start at 8.30pm; tickets are available online. Seating is not allocated, so get in early to secure a good seat.

☆ Stephansdom & the Historic Centre

Jazzland LIVE MUSIC
(Map p68; ☎01-533 25 75; www.jazzland.at; 01, Franz-Josefs-Kai 29; cover €11-20; ⏲7pm-1am Mon-Sat mid-Aug–mid-Jul, live music from 9pm; 🚋1, 2, 31 Schwedenplatz, Ⓤ Schwedenplatz) Buried in a 500-year-old cellar beneath **Ruprechtskirche** (St Rupert's Church; Map p68; ☎01-535 60 03; www.ruprechtskirche.at; 01, Ruprechtsplatz 1; ⏲10am-noon Mon & Tue, 10am-noon & 3-5pm Wed, 10am-5pm Thu & Fri, 11.30am-3.30pm Sat; 🚋1, 2 Schwedenplatz, Ⓤ Schwedenplatz), Jazzland is Vienna's oldest jazz club, dating from 1972. The music covers the whole jazz spectrum, and features both local and international acts. Past performers have included Ray Brown, Teddy Wilson, Big Joe Williams and Max Kaminsky. Arrive early as it doesn't take reservations.

Metro Kinokulturhaus CINEMA
(Map p68; ☎01-512 18 03; www.filmarchiv.at; 01, Johannesgasse 4; film tickets €8.50, exhibition tickets €7.50, combined ticket €13; ⏲3-9pm; Ⓤ Stephansplatz) Part of the Austrian Film Archive, with a collection that includes 200,000 films, two million photographs and stills, 50,000 programs and 16,000 posters, the Metro Kinokulturhaus is a showcase for exhibitions. The restored cinema here was first converted for screenings in 1924 and retains its wood panelling and red-velvet interior; it shows historic and art-house Austrian films (in German).

Gartenbaukino CINEMA
(Map p68; ☎01-512 23 54; www.gartenbaukino.at; 01, Parkring 12; tickets €9-12.50; 🚋2, Ⓤ Stubentor, Stadtpark) With an interior dating from the 1960s, this cinema seats a whopping 736 people, and is packed during Viennale Film Festival (p97) screenings. Its regular screening schedule is filled with art-house films, often in their original language (including English) with German subtitles.

ℹ ENTERTAINMENT TICKETS

The state ticket office, **Bundestheaterkassen** (Map p68; ☎01-514 44 7880; www.bundestheater.at; 01, Operngasse 2; ⏲8am-6pm Mon-Fri, 9am-noon Sat & Sun; Ⓤ Stephansplatz), only sells tickets to federal venues: Akademietheater, Burgtheater, Staatsoper and Volksoper. No commission is charged. Staatsoper tickets are available here two months prior to the performance date. Tickets can also be booked online or by phone. The **Info unter den Arkaden** (Map p68; www.bundestheater.at; 01, Herbert-von-Karajan-Platz 1; ⏲9am-2hr before performance begins Mon-Fri, 9am-noon Sat Sep-Jun) branch is located on the Kärntner Strasse side of the Staatsoper.

The **Wien-Ticket Pavillon** (Map p68; ☎01-588 85; www.wien-ticket.at; 01, Kärntner Strasse; ⏲10am-7pm; 🚋D, 1, 2, 71 Kärntner Ring/Oper, Ⓤ Karlsplatz) charges anything from no commission up to a 12% levy. It sells tickets for all venues except the Staatsoper, Burgtheater and Volksoper.

Standing-Room Tickets

You can get a taste of high culture for next to nothing with a little advance planning. Among the best culture deals are the standing-room tickets at the city's stately 19th-century concert halls. Standing-room tickets (€4 to €10) for opera productions at the Staatsoper (p114) are sold 80 minutes before the performance at the venue box office. Arrive two to three hours ahead; there's a limit of one ticket per person.

To see the Vienna Philharmonic Orchestra perform in the Musikverein's (p114) lavishly gilded Grosser Saal, you can book standing-room tickets (€7 to €15) up to seven weeks ahead.

DON'T MISS

VIENNA BOYS' CHOIR

Founded by Maximilian I in 1498 as the imperial choir, the Wiener Sängerknaben (Vienna Boys' Choir) is the most famous of its type in the world. The experience will be very different depending on where you see the performance. The most formal occasions are held in the Burgkapelle, where the focus is obviously on sacral music. Performances at other venues might range from pop through to world music. Regardless of the setting and style of the performance, the beauty and choral harmony of the voices remains the same.

Performances

The choir sings during Sunday Mass in the **Burgkapelle** (Royal Chapel; Map p68; 01-533 99 27; www.hofmusikkapelle.gv.at; 01, Schweizerhof; 10am-2pm Mon & Tue, 11am-1pm Fri; D, 1, 2, 71 Burgring, U Herrengasse) in the Hofburg, but occasional concerts are also given during the week at other venues in Vienna and elsewhere. Sunday performances in the Burgkapelle are held from mid-September to June at 9.15am. Other venues where you can hear the choir include **MuTh** (Map p102; 01-347 80 80; www.muth.at; 02, Obere Augartenstrasse 1e; Vienna Boys' Choir Fri performance €39-89; box office 4-6pm Mon-Fri & 1hr before performance; U Taborstrasse), the choir's dedicated hall in Augarten, which hosts regular Friday-afternoon performances.

The Vienna Boys' Choir website (www.wienersaengerknaben.at) has links to the venues alongside each performance date.

Tickets

Book tickets through the individual venue. Tickets for the Sunday performances at Burgkapelle cost €10 to €36 and can be arranged through the Burgkapelle's **booking office** (Map p68; 01-533 992 711; tickets €11-37) by sending an email or fax. It's best to book about six weeks in advance.

For orders under €60, you pay cash when you pick up your tickets, which can be done from 11am to 1pm and 3pm to 5pm at the chapel's booking office in the Schweizerhof of the Hofburg on the Friday before the performance. You can also pick them up between 8.15am and 8.45am on the Sunday, but this is less advisable as queues are long. If your order amounts to €60 or more, you will be sent the bank details for transferring the money. Credit cards and cheques aren't accepted. Seats costing €10 do not afford a view of the choir itself.

Tickets for a free *Stehplatz* (standing-room space) are available from 8.30am. Uncollected tickets are also resold on the day from 8am. The queues for these and for standing-room tickets are long, so arrive very early – around 7am – and be prepared to wait.

☆ Karlsplatz & Around Naschmarkt

★Staatsoper OPERA

(Map p68; 01-514 44 7880; www.wiener-staatsoper.at; 01, Opernring 2; tickets €14-287, standing room €4-10, tour adult/child €9/4; D, 1, 2, 62, 71 Kärntner Ring/Oper, U Karlsplatz) The glorious Staatsoper is Vienna's premier opera and classical-music venue. Productions are lavish, formal affairs, where people dress up accordingly. In the interval, wander the foyer and refreshment rooms to fully appreciate the gold-and-crystal interior. Opera is not performed here in July and August (though tours still take place). Tickets can be purchased up to two months in advance.

★Musikverein CONCERT VENUE

(Map p95; 01-505 81 90; www.musikverein.at; 01, Musikvereinsplatz 1; tickets €15-105, standing room €7-15; box office 9am-8pm Mon-Fri, to 1pm Sat Sep-Jun, 9am-noon Mon-Fri Jul & Aug; U Karlsplatz) The opulent Musikverein holds the proud title of the best acoustics of any concert hall in Austria, which the Vienna Philharmonic Orchestra embraces. The lavish interior can be visited by 45-minute guided tour (in English; adult/child €8.50/5) at 1pm Tuesday to

Saturday. Smaller-scale performances are held in the Brahms Saal. There are no student tickets.

Theater an der Wien THEATRE

(Map p82; ☎01-588 85-111; www.theater-wien.at; 06, Linke Wienzeile 6; tickets €5-165; ⊙box office 10am-6pm Mon-Sat, 2-6pm Sun; U Karlsplatz) The Theater an der Wien has hosted some monumental premiere performances, including Beethoven's *Fidelio,* Mozart's *The Magic Flute* and Johann Strauss II's *Die Fledermaus*. These days, besides staging musicals, dance and concerts, it's reestablished its reputation for high-quality opera.

Student tickets go on sale 30 minutes before shows; standing-room tickets are available one hour prior to performances.

☆ The Museum District & Neubau

★**Burgtheater** THEATRE

(National Theatre; Map p68; ☎01-514 44 4140; www.burgtheater.at; 01, Universitätsring 2; seats €7-61, standing room €3.50, tours adult/child €7/3.50; ⊙box office 9am-5pm Mon-Fri, closed Jul & Aug, English tours 3pm daily Jul & Aug, 3pm Fri-Sun Sep-Jun; D, 1, 71 Rathausplatz/Burgtheater) The Burgtheater hasn't lost its touch over the years – this is one of the foremost theatres in the German-speaking world, staging some 800 performances a year, from Shakespeare to modern works. The theatre also runs the 500-seater **Akademietheater**, which was built between 1911 and 1913.

Tickets at the Burgtheater and Akademietheater are sold for a 25% discount an hour before performances. Advance bookings are recommended, although, depending on the performance, some last-minute tickets may be available.

Volkstheater THEATRE

(Map p82; ☎01-521 11-400; www.volkstheater.at; 07, Arthur-Schnitzler-Platz 1; tickets €9-55; ⊙box office 10am-7.30pm Mon-Sat; U Volkstheater) With a seating capacity close to 1000, the Volkstheater is one of Vienna's largest theatres. Built in 1889, the interior is suitably grand. While most performances are of translated works (anything from Ingmar Bergman to Molière), only German-language shows are staged. Advance bookings are necessary; students can buy unsold tickets for €5 one hour before performances start.

Vienna's English Theatre THEATRE

(Map p72; ☎01-402 12 60-0; www.englishtheatre.at; 08, Josefsgasse 12; tickets €24-47; ⊙box office 10am-7pm Mon-Fri, 5-7pm Sat performance days, closed Jul–mid-Aug; 2 Rathaus, U Rathaus) Founded in 1963, Vienna's English Theatre is the oldest foreign-language theatre in Vienna (with the occasional show in French or Italian). Productions range from timeless pieces, such as Shakespeare, to contemporary works and comedies. Students receive a 20% discount and are eligible for standby tickets (€10), which go on sale 15 minutes before showtime.

Tanzquartier Wien DANCE

(Map p82; ☎01-581 35 91; www.tqw.at; 07, Museumsplatz 1; tickets €10-57; ⊙box office 10am-4.30pm mid-Jul–Aug, 9am-7.30pm Mon-Fri, 10am-7.30pm Sat Sep–mid-Jul; U Museumsquartier, Volkstheater) Tanzquartier Wien, located in the MuseumsQuartier (p73), is Vienna's first dance institution. It hosts an array of local and international performances with a strong experimental nature. Students receive a €10 discount on advance tickets. Unsold tickets (€5) go on sale 15 minutes before showtime.

☆ Alsergrund & the University District

Volksoper OPERA

(People's Opera; Map p72; ☎01-513 15 13; www.volksoper.at; 09, Währinger Strasse 78; ⊙10am-7pm Sep-Jun; U Währinger Strasse) Offering an intimate experience, the Volksoper specialises in operettas, dance performances, musicals and a handful of standard, heavier operas. Standing and impaired-view tickets cost €3 to €10 and, like many venues, there is a plethora of discounts and reduced tickets for sale 30 minutes before performances. The Volksoper closes for July and August.

B72 LIVE MUSIC

(www.b72.at; 08, Hernalser Gürtel 72; ⊙8pm-4am Sun-Thu, to 6am Fri & Sat; 44 Hernalser Gürtel, U Alser Strasse) Fringe live acts, alternative beats and album launches are the mainstay of B72's entertainment line-up, which all attract a predictably youthful crowd. Its tall glass walls and arched brick interior are typical of most bars along the Gürtel, as is the happy grunginess. Its name comes from its location, Bogen 72.

☆ Schloss Belvedere to the Canal

★Radiokulturhaus CONCERT VENUE

(Map p95; ☎01-501 703 77; http://radiokulturhaus.orf.at; 04, Argentinierstrasse 30a; tickets €19; ⊙box office 4-7pm Mon-Fri; 🚊D Plösslgasse, Ⓤ Taubstummengasse) The line-up swings from classical concerts to jazz quartets and cabaret at the Radiokulturhaus. Housed in several performance venues including the Grosser Sendesaal (home to the Vienna Radio Symphony Orchestra and the Klangtheater, the latter used primarily for radio plays), this is one of Vienna's cultural hotspots.

The venue also presents dance, lectures and literary readings as well as low-key performances in its cafe.

★Konzerthaus CONCERT VENUE

(Map p95; ☎01-242 002; www.konzerthaus.at; 03, Lothringerstrasse 20; ⊙box office 9am-7.45pm Mon-Fri, 10am-2pm Sat, plus 45min before performance; 🚊D Gusshausstrasse, Ⓤ Stadtpark) The Konzerthaus is a major venue in classical-music circles, but throughout the year ethnic music, rock, pop or jazz can also be heard in its hallowed halls. Up to three simultaneous performances, in the Grosser Saal, the Mozart Saal and the Schubert Saal, can be staged; this massive complex also features another four concert halls.

Arena Wien LIVE MUSIC

(http://arena.wien; 03, Baumgasse 80; tickets around €15; Ⓤ Erdberg, Gasometer) A former slaughterhouse turned music and film venue, Arena is one of Vienna's quirkier places for seeing live acts. Hard rock, rock, metal, reggae and soul (along with cinema) fill its outdoor stage from May to September; in winter bands play in one of its two indoor halls. Regular events include the monthly German–British 1970s New Wave bash 'Iceberg'.

Kursalon CLASSICAL MUSIC

(Map p68; ☎01-512 57 90; www.kursalonwien.at; 01, Johannesgasse 33; tickets €45-99, concert with 3-course dinner €79-133, with 4-course dinner €84-138; 🚊2 Weihburggasse, Ⓤ Stadtpark) Fans of Strauss and Mozart will love the performances at Kursalon, which holds daily evening concerts at 8.15pm devoted to the two masters of music in a splendid, refurbished Renaissance building. Also popular is the concert and dinner package (three- or four-course meal, excluding drinks, at 6pm, followed by the concert) in the equally palatial on-site restaurant.

☆ Prater & East of the Danube

Kino wie noch nie CINEMA

(Map p102; www.kinowienochnie.at; 02, Augarten; adult/student tickets €8.50/7; Ⓤ Taborstrasse) Every summer the Augarten plays host to this two-month open-air cinema, which screens a mixed bag of art-house, world, cult and classic films.

Shopping

With a long-standing history of craftsmanship, this elegant city has recently spread its creative wings in the fashion and design world. Whether you're browsing for hand-painted porcelain in the Innere Stadt, new-wave streetwear in Neubau or epicurean treats in the Freihausviertel, you'll find inspiration, a passion for quality and an attentive eye for detail.

The Hofburg & Around

★J&L Lobmeyr Vienna HOMEWARES

(Map p68; www.lobmeyr.at; 01, Kärntner Strasse 26; ⊙10am-7pm Mon-Fri, to 6pm Sat; Ⓤ Stephansplatz) Reached by a beautifully ornate wrought-iron staircase, this is one of Vienna's most lavish retail experiences. The collection of Biedermeier pieces, Loos-designed sets, fine/arty glassware and porcelain on display here glitters from the lights of the chandelier-festooned atrium. Lobmeyr has been in business since 1823, when it exclusively supplied the imperial court.

★Zuckerlwerkstatt FOOD & DRINKS

(Map p68; www.zuckerlwerkstatt.at; 01, Herrengasse 6-8; ⊙10am-6pm Mon-Fri, 9am-5pm Sat; Ⓤ Herrengasse) Long-lost recipes for traditional sweets and all-natural ingredients including Austrian sugar (produced from sugar beet) are used by this 'sugar workshop'. Its pillow-shaped striped silk candies, sugar drops, fruit jellies, lollipops, candy canes and boiled sweets are enticingly displayed in glass jars.

Dorotheum ANTIQUES

(Map p68; www.dorotheum.com; 01, Dorotheergasse 17; ⊙10am-6pm Mon-Fri, 9am-5pm Sat; Ⓤ Stephansplatz) The Dorotheum is among the largest auction houses in Europe, and for the casual visitor it's more like a museum, housing everything from antique toys and tableware to autographs, antique guns and, above all, lots of quality paintings. You can bid at the regular auctions held here; otherwise just drop by and enjoy browsing.

Freytag & Berndt BOOKS

(Map p68; www.freytagberndt.com; 01, Wallnerstrasse 3; ⏲9.30am-6.30pm Mon-Fri, to 6pm Sat; 🚌1A, 2A Michaelerplatz, Ⓤ Herrengasse) The ultimate place to inspire wanderlust, Freytag & Berndt has an extensive collection of guides and maps (many in English) to Vienna, Austria (including some superbly detailed walking maps) and destinations around the globe.

Stephansdom & the Historic Centre

Cuisinarum HOMEWARES

(Map p68; www.cuisinarum.at; 01, Singerstrasse 14; ⏲9.30am-6.30pm Mon-Fri, to 6pm Sat; Ⓤ Stephansplatz) Everything you need to cook Austrian cuisine is here: specialised cookware such as a *Spätzle Sieb* (a metal press to make *Spätzle* noodles); pots, pans and casserole dishes from Austrian manufacturer Riess; Austrian cookbooks (in English and German); and cookie cutters and cake moulds in Viennese and Austrian designs.

Altmann & Kühne CHOCOLATE

(Map p68; www.altmann-kuehne.at; 01, Graben 30; ⏲9am-6.30pm Mon-Fri, 10am-5pm Sat; Ⓤ Stephansplatz) This small, charming shop is the flagship of century-old chocolatier Altmann & Kühne, which produces handmade chocolates and sweets. It's located behind a modernist facade designed by Josef Hoffmann, a founding member of the visual arts collective Wiener Werkstätte. Hoffmann also designed the interior as well as the iconic packaging: miniature hat boxes, luggage trunks, glass cabinets, bookshelves and baroque buildings.

Karlsplatz & Around Naschmarkt

Blühendes Konfekt FOOD

(Map p82; ☎0660 341 1985; www.bluehendes-konfekt.com; 06, Schmalzhofgasse 19; ⏲10am-6.30pm Wed-Fri, by reservation Mon & Tue; Ⓤ Zieglergasse, Westbahnhof) Violets, forest strawberries and cherry blossom, mint and oregano – Michael Diewald makes the most of what grows wild and in his garden to create confectionery that fizzes with seasonal flavour. Peek through to the workshop to see flowers and herbs being deftly transformed into one-of-a-kind bonbons and minibouquets that are edible works of art. Cash only.

Beer Lovers DRINKS

(Map p82; www.beerlovers.at; 06, Gumpendorfer Strasse 35; ⏲11am-8pm Mon-Fri, 10am-5pm Sat; Ⓤ Kettenbrückengasse) A wonderland of craft beers, this emporium stocks over 1000 labels from at least 125 different breweries in more than 70 styles, with more being sourced every day. Tastings are offered regularly, and cold beers are available in the walk-in glass fridge and in refillable growlers. It also stocks craft ciders, small-batch liqueurs and boutique nonalcoholic drinks such as ginger beers.

Teuchtler Records MUSIC

(Map p82; ☎01-586 21 33; www.schallplatten-ankauf-wien.com; Windmühlgasse 10; ⏲1-6pm Mon & Fri, 10am-1pm Sat; Ⓤ Neubaugasse) Film fans will recognise Teuchtler Records from Richard Linklater's classic 1995 Vienna homage *Before Sunrise* – the promotional poster still hangs prominently above the till. It jostles for pride of place amongst autographed headshots of jazz stars, punk-rock record posters and vintage gramophone

SHOPPING STREETS

Kärntner Strasse The Innere Stadt's main shopping street and a real crowd-puller.

Kohlmarkt A river of high-end glitz, flowing into a magnificent Hofburg view.

Neubau Track down the city's hottest designers along boutique-clogged streets like Kirchengasse, Lindengasse and Neubaugasse.

Mariahilfer Strasse Vienna's mile of high-street style, with big names and crowds.

Freihausviertel Lanes packed with home-grown fashion, design and speciality food stores, south of Naschmarkt.

Theobaldgasse Hole-in-the-wall shops purvey everything from fair-trade fashion to organic food.

LOCAL KNOWLEDGE

VIENNESE HONEY

Some 5000 bee colonies and 600 bee-keepers harvest honey within Vienna's city limits, including on the rooftops of the *Rathaus*, Staatsoper, Kunsthistorisches Museum Vienna, Secession and several hotels. The fruits of their labour are sold at specialist honey boutique **Wald & Wiese** (Map p68; www.waldundwiese.at; 01, Wollzeile 19; 10am-6.30pm Mon-Fri, to 5pm Sat; U Stephansplatz), which also sells honey-based beverages including mead, honey-and-whisky liqueur and grappa, along with beeswax candles, hand creams, toothpaste, royal jelly...

players. This is a musical cave of wonders covering everything from the Beatles to rare opera recordings.

★**Gabarage Upcycling Design** DESIGN
(Map p82; www.gabarage.at; 04, Schleifmühlgasse 6; 10am-6pm Mon-Thu, 7pm Fri, 11am-5pm Sat; U Taubstummengasse) Recycled design, ecology and social responsibility underpin the quirky designs at Gabarage. Old bowling pins become vases, rubbish bins get a new life as tables and chairs, advertising tarpaulins morph into bags, and traffic lights are transformed into funky lights.

The Museum District & Neubau

★**Die Werkbank** DESIGN
(Map p82; www.werkbank.cc; 07, Breite Gasse 1; 1-6.30pm Tue-Fri, 11am-5pm Sat; 49 Volkstheater) Furniture, lamps, rugs, vases, jewellery, watches, graphic art, bags, even bicycles are among the creations you might find on display at 'The Workbench'. This all-white space operates as a design collective, where some of Vienna's most innovative designers showcase their works.

Runway FASHION & ACCESSORIES
(Map p82; www.runwayvienna.at; 07, Kirchengasse 48; 11am-12.30pm & 1-6.30pm Tue-Fri, to 6pm Sat; 46 Strozzigasse) Runway is a launching pad for up-and-coming Austrian fashion designers, whose creations sit alongside those of their established compatriots. Framed by arched windows, the whitewashed space showcases the direction of Viennese womenswear today through its rotating racks of clothes and accessories.

Schokov CHOCOLATE
(Map p82; www.schokov.com; 07, Siebensterngasse 20; noon-6.30pm Mon-Fri, 10am-6pm Sat; 49 Siebensterngasse) Thomas Kovazh turned his chocolate-making dream into reality when he opened this sleek gallery-style shop. Today, Schokov sells some of Vienna's best pralines and truffles (over 200 varieties). Chilli, lavender, sea-salt, potato and pepper chocolate – you'll find them all in bar form here, alongside top Austrian brands like Zotter and Scharffen Berger. A 1½-hour, 20-chocolate-tasting workshop (English available) costs €29.

Alsergrund & the University District

Palais Ferstel SHOPPING CENTRE
(Map p68; 01, Strauchgasse 4; 10am-7pm Mon-Sat; U Herrengasse) With its hexagonal skylight, allegorical sculptures and beautifully lit arcades in Italian Renaissance style, Palais Ferstel hearkens back to a more glamorous age of consumption. Opened in 1860, it sidles up to the ever-grand **Café Central** (Map p68; www.cafecentral.wien; 01, Herrengasse 14; 7.30am-10pm Mon-Sat, from 10am Sun; ; U Herrengasse) and likewise bears the hallmark of architect Heinrich von Ferstel, the Habsburgs' blue-eyed boy in the mid-19th century.

Today it shelters upmarket delis, jewellers and chocolatiers; pop in for a mosey even if you have no intention of buying.

Bauernmarkt Yppenplatz MARKET
(16, Yppenplatz; 8am-1pm Fri & Sat; 44 Yppengasse, Neulerchenfelder Strasse, U Josefstädter Strasse) *Bauern* (farmers) join the usual market traders every Friday and Saturday morning, when local farmers come to town to sell their meats, dairy, fruit and vegetables, as do artisan producers from around Vienna and occasionally as far afield as Styria, Carinthia and Slovenia.

Brunnenmarkt MARKET
(16, Brunnengasse; 6am-6.30pm Mon-Fri, to 5pm Sat; 2 Neulerchenfelder Strasse, U Josefstädter

Strasse) Over 170 stalls fill the area between Thaliastrasse and Ottakringer Strasse every Saturday in what is Vienna's largest street market. It's an enthralling sprawl of Turkish grocers, fruit and vegetable producers and tack, which gradually and almost imperceptively flows into the happily hipster Yppenplatz market.

Prater & East of the Danube

Karmelitermarkt MARKET

(Map p102; 02, Karmelitermarkt; ⏲6am-7.30pm Mon-Fri, to 5pm Sat; 🚊2 Karmeliterplatz, Ⓤ Taborstrasse) A market with a long tradition, the Karmelitermarkt reflects the ethnic diversity of its neighbourhood. Set in an architecturally picturesque square, the market springs to life when the midday lunching locals descend on its terrific array of places to eat. Fruit and vegetable stalls share the marketplace with butchers selling kosher and halal meats.

Stilwerk Wien DESIGN

(Map p102; www.stilwerk.de/wien; 02, Praterstrasse 1; ⏲10am-7pm Mon-Fri, to 6pm Sat; 🚊2 Marienbrücke, Ⓤ Schwedenplatz) Plug into Vienna's contemporary-design scene at this cluster of concept and interior stores in the glass-clad Design Tower.

Schloss Schönbrunn & Around

Die Schwalbe FASHION & ACCESSORIES

(☎01-952 98 40; www.die-schwalbe.at; 15, Reindorfgasse 38; ⏲noon-6.30pm Mon, 10.30am-6.30pm Tue & Wed, 10.30am-7pm Thu & Fri, 10am-5pm Sat; 🚌52, 60 Rustengasse) 'Eco-urban steetwear' here spans hoodies and pullovers to T-shirts, jackets, shorts and pants, plus accessories such as beanies, caps and scarves from small-scale labels including Blueberry Rockster, Habu San, hemp-based HoodLamb and PlazmaLab. There's an in-house piercing lounge.

1130Wein FOOD & DRINKS

(Map p101; www.1130wein.at; 13, Lainzerstrasse 1; ⏲10am-7pm Mon-Fri, to 3pm Sat; Ⓤ Hietzing) Pop into this neighbourhood *Vinothek* for tastings with the delightful Robert Sponer-Triulzi, who stocks a huge range of interesting, top-quality (though not always expensive) wines from all over Austria. He'll challenge you with a new varietal or two and make sure you come away with a drop you'll love. There are chilled whites if you're picnicking.

ℹ Information

DISCOUNT CARDS

Vienna Card (Die Wien-Karte; 24/48/72hr €17/25/29) Unlimited travel on the public-transport system (including night buses) and hundreds of discounts at selected museums, cafes, *Heurigen*, restaurants and shops across the city, and on guided tours and the City Airport Train (CAT). The discount usually amounts to 5% to 25% off the normal price. It can be purchased online or at Tourist Info Wien, the Airport Information Office and many concierge desks at the top hotels.

MEDICAL SERVICES

Vienna's main hospital, **Allgemeines Krankenhaus** (☎01-40 40 00; www.akhwien.at; 09, Währinger Gürtel 18-20; Ⓤ Michelbeuern-AKH), better known as AKH, has a 24-hour Accident & Emergency department.

Nachtapotheken (night pharmacies) rotate; check www.nachtapotheke.wien for locations and opening times.

TOURIST INFORMATION

Tourist Info Wien (Map p68; ☎01-245 55; www.wien.info; 01, Albertinaplatz; ⏲9am-7pm; 📶; 🚊D, 1, 2, 71 Kärntner Ring/Oper, Ⓤ Stephansplatz) Vienna's main tourist office, with a ticket agency, hotel booking service, free maps and every brochure under the sun.

Airport Information Office (www.wien.info; Vienna International Airport; ⏲7am-10pm) Full services, with maps, Vienna Card and walk-in hotel booking. Located in the arrival hall.

Jugendinfo (Vienna Youth Information; Map p68; ☎01-4000 84 100; www.wienxtra.at/jugendinfo; 01, Babenbergerstrasse 1; ⏲2.30-6.30pm Mon-Fri; 🚊D, 1, 2, 71 Burgring, Ⓤ Museumsquartier) Offers various reduced-priced event tickets for 14- to 26-year-olds. Staff can tell you about events around town.

Rathaus Information Office (Map p72; ☎01-502 55; www.wien.gv.at; 01, Rathaus; ⏲7.30am-6pm Mon-Fri; 🚊D, 1, 2, 71 Rathausplatz/Burgtheater, Ⓤ Rathaus) Vienna's City Hall provides information on social, cultural and practical matters, and is geared as much to residents as to tourists. There's a useful info screen.

Getting There & Away

AIR

Located 19km southwest of the city centre, **Vienna International Airport** (VIE; 01-700 722 233; www.viennaairport.com;) operates services worldwide. Facilities include restaurants and bars, banks and ATMs, money-exchange counters, supermarkets, a post office, car-hire agencies and two left-luggage counters open 5.30am to 11pm (per 24 hours €4 to €8; maximum six-month storage).

Bratislava, Slovakia's capital, is only 60km east of Vienna, and **Bratislava Airport** (BTS; 02-3303 3353; www.bts.aero; Ivanská cesta), serving Bratislava, makes a feasible alternative to flying into Austria.

BOAT

The Danube is a traffic-free access route for arrivals and departures from Vienna. Eastern Europe is the main destination; **Twin City Liner** (Map p68; 01-904 88 80; www.twincity liner.com; 01, Schiffstation, Schwedenplatz; one-way adult €30-35; 1, 2 Schwedenplatz, U Schwedenplatz) connects Vienna with Bratislava in 1½ hours.

Slovakian ferry company **LOD** (in Slovakia 421 2 529 32 226; www.lod.sk; Vienna departure point 02, Schiffstation Reichsbrücke, Handelskai 265; one way/return €24/39; late Apr-early Oct; U Vorgartenstrasse) runs hydrofoils between Bratislava and Vienna (1½ hours) five to seven days per week from late April to early October. The season can vary depending on weather conditions.

BUS

Eurolines (www.eurolines.eu) Has bus routes connecting Austria with the rest of Europe. Its main terminal is at the U3 U-Bahn station Erdberg but some buses stop at Südtiroler Platz by Vienna's *Hauptbahnhof* (main train station).

FlixBus (www.flixbus.com) Serves destinations across Europe. Buses use the terminal at the U3 U-Bahn station Erdberg.

TRAIN

Austria's train network is a dense web reaching the country's far-flung corners and beyond. The system is fast, efficient, frequent and well used. Österreiche Bundesbahn (ÖBB; www.oebb.at) is the main operator, and has information offices at all of Vienna's main train stations. Tickets can be purchased online, at ticket offices or from train-station ticket machines. Long-distance train tickets can be purchased onboard but incur a €3 service charge. Tickets for local, regional and intercity trains must be purchased before boarding.

International trains include a growing network of overnight trains; see www.night-trains.com.

The website www.seat61.com has up-to-date rail information.

Getting Around

TO/FROM THE AIRPORT

The **City Airport Train** (CAT; www.city airporttrain.com; single/return €11/19; 1 Landstrasse-Wien Mitte, U Landstrasse) leaves the airport every 30 minutes from 6.09am to 11.39pm, 365 days. The cheaper but slower S7 suburban train (€4.20, 37 minutes) also runs every 30 minutes from 5.18am to 12.18am from the airport to Wien-Mitte.

Vienna Airport Lines (517 17; www.vienna airportlines.at) has three services connecting different parts of Vienna with the airport. The most central is the **Vienna Airport Lines bus stop** (Map p68; 01, Morzinplatz) at Morzinplatz/Schwedenplatz (bus 1185; one way/return €8/13, 20 minutes), running via the Wien-Mitte train station.

A taxi to/from the airport costs between €25 and €50. The yellow Taxi 40100 in the arrivals hall (near the bookshop) has a fixed airport rate of €36. **C&K Airport Service** (01-444 44; www.cundk.at) has rates starting at €33.

An Uber (www.uber.com) between the airport and city centre costs around €21 to €29.

Slovaklines (www.slovaklines.sk) in conjunction with Eurolines runs buses between Bratislava Airport and Vienna International Airport and on to Südtiroler Platz at Vienna's *Hauptbahnhof* (one way/return €10/20, 90 minutes, hourly or better).

Buses leave outside the Bratislava Airport arrival hall between 8.30am and 9.35pm daily, and from Südtiroler Platz at Vienna's *Hauptbahnhof* between 8.30am and 9.35pm daily.

BICYCLE

Vienna is a fabulous place to get around by bike. Bicycles can be carried free of charge on carriages marked with a bike symbol on the S-Bahn and U-Bahn from 9am to 3pm and after 6.30pm Monday to Friday, after 9am Saturday and all day Sunday. It's not possible to take bikes on trams or buses. The city also runs the **Citybike Wien** (Vienna City Bike; www.citybikewien.at; per 1/2/3hr free/€1/2, per hour thereafter €4) shared-bike program, with bike stands scattered throughout the city.

CAR & MOTORCYCLE

You may consider hiring a car to see some of the outer sights but in Vienna itself it's best to stick with the excellent public-transport system.

PUBLIC TRANSPORT

Vienna's comprehensive and unified public-transport network is one of the most efficient in Europe. Flat-fare tickets are valid for trains, trams, buses, the underground (U-Bahn) and the S-Bahn regional trains. Services are frequent and you rarely have to wait more than 10 minutes.

Transport maps are posted in all U-Bahn stations and at many bus and tram stops. Free maps are available from **Wiener Linien** (☎ 01-790 91 00; www.wienerlinien.at), located in U-Bahn stations. The Karlsplatz, Stephansplatz and Westbahnhof information offices are open 6.30am to 6.30pm Monday to Friday and 8.30am to 4pm Saturday and Sunday. Those at Schottentor, Praterstern, Floridsdorf, Philadelphiabrücke and Erdberg are closed at weekends.

TAXI

Taxis are reliable and relatively cheap by Western European standards. City journeys are metered; the minimum charge is roughly €3.80 from 6am to 11pm Monday to Saturday and €4.30 any other time, plus a per-kilometre fee of €1.42. A telephone reservation costs an additional €2.80. A tip of 10% is expected. Taxis are easily found at train stations and taxi stands all over the city. To order one, contact **Taxi 40100** (☎ 01-401 00; www.taxi40100.at) or **31300 Taxi** (☎ 01-313 00; www.taxi31300.at). These accept common credit and debit cards (check before hopping in, though). Uber operates in Vienna.

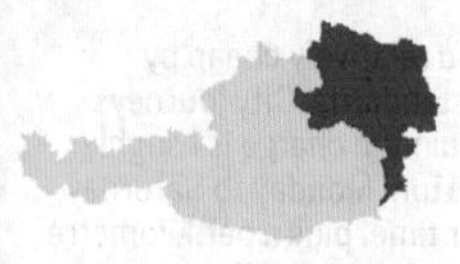

Lower Austria & Burgenland

Includes ➡

Best Places to Eat

- ➡ Zur Dankbarkeit (p157)
- ➡ Zum Kaiser von Österreich (p129)
- ➡ Restaurant Loibnerhof (p132)
- ➡ Weingut Gabriel (p155)
- ➡ Gut Drauf at Gut Oggau (p155)

Best Places to Stay

- ➡ Gut Purbach (p156)
- ➡ Burg Bernstein (p152)
- ➡ Hotel Looshaus (p146)
- ➡ Seewirt (p157)
- ➡ St Martins Therme & Lodge (p157)
- ➡ Raffelsberger Hof (p129)

Why Go?

Encircling Vienna, Lower Austria is a cradle of Austrian civilisation and a region offering visitors one of the country's most lively cultural landscapes. Outdoor activities, some worthwhile museums, world-class wines, hearty food and a glimpse into the age of the Romans at Carnuntum make leaving the capital for a day or longer an attractive prospect.

And naturally everyone's heard of the Danube River (Donau), which cuts a picturesque valley, the Wachau, through the region's northwest. A place of magnificent natural beauty, this is truly a European highlight for its vineyards, castles, abbeys and medieval villages.

To the south of the capital, undervisited Burgenland is all but the typical Austria of the holiday brochures; you won't find soaring mountains, glacial lakes and bombastic architecture here, just bucolic flatlands spread like a well-tenderised schnitzel around the jewel in its crown – Neusiedler See – a shallow mecca for water-sports fans and paddling toddlers alike.

When to Go

- ➡ Visit Burgenland, especially the Neusiedler See region in the north, between April and October.
- ➡ From November to March, Burgenland goes into low-season hibernation and its prime attraction – the outdoors – becomes cold, grey and windswept.
- ➡ Visit Lower Austria during the April to October warm season, when the Wachau is often bathed in a soft light and you can make the most of the Danube River and its sights and activities.
- ➡ Autumn is the best time to enjoy wine in the Wachau, and from 11 November (St Martin's Day) each year young wine is sold.

LOWER AUSTRIA

Providing popular day-trip material from Vienna, Lower Austria possesses the country's most vibrant cultural landscape, a combination of vineyards and art, monasteries and low wooded hills. Through this enchanting scene flows the mighty Danube which forms the famous Wachau – one of Europe's most fascinating valleys, watched over by castles and medieval villages.

Getting There & Away

Much of Lower Austria has excellent autobahn, rail and bus connections to the rest of the country. Travelling through the province can be done mostly by rail, but the Waldviertel north of the Danube and the Mostviertel south of the Danube have limited train connections. Here it's better to have your car or bicycle, or use local buses.

The Danube Valley

The Danube, which enters Lower Austria from the west near Ybbs and exits in the east near Bratislava, Slovakia's capital, carves a picturesque path through the province's hills and fields. Austria's most spectacular section of the Danube is the dramatic stretch of river between Krems an der Donau and Melk, known as the **Wachau**. Here the landscape is characterised by vineyards, forested slopes, wine-producing villages and imposing fortresses at nearly every bend. The Wachau is today a Unesco World Heritage site, due to its harmonious blend of natural and cultural beauty.

Getting Around

BICYCLE

A wonderfully flat cycle path runs along both sides of the Danube between Vienna and Melk, passing through Krems, Dürnstein, Weissenkirchen and Spitz on the northern bank. Many hotels and *Pensionen* (guesthouses) are geared towards cyclists, and most towns have at least one bike-rental and -repair shop.

For more information, pick up a free copy of *The Donauradweg – Von Passau bis Bratislava* (from tourist offices), which provides details of distances, hotels and tourist information offices along the entire route.

BOAT

A popular way of exploring the region is by boat, particularly between Krems and Melk (through the Wachau); it's also possible to travel from Passau (in Germany) to Vienna. The most convenient time to take a boat trip on the Danube is between May and September, when boat companies operate on a summer schedule. Children receive a 50% discount.

Brandner (☎ 07433-25 90 21; www.brandner.at; Ufer 15, Wallsee) Services the Krems–Melk route one to two times daily from mid-April to late October; stops include Spitz.

DDSG Blue Danube (☎ 01-588 80; www.ddsg-blue-danube.at; Handelskai 265, Reichsbrücke, Vienna; Ⓜ Vorgartenstrasse) Operates boats between Krems and Melk, stopping in at Dürnstein and Spitz, from April to October. Bikes can be taken on board all boats for free.

CAR

The roads on both sides of the Danube between Krems and Melk, where the B3 and the B33 hug the contours of the river, lend themselves well to touring. Bridges taking motor vehicles cross the river at Krems (two crossing points), Melk, Pöchlarn and Ybbs.

Krems an der Donau

☎ 02732 / POP 24,600

Krems, as it's known to its friends, is the gateway to the Wachau and one of the prettiest towns sitting astride the Danube. A region-driven food scene; an intact historical centre; top-quality Grüner Veltliner and riesling whites from local vineyards; and high-calibre museums attract the summer crowds, but the rest of the year things quieten down a notch. Aimless wandering is the way to go, dipping into churches and museums, strolling the banks of the Danube and sampling wines.

Krems has three parts: Krems to the east, Stein (formerly a separate town) to the west, and the connecting suburb of Und. Hence the local witticism: *Krems und Stein sind drei Städte* (Krems and Stein are three towns).

Sights

The big attraction in Krems is the Kunstmeile (Art Mile), 1.6km of arty institutions stretching from the Minoritenkirche to the Dominikanerkirche. There are eight attractions visitors can access, each one with its own tickets and opening times (these are all similar) but a single combi ticket (€18) available from the tourist office and selected venues covers them all.

Lower Austria & Burgenland Highlights

❶ **Danube Valley** (p130) Wandering, cycling or driving the cultural landscape of the Wachau.

❷ **Krems an der Donau** (p123) Walking the Kunstmeile, exactly a mile of art in many forms.

❸ **Rust** (p154) Sipping wines in one of the pretty *Heurigen* (wine taverns).

❹ **Stift Melk** (p134) Going baroque at Melk's magnificent monastery on the banks of the Danube.

❺ **Neusiedler See** (p153) Making a splash in Austria's slurping steppe lake.

❻ **Semmeringbahn** (p147) Riding the footplate of this remarkable feat of Habsburg engineering in Semmering.

❼ **Neusiedler See-Seewinkel National Park** (p157) Twitching at your leisure in Seewinkel's haven for birdlife.

❽ **Dürnstein** (p130) Exploring this pretty Danube village and scrambling up to the castle where Richard the Lionheart was kept captive.

❾ **Schneeberg** (p145) Hiking or catching the train up Lower Austria's highest peak.

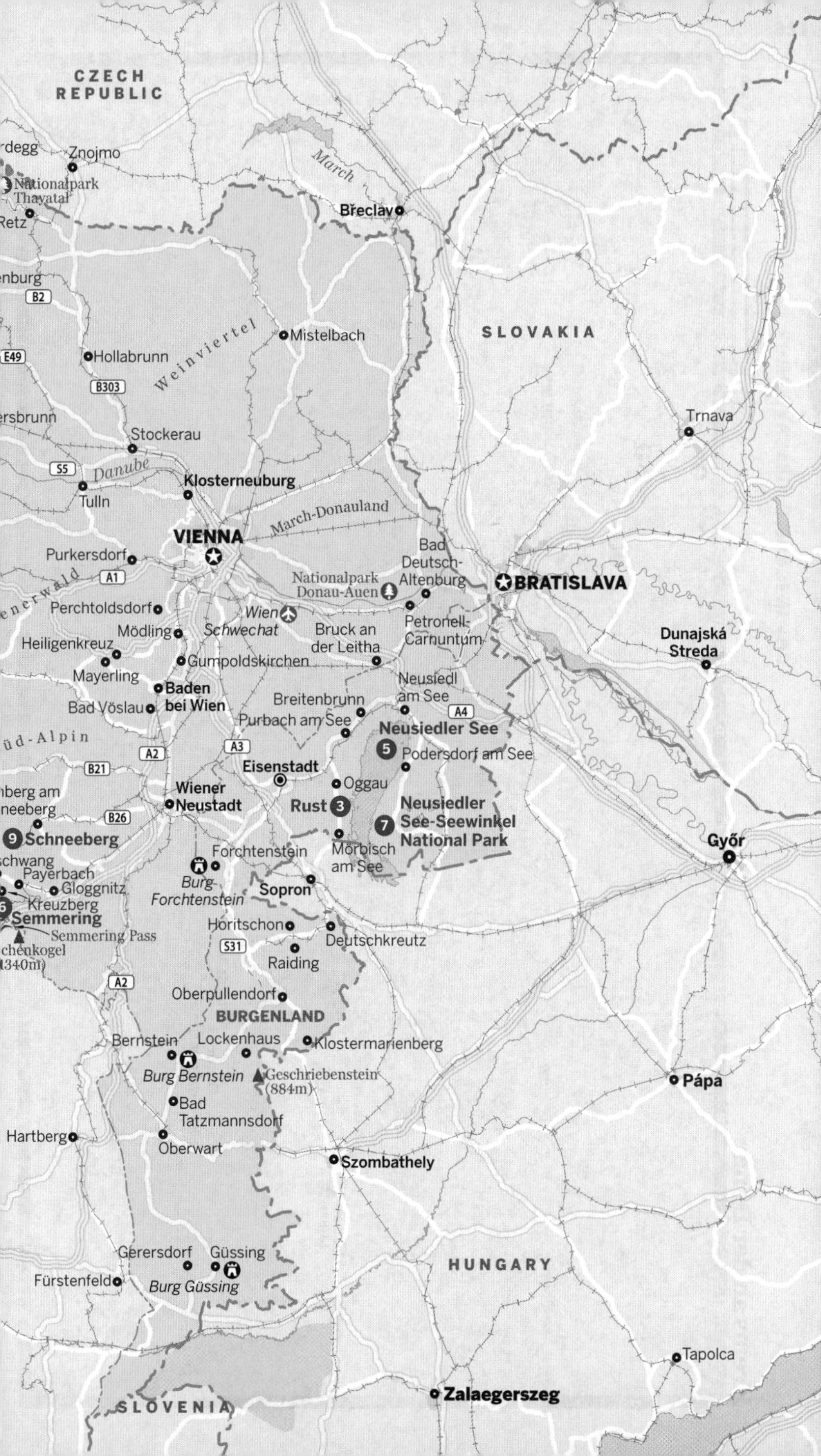
CZECH REPUBLIC
Znojmo
Nationalpark Thayatal
Retz
B2
Hollabrunn
E49
B303
Weinviertel
Mistelbach
March
Břeclav
SLOVAKIA
Trnava
Stockerau
S5
Danube
Tulln
Klosterneuburg
March-Donauland
VIENNA
Purkersdorf
A1
Nationalpark Donau-Auen
Bad Deutsch-Altenburg
BRATISLAVA
Perchtoldsdorf
Wien Schwechat
Mödling
Bruck an der Leitha
Petronell-Carnuntum
Dunajská Streda
Heiligenkreuz
Gumpoldskirchen
Mayerling
Baden bei Wien
Bad Vöslau
Breitenbrunn
Neusiedl am See
Purbach am See
A4
Neusiedler See
A2
A3
5
Podersdorf am See
B21
Eisenstadt
Oggau
Wiener Neustadt
Rust
3
Neusiedler See-Seewinkel National Park
7
B26
9 Schneeberg
Forchtenstein
Mörbisch am See
Győr
Payerbach
Gloggnitz
Burg Forchtenstein
Sopron
Kreuzberg
Semmering
Semmering Pass
Horitschon
Deutschkreutz
S31
Raiding
A2
Oberpullendorf
BURGENLAND
Bernstein
Lockenhaus
Klostermarienberg
Burg Bernstein
Geschriebenstein (884m)
Pápa
Bad Tatzmannsdorf
Hartberg
Oberwart
Szombathely
Gerersdorf
Güssing
HUNGARY
Fürstenfeld
Burg Güssing
Tapolca
SLOVENIA
Zalaegerszeg

Krems an der Donau

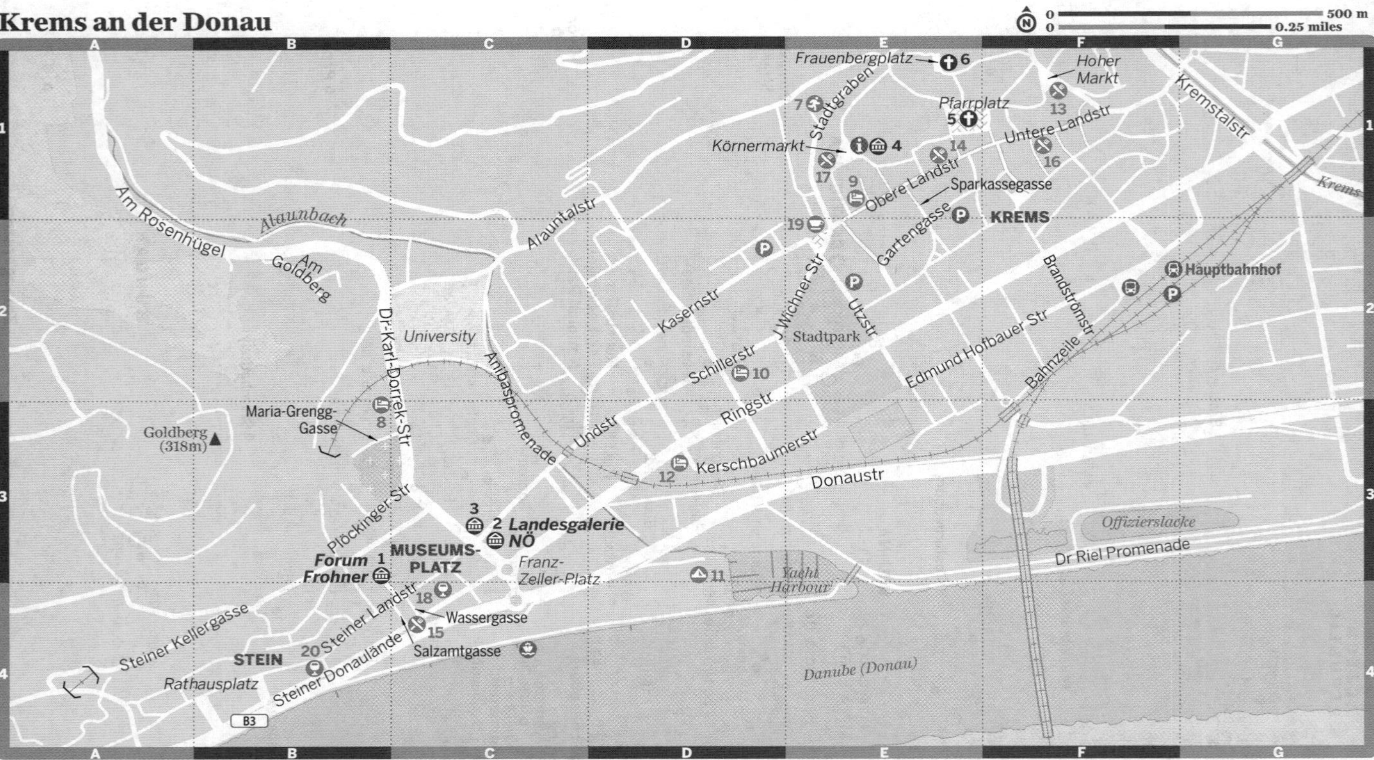

Krems an der Donau

Top Sights
1 Forum Frohner B3
2 Landesgalerie NÖ C3

Sights
Karikaturmuseum .... (see 2)
3 Kunsthalle Krems C3
4 Museum Krems E1
5 Pfarrkirche St Veit E1
6 Piaristenkirche E1

Activities, Courses & Tours
7 Weingut der Stadt Krems E1

Sleeping
8 Arte Hotel Krems B3
9 Hotel Alte Poste E1
10 Hotel Unter den Linden D2
11 ÖAMTC Donaupark Camping D3
12 Radfahrerherberge Krems D3

Eating
13 Jell F1
14 MOYOme E1
15 Salzstadl C4
16 Schwarze Kuchl F1
17 Zum Kaiser von Österreich E1

Drinking & Nightlife
18 Piano C4
19 Stadtcafe Ulrich E2
20 Weinstein B4

Shopping
Volkskultur .... (see 20)

★Landesgalerie NÖ — GALLERY

(02732-908 010; www.landesgalerie-noe.at; Museumsplatz 1; adult/child €10/3.50; 10am-6pm Tue-Sun) From one side it looks like a squashed cube, from the other as though it's about to topple over – welcome to the latest addition to Krems' Kunstmeile: a bold, 21st-century statement in grey aluminium tiles that looms over the newly created Museumsplatz like an alien spacecraft. It's a more than apt setting for the ever-changing exhibitions of edgy modern art and contemporary installations inside, and gives focus to the 'Art Mile' that had been missing up until it opened in 2019.

★Forum Frohner — GALLERY

(Kunstmeile; 02732-908 010; www.forum-frohner.at; Minoritenplatz 4; adult/child €5/4; 11am-7pm Tue-Sun) Part of Krems' Kunsthalle network, this contemporary white cube is named after the artist Adolf Frohner and is housed in the former Minorite monastery. It has an impressive calendar of conceptual work, both international and Austrian.

Kunsthalle Krems — GALLERY

(www.kunsthalle.at; Museumsplatz 5; adult/child €10/3.50; 10am-6pm Tue-Sun) One of the main attractions on Krems' Kunstmeile, the Kunsthalle has a program of changing exhibitions. These might be mid-19th-century landscapes or hard-core conceptual works, but are always well curated.

Stift Göttweig — MONASTERY

(Göttweig Abbey; 02732-855 81-0; www.stiftgoettweig.at; Furth bei Göttweig; adult/child €8.50/5; 10am-6pm Apr-Oct) Founded in 1083, the abbey was devastated by fire in the early 18th century and so sports an impressive baroque interior. It's still a working monastery today. Aside from the sublime view back across the Danube Valley from its garden terrace and restaurant, the abbey's highlights include the Imperial Staircase with a heavenly ceiling fresco painted by Paul Troger in 1739, and the over-the-top baroque interior of the Stiftskirche, which has a Kremser Schmidt work in the crypt.

Fully guided tours take in the abbey's Imperial Wing, church and summer vestry; shorter tours explore either the Imperial Wing or the church and vestry.

The best way to reach Göttweig is by train from Krems (10 minutes, hourly), though it's a steep walk uphill from the village station.

Piaristenkirche — CHURCH

(Frauenbergplatz; dawn-dusk) Reached by a covered stairway (Piaristenstiege) from Pfarrplatz, Krems' most impressive church has a wonderful webbed Gothic ceiling and huge, austerely plain windows. It's most atmospheric after dark, when you can best imagine the spectacle of the massive baroque altar for the 18th-century parishioners.

Karikaturmuseum — MUSEUM

(02732-908-010; www.karikaturmuseum.at; Museumsplatz 3; adult/child €10/3.50; 10am-6pm) Austria's sole caricature museum occupies a suitably tongue-in-cheek chunk of purpose-built architecture, its spiky facade tearing the blue Austrian sky. Changing exhibitions and a large permanent collection of caricatures of prominent Austrian and international figures make for a fun diversion if the other art in the Kunstmeile gets too heavy.

Pfarrkirche St Veit CHURCH
(Pfarrplatz 5; ⌚dawn-dusk) Known as the 'Cathedral of the Wachau', the large baroque parish church boasts colourful frescos by Martin Johann Schmidt, an 18th-century local artist who was also known as Kremser Schmidt. The baroque building is the work of Cipriano Biasino, who worked on several churches in the Wachau, including the abbey church at Stift Göttweig (p127). The cool single nave has many examples of *trompe l'œil*, lending it 3D features it doesn't have, and is peppered with gilt cherubs and laurel wreathes.

Museum Krems MUSEUM
(www.museumkrems.at; Körnermarkt 14; admission €7.50; ⌚10am-6pm mid-Apr–Oct; P) Housed in a former Dominican monastery, this museum has collections of religious and modern art, including works by Kremser Schmidt, as well as winemaking artefacts and a section on the famous Krems mustard.

Activities

Weingut der Stadt Krems WINE
(☎02732-801 441; www.weingutstadtkrems.at; Stadtgraben 11; ⌚9am-noon & 1-5pm Mon-Fri, 9am-noon Sat) This city-owned vineyard, yielding 200,000 bottles per year, mostly Grüner Veltliner and riesling, offers a wide variety of wine for tasting and purchase.

Sleeping

ÖAMTC Donaupark Camping CAMPGROUND €
(☎02732-844 55; www.donauparkcamping-krems.at; Yachthafenstrasse 19; camp sites per adult/child/car €6.30/3.30/5, per tent €5-9; ⌚Apr-Oct; P 📶) Surprisingly centrally located and well-maintained campsite alongside the Danube with cycle hire and a snack bar.

Radfahrerherberge Krems HOSTEL €
(☎02732-834 52; www.oejhv.at; Ringstrasse 77; dm €20; ⌚Apr-Oct; P 📶) This popular Hostelling International (HI) hostel is well geared for cyclists; it features a garage, an on-site bicycle-repair service and packed lunches. Dorms are clean but basic.

Arte Hotel Krems DESIGN HOTEL €€
(☎02732-71123; www.arte-hotel.at; Dr-Karl-Dorrek-Strasse 23; s/d €105/157; P 📶) The art of the title might be a stretch, but what you do get here are large, well-designed rooms with open-plan bathrooms, all scattered with 1960s-tilting furniture and big, bright patterns. There's a separately owned wellness studio in the building, and a decent grill restaurant in the same complex.

Hotel Unter den Linden HOTEL €€
(☎02732-821 15; www.udl.at; Schillerstrasse 5; s/d from €72/98; P 📶) This big, family-run hotel has knowledgeable and helpful owners, modern, parquet-floored rooms and a convenient location. Its mix of historic and streamlined modern works well throughout, and breakfast is taken in the folksy dining room. Book ahead.

Hotel Alte Poste HOTEL €€
(☎02732-822 76; www.altepost-krems.at; Obere Landstrasse 32; s €42-65, d €72-100; 📶) If you are on a budget and want to stay centrally, the 23 rooms at this historic 500-year-old post inn by the Steinertor (the medieval gateway into the old town) are for you. Basic but well-kept, rooms are gathered around an enchanting courtyard. Immaculate bathrooms are shared and rates include breakfast.

Eating

Salzstadl AUSTRIAN €
(☎02732-703 12; www.salzstadl.at; Steiner Donaulände 32; mains €5-15; ⌚11am-3pm & 6-11pm; 📶) Housed in an old salt store, this well-established restaurant has been banging down local favourites such as pike-perch, goulash and grilled chicken for over 20 years. It also doubles as a theatre/music venue with live jazz and other genres taking to the stage at least once a month. Check the website for the programme.

MOYOme BISTRO €
(☎0664 514 4686; www.moyome.com; Obere Landstrasse 10; mains €5-9; ⌚8am-7pm Mon-Fri, 8.30am-5pm Sat, 9am-5pm Sun; 📶) Proving that locally sourced doesn't have to mean pricey, this bistro that spills out onto pedestrianised Obere Landstrasse is full from start to finish. The all-day breakfasts are a hit, as are the light lunches and cheap drinks. Caters well for vegetarians, too.

Schwarze Kuchl AUSTRIAN €
(www.schwarze-kuchl.at; Untere Landstrasse 8; mains €4-15; ⌚9am-7.30pm Mon-Fri, to 6pm Sat) For some good, filling local food, a 9am beer or a salady lunch, head to this Krems institution on the main drag through town where you can enjoy veal goulash, apricot-filled

WORTH A TRIP

WEISSENKIRCHEN

Weissenkirchen, 12km from Krems, has a laid-back elegance as well as historic cache, but somehow eludes the crowds. The main attraction is the fortified Gothic parish church, and below it, the charming Teisenhoferhof arcaded courtyard, with a covered gallery and lashings of flowers and dried corn. Directly below the church, the tiny, pretty **Wachau Museum** (☎02715-22 68; www.weissenkirchen.at; Weissenkirchen 32; adult/child €6/2.50; ⏲10am-5pm Tue-Sun Apr-Oct) showcases artists of the Danube School.

Weissenkirchen has boat and train connections to Dürnstein, but the easiest way to reach the village from there is by local bus (eight minutes, 18 daily). If you fancy overnighting here, the exceptionally atmospheric **Raffelsberger Hof** (☎02715-22 01; www.raffelsbergerhof.at; Freisingerplatz 54; s/d from €98/138; ⏲mid-Apr–Nov; P) occupies a gently modernised Renaissance castle.

pancakes and Waldviertel potato-and-beef hotpot *(Gröstl)* while warming your toes on the huge tiled oven. Spills out among the shoppers on busy days.

Jell AUSTRIAN €€
(www.amon-jell.at; Hoher Markt 8-9; mains €15-30; ⏲11am-2pm & 6-10.30pm Tue-Fri, from 2pm Sat & Sun; P) Occupying a gorgeous stone house, Jell is hard to beat for a rustic atmosphere and fine wine from its own vineyard. Its friendly staff also adds to a great regional experience, making this one of the best dinner spots in town. Also has a terrace for warm-weather dining. Located just east of Pfarrkirche St Veit.

★Zum Kaiser von Österreich AUSTRIAN €€€
(☎0800 400 171 052; www.kaiser-von-oesterreich.at; Körnermarkt 9; menus €42.50-72.50, cover €4.60; ⏲6-11pm Tue-Sat) The 'Emperor of Austria' is one of Krems' most well-loved upmarket restaurants. Interiors recall a hunting lodge, which sets the scene for menus built around the region's bounty of game, from deer to pheasant to rabbit. Other hyperlocal ingredients like Wachau apples and apricots, wild herbs and mushrooms, Waldviertel fish and Weinviertel pumpkins are also used in the finely crafted, imaginative dishes.

The kitchen is happy to cater for vegetarians and those with allergies – just let the staff know when you book, which you must if you ever want to get a table here.

Drinking & Nightlife

Piano BAR
(www.piano-krems.at; Steiner Landstrasse 21; ⏲5pm-2am Mon-Sat, to midnight Sun; 📶) An assorted crowd of students, local office workers and mellow jazz types pack in tightly at this lively and off-beat pub. It does a couple of local sausage snacks and sandwiches to go with its expertly assembled selection of beers. One of the last places to close in otherwise quiet Krems.

Weinstein WINE BAR
(☎0664 1300 331; www.weinstein.at; Steiner Donaulände 56; ⏲from 5pm Mon-Sat) A Danube-facing, columned wine bar that stocks a comprehensive lineup of local wines by the glass. The kitchen turns out good drinking food, say carpaccio in summer or a house burger in winter.

Stadtcafe Ulrich CAFE
(☎02732-820 94; Südtirolerplatz 7; ⏲7am-11pm Mon-Thu, to midnight Sat, 9am-11pm Sun; 📶) Krems' busiest cafe is this elegantly high-ceilinged, open-all-hours Viennese job next to the Steinertor. The coffee and strudel here makes a great breakfast and there's a small terrace out front.

Shopping

Volkskultur GIFTS & SOUVENIRS
(☎02732-850 15 15; www.volkskultureuropa.org; Haus der Regionen, Steiner Donaulände 56; ⏲10am-noon & 1-6pm Mon-Sat) A wonderfully kitsch- and junk-free showcase of quality Austrian craftsmanship, spanning traditional clothing, fabrics, scarves, jewellery and kitchenware. Look out for the iconic Riess enamelware with folk patterns, apricot specialities and glass paintings.

Information

Krems Tourismus (☎02732-826 76; www.krems.info; Körnermarkt 14; ⏲10am-6pm Mon-Sat, to 4pm Sun mid-Apr–mid-Oct, 9am-5pm Mon-Fri mid-Oct–mid-Apr) Helpful office well stocked with info and maps.

Getting There & Away

For boats, the **river station** is near Donaustrasse, about 1.5km west of the train station. Brandner (p123) operates pleasure boats from here to Spitz and Melk; see the website for exact timetables.

Frequent daily trains connect Krems with Vienna (€18.40, 70 minutes) and Tulln (€10.30, 39 minutes).

Wachau Linien (www.vor.at) buses for the Wachau leave from near the *Hauptbahnhof* (main train station).

Parking costs €4 a day and the most convenient car park for the centre is at Südtirolerplatz.

Dürnstein

02711 / POP 875

The pretty town of Dürnstein, on an impossibly photogenic curve in the Danube, is not only known for its beautiful buildings but also for the castle above the town where Richard I of England, yes, the Lionheart, was once imprisoned.

Busy with visitors in summer, Dürnstein completely shuts up shop over the winter.

Sights

Domäne Wachau WINERY

(02711-371; www.domaene-wachau.at; Dürnstein 107; 10am-5pm Mon-Sat Apr-Oct, closed Sat Nov-Mar) If you're intent on tasting the best of what the Wachau has to offer, it's a good idea to do a broad range of vineyards, from the innovative family-run operations to the big boys such as Domäne Wachau, one of the region's most well-known producers internationally.

A large, modern tasting room is set back from the river and staffed by an army of keen young assistants. It also stocks some nice local food products if wine's not your thing.

Kuenringerburg CASTLE

FREE Kuenringerburg, the castle high on the hill above the town, is where Richard the Lionheart was incarcerated from 1192 to 1193. His crime was insulting Leopold V; his misfortune was to be recognised despite his disguise when journeying through Austria on his way home from the Holy Lands. His liberty was granted only upon payment of an enormous ransom of 35,000kg of silver (this sum partly funded the building of Wiener Neustadt).

Driving & Cycling Tour
The Danube Valley

Starting and ending in Krems, this 150km tour should take a full day.

From the Krems-Stein roundabout in **1 Krems an der Donau**, take the B3 southwest towards Spitz. About 3km from Krems-Stein you approach the small settlement of **2 Unterloiben**, where on the right you can see the Franzosendenkmal (French Monument), erected in 1805 to celebrate the victory of Austrian and Russian troops here over Napoleon. Shortly afterwards the lovely town of **3 Dürnstein**, 6km from Krems, comes into view with its blue-towered Chorherrenstift backed by Kuenringerburg, the castle where Richard the Lionheart was imprisoned in 1192.

The valley is punctuated by picturesque terraced vineyards as you enter the heart of the Wachau. In **4 Weissenkirchen**, 12km from Krems, you'll find a pretty fortified parish church on the hilltop. The Wachau Museum here houses work by artists of the Danube School.

A couple of kilometres on, just after Wösendorf, you find the church of **5 St Michael**, in a hamlet with 13 houses. If the kids are along for this ride, now's the time to ask them to count the terracotta hares on the roof of the church (seven, in case they're not reading this!).

Some 17km from Krems, the pretty town of **6 Spitz** swings into view, surrounded by vineyards and lined with quiet, cobblestone streets. Some good trails lead across hills and to *Heurigen* (wine taverns) here (start from the church).

Turn right at Spitz onto the B217 (Ottenschläger Strasse). The terraced hill on your right is 1000-Eimer-Berg, so-named for its reputed ability to yield 1000 buckets of wine each season. On your left, high above the valley opening, is the castle ruin Burgruine Hinterhaus. Continue along the B217 to the mill wheel and turn right towards **7 Burg Oberranna**, 6km west of Spitz in Mühldorf is surrounded by woods and overlooks the valley.

From here, backtrack down to the B3 and continue the circuit. The valley opens up and on the left, across the Danube, you glimpse the ruins of Burg Aggstein.

8 Willendorf, located 21km from Krems, is where the 25,000-year-old Ve-

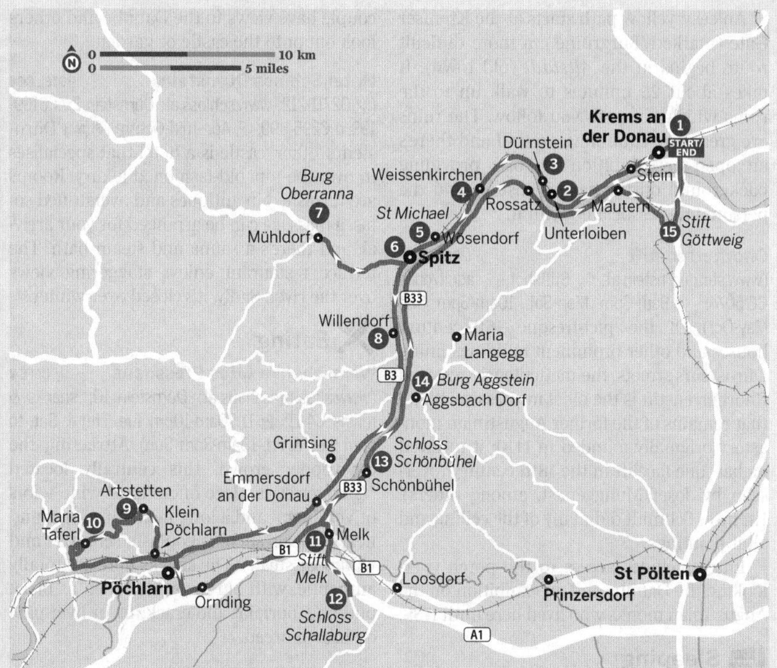

nus of Willendorf was discovered. It is today housed in the Naturhistorisches Museum in Vienna. Continuing along the B3, the majestic Stift Melk rises up across the river. There's some decent swimming in the backwaters here if you're game to dip into the Danube.

At Klein Pöchlarn, a sign indicates a turn-off on Artstettner Strasse (L7255): follow it for 5km to 9 **Artstetten**, famous for its many onion domes and castle. From here, the minor road L7257 winds 6.5km through a sweeping landscape to 10 **Maria Taferl** where the baroque church Pfarr-und Wallfahrtskirche Maria Taferl rises high above the Danube Valley.

Head 6km down towards the B3. Turn left at the B3 towards Krems and follow the ramp veering off to the left and across the river at the Klein Pöchlarn bridge. Follow the road straight ahead to the B1 (Austria's longest road) and turn left onto this towards Melk.

This first section along the south bank is uninteresting, but it soon improves. Unless the weather isn't playing along, across the river you can make out Artstetten in the distance, and shortly must-see 11 **Stift Melk** (p134) will rise up ahead, its celebrated monastery emerging in golden shimmering splendour.

From Stift Melk, a 7km detour leads south to the splendid Renaissance castle of 12 **Schloss Schallaburg** (p135). To reach the castle from the abbey in Melk, follow the signs to the *Bahnhof* (train station) and Lindestrasse east, turn right into Hummelstrasse/Kirschengraben (L5340) and follow the signs to the castle.

Backtrack to the B33. Be careful to stay on the south side of the river. When you reach the corner of Abt-Karl-Strasse and Bahnhofstrasse, go right and right again at the river. Follow the B1 for 4km to 13 **Schloss Schönbühel**, a 12th-century castle standing high on a rock some 5km northeast of Melk. Continue along this lovely stretch of the B33 in the direction of Krems. About 10km from Schloss Schönbühel the ruins of 14 **Burg Aggstein** (www.ruineaggstein.at; Aggsbach Dorf; adult/child €6.90/4.90; ⏲9am-6pm Apr-Oct) swing into view. This 12th-century hilltop castle was built by the Kuenringer family and now offers a grand vista of the Danube.

About 27km from Melk some pretty cliffs rise up above the road. From Mautern it's a detour of about 6km to 15 **Stift Göttweig** (p127), another bombastic monastery. From here, make your way back to Krems.

An easy, yellow path starts at the Kremser Gate (marked 'Burgruine'); a more difficult route begins in the *Altstadt* (old town). It takes about 25 minutes to walk up to the ruins whichever path you follow. The ruins are great for scrambling around and there's an open-air exhibition of sorts providing background on the castle's history and the personalities associated with it.

Chorherrenstift MONASTERY
(www.stiftduernstein.at; Stiftshof; adult/child €6.50/4; 9am-6pm Mon-Sat, 10am-6pm Sun May-Oct) Of the picturesque 16th-century houses and other prominent buildings lining Dürnstein's streets, the meticulously restored Chorherrenstift is the most impressive. It's all that remains of the former Augustinian monastery originally founded in 1410; it received its baroque facelift in the 18th century (overseen by Josef Munggenast, among others). Kremser Schmidt did many of the ceiling and altar paintings.

Entry includes access to the porch overlooking the Danube and an exhibition on the Augustinian monks who lived here until 1788.

Sleeping

Pension Böhmer GUESTHOUSE €
(02711-239; Hauptstrasse 22; s €45, d €55-68; P) This small pension in the heart of town has comfortable rooms that overlook the main street. Downstairs there's a couple of atmospheric rooms and a cobbled entrance that is perfect for a leisurely wine. The Böhmer can also sort you out for the best local apricot schnapps and jams.

Hotel Sänger Blondel HOTEL €€
(02711-253; www.saengerblondel.at; Klosterplatz/Dürnstein 64; s €83-93, d €126-146; P) Arguably Dürnstein's best-value option, this welcoming hotel has generously sized rooms furnished in light woods, some with sofas. A couple have views to the Danube and others look out onto the castle or garden.

Hotel Schloss Dürnstein HOTEL €€€
(02711-212; www.schloss.at; Dürnstein 2; s €169-199, d €295-399; Apr–mid-Oct; P) Dürnstein's 'other' castle is a hotel that specialises in over-the-top, old-fashioned luxury. Rooms are furnished in antiques and overstuffed sofas, a massage can be arranged for your arrival, and there's a sauna and steam bath. The terrace restaurant enjoys staggering views over the river. Sadly, it's closed over winter.

A HIKE FROM DÜRNSTEIN

After visiting the Kuenringerburg (p130), in which Richard the Lionheart was incarcerated, hike the Schlossbergweg (marked green) from there to Fesselhütte, about one hour by foot from the castle, to enjoy sausage, soup or wine at this forest tavern. A road also leads up here from Weissenkirchen.

Eating

Weinschenke Altes Presshaus CAFE €
(www.altes-presshaus.at; Dürnstein 10; snacks & mains €4-11; 11.30am-10pm Tue, Thu & Sat, to 5pm Wed & Fri, 10am-3pm Sun) Attracting the day-tripper crowd, this centrally located *Heuriger*-style place offers local wine – lots of Veltliner – and a long menu of snacks and hearty meals such as goulash, schnitzel and wild boar steaks. The snacks here are totally authentic, with old favourites such as black pudding, pork fat and crackling or liver pâté on brown bread.

Fesselhütte AUSTRIAN €
(02732-41 277; www.fesslhuette.at; Dürsteiner Waldhütten 23; mains €8-13; 9.30am-6pm Tue-Sun Apr-Oct) This lovely, old, forest dining room has a selection of platters, a hot lunch dish and homemade cakes and pastries. Sit out in the garden with a glass of wine from a Wachau vineyard. It's on several hiking routes and is a great place to take a break.

★ **Restaurant Loibnerhof** AUSTRIAN €€
(02732-828 90; www.loibnerhof.at; Unterloiben 7; mains €15-26; 11.30am-midnight Wed-Sun;) Situated 1.5km east of Dürnstein's centre, this traditional, family-run restaurant inside a Biedermeier, 400-year-old vaulted cellar serves up creative takes on Waldviertel cooking. In summer, there are tables out in the family's orchard. Take away the house nut schnapps, apricot jam or foie gras parfait.

Information

High visitor numbers didn't stop Dürnstein scrapping its tourist office in 2013 – try the **Rathaus** (Town Hall; 02711-219; www.duernstein.at; Hauptstrasse 25; 8am-noon Mon & Fri, 8am-noon & 1-6pm Tue, 8am-1pm Thu), which also has some information.

WORTH A TRIP

MARIA TAFERL & ARTSTETTEN

Located off the river on the northern side of the Danube in the Waldviertel, the small town of Maria Taferl is famous for its church looming high above the Danube Valley. The baroque **Pfarr-und Wallfahrtskirche Maria Taferl** (Parish & Pilgrimage Church; www.basilika.at; Maria Taferl 1; ⏲7am-8pm) was created by Jakob Prandtauer (of Melk fame), and has two onion domes and dark dome frescoes. Its altar is a complex array of figures in gold.

About 6km east of Maria Taferl and about the same distance from the Danube is Artstetten, famous for its castle. Built from the ruins of a 13th-century medieval castle and tinkered with for 700 years, **Artstetten Castle** (www.schloss-artstetten.at; Artstetten 1; adult/child €9/5.70; ⏲9am-5.30pm Apr-Oct; P) gained fame and glory after passing into the hands of the Habsburgs in the early 19th century, winding up in the possession of Archduke Franz Ferdinand. Inside is a museum devoted to the luckless heir, displaying photos and stories of his and his Czech wife's lives at the castle and their fateful trip to Sarajevo where his assassination kicked off WWI. The pair were buried in the family tomb, the *Familiengruft*, quite a place of pilgrimage for Habsburg fans.

The two destinations make for an interesting stop-off for those with their own car.

Getting There & Away

Brandner (www.brandner.at) boats connect Dürnstein with Krems (20 to 30 minutes) once or twice daily from mid-April to late October.

Dürnstein is linked to Melk (45 minutes, hourly) and Krems (25 minutes, 18 daily) by bus. The main stop is at the large car park south of the town. This is by far the most convenient way to travel.

Dürnstein's train station is called Dürnstein-Oberloiben, with connections to Krems (17 minutes, three daily) and Weissenkirchen (seven minutes, three daily).

Spitz

☎02713 / POP 1600

Sitting pretty on the north bank of the Danube, Spitz is a pleasant town that doesn't get quite as choked with day trippers as nearby Dürnstein does. It has a picturesque old-town centre, and offers some good hiking in the surrounding forests and vineyards. To reach the old town, turn left after leaving the station then head right up Marktstrasse to Kirchenplatz. Six kilometres west of Spitz, Mühldorf is home to the castle Burg Oberranna (not open to the public).

Hotel Mariandl HOTEL **€€**

(☎02713 23 11; www.hotel-mariandl.at; Kremserstrasse 2; d €105-140; P 📶) Located near the train station, the delightful Mariandl is housed in a late-19th-century villa and offers a range of rooms, from elegant, antique-sprinkled quarters to rather bog-standard, 21st-century bedrooms. There's an excellent restaurant on the premises where the breakfast buffet is laid out.

This hotel has two unexpected extras: guests can watch classic old Austrian films in a period cinema and peruse the owner's museum dedicated to actor and director, Gunther Philipp.

Information

The **tourist office** (☎02713-23 63; www.spitz-wachau.com; Mittergasse 3a; ⏲9am-1pm & 2-6pm Mon-Sat Apr-Oct), situated 400m west of the station, has excellent free maps of the town, with hiking trails marked, and maintains a comprehensive *Heuriger* calendar. Note it has unspecified and irregular hours in low season.

Tourismusverband Wachau Nibelungengau (☎02713-300 60 60; www.wachau.at; Schlossgasse 3; ⏲9am-4.30pm Mon-Thu, to 2.30pm Fri) has comprehensive information on the Wachau and the surrounding area.

Getting There & Away

Trains connect Spitz and Krems (35 minutes, three daily) but the bus (35 minutes, 20 daily) is a better option. Buses stop outside the train station.

Hire a bike from **Wachau Touristik Bernhardt** (☎02713-022 22; www.wachau-touristik.at; Bahnhofstrasse 6; per day €15) to explore the surrounding area on two wheels.

Feuersbrunn

About 10km east of Krems near the road to Tulln stands Schloss Grafenegg, a mid-19th-century historicist fantasy that's now a venue for exhibitions and concerts as well as a museum. Two kilometres away, the hamlet of Feuersbrunn is home to a couple of the region's best eating and sleeping options.

Schloss Grafenegg CASTLE
(www.grafenegg.com; Grafenegg 10; adult/child €6/4; ⊙11am-5pm Tue-Sun Mar–mid-Dec; P) About 6km south of Diendorf is this historicist castle with the look and feel of an ornate Tudor mansion set in English woods, although look a little closer and you'll spot faux Gothic, baroque and Biedermeier elements. Entrance is by guided tour only, which includes the library and staterooms which are devoid of furniture as the castle was partially destroyed during its time as Red Army headquarters after WWII. The manicured 19th-century gardens are perfect for a picnic.

Hotel Villa Katharina HOTEL €€
(☎02738-229 80; www.moerwald.at/hotel-villa-katharina; Kleine Zeile 10; s €90-100, d €150-180; P) This small, pretty, country hotel has simple, light and stylish rooms set among the vines, each spritzed with colours that reflect the wine-growing region. Its attached **Restaurant Zur Traube** (www.moerwald.at/restaurant-zur-traube; Kleine Zeile 13-17; mains €13-34; ⊙noon-3pm & 6-10pm, closed Mon-Wed Jul & Aug;) is something of a destination in itself.

Restaurant & Hotel Schloss Grafenegg AUSTRIAN €€
(☎02735-2616-0; www.moerwald.at/restaurant-schloss-grafenegg-2; Grafenegg 12; mains €13-30; ⊙10am-10pm Wed-Sun Easter-Dec; P) This traditional hotel restaurant, with an atmospherically retro interior, is owned by celebrity chef and winemaker Toni Mörwald and is known for its attention to detail. The menu is an almost purely Austrian affair, with the occasional intruder such as foie gras making the cut.

Getting There & Away

To reach Schloss Grafenegg from Vienna, take the train to nearby Wagram-Grafenegg (€15, 50 minutes, around nine daily) and walk 2km northeast to the castle or take a taxi. It's about a 40- to 50-minute drive from Vienna.

Melk

☎02752 / POP 5250

With its blockbuster abbey-fortress set high above the Danube, Melk is undoubtedly a high point of any visit to the region and a popular stop-off. Separated from the river by a stretch of woodland, this alluring town makes for an easy and rewarding day trip from Krems or even Vienna.

Melk is one of the most popular destinations in Austria, so you certainly won't be alone on its cobbled streets. It's also one of the few places in the Wachau that has a pulse in winter, making it a year-round option.

Sights

★**Stift Melk** ABBEY
(Benedictine Abbey of Melk; www.stiftmelk.at; Abt Berthold Dietmayr Strasse 1; adult/child €12.50/6.50, with guided tour €14.50/8.50; ⊙9am-5.30pm, tours 10am-4pm Apr-Oct) Of the many abbeys in Austria, Stift Melk is the most famous. Possibly Lower Austria's finest, the monastery church dominates the complex with its twin spires and high octagonal dome. The interior is baroque gone barmy, with a riot of chubby cherubs, barley-sugar twirls and polished faux marble. The theatrical high-altar scene, depicting St Peter and St Paul (the church's two patron saints), is by Peter Widerin. Johann Michael Rottmayr created most of the ceiling paintings, including those in the dome.

Historically, Melk was of great importance to the Romans and later to the Babenbergs, who built a castle here. In 1089 the Babenberg margrave Leopold II donated the castle to Benedictine monks, who converted it into a fortified abbey. Fire destroyed the original edifice, which was completely baroque-ified between 1702 and 1738 according to plans by Jakob Prandtauer and his disciple, Josef Munggenast. It's claimed nine million bricks were used to create the 500 rooms – don't worry though, you don't have to visit them all! (Most of the complex is taken up by a school, monks' quarters and offices.)

Besides the monastery church, highlights include the **Bibliothek** (library) and the **Marmorsaal** (Marble Hall); both have amazing trompe-l'œ-painted tiers on the ceiling (by Paul Troger) to give the illusion of greater height, and ceilings are slightly curved to aid the effect. Eleven of the imperial rooms, where dignitaries (including

Napoleon) stayed, are now used as a somewhat overcooked concept museum.

Before or after a tour of the main complex, take a spin around the **Nordbastei** (north bastion), where you'll discover some quirky temporary exhibitions, a viewing terrace and the Stift's gift shop.

English tours run at 10.55am and 2.55pm as well as 2pm May to September.

Schloss Schallaburg PALACE

(02754-6317; www.schallaburg.at; Schallaburg 1; adult/child €11/3.50; 9am-5pm Mon-Fri, to 6pm Sat & Sun mid-Mar–Oct) This palace is famous not only for its stunning architecture but also for the innovative exhibitions it houses, along with its lovely gardens. A wonderful curio are the 400 terracotta sculptures, completed between 1572 and 1573, the largest of which support the upper-storey arches of the palace. The excellently curated yearly shows are thematically conceived, and can cover anything from world handicrafts to The Beatles.

Combined tickets with Stift Melk cost €21. To reach Schallaburg, take the shuttle bus (€2.30) that leaves Melk train station at 9.30am, 10.30am, 12.30pm and 2.45pm.

Sleeping

Hotel Wachau HOTEL €€

(02752-525-31; www.hotel-wachau.at; Am Wachberg 3; s €80-99, d €129-149; P) Bright, clean rooms with fancy names run the gamut between modern business and Austrian twee at this hotel 2km southeast of the train station. The restaurant here turns out well-prepared regional cuisine.

Hotel Restaurant Zur Post HOTEL €€

(02752-523 45; www.post-melk.at; Linzer Strasse 1; s €65-90, d €120-140, f €155-180; P) A bright and pleasant hotel in the heart of town offering 25 large, comfortable rooms in plush colours with additional fancy touches such as brass bed lamps. There's a sauna, facilities for massages and free bike use for guests. The understatedly stylish restaurant offers mainly no-nonsense Austrian classics.

Eating

Zum Fürsten INTERNATIONAL €

(02752-523 43; Rathausplatz 3; mains €6-12; 10.30am-11pm;) Right at the foot of the Stift, this popular cafe serving pastas, strudel, chilli con carne and other international dishes.

Zur Post AUSTRIAN €€

(02752-523 45; Linzer Strasse 1; mains €14-20; 11.30am-10pm, closed Sun evening & Mon;) This traditional and understated restaurant is in the hotel of the same name on Melk's main drag. *Tafelspitz* (prime boiled beef), *Wiener Schnitzel* (breaded veal cutlet), local venison and organic lamb grace the menu, which also features vegetarian options.

Information

Melk Tourist Office (02752-511 60; www.stadt-melk.at; Kremser Strasse 5; 9.30am-5pm Mon-Sat, 10am-2pm Sun Apr & Oct, 9.30am-6pm Mon-Sat, 9.30am-3.30pm Sun May-Sep, shorter hours rest of year) has all you need to know about the town and the valley either side.

Getting There & Away

Boats operated by Brandner (p123) leave from the canal by Pionierstrasse, 400m north of the abbey, for Krems and Spitz.

Wachau Linien (p129) runs buses along the Danube Valley between Melk and Krems (€9.20, one hour, hourly).

Wachau Touristik Bernhardt (p133) rents bicycles from the ferry station in Melk and from the train station in Spitz.

There are regular train services to Melk from St Pölten (€5.70, 15 to 23 minutes, twice hourly), Vienna (€18.40, 50 minutes, twice hourly) and Salzburg (€45.10, 2½ hours with a change in St Pölten or Amstetten, at least hourly).

Tulln

02272 / POP 15,700

Tulln, the home town of painter Egon Schiele and situated 30km northwest of Vienna on the Danube, has a couple of interesting museums and can be easily visited on a day trip from Vienna or Krems.

Sights

Egon Schiele Museum MUSEUM

(www.schielemuseum.at; Donaulände 28; adult/child €5.50/3.50; 10am-5pm Tue-Sun Apr-Oct) The Egon Schiele Museum, housed in a former jail near the Danube, vividly presents the story of the life of the Tulln-born artist. It presents around 100 of his paintings and sketches, and a mock-up of the cell where he was briefly imprisoned, when he fell foul of the law in 1912 and over 100 of his erotic drawings were seized. Schiele-themed temporary exhibitions add more flesh to the bones.

Egon Schiele Birthplace MUSEUM
(Bahnhofstrasse 69, Hauptbahnhof Tulln; €2; 9am-8pm Apr-Oct, to 5pm Nov-Mar) This interpretive, interactive museum is based in a touching recreation of Egon Schiele's actual birthplace and family home. The son of the local station master Adolf Schiele, Egon Schiele spent the first 11 years of his life, from 1890, in the apartment at the train station that came with his father's job. The exhibition looks at his childhood and the influences he was exposed to as a boy.

Museum im Minoritenkloster MUSEUM
(Minoritenplatz 1) This city-promoted museum space features some excellent changing exhibitions based around mostly Austrian artists. Schiele has made a couple of appearances (surprise, surprise). Admission prices and opening times vary according to exhibition. It adjoins the Minorite church.

Minoritenkirche CHURCH
(Minoritenplatz 1; 8am-7pm) Alongside the tourist office, the rococo Minorite church from 1739 is decorated with magnificent ceiling frescoes dedicated to St Johannes Nepomuk.

Pfarrkirche St Stephan CHURCH
(Wiener Strasse 20; 7.30am-7.30pm) This parish church combines Gothic and baroque elements, along with the wonderful 13th-century frescoed Romanesque funerary chapel.

Sleeping & Eating

Junges Hotel Tulln HOSTEL €
(02272-651 65 10; www.tulln.noejhw.at; Marc-Aurel-Park 1; dm/s/d €25/37/56; P) Bright, cheaply furnished youth hostel near the Danube catering for seminar guests as well as tourists. Dorms sleep between four and eight guests. Note that reception is closed mornings at weekends.

Donaupark Camping CAMPGROUND €
(02272-652 00; www.campingtulln.at; Donaulände 76; camp sites per adult/tent & car €9/7; Apr–mid-Oct;) Great campground conveniently located just east of the centre on the river and alongside a pretty forest.

Hotel Nibelungenhof HOTEL €€
(02272-626 58; www.nibelungenhof.info; Donaulände 34; s €69-81, d €122-138; P) Situated along the Danube River with a lovely terrace garden and cafe-restaurant downstairs, this beautifully kept hotel has individually furnished rooms in bright and attractive colours, and with antique-style furniture. The lounge has a large library of books and a proper open fire.

Gasthaus zur Sonne AUSTRIAN €€
(02272-646 16; Bahnhofstrasse 48; mains €9-25; 11.30am-1.30pm & 6-9pm Tue-Sat;) This traditional, quite formal restaurant serves excellent versions of trad dishes such as goulash and veal liver in a balsamic vinegar. Reserve ahead – it's popular.

Information

The **tourist office** (02272-675 660; www.tulln.at; Minoritenplatz 2; 9am-6pm Mon-Fri, 10am-6pm Sat & Sun Apr-Oct, 9am-3pm Mon-Fri Nov-Mar) is one block north of Hauptplatz from the fountain end.

Getting There & Away

Several regional and S-Bahn trains each hour connect Tulln with Vienna's Franz-Josefs-Bahnhof (€9.30, 30 to 45 minutes) and hourly trains go to Krems (€10.30, 39 minutes).

Getting Around

Tulln and its tourist office are well set up for cyclists, as the Danube cycleway runs alongside the river on the town's northern border. Tulln has numerous Leihradl stations where you can hire a bicycle.

Waldviertel & Weinviertel

The Waldviertel (Woods Quarter) is a hugely underrated and highly picturesque region of rolling hills and rural villages, and while there isn't actually much forest to speak of, there are a number of fine attractions and retreats. The Kamptal wine region in particular is a great place for escaping the tourist crowds.

Forming a broad swath across Lower Austria north of the Danube, the Waldviertel begins near Krems and the Kamptal in the east (the latter borders the largely agricultural and winemaking region, the Weinviertel or 'Wine Quarter') and ends at the Czech border in the north and west. The highlight in these parts is definitely the Nationalpark Thayatal, a small protected area that extends along both sides of the Czech–Austria border.

Drosendorf

02915 / POP 1200

Situated on the northern fringe of the Waldviertel, hard on the Czech border, the lovely fortressed town of Drosendorf is often overlooked by the Viennese – it's simply too far-flung. Yet, with a completely intact town wall, it is a unique and beautiful town and one well worth the trouble it takes to reach it. A fortress walk begins at the information service; it passes the castle, a mostly baroque structure on top of Romanesque foundations, and exits through the Hornertor, the main gate in the southeast, dating from the 13th to 15th centuries. Cross the moat and follow the wall clockwise.

MOKA CAFE €

(02915-22 27; www.moka.at; Hauptplatz 5; mains €5-12; 9am-6pm Thu-Mon Apr-Oct) The rather knowingly nostalgic MOKA just doesn't do poppy-seed cake, but a whole range of poppy-seed cakes. These include white poppy seed, poppy seed with almond or chocolate-topped versions alongside the traditional darkly fragrant one. The coffee here is spot on, plus there's a spritz menu and a terrace for summer days. And yes, this is cake that's worth a detour.

Information

The weekday-only **information service** (02915-232 10; Schlossplatz 1; 8am-4.30pm Mon-Thu, to 12.30pm Fri) is the best place to start when visiting Drosendorf.

An information stand with a useful walk-by-numbers brochure (in German) as well as an accommodation list is situated on Hauptplatz, inside the walls.

Getting There & Away

To reach Drosendorf from Vienna (Praterstern station), take the train leaving every two hours to Retz (€17.30, 70 minutes), making sure it connects with one of several buses on weekdays (€7, one hour). The only way into the Czech Republic from here is to backtrack to Retz, from where there are trains to Znojmo, or hike (or take a taxi) 6km to the first village (Vratěnín) on the other side of the border, from where there are buses further into Moravia.

Langenlois

02734 / POP 7600

The pretty but hard-working town of Langenlois is at the centre of the winegrowing Kamptal. Lush lowlands meet gently rolling hills and vines stretch in rows as far as the eye can see. White wines – Grüner Veltliner, riesling, Welschriesling and Weissburgunder in particular – reach stellar heights here, and the town square is full of *Vinothek* (wine merchants) and seemingly every lane and road is lined with *Heurigen* or cellar doors.

★ Weingut Hirsch WINE

(02735-24 60; www.weingut-hirsch.at; Hauptstrasse 76, Kammern) Johannes Hirsch and his family make some of Austria's most elegant and uncompromising wines. Grapes are grown using biodynamic farming methods, picked by hand and, uniquely for this region, soft pruned; wine is a fruitful combination of modern and traditional 'slow' practices in the cellar. The winery concentrates on Grüner Veltliner and riesling only, and each of the wines comes from a single vineyard.

A short drive from Langenlois centre in the hamlet of Kammern, this winery does tastings by appointment only, so it's worth planning ahead to visit.

Loisium Weinwelt WINE

(www.loisium.at; Loisium Allee 2; 90min audio tour €13.50; 10am-7pm) Loisium Weinwelt is a paean to Langenlois' long history of wine growing as well as its present and future. It's something of an architectural statement too, set within an aluminium cube designed by New York architect Steven Holl. Multilingual audio tours set off every 30 minutes and lead you through a 1.5km network of ancient and very deep tunnels where wine is stored.

You can also taste and buy regional wines upstairs, and there is a produce shop and cafe too.

Loisium Hotel HOTEL €€

(02734-77 100-0; www.loisium.at; Loisium Allee 2; d €144-203; P ⊖ @ ≋) This contemporary hotel set among the vines has large, light and modern rooms. Bathrooms have a pared-back glamour and all rooms have balconies. There's a great restaurant and bar on-site but the highlight is the spa, with a large sauna and steam room area and a very pleasant 20m heated outdoor pool (it's open all year too).

Massages and other spa treatments use either Aveda or wine-sourced products.

Information

Ursin Haus (☎02734-20 00; www.langenlois.at; Kamptalstrasse; ⏰10am-6pm) wine emporium does double duty as the town's tourism information service point. It has comprehensive lists of all the town's wine offerings including seasonal *Heurigen*, cellar doors and restaurants. The main tourist website also lists these and has a downloadable map of the Langenlois Wine Route.

Getting There & Away

Langenlois is best reached by car, but there are regular train connections from Vienna (one to 1½ hours, €17.30, change in Hadersdorf/Kamp) and buses run from Krems (40 minutes, €4.60).

Nationalpark Thayatal

Tight against the border of Austria and the Czech Republic (a stretch of the old Iron Curtain) in the northwestern reaches of the Weinviertel is Austria's smallest national park, the Thayatal. This unique piece of landscape is one of Central Europe's last natural valleys and is actually two parks; its other half, Podyjí National Park, is located across the border. Of the 3000 plant species found in Austria, about 1300 occur in Thayatal. The landscape consists of a deep canyon cut by the Thaya River (the Dyje in Czech), numerous rock formations, steep slopes, some dry grassland and meadows, and large stretches of gnarled primeval forest. Walking is by far the most popular activity here, with trails sometimes crossing from one country into the next and back again.

Nationalparkhaus MUSEUM
(Nationalpark Thayatal; ☎02949-700 50; www.np-thayatal.at; Hardegg; ⏰9am-6pm mid-Mar–Sep, 10am-5pm Oct) The Nationalparkhaus, near Hardegg, has loads of information and an exhibition on the park's various ecosystems and animal residents, including wildcats, storks and lizards. Hardegg, the natural jump-off point for the park, is not easy to get to without your own transport.

★**Schloss Starrein** APARTMENT €€
(☎0664 13 12 333; www.gutstarrein.org; Starrein 1; apt €85; P 📶) A short drive from the national park, in the heart of Weinviertel farmland, young owners Peter and Sabine have one guest apartment in the family Schloss. On the top floor of a semirestored and extremely atmospheric 12th-century and Renaissance castle, it's a beautiful, airy and generous space, simply and stylishly decorated with a well-equipped kitchen and super-comfortable bed. One 'window' looks over the castle's exquisite original chapel, others look onto the fields beyond.

Getting There & Away

Without your own wheels, the park is best approached by train from Vienna to Retz (€17.30, 70 minutes), from where you take a bus to Pleising, then another to Hardegg. It's far easier with a car. From the Czech side you can walk into the park from the town of Znojmo.

Wienerwald

The Wienerwald (Vienna Woods) encompasses gentle wooded hills to the west and southwest of Vienna, as well as the wine-growing region directly south of the capital. For the Viennese, it's a place for walking, climbing and mountain biking.

Sights & Activities

Attractive settlements, such as the grape-growing towns of **Perchtoldsdorf** and **Gumpoldskirchen**, speckle the Wienerwald. Picturesque **Mödling**, only 15km south of Vienna, was once favoured by the artistically inclined: Beethoven's itchy feet took him to Hauptstrasse 79 from 1818 to 1820, and Austrian composer Arnold Schönberg stayed at Bernhardgasse 6 from 1918 to 1925.

About 20km from Mödling is **Heiligenkreuz** (☎02258-8703; www.stift-heiligenkreuz.at; Heiligenkreuz 1; adult/child €9.50/5.50; ⏰tours 10am, 11am, 2pm, 3pm & 4pm Mon-Sat, 11am, 2pm, 3pm & 4pm Sun), home of a 12th-century Cistercian abbey. **Mayerling**, which lies 6km southwest of Heiligenkreuz, is unremarkable now, but the tragic royal murder-suicide that occurred here in 1889 still draws visitors to the site.

Between Mayerling and Weissenbach-Neuhaus, situated about 5km from both on the L4004 and accessible from the Schwarzensee parking area and bus stop, is Peilstein (716m), with rock climbing on the **Peilstein Klettersteig** (www.bergsteigen.com). This is one of the most picturesque climbs in the region and a favourite among the Viennese. Peilsteinhaus, a hut and restaurant with a kids' playground, can be reached by **hiking trails** via Mayerling from Heiligenkreuz (16km, 4½ hours to Peilstein). From the Schwarzensee/Peilstein bus stop, it's a half-hour hike and from Weissenbach it takes 1½ hours.

Information

For trip planning and more information on the region, visit www.wienerwald.info.

The **Tourismus Information Mödling** (☎ 02236-400-27; www.moedling.at; Kaiserin Elisabeth-Strasse 2; ⏲ 9am-5pm Mon-Fri) office is a useful place to pick up maps and other info.

Getting There & Away

To really get under the skin of this region, it's best to have your own bicycle or car, but trains and buses will carry you to the main centres. The main road through the area is the A21 that loops down from Vienna, passes by Heiligenkreuz, then curves north to join the A1 just east of Altlengbach.

Bus connections are from Baden bei Wien to Heiligenkreuz (€2.50, 20 to 30 minutes, seven daily on weekdays) or from Baden to Schwarzensee (€6, one hour, six daily Monday to Saturday).

To get here by train, take the S1 or S2 from Vienna Meidling via Perchtoldsdorf (€4.20, 11 minutes, four hourly) to Gumpoldskirchen (€4.70, 28 minutes, hourly).

Baden bei Wien

☎ 02252 / POP 24,800

With its sulphurous mineral springs and lush green parks, gardens and woods, this spa town on the eastern fringes of the Wienerwald is a picturesque anachronism. Baden has a long history of receiving notable visitors; the Romans came here to wallow in the medicinal waters, Beethoven blew into town in the hope of a cure for his deafness, and in the early 19th century it flourished as the favourite summer retreat of the Habsburgs. Much of the town centre is in the 19th-century Biedermeier style. Note that Baden goes into virtual hibernation between October and March.

The centre is about 15 minutes by foot from the train station. Follow Kaiser-Franz-Joseph-Ring west and turn right into Wassergasse.

Sights

★ Arnulf Rainer Museum — MUSEUM

(www.arnulf-rainer-museum.at; Josefsplatz 5; adult/child €6/3; ⏲ 10am-5pm Tue-Sun) Located inside the former Frauenbad (Women's Bathhouse) near the tram terminus, this interesting museum showcases the work of its namesake Arnulf Rainer, who was born in Baden in 1929. A recalcitrant art-school dropout, he began painting in a surrealist style before developing his idiosyncratic multimedia and performance works.

This includes the infamous painting with chimpanzees episode where Rainer attempted to mimic the work of a number of painting apes only to be chased by one of his unwilling collaborators. The museum has retained the delightful marble features of the Biedermeier bathhouse from 1815, making it all the more worth a visit. Exhibitions change twice a year.

Kurpark — PARK

The *Kurpark* is a magnificent setting for a stroll or as a place to repose on the benches in front of the bandstand, where free concerts are held from May to September. Attractive flower beds complement monuments to famous artists (Mozart, Beethoven, Strauss, Grillparzer etc). Near the southern entrance to the park, the Undine-Brunnen (fountain) is a fine amalgam of human and fish images.

Dreifaltigkeitssäule — MONUMENT

(Hauptplatz) This monument on Hauptplatz to the Holy Trinity, dating from 1714, is one of Austria's weirdest. It's a dribbly affair, like cake left out in the rain plus a bit of baroque styling.

Rollett Museum — MUSEUM

(☎ 02252-8680 0580; www.rollettmuseum.at; Weikersdorfer Platz 1; adult/child €4/2.50; ⏲ 3-6pm Wed-Mon) The Rollett Museum covers important aspects of the town's history. The most unusual exhibit is the collection of skulls, busts and death masks amassed by the founder of phrenology, Josef Gall (1752–1828), who sparked the craze of inferring criminal characteristics from the shape of one's cranium. Not pleasant. The museum is southwest of the town centre and just off Weilburgstrasse (a five-minute walk southeast of the Thermalstrandbad).

Activities

Thermalstrandbad — SWIMMING

(Helenenstrasse 19-21; all day adult/child €9.60/4.30; ⏲ 8.30am-7.30pm May-Sep) A purpose-built functionalist building from 1926 houses this pool complex and includes a strip of precious shipped-in sand. The building itself is worth a peek, but it's also a pleasant place to while away an afternoon on the grass or having a splash. At times you do get a fair whiff of Baden's signature 'poached egg' smell – from the sulphur contained in its healing waters – but it's not always that obvious.

Kronprinz-Rudolf-Weg CYCLING

Cycling or hiking the 12km Kronprinz-Rudolf-Weg along the Schwechat River to Mayerling is a good summer alternative to museums or the baths. The tourist office has a free trail description (in German) and bikes can be hired in town. The trail can be combined with a 6km return northern branch trail to Heiligenkreuz.

Römertherme SPA

(Roman Baths; 02252-450 30; www.roemertherme.at; Brusattiplatz 4; 3hr/all day €14.60/18.30; 10am-10pm) Römertherme is a modern wellness-focused baths with a number of therapeutic pools and a large range of treatments. Admission at weekends is slightly more expensive.

Sleeping & Eating

Villa Inge PENSION €

(02252-431 71; www.pensioninge.cz; Weilburgstrasse 24-26; s/d €32/53; Apr-Oct; P ❄ ☎) This large villa is set alongside the river close to the Thermalstrandbad. Rooms are spacious and the breakfast room is lovely and bright, looking out to the garden. It offers good value for Baden, especially for its family apartment (from €100).

★**Hotel Schloss Weikersdorf** HOTEL €€

(02252-48 301 0; www.hotelschlossweikersdorf.at; Schlossgasse 9-11; s/d from €80/100; P ☎) For the total Baden experience, look no further than this ultra-padded hotel set in beautiful gardens. Rooms are smart and some have balconies, and there are massage services, relaxation coves, lounges and other wellness facilities. It also has three places to eat, including the Rosenkavalier restaurant, one of Baden's best.

Hotel Herzoghof HOTEL €€

(02252-872 97; www.hotel-herzoghof.at; Kaiser-Franz-Ring 10; s/d €100/149; P ☎) This central hotel opposite the *Kurpark* offers simple, modern rooms and good value for money. There's a sauna and steam bath on-site.

Cafe Central CAFE

(Hauptplatz 19; 8am-8pm; ☎) The town's Hauptplatz standard is a delightful old dame with a gem of a mid-20th-century interior and formal waiters serving Austrian classics.

Information

Baden Tourismus (02252-8680 0600; www.baden.at; Brusattiplatz 3; 9am-6pm Mon-Sat, to 3pm Sun May-Sep, to 5pm Mon-Fri Oct-Apr) can help out with most things spa- and nonspa-related.

Getting There & Away

Bus 360 departs every 30 to 60 minutes (€5.80, 40 minutes) from the Oper in Vienna. In Baden, bus 362 runs between the Thermalstrandbad and Bahnhof via the centre.

Regional and S-Bahn trains connect Baden with Vienna Meidling (€5.80, 20 minutes, three times hourly).

A *Lokalbahn* tram (€5.80, one hour, every 15 minutes, 40 minutes) connects the Oper in Vienna with Josefsplatz in Baden.

Baden bei Wien is just off the A2 motorway heading south from Vienna.

March-Donauland

Stretching from the eastern city limits of Vienna to the border with Slovakia, the March-Donauland is dominated by the Danube and its natural flood plains, a flat area dotted with industry throughout the pretty, if not particularly inspiring, countryside. Carnuntum, an important Roman camp during the days of the Roman Empire, and the Nationalpark Donau-Auen are the attractions here and make for interesting day trips from Vienna and the Slovak capital Bratislava, which has vastly cheaper accommodation. Both have easy transport links.

Nationalpark Donau-Auen NATIONAL PARK

(www.donauauen.at; Schlossplatz 1, Orth an der Donau; 9am-6pm mid-Mar–Sep, to 5pm Oct) Nationalpark Donau-Auen is a thin strip of natural flood plain on either side of the Danube, running from Vienna to the Slovak border. Established as a national park in 1997, it was the culmination of 13 years of protest and environmentalist action against the building of a hydroelectric power station in Hainburg an der Donau. You'll find plentiful flora and fauna, including 700 species of fern and flowering plants, and a high density of kingfishers (feeding off the 50 species of fish).

Information

The **Nationalparkhaus Wien-lobAU** (01-4000-49495; www.donauauen.at; Dechantweg 8, Vienna; 10am-6pm Wed-Sun Mar-Oct) is the information centre for the Donau-Auen National Park and is located in Vienna.

Getting There & Away

Vienna's backyard is serviced by regular trains and buses and is criss-crossed with cycle paths. You're also only a quick hop from the Slovakian capital of Bratislava here, which can be reached by train and bus.

Petronell-Carnuntum & Around

☎02165 / POP 1240

The Roman town of Carnuntum was the most important political and military centre in the empire's northeast, once known as Upper Pannonia; with a population of 50,000 people at its peak, it made Vienna look like a village in comparison. The town developed around 40 CE but was abandoned some 400 years later. The main sights are spread between the modern-day settlement Petronell-Carnuntum, the larger spa town of Bad Deutsch-Altenburg about 4km away, and Hainburg an der Donau, another 4km east of this. Allow at least half a day to see everything.

Sights

Freilichtmuseum Petronell RUINS

(www.carnuntum.at; Hauptstrasse 1a, Petronell-Carnuntum; adult/child €12/6; 9am-5pm mid-Mar–mid-Nov) The open-air museum is the major attraction in Petronell-Carnuntum itself and lies on the site of the old civilian town. It includes ruins of the public baths and a totally reconstructed temple of Diana. Strapping young actors lead happily kitsch tours in tunics and togas, and you can buy replicas of Roman sandals and clothing here for your next toga party. The museum is very touristy, but nevertheless interesting and fun; descriptions everywhere are in *Lingua Anglica*.

Museum Carnuntinum MUSEUM

(www.carnuntum.at; Badgasse 40-46, Bad Deutsch-Altenburg; adult/child €12/6; 9am-5pm mid-Mar–Nov) This museum of archaeological finds is the largest of its kind in Austria, having amassed an incredible 3300 Roman treasures in its century-long existence. The museum's highlight, *Tanzende Mänade* (Dancing Maenad), a marble figure with a most perfect bum, is usually displayed here.

Amphitheater Bad Deutsch-Altenburg RUINS

(www.carnuntum.at; Wienerstrasse 52, Petronell-Carnuntum; 9am-5pm mid-Mar–mid-Nov) FREE This grass-covered amphitheatre formerly seated 15,000. It now hosts a theatre festival over summer.

Sleeping

Hotel-Gasthof Stöckl HOTEL €

(☎02165-623 37; www.gasthof-stoeckl.at; Hauptplatz 3, Bad Deutsch-Altenburg; s/d from €50/76; P) The area's best deal is this comfortable, centrally located hotel with a solar-heated outdoor pool, and a sauna and steam bath. The restaurant is a welcome refuge after a day at the Roman ruins.

★**Hotel Altes Kloster** HOTEL €€

(☎02165-640 20; www.alteskloster.at; Fabriksplatz 1, Hainburg an der Donau; s/d €70/160; P) A modern and cleanly stylish hotel has taken over this 17th-century monastery in the historic old town of Hainburg. Rooms are large and soothing, and there's a spa area for guests with sauna, steam bath and infrared cabin. The half-board option (room rate plus €21; full board: room rate plus €28) is quite good value; the hotel's restaurant is one of the better ones around here.

Information

The two information points serving the area are the **Bad Deutsch-Altenburg Tourist Office** (☎02165-629 00; www.bad-deutsch-altenburg.gv.at; Erhardgasse 2; 8am-noon & 1-7pm Mon, 8am-noon Tue-Thu, 8am-1pm Fri) and the **Petronell-Carnuntum Tourist Office** (☎02163-337 70; www.carnuntum.at; Hauptstrasse 1a; 9am-5pm mid-Mar–mid-Nov) at the open-air museum.

Getting There & Away

There are hourly S-Bahn departures from Wien-Mitte for Petronell-Carnuntum, Bad Deutsch-Altenburg (both €10.40, one hour) and Hainburg an der Donau (€11.60, one hour).

When driving, take the A4 from Vienna then turn onto regional road 9 heading towards Bratislava.

The cycle path from Vienna goes along the north bank of the Danube, crosses to the south near Bad Deutsch-Altenburg, and continues into Slovakia.

St Pölten

☎02742 / POP 52,100

A destination few may even notice as they scream through on their way from Vienna to Salzburg, St Pölten may be Lower Austria's capital but it retains a drowsy atmosphere. Though no beauty, it has a quaint-ish *Altstadt* contrasted by the new,

St Pölten

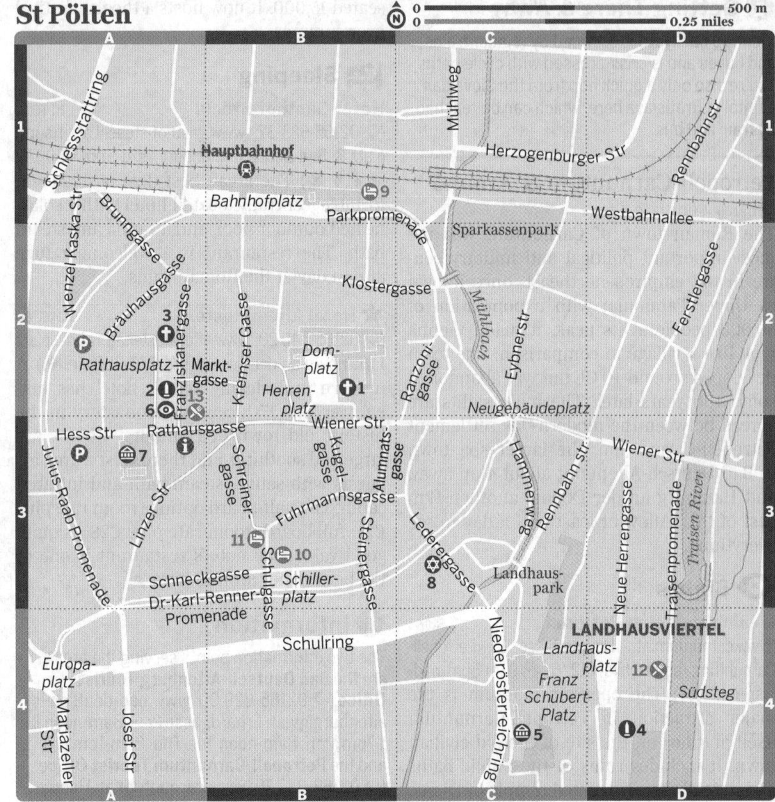

St Pölten

Sights

1	Dom	B2
2	Dreifaltigkeitssäule	A2
3	Franziskanerkirche	A2
4	Klangturm	D4
5	Landesmuseum	C4
6	Rathausplatz	A2
7	Stadtmuseum	A3
8	Synagoge	C3

Sleeping

9	Jugendherberge St Pölten	B1
10	Metropol	B3
11	Stadthotel Hauser Eck	B3

Eating

12	Landhaus Stüberl	D4
13	Schau.Spiel	A2

oh-so-21st-century Landhausviertel (State Parliament Quarter). Most visit on their way elsewhere but the town is worth a halt for its museums and cathedral.

History

The borders of Lower Austria were drawn by the Babenberg rulers in the 13th century, but in 1278 the region and empire-to-be fell to the Habsburgs. In a strange twist of fate – an ailing economy in the 1920s stalled the decision to give Lower Austria its own capital, and later the Nazis favoured making Krems the capital – St Pölten became capital of Lower Austria only in 1986, ending a long-running situation in which Lower Austria was administered geographically from Vienna, but was in fact a separate province. Ironically, it happens to have the oldest known municipal charter – granted in 1159.

The *Altstadt* is noted for its baroque buildings: baroque master Jakob Prandtauer lived and died in the city.

Sights

Rathausplatz SQUARE

The Rathausplatz is a pretty town square lined with cafes and eye-catching pastel-coloured buildings. It is dominated by the **Rathaus** (town hall) on its southern side, which has a baroque facade (1727) designed by Joseph Munggenast. On the northern fringe is the **Franziskanerkirche** (Rathausplatz 12; dawn-dusk), completed in 1770 with a grandiose altar offset by side-altar paintings by Kremser Schmidt. Between the two is the tall **Dreifaltigkeitssäule** (Trinity Column), from 1782, a captivating white, oversized swirl of motifs, built partly to mark the passing of the plague.

Synagoge SYNAGOGUE

(Dr-Karl-Renner-Promenade 22; 9am-3pm Mon-Fri) St Pölten's main synagogue dates from 1912 and has attractive art-nouveau features. The Nazis laid it to waste during the pogroms of 1938 and the building ended up in the hands of the city council, which used it as a camp for Russian forced-labour victims before the Red Army arrived and turned it into a grain store. Today, it houses an institute for Jewish history.

Dom CATHEDRAL

(Domplatz 1; dawn-dusk) Jakob Prandtauer was one of the most prominent architects of the baroque era, and the cathedral, his masterpiece of baroque rebuilding in St Pölten, has an impressive interior with lashings of fake marble and gold, augmented by frescoes by Daniel Gran. While exploring the cathedral, be sure to visit the cloister with its old gravestones.

Stift Herzogenburg ABBEY

(02782-83112 13; www.stift-herzogenburg.at; Herzogenburg; adult/child €9/7; tours 11am, 2pm, 3.30pm Apr-Oct; P) A short drive or train ride from town, Stift Herzogenburg is one of the Danube's baroque gems. You'll need to take a tour (book in advance for an English-speaking guide), which takes in the *Stiftskirche* (monastery church) and a painting collection that includes local Gothic panel works, stained glass and some unusually nonreligious baroque paintings.

Landesmuseum MUSEUM

(02742-90 80 90; www.landesmuseum.net; Franz-Schubert-Platz 5; adult/child €9/4.50; 9am-5pm Tue-Sun) The Lower Austria State Museum houses an interesting collection on the history, art and environment of the region. A wave made from glass, frozen in movement above the entrance, sets the mood, and indeed water is a theme throughout. The highlight of the art collection spanning the Middle Ages to the present is the 13th-century Lion of Schöngrabern.

The museum is situated in the Landhausviertel, a modern conflux of state buildings alongside the river.

Stadtmuseum MUSEUM

(02742-333 2643; www.stadtmuseum-stpoelten.at; Prandtauerstrasse 2; adult/child €5/2; 10am-5pm Wed-Sun) The City Museum is expertly curated and well worth a visit. Its permanent collection focusing on art nouveau in St Pölten is on the 1st floor, and a section on the ground floor is devoted to local archaeological treasures. Admission includes temporary exhibitions that are usually very worthwhile.

Klangturm TOWER

(Landhausplatz; 8am-6pm Mon-Sat, 9am-5pm Sun) FREE For a bird's-eye view of the Landhausviertel, take the lift to the top of this tower, which often stages temporary art exhibitions.

Sleeping

Jugendherberge St Pölten HOSTEL €

(02742-321 96; www.oejhv.at; Bahnhofplatz 1a; dm/s/d €21/29/50; @) This year-round youth hostel is about as convenient to the train station as it gets – it's all but in the same building. It's spotlessly clean and rates include a basic buffet breakfast.

Stadthotel Hauser Eck HOTEL €€

(02742-733 36; www.hausereck.at; Schulgasse 2; s €43-55, d €120-140;) This well-maintained hotel inside a rambling art-nouveau corner building (hence the name) in the historical part of town is arguably St Pölten's best deal, especially for solo travellers. The 28 rooms are well fitted out, if sometimes on the snug side, and bathrooms are kept sparklingly clean.

Metropol HOTEL €€

(02742-707 00; www.hotel-metropol.at; Schillerplatz 1; s €92-108, d €142-158; P) Cosy, quite upmarket and aimed firmly at a business and weekend culture clientele, the Metropol is not cheap (especially not the economy rooms), but for these prices you do get free use of the sauna, steam bath and infrared lamps. Its restaurant serves up steak and good business-trip-type meals.

Eating

Landhaus Stüberl AUSTRIAN €
(☎02742-24524; www.landhausstueberl.at; Landhausboulevard 27; breakfast €5-7, lunch menu €8, mains €8.50-14; ⏰7.30am-7pm Mon-Thu, to 5pm Fri; 📶) The name suggests a traditional tavern, but this postmillenium eatery in the Landhausviertel is anything but, and is aimed firmly at lunching bureaucrats (hence the opening hours) from the nearby Landtag and culture managers who come here to finger their devices and 'touch base'. The food is Italo-Austrian and can be picked at indoors or on the terrace overlooking the Traisen River.

★**Schau.Spiel** INTERNATIONAL €€
(☎02742-43742; www.schauspiel.at; Rathausgasse 1; mains €9-20; ⏰7.30am-midnight Mon-Wed, to 1am Fri & Sat, 9am-4pm Sun; 📶) Breakfast or brunch, dinner or drinks, this impressive, 21st-century restaurant-bar does it all right in the centre of town. The range of food on offer means there's something for everyone, even vegans, and the atmosphere here is always lively. Good place to come if your hotel or guesthouse doesn't do breakfast.

Information

The municipal **tourist office** (☎02742-353 354; www.st-poelten.gv.at; Rathausplatz 1; ⏰8am-noon & 1-5pm Mon-Fri, 9am-5pm Sat, 10am-5pm Sun Apr-Oct, closed Sat & Sun Nov-Mar) hands out maps and other information on the town and surrounding area.

Getting There & Away

St Pölten has good road connections: the east–west A1/E60 passes a few kilometres south of the city and the S33 branches north from there, bypassing St Pölten to the east, and continuing to Krems.

Trains run around three times an hour from Vienna Westbahnhof to St Pölten (€13.80, 30 minutes). There are also hourly direct trains to Krems (€6.90, 36 minutes), twice-hourly departures for Melk (€5.70, 15 to 25 minutes) and at least four a day to Mariazell (€18, 2½ hours).

Süd-Alpin

The southern corner of Lower Austria known as the Süd-Alpin (Southern Alps) has some of the province's most spectacular landscapes. Here the hills rise to meet the Alps, peaking at Schneeberg (2076m), a mountain popular among the Viennese for its skiing and hiking possibilities. Nearby Semmering has long been a favourite of the capital's burghers, due mainly to its crisp alpine air. One of the greatest highlights of the area, though, is the journey here; the winding railway over the Semmering Pass has been designated a Unesco World Heritage site.

Wiener Neustadt

☎02622 / POP 44,800

Though slightly off the tourist trail, Wiener Neustadt is worth a halt for its cathedral and main square, plus its low-key, authentic feel that's a long way from the region's tourist spots.

The town used to be known simply as Neustadt (New Town) or Nova Civitas and was built by the Babenbergs in 1194 with the help of King Richard the Lionheart's ransom payment (so if you're English, those town walls, by rights, belong to you!). It became a Habsburg residence in the 15th century during the reign of Friedrich III. His famous AEIOU (*Alles Erdreich Ist Österreich Untertan;* Everything in the world is subservient to Austria) engraving can be found throughout the city. The town was severely damaged in WWII (only 18 homes were left unscathed), so what you see today is mainly a postwar rebuild.

Sights

Hauptplatz SQUARE
The town's main piazza is closed off on one side by the **Rathaus**, which is something of a hybrid of styles. It began life as a Gothic building, was given some Renaissance flourishes from the late 16th century, and then when imitations came into vogue from the early 19th century, a neo-Gothic spire was tacked onto it. In the centre of the square is the **Mariensäule** (Column of Mary) from 1678, flanked by a group of woe-begotten saints.

Dom CATHEDRAL
(Domplatz; ⏰dawn-dusk) This cathedral runs an architectural gamut from the Romanesque (it dates from the late 13th century) to the Gothic and beyond to the baroque. The simplicity of the facade and clear lines are striking from the outside, but inside it will drive those who love the symmetry of the Romanesque style to despair as the nave is noticeably out of kilter with the sanctuary.

Fifteenth-century wooden apostles peer down from pillars and there's a baroque high altar and pulpit. To visit the Turmmuseum, a free-standing tower that provides grand views over the city's rooftops, you need to ask inside the Stadtmuseum. Someone will take you up there, but only in good weather.

Neukloster CHURCH
(Ungargasse; ⌚ dawn-dusk) This church's claim to fame is as the venue for the very first performance of Mozart's Requiem in 1793. Architecturally, the 14th-century church is fairly straight up and down Gothic, with a vaulted ceiling and high windows, but the interior has had a major baroque do-over. The clash of styles leaves a little to be desired; the most attractive features are the tranquil cloisters, reached by an unmarked door on the right and sporting a Renaissance-era well.

Museum St Peter an de Sperr MUSEUM
(☎ 02622-373 951; www.museum-wn.at; Johannes-von-Nepomuk-Platz 1) Partly housed in the former St Peter's monastery and partly in a new, connected building, the city museum reopened in 2020 after undergoing a complete renovation.

Militärakademie CASTLE
(Military Academy; Burgplatz 1) FREE Dating from the 13th century, this former castle was turned into a military academy in the mid-18th century (founded by Empress Maria Theresia) and was even commanded by the young Rommel in his pre-'Desert Fox' days. The academy was completely rebuilt after WWII, and its real highlight is **St-Georgs-Kathedrale**, with a fine late-Gothic interior. Maximilian I, who was born in the castle, is buried under the altar. Entry to the church is on the south side (register with the guard).

The eastern wall of the church is packed with heraldic coats of arms dating from 1453 and was the only part of the building to survive WWII unscathed. The relief depicts a genealogy of Austrian rulers. Only 19 of the heraldic arms are real – the rest were invented by Peter von Pusica, the artisan who created it.

Sleeping & Eating

Hotel Freizeittempel BOUTIQUE HOTEL €€
(☎ 02622-20 720; www.freizeittempel.at; Wiener Strasse 109; s/d €59/91; P 📶) The 'Leisure Temple' is Wiener Neustadt's most characterful place to unpack with 14 imaginatively themed rooms, a decent buffet breakfast and fitness/wellness facilities. Rooms take you from Mexico to Indonesia, from industrial teenager pad to an attempted country house. Located north of the town centre near Wiener Neustadt Nord train station.

Hartig's AUSTRIAN €
(☎ 02622-22 258; www.hartigs-heurigen.at; Domplatz 2; mains €8-16; ⌚ 11.30am-midnight Mon-Sat, to 9pm Sun; 📶) In the shadow of the Dom, this *Gasthöfe* (restaurant) serves a range of Austrian classics in a *Beisl* (bistro pub) atmosphere. The beer garden out the back is one of the most pleasant in town.

Zum Weissen Rössl BISTRO €
(☎ 02622-23 304; www.weisses-roessel.gusti.at; Hauptplatz 3; mains €9-15; ⌚ 8am-10pm Mon-Sat, 11am-3pm Sun; 📶) This cosily curtained eatery, tucked away beneath the arcading of the *Rathaus*, serves affordable Austrian classics, including a choice of a small or large goulash. There's outdoor seating on Hauptplatz.

Information

Tourist Office (☎ 02622-373 311; www.wiener-neustadt.gv.at; Hauptplatz 1-3, Altes Rathaus; ⌚ 6.30am-7pm Mon-Fri, 8am-1pm Sat) Stocks a free English-language booklet, *Cultural Promenade*, describing the central sights and giving their locations on a map.

Getting There & Away

Several trains each hour connect Wiener Neustadt with Vienna Meidling (€11.60, 30 to 50 minutes). Postbus services depart from the northern end of Wiener Neustadt train station.

Wiener Neustadt is just off the main A2 motorway heading south from Vienna.

Schneeberg, Raxalpe & Höllental

To the north of Semmering are two of Lower Austria's highest peaks: Schneeberg (2076m) and Raxalpe (2007m). The area is easily reached by train from Vienna, making it a popular hiking destination. The trailhead for hiking or taking the cogwheel railway is Puchberg am Schneeberg.

On the southern side of Schneeberg is the scenic Höllental (Hell's Valley), a deep, narrow gorge created by the Schwarza River.

From Hirschwang, a small village in Höllental, the **Raxseilbahn** (☎02666-524 97; www.raxseilbahn.at; one way/return €16.50/28) cable car ascends the Raxaple to 1547m and hiking trails. The Raxseilbahn is the site of Austria's first cable car, built in 1926.

Activities

Schneebergbahn RAIL
(www.schneebergbahn.at; Bahnhofplatz 1, Puchberg am Schneeberg; one way/return €28/38; ⏲late Apr-late Oct) The Schneebergbahn leaves from Puchberg am Schneeberg and takes about an hour on the Salamander (a train, for some reason, painted as a salamander); check the website for the latest timetable.

Sleeping & Eating

Gasthof Pension Schmirl GUESTHOUSE €
(☎02636-2277; www.schmirl.at; Muthenhofer Strasse 8, Puchberg am Schneeberg; s/d €36/72; P ⊖ ᯤ) On the edge of town near the railway, fulfil your alpine dreams at Gasthof Pension Schmirl. Some of the comfortable, modern rooms have balconies; in others you can psyche yourself for the stiff climb ahead with widescreen views of the Schneeberg.

Damböckhaus HUT €
(☎02636-22 59; www.damboeckhaus.at; Hochschneeberg 8, Puchberg am Schneeberg; tw €66; ⏲May-Oct; ᯤ) High on the plateau at over 1800m, this super-homey hut is tended to with love by hosts Willi and Gisi. Rooms only provide the basics but are clean and comfortable, and there are filling meaty mains and homemade desserts for posthike appetites.

Baumgartenhütte HUT €
(☎072099 1234; www.schneebergbahn.at; Hochschneeberg 5, Puchberg am Schneeberg; ⏲daily when train runs) A cosy mountain hut along the rail line; known for its good home cooking.

★**Hotel Looshaus** HISTORIC HOTEL €€
(☎02666-529 11; www.looshaus.at; Kreuzberg 60, Payerbach; s/d €60/104, without bathroom €53/90; P ᯤ) Although most of the guests here are likely to be Viennese on quick mountain breaks, this hotel is also something of an architectural pilgrimage site for those with a fascination for 20th-century design. It's a late work by Alfred Loos, a private country home that was completed in 1930. It's been a hotel and run by the same family since 1959.

Berghaus Hochschneeberg HUT €€
(☎02636-22 57; www.berghaushochschneeberg.at; Hochschneeberg 6, Puchberg am Schneeberg; s/d €42/84) A lovely bit of old Austria, with gently ageing, antique-dotted rooms and traditional food in the restaurant, Berghaus Hochschneeberg is at mountain train station Bergstation. Half-board can be had for another €12 per night.

Hotel Marienhof HOTEL €€
(☎02666-529 95; www.marienhof.at; Hauptstrasse 71-73, Reichenau; s/d €104/172; P ᯤ ≋) The Marienhof is a rambling grand dame of a hotel with an old-world restaurant, clubby bars and a lovely garden terrace. Rooms have high ceilings, lots of upholstery and swaggy curtains.

Hengsthütte AUSTRIAN €€
(☎02636-21 03; www.hengsthuette.at; Hochschneeberg 1, Puchberg am Schneeberg; ⏲8am-8pm Wed-Sun Apr-Oct, Sat & Sun Nov-Mar; ᯤ) This eating-only, wood-clad mountain hut, along the rail line, serves up mountain favourites like pork and dumplings and apple cake, along with wines and organic juices.

Information

The Puchberg am Schneeberg **tourist office** (☎02636-22 56; www.puchberg.at; Sticklergasse 3, Puchberg am Schneeberg; ⏲9am-noon & 2-4.30pm Mon-Thu, 9am-noon Fri) can tell you about hiking conditions on Schneeberg. From May to October, it also operates a window at the train station from 8am to 4pm.

Getting There & Away

A change in Wiener Neustadt is required to reach Puchberg am Schneeberg from Vienna Meidling (€17.30, one hour 20 minutes, hourly). Hirschwang (€20, two hours) is only a little harder to get to from Vienna; a train must first be taken to Payerbach, from where hourly buses run up the Höllental valley.

Semmering

☎02664 / POP 600

With its clean air and grandiose peaks rising out of deeply folded valleys, Semmering is a popular alpine resort for the Viennese, especially among an older audience who come to this spa town in summer for peaceful walks or to ride the dramatic railway (it gets younger when it's time to hit the ski pistes). There's no real centre to this low-key resort: it's mostly ranged along Hochstrasse, which forms an arc behind the train station.

Activities

This is good hiking country, and there's a nice alpine golf course. It's an easy if not particularly hard-core ski destination for the Viennese too.

Hiking

Towering over Semmering to the south is the **Hirschenkogel** ('Zauberberg'; 1340m), where a modern cable car (one way/return €12/16.50) whisks walkers or skiers to the top. The tourist office nd Infostelle have maps and brochures on walks.

Two fairly easy trails follow the scenic route of the Semmeringbahn, starting behind the train station. One follows the line for 17km to Mürzzuschlag in Styria, where frequent trains chug you back to Semmering, and a second leads to Breitenstein and Klamm (Lower Austria), 9.5km and 15km respectively from the start. At Klamm, the trail divides and one route leads to Payerbach (21km from the start) and another to Gloggnitz (23km from the start).

Skiing

The tourist office can provide information on ski schools. A winter skiing day pass for the Hirschenkogel cable car costs €34. Regional skiing day passes are also available for €36.50.

Cycling

In the summer months the tourist office rents bicycles (per 24 hours €12).

DON'T MISS

SEMMERING PASS BY TRAIN

For its time, it was an incredible feat of engineering and it took more than 20,000 workers' years to complete. Even today, it never fails to impress with its switchbacks, 15 tunnels and 16 viaducts. This is the **Semmeringbahn** (Semmering Railway; www.semmeringbahn.at), a 42km stretch of track that begins at Gloggnitz and rises 455m to its highest point of 896m at Semmering Bahnhof.

Completed in 1854 by Karl Ritter von Ghega, the Semmering line was Europe's first alpine railway; due to its engineering genius, it gained Unesco World Heritage status in 1998. It passes through some impressive scenery of precipitous cliffs and forested hills en route; the most scenic section is the 30-minute stretch between Semmering and Payerbach.

From Vienna, most express services heading to Graz stop at Mürzzuschlag, from where you take a regional train to Semmering (€22.40, 1¾ hours).

Sleeping & Eating

Pension Löffler GUESTHOUSE €

(☎02664-23 04; www.pension-loeffler.at; Hochstrasse 20; s/d €57/77; 📶) A good choice if you're here for the skiing, with just a short walk to the runs and Semmering's limited après-ski action. Rooms are basic but comfortable, and there's a good restaurant and cafe downstairs.

★**Panorama Hotel Wagner** HOTEL €€

(☎02664-25 12; www.panoramahotel-wagner.at; Hochstrasse 267; s €40-155, d €65-170; P @ 📶) 🍃 The Wagner family look after body and mind at this seriously ecofriendly hotel: rooms have untreated wood furniture, natural cotton bedding and grand views of the valley. Felt slippers are provided so you leave the dust of the street behind you. A pretty garden, a well-stocked library with hammocks, a sauna, a spa and massage facilities make chilling out easy.

The highly rated and, yes, panoramic restaurant uses organic ingredients as much as possible. You can also pick up supplies here at the well-stocked organic shop.

Hotel-Restaurant Belvedere HOTEL €€

(☎02664-22 70; www.belvedere-semmering.at; Hochstrasse 6; s/d from €48/92; P 🏊) The family-run Belvedere has simple alpine decor, rooms with balconies, and extras such as a small swimming pool, a sauna and a large garden and patio area. Doubles with connecting doors are suitable for families. It's close to Semmering train station as well as some good hiking trails.

Information

Infostelle Bahnhof (☎02664-845 20; www.semmeringbahn.at; ⏲9am-3pm May-Oct) Run by railway enthusiasts and stocks material on the Semmeringbahn and the town itself.

Tourismusbüro Semmering (☎02664-200 25; www.semmering.at; Hochstrasse 1; ⏲8am-4pm Mon-Fri, 9am-noon Sat) General info for the area.

ℹ Getting There & Away

If you're driving, consider taking the small back road northwest of Semmering to Höllental via Breitenstein; the road winds its way down the mountain, passing under the railway line a number of times and taking in the spectacular scenery you see on the train trip.

Semmering has train connections with Breitenstein (€2.30, nine minutes), Klamm (€2.30, 15 minutes), Payerbach (€3.40, 30 minutes) and Gloggnitz (change in Payerbach; €6, 40 minutes). At least five direct EuroCity (EC) and InterCity (IC) trains between Graz (€20.60, one hour 20 minutes) and Vienna (€22.40, 1¼ hours) stop at Semmering.

BURGENLAND

Flat as a topographically challenged pancake, Burgenland is all about the Neusiedler See – a bucolic lake that attracts flocks of splashing holidaymakers and European birds. Away from the water fun, wine is the other main draw here, the region producing some of Austria's finest reds and whites. As far as urban pleasures go, the capital Eisenstadt possesses Burgenland's grandest castle with a strong Haydn association.

History

In the 10th century the area fell into the hands of Hungary, but German-speaking peasants gradually settled land between the Hungarian villages. The arrival of the Turks in the 16th century quashed both the Hungarians and the Austrian-Germans, and devastated the local population. Landlords, without anyone to tend their farms, invited substantial numbers of Croats to settle, laying the foundations for the area's Hungarian and Croatian influences today – around 10% of the population is Croatian, and Croatian, along with Hungarian, is a recognised local language; a few small towns in middle Burgenland bear Croatian signage.

With the demise of the Habsburg empire after WWI, Austria lost control of Hungary, but it eventually managed to retain the German-speaking western region of Hungary under the Treaty of St Germain. The new province of Burgenland was born, named for the 'burg' suffix of the four western Hungarian district names at that time – Pressburg (Bratislava), Wieselburg (Moson), Ödenburg (Soporn) and Eisenburg (Vasvär). As Hungary was loath to lose Ödenburg (Sopron), a controversial plebiscite held in December 1921 resulted in Sopron remaining Hungarian. Burgenland lost its natural capital, and Eisenstadt became the new *Hauptstadt*.

ℹ Getting There & Away

The A2 autobahn, heading south from Vienna towards Graz and Carinthia, runs parallel to the western border of Burgenland. Its many exits provide quick, easy access to much of the province. The A4 leads to Neusiedl am See. Eisenstadt and the northern extension of Neusiedler See are easily reached by train and bus from Vienna and Lower Austria.

ℹ Getting Around

Lower and Middle Burgenland are mostly served by buses, but Sunday services are patchy or nonexistent. Hiring a car means you'll see a lot more.

THE WINES OF BURGENLAND

The wine produced throughout this province is some of the best in Austria, due in no small part to the 300 days of sunshine per year, rich soil and excellent drainage. Although classic white varieties have a higher profile, the area's reds are more unusual, and the finest of the local wines is arguably the red *Blaufränkisch*, whose 18th-century pedigree here predates its arrival in the Danube region and Germany.

Middle Burgenland, especially around the villages of Horitschon and Deutschkreutz, has a long tradition of Blaufränkisch, which is also at home in southern Burgenland.

Sweet wines are also produced here. Don't miss the chance to taste *Schilfwein*, made by placing the grapes on reed (*Schilf*) matting, at Weingut Gerhard Nekowitsch (p157).

Austria's smallest wine region, the Neusiedler See, is also known for its innovative and pioneering wine producers, many of them opting to create biodynamic, natural or minimum-intervention wines. This booming and often youthful scene makes for some great – and far more local and laid-back – wine experiences than those along the Danube. One of the best ways to go tasting here is to hire a bicycle in Neusiedl am See and pedal south through the vineyards towards the national park.

BICYCLE

Burgenland is a cyclist's dream. Much of the landscape is flat or has gently rolling hills and is criss-crossed with well-marked cycle paths. Local tourist offices can supply cycle maps. From Neusiedl am See, the 135-km Neusiedler See bike trail leads south, crossing into Hungary (bring your passport) for 38km before the path re-emerges in Austria, just south of Mörbisch am See on the western side of the lake.

Nextbike (www.nextbike.at) Has around 16 stations around the Neusiedler See and in Eisenstadt where you can hire and drop off a rented bicycle. The website explains the steps and how to register (which you need to do in advance on the website).

Fahrräder Bucsis (☎02167-207 90; www.fahrraeder-bucsis.at; train station, Neusiedl am See; per day €15; ⏲8.30am-7pm Mar–mid-Oct) The bike path begins at its door.

Eisenstadt

☎02682 / POP 14,300

The small, elegant capital of Burgenland is best known for its most famous former resident, 18th-century musician and composer Joseph Haydn. Watched over by a wonderful palace, there are a couple of good museums and some pretty streets to wander. It's an easy day trip from Vienna or a more affordable base than the Neusiedler See towns for touring the vineyards.

Sights & Activities

★Schloss Esterházy PALACE

(www.esterhazy.at; Esterházyplatz 1; adult/child €12/6; ⏲10am-5pm mid-Mar–Apr & Oct, 10am-6pm May-Sep, 10am-5pm Fri-Sun Nov–mid-Mar; P) Schloss Esterházy, a giant, ochre castle-palace that dominates Esterházyplatz, is by far Eisenstadt's most compelling attraction. Dating from the 14th century, the *Schloss* received a baroque makeover and a later one in neoclassical style. Many of the 256 rooms are occupied by the provincial government, but around 25 can be viewed on tours. The regular tour covers about seven rooms, giving you an insight into the history of the palace and the lives of the people who inhabited it.

Österreichisches Jüdisches Museum MUSEUM

(Jewish Museum of Austria; ☎02682-651 45; www.ojm.at; Unterbergstrasse 6; adult/child €5/3; ⏲10am-5pm Tue-Sun May-Oct) Situated in the former Judengasse – a street where Eisenstadt's Jewish population lived in the Middle Ages – this museum has a permanent exhibition illustrating the rituals and lifestyle of Eisenstadt's Jewish community. Descriptions are in German and Hebrew.

Part of the museum is the private synagogue of Samson Wertheimer, who was born in Worms in Germany in 1658 and rose to the position of rabbi in Hungary. He financed the synagogue, and it was one of the few to survive after 1938.

Bergkirche CHURCH

(☎02682-626 38; www.haydnkirche.at; Haydnplatz 1; adult/child €6/3; ⏲9am-5pm Apr-Oct) This unusual, lumpy church, its exterior bedecked in life-size disco-dancing angels and saints, contains the white-marble tomb with Haydn's remains. It began life as a small chapel and in 1701 was transformed into a bizarre representation of Calvary, the mountain outside Jerusalem upon which Christ is thought to have been crucified.

The church is free but you have to pay admission to see the tomb and the view from this high-flying location.

Haydn-Haus MUSEUM

(www.haydnhaus.at; Josef-Haydn-Gasse 21; adult/child €5/4.50; ⏲9am-5pm Mon-Sat, from 10am Sat & Sun) Situated in a house dating from the early 18th century, this museum dedicated to Haydn was where the great composer lived from 1766 to 1778.

Probably one for Haydn fans only, the collection offers an insight into his private life and has reconstructed rooms with furniture from the era. Original portraits cover the walls, and there are some rare exhibits such as a fortepiano that was made in Eisenstadt.

Landesmuseum MUSEUM

(☎02682-719 4000; www.landesmuseum-burgenland.at; Museumgasse 1-5; adult/child €6/5; ⏲9am-5pm Tue-Fri, from 10am Sat & Sun) The Landesmuseum plunges you deep into the local history of the region, seemingly all at once, including a collection of Roman mosaics, ancient artefacts, winemaking equipment and some interesting propaganda posters from the 1920s.

There's also a room devoted to Franz Liszt, replete with a warty death mask of the Hungarian composer.

Eisenstadt

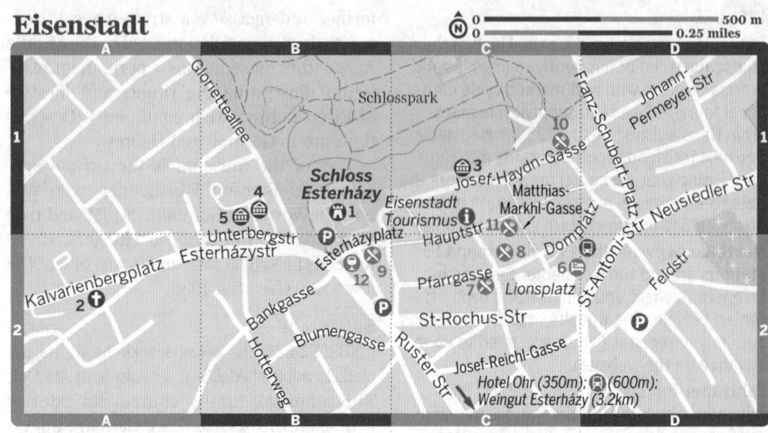

Eisenstadt

Top Sights
1 Schloss Esterházy B1

Sights
2 Bergkirche A2
3 Haydn-Haus C1
4 Landesmuseum B1
5 Österreichisches Jüdisches Museum ... B1

Sleeping
6 Hotel-Pension Vicedom C2

Eating
7 Haydnbräu C2
8 Kredenz C2
9 Restaurant Henrici B2
10 Ruckendorfer C1
11 Weinschwein C1

Drinking & Nightlife
12 Selektion Vinothek Burgenland B2

Weingut Esterházy WINE

(www.esterhazywein.at; Trausdorf 1, Trausdorf; 10am-6pm Apr-Oct, closed Sun Nov-Mar) Located 10 minutes' drive out into the countryside from the centre of Eisenstadt, this large-scale cellar door is a gateway to the Neidlersee wine district. One of the region's largest producers, Esterházy wines are still made by the ancient, once-noble, local family. These are beautiful wines, which despite their reach and stylish contemporary labels are far from commercial or bland.

You can taste casually here or opt for a tour and more extensive tasting complete with local snacks (€14).

Festivals & Events

Herbstgold MUSIC

(www.herbstgold.at; Sep) Essentially a revamped Haydn Festival (its name until 2017) with most concerts of classical music taking place in the Haydn Hall and a couple of jazz, Balkan and Roma bands striking up elsewhere. It's Eisenstadt's biggest festival of the year and lasts for 10 days.

Sleeping

Hotel Ohr HOTEL €€

(02682-624 60; www.hotel-ohr.at; Rusterstrasse 51; s €70, d €99-185; P) In the south of town, the Ohr is a large family-run hotel with basic, slightly ageing but reasonably priced quarters. There are two distinct classes of room with quite a price hike for the admittedly better four-star section. Its rustic-styled restaurant is a godsend at the end of a long day's exploration; otherwise there's a new supermarket right next door.

Hotel-Pension Vicedom PENSION €€

(02682-642 22; www.vicedom.at; Vicedom 5; s/d €67/133; P) While this might sound like a downtown hipster bolthole, it's in fact a three-star guesthouse with contemporary if slightly frugal rooms in a 21st-century building in a central location. The buffet breakfast is better than average for this price range and bathrooms gleam.

Eating

Weinschwein AUSTRIAN €
(www.hofpassage.at; Hofpassage; mains €7-14; ⊙10am-3pm Wed & Sun, to 11pm Thu-Sat;) Entering the Hofpassage, a pretty courtyard off Hauptstrasse, you are greeted by a large plastic pig, but have no fear – this is no rural-themed, knickknack restaurant but a trendy, clean-cut *Heuriger*-type cafe with heaps of informal al fresco seating, a menu of old favourites plus the odd Spanish intruder.

Kredenz INTERNATIONAL €
(www.kredenz.at; Pfarrgasse 33; mains €9-18; ⊙11.30am-2pm Mon-Fri, plus 6-10pm Wed & Thu, 6pm-2am Fri & Sat;) With the door stickers to prove its foody Kredenzials, this courtyard bistro-style eatery serves a brief menu of internationally flavoured dishes but it does them well. Good for both a quick, cheap lunch between sights or a romantic al fresco dinner.

Restaurant Henrici AUSTRIAN €€
(www.henrici.at; Esterházyplatz 5; mains €12-39; ⊙11am-10pm Mon-Fri, 9am-10pm Sat, 9am-5pm Sun;) This smart restaurant shares the former gatehouse of Schloss Esterházy with its sister wine bar **Selektion** (☎02682-633 45; www.selektion-burgenland.at; Esterházyplatz 4; ⊙11am-10pm Mon-Wed, to midnight Thu-Sat, 5-10pm Sun). It's an atmospheric space to graze or dine, with a crowd-pleasing menu of burgers, pasta, Mediterranean-style fish dishes or local specialities such as the Esterházy-Rostbraten – roast beef with potato *Spätzle* – and the Esterházy-Cream Cake.

Ruckendorfer ALPINE €€
(☎02682-64688; www.ruckendorfer.com; Joseph-Haydn-Gasse 43; mains €10-20; ⊙10am-2pm & 7.30-11pm Tue-Sat, 10am-3pm Sun;) With its slick interior, dreamily tranquil garden, Austro-Italian menu and location in a rapidly modernising part of town, this is a good choice for a stylish but inexpensive lunch or a more formal dinner. Popular with office workers at midday and couples in the evenings.

Haydnbräu AUSTRIAN €€
(www.haydnbraeu.at; Pfarrgasse 22; mains €11-18; ⊙9.30am-11pm;) Duck into this microbrewery and restaurant for some of the best-value eating in town. Culinary classics such as schnitzel and goulash are complemented by seasonal dishes. The generous lunch menu is a steal at €7.40 and the snack menu has small portions suitable for kids.

Information

The **tourist office** (☎02682-673 90; www.eisenstadt-leithaland.at; Hauptstrasse 21; ⊙9am-4.30pm Mon-Fri, to 1pm Sat Apr-Oct, closed Sat Nov-Mar) is handily located on the main shopping street not far from the palace.

Getting There & Away

Hourly direct buses to Eisenstadt's **main bus station** (Domplatz) leave from Vienna's Südtiroler Platz (€11.60, one hour 20 minutes). Direct trains also leave hourly from the *Hauptbahnhof* (€11.60, one hour 10 minutes). There's plenty of parking in Eisenstadt and even the *Schloss* has its own (pricey) underground car park.

WORTH A TRIP

BURG FORCHTENSTEIN

Straddling a dolomite spur some 20km southwest of Eisenstadt, **Burg Forchtenstein** (www.esterhazy.at; Melinda Esterházy-Platz 1; each attraction adult/child €12/10, highlight tour €18/16; ⊙10am-6pm late Mar-Oct) is one of Burgenland's most imposing castles, with a grand view from its ramparts. This stronghold was built in the 14th century and enlarged in 1635 by the Esterházys, who still own it today.

The castle's highlights include a museum dedicated to an impressive collection of armour and weapons, portraits of regal Esterházys in the Ahnengalerie and spoils from the Turkish wars (the castle curators will proudly tell you Forchtenstein was the only castle in the area not to fall to the Turks). Its *Schatzkammer* (treasury) contains a rich collection of jewellery and porcelain.

During summer the small town of Wiesen, about 5km north of Forchtenstein, morphs into Austria's version of Glastonbury. The series of **festivals** (www.wiesen.at) between May and August hosted here is the biggest in the country and ranges across the musical spectrum.

To reach Wiesen, take any train from Vienna Meidling towards Wiener Neustadt and change there to either another train or bus (€13.80, one hour).

WORTH A TRIP

BERNSTEIN & BAD TATZMANNSDORF

Bernstein, 15km west of Lockenhaus, is dominated by the impressive **Burg Bernstein** (Bernstein Castle; ☎03354-63 82; www.burgbernstein.at; Schlossweg 1; s €95-190, d €190-380; ⊙late Apr–mid-Oct; P 📶), now a hotel. This ancient *Schloss* (castle) is everything you want in a destination hotel. The building's foundations date from 1199, and it retains much of its premodern atmosphere, with a beautiful internal courtyard and a tumbling, artfully wild garden and moat beyond.

In Bernstein town centre, the small **Felsenmuseum** (☎03354-66 20; www.felsenmuseum.at; Hauptplatz 5; €8; ⊙9am-6pm Mar-Oct, to 5pm Nov & Dec, closed Jan & Feb) concentrates its displays on the gemstone serpentine and its local mining (it was first mined in the town in the mid-19th century). You'll also find a cool little all-day **cafe** (☎03354-200 23; www.kantine48.at; Badgasse 48; mains €8-12; ⊙10am-10pm daily, hours vary) down by the lake where you can have lunch or dinner.

If your body needs a bit of a service after several days of sightseeing, make a halt at the spa town of Bad Tatzmannsdorf, 15km south of Bernstein, and take the waters at the large, modern **Burgenland Therme** (☎03353-89 90; www.burgenlandtherme.at; Am Thermenplatz 1; day card adult/child €26/16.50; ⊙9am-10pm Sun-Thu, to 12.30am Fri, to 11pm Sat) spa complex, currently operated by Aviva. In summer the natural outdoor swimming pond is the best spot and there are myriad wellness procedures you can undergo.

Next to the Burgenland Therme, the small but rewarding **Südburgenländisches Freilichtmuseum** (www.freilichtmuseum-badtatzmannsdorf.at; Josef Hölzel-Allee; €2; ⊙9am-6pm; P) is filled with thatched buildings from 19th-century Burgenland.

The main **tourist office** (☎03353-70 15; www.bad.tatzmannsdorf.at; Joseph-Haydn-Platz 3, ⊙8am-5.30pm Mon-Fri, 9.30am-2.30pm Sat) for the area is located at Bad Tatzmannsdorf. You'll need your own car to reach both of these places comfortably.

Güssing

☎03322 / POP 3820

Güssing, 40km south of Bad Tatzmannsdorf, is a peaceful town on the banks of the Strembach River. The main draws here are the fairy-tale castle and an open-air museum. Although small, you could easily spend an entire day here exploring.

Burg Güssing CASTLE
(☎03322-434 00; www.burgguessing.info; Batthyanystrasse 10; adult/child €7.50/4; ⊙9am-5pm Tue-Sun Easter–mid-Nov; P) The arresting Burg Güssing rises dramatically over the river and town. The castle, which is a mix of ruins and ongoing renovations, contains plenty of weapons that once belonged to the invading Turks and Hungarians, striking portraits from the 16th century and a tower with 360-degree views. There are also wide-screen vistas from the ramparts.

Freilichtmuseum MUSEUM
(☎03328-32255; www.freilichtmuseum-gerersdorf.at; Gerersdorf bei Güssing 66, Gerersdorf; adult/child €5.50/3; ⊙10am-6pm Tue-Sun Apr–mid-Oct, to 4pm mid-Oct–mid-Nov; P) A pleasant detour can be had at this museum, 5km west of Güssing, exploring the 30-odd buildings and their traditional furniture and fittings, thatched roofs and chunky beams, which capture the rural culture of Burgenland in the 18th and 19th centuries. Hosts concerts and events over the summer.

Burg Güssing AUSTRIAN €€
(☎03322-425 79; www.burgrestaurant.net; Batthyanystrasse 10; mains €12.50-25; ⊙10am-5pm Mon-Fri, to 10pm Sat, to 4pm Sun Mar-Dec) Enjoy a menu of traditional dishes as well as burgers at this castle restaurant. The dining room holds 300 diners, prices are reasonable and there's a large wine cellar.

ℹ Information

Tourist Office (☎03322-440 03; www.suedburgenland.info; Hauptplatz 7; ⊙9am-noon & 1-4pm Mon-Fri)

ℹ Getting There & Away

Every one to two hours daily, direct buses connect Güssing (€8, 45 to 70 minutes) with Oberwart. On weekdays and Saturday, several direct buses connect Güssing and Gerersdorf (€2.50, 10 minutes).

Getting Around

A 100m **funicular railway** (Schrägaufzug; one-way/return €2/4; ⏲10am-5pm Tue-Sun Easter-Oct) with tiny cabins helps those with weary legs to reach the castle.

Lockenhaus

03353 / POP 2000

Lockenhaus, in the centre of Burgenland, is famous for its castle or, more accurately for its former resident Elizabeth Bäthory (the 'Blood Countess'). Some 13km east of Lockenhaus is the tiny village of Klostermarienberg, home to a now-defunct monastery housing a museum dedicated to dogs.

Burg Lockenhauf CASTLE

(02616-239 40; www.ritterburg.at; Günserstrasse 5; adult/child €9/4; ⏲9am-6pm May-Oct, reduced hours winter) Lockenhaus is famous for its castle, or more accurately, for its former resident Elizabeth Bäthory. Better known as the 'Blood Countess', she has gone down in history for her reign of terror early in the 17th century, when she reputedly tortured and murdered over 600 mainly peasant girls and women for her own sadistic pleasure. The castle has long been cleansed of such gruesome horrors but still contains the requisite and rather impressive torture chamber, complete with an iron maiden.

In addition to being a tourist attraction, the castle also houses hotel rooms and a restaurant.

Europäisches Hundemuseum MUSEUM

(02611-2292; Klostermarienberg; €5; ⏲2-5pm Sun May-Aug; P) The Europäisches Hundemuseum is Europe's only museum dedicated to our four-legged friends. The oddball collection of dog paraphernalia includes paintings, statues and intriguing photos of dogs dressed for war during WWI and WWII, complete with gas masks. Take a few minutes to visit the monastery's crypt, a chamber containing archaeological finds dating from the 13th and 14th centuries. Note the very limited opening times.

Burghotel Lockenhaus HISTORIC HOTEL €€

(02616-23 94; www.ritterburg.at; s/d €99/137; P) Burghotel Lockenhaus has antique furnished rooms, and a sauna. Breakfast costs €8; there's an extra €15 supplement for heating from October to March. Apartments with kitchenettes attached to the castle wall are also available (€161, including breakfast).

Getting There & Away

You're better off with your own transport in this region as bus connections can be thin. Three direct weekday buses connect Lockenhaus and Eisenstadt (€14, 1½ hours). On weekdays hourly and on Saturday two-hourly direct buses go north from Oberwart (where there's a train station) to Bad Tatzmannsdorf (€2.50, five minutes); from Oberwart to Bernstein (€5, 30 minutes, every one to three hours) or Lockenhaus (€6.80, one hour, twice each weekday) is also manageable.

Neusiedler See

Neusiedler See, Europe's second-largest steppe lake, is the lowest point in Austria. Fortunately, that lowliness does not extend to metaphor – it's in fact a delight. The lake's average depth is 1.5m, which means the water warms quickly in summer. Add to this the prevailing warm winds from the northwest, and you have a landlocked Austrian's dream come true (almost).

Another feature of the region are the acres of vineyards, making some of Austria's most sought-after and innovative wines. Rust, on the western shore of the lake, is a perfect place to sample wine in a *Heuriger*, a quintessential experience in the region.

Information

Neusiedler See Tourismus (02167-86 00; www.neusiedlersee.com; Obere Hauptstrasse 24, Neusiedl am See; ⏲8am-5pm Mon-Fri) The main information centre for the entire lake region.

Getting There & Away

There are hourly trains from Vienna Südbahnhof to Neusiedl am See and from there bus or regional rail connections to all of the larger towns. You can also arrange car and driver day trips from Vienna via the Neusiedler See tourist office.

NEUSIEDLER SEE CARD

If you are staying overnight in Eisenstadt or in towns on the Neusiedler See, make sure you get the Neusiedler See Card (www.neusiedlersee.com), which gives you free transport on buses and trains around the lake and on town buses, as well as free or discount admission to many sights. Take the registration form given to you by your hotel to an issuing office (tourist offices are the easiest) and you'll be given the card free for the duration of your stay.

Getting Around

From late spring to early autumn, ferries connect Illmitz with Mörbisch, Rust and Fertörákos in Hungary; Rust with Podersdorf, Breitenbrunn and Fertörákos; and Breitenbrunn with Podersdorf. See www.neusiedlersee.com for current schedules and prices.

Bus connections are frequent, and Purbach and Neusiedl am See are linked by regional train services.

Rust

02685 / POP 1900

Rust, 14km east of Eisenstadt, is one of the most agreeable towns that cluster around the Neusiedler See. Its reed shoreline and hidden boatsheds give it a sleepy, swampy feel on a steamy day, and in the summer months storks glide lazily overhead and clack their beaks from rooftop roosts (web cams at www.rust.at follow their every move).

Dozens of storks make their homes on chimneys in town, although it's wine, not storks, that has made Rust prosperous. In 1524 the emperor granted local vintners the right to display the letter 'R' (a distinctive insignia as a mark of origin from Rust) on their wine barrels and today the corks still bear this mark. It's best to sample this history in one of the town's many *Heurigen*.

Sights

Katholische Kirche CHURCH

(Haydengasse; 10.30am-noon & 2.30-5pm Mon-Sat, 3-5pm Sun) The church's tower is a good vantage point for observing storks' nests and the priest doesn't seem to mind. It's located at the eastern end of Rathausplatz.

Fischerkirche CHURCH

(Rathausplatz 16; dawn-dusk Apr-Oct) At the opposite end of Rathausplatz from the Katholische Kirche, this is the oldest church for miles around, built between the 12th and 16th centuries.

Activities

Seebad Rust SWIMMING

(www.seebadrust.at; Ruster Bucht 2; adult/child €5.50/3; 9am-7pm May–mid-Sep) Access to the lake and bathing facilities is 1km down the reed-fringed Seepromenade. The swimming here is an acquired taste, very reedy but ultimately refreshing. There are slides, grassy areas and a number of bars, cafes and restaurants too.

Sleeping

Storchencamp Rust HOSTEL, CAMPGROUND €

(02685-595; www.gmeiner.co.at; Ruster Bucht 2; s/d €40/60, camp sites per adult/child/tent/car €8/5/7/5.50;) This friendly hostel right on the harbour forms part of the bathing complex and has modern, clean rooms. You can also stay in a teepee for €17 per night.

It operates a popular, friendly 200-pitch campground, which has a large children's playground, cheap bike rental, close proximity to the lake and free access to the bathing area. The campground is only open April to October.

Hotel Sifkovits HOTEL €€

(02685-276; www.sifkovits.at; Am Seekanal 8; s/d €87/156; high season only;) Close to the centre of town, the 25-room Sifkovits is a fine, family-run hotel with no-frills rooms, a lift and extras like its downstairs lounge with a bowl of fruit and a refrigerator stocked with free mineral water. It also has a good restaurant and a soothing garden.

★**TiMiMoo Boutique Hotel Bürgerhaus** BOUTIQUE HOTEL €€€

(02685-6162; http://timimoo.at; Hauptstrasse 1; ste €275-310;) With spiral staircases inside a 1537 former bakery and Biedermeier-style rooms with vaulted ceilings and drapes around the beds, this sweetly nostalgic hotel is pretty and cluttered with antiques faux and real, creating an impressive place to stay. The theme continues out in the extensive gardens, service is top-notch and children are superbly catered for.

Its restaurant (closed Monday) serves rustic regional specialities and local wines out in the garden.

Eating

Peter Schandl AUSTRIAN €

(www.buschenschankschandl.at; Hauptstrasse 20; mains €8-15; 4pm-late Mon & Thu-Fri, from 11am Sat & Sun mid-Mar–Nov, also 4pm-late Wed Jul-Sep;) Set in an 18th-century town house, and with a shaded courtyard, noted winemaker Peter Schandl serves up a menu that's beyond usual cellar-door fare. Seasonal offerings might include a cream soup of pumpkin with ginger and roasted pumpkin seeds, a peppery, coarse liver sausage and cucumber-mustard relish or a meatloaf with cabbage. Just off Rathausplatz.

Weingut Gabriel BUFFET €
(www.weingut-gabriel.at; Hauptstrasse 25; cold platters €14; ⏰ from 4pm Thu & Fri, from 2pm Sat & Sun Apr-Oct; 👪) If you are going to eat anywhere in Rust, make it this rustic wine spot on the main street. Not only is the pay-by-weight buffet brimming with delicious sausage and cold cuts, the wine is good and, in season, the idyllic cobblestone courtyard is a wonderful vantage point to observe the local storks.

Drinking & Nightlife

★ **Gut Drauf at Gut Oggau** WINERY
(☎0664 2069 298; www.gutoggau.com; Hauptstrasse 31, Oggau; ⏰ noon-10pm Thu-Sun May-Aug, 4-10pm Fri, noon-10pm Sat & Sun Feb-Apr & Sep; 📶) It's worth planning ahead to visit this wonderful cellar door, a few kilometres north of Rust, in the hamlet of Oggau. Young winemakers Eduard Tscheppe and Stephanie Tscheppe-Eselböck create highly individual, biodynamic and minimal-intervention wines for their gorgeous, new-school *Heuriger*. Apart from their own wines, they also offer a selection of reasonably priced vintages from like-minded Austrian and Italian producers.

Information

Tourist Office (☎02685-502; www.rust.at; Conradplatz 1, Rathaus; ⏰ 9am-noon & 1-4pm Mon-Fri, 9am-6pm Sat, to noon Sun) Has a list of wine growers offering tastings, plus hotels and private rooms in the town.

Getting There & Away

Hourly buses connect Eisenstadt and Rust (€3.80, 25 minutes). For Neusiedl am See (€3.80, 40 minutes, every one to two hours), change to the train at Schützen am Gebirge train station. Ferries cross the lake to Podersdorf, Breitenbrunn and Fertörákos.

Mörbisch am See

☎02685 / POP 2300

Mörbisch am See is a sleepy community 6km south of Rust and only a couple of kilometres shy of the Hungarian border. Soaking up the relaxed atmosphere and taking in quaint whitewashed houses with hanging corn and flower-strewn balconies is the order of the day here.

Seefestspiele PERFORMING ARTS
(www.seefestspiele-moerbisch.at) The town's sleepy mood changes dramatically during the evening from mid-July to August with this summer operetta festival that attracts some 200,000 people each year.

Oper im Steinbruch PERFORMING ARTS
(www.operimsteinbruch.at; ⏰ mid-Jul–mid-Aug) The Opern Festspiele is an opera festival held in an old Roman quarry near St Margareten, around 7km northwest of Mörbisch.

Information

The local **tourist office** (☎02685-8430; www.moerbischamsee.at; Hauptstrasse 23; ⏰ 9am-5pm Jul & Aug, shorter hours rest of year, closed Sat & Sun Nov-Mar) can advise on accommodation, the festivals and lakeside facilities, and give you a list of *Heurigen*.

Getting There & Away

Frequent buses go to Mörbisch via Rust from Eisenstadt (€3.80, 35 minutes). A foot- and cycle-only border crossing into Hungary, 2km south of Mörbisch, is handy for those circumnavigating the lake. Border checks are rare, but take your passport just in case. Alternatively, jump on the ferry across the lake to stay within Austria.

Purbach am See

☎02683 / POP 2835

Most agree that little Purbach am See is one of the prettiest towns on the Neusiedler See, its small, compact centre filled with squat houses and still protected by bastions and three gates – reminders of the Turkish wars. While there isn't a whole load to see in the town – nor has it direct access to Neusiedler See – it's nice to soak up the slow pace of life and wander from one wine cellar to the next along historic Kellergasse and Kellerplatz, both outside the town's walls.

Activities

Although Purbach isn't located directly on the lake shore, it's inside a nature reserve and has reed banks that invite exploration on a bicycle ride or an easy walk. Kirchengasse/Gartengasse, one block north of the tourist office, leads down to the reeds, and from there a 2.5km path follows a canal out to the lake. An alternative ride or walk is to follow the Kirschblutenradweg (B12) north along the reeds to Breitenbrunn (about 4.5km), turn right onto the Schilflehrpfad (Reed Educational Path) and follow that out to the lake (about 3km), where there's lake swimming. Hire bikes from the camping ground (p156) or ask at the tourist office (p156).

Sleeping & Eating

Gasthof zum Türkentor GUESTHOUSE €
(02683-34 00; www.foltin.at; Hauptgasse 2; s/d €45/70; P 📶) This sweet old-fashioned guesthouse is actually situated within the old city wall, at the entrance to the historic part of town. Rooms are basic but clean and a godsend for those on any kind of budget. No-nonsense restaurant on the premises.

Storchencamp Camping Purbach & Jugendherberge CAMPGROUND €
(02683-55 38; www.gmeiner.co.at; Türkenstrasse 13; pitches per adult/tent €6/3.50, dm €23; Apr-Oct; @ 📶) This well-run camping ground on the edge of the reed beds has all the facilities you would expect plus a cheap hostel. Popular with sports clubs due to its facilities.

★ **Gut Purbach** HOTEL €€€
(02683-560 86; www.gutpurbach.at; Hauptgasse 64; r/ste €195/295; 📶) This is arguably the 'See's most stylish sleeping choice. Five rooms, including one suite, mix beautiful old bones with rustic antiques and contemporary design pieces. No two rooms are the same but they all have large, incredibly comfortable beds. You're also well placed for Max Stiegl's wonderful on-site restaurant.

The menu includes goat from Stiegl's own farm, pigs from nearby pastures and fish fresh from the lake.

Fossil AUSTRIAN €€
(02683-210 25; www.restaurant-fossil.at; Kellergasse 6; mains €10-20; noon-10pm Thu-Sun; 📶) In a converted wine cellar, Purbach's top place to eat is a 21st-century, gourmet-style affair where plates are stacked with seasonal, local food in imaginative ways, all paired with wines. Menus change according to the time of year.

Information

The **tourist office** (02683-5920; www.purbach.at; Am Kellerplatz 1; 9am-7pm) has information on accommodation and wine experiences.

Getting There & Away

Purbach has direct train connections with Neusiedl am See (€3.80, 11 minutes, hourly), Eisenstadt (€3.80, 15 minutes, hourly) and Vienna's *Hauptbahnhof* (€13.60, one hour, hourly), and direct bus connections with Eisenstadt (€3.80, 20 minutes, at least one every two hours). From Rust, get off in Schützen am Gebirge (centre) and walk 300m to the train station to change to a regional train.

Podersdorf am See

02177 / POP 2100

Podersdorf am See, on the eastern shore, is the only town that can truly claim to be totally *Am See* (on the lake). This fact, combined with a reed-free location, is the possible reason it's become the most popular holiday destination in the Neusiedler See region and Burgenland.

Activities

St Martins Therme & Lodge Spa Resort SPA
(02172-205 00; www.stmartins.at; Im Seewinkel 1, Frauenkirchen; day tickets adult/child €28/17; 9am-10pm) In Frauenkirchen, 8km southeast from Podersdorf, you can take the cure at this modern spa resort fed by hot springs. Set in an interesting wetlands landscape, you can also swim outdoors in the lake fed by mineral springs. Nonguests are welcome to visit the extensive spa facilities.

Book ahead at the hotel for free pick-up from Frauenkirchen train station if arriving by rail or bus. St Martins can also be easily reached by bike on a detour from the main bike path (there's a Nextbike station at the spa and others at the train station and the basilica in Frauenkirchen; see www.nextbike.at).

Mission to Surf WATER SPORTS
(0680 234 6529; www.surf-schule.at) This professional outfit has equipment for hire and offers kite-surfing courses.

Surf & Segelschule Nordstrand WATER SPORTS
(0664 277 6140; www.nordstrand.at; Seeufergasse 17) Rents out sailing boats and holds weekday sailing courses.

Sleeping

Strandcamping CAMPGROUND €
(02177-22 79; www.podersdorfamsee.at; Strandplatz 19; pitch per adult/tent €9/6; mid-Mar–mid-Nov; 📶) Right by the beach, this popular, well-regimented camping ground is one of the largest around and has plenty of shade from the sweltering heat in high summer. Book well ahead for July and August.

★ **Seewirt** HOTEL €€

(☎02177-24 15; www.seewirtkarner.at; Strandplatz 1; s €70-100, d €120-200; P ⊖ 📶) Having bagged a prime spot right next to the ferry terminal and beach, the four-star Seewirt fills up quickly. Rooms are crisp, fuss-free and full of sea-refracted light, and the restaurant serves no-nonsense Austrian fare.

Hotel-Restaurant Pannonia HOTEL €€

(☎02177-22 45; www.pannonia-hotel.at; Seezeile 20; s €51-79, d €102-160; P ⊖ 📶 ⊠) Set a short stroll from the waterfront, this smart hotel sports 21st-century furnishings and a large grassy area where children can play. The owners run a second hotel across the road with family rooms. The restaurant has a wine list the size of a short novel and serves seasonal dishes such as venison carpaccio on wild-garlic pesto with tomatoes.

Steiner B&B €€

(☎02177-2790; www.steinergg.at; Seestrasse 33; s/d €42.50/88; P 📶) This central *Gästehaus* (guesthouse) has welcoming staff, a tranquil, homely atmosphere and spartanly clean, basic and well-maintained rooms with bathrooms of recent vintage. Some rooms have balconies and there's a pleasant outdoor space where the kids can play.

St Martins Therme & Lodge SPA HOTEL €€€

(☎02172-205 00; www.stmartins.at; Im Seewinkel 1, Frauenkirchen; d €209-319; P ⊖ @ 📶) In Frauenkirchen, 8km inland from Podersdorf, this modern resort has luxurious rooms with views over the wetlands. It's a large place and occasionally can be full of conference-goers. Book ahead for free pick-up from Frauenkirchen train station if you're arriving by train or bus.

Eating

Heuriger & Vinothek Fabian AUSTRIAN €

(☎699-119 503 13; www.sloboda.at; Alte Satz; mains €7.20-9.20; ⊙noon-9.30pm Apr-Oct; 📶) One of the best places for a light lunch of local cheese or venison sausages or an evening wine tasting with something more substantial (schnitzel, goulash) is this modern *Heuriger* south of the town centre. Owner Fabian Sloboda has gathered together tens of the region's best wines and pairs them with tasty treats.

★ **Zur Dankbarkeit** AUSTRIAN €€

(☎02177-22 23; www.dankbarkeit.at; Hauptstrasse 39; mains €9-19; ⊙11.30am-9pm Thu-Sun, daily Jul & Aug, closed Nov-Jan; 📶) This lovely old restaurant has been serving some of the best regional cooking around for over two decades. The inner garden, with its trees and country ambience, is the ideal spot to knock back some local wine.

Drinking & Nightlife

Weinklub 21 WINE BAR

(www.weinclub21.at; Seestrasse 37; tastings €6-13; ⊙9am-noon & 4-9pm May-Sep) This excellent *Vinothek* represents 15 wine producers in the town and region; it holds regular tastings and wine-themed events.

Information

The local **tourist office** (☎02177-2227; www.podersdorfamsee.at; Hauptstrasse 4-8; ⊙8am-4.30pm Mon-Fri, 9am-4.30pm Sat, 9am-noon Sun Mar-Oct) can help out with anything from public transport info to accommodation advice.

Getting There & Away

Buses leave hourly or two-hourly connecting Neusiedl and Podersdorf (€3.80, 16 minutes). Ferries connect Podersdorf with Rust and Breitenbrunn on the western shore.

Seewinkel

☎02175

Seewinkel is the heart of the **Neusiedler See-Seewinkel National Park**, and a grassland and wetland of immense importance to birds and other wildlife. The vineyards, reed beds, shimmering waters and constant birdsong make this an enchanting region for an excursion. This is an excellent area for birdwatching and explorations on foot or by bicycle.

The town of **Illmitz**, 4km from the lake, is surrounded by the national park and makes for a good base. Staff at its tourist office can provide information on the region.

Weingut Gerhard Nekowitsch WINE

(☎02175-20 39; www.weinbau-nekowitsch.at; Urbanusgasse 2, Illmitz) Sweet dessert wines are enjoying a renaissan7ce in Austria. *Eiswein* (wine made from grapes picked late and shrivelled by frost) and selected late-picking sweet or dessert wines are being complemented by *Schilfwein*, made by placing the grapes on reed *(Schilf)* matting so they shrivel in the heat. The guru of *Schilfwein* is Gerhard Nekowitsch from Weingut Gerhard Nekowitsch; sample it here.

Arkadenweingut-Gästehaus GUESTHOUSE €
(☎02175-33 45; www.arkadenweingut-heiss.at; Obere Hauptstrasse 20, Illmitz; s/d €37/74; P⊖) This simple guesthouse is set in a lovely arcaded homestead in the centre of Illmitz. Rooms aren't fancy but are comfortable and spotless.

Waidhofen an der Ybbs Tourist Office TOURIST INFORMATION
(☎07442-93 049; www.waidhofen.at; Schlossweg 2, Waidhofen an der Ybbs; ⊙9am-1pm & 2-5pm Tue-Sat, 9am-1pm Sun May-Sep) Staff have information on the town and the eight mountain-bike trails of varying degrees of difficulty around Waidhofen.

Information

The **Nationalparkhaus** (☎02175-3442; www.nationalpark-neusiedlersee-seewinkel.at; ⊙8am-5pm Mon-Fri, 10am-5pm Sat & Sun, closed Sat & Sun Nov-Mar) is the place to pick up maps and heaps of other info on the Seewinkel.

The local **tourist office** (☎02175-2383; www.illmitz.co.at; Obere Hauptstrasse 2-4; ⊙8am-noon & 1-4.30pm Mon-Fri, 9am-noon & 1-4pm Sat, 9am-noon Sun, closed Sat & Sun Dec-Feb) deals with accommodation and regional information.

Getting There & Away

Illmitz is connected with Möbisch, Rust and Fertörákos (in Hungary) by ferry and Neusiedl am See by hourly buses (€6.80, 30 minutes).

Upper Austria

Includes ➡

Best Places to Eat

➡ Cafe Jindrak (p165)

➡ Lukas Restaurant (p178)

➡ Freistadt Brauhaus (p177)

➡ Knapp am Eck (p172)

➡ Löwenkeller (p175)

Best Places to Stay

➡ Hotel am Domplatz (p164)

➡ Hotel Christkindlwirt (p171)

➡ Hotel Goldener Adler (p176)

➡ arte Hotel (p164)

➡ Baumhotel (p175)

➡ Landhotel Stockerwirt (p174)

Why Go?

Unfolding across the gently undulating countryside, this under-the-radar region has a taste of all that is great about Austria. For starters, there's the mighty Danube (Donau) and a rich musical heritage, old-world coffee houses and castle-topped medieval towns, and resplendent Augustinian abbeys and spas.

Beyond the high-tech museums and avant-garde galleries of Linz lies a land in miniature filled with surprises: from rustic farmhouses serving home-grown *Most* (cider) to the limestone pinnacles of the Kalkalpen, where the elusive lynx roams, and picturesque towns such as Steyr and Schärding, painted in a palette of ice cream–coloured hues. Whether you're among the mist-shrouded hills rippling towards the Czech Republic or wheat fields fading into a watercolour distance at dusk, you'll find these landscapes have a quiet, lingering beauty of their own.

When to Go

➡ Summer is a fine time to cycle along the Danube and through the countryside. Come in September for cutting-edge technology festivals and free riverside concerts in Linz. Rooms are at a premium from June to September, so book ahead.

➡ Autumn is perfect for crisp walks through the forests. Room rates fall from October, along with visitor numbers.

➡ Winter brings glittering Christmas markets galore. From early December to mid-April, cross-country skiers glide through the Nationalpark Kalkalpen, while downhill skiers carve up the slopes at Wurzeralm and Hinterstoder.

➡ The spring shoulder season from March to May is a great time to see the orchards in blossom and to celebrate Schubert in Steyr.

Upper Austria Highlights

1. **Ars Electronica Center** (p161) Playing with pixels and conversing with robots at Linz' tech and digital media centre.

2. **Steyr** (p169) Falling for the storybook lanes and fast-flowing rivers of the old town.

3. **Baumkronenweg** (p175) Walking (and sleeping) high above the treetops in Kopfing.

4. **Nationalpark Kalkalpen** (p173) Hiking through the rugged wilderness of Austria's second-biggest national park.

5. **Stift Kremsmünster** (p175) Admiring the baroque stucco and frescoes in this Benedictine abbey from 777.

6. **Augustiner Chorherrenstift** (p168) Catching an organ concert in the sublime Stiftsbasilika of St Florian's Augustinian abbey.

7. **Mauthausen Memorial** (p169) Exploring the past at a former concentration camp

8. **Stift Engelszell** (p178) Sampling monk-made beers and cheeses at Austria's only Trappist brewery.

Getting There & Around

AIR

Blue Danube Airport Linz (LNZ; 07221-6000; www.linz-airport.com; Flughafenstrasse 1, Hörsching) Year-round, there are flights to Vienna, Frankfurt and Düsseldorf, plus several other European cities in summer.

CAR & MOTORCYCLE

The A1 autobahn runs east–west to Vienna and Salzburg; the A8 heads northwest to Passau and the rest of Germany; and the A9 runs south into Styria. From Linz, the S10 runs north to Prague.

PUBLIC TRANSPORT

Upper Austria's bus and train services are covered by the **Oberösterreichischer Verkehrsverbund** (www.ooevv.at). Prices depend on the number of zones you travel (one zone costs €2.30). As well as single tickets, daily, weekly, monthly and yearly passes are available. Express trains between Vienna and Salzburg pass through Linz and much of southern Upper Austria, and there are also express trains heading south from Linz to St Michael in Styria, from where connections to Klagenfurt and Graz are possible.

LINZ

0732 / POP 204,845

'In Linz beginnt's' (it begins in Linz) goes the Austrian saying, and it's spot on. This is a city on the move, with its finger on the pulse of the country's technology industry. Daring public art installations, a burgeoning cultural scene, a cyber centre and a cutting-edge gallery that looks freshly minted for a sci-fi movie all signal tomorrow's Austria.

Linz seized the reins as European Capital of Culture in 2009, and in 2014 Austria's third-largest city became a Unesco City of Media Arts. Sitting astride the Danube, Linz is not only a contemporary hub but also harbours a charming *Altstadt* (old town) filled with historic baroque architecture.

History

Linz was a fortified Celtic village when the Romans took over and named it Lentia. By the 8th century, when the town came under Bavaria's rule, its name had changed to Linze, and by the 13th century it was an important trading town for raw materials out of Styria. In 1489 Linz became the imperial capital under Friedrich III until his death in 1493.

Like much of Upper Austria, Linz was at the forefront of the Protestant movement in the 16th and 17th centuries. With the Counter-Reformation, however, Catholicism made a spectacular comeback. The city's resurgence in the 19th century was largely due to the development of the railway, when Linz became an important junction.

Adolf Hitler was born in nearby Braunau am Inn and spent his schooldays here. His Nazi movement built massive iron and steel works, which still employ many locals. After WWII Linz was at the border between the Soviet- and US-administered zones. Since 1955 Linz has flourished into an important industrial city, port and provincial capital.

Sights

★Lentos GALLERY

(www.lentos.at; Ernst-Koref-Promenade 1; adult/child €8/4.50; 10am-6pm Tue, Wed & Fri-Sun, to 9pm Thu) Overlooking the Danube, the rectangular glass-and-steel Lentos is strikingly illuminated by night. The gallery guards one of Austria's finest modern-art collections, including works by Warhol, Schiele, Klimt, Kokoschka and Lovis Corinth, which sometimes feature in the large-scale exhibitions. Download Lentos' app from the website, or rent a multimedia guide (€2).

★Mariendom CATHEDRAL

(Neuer Dom; www.dioezese-linz.at; Herrenstrasse 26; 7.30am-7pm Mon-Sat, 8am-7.15pm Sun) Also known as the Neuer Dom, this neo-Gothic giant of a cathedral lifts your gaze to its riot of pinnacles, flying buttresses and filigree-traceried windows. Designed in the mid-19th century by Vinzenz Statz of Cologne Dom fame, the cathedral sports a tower whose height was restricted to 134m, so as not to outshine Stephansdom in Vienna. The interior is lit by a veritable curtain of stained glass, including the Linzer Fenster, depicting scenes from Linz' history.

★Ars Electronica Center MUSEUM

(www.aec.at; Ars-Electronica-Strasse 1; adult/child €9.50/7.50; 9am-5pm Tue, Wed & Fri, to 7pm Thu, 10am-6pm Sat & Sun) The technology, science and digital media of the future are in the spotlight at Linz' biggest crowd-puller. In the labs you can interact with robots, animate digital objects, print 3D structures, turn your body into musical instruments and (virtually) travel to outer space. Kids love it. Designed by Vienna-based architectural firm Treusch, the centre resembles a futuristic ship by the Danube after dark, when its LED glass skin kaleidoscopically changes colour.

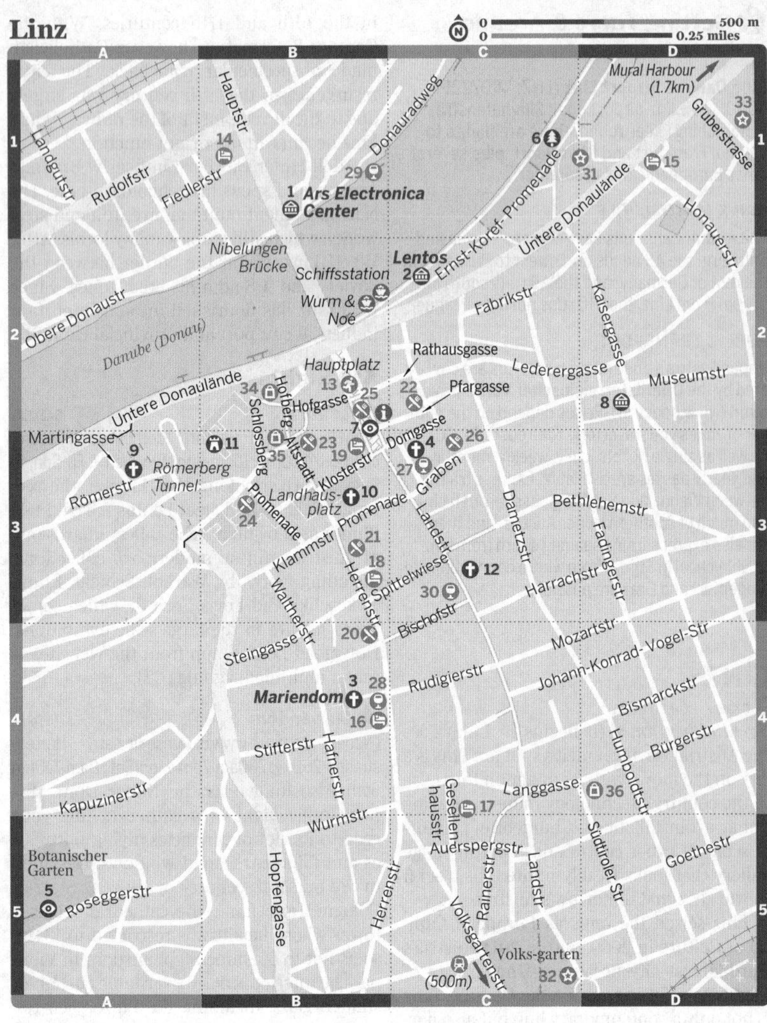

Mural Harbour

PUBLIC ART

(www.muralharbor.at; Industriezeile 40; guided tours walk/cruise/combination €18/30/55, 1hr street-art workshop €10) Street art comes into its own on the graffiti-blasted industrial facades in Linz' harbourside Hafenviertel. You'll find eye-catching, larger-than-life works from the likes of Roa (Belgium), Lords (USA), Aryz (Spain) and a host of Austrian artists. For more insider info, join one of the regular walks, workshops or cruises; combination tours include stencil and spray-can classes (you can also take classes separately). Visit the website for times and dates.

Landesgalerie

GALLERY

(www.landesgalerie.at; Museumstrasse 14; adult/child €6.50/4.50; 10am-6pm Tue, Wed & Fri-Sun, to 9pm Thu) Housed in a sumptuous late-19th-century building, the Landesgalerie focuses on 20th- and 21st-century paintings, photography and installations. The rotating exhibitions often zoom in on works by Upper Austrian artists, such as Alfred Kubin's expressionist fantasies and Valie Export's shocking Viennese Actionism–inspired pieces. The open-air **sculpture park** contrasts modern sculpture with the gallery's neoclassical architecture.

Linz

Schlossmuseum CASTLE

(www.landesmuseum.at; Schlossberg 1; adult/child €6.50/4.50; 10am-6pm Tue, Wed & Fri-Sun, to 9pm Thu) Romans, Habsburg emperors, fire – Linz' castle has seen the lot. Enjoy the panoramic city views before delving into its museum's trove of treasures, gathered from abbeys and palaces over the centuries. The collection skips through art, archaeology, historical weapons and instruments, technology and folklore. The Gothic ecclesiastical paintings are a real highlight.

Hauptplatz SQUARE

Street performers entertain the crowds, trams rumble past and locals relax in pavement cafes on the city's centrepiece square, framed by ornate baroque and pastel-coloured Renaissance houses. The square's **Dreifaltigkeitssäule** (Trinity Column) – a 20m pillar of Salzburg marble carved in 1723 to commemorate the town's deliverance from war, fire and plague – glints when it catches the sunlight.

Martinskirche CHURCH

(www.dioezese-linz.at; Römerstrasse 21; 9am-7pm Mon-Sat, 10am-7pm Sun May-Sep, to 5pm Oct-Apr) One of Austria's oldest churches, Martinskirche was first mentioned in 799. Inside are Roman inscriptions and a kiln, and a painting believed to date from the early 13th century of the famous *Volto Santo* sculpture in Lucca, Italy.

Alter Dom CATHEDRAL

(www.dioezese-linz.at; Domgasse 3; 7am-6.30pm Mon-Wed & Fri, to 6pm Thu, to 5pm Sat & Sun) The twin towers of this late-17th-century cathedral dominate Linz' skyline. With its stuccowork, pink-marble altar and gilt pillars, the interior is remarkably ornate. Famous local lad Anton Bruckner served as organist here from 1856 to 1868.

Minoritenkirche CHURCH

(Church of the Minor Friars; www.dioezese-linz.at; Promenade 24; 9am-7pm May-Sep, to 5pm Mon-Sat, 10am-5pm Sun Oct-Apr) Founded in 1236 and redesigned in rococo style with delicate pink stucco, this church contains altar paintings by Bartolomeo Altomonte.

Ursulinenkirche CHURCH

(www.dioezese-linz.at; Landstrasse 31; 7am-7pm) This baroque, twin-domed church was a former nunnery and features altar paintings by the prolific Martin Altomonte.

Donaupark PARK

(Ernst-Koref-Promenade; 24hr) Next to Lentos on the southern bank of the Danube is the Donaupark, the city's green escape vault. Modern sculptures rise above the bushes in the well-tended gardens, which are a magnet for walkers, joggers, skaters, picnickers and city workers seeking fresh air in summer.

Botanischer Garten GARDENS
(www.botanischergarten.linz.at; Roseggerstrasse 20; adult/child €3.50/2.50; ⊙7am-7pm Apr-Sep, 9am-5pm Mar & Oct, to 4pm Nov-Feb) These peaceful botanical gardens, 1.7km southwest of the centre, nurture 10,000 species, from native alpine plants to orchids, rhododendrons, tropical palms and one of Europe's largest cacti collections. Concerts and exhibitions take place here throughout the year.

Activities

Pöstlingbergbahn HERITAGE RAILWAY
(www.linzag.at; Hauptplatz; adult/child return €6.40/3.20; ⊙6am-10.30pm Mon-Sat, 7.30am-10pm Sun Apr-Oct, 6am-8.30pm Mon-Sat, 7.30am-8.30pm Sun Nov-Mar) It's a gentle hike to the top of **Pöstlingberg**, or a precipitous 20- to 30-minute ride aboard the narrow-gauge Pöstlingbergbahn. It's Austria's – and one of the world's – steepest adhesion railway (running on electricity alone, rather than cables and pulleys).

Festivals & Events

Pflasterspektakel CARNIVAL
(www.pflasterspektakel.at; ⊙mid-Jul) Musicians, jugglers, actors, poets, fire-breathers and acrobats from across Europe descend on Linz for this three-day street festival, with performances throughout the city.

Ars Electronica Festival CULTURAL
(www.aec.at; ⊙early Sep) This innovative five-day event showcases cyber-art, music written and performed by computers, and other marriages of technology and art at venues across town.

Brucknerfest MUSIC
(www.brucknerhaus.at; ⊙mid-Sep–late Oct) Linz pays homage to native son Anton Bruckner with classical music during this six-week festival held at the Brucknerhaus (p166).

Voestalpine Klangwolke MUSIC
(www.klangwolke.at; Donaupark; ⊙mid-Sep) Modern, classical, children's musicals – it's all in the mix at this free concert series spread over a week in mid-September in the Donaupark (p163).

Sleeping

etagerie APARTMENT €
(☎0732-323 000; www.etagerie.com/linz; Untere Donaulände 62-64; 3-/5-/7-person apt from €67/88/129; 📶) Bearing the imprint of cutting-edge architectural firm Urbanauts, these super-slick apartments in the former workers' quarters of the tobacco factory sport parquet floors, vintage furniture and a clean aesthetic. Three sizes (medium, large and extra-large) sleep up to three, five and seven people respectively. It's right near the river and Lentos; from the *Hauptbahnhof* (main train station), take bus 12 to Haltestelle Parkbad.

★**Hotel am Domplatz** DESIGN HOTEL €€
(☎0732-773 000; www.hotelamdomplatz.at; Stifterstrasse 4; d/ste from €159/325; P❄📶) Adjacent to the neo-Gothic Mariendom (p161; ask for a room overlooking the cathedral), this glass-and-concrete cube filled with striking metal sculptures has 69 streamlined, Nordic-style white and blond-wood rooms with semiopen bathrooms, and two suites. Wind down with a view in the rooftop spa. In fine weather, head to the cathedral-facing terrace for breakfast (€19), which includes a glass of bubbly.

arte Hotel DESIGN HOTEL €€
(☎0732-733 733; www.arte-linz.at; Fiedlerstrasse 6; d/studio/ste from €116/135/165; P❄@📶) Austrian architect Isa Stein has left her avant-garde imprint on this hotel, from the lobby's moulded furnishings to UFO-style lighting. Each of the hotel's minimalist rooms spotlights an aspect of Linz' arts scene, and features clean lines, hardwood floors, coffee-making facilities and bespoke pieces by local creatives; there's a choice of open-plan or enclosed bathrooms. Some rooms have balconies.

Hotel Kolping HOTEL €€
(☎0732-661 690; www.hotel-kolping.at; Gesellenhausstrasse 5; s/d from €89/117; P❄📶) Hidden down a backstreet in central Linz, Kolping has bright, spotless pine-furnished rooms and attentive service. The breakfast buffet (included in the rate) is among the best in town with locally sourced organic produce including farmyard eggs, regional cheeses and fresh seasonal fruit. Packed lunches can be arranged by request.

Hotel Schwarzer Bär HOTEL €€
(☎0732-772 477; www.linz-hotel.at; Herrenstrasse 11; s/d/ste from €89/109/169; P❄📶) The birthplace of acclaimed tenor Richard Tauber (1891–1948), the 'Black Bear' is run by the friendly Nell family. Overlooking a courtyard,

the 54 rooms and suites have been made-over in monochrome hues and parquet; some even sport waterbeds. The wood-panelled restaurant dishes up Austrian classics; views extend from its rooftop bar.

Wolfinger HISTORIC HOTEL €€
(☎0732-773 29 10; www.hotelwolfinger.at; Hauptplatz 19; s/d/tr/q from €88/114/138/165; P@📶) This 15th-century hotel on the main square has an air of old-world grandeur. Archways, stucco and period furniture lend its 50 rooms character; those at the back are quieter and some have balconies. Children are warmly welcomed.

Eating

★Cafe Jindrak CAFE €
(www.jindrak.at; Herrenstrasse 22; dishes €3-8.80; ⊙8am-6pm Mon-Sat, 8.30am-6pm Sun) Join the cake-loving locals at this celebrated cafe – the original shop (1929) of a now nine-strong chain that produces over 100,000 of its famous *Linzer Torte* each year made to its family recipe. You'd need a huge fork (and appetite) to tackle the torte that set a Guinness World Record in 1999, measuring 4m high and weighing 650kg.

Wirt am Graben AUSTRIAN €
(☎0732-772 975; www.wirt.amgraben.at; Graben 24; mains €11-20, 2-course lunch menu €10.20-11.20; ⊙kitchen 11.30am-2.30pm & 6-9pm Mon-Sat, bar 11am-11pm Mon-Sat; 📶) This enticingly boho bar-restaurant spills out into a tree-shaded courtyard in summer. Come for the chilled vibes and creative Slow Food made with local organic, seasonal ingredients. The changing menu keeps things delightfully simple with such dishes as local lamb bratwurst with potato pancakes and sauerkraut, and daily vegetarian and gluten-free choices.

Deli Linz CAFE €
(www.deli-linz.at; Herrenstrasse 7; dishes €5-12; ⊙9am-8pm Mon-Sat; 📶🌱) Breakfast and lunch bowls, tacos, burgers and open-faced toasties at this hip cafe are made with vegetarian, vegan or organic meat ingredients, including superfoods such as quinoa, kale, spirulina and hemp seeds, while fresh juices include beetroot, apple and celery. A two-course lunch menu costs €7.50. Dine in its vaulted interior or on the partially covered terrace.

DON'T MISS

LINZER TORTE

Old-style cafes such as Cafe Jindrak and k.u.k. Hofbäckerei are atmospheric places to try the classic *Linzer Torte*. Made to a recipe dating from 1653 with hazelnuts, spices and tangy redcurrant jam, the multilayered cake is the greatest rival to Vienna's *Sacher Torte*.

Promenadenhof AUSTRIAN €
(☎0732-777 661; www.promenadenhof.at; Promenade 39; mains €8-21.50; ⊙kitchen 11am-10pm Mon-Sat, bar 5pm-2am Mon-Sat) Promenadenhof enjoys a loyal following for spot-on Austrian fare such as *Tafelspitz* (prime boiled beef) and Styrian-style chicken salad, complemented by over 100 mostly Austrian wines. There are vaulted *Stuben* (parlours) and a beer garden.

k.u.k. Hofbäckerei CAFE €
(Pfarrgasse 17; dishes €3-6; ⊙6.30am-6.30pm Mon-Fri, 7am-12.30pm Sat) The Empire lives on at this gloriously frozen-in-time cafe in a timber-framed building dating from 1371. Here Fritz Rath bakes some of the best *Linzer Torte* in town – rich, spicy and with a wonderful crumbly lattice pastry. In summer, the best seats are in the shady courtyard.

Stadtmarkt MARKET
(www.stadtmarkt-linz.at; Hauptplatz; ⊙9am-2pm Tue & Fri) 🌿 Put together a picnic from the 25-plus stalls at Linz' twice-weekly farmers market.

Verdi AUSTRIAN €€
(☎0732-733 005; www.verdi.at; Pachmayrstrasse 137; mains €17-33, 6-course menu €85; ⊙5-11pm Tue-Sat) Linz spreads out picturesquely before you from Verdi, 5km north of the city centre. Chef Erich Lukas prepares seasonal dishes with panache and precision, such as quail breast with herby risotto and venison with truffle gnocchi, and, to finish, walnut-crusted, caramelised banana with dark-chocolate ganache.

Cubus FUSION €€
(☎0732-944 149; www.cubus.at; Ars-Electronica-Strasse 1; mains €15-25; ⊙kitchen 11am-2pm & 5-10pm Tue-Thu, 9am-10pm Fri & Sat, to 3pm Sun, bar to midnight Tue-Thu, to 1am Fri & Sat; 📶) On

LINZ CARD

The Linz Card (one day adult/child €18/15, three days €30/25) covers unlimited use of public transport; entry to major museums including the Ars Electronica Center, Schlossmuseum, Lentos and the Landesgalerie; plus discounts on other sights, city tours and river cruises. The three-day card also includes a round trip on the Pöstlingbergbahn. Buy the Linz Card at the tourist office, airport, museums and some hotels.

the 3rd floor of the Ars Electronica Center (p161), this glass cube looking over the Danube to the south bank glows purple after dark. Seasonally inspired food (grilled zander with polenta; schnitzel with green herb sauce) is fresh and contemporary; the two-course weekday-only lunch is a snip at €9.50. After dark, linger over a cocktail and dazzling skyline views.

Muto BISTRO €€€
(☎0732-770 377; www.mutolinz.at; Altstadt 7; 5-/7-course menu vegetarian €52/65, meat & fish €60/75; ⏰6-9pm Wed-Sat; ✍) *Muto* is Latin for 'transform', which is what the culinary wizards achieve in the kitchen. Meat- and fish-based menus might include smoked quail with hazelnut foam and morrel gel, or zander with pea and wild garlic sorbet and a squid ink alpine cheese crisp, while vegetarian menus feature dishes like roast kohlrabi with pressed cucumber cubes and pickled black radish.

Drinking & Nightlife

★Paul's BAR
(www.pauls-linz.at; Herrenstrasse 36; ⏰11am-1am Mon-Fri, 2pm-1am Sat; 📶) Facing the monumental Mariendom cathedral, this A-line building's facade is split down the middle: half is stone, the other half is fronted by floor-to-ceiling glass that's lit up in vivid red at night. Austrian beers include organic and gluten-free varieties, and Paul's own pale ale, brewed by Salzburg's Hofbräu Kaltenhausen; there are also Austrian wines by the glass and bottle.

Salonschiff Fräulen Florentine BAR
(www.frl-florentine.at; Donauradweg; ⏰2pm-3am Mon-Fri, noon-3am Sat, to 1am Sun; 📶) Permanently moored on the Danube across from Linz' historic centre, with stunning sunset and night-time views, this vast boat bar has a huge, sunny upper deck, and a cosy, portholed lounge below. Wines and beers are from Austria and Germany only. Live music plays most weekends year-round and occasionally during the week in summer.

Boiler Room COCKTAIL BAR
(www.boiler-room.at; Domgasse 5; ⏰6-11pm Wed & Thu, 7pm-4am Fri & Sat, closed Aug; 📶) Below Linz' streets, this classy bar occupies an elongated vaulted cellar. Craft cocktails change seasonally; creations might include the CHM (lime- and spruce-infused vodka, raspberry purée, white chocolate syrup, apple juice and smoked chilli) or vividly coloured Green Poison Daiquiri (basil-infused gin, nettle-infused rum and lime juice). DJs spin until late.

Stiegelbräu zum Klosterhof MICROBREWERY
(www.klosterhof-linz.at; Landstrasse 30; ⏰9am-midnight) Go straight for the freshly tapped Stiegl beer at the cavernous Klosterhof, dating from 1929. Centred on a huge fountain, the chestnut tree–shaded beer garden has space for 1350 thirsty punters. Catch live music every night in summer and most weekends in winter.

☆ Entertainment

Tabakfabrik CULTURAL CENTRE
(www.tabakfabrik-linz.at; Peter-Behrens-Platz 1-15) A shining example of Linz' cultural renaissance is this cultural centre, lodged in what was once a tobacco factory. Check the website program for details of upcoming events from exhibitions to readings, film screenings, concerts and party nights.

Brucknerhaus LIVE MUSIC
(☎0732-775 230; www.brucknerhaus.at; Untere Donaulände 7) Linz' premier music venue stages top-drawer classical and jazz concerts in two halls; the largest accommodates 1570 people, and the smaller 392. There is a dedicated program for kids of different ages ('mini' and 'midi' music).

Musiktheater THEATRE
(☎0732-7611-400; www.landestheater-linz.at; Am Volksgarten 1) Designed by London-based architect Terry Pawson and opened in 2013, Linz' Musiktheater is a strikingly geometric opera house with a capacity of 1000. It's the city's main stage for operas, operettas, ballets, musicals and children's productions.

Shopping

★Markthalle FOOD & DRINKS

(www.markthall12.at; Altstadt 12; ⏲7am-8pm Mon & Tue, to 11pm Wed-Fri, 9am-8pm Sat & Sun) An apricot-coloured former salt warehouse now houses this spectacular gourmet emporium selling all-Austrian products from small producers. Browse for Salzkammergut gins, liqueurs and wines; Innviertel jams, chutneys, salt and alpine herbs; Mühlviertel mustard and beers; Tyrol and Carinthia cheeses; and charcuterie from Linz' surrounds. It's ideal for packing a picnic; there's also a fabulous organic cafe to dine on-site.

Vinyl Corner MUSIC

(www.vinylcorner.at; Bürgerstrasse 14; ⏲11am-6pm Mon-Fri, 9am-3pm Sat) Traditional Austrian folk, French *chansons* à la Édith Piaf, funk, jazz, rock, reggae, metal, rap, classical, cabaret...you name it, this collector's dream has it on vinyl. It also sells posters, turntables and cleaning kits.

A/T Store DESIGN

(www.facebook.com/AT.STORE.LINZ; Hofburg 10; ⏲10am-6pm Mon-Fri, to 3pm Sat) Most of the products at this hip little concept store are made by Austrian designers, while a handful of others from Scandinavia and the Netherlands share the same minimalist aesthetic. Fashion (women's and men's), shoes, watches and jewellery sit alongside perfumes, hand and body lotions, and gourmet items such as ice creams, preserves and alpine herb and spice packs.

Information

Kepler Universitäts Klinikum (Kepler University Hospital; ☎05 7680 82-0; www.kepleruniklinikum.at; Krankenhausstrasse 9) The main hospital, 1km east of the centre, with a 24-hour Accident & Emergency Department.

Tourist Information Linz (☎0732-7070 2009; www.linztourismus.at; Hauptplatz 1; ⏲9am-7pm daily May-Sep, to 5pm Mon-Sat, 10am-5pm Sun Oct-Apr) Brochures, accommodation listings and Upper Austria information are available here.

Getting There & Away

AIR

Blue Danube Airport Linz (p161) is 12km southwest of town. A direct shuttle bus service, bus 601, connects the *Hauptbahnhof* (€3.30, 22 minutes) with the airport hourly from 5am to 8.30pm Monday to Friday, with fewer services at weekends. Alternatively, there are hourly train connections between Linz and Hörsching (10 minutes, €2.40), a three-minute ride from the airport by free shuttle bus. Use the free phone at the station to dial 0800 20 66 00 for a pick-up. The service is very reliable and runs daily from 5am to 11pm.

BOAT

The **Schiffsstation** (Untere Donaulände 1) is on the south bank next to the Lentos Kunstmuseum. From late April to October, **Wurm & Noé** (☎0732-783 607; www.donauschifffahrt.eu; Untere Donaulände 1) sends boats westwards to Passau, Germany (one way €27, 6½ hours, 2.20pm Tuesday to Thursday, Saturday and Sunday; 2.20pm Saturday early October), and east to Krems (€40, 7¼ hours, 9am Saturday), from where buses and trains run to Vienna.

BUS

Regional buses depart from stands at the main bus station adjacent to the *Hauptbahnhof*.

TRAIN

Linz is on the main rail route between Vienna (€37.40, 1¼ hours) and Salzburg (€28.60, 1¼ hours); express trains run twice hourly in both directions.

Four direct trains depart daily for Prague (€51.40, four hours). Tickets are sold at www.oebb.at.

Getting Around

BICYCLE

Linz is a major stop on the **Danube Cycle Path** (www.danube-cycle-path.com) and has over 200km of bicycle routes. Bikes are available for hire at **Donau Touristik** (☎0732-2080; www.donaureisen.at; Lederergasse 4-12; mountain bike hire per day/week €15/79, electric bike €20/160; ⏲8am-6pm daily May-Sep, 9am-4.30pm Mon-Thu, to 1pm Fri, to 3pm Sat & Sun Apr & Oct).

CAR & MOTORCYCLE

One-way systems, congested roads and pricey parking make public transport preferable to driving in central Linz, although a car is a definite plus if you're keen to explore more of Upper Austria. Major car hire firms have desks at the airport and *Hauptbahnhof*.

PUBLIC TRANSPORT

Linz AG (www.linzag.at) has an extensive bus and tram network. Single tickets (€1.20), day passes (€4.50) and weekly passes (€14.70) are available from pavement dispensers, *Tabakladen* (tobacconist) shops and the *Hauptbahnhof*. Drivers don't sell tickets – buy and validate your tickets before you board.

AROUND LINZ

St Florian

07224 / POP 6175

Unassuming St Florian, a market town 18km southeast of Linz, hides one of Austria's finest Augustinian abbeys. Supposedly buried under the abbey, St Florian was a Roman officer who converted to Christianity and was subsequently tortured and drowned in the Enns River in the year 304 for his beliefs. Legend has it that Florian, the patron saint of firefighters and of Upper Austria, saved a burning village with a single water-filled bucket. In many Austrian churches, he's depicted as a Roman warrior dousing flames with a bucket of water.

Sights

★Augustiner Chorherrenstift ABBEY

(www.stift-st-florian.at; Stiftstrasse 1; tours €10.50; tours 11am, 1pm & 3pm May–mid-Oct) Rising like a vision above St Florian, this abbey dates at least to 819 and has been occupied by the Canons Regular, living under Augustinian rule, since 1071. Today its imposing yellow-and-white facade is overwhelmingly baroque.

You can only visit the abbey's interior by guided tour, which takes in the resplendent apartments adorned with rich stuccowork and frescoes. They include 16 emperors' rooms (once occupied by visiting popes and royalty) and a galleried library housing 150,000 volumes.

The opulent **Marble Hall** pays homage to Prince Eugene of Savoy, a Frenchman who frequently led the Habsburg army to victory over the Turks. Prince Eugene's Room contains an amusing bed featuring carved Turks, which gives a whole new meaning to the idea of sleeping with the enemy!

A high point of the tour is the **Altdorfer Gallery**, displaying 14 paintings by Albrecht Altdorfer (1480–1538) of the Danube School. The sombre and dramatic scenes of Christ and St Sebastian reveal a skilful use of chiaroscuro. Altdorfer cleverly tapped into contemporary issues to depict his biblical scenes (for example, one of Christ's tormentors is clearly a Turk).

The **Stiftsbasilika** (open 6.30am to dusk) is an exuberant affair: its altar is carved from 700 tonnes of pink Salzburg marble and the huge, gilded 18th-century organ, with 7343 pipes, was Europe's largest at the time it was built.

Alongside Anton Bruckner's simple tomb in the **crypt** are the remains of some 6000 people believed to be Roman, which were unearthed in the 13th century. Stacked in neat rows behind a wrought-iron gate, their bones and skulls create a spine-tingling work of art.

OÖ Feuerwehrmuseum MUSEUM

(Fire Brigade Museum; www.feuerwehrmuseum-stflorian.at; Stiftstrasse 2; adult/child €5/free; 10am-noon & 2-5pm Tue-Sun May-Oct) Opposite the abbey, this is a child's dream of a museum and an ode to St Florian, patron saint of firefighters. The collection comprises historic fire engines, hoses and other paraphernalia.

Sleeping & Eating

Landgasthof zur Kanne GUESTHOUSE €€

(07224-4288; www.gasthof-koppler.at; Marktplatz 7; s/d €58/94; P) This yellow-fronted 14th-century guesthouse on the main square scores points for its clean, snug rooms and its restaurant (open Wednesday to Sunday), which serves fresh produce from the Koppler family's farm.

Zum Goldenen Löwe AUSTRIAN €

(07224-8930; www.goldenerloewe-wimhofer.at; Speiserberg 9; mains €7.50-16; 11.30am-10pm Thu-Mon) The sound of the chef pounding humongous schnitzels welcomes you to this wood-panelled restaurant opposite the abbey gates. The sunny beer garden out back overlooks rolling countryside. Weekday lunch specials go for €8.50.

ST FLORIAN'S HEAVENLY MUSIC

Famous Austrian Romantic composer Anton Bruckner was born 8km from St Florian in the village of Ansfelden in 1824. A choirboy in St Florian and church organist from 1850 to 1855, he was buried in the crypt below his beloved organ in 1896. Indeed the Augustiner Chorherrenstift abbey has a long musical tradition, associated with names such as Schubert and Michael Haydn, and is world famous for its resident boys' choir, the St Florianer Sängerknaben; see www.florianer.at for concert dates.

MAUTHAUSEN

Mauthausen's status as a quarrying centre prompted the Nazis to site KZ Mauthausen concentration camp here. Prisoners were forced into slave labour in the granite quarry and many died on the *Todesstiege* (stairway of death) leading from the quarry to the camp. Some 100,000 prisoners died or were executed on site between 1938 and 1945. The camp has been turned into the emotive **Mauthausen Memorial** (☎07238-2269-0; www.mauthausen-memorial.org; Erinnerungsstrasse 1, Mauthausen; ⏲9am-5.30pm Mar-Oct, to 3pm Tue-Sun Nov-Feb), which tells its history, and that of other camps such as those at Ebensee and Melk.

Visitors can walk through the remaining living quarters (each designed for 200, but housing up to 500) and see the disturbing gas chambers. The former Sick Quarters now shelters most of the camp's harrowing material – charts, artefacts and many photos of both prisoners and their SS guards. It is a stark and incredibly moving reminder of human cruelty.

Guided tours lasting two hours take place in English at 10am from March to October. An audio guide costs €3.

Bus 360 from Linz (€5.50, 50 minutes, hourly) drops you at the Mauthausen OÖ Linzer Strasse/Hauptschule stop, from where it's a steep 1.5km walk northwest to the memorial.

Trains link Linz with Mauthausen (€5.50, 30 minutes, hourly), most requiring a change in St Valentin. Mauthausen Memorial is 4km northwest of the train station (follow the KZ Mauthausen signs), around an hour's walk, of which the final 1.5km is uphill.

✩ Entertainment

Augustiner Chorherrenstift Concerts CLASSICAL MUSIC
(tickets €6; ⏲2.30pm Mon, Wed-Fri & Sun mid-May–mid-Oct) To hear the organ of the Stiftsbasilika in full swing, time your visit to attend one of the 25-minute concerts.

ℹ Getting There & Away

St Florian (officially Markt St Florian) is not accessible by train. Buses depart frequently from the main bus station at Linz' *Hauptbahnhof* (€3.30, 30 minutes, up to three per hour Monday to Saturday, fewer Sunday).

THE TRAUNVIERTEL

The rolling green landscapes of the Traunviertel are less about sightseeing and more about easing into country life – whether hiking in the forest, skiing in the mountains, sampling homemade *Most* in the apple orchards or bedding down in a rambling *Vierkanter* farmhouse.

Steyr

☎07252 / POP 38,330

Franz Schubert called Steyr 'inconceivably lovely' and was inspired to pen the sprightly *Trout Quintet* here. And lovely it is: on the confluence of the swiftly flowing Enns and Steyr Rivers, the postcard-like old town of cobbled lanes and candy-hued baroque houses is one of Upper Austria's most attractive.

Sights

Schlosspark PARK
(Blumauergasse) Footpaths through this quiet park lead to baroque **Schloss Lamberg**, sitting pretty between the confluence of the Enns and Steyr Rivers. A steep passageway next to the **Bummerlhaus** (Stadtplatz 32), with overhanging arches, squeezes through the old city walls and climbs up to cobbled Berggasse and the park.

Museum Arbeitswelt MUSEUM
(☎07252-773 51-0; www.museum-steyr.at; Wehrgrabengasse 7; adult/child €7/5; ⏲9am-5pm Tue-Sun early May–mid-Dec) Housed in a converted factory by the river, this excellent museum delves into Steyr's industrial past with exhibits on working-class history, forced labour during WWII and the rise of the Socialist Party.

Stadtpfarrkirche CHURCH
(www.dioezese-linz.at; Brucknerplatz 4; ⏲8am-6pm) The spire of this Gothic church is one of Steyr's most visible landmarks. The church shares features with Stephansdom in Vienna and the same architect, Hans Puchsbaum.

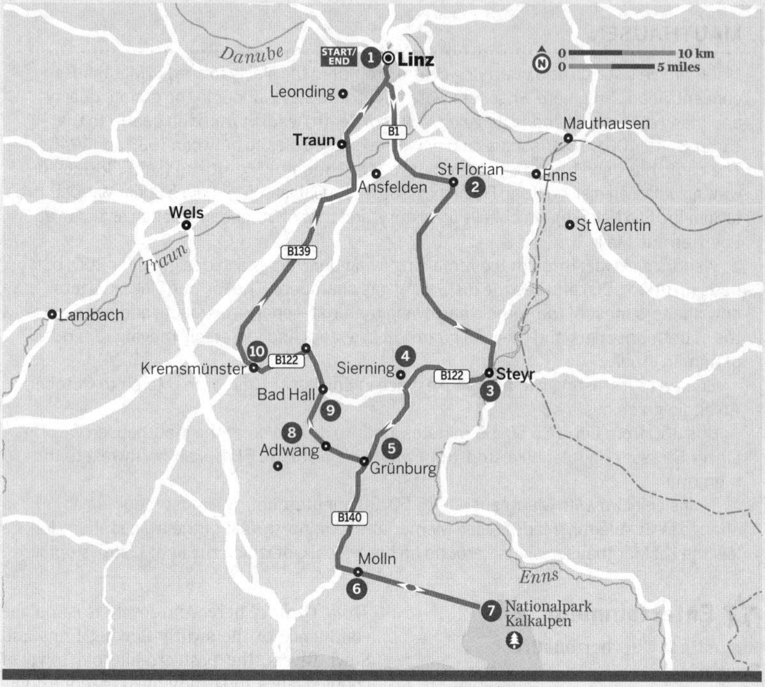

Driving Tour
Upper Austria Highlights

START LINZ
END LINZ
LENGTH 140KM; ONE DAY

This off-the-beaten-track drive meanders through the region's bucolic landscapes to resplendent abbeys, rustic villages, spa towns and limestone mountains. It's particularly beautiful in autumn, when the apple trees are laden and the forests are russet and gold.

After you've seen high-tech developments and magnificent architecture in 1 **Linz** (p161), head south along the B1. The city's industrial fringes soon give way to low-rise hills and meadows. Stop in 2 **St Florian** (p168) to explore its Augustinian abbey, a masterpiece of baroque art and the final resting place of Romantic composer Anton Bruckner.

Continue south on minor roads through patchwork fields studded with *Vierkanthof*, huge farmhouses with inner courtyards, to riverside 3 **Steyr** (p169), the picture-book town that inspired Schubert's *Trout Quintet* and a relaxed place for lunch. Rahofer, on the main street, has a cafe, a restaurant serving classic Austrian cuisine, and a delightful sheltered courtyard. Afterwards, take a stroll through Steyr's pastel-shaded streets.

Follow the emerald-tinted Steyr River west along the B122 to 4 **Sierning**, dominated by its Renaissance castle. From here, the B140 shadows the river south to the pretty church-topped town of 5 **Grünburg**, nestled in wooded hills. It's just a 15-minute drive south to 6 **Molln**, the northern gateway to the spectacular limestone peaks, waterfalls and wilderness of 7 **Nationalpark Kalkalpen** (p173). Get information on local walks at Molln's national park visitor centre.

Refreshed by the mountain air, head north, passing Grünburg and swinging west along a country road to tiny 8 **Adlwang**. Here Gangl farmhouse is a good stop for home-grown apple juice and *Most*. Just north sits the spa town of 9 **Bad Hall** (p172), where you can bathe in its fabled healing waters at Mediterrana Therme. A short drive west along the B122 leads to 10 **Kremsmünster** (p175), whose opulent Benedictine abbey harbours an incredible library and observatory. Go back to Linz via the scenic villages lining the B139.

Michaelerkirche CHURCH
(www.dioezese-linz.at; Michaelerplatz 1; ⌚8am-6pm) Just north of the Steyr River, this twin-towered baroque church is embellished with a fresco of St Michael and the fallen angels.

Franz Schubert's House HISTORIC BUILDING
(Stadtplatz 16) Look out for this fine house on the square, where Schubert was inspired to compose the *Trout Quintet*.

Festivals & Events

Musik Festival Steyr MUSIC
(www.musikfestivalsteyr.at; ⌚late Jul–mid-Aug) Classical music is the mainstay of this two-week festival, but it also sees brass bands, opera, theatre and outdoor cinema screenings, as well as a children's theatre workshop.

Schubert@Steyr MUSIC
(www.schubertatsteyr.at; ⌚mid-Oct) Every year, the town pays homage to the composer at the three-day Schubert@Steyr festival at churches and outdoor stages throughout town.

Christkindl Seasonal Post Office CHRISTMAS
(www.christkindl.at; Christkindlweg 6, Christkindl; ⌚10am-5pm 25 Nov-6 Jan) If you're in Steyr around Christmas, head for the suburb of Christkindl, west of the old town, which shares its name with the winged Christkind ('Christ Child'; affectionately known as Christkindl, who delivers children's presents under the Christmas tree on 24 December). During the festive season, a special post office handles the almost two million letters posted around the world.

Sleeping

Gasthof Bauer PENSION €
(☎07252-544 41; www.bauer-gasthof.at; Josefgasse 7; s/d €46/82; P 🛜) Run by the same family since 1880, this cosy 14-room pension sits on a little Steyr river island. The rooms are simple but comfy, and there's a leafy chestnut-shaded garden and a restaurant (open Wednesday to Sunday, mains €8 to €13) serving fresh fare such as locally caught trout. It's a 1km walk northwest of the Stadtplatz. Cash only.

Camping am Fluss CAMPGROUND €
(☎07252-780 08; www.campingamfluss.at; Kematmüllerstrasse 1a; camp sites per adult/child/tent €6.50/3/3; P 🛜) On the banks of the Enns, 3.3km northeast of the centre, this tree-shaded campground has 50 pitches, a playground, activities such as canoeing and tennis, plus repair facilities and bike storage for cyclists. Take bus 1 from the centre.

★ **Hotel Christkindlwirt** HOTEL €€
(☎07252-521 84; www.christkindlwirt.at; Christkindlweg 6, Christkindl; s/d from €83/120; P 🛜) Tucked behind the church in Christkindl, this boutique hotel has contemporary, warm-coloured rooms, many with balconies overlooking the river. Candles create a restful feel in the grotto-like spa, which has a sauna, a steam room and treatments such as shiatsu massage. The panoramic terrace of its restaurant (mains €12.50 to €27) has sweeping valley views.

Minichmayr HOTEL €€
(☎07252-534 10; www.hotel-minichmayr.at; Haratzmüllerstrasse 1-3; s/d from €86/128; 🛜) At the confluence of the Steyr and Enns Rivers, this 500-year-old property has fresh, modernised rooms with light cream tones that are elegant in their simplicity, and a superb Austrian restaurant (mains €9.50 to €16) with intricately carved honey-coloured wood panelling and stupendous town and river views. Views also extend from the upstairs spa sheltering a Jacuzzi and steam room.

Stadthotel Styria HISTORIC HOTEL €€
(☎07252-515 510; www.stadthotel-steyr.at; Stadtplatz 40; s/d/ste from €97/148/196; P 🛜) Steyr's most historic hotel occupies a 400-year-old town house right on the Stadtplatz. Many of the rooms have original features, from period furnishings to beams; a frescoed breakfast room overlooks the rooftops. Rooms at the rear of the building are more modern but two have large private terraces. There's a sauna and hammam for guests' use.

Gasthof Alpenblick HOTEL €€
(☎07259-2552; www.gasthof-alpenblick.at; Frauenhofenstrasse 23, Sierning; s/d from €51/88; P 🛜) Most of the 16 shiny, spacious rooms at this modern guesthouse have balconies that take advantage of the surrounding mountains. Its *Vinothek* (wine shop) sells local wines and liqueurs; you can also try them at its excellent restaurant (open Friday to Tuesday; mains €9 to €22), which has several vegetarian options such as root-vegetable strudel. It's 10km west of Steyr.

Eating

★Knapp am Eck BISTRO €€
(☎07252-762 69; www.knappameck.at; Wehrgrabengasse 15; mains €11-25; ⏰11am-2pm & 6-11pm Tue-Sat) A cobbled lane shadows the Steyr River to this locavore bistro, which utilises organic, seasonal produce to create dishes such as tender lamb with polenta, and sage-stuffed pork. By night, candles and lanterns illuminate the ivy-covered walls, trailing roses and chestnut trees in the garden. Its three-course lunch (midweek only) costs €21.

Rahofer AUSTRIAN €€
(☎07252-546 06; www.restaurant-rahofer.at; Stadtplatz 9; restaurant mains €14.50-28.50, cafe dishes €2.80-4.50; ⏰restaurant 11.30am-1.30pm & 6.30-9.30pm Tue-Sat, cafe 9am-6.30pm Tue-Thu & Sat, to 11pm Fri) In the centre of Steyr, Rahofer has a classic cafe across from the Enns River, a traditional restaurant opening off the Stadtplatz, and, between them, a lovely sheltered courtyard that's filled with tables in summer. Cakes such as *Gugelhupf* (yeast-based cake baked in a circular mould) are served at its cafe; Austrian fare at its restaurant includes *Tafelspitz*.

Orangerie im Schlosspark EUROPEAN €€
(☎07252-740 74; www.orangerie-steyr.at; Blumauergasse 1; mains €15-25; ⏰11.30am-10pm Thu-Mon May-Sep, 11.30am-2pm & 5.30-10pm Thu-Mon Oct-Apr;) This beautifully converted 18th-century orangery opens onto a leafy terrace facing the Schlosspark. The kitchen prepares fresh, seasonal dishes ranging from chanterelle tagliatelle to roast guinea fowl with sweet potato and asparagus. During the week, its two-course lunch menus (€8.50 to €10.50) always offer a vegetarian option.

Gasthof Mader AUSTRIAN €€
(☎07252-533 58; www.mader.at; Stadtplatz 36; mains €13-31, 3-/4-/5-course dinner menus €33.50/40.50/50; ⏰kitchen 5-10pm Mon, 8am-10pm Tue-Sat, to noon Sun, bar to midnight Mon-Sat) With its Gothic vaults, frescoed *Schubertstüberl* (parlour) and arcaded inner courtyard, Mader is historic dining at its best. Specialities such as crisp roast pork with dumplings or trout served with parsley potatoes figure on the thoroughly Austrian menu. Sunday's all-you-can-eat buffet brunch costs €22. Upstairs are a dozen comfortable rooms (single/double/family €99/142/166).

Drinking & Nightlife

Strandbar BAR
(☎0660 569 5980; https://strandbar.business.site; Roseneggstrasse 16; ⏰9am-9pm mid-May–mid-Sep) During summer, head 3.5km west of town to this local secret, a wooden shack hidden in the forest footsteps from a white-sand beach on the Steyr River. Sit at its outdoor picnic tables to down regional Zipfer beers and dine on whole fish (pike or zander), pork and beef ribs grilled on the barbecue (mains €6.50 to €13).

Information

The **tourist office** (☎07252-532 29-0; www.steyr.info; Stadtplatz 27; ⏰9am-6pm Mon-Fri, to noon Sat) is on the main square in the *Rathaus* (town hall).

Getting There & Away

BUS

City and regional buses depart from the *Hauptbahnhof*, a 200m walk east of the old town via a pedestrian footbridge across the Enns River.

CAR & MOTORCYCLE

Steyr is on the B115, the road branching from the A1 and running southeast to Leoben.

TRAIN

Direct trains link Steyr with Linz (€8.80, 55 minutes, hourly Monday to Saturday, fewer Sunday). Most trains for Wels (€13.80, 1½ hours, hourly Monday to Saturday, fewer Sunday) require a change in St Valentin.

Bad Hall

☎07258 / POP 5295

A sleepy spa town 18km west of Steyr, Bad Hall's big draw is the Mediterrana Therme, hailed for the waters' therapeutic properties.

Kurpark PARK
(⏰dawn-dusk) Opposite the Mediterrana Therme, this 34-hectare park features exotic and native woodlands, aromatic gardens, blooming flower beds and regularly changing art installations. There are 40km of trails, and playgrounds for the kids. To inhale the spa's iodised salt for free, head for the central pavilion, where 1000L of the stuff filters through twig walls every hour.

Mediterrana Therme SPA
(www.eurothermen.at; Kurhausstrasse 10; day ticket adult/child €21.50/16; ⏰9am-midnight) The iodine-rich, 40°C waters that gush from Bad

Hall's thermal springs are hailed for their therapeutic properties. Outside there are massage jets and mountain views, while inside an iodine steam room, a columned Roman bath and whirlpools pummel you into a blissfully relaxed state. A splash pool keeps tots amused.

Ferienhof Gangl FARMSTAY €
(☎07258-40 18; Mandorferstrasse 28, Adlwang; d/apt €86/144; P) Leopold Höllhuber sells award-winning potent schnapps, along with apple juice and *Most* at Gangl, a courtyard-facing *Vierkanter* farmhouse with pine-furnished rooms where you can also spend a very comfortable night. Kids can romp about in the playground.

Information

The **tourist office** (☎07258-7200-0; www.badhall.at; Kurpromenade 1; ⏰8am-5.30pm Mon-Fri, 9am-noon & 1.30-5.30pm Sat, 2-5.30pm Sun Apr-Oct, shorter hours Nov-Mar) is 200m southeast of the Mediterrana Therme.

Getting There & Away

Buses link Bad Hall with Steyr (€5.50, 35 minutes, hourly Monday to Saturday, every two hours Sunday).

Nationalpark Kalkalpen

This little-known, almost untouched wilderness of rugged limestone mountains, high moors and over 80% spruce, fir and beech forest is home to the elusive golden eagle and lynx. Bordering Styria, this is Austria's second-largest national park (after Hohe Tauern) at 208 sq km. Its valleys and gorges cut through classic alpine landscapes, dominated by **Hoher Nock** (1963m).

Activities

Nationalpark Kalkalpen is a paradise for hikers, cyclists and rock climbers in summer and cross-country skiers in winter. Kompass map 70 (1:50,000) covers the park and its trails in detail. Other activities in the park's vicinity include paragliding, white-water rafting and caving.

Wurbauer Kogel OUTDOORS
(☎07564-5275; www.wurbauerkogel.at; Kühbergstrasse 2, Windischgarsten; toboggan or Alpine Coaster per ride €6.50, incl chairlift €9.50, mountain-bike trail pass/bike hire per 4hr €25/50; ⏰9am-6pm May-Oct) Activity base Wurbauer Kogel has a 1400m-long toboggan, reaching speeds of up to 80km per hour, and a gentler 800m-long Alpine Coaster reaching 40km per hour. Also here are four downhill mountain-bike trails, including ramps, drops and wall rides, plus hiking trails, via ferrata, and a six-storey (21m) panoramic tower overlooking the national park.

Pro Adventures ADVENTURE SPORTS
(☎0664 4412 111; www.pro-adventures.com; Gaisriegl 8, Vorderstoder; ⏰by reservation) Pro Adventures runs a diverse range of guided activities, among them white-water rafting (per day €79), river snorkelling (per half-day €55), via ferrata (per day €79) and caving (per half-day from €45), and hires canoes (per day €55). Multiday courses include igloo building (per two days €150) and hiking/cross-country skiing tours (from €299). Confirm meeting points when booking.

Mountain-hut accommodation can be arranged; ask for seasonal prices.

Flugschule ADVENTURE SPORTS
(☎0664 300 1410; www.fliegmit.at; Mitterstoder 57, Hinterstoder; 20min tandem flight €140, 2-day training course €600; ⏰by reservation) This flying school runs paragliding and hang-gliding tandem flights, and intensive instruction courses (in English and German) so you can fly solo. Flights mostly take place in the Hinterstoder ski resort area but also go to Nationalpark Kalkalpen; confirm the meeting point when you book.

Wurzeralm SKIING
(www.hiwu.at; Pyhrn 33, Wurzeralm; day pass adult/child €41.50/21.50; ⏰lifts 8.30am-4.30pm Dec-early Mar) A cable car whisks you from Wurzeralm's car park to the ski area, sitting between 800m and 1870m, where 22km of slopes are serviced by seven ski lifts. There's a play/training area for kids. Lifts don't operate in summer, but you can still hike here.

Hinterstoder SKIING, HIKING
(www.hiwu.at; Hinterstoder 21, Hinterstoder; day pass adult/child €44.50/23; ⏰8.30am-4.30pm Dec-late Mar, 8.45am-4.30pm late May–mid-Oct) Against a spectacular backdrop of rugged peaks, between 600m and 2000m, Hinterstoder offers 40km of ski slopes served by 14 lifts. Summer activities include via ferrata, hiking through alpine meadows and mountain biking (though note not all lifts accommodate bikes).

Sleeping & Eating

Landhotel Stockerwirt HOTEL €€
(☎07564-821 400; www.stockerwirt.net; Vorderstoder 2, Vorderstoder; d/ste from €130/164; P 📶 🏊) Glorious alpine views surround Stockerwirt, even from the heated indoor pool and sauna area, framed by a wall of glass. Rooms are split between an old-fashioned chalet-style building and state-of-the-art modern building; most rooms in both buildings have balconies. Local hunters, farmers and foragers supply its restaurant (closed Mondays), which has summer barbecues in the gardens. It's 30km south of Molln.

Hotel Freunde der Natur HOTEL €€
(☎07563-681; www.naturfreundehotel.at; Wiesenweg 7, Spital am Pyhrn; s/d from €67/105; P 📶) Handily positioned for Wurzeralm and the Nationalpark Kalkalpen, this 70-room chalet-style property overlooking the mountains offers great facilities including a spa area with saunas and a steam room, a drying room and ski storage, as well as family-friendly amenities such as a playground, a kids' menu at the traditional Austrian restaurant, and interconnecting rooms.

Das Rössl AUSTRIAN €€
(☎07562-205 55; www.dasroessl.at; Hauptstrasse 9, Windischgarsten; mains €11-17; ⊙kitchen 11am-2pm & 5-10pm Mon, Tue & Thu-Sat, 11am-8pm Sun, bar 11am-midnight Mon, Tue & Thu-Sat, 11am-11pm Sun; 👪) The pick of places to dine in charming Windischgarsten, this oyster-grey guesthouse cooks up hearty dishes including rib-eye steak, riesling-marinated pork and river trout. Carb-loading for outdoor adventures isn't a problem – every main comes with potato salad. Upstairs are 26 simple but comfortable rooms (doubles from €84); breakfast is available every day for overnight guests and included in the rate.

Information

For more information on activities, visit the ultramodern **Nationalpark Zentrum Molln** (☎07584-3651; www.kalkalpen.at; Nationalparkallee 1, Molln; ⊙9am-4pm Mon-Fri, to 2pm Sat & Sun May-Oct, shorter hours rest of year), near the northern entrance to the park, or **Tourismusverband Pyhrn-Priel** (☎07562-526 699; www.urlaubsregion-pyhrn-priel.at; Hauptstrasse 28, Windischgarsten; ⊙8am-5pm Mon-Fri, 9am-noon Sat & Sun May-Oct, shorter hours Nov-Apr), to the south of the park. Staff at both information centres can arrange guided tours in English.

Getting There & Away

Direct buses run from Steyr to Molln (€6.50, 50 minutes, seven daily) and on to Windischgarsten (€7.10, one hour). From Windischgarsten local buses run to Hinterstoder and Wurzeralm during the skiing and hiking seasons.

To really get out and explore the area, however, you'll need your own wheels.

Wels

☎07242 / POP 61,235

Settled since the Neolithic era and a strategic Roman stronghold, Wels is the largest town in the Traunviertel. While there are few real sights, this is a handy base for exploring rural Upper Austria. The centre is a pleasure to stroll through, with a clutch of Renaissance and baroque town houses hiding inner courtyards and walled gardens. In summer the town springs to life with markets and open-air concerts.

Sights

Stadtplatz HISTORIC SITE
Wels' main square is framed by slender town houses, many of which conceal arcaded inner courtyards. Particularly attractive is the ivy-clad courtyard at No 18, nurturing palms, rhododendrons and Japanese umbrella trees. At the front, glance up to spy the 2000-year-old **Römermedallion** (Roman medallion) relief.

Nearby at No 24, the Renaissance **Haus der Salome Alt** sports a trompe l'oeil facade and takes its name from one-time occupant Salome Alt, mistress of Salzburg's most famous prince-archbishop, Wolf Dietrich von Raitenau.

The stout **Ledererturm** (Tanner's Tower), built in 1326, overshadows the western end of the Stadtplatz and is the last remnant of the town's fortifications.

Burg Wels CASTLE
(www.wels.at; Burggasse 13; adult/child €4.70/2.10; ⊙10am-5pm Tue-Fri, 2-5pm Sat, 10am-4pm Sun) Set around a quiet, geranium-filled garden, this castle is where Emperor Maximilian I drew his last breath in 1519. The folksy museum contains everything from cannonballs to Biedermeier costumes. Must-sees include the horse-drawn cider press and the circular room that's a shrine to baking, with walls smothered in animal- and flower-shaped pastries and gigantic pretzels.

Stadtpfarrkirche CHURCH

(www.dioezese-linz.at; Pfarrgasse 27; ⌚8am-6pm) Built in the 14th century on the site of a wooden chapel first mentioned in 888, the refreshingly simple Stadtpfarrkirche is noteworthy for its Gothic stained glass.

Sleeping

Boutique Hotel Hauser BOUTIQUE HOTEL €€

(☎07242-454 09; www.hotelhauser.com; Bäckergasse 7; s/d from €96/123;) With its polished service, clean-lined contemporary rooms and seasonal rooftop pool, sauna and terrace, this central boutique hotel outshines most of Wels' midrangers. Organic and regional produce, homemade cakes and jams spice up the breakfast buffet, and guests can refresh with free tea and fruit throughout the day.

Hotel Ploberger HOTEL €€

(☎07242-629 41; www.hotel-ploberger.at; Kaiser-Josef-Platz 21; s/d from €106/141; P) In the heart of town, Hotel Ploberger has 92 fresh, contemporary rooms in monochrome hues, some with comforts such as Nespresso coffeemakers. The sauna and open fire keep things cosy in winter.

Eating

★**Löwenkeller** INTERNATIONAL €€

(☎07242-797 85; www.loewenkeller.at; Hafergasse 1; mains €17-32, 2-/3-course lunch menus €10.90/14.90, 3-/4-/5-course dinner menus €45/50/56; ⌚11.30am-2pm & 6-10pm Tue-Fri, 6-10pm Sat) With its exposed stone, starchy white linen and polished service, Löwenkeller is by far the most sophisticated restaurant in town. Dishes such as poached trout with wild garlic risotto, roast guinea fowl with locally picked forest mushroom sauce, and salt-baked Upper Austrian lamb with semolina dumplings are presented with flair, and paired with Austrian wines from the cellar.

Gasthaus zur Linde AUSTRIAN €€

(☎07242-460 23; www.gasthaus-zur-linde.at; Ringstrasse 45; mains €8-17; ⌚11.30am-2pm & 5.30-9.30pm Tue-Sat;) Sizzling and stirring for the past 200 years, this family-run place radiates old-fashioned warmth. It dishes up Austrian classics alongside seasonal treats such as asparagus in spring and game in autumn, with four vegetarian dishes to choose from each day. The weekday two-course lunch menu is great value at €9.20.

WORTH A TRIP

ABOVE THE TREETOPS

Tarzan wannabes can take a head-spinning walk above the treetops at **Baumkronenweg** (www.baumkronenweg.at; Knechtelsdorf 1, Kopfing; adult/child €11/7.50; ⌚10am-6pm Apr-early Nov), a canopy boardwalk in Kopfing, 21km east of Schärding. Stretching 2.5km, the raised path snakes above misty spruce trees and passes lookout towers, rope bridges and platforms that afford bird's-eye perspectives over the forest. You can sleep among the trees at the **Baumhotel** (☎07763-228 90; www.baumkronenweg.at; half-board adult/child from €81/70; P).

Information

Information on the city is available from the **tourist office** (☎07242-235-0; www.wels.at; Stadtplatz 44; ⌚9am-noon & 12.30-5pm Mon-Thu, to 1pm Fri) on the Stadtplatz.

Getting There & Away

Trains and buses arrive at the *Hauptbahnhof*, 1.25km north of the Stadtplatz.

The town is on the InterCity (IC) and EuroCity (EC) express rail route between Linz (€5.50, 15 minutes, up to six hourly) and Salzburg (€23.30, one hour, hourly). Other regular services include Passau (Germany; €16, one hour, up to three per hour) and Vienna (€34.90, 1¾ hours, up to three per hour).

Kremsmünster

☎07583 / POP 6585

Kremsmünster would be just another working Austrian town were it not for its majestic Benedictine abbey, looming large above the fertile Krems Valley.

Sights

★**Stift Kremsmünster** ABBEY

(☎07583-5275-0; www.stift-kremsmuenster.at; Stift 1; tours adult/child €8/3; ⌚tours by reservation 10am, 11am, 2pm, 3.30pm & 4pm May-Oct, 11am, 2pm & 3.30pm Nov-Apr) Kremsmünster's enormous Benedictine abbey dates from 777, but was given a baroque facelift in the 18th century. Elaborate stucco and frescoes shape the long, low **Bibliothek** (library), where shelves creak under 160,000 volumes, and the **Kaisersaal** (Emperor's Hall). The most prized piece in the **Schatzkammer** (treasury) is the gold Tassilo Chalice, which the Duke of Bavaria donated to the monks in about 780. You can visit all three on a one-hour guided tour (available in English).

Stiftskirche CHURCH
(Stift 1; ⌚8am-6pm) You don't have to tour the Stift Kremsmünster (p175) to enter its Stiftskirche. The marvellously over-the-top baroque church is criss-crossed with white stuccowork, draped in Flemish tapestries and festooned with dark, brooding paintings.

Eating

Schupf'n AUSTRIAN €
(☎07258-7073; www.schupfn.at; Oberro 10, Rohr im Kremstal; mains €10-15; ⌚11am-8.30pm Fri-Sun; 👪) Overlooking farmland 5km east of Kremsmünster, rustic Schupf'n has a wood-lined dining room where welcoming staff in traditional Austrian dress serve up robust dishes made from local farm produce, such as pork fillet with sauerkraut and sour cream sauce, *Käsespätzle* noodles with Mondsee cheese, and roast onion and *Mostschober* (sponge soaked with spiced apple cider) for dessert.

Getting There & Away

Direct trains link Kremsmünster with Linz (€7.40, 40 minutes, hourly).

Buses serve Bad Hall (€3.30, five minutes, up to three per hour Monday to Saturday, hourly Sunday) and Wels (€4.50, 30 minutes, seven daily Monday to Saturday only).

THE MÜHLVIERTEL

The Mühlviertel is a remote, beautiful region of misty granite hills, thick woodlands and valleys speckled with chalk-white *Steinbloass* farmhouses. The scenery is redolent of the not-so-distant Czech Republic. This corner of Upper Austria is well worth a visit for its Gothic architecture, warm-hearted locals, and total peace and quiet.

Freistadt

☎07942 / POP 7910

Just 10km from the Czech border as the crow flies, Freistadt has some of the best-preserved medieval fortifications in Austria. Stroll through the town's narrow streets to gate towers and the gardens that have taken root in the original moat.

Sights

Schlossmuseum MUSEUM
(☎07942-722 74; www.museum-freistadt.at; Schlosshof 2; adult/child €6/2; ⌚9am-5pm Mon-Fri, 2-5pm Sat & Sun Jun-Sep, 9am-noon & 2-5pm Mon-Fri, 2-5pm Sat & Sun Oct-May) The city's 14th-century castle, with a square tower topped by a tapering red-tiled roof, harbours this museum, exhibiting 600 works of engraved painted glass, as well as local ceramics, crafts and folklore displays. Climb the 50m Bergfried tower for far-reaching views over Freistadt.

Stadtmauern WALLS
Freistadt's *Altstadt* sits within its sturdy 14th-century city walls complete with gate towers such as the medieval **Linzertor** and skeletal **Böhmertor**, which reflect its past need for strong defences as an important staging point on the salt route to Bohemia. The moat encircling the town is now given over to gardens and allotments.

Hauptplatz SQUARE
Freistadt's focal point is the elongated Hauptplatz, jammed between the old city walls. The square has some ornate buildings and a Gothic **Stadtpfarrkirche** (Parish Church; www.dioezese-linz.at; Hauptplatz; ⌚8am-6pm) capped with a baroque tower. Some of the houses along Waaggasse, just west of the Hauptplatz, are embellished with sgraffito mural designs.

Sleeping & Eating

Pension Pirklbauer PENSION €
(☎07942-724 40; www.pension-pirklbauer.at; Höllgasse 2-4; s/d from €32/52) Nudging up against medieval Linzertor is this charmingly old-school pension. Christine is a dab hand at making her guests feel at home, whether on the rooftop terrace overlooking the town's garden-filled moat or in the country-cottage rooms with pine wood, floral fabrics and squeaky-clean bathrooms.

Hotel Goldener Adler HISTORIC HOTEL €€
(☎07942-207 990; www.hotels-freistadt.at; Salzgasse 1; s/d/tr €68/110/147; P 📶) Polished stone slabs, wrought-iron banisters and vaulted passages crammed with antique wagons and spinning wheels hint at this hotel's 700-year history (it's the 1841 birthplace of artist Karl Kronberger). Some of the 30 rooms have four-poster beds. Unwind in the sauna and whirlpool, or tuck into the famous beer-marinated Bohemian pork shoulder in the beer garden (mains €8 to €16).

LOCAL KNOWLEDGE

COMMUNAL BREWERY

Freistadt is a *Braucommune*, a town where the citizens actually own their brewery – when you buy a house, you automatically buy a share of your favourite tipple. Ownership is limited to the 149 households within the town walls, but if you have the spare change and *really* like your beer, properties sell for upwards of €400,000. Realistically, the brewery cannot be taken over, as the business would have to buy the whole town in order to take control.

The arrangement started way back in 1777 when the brewery opened. In the ensuing centuries the lucky owners would receive their share of the profits in liquid form, which would be distributed in *Eimer Bier* containers holding 56L. Each owner might get up to 130 containers! Nowadays, for better or worse, owners get a cash payment of equivalent value (which, on Friday and Saturday nights, often goes straight back to the brewery).

Practically every bar in town serves the local brew, including the **Freistadt Brauhaus** (☎07942-727 72; www.freistaedter-bier.at; Brauhausstrasse 2; mains €10.50-15; ⏲kitchen 9am-11pm, bar to midnight), so it's not hard to see why the brewery remains a profitable business. If you'd like to learn more about Freistadt beer and stock up, nip into the **brewery shop** (www.freistaedter-bier.at; Brauhausstrasse 2; ⏲8am-5pm Mon-Fri, 9am-noon Sat).

Gasthaus Ratsherrnstube AUSTRIAN €€
(☎07942-724 39; www.ratsherrnstube-freistadt.stadtausstellung.at; Hauptplatz 1; mains €9-16; ⏲kitchen 9am-11pm Tue-Sun, bar to midnight; 👪) Right on Freistadt's main square, with terrace tables in summer, this large, traditional guesthouse turns out hearty Austrian fare including seven different schnitzels, paprika-spiced *Müllerwurst* sausage with sauerkraut, pan-fried zander with parsley potatoes and *Käsenocken* (cheese dumplings). Children can order smaller versions of adults' dishes.

Drinking & Nightlife

★**Suchan** COFFEE
(www.suchan-freistadt.com; Pfarrplatz 3; ⏲8am-3pm Wed-Sun, 9am-noon Sun) Suchan's coffee has become so popular throughout Austria and even Berlin that it's expanded its roasting operation just outside town, using unmixed (single-origin), slow-drum and air-cooling techniques. All beans are organic and sourced from small-scale fair-trade farms. Along with coffee, its light, bright cafe serves breakfast, lunch and cakes, which you can enjoy on the sunny terrace in summer.

Information

The **Mühlviertler Kernland Tourist Office** (☎07942-757 00; www.muehlviertel.at/wo/region-freistadt; Waaggasse 6; ⏲8.30am-12.30pm & 1-5pm Mon-Fri) provides information on the town and its surrounds.

Getting There & Away

Freistadt is on a direct rail route from Linz (€9.70, one hour, every two hours). This line then wriggles its way to Prague (€19, 3¼ hours, four direct services daily), 205km north; Czech rail fares are lower than those in Austria, so you can save money by waiting and buying (in Czech currency, koruna) your onward tickets once you've crossed the border.

Frequent trains travel between Freistadt and Kefermarkt (€2.50, 10 minutes, up to two per hour).

The B310, which connects to the A7 motorway to Linz, runs adjacent to the walled centre and then continues its way northwards towards Prague.

THE INNVIERTEL

Ping-ponged between Bavaria and Austria over the centuries, the Innviertel is a fertile farming region sliced in two by the Inn River, whose banks are a drawcard for cyclists in summer. There's beautiful baroque and Gothic architecture, most notably in Schärding.

Schärding

☎07712 / POP 5255

Schärding is a storybook-pretty town on the Inn, with peaceful riverfront walks and a baroque centre studded with merchants' houses in myriad sugared-almond shades, including the identically gabled properties lined up along the Silberzeile (Silver Row).

WORTH A TRIP

TRAPPIST BREWS

The little riverside village of Engelhartszell an der Donau is home to one of only eight licensed Trappist breweries outside Belgium, and the only one in Austria. At the 1293-founded abbey **Stift Engelszell** (www.stift-engelszell.at; Stiftstrasse 6; ⌚church 8am-7pm Apr-Oct, to 5pm Nov-Mar, shop 9am-5pm Apr-Oct, shorter hours rest of year), you can purchase monk-made brews (dark Gregorius, amber Benno and blond Nivard); the shop also sells apple juice, liqueurs and cheeses produced here by the monks. Adjoining the shop is the abbey's gorgeous rococo church, completed in 1764.

Hotel Forstinger HOTEL €€
(☎07712-2302-0; www.hotel-forstinger.at; Unterer Stadtplatz 3; s/d/apt from €89/161/189; P❄📶) Standing head and shoulders above most places in town is antique-meets-modern Hotel Forstinger, with a choice of tastefully appointed rooms with either a contemporary aesthetic or period features. Family-friendly apartments sleeping up to four people come with kitchenettes; some have roof terraces. Organic breakfasts include vegetarian and vegan options, and are served in the flower-filled garden or glass conservatory.

★**Lukas Restaurant** AUSTRIAN €€€
(☎0664 341 3285; www.lukas-restaurant.at; Unterer Stadtplatz 7; 4-/6-course menu €75/99, with wines €113/167; ⌚6pm-midnight Tue-Sat) 🍃 White walls, bare floorboards, sheepskin-covered chairs and copper lighting set the stage for chef Lukas Kienbauer's innovative Austrian cuisine. In the full-length open kitchen, he utilises local meat, river fish and plants grown on his farm or foraged nearby in no-choice menus that might feature spruce macarons, nettle-wrapped zander parcels with wild thyme foam, and alpine honey–marinated pork belly.

ℹ Information

The **tourist office** (☎07712-4300-0; www.schaerding.at; Innbruckstrasse 29; ⌚10am-5pm Mon-Fri, 9am-noon Sat), near the bridge spanning the river into Germany, has a bike service point with pumps, repair kits and an electric charging point.

ℹ Getting There & Away

If you have your own transport, the approach to Schärding from Linz, via Engelhartszell along the Danube, is beautiful and certainly off the beaten track.

From April to October, an even more leisurely alternative is a one-hour **boat trip** (☎07712-7350; www.innschifffahrt.at; Leonhard-Kaiser-Weg 1; one way adult/child €10/5, return €14/7; ⌚11am & 2pm Tue-Sun Apr-Oct) between Ingling (across the river from Passau, Germany) and Schärding. Bikes are transported for free.

Trains connect Schärding with Linz (€16, 1¼ hours, five direct services Monday to Saturday, four Sunday).

Geinberg

In the heart of rural Upper Austria, it's a surreal experience to soak in a bath-warm Caribbean saltwater lagoon, as underwater music plays and palms sway at one of Austria's top spas, **Therme Geinberg** (☎07723-8501; www.therme-geinberg.at; Thermenplatz 1; day ticket adult/child Mon-Fri €26.70/19.60, Sat & Sun €28.40/21.30; ⌚9am-10pm Sat-Thu, to 11pm Fri May-Sep, 9am-10pm Sun-Thu, to 11pm Fri & Sat Oct-Apr). Saunas imitate a starry sky or smell deliciously of coconuts. After a steam, the icy sleet shower is an abrupt shock. Luxury accommodation is available (doubles from €318).

Its five pools with fresh water, thermal spring water and saltwater span 3000 sq metres, with a temperature range of between 26°C to 36°C, along with spa treatments (including massages), and several restaurants and cafes.

Trains link Geinberg with Schärding (€9.70, 1½ hours, five daily), which requires a change in Neumarkt-Kallham and/or Ried im Innkreis, which has connections to Linz.

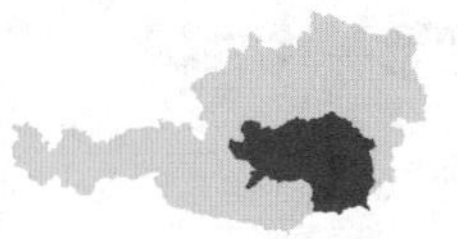

Styria

Includes ➡

Best Places to Eat

- Aiola Upstairs (p188)
- Der Steirer (p188)
- El Pescador (p188)
- T.O.M R (p194)
- Die Weinerei im Baderhaus (p197)
- Landhauskeller (p188)

Best Places to Stay

- Baderhaus (p197)
- Hotel Wiesler (p186)
- Schlossberg Hotel (p186)
- Loisium Südsteiermark (p192)
- Stadthotel Brunner (p204)
- JUFA Hotel Schloss Röthelstein (p201)

Why Go?

Austria's second-largest province is a picturesque combination of culture, architecture, rolling hills, vine-covered slopes and mountains. Graz, Austria's second-largest city, is Styria's photogenic and fabulously relaxed capital. Head south from Graz and you're in wine country, dubbed 'Styrian Tuscany'. This is also the land of *Kürbiskernöl* – the strong, dark pumpkin-seed oil ubiquitous in Styrian cooking.

The eastern stretch of Styria is dotted with rejuvenating thermal spas and centuries-old castles. If you're a fan of the former, Bad Blumau is a mandatory stop, not only to take the waters but also to appreciate its unusual architecture, designed by Friedensreich Hundertwasser. If you prefer castles, Schloss Riegersburg is one of Austria's best.

In the north and west, Styria's landscape changes to cold, fast-flowing alpine rivers, towering mountains and carved valleys. Highlights are Admont Abbey, charming Murau and Erzberg's open-cast mine. The very northwestern reaches of Styria stretch into Salzkammergut.

When to Go

- Summer has perfect weather for outdoor activities like cycling, hiking on mountain trails and open-air swimming. Come between June and September to make the most of the sunshine and warmth.
- The grape harvest occurs in early autumn, so September and October are ideal for taking in festivals along the Styrian wine roads.
- December to February is when the ski fields swing into action (although there is glacier skiing year-round).

Styria Highlights

❶ **Graz** (p181) Admiring Schloss Eggenberg, the capital's stunning Renaissance palace and museum, before exploring the city's smart restaurants, lively bars and late-night caverns.

❷ **Benedictine Abbey** (p200) Wandering Admont's spectacular baroque abbey and its library – the largest in the world.

❸ **Erzberg** (p199) Tripping underground, or overground, at Eisenerz' ironworks and mine.

❹ **Schladming** (p202) Hiking the trails or glacier gazing around this laid-back alpine resort.

❺ **Wine Roads** (p192) Tasting your way through 'Styrian Tuscany', the vineyards of southern Styria.

❻ **Genuss Regal Vinofaktur** (p193) Sampling local produce in Vogau and getting to know your Grauburgunder from your Grüner.

❼ **Johnsbach** (p201) Discovering the strange and touching beauty of one of Austria's earliest mountain-climbing centres.

Getting There & Away

BUS

Styria's bus services offer extended transport options beyond the main train line hubs. For timetables and routes, the website www.postbus.at is the place to start. Services fanning out of Graz depart from the central bus station (p190). Bus departures to Mariazell, which isn't on the train line, are integrated with train arrivals at Bruck an der Mur. To Eisenerz, integrated bus services leave from Leoben. For Admont and the Gesäuse, the towns of Liezen and Hieflau form the main bus-transfer points. Österreiche Bundesbahn (ÖBB) railway buses connect Graz' *Hauptbahnhof* (main train station) and Klagenfurt.

CAR

The A2, from Vienna to Villach in Carinthia, runs through southern Styria, passing just below Graz, while the A9 runs an almost north–south course through the middle of Styria, making it straightforward to travel from Linz and Salzburg to Graz. The A9 also connects Graz with Slovenia, 40km to the south.

TRAIN

Styria's train lines are relatively sparse; the main line between Carinthia and Vienna passes well north of Graz through the region's main railhead, Bruck an der Mur. Direct trains connect Graz and Salzburg, whereas travelling to Linz generally involves backtracking to Vienna. Check out the website www.oebb.at for information.

Getting Around

Regional and city transport is run by **Verbund Linie** (050 678 910; www.verbundlinie.at) and is based on a system of zones and time tickets. Tickets can be bought from machines for one to 22 zones; the price rises from a single trip in one zone (€2.40, valid for one hour) to 24-hour passes for one (€5.30) or multiple zones (eg €8.60 for four zones to Bärnbach). Weekly and monthly passes are also available.

In Graz, **Mobilzentral** (050 678 910; www.mobilzentral.at; Jakoministrasse 1; 8am-6pm Mon-Fri, 9am-1pm Sat; 1, 3, 4, 5, 6, 7, 13 Jakominiplatz) is a useful store of information on Styrian regional buses.

GRAZ

0316 / POP 286,290

Austria's second-largest city is its most relaxed and an instant heart-stealer, with abundant parkland, a sea of red rooftops and a narrow but fast-flowing river loudly gushing through its centre. A very beautiful bluff – connected to the centre by steps, a funicular and a glass lift – is the city's signature attribute. Architecturally, Graz hints at nearby Italy with its Renaissance courtyards and baroque palaces. That said, there's a youthful energy here too, with a handful of edgily modern buildings, a vibrant arts scene and upbeat, student-fuelled nightlife. This extends to both sides of the Mur, although the Lend district, across from the historic centre, skews young and edgy.

Sights

★ Kunsthaus Graz — GALLERY

(0316-8017 92 00; www.museum-joanneum.at; Lendkai 1; adult/child €9.50/3.50; 10am-5pm Tue-Sun; 1, 3, 6, 7 Südtiroler Platz) Designed by British architects Peter Cook and Colin Fournier, this world-class contemporary-art space is known as the 'friendly alien' by locals. The building is signature Cook, a photovoltaic-skinned sexy biomorphic blob that is at once completely at odds with its pristine historic surroundings but sits rather lyrically within it as well. Exhibitions, which usually change every three to four months, focus on contemporary arts and themes, often on issues relating to current political, social and cultural life.

★ Schloss Eggenberg — PALACE

(0316-8017 95 32; www.museum-joanneum.at; Eggenberger Allee 90; adult/child €15/6; tours hourly 10am-4pm, except 1pm Tue-Sun Apr-Oct, exhibitions 10am-5pm Tue-Sun Apr-Oct; 1 Schloss Eggenberg) Graz' elegant palace was created for the Eggenberg dynasty in 1625 by Giovanni Pietro de Pomis (1565–1633) at the request of Johann Ulrich (1568–1634). Admission is via a highly worthwhile guided tour during which you learn about the idiosyncrasies of each room, the stories told by the frescoes and about the Eggenberg family itself.

Johann Ulrich rose from ordinariness to become governor of Inner Austria in 1625, at a time when Inner Austria was a powerful province that included Styria, Carinthia, and parts of Slovenia and northern Italy. His baroque palace was built on a Gothic predecessor (which explains an interesting Gothic chapel in one section of the palace, viewed from a glass cube) and has numerous features of the Italian Renaissance, such as the magnificent courtyard arcades.

The guided tour (available in English or German) takes you through the 24 *Prunkräume* (staterooms), which, like everything else in the palace and gardens, are based on astronomy, the zodiac, and classical or religious mythology. The tour either ends or starts at the **Planet Hall**, which is a riot of white stuccowork and baroque frescoes. The ticket for the tour (State Room Ticket) also allows you to visit the Schloss Eggenberg Museums and the rest of the 18 Joanneum museums within a 24-hour period from the time of purchase.

Schloss Eggenberg Museums — MUSEUM

(Alte Galerie & Museums; 0316-8017 97 70; www.museum-joanneum.at/alte-galerie; Eggenberger Allee 90; adult/child €9.50/3.50; 10am-5pm

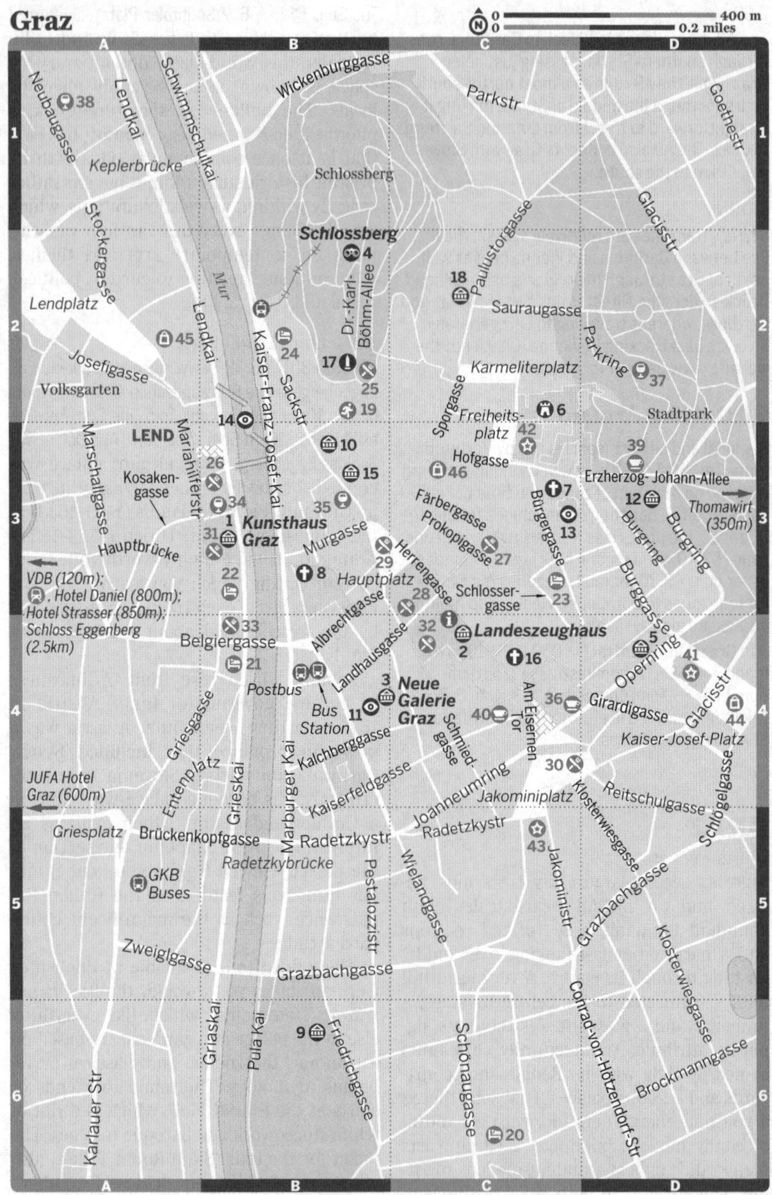

Tue-Sun Apr-Oct, Alte Galerie from mid-Apr; 🚊1 Schloss Eggenberg) Graz' Schloss Eggenberg (p181) and park grounds are home to an ensemble of excellent museums, including the **Alte Galerie** (Old Gallery), with its outstanding collection of paintings from the Middle Ages to the baroque. Also very worthwhile are the **Archaeological Museum** housing relics from prehistory to classical times, and the **Coin Collection**.

Just a few of the highlights in the Alte Galerie are works by Lucas Cranach the

Graz

Top Sights
1 Kunsthaus Graz ... B3
2 Landeszeughaus ... C4
3 Neue Galerie Graz ... B4
4 Schlossberg ... B2

Sights
5 Atelier Jungwirth ... D4
6 Burg ... C2
7 Domkirche ... C3
8 Franziskaner Kirche ... B3
9 FRida & FreD ... B6
10 Grazmuseum ... B3
11 Joanneumsviertel ... B4
12 Künstlerhaus Graz ... D3
13 Mausoleum of Ferdinand II ... C3
14 Murinsel ... B2
15 Museum für Geschichte ... B3
Naturkundemuseum ... (see 3)
16 Stadtpfarrkirche ... C4
17 Uhrturm ... B2
18 Volkskundemuseum ... C2

Activities, Courses & Tours
19 Fairytale Express Graz ... B2
Schlossberg Slide ... (see 19)

Sleeping
20 Augarten Hotel ... C6
21 Hotel Weitzer ... B4
22 Hotel Wiesler ... B3
23 Hotel zum Dom ... C3
24 Schlossberg Hotel ... B2

Eating
25 Aiola Upstairs ... B2
26 Caylend ... B3
Der Steirer ... (see 21)
27 Eckstein ... C3
28 El Pescador ... C3
29 Fast-Food Stands – Hauptplatz ... B3
30 Fast-Food Stands – Jakominiplatz ... C4
31 Kunsthauscafé ... B3
32 Landhauskeller ... C4
33 Mangolds ... B4

Drinking & Nightlife
34 Cafe Centraal ... B3
Dom im Berg ... (see 19)
35 Freiblick Tagescafe ... B3
36 Operncafé ... C4
37 Parkhouse ... D2
38 p.p.c. ... A1
39 Promenade ... D3
40 Tribeka ... C4

Entertainment
41 Opernhaus ... D4
42 Schauspielhaus ... C3
43 Stockwerk Jazz ... C5

Shopping
44 Farmers Market – Kaiser-Josef-Platz ... D4
45 Farmers Market – Lendplatz ... A2
46 Hofbäckerei Edegger-Tax ... C3

Elder, Martin Johann Schmidt and Pieter Brueghel the Younger. In a clever touch, each room has been individually coloured to highlight and complement the dominant tones of the paintings displayed in them. While the Coin Collection is more of eclectic interest (magnifying glasses on the case help to see the coins close up), the Archaeological Museum houses the exceptional Strettweg Chariot and a bronze mask, both dating from the 7th century BC, as well as a collection of Roman finds in the province.

Schloss Eggenberg Parkland GARDENS
(www.museum-joanneum.at; Eggenberger Allee 90, Schloss Eggenberg; adult/child €2/1; 8am-7pm Apr-Oct, to 5pm Nov-Mar; 1 Schloss Eggenberg) Lending Graz' Schloss Eggenberg broad splashes of green, these palace gardens are a relaxing place for whiling away the time amid squawking peacocks and deer that roam among Roman stone reliefs. It includes the **Planetengarten** (Planet Garden) based on the same Renaissance theme of planets you find inside the palace itself.

★**Landeszeughaus** MUSEUM
(Styrian Armoury; 0316-8017 98 10; www.museum-joanneum.at; Herrengasse 16; adult/child €9/3; 10am-5pm Tue-Sun Apr-Oct, 11am-3pm Tue-Sun Nov-Mar; 1, 3, 4, 5, 6, 7 Hauptplatz) If you have a passion for armour and weapons, you'll especially enjoy the Landeszeughaus, where more than 30,000 pieces of glistening weaponry are housed. The exhibition is one of Graz' most interesting and the largest of its kind in Austria and, by its own account, in the world. Expect to see a range of weapons from the 15th to 18th centuries. Admission from November to March is only on tours, which are held in German (11am, 2pm) and in English (12.30pm).

★**Schlossberg** VIEWPOINT
(one way €2.40; 4, 5 Schlossbergplatz) FREE Rising to 473m, Schlossberg is the site of the original fortress where Graz was founded and is marked by the city's most visible icon – the **Uhrturm** (Clock Tower; 4, 5 Schlossplatz/Murinsel) FREE. Its wooded slopes can be reached by a number of bucolic and

GRAZ' MUSEUMS

Most of Graz' museums are under the umbrella of the Universalmuseum Joanneum with almost 20 locations throughout the city. Three museums are located inside the Joanneumviertel complex, an interesting and eye-catching building that is partially below ground.

Admission with a **24-hour ticket** (adult/child/family €15/6/30) allows you to visit the entire museum ensemble over two days (but within 24 hours). The major sites are Schloss Eggenberg (p181), Kunsthaus Graz (p181), Landeszeughaus (p183), Museum für Geschichte, and Naturkundemuseum and the Neue Galerie Graz, the latter two both in the Joanneumsviertel.

An alternative is the **48-hour ticket** (adult/child/family €21/9/42), available from any of the museums. Family tickets, valid for two adults and children under 14, also offer significant discounts.

strenuous paths, but also by lift or Schlossbergbahn funicular. It's a brief walk or take tram 4 or 5 to Schlossplatz/Murinsel for the lift. A fun way of getting back down is on the **Schlossberg Slide** (The Slide; 0316-82 90 28; www.schlossbergrutsche.at; adult/child plus lift ticket €6.60/6.10; 10am-7pm).

To avoid a walk back late at night, bear in mind that the lift operates from 8am to 12.30am daily, and the funicular from 9am to midnight from Sunday to Wednesday and until 2am from Thursday to Saturday.

Joanneumsviertel NOTABLE BUILDING
(www.museum-joanneum.at; 1, 3, 4, 5, 6, 7 Hauptplatz) This historic building contains a number of museums, including the Neue Galerie Graz and the Naturkundemuseum, along with a couple of recently redesigned public spaces that are used for summer events.

★Neue Galerie Graz GALLERY
(0316-8017 91 00; www.museum-joanneum.at; Joanneumsviertel; adult/child €9.50/3.50; 10am-5pm Tue-Sun; 1, 3, 4, 5, 6, 7 Hauptplatz) The Neue Galerie is the crowning glory of the three museums inside the Joanneumsviertel complex. The collection of works on level 0 is the highlight, which is regularly curated from visual arts works since 1800. It also has changing exhibitions on level 1, and a section about Styrian artists; finally, the Bruseum (a separate museum) on level 0 is dedicated to the Styrian artist Günter Brus and his followers.

Naturkundemuseum MUSEUM
(Museum of Natural History; 0316-8017 90 00; www.museum-joanneum.at; Joanneumsviertel; adult/child €9.50/3.50; 10am-5pm Tue-Sun; ; 1,3, 4, 5, 6, 7 Hauptplatz) Located inside the Joanneumsviertel complex of museums, the Museum of Natural History has an excellent section on geology, with an interesting collection of stone slabs from different parts of the world. Butterfly buffs will find more than enough Lepidoptera pinned to the boards here.

Atelier Jungwirth GALLERY
(0316-81 55 05; www.atelierjungwirth.com; Opernring 12; 2-5pm Wed-Fri, 11am-3pm Sat; 1, 3, 4, 5, 6, 7, 13 Jakominiplatz) Graz' most compelling contemporary art space specialises in photography. A calendar of shows spans reportage, fashion and more conceptual work, and features some stellar international names like Paolo Roversi.

Domkirche CHURCH
(0676 8742 68 25; www.domgraz.at; Burggasse 3; dawn-dusk; 1, 3, 4, 5, 6, 7 Hauptplatz) The Domkirche dates from the 15th century, and became a cathedral in 1786. The interior combines Gothic and baroque elements, with reticulated vaulting on the ceiling; its highlights are Conrad Laib's panel painting *Crucifixion in the Throng* (1457) and the faded *Gottesplagenbild* fresco on the cathedral's exterior, which dates from 1485. The fresco depicts life in the early 1480s, when Graz was besieged by its triple tragedy of Turkish invasion, the plague and locusts.

Stadtpfarrkirche CHURCH
(0316-82 96 84; Herrengasse 23; dawn-dusk; 1, 3, 4, 5, 6, 7 Hauptplatz) Rising up on Herrengasse between the main square and Jakominiplatz, the town parish church stands out for its attractive baroque exterior. Inside, the post-WWII stained-glass window by Salzburg artist Albert Birkle has a controversial anomaly: the fourth panel from the bottom on the right (left of the high altar) clearly shows Hitler and Mussolini looking on as Christ is scourged.

Murinsel BRIDGE

(🚸; 🚋4, 5 Schlossplatz/Murinsel, 🚋1, 3, 6, 7 Südtiroler Platz) Murinsel is a constructed island-cum-bridge of metal and plastic in the middle of the Mur. This modern floating landmark contains a cafe, a kids' playground and a small stage. Even if you don't stop in, it's a great little detour that brings you up close to the fast-flowing river.

Künstlerhaus Graz GALLERY

(☎0316-74 00 84; www.km-k.at; Burgring 2; adult/child €4/2; ⊙10am-6pm Tue & Wed, Fri-Sun, to 8pm Thu; 🚌30 Tummerlplatz) The city's edgiest contemporary-art institution calls itself a 'Halle für Kunst & Medien' – art and media – and presents a program of installation, performance and video from both international names and emerging Styrian artists. Set in the green of the Stadtpark, it's also an impressive piece of modernist architecture – a 1952 Leo Scheu – that was given a contemporary renovation in 2013. Look out for launches, films and performances (see events on the website).

Museum für Geschichte MUSEUM

(Museum of History; ☎0316-8017 98 00; www.museum-joanneum.at; Sackstrasse 16; adult/child €9.50/3.50; ⊙10am-5pm Wed-Sun; 🚋1, 3, 4, 5, 6 ,7 Hauptplatz) The Museum of History is housed inside the baroque Palais Herberstein, which has an elegant staircase dating from 1757 and stately rooms. Exhibits in the permanent **Schaudepot** section are selected from a collection of 35,000 objects, mostly from the applied arts, including monstrances and musical instruments. There's also a permanent multimedia section here taking in photography and film. On top of this it has long-running special exhibitions and also shorter ones of specific themes. See the website for current exhibitions.

Franziskaner Kirche CHURCH

(☎0316-82 71 72; www.franziskaner-graz.at; Franziskanerplatz 14; ⊙8-11am & 2-5pm Mon-Fri; 🚋1, 3, 4, 5, 6, 7 Hauptplatz) This church and monastery was founded by the Franciscan order in 1239. Its 14th-century chancel was rebuilt in a contemporary style after being gutted by an Allied bomb during WWII. The main reason to visit, however, is the serene, silent, rose-filled monastery garden, still surrounded by its original Gothic cloisters.

Grazmuseum MUSEUM

(☎0316-872 76 00; www.grazmuseum.at; Sackstrasse 18; adult/child €5/3; ⊙10am-6pm Thu-Tue, to 8pm Wed; 🚋1, 3, 4, 5, 6, 7 Hauptplatz) This small museum has a permanent collection featuring objects from city history, complemented by changing exhibitions. Check the website for what's currently on.

Mausoleum of Ferdinand II MAUSOLEUM

(☎0316-804 18 90; www.domgraz.at; Burggasse 2; tours adult/child €7/2.50; ⊙visits by prior arrangement; 🚋1, 3, 4, 5, 6, 7 Hauptplatz) The mannerist-baroque Mausoleum of Ferdinand II was designed by Italian architect Pietro de Pomis and begun in 1614; after Pomis' death the mausoleum was completed by Pietro Valnegro, while Johann Bernhard Fischer von Erlach chipped in with the exuberant stuccowork and frescoes inside. Ferdinand (1578–1637), his wife and his son are interred in the crypt.

Burg CASTLE

(Hofgasse; 🚌30 Schauspielhaus, 🚋1, 3, 4, 5, 6, 7 Hauptplatz) Graz' 15th-century Burg today houses government offices. At the far end of the courtyard, on the left under the arch, is an ingenious double staircase (1499) – the steps diverge and converge as they spiral. It adjoins **Stadtpark**, the city's largest green space.

Volkskundemuseum MUSEUM

(Folk Life Museum; ☎0316-8017 99 00; www.museum-joanneum.at; Paulustorgasse 11-13a; adult/child €7/2.50; ⊙2-6pm Wed-Sun Apr-early Jan; 🚌30 Paulustor, 🚋1, 3, 4, 5, 6, 7 Hauptplatz) The Folk Life Museum is devoted to folk art and social history. Highlights include 2000 years of traditional clothing in an exhibition that brings together ways of life with clothing and belief.

Österreichisches Freilichtmuseum MUSEUM

(Austrian Open-Air Museum; ☎03124-537 00; www.freilichtmuseum.at; Stübing; adult/child/family €11.50/5.50/29; ⊙9am-4pm Apr-Oct) Located some 15km northwest of Graz and

GRAZ GUIDED TOURS

Graz Tourismus (p190) offers a number of walking tours, including a walking tour of the historic centre (€13.50/7 per adult/child) in German and English at 2.30pm daily year-round.

GRAZ FOR CHILDREN

With its green spaces, playgrounds and relaxed atmosphere, Graz is made for children. The creation of **FRida & FreD** (☎0316-872 77 00; www.fridaundfred.at; Friedrichgasse 34; one exhibition adult/child/family €5.50/5.50/16; ⏰9am-5pm Mon, Wed & Thu, to 7pm Fri, 10am-5pm Sat & Sun, closed late Feb-late Mar; 🚸; 🚌34, 34E Museum der Wahrnehmung), Graz' first museum devoted to children, makes it even better. This small but fun-packed museum is aimed at kids up to the age of 12, and hosts workshops, exhibitions and theatre. It has loads of hands-on tasks and interactive displays.

The **Fairytale Express Graz** (Schlossberg Cave Railway; ☎0316-872 77 22; www.grazermaerchenbahn.at; Schlossbergplatz; adult/child €8.50/6.50; ⏰10.30am-5.30pm, closed 1st Mon of month; 🚸; 🚋4, 5 Schlossbergplatz/Murinsel), the longest grotto railway in Europe, is another highlight for the little 'uns. The 20-minute-long railway ride takes you past fairy-tale scenes in tunnels once used as a refuge from Allied bombings during WWII.

One of the latest attractions for children (and adults, actually) is the Schlossberg Slide (p184), a 175m slide that spirals down from Schlossberg to the foot of the cliff.

consisting of about 100 Austrian farmstead buildings, the Austrian Open-Air Museum in Stübing is ideal for a family outing. The museum is about a 20-minute walk from the Stübing train station; turn left out of the train station and pass over the tracks, then under them before reaching the entrance. Hourly trains make the journey from Graz (€4.50, 15 minutes).

Festivals & Events

Styriarte MUSIC

(☎0316-82 50 00; www.styriarte.com; ⏰Jun & Jul) Classical festival featuring almost continuous concerts. Some concerts are held in Renaissance courtyards and are free.

La Strada Graz CULTURAL

(www.lastrada.at; ⏰late Jul-early Aug) An outdoor summer arts festival with street theatre, dance, puppet theatre and 'nouveau cirque'.

Lange Tafel FOOD & DRINK

(www.graztourismus.at; Hauptplatz; ⏰Aug) Every August, Graz throws one heck of a banquet when it hosts the 'Long Table', where the historic centre becomes one big open-air dinner party for some 750 guests. The aim is to show off regional produce to best effect in a tasting menu paired with some excellent wines. Contact the tourist office (p190) for tickets.

Steirischer Herbst PERFORMING ARTS

(www.steirischerbst.at; ⏰Oct) An ambitious, sometimes edgy festival of new music, theatre and film, plus exhibitions and art installations.

Sleeping

JUFA Hotel Graz HOSTEL €

(☎0316-70 83 210; www.jufa.eu/hotel/graz; Idlhofgasse 74; s/d €69/79; P⊖❄@📶; 🚌31, 32, 33 Lissagasse) This clean and comfortable HI hostel is located about 800m south of the main train station and can be easily reached by bus from Jakominiplatz. No dorms, but there are four-person rooms that make the rates more affordable.

Hotel Strasser HOTEL €

(☎0316-71 39 77; www.hotelstrasser.at; Eggenberger Gürtel 11; s/d/tr €69/89/100; P⊖📶; 🚋1, 3, 6, 7 Hauptbahnhof) Hotel Strasser's well-priced rooms have parquetry floors and high ceilings; some, including the single, are cosily wood-lined. Breakfast is not usually included in the rates and costs €8.90.

★**Hotel Wiesler** HOTEL €€

(☎0316-70 66-0; www.hotelwiesler.com; Grieskai 4; d €141-246; P⊖@📶; 🚋1, 3, 6, 7 Südtiroler Platz) The riverside Wiesler, a *Jugendstil* (art nouveau) gem from 1901, has been transformed into Graz' most glamorous hotel, complete with oriental-style spa. Hotelier Florian Weltzer has shaken up everything, including the notion of room categories, and ensured that this is a luxury experience that is far from stuffy.

★**Schlossberg Hotel** HOTEL €€

(%0316-807 00; www.schlossberg-hotel.at; Kaiser-Franz-Josef-Kai 30; s/d from €120/160; piWs; j4, 5 Schlossbergbahn) Central but just removed from the action, four-star Schlossberg is blessed with a prime location tucked below its namesake. Rooms are well sized, individually decorated and have an eccentric elegance. The hotel brings together three historic buildings so even the architecture is gently idiosyncratic. A small rooftop pool and vertiginous terraced garden make a stay here completely memorable. Breakfast isn't included in the rates.

Hotel Daniel HOTEL €€
(☎0316-71 10 80; www.hoteldaniel.com; Europaplatz 1; d Smart €78-130, Loggia €92-150, Loft Cube €295-530; P ⊖ ❄ @ ☎; 🚊1, 3, 6, 7 Hauptbahnhof) The Daniel's rooms are well designed and super-simple, and while its small 'smart' rooms scrape into budget territory, it also offers the super-exclusive loft cube on the roof if you're looking for something out of the ordinary. The lobby area is a lot of fun – a great space in which to work or just hang out.

Augarten Hotel HOTEL €€
(☎0316-208 00; www.augartenhotel.at; Schönaugasse 53; s €125-175, d €140-200; P ⊖ ❄ ☎ ≋; 🚊4, 5 Finanzamt) Augarten is decorated with the owner's private art collection, which includes works by Maria Lassnig, Franz West and Martin Kippenberger. All rooms are bright and modern, and have something of a masculine edge, though not overbearingly so. The larger rooms are worth it, with windows on two walls in some and a luxurious spaciousness.

Hotel Weitzer HOTEL €€
(☎0316-70 30; www.hotelweitzer.com; Grieskai 12; s €122-175, d €139-197; P ⊖ @ ☎; 🚊1, 3, 6, 7 Südtiroler Platz) A big, busy but friendly hotel that retains its family-run origins, rooms here are decorated in a crisp, smart style. The hotel's lovely old bones banish the bland. There are good eating options on-site, and sauna and fitness facilities.

Hotel zum Dom HOTEL €€
(☎0316-82 48 00; www.domhotel.co.at; Bürgergasse 14; s €100-160, d €145-175; P ⊖ ❄ ☎; 🚌30 Palais Trauttmansdorff/Urania, 🚊1, 3, 4, 5, 6, 7 Hauptplatz) Ceramics and other objects feature throughout the Hotel zum Dom, whose individually furnished rooms are traditional but far from bland. Bonus: they come either with steam/power showers or whirlpools; one even has a terrace whirlpool. Prices vary considerably; check online.

Eating

Kunsthauscafé INTERNATIONAL €
(☎0316-71 49 57; www.kunsthauscafe.co.at; Südtiroler Platz 2; mains €7-16.50; ⏰9am-midnight Mon-Thu, to 2am Fri & Sat, to 8pm Sun; 🚊1, 3, 6, 7 Südtiroler Platz) A happy, young crowd fills the long tables here for a menu that incorporates burgers (from big beef to chickpea), creative salads and international flavours from noodle bowls to steak tartare with skinny fries. It's very, very loud – but fun if you're in the mood. The lunch special goes for just €6.80.

Mangolds VEGETARIAN €
(www.mangolds.at; Griesgasse 11; meals €8-15; ⏰11am-7pm Mon-Fri, to 4pm Sat; 🖉 👪; 🚊1, 3, 6, 7 Südtiroler Platz) 🍃 Tasty vegetarian patties, rice dishes and more than 40 different salads are served at this pay-by-weight vegetarian cafeteria. It's an appealing place to while away a few hours over coffee and cake too.

★ **Thomawirt** BISTRO €€
(☎0316-32 86 37; www.thomawirt.at; Leonhardstrasse 40-42; lunch menu €6.90 & €7.90, mains €7.80-17.90; ⏰9am-1am; 🖉 🐾; 🚊7 Merangasse) This neo-*Beisl* (bistro pub) in the uni quarter serves a lunch special weekdays from 11am, and other excellent lunch and dinner dishes ranging from Styrian classics to (expensive) steaks and vegetarian mains until 1am. As well as serving great pub food, Thomawirt has a cafe where you can order the same restaurant dishes; there's occasional live music in a lounge-bar.

FARMERS MARKETS & FOOD STANDS

➡ There are plenty of cheap eateries near Graz University (trams 1 and 7), particularly on Halbärthgasse, Zinzendorfgasse and Harrachgasse.

➡ The freshest fruit and vegetables are at the farmers markets on **Kaiser-Josef-Platz** (⏰6am-1pm Mon-Sat; 🚊1, 7 Kaiser-Josef-Platz) and **Lendplatz** (⏰6am-1pm Mon-Sat; 🚊1, 3, 6, 7 Südtiroler Platz), which also have brilliant little food stands.

➡ For fast-food stands, head for **Hauptplatz** (🚊1, 3, 4, 5, 6, 7 Hauptplatz) and **Jakominiplatz** (🚊1, 3, 4, 5, 6, 7, 13 Jakominiplatz), open daily well into the night, some till late.

★El Pescador SEAFOOD €€
(☎0316-82 90 30; www.elpescador.at; Landhausgasse 6; mains €21-32; ⏲11.30am-midnight Mon-Sat; 🚋1, 3, 4, 5, 6, 7 Hauptplatz) A veritable wave of seafood scents will strike you when you enter this place, which serves a range of delicious specialities from the seas, heavily influenced by Dalmatian cooking but also leaning towards Italy. There's a catch of the day between 11.30am and 5pm to complement the menu. The atmosphere is modern without losing its homeliness, with wooden tables and friendly staff.

★Der Steirer AUSTRIAN €€
(☎0316-70 36 54; www.der-steirer.at; Belgiergasse 1; weekday lunch menu €8.90, mains €11.50-24; ⏲11am-midnight; 🖉; 🚋1, 3, 6, 7 Südtiroler Platz) This neo-*Beisl* and wine bar has a beautiful selection of Styrian dishes, including great goulash, crispy *Backhendl* (fried breaded chicken) and seasonal game dishes, all done in a simple, contemporary style. Its Styrian tapas concept is a nice way to sample local flavours.

★Landhauskeller AUSTRIAN €€
(☎0316-83 02 76; www.landhaus-keller.at; Schmiedgasse 9; mains €17-36; ⏲noon-1am Mon-Wed, to 2am Thu-Sat; 🖉; 🚋1, 3 ,4, 5, 6, 7 Hauptplatz) What started as a spit-and-sawdust pub in the 16th century has evolved into a darkly atmospheric, super-stylish restaurant serving modern takes on Styrian or national specialities. As well as favourites like *Tafelspitz* (prime boiled beef), you'll find some vegetarian options and ragout, and the full range of meats, plus seafood, all prepared creatively.

★Aiola Upstairs INTERNATIONAL €€
(☎0316-81 87 97; http://upstairs.aiola.at; Schlossberg 2; pasta €16-17.50, mains €19.90-34; ⏲9am-midnight; 📶🖉; 🚋4, 5 Schlossbergplatz/Murinsel for lift) This cracking restaurant atop Schlossberg (p183) has fabulous views from both its glass box interior and summer terrace. Even better, the cooking up here is some of the city's best, with chefs putting a novel spin on regional, seasonal and global ingredients in a skilful act that takes you through ravioli and gnocchi to a selection of red meat and fish specialities, and a vegan curry.

Caylend FUSION €€
(☎0316-71 15 15; http://caylend.at; Stigergasse 1; mains €13-29; ⏲4pm-midnight Wed-Fri, noon-midnight Sat & Sun; 🚋1, 3, 6, 7 Südtiroler Platz) Backlighting, a streamlined design and primary colours lend a contemporary feel to this vaulted, wood-floor bistro and wine bar, with ever-exciting fusion cuisine. Dishes range from the Austro-exotic such as 24-hour-smoked pork belly with wild garlic and cream cheese, to the Australo-exotic kangaroo steaks (albeit with *Spätzle*) and beef flaps 'Caylend style'. There's a huge selection of Austrian wines to match.

Eckstein INTERNATIONAL €€
(☎0316-82 87 01; www.eckstein.co.at; Mehlplatz 3; mains €18-31; ⏲11am-midnight; 🚋1, 3 ,4, 5, 6, 7 Hauptplatz) Eckstein has been a long-time presence on the Graz eating scene, but has more recently reinvented itself with a smaller and more selective international menu. This does a culinary loop through Italian antipasti, stops off for some Styrian fare, and moves on to internationally popular meat and fish dishes. It has outdoor summer seating on Mehlplatz for those warm days and nights.

Drinking & Nightlife

★Promenade CAFE
(☎0316-813 840; http://promenade.aiola.at; Erzherzog-Johann-Allee 1; ⏲9am-1am Mon-Thu, to 2am Fri & Sat, to midnight Sun; 📶; 🚌30 Schauspielhaus) Delightful Promenade is a Graz institution. Run by the people behind the legendary Aiola, it's a pretty, modern take on the traditional coffee house. On a tree-lined avenue in the Stadtpark, it's the perfect place for weekend breakfasts – eggs or savoury plates – or for an afternoon spritz and a few of the smart little tapas-style dishes.

Parkhouse BAR
(☎0316-811 326; www.parkhouse.at; Stadtpark 2; ⏲10am-2am Mar-Oct, 9pm-2am Fri & Sat Nov-Feb; 🚌30 Kameliterplatz) A super laid-back bar in a lovely rotunda-style building in the park, perfect for an early or late drink. Check the website for details of DJs or live music.

Operncafé CAFE
(☎0316-83 04 36; www.operncafe.at; Opernring 22; coffee & cake €9; ⏲7.30am-11pm Fri & Sat, to 9pm Sun-Thu; 📶; 🚋1, 3, 4, 5, 6, 7, 13 Jakominiplatz) This traditional cafe does old school beautifully with homemade pastries, lots of things to read and pleasant, suited waiters who have found a calling in life.

Freiblick Tagescafe ROOFTOP BAR

(☎0316-83 53 02; www.freiblick.co.at; Kastner & Öhler, Sackstrasse 7-11; ⊙9.30am-7pm Mon-Fri, to 6pm Sat; 📶; 🚊1, 3, 4, 5, 6, 7 Hauptplatz) This huge rooftop terrace cafe-bar tops the Kastner & Öhler department store and has the best view in the city. Enjoy the clouds and rooftops over a breakfast platter and coffee or a lunchtime soup or salad. Or stop by in the afternoon for something from the Prosecco spritz menu or a Hugo Royal – Moët Chandon splashed with elderflower (€15).

Tribeka COFFEE

(☎0316-26 97 64; www.tribeka.at; Kaiserfeldgasse 6; ⊙7am-8pm Mon-Fri, from 8am Sat & Sun; 📶; 🚊1, 3, 4, 5, 6, 7 Hauptplatz) This branch of the popular Graz chain is an early-morning coffee must if you're in need of 'good' coffee in the centre. Big windows and a raised streetside terrace fill up with freelancers and there's a good range of brownies, cheesecake and pastries for sustenance.

p.p.c. CLUB

(☎0316-8141 4133; www.popculture.at; Neubaugasse 6; ⊙from 10pm Wed-Sat; 🚊4, 5 Kepplerbrücke) One of Graz' most popular dance places with a wide range of performers and theme nights each week ranging from hip-hop and RnB through to reggae, dancehall and metal. Check the website for upcoming gigs.

Dom im Berg CLUB

(☎0316-8008 90 00; www.spielstaetten.at; Schlossbergplatz; 🚊4, 5 Schlossplatz/Murinsel) The tunnels under Schlossberg were once used as air-raid shelters. Today, some of them have been refashioned into a large arts-clubbing venue. See the website for variable opening times and prices.

Cafe Centraal PUB

(www.centraal.at; Mariahilferstrasse 10; ⊙8am-2am; 📶; 🚊1, 3, 6, 7 Südtiroler Platz) This traditional bar and *Beisl* with a dark-wood interior and outside seating has an alternative feel and super-cheap eats from breakfast onwards.

☆ Entertainment

Opernhaus OPERA

(☎0316-8000; www.oper-graz.com; Kaiser-Josef-Platz 10; ⊙closed early Jul-late Aug; 🚊1, 7 Kaiser-Josef-Platz) A visit to the opera here is also stepping foot into an opulent neobaroque and neorococo backdrop splashed in gold, white and red tones. There's space for over 1200 people in its towering main auditorium. The company itself has received numerous accolades over the years. See the website for performances and prices.

Schauspielhaus THEATRE

(☎0316-8000; www.schauspielhaus-graz.com; Hofgasse 11; ⊙closed early Jul-late Aug; 🚌30 Schauspielhaus, 🚊1, 3, 4, 5, 6, 7 Hauptplatz) Graz' main venue for theatre. See the website for dates and prices.

Stockwerk Jazz JAZZ

(☎0676 315 95 51; http://stockwerkjazz.mur.at; Jakominiplatz 18; ⊙4pm-1am Mon-Sat, to midnight Sun; 📶; 🚊1, 3, 4, 5, 6, 7, 13 Jakominiplatz) In addition to being Graz' premier jazz bar for home-grown artists and international acts, this is also a great place to have a drink. It has rustic wooden features and a summer rooftop terrace.

WORTH A TRIP

ROGNER BAD BLUMAU

East Styria is well known throughout Austria for its thermal springs and spa centres. Fans of Friedensreich Hundertwasser's unique architecture won't want to miss **Rogner Bad Blumau** (☎03383-51 00; www.blumau.com; Bad Blumau; adult/child Mon-Fri €45/26, Sat & Sun €54/31, admission after 5pm €32.90/22.90; ⊙9am-11pm), near the town of Bad Blumau, 50km east of Graz. Facilities include a Finnish sauna and steam baths, large outdoor mineral lakes, its AlphaSphere23 with sound, light and movement effects, plus a range of massages and treatments.

The complex is in Hundertwasser's idiosyncratic organic style with spacial and decorative trademarks like uneven floors, grass on the roof, colourful ceramics and golden spires. If you're thinking of staying in the hotel, accommodation includes entry to the spa. Trains connect Graz with Bad Blumau every two hours (€18,60, two hours).

Shopping

Hofbäckerei Edegger-Tax FOOD

(☎0316-8302 300; www.hofbaeckerei.at; Hofgasse 6; ⏰7am-6pm Mon-Fri, to 1pm Sat; 🚊1, 3, 4, 5, 6, 7 Hauptplatz) The extravagantly carved neo-baroque oak facade of this historic bakery comes complete with a gold-plated double eagle above the entrance, testament to its one-time imperial patronage. Inside you'll find bread, the Styrian nutty-filled pastry *Panthertatzen* (panther's claw), as well as pumpkin-seed and vanilla croissants and a cornucopia of sweet nutty biscuits. Everything is beautifully packaged.

VDB FOOD & DRINKS

(☎0316-71 48 84; www.vdb.co.at; Annenstrasse 25; ⏰10am-6pm Mon-Fri, 9am-1pm Sat; 🚊1, 3, 5, 6, 7, 13 Roseggerhaus) Manfred van den Berg has collected a wonderful assortment of spices as well as producing a couple of house-blend gins. Stock up on olive oils, chocolates, jams and pumpkin-seed products.

Information

Graz Tourismus (☎0316-807 50; www.graztourismus.at; Herrengasse 16; ⏰10am-5pm Jan-Mar & Nov, to 6pm Apr-Oct & Dec; 📶; 🚊1, 3, 4, 5, 6, 7 Hauptplatz) Graz' main tourist office, with loads of free information on the city, and helpful and knowledgeable staff. Also provides free buggy (stroller) and wheelchair rental.

Getting There & Away

AIR

Graz Airport (GRZ; ☎0316-290 21 72; www.flughafen-graz.at) is 10km south of the town centre, just beyond the A2 and connected by train and bus with the *Hauptbahnhof*. Direct connections with Graz include to/from Berlin Tegel (Germany) with easyJet (www.easyjet.com) and to/from Vienna, Zürich (Switzerland) and Stuttgart (Germany) with Eurowings (www.eurowings.com). KLM, Swiss and Turkish Airlines have regular direct flights to the Netherlands, Switzerland and Turkey respectively. **Austrian Airlines** (☎05 1766 1000; www.austrian.com) has flights to/from Düsseldorf and Stuttgart (Germany), Vienna and Salzburg. **Lufthansa** (☎0810 1025 8080; www.lufthansa.com) has frequent flights to Frankfurt am Main, Munich and Stuttgart in Germany.

Facilities at the airport include an **information desk** (☎0316-290 21 72; www.flughafen-graz.at; ⏰5am-10.30pm; 📶), free internet terminals and wi-fi inside the security zone, and a bank with an ATM in arrivals on the ground floor.

BUS

Postbus (☎050 678 910, 05 17 17; www.postbus.at) services depart from outside the *Hauptbahnhof* and from the **bus station** (Andreas-Hofer-Platz; 🚊1, 3, 6, 7 Südtiroler Platz) at Andreas-Hofer-Platz to all parts of Styria. Frequent direct **GKB buses** (☎0316-59 87-0; www.gkb.at; 🚊1, 3, 6, 7 Südtiroler Platz) run to Bärnbach (€8.60, 50 minutes) daily. All leave from Griesplatz. Six direct ÖBB buses daily (€31, two hours) leave for Klagenfurt from the *Hauptbahnhof*.

CAR

Companies include **Avis** (☎0316-81 29 20; www.avis.com; Reinighausstrasse 66; 🚊7 Karl-Morre-Strasse), **Hertz** (☎0316-82 50 07; www.hertz.com; Andreas-Hofer-Platz 1; 🚊1, 3, 6, 7 Südtiroler Platz), **MegaDrive** (☎050 105 4130; www.megadrive.at; Keplerstrasse 93-95; 🚊1, 3, 5, 6, 7, 13 Eggenberger Gürtel) and **Sixt** (☎0150 526 40 04; www.sixt.at; Kärntner Strasse 44; 🚌Don Bosco). Most have airport pick-up as well.

Note that much of Graz is a *Kurzparkzone* (short-term parking zone); tickets are available from parking machines (€1 per 30 minutes, maximum three hours in most blue zones). Green zones are in outer suburbs, are cheaper and have no time limit. See www.graz.at for zone maps.

TRAIN

Trains to Vienna depart hourly (€40, 2½ hours), and four daily go to Salzburg (€52, four hours). Most trains running north or west go via Bruck an der Mur (€12.60, 30 to 45 minutes, every 30 minutes), a main railway junction with more frequent services. Trains to Klagenfurt (€43, three hours, five daily) require a change in Bruck an der Mur.

International direct train connections from Graz include Zagreb (€44, four to 6½ hours), Ljubljana (€31.90, 3½ hours), Szentgotthárd (€16.60, 1½ hours) and Budapest (€56.40 to €79, 5½ hours).

Getting Around

BICYCLE

Rental is available from **Bicycle** (☎0316-82 13 57; www.bicycle.at; Körösistrasse 5; per 24hr €14, Fri-Mon €24, per week €65; ⏰9am-5pm Mon-Fri; 🚊4, 5 Keplerbrücke), and Mobilzentral (p181) has city rental bicycles for €15 per day or €70 per week. **Fahrradverleih am Hauptbahnhof** (www.bicycle.at; Europaplatz 4, Hauptbahnhof; city bikes per half-day/24hr/weekend/week €9/14/24/65; ⏰8am-6pm Mon-Fri, 9am-noon & 5-7pm Sat & Sun, shorter winter hours; 🚊1, 3, 6, 7 Hauptbahnhof) is run by Bicycle and has mountain bikes, e-mountain bikes and e-trekking bikes.

PUBLIC TRANSPORT

Graz has one zone (zone 101). Single tickets (€2.40) for buses and trams are valid for one hour, but you're usually better off buying a 24-hour pass (€5.30). Ten one-zone tickets cost €20.60, and weekly/monthly passes cost €14.80/49.50. Tickets can be purchased from machines on trams or from pavement ticket machines, and from *Tabak* (tobacconist) shops. Bus tickets can be bought from drivers, although in the longer term machines will also be installed in buses.

Tram

Trams 1, 3, 6 and 7 connect Jakominiplatz with the *Hauptbahnhof* every five to 20 minutes from around 5am to early evening Monday to Saturday. After that trams 1 and 7 do the run alone until services end just before midnight.

TAXI

Call 0316-2801, 0316-878, 0316-889 or 0316-222.

SOUTHERN STYRIA

Southern Styria is known as *Steirische Toskana* (Styrian Tuscany), and for good reason. Not only is this wine country, but the landscape is reminiscent of Chianti, with gentle rolling hills cultivated with vineyards or patchwork farmland, dotted with small forests where deer roam. It's also famous for *Kürbiskernöl,* the rich pumpkin-seed oil generously used in Styrian cooking.

Deutschlandsberg

☎03462 / POP 11,600

In the heart of the Schilcher wine region, Deutschlandsberg is a bustling little town dominated by a well-restored castle with museum.

Burg Museum Archeo Norico MUSEUM

(☎03462-56 02; www.burgmuseum.at; Burgplatz 2; adult/child €9/4; ⏲10am-6pm Tue-Sun mid-Mar–Nov) You will find four thematic exhibits at this castle museum covering ancient history, the Celts, historical weapons and antique jewellery. The extensive collection, whose highlights include a delicate gold necklace from the 5th century BC, takes about 1½ hours to see. As with any good castle, there's a torture chamber in the underground vaults. It's some 25 minutes' walk uphill from the town centre.

Burg Hotel HOTEL €€

(☎03462-56 56-0; www.burghotel-dl.at; Burgplatz 1; s €68-90, d €130-142; P ⊖ 📶) For sleeping arrangements, look no further than the Burg Hotel, which is located in the castle. Its crowning glory is the tower suite (€250 per night); rooms are more modern than old-world style, but are sweetly fancy, large, peaceful and have views of the woods.

JUFA Hotel Deutschlandsberg HOSTEL €€

(☎05 7083 260; www.jufa.eu/hotel/deutschlandsberg; Burgstrasse 5; s/d/tr/q/apt €53/85/125/155/215; P ⊖ @ 📶) Rooms in this hostel are modern, clean and nicely decorated in pastel tones, each with its own bathroom. Apartments have two rooms and sleep up to five people. It's set in a vineyard at the foot of the road that winds up to the castle. It also rents e-bikes/mountain bikes from €10/8 per day.

Marmeladenfleck CAFE €

(☎0650 440 96 70; www.marmeladenfleck.com; Untererplatz 1; lunch mains €5.50-7.50; ⏲8am-4pm Tue, Thu & Fri, to 7pm Wed, 9am-2pm Sat & Sun) This simple, cosy cafe with outdoor seating in summer serves a daily, freshly prepared lunch dish and is a place to watch the world go by, while sipping one of the six craft beer varieties from the Carinthian Schleppe brewery. Check the website for the current dish but it might be anything from a vegetarian soup to a salmon pasta dish.

ℹ Information

Tourist Office (☎03462-75 20; www.schilcherland.at; Hauptplatz 34; ⏲9am-4pm Mon-Fri, to noon Sat Apr-Oct, to 2pm Mon-Fri Nov-Mar) A good source of information on the town and environs.

ℹ Getting There & Away

Hourly trains (€10.60, 45 minutes) connect Graz and Deutschlandsberg. The **JUFA Hotel Deutschlandsberg** (☎05 7083 260; www.jufa.eu/hotel/deutschlandsberg; Burgstrasse 5; e-bikes/mountain bikes per day from €10/8) rents out bikes to guests and nonguests alike.

Ehrenhausen

☎03453 / POP 2560

The picturesque town of Ehrenhausen, near the A9 connecting Graz with the Slovenian border, makes a fine base for exploring the vineyards of southern Styria. The town is little more than one street of

STYRIAN WINE ROADS

The *Weinstrassen* (wine roads) of southern Styria comprise an idyllic bundle of winding roads criss-crossing a picturesque landscape that is reminiscent of Tuscany. The region is at its best about two weeks after the grape harvest (usually September), when *Sturm* (young wine) is sold. The **Weinlesefest** (Wine Harvest Festival; ☎03454-7060 300; www.rebenland.at; tickets €10; ⏲last weekend in Sep) takes place in Leutschach on the last weekend in September, with lots of wine and song.

The main towns in the region are Ehrenhausen, Gamlitz and Berghausen in the north, and the town of Leutschach in the west, less than 20km away but best reached via a serpentine route partly along the Slovenian border. Villages and clusters of vineyards rather than fully fledged towns dot the region, some of these offering picturesque and romantic places to stay overnight. Less rural accommodation is available in the Ehrenhausen. On weekends in September and October accommodation is usually booked out. During the week and at other times it's usually fine if you're flexible.

To explore further, from Leutschach a road veers left at the top of the main street. This leads to Eichberg-Trautenburg, a pretty region with numerous *Buschenschenken* (wine taverns) and narrow sealed roads. A walking trail (560) goes through forest, across meadows and partly alongside the road.

Regions along and south of the Alte Weinstrasse are more remote, while to the north the slopes of the Sausal range make for a very pretty patchwork of vines and small forests. Here too are a growing number of *Buschenschenken,* but often without the crowds.

Tourismusverband Die Südsteirische Weinstrasse (☎03454-70 70; www.suedsteirischeweinstrasse.com; Arnfelser Strasse 10; ⏲9am-5pm Mon-Fri) in Leutschach has information on the wine roads.

Cycling the Wine Roads

One of the most enjoyable ways of seeing the region is by bike. Fahrradverleih am Hauptbahnhof (p190) in Graz rents out trekking and mountain bikes by the day or week for longer trips, and Bicycle (p190), also in Graz, rents out city bikes. Take the train to Ehrenhausen and set out from there. The JUFA Hotel Deutschlandsberg (p191) rents out e-bikes and mountain bikes to both guests and nonguests, whereas in Leutschach there is also e-bike hire from the tourist office. Gut Pössnitzberg outside Leutschach is one place where you can also pick up e-bikes for a local spin, although hotel guests get preference here.

pastel-coloured houses dominated by the baroque **Pfarrkirche** (Hauptplatz; ⏲dawn-dusk) and the yellow and white mausoleum of Ruprecht von Eggenberg.

Sights

Mausoleum MAUSOLEUM

Follow the path on the right of Ehrenhausen's *Rathaus* (town hall) up to the mausoleum of Ruprecht von Eggenberg (1546–1611), hero of the Battle of Sisak against the Turks and the local offshoot of the same family that built Schloss Eggenberg in Graz.

Sleeping & Eating

★**Loisium Südsteiermark** HOTEL, SPA €€

(☎03453-288 00; www.loisium-suedsteiermark.at; Am Schlossberg 1a; s/d €135/176; P ⊜ 🛜 ≋) A sister hotel to the original Loisium resort in the Kamptal, Loisium Südsteiermark ups the luxury ante in the south. Contemporary architecture, simple and stylish rooms, vineyard views and a seriously relaxing Aveda spa make this a hard place to leave but a delicious place to come back to after a hard day of wine tasting.

★**Die Weinbank** AUSTRIAN €€€

(☎03453-222 91; www.dieweinbank.at; Hauptstrasse 44; Wirtshaus mains €18-35, menu €56, restaurant menus €98-125; ⏲Wirtshaus 11am-10pm Wed-Sun, restaurant noon-1.30pm Thu-Sun, 7-9pm Wed-Sun) The brainchild of chef Gerhard Fuchs and sommelier Christian Zach, Die Weinbank brings together exquisite cuisine with an extraordinary range of local wines, which are served in the less formal Wirtshaus and in the restaurant. Topping this off is the *Vinothek*, where you can buy the wines along with gourmet foods such as Mangalitza ham.

Shopping

Genuss Regal Vinofaktur FOOD & DRINKS
(03453-406 77-0; www.genussregal.at; An der Mur 13, Vogau; 9am-6pm) While the *Weinstrasse* can seem impossibly rustic in places, this gourmet superstore is symbolic of Styria's rising status as a food and wine mecca. With its precariously stacked shipping containers outside, it's certainly hard to miss. If you're short on time for cellar door visits, you can stock up on most of the local producers here.

Information

Tourist Office (0664 857 04 08, 03453-222 51; www.ehrenhausen-gv.at; Hauptstrasse 29/7; 9am-noon & 12.30-5pm Mon-Fri, to noon Sat) Has a list of *Buschenschenken* (wine taverns) and the opening times. It also has very comprehensive accommodation lists and can help with organising a private tour of the town's mausoleum and Pfarrkirche.

Getting There & Away

Hourly trains (€10.60, 48 minutes) run from Graz to Ehrenhausen. The train station is about four minutes' walk east of Hauptplatz.

Leutschach

03454 / POP 3725

Leutschach is home to some of Styria's best-known wine producers. The town has the character of a cluster of vineyards and cellar doors set among rolling hills and winding roads.

Gut Pössnitzberg HOTEL €€
(03454-205; www.poessnitzberg.at; Pössnitz 168; s €92-107, d €194-214;) Set on a particularly fetching bend of the road 5km southeast of Leutschach, this *'Weinhotel'* mixes contemporary architecture with Styrian style and hospitality. Rooms are designed for maximum relaxation with large bathrooms and the occasional in-room Jacuzzi; there's also a beautiful elevated pool area. Sunday to Thursday and off-season, prices are much lower.

It's a great spot for touring the neighbouring wineries, but with its own tasting room, wine bar and well-regarded **Kreuzwirt** (03454-205; www.poessnitzberg.at/kreuzwirt; Pössnitz 168; mains €15-26.50; 5-9pm Mon-Fri, noon-9pm Sat) restaurant, a highly satisfying *Weinstrasse* experience can be had by just staying put too.

Bus 605 to Pössnitz Kreuzwirt (€2.40, 12 minutes, several on weekdays) brings you here. The hotel also rents e-bikes per full/half-day for €28/16.

Tscheppes Lang-Gasthof HOTEL €€
(03454-246; www.langgasthof-tscheppe.at; Hauptplatz 6; s/d €73/112;) A popular four-star hotel with spa facilities and a Finnish sauna, known for its herbal bath filled with hops (this is also a big hop-growing district). Rooms are bright, decorated in light tones, and with nicely sized bathrooms. The restaurant (mains €9.80 to €19.20; closed Wednesday and Thursday) serves traditional Austrian cuisine, with locally sourced beef, some of it organic.

Information

Tourist Office (03454-7070 340; www.rebenland.at; Arnfelser Strasse 1; 9am-noon & 2-5pm Mon-Fri, 10am-1pm Sat) Has a free *Freizeitkarte* with hiking trails and *Buschenschenken* marked (opening times included). There are brochures and maps outside when the office is closed. This is also a pick-up point for e-bikes.

Getting There & Away

Plan ahead and take the train from Graz to Leibnitz (€8.60, 38 minutes), then bus it to Leutschach (€8.60, 45 minutes), or use the train-bus connection from Graz via Kaindorf/Sulm Bahnhof to Leutschach (€16.60, 1½ hours).

Getting Around

Having your own wheels is useful if you want to visit the wineries or explore the villages.

E-bikes (03454-70 70; www.suedsteirischeweinstrasse.com; Arnfelser Strasse 1; e-bike per day €27, e-mountain bike €32; 9am-noon Mon-Fri, 10am-1pm Sat mid-Apr–late Oct) can be reserved online in advance then collected from Tourismusverein Leutschach an der Weinstrasse.

Riegersburg

☎03153 / POP 4920

Riegersburg, situated almost 40km east of Graz amongst gently rolling hills, is in a small region known as Steirisches Vulkanland (Styrian Volcano Land). This is part of an ancient volcanic belt stretching from Slovenia to the Carpathian Mountains. In terms of attractions, there's not much to the town centre itself. Its big drawcard is the hilltop castle, Burg Riegersburg, which now plays host to a trio of museums, an adventure climbing park and a falconry centre.

Burg Riegersburg CASTLE
(☎03153-82 131; www.dieriegersburg.at; Riegersburg 1; adult/child/family €19/11/45; ⏲9am-6pm May-Sep, 10am-6pm Apr & Oct) Perched on a 200m-high rocky outcrop and offering spectacular views over the countryside, this hugely impressive 12th-century castle was built for protection from invading Hungarians and Turks. Today it houses a **Hexenmuseum** on witchcraft, a **Burgmuseum** featuring the history of the Liechtenstein family, who acquired it in 1822, and an impressive collection of weapons in the **Waffenmuseum**.

A cable car on the north side whisks you up in 90 seconds (return €6).

Schloss Kapfenstein HOTEL €€
(☎03157-30 03 00; www.schloss-kapfenstein.at; Kapfenstein 1; s €109-133, d €158-206; ⏲closed mid-Dec–Feb; P ⊖ ᯤ) If you have your own transport, consider stopping in at the beautifully located Schloss Kapfenstein, a hotel-restaurant 17km south of Riegersburg. The elegantly furnished rooms vary in style, but many have historic touches and views across the surrounding landscape. The restaurant serves delightful Styrian cuisine on terraces and in its outer courtyard overlooking the valley. Friday-to-Sunday accommodation packages are possible.

Seehaus AUSTRIAN €€
(☎03153-721 06; www.seehaus-riegersburg.at; Riegersburg 205; mains €9.50-17; ⏲9am-10pm Mon-Sat, to 9pm Sun) This restaurant, located alongside the local swimming lake a few minutes' walk southeast of the centre, serves a broad sweep of simple Austrian fare as well as a few burgers and Mediterranean dishes. Its waterside location makes it popular.

ℹ Information

Tourist Office (☎03153-86 70; www.riegersburg.com; Riegersburg 26; ⏲8.30am-3pm Mon-Fri, info foyer 5.30am-midnight) For more information on the *Schloss* (castle) and other activities.

ℹ Getting There & Away

Frequent trains run from Graz to nearby Feldbach (€10.60, one hour), and from there four direct weekday buses head for Riegersburg (€2.40, 20 minutes). The last bus back is at around 6pm; check before setting out.

The Sausal

This hilly region to the northwest of Ehrenhausen is a quieter and gentler alternative to the well-trodden wine routes. Its cellar doors often look over terraced vineyards from the top of a ridge, making for some beautifully elevated settings and tastings with a view.

Weingut Schauer GUESTHOUSE €€
(☎03456-35 21; www.weingut-schauer.at; Greith 21, Kitzeck/Greith; d €184-200; ⏲Mar-late Nov; P ⊖ ᯤ) This vineyard is perched on a hilltop at over 500m, north of Kitzeck in the settlement of Greith. Rooms are furnished in light colours, with wooden floorboards, and breakfast includes homemade bread and local organic produce.

★**T.O.M. R** INTERNATIONAL €€€
(☎0660 400 87 34; www.tomr.at; St Andrä im Sausal 1, St Andrä im Sausal; Sat only 10-course lunch €85, Wed-Sat 10-course dinner €115, 6-course Sun brunch €55; ⏲6.30-11pm Wed-Sat, 12.30-3pm Sat, 11am-3pm Sun) T.O.M. R, located in the village of St Andrä im Sausal, 20km north of Leutschach, has long been southern Styria's dining hotspot. Tom Riederer and partner Katarina run their venture in a former rectory – a light, elegant fine-dining space with a few upstairs rooms for overnight stays. Riederer's cooking is exacting and highly visual, and there's Styrian warmth and easiness here.

Zur Hube MEDITERRANEAN €€€
(☎0664 2211 242; www.zurhube.at; Sausal 51, Pistorf/Gleinstätten; 3-/4-course menu €49/62; ⏲from 6pm Fri & Sat; P) Plan and reserve ahead for this small gourmet restaurant deep in the Sausal. The cuisine, expertly prepared by owner and chef Gingi Peez-Petz, very much has a Mediterranean swing, and

the menus are seasonal, drawing on Slovenian, Italian, Croatian and other influences. You can voyage into the wine cellar yourself to pick your vintage.

Felber Jörgl WINERY

(☎03456-31 89; www.felberjoergl.at; Höch 47, Kitzeck im Sausal; ⏲1-9pm Fri-Tue) Half of the fun in the Sausal is driving the scenic roads and trying whichever places take your fancy. This beautifully sited cellar door is a good place to start with a range of mostly white wines and excellent meat and cheese plates.

Getting There & Away

A lack of public transport and the spread-out nature of the vineyards make this a destination best done by car or bicycle.

NORTHERN STYRIA

Heading north from Graz the landscape of Styria begins to change; gentle hills and flat pastures are replaced by jagged mountains, virgin forests, deep valleys and cold, clear mountain streams. This is also the region's industrial heartland, where for centuries iron ore mining was the backbone of the economy. Two cultural highlights are the pilgrimage church of Mariazell and the abbey of Admont.

Mariazell

☎03882 / POP 3815

Mariazell, situated on the lower reaches of the Eastern Alps, is one of Austria's icons. It offers opportunities for hiking, mountain biking and skiing, but what makes Mariazell so well known is its status as Austria's most important pilgrimage site. Its basilica, founded in 1157, holds a sacred statue of the Virgin, and busloads of Austrians flock to the site on warm weekends in summer and for Assumption (15 August) and Mary's name day (8 September). The mountain above town, **Bürgeralpe** (1270m), has a couple of restaurants and a small museum, and is the town's outdoor playground.

Sights

★**Basilika** CHURCH

(☎03882-259 50; Kardinal Eugen Tisserant Platz 1; ⏲8am-8pm) Mariazell's basilica, a pilgrimage church, is famed for its small but exquisite chapel, known as the Gnadenkapelle (Chapel of Grace). This gold and silver edifice houses the Romanesque statue of the Madonna, whose healing powers reputedly helped King Louis of Hungary defeat the Turks in 1377. Except for two days each year, she's dressed up rather doll-like in her *Liebfrauenkleid* (dress of Our Lady). The interesting **Schatzkammer** (Treasury; adult/child €4/1; ⏲10am-3pm Tue-Sat, 10am-4pm Sun May-Oct) in the upper galleries contains votive offerings spanning six centuries, especially naive-style paintings.

Erlebniswelt Holzknechtland MUSEUM

(www.buergeralpe.at; Bürgeralpe; entry & cable car/chairlift adult/child €19.90/12.70, entry museum adult/child €9.20/6.10; ⏲9.30am-5pm May-early Oct, closed Mon May-early Jun) This outdoor museum for children on Bürgeralpe is devoted to wood and all its wonderful uses.

The museum is accessible either via the Bürgeralpe Cable Car or alternatively by **chairlift** (☎03882-25 55) from St Sebastian.

Activities

Bürgeralpe HIKING, SKIING

(www.buergeralpe.at) This mountain is a great starting or finishing point for hiking in the summer months, and also has skiing in winter. The **cable car** (☎03882-25 55; www.buergeralpe.at) operates year-round. The resort has an artificial lake used as a setting for special events. During winter, adult/child ski passes cost €35.50/30 per day and €181.50/153.50 weekly.

The chairlift in St Sebastian provides an alternative way to ascend the mountain if the cable car isn't operating due to maintenance.

BikeAlps MOUNTAIN BIKING

(☎03882-25 55; www.buergeralpe.at/sommer/bikealps; Bürgeralpe; ⏲9.30am-5pm May-early Oct, closed Mon May-early Jun) BikeAlps is a set of downhill trails for mountain bikers and has runs suitable for professionals as well as novices. Some of the stuff is quick, rough and dirty, some of it tame family fun. It operates in conjunction with the chairlift in St Sebastian and the **BikeStore.cc** (☎03842-470 44 21; www.freeride-coach.com/verleihtestcenter/bike-verleih; St Sebastian, Chairlift valley station; downhill bike plus protection full day €90, plus adult/child €28/16 for day ticket on chairlift; ⏲9.30am-5pm May-early Oct, closed Mon May-early Jun), which rents out the bikes. Check www.buergeralpe.at website for times, which very much depend on weather.

Mariazell

Top Sights
1 Basilika B2

Activities, Courses & Tours
2 Bürgeralpe Cable Car A1

Sleeping
3 Goldene Krone A2
4 Hotel Drei Hasen A2

Eating
5 Brauhaus Mariazell A2

Erlaufsee OUTDOORS
This small lake, lying a few kilometres northwest of the town, reaches about 22°C in summer and, apart from swimming, offers good opportunities for windsurfing and scuba diving; contact addresses for water sports are listed in the booklet *Mariazellerland von A-Z,* available at the tourist office.

An easy four-hour *Rundwanderweg* (circuit trail) runs past the lake and south through forest back into Mariazell; alternatively, you can take the steam **Museumstramway** (www.museumstramway.at; one way/return adult €8/12, child €3/4), which runs at weekends and holidays from early June to late October.

Sleeping & Eating

JUFA Hotel Mariazell HOSTEL €
(05 7083 390; www.jufa.eu/hotel/erlaufsee; Erlaufseestrasse 49, St Sebastian; s €47, tw & d €74; P @) This hostel has a quiet location about halfway between Mariazell and Erlaufsee, set back from the main road in the settlement of St Sebastian. Rooms are clean and bright, with large windows mostly looking out to a grassy area. They have their own bathrooms and safe, and there's a sauna, solarium and fitness room on-site.

Campingplatz Erlaufsee CAMPGROUND €
(03882-49 37; www.st-sebastian.at; St Sebastian; camp sites per adult/child/tent/car €5/2.5/4/3; May–mid-Sep; P) A small camping ground in St Sebastian on the Erlaufsee, flanked by pine trees. Bus 197 runs regularly to St Sebastian from the bus station.

Lurgbauer FARMSTAY €€
(03882-37 18; www.lurgbauer.at; Lurg 1, St Sebastian; r €152-228; restaurant noon-2pm & 6-11pm Wed-Sat, noon-3pm Sun May-Oct, closed Mon-Thu Nov-Apr; P) Located 6km north of Mariazell and reached via an unsealed road, Lurgbauer is a functioning *Bauernhof* (farm) with six delightful rooms and a good restaurant. The highlight is the chalet, a 200-year-old wooden former storehouse, today with a sauna overlooking the meadows. A guesthouse and a wellness room complete the range.

Goldene Krone HOTEL €€
(03882-25 83; www.mariazell.at/krone; Grazer Strasse 1; s €46-57, d €92-114;) Goldene Krone's big and bright rooms have a homely feel, which is complemented by a Finnish sauna and billiard room (also with table football). The ground floor has an excellent midrange restaurant featuring traditional Austrian cuisine and streetside seating.

Hotel Drei Hasen HOTEL €€
(03882-24 10; www.dreihasen.at; Wiener Strasse 11; s/d/ste €80/130/180; closed mid-Mar–mid-Apr & Nov; P) This comfortable hotel has some of the most pleasant rooms in town, with the added bonus of a sauna, relaxation room and sun deck. Some rooms have connecting doors for families. The first-class restaurant (mains €9 to €30) specialises in seasonal game dishes.

Brauhaus Mariazell AUSTRIAN €€
(03882-25 23; www.bierundbett.at; Wiener Strasse 5; mains €11-28; 10am-2pm & 5-11pm

Wed-Sat, 10am-2pm Sun;) This lovely, rustic microbrewery has some of the best Styrian cuisine in these parts and brews its own light and dark beer. There's a garden out back and upstairs accommodation (rooms from €75 per person).

Information

Tourist Office (03882-23 66; www.mariazell-info.at; Hauptplatz 13; 9am-5.30pm Mon-Fri, to 4pm Sat, to 12.30pm Sun, closed Sat & Sun Apr & Nov, closed Sun Oct-Mar) Has a town map and brochure with walking trails marked; doesn't book rooms but has accommodation listings.

Getting There & Away

A narrow-gauge train departs from St Pölten, 84km to the north, every two to three hours to Mariazell train station, 15 minutes by foot north of the centre. It's a slow trip (€18, 2½ hours), but the scenery is spectacular for the last hour approaching Mariazell. Bus is the only option for further travel from Mariazell into Styria; four direct buses run daily to/from Bruck an der Mur (€12.60, 1½ hours), with train connections to/from Graz (€22.30, 2¼ hours). There is also one early-morning and one afternoon direct bus each way daily between Vienna (Südtiroler Platz) and Mariazell (€26, three hours).

The steam Museumstramway runs to the Erlaufsee at weekends and holidays from early June to late October. The easiest place to pick it up is at Mariazell Bahnhof.

Bruck an der Mur

03862 / POP 15,885

Bruck, at the confluence of the Mur and Mürz Rivers, is the Mur Valley's first real town and an important railway junction for Styria. Attractions are limited, but if you're breaking a journey here there are a few interesting things to see.

Sights

Koloman-Wallisch-Platz SQUARE

The town square, host to a food and flower market on Wednesday and Saturday, is graced by the *Rathaus*, with an attractive arcaded courtyard; Kornmesserhaus (1499) brings together Gothic and some Renaissance features and was based on the design of a Venetian palace. Other historic highlights include the art-nouveau facade at No 10 and the fine Renaissance-style wrought-iron well created by Hans Prasser in 1626.

Schloss Landskron RUINS

Several paths wind up to this castle, where local nobility held court until fire ravaged it along with the rest of the town in 1792. The population helped itself to the stone to rebuild their houses, and today all that remains is a clock tower and a couple of cannons captured from the French.

Pfarrkirche CHURCH

(Kirchplatz; dawn-dusk) This 15th-century Gothic church is on the way up to the castle ruins.

Sleeping & Eating

★Baderhaus PENSION €

(03862-573 01; www.baderhaus.at; Ringelschmiedgasse 7; s/d/apt €50/85/95;) Baderhaus quite literally used to be the local bathhouse, and you can still see the soot marks on some of the bricks salvaged from one of the city fires in the 13th century. The heritage of the house can be found everywhere, in each uniquely furbished room, many with bathtubs and all with wooden floors.

★Die Weinerei im Baderhaus AUSTRIAN €€

(03862-563 25; www.weinerei-baderhaus.at; Schiffländ 15; mains €11.90-26.80; 11.30am-midnight Tue-Sat) The dishes in this exquisite restaurant change quite frequently according to season, but expect local classics that have been very well prepared and are elegantly presented in one of Bruck's oldest buildings. It has outdoor seating, a bar area and a strong selection of wines from Austria, France and southern Europe.

Gasthof Post Riegler AUSTRIAN €€

(03862-549 04; www.restaurant-riegler.at; Koloman Wallisch-Platz 11; mains €8.50-28.50; 9am-11pm Wed-Sat) Riegler is the most popular of the traditional restaurants in town and has outdoor seating on a terrace overlooking the Mur River in summer.

Information

Tourist Office (03862-306 01; www.tourismus-bruckmur.at; Herzog-Ernst-Gasse 2; 8am-12.30pm & 1.30-5pm Mon-Fri) Located inside the Kornmesserhaus, with the entrance from Herzog-Ernst-Gasse. Has useful town and environs maps with some walking trails.

Getting There & Away

Along with Leoben, Bruck is the region's main rail hub; fast trains to Graz (€12.60, 45 minutes, hourly) pass through here. Other direct trains go hourly to Klagenfurt (€35.60, two hours) and hourly to Vienna (€32.10, 1¾ hours). By road, the main autobahn intersect southeast of town. If you're planning to cycle in the region, the tourist office has useful maps. Four direct buses run daily to/from Mariazell (€12.60, 1½ hours). Postbus services arrive and depart next to the train station.

Leoben

03842 / POP 24,650

Unprepossessing Leoben reveals a few surprises once you dig down into its modest urban soul, and an interesting museum quarter is one very good reason to prolong a visit here between trains. A centre for metallurgical industries and home to Gösser beer, the town achieved ultimate fame with the peace treaty signed here in 1797 by Napoleon and Emperor Franz II.

Like Eisenerz further north, Leoben has been shaped by the mining industry, and is the 'gateway' to the **Steirische Eisenstrasse** (Styrian Iron Road). This winds for about 100km through a landscape that is often impossibly rugged, especially just outside Eisenerz where it becomes precipitous and crosses a bridge with spectacular views to that town. Today, Leoben is also home to a renowned University of Mining.

Sights

Hauptplatz SQUARE

Dating from the 13th century, this long, rectangular square has an attractive **Pestsäule** (Plague Column; 1717). Many of the elegant facades lining the square were created in the 17th century, including the 1660-built **Hacklhaus** (Hauptplatz 9).

MuseumsCenter Leoben MUSEUM

(03842-406 24 08; www.museumscenter-leoben.at; Kirchgasse 6; adult/child/family €5/3.50/11, special exhibitions €10/5/20, combined Kunsthalle €13/7/26; 10am-5pm Tue-Sat, longer hours during Kunsthalle exhibitions) This is the cultural heart of Leoben. The complex has an interesting *Schienen der Vergangenheit* (Tracks of the Past) section telling the history of Leoben and its industries, starting with the present and working back in time, and a large section, the **Kunsthalle** (exhibitions adult/child/family €10/5/20, combined ticket with Schienen der Vergangenheit adult/child/family €13/7/26; 9am-6pm), with special exhibitions, which are held every two years over a period of about seven or eight months and focus on a particular theme. Check the website for information on current or upcoming ones.

Pfarrkirche St Xaver CHURCH

(Kirchplatz 1; 8am-7pm) The simple exterior of this early baroque edifice, built in 1665 as a Jesuit church, belies a complex interior of white walls and black-and-gold baroque altars.

Altes Rathaus HISTORIC BUILDING

(Hauptplatz 1) Leoben's connection with the iron industry is seen in the curious town motif displayed on the Altes Rathaus facade, which shows an ostrich eating horseshoes.

Activities

Asia Spa SPA

(03842-245 00; www.asiaspa.at; In der Au 3; 4hr spa adult/child €11/6, 4hr sauna adult €23.50; spa & sauna 9am-9pm) Leoben's spa centre has various pools and saunas, and offers massages and treatments. There's a 25m swimming pool for sport swimming. Note that children under 16 may not enter the sauna.

Sleeping & Eating

Pension Jahrbacher PENSION €

(664 883 588 82; www.pension-leoben.at; Kirchgasse 14; s/d/tr €48/87/135;) This small, centrally located pension has the advantage of being right next to **Cafe am Schwammerlturm** (03842-436 00; www.jahrbacher.at; Homanngasse 11; 1-10pm Sun-Thu, to 2am Fri & Sat), a tiny cafe with big views, perched atop the circular city tower. Furnishings are quite plain but rooms are comfortable. Book ahead for the pension; if no one answers the door, drop by the adjacent antique shop or the cafe.

Gasthof zum Greif PENSION €€

(03842-214 86; www.zum-greif.at; Waasenstrasse 5; s €69, d €98-129; P) This family-run pension has 13 rooms in all, including three on the top floor that have vaulted ceilings. Expect wooden floors, quite an olde-worlde atmosphere but also some modern furnishings. A lift makes two of the rooms accessible for those in wheelchairs. It's just a hop, step and jump from the centre.

★ Stadt Meierei AUSTRIAN €€
(☎03842-446 03; www.stadt-meierei.at; Homanngasse 1; lunch menu €9.90, mains €17-30; ⏲10am-11pm Tue-Sat) Run by chef Martin Neuretter and *chef de rang* and sommelier Isabella Pichler, this restaurant offers quality cuisine from a menu featuring lamb, beef, poultry and fish specialities. The atmosphere has something of a neo-*Beisl* feel about it, and the service is friendly. Dishes are complemented by a small but excellent selection of Austrian white and red wines.

Information

Tourismusverband Leoben (☎03842-481 48; www.tourismus-leoben.at; Hauptplatz 3; ⏲9am-5pm Mon-Fri) Main information centre for Leoben; stocks a *Welcome to Leoben* booklet with useful listings. Its free Leoben map also includes a great environs map with hiking trails.
Stadt Information Leoben (☎03842-802 16 03; www.leoben.at; Hauptplatz 12; ⏲8am-4pm Mon-Thu, to 1pm Fri) Community and event information centre with some brochures.

Getting There & Away

Frequent buses run to Eisenerz (€8.60, one hour). Leoben is 16km west of Bruck an der Mur (€4.50, 15 minutes, hourly) and on the main rail route to Klagenfurt (€33.10, two hours, every two hours). Direct InterCity (IC) trains run every two hours to Schladming (€25.40, 1¾ hours). The town centre is a 10-minute walk from Leoben's *Hauptbahnhof*: cross the Mur and follow Franz-Josef-Strasse.

Eisenerz

☎03848 / POP 4050

Eisenerz, nestled at the foot of the extraordinary Erzberg (Iron Mountain), is one of the important stops along the Steirische Eisenstrasse. This unusual peak has been completely denuded by open-cast stope mining and resembles a step pyramid. The outcome is eerie and surprisingly beautiful, with its orange and purple shades contrasting with the lush greenery and grey crags of surrounding mountains.

Sights

Erzberg MUSEUM
(☎03848-32 00; www.abenteuer-erzberg.at; Erzberg 1; tours adult/child €18/9, combined tours €32/16, Hauly explosion tour €27/15; ⏲tours 8.30am-3pm May-Oct, advance booking recommended; P 👪) Eisenerz' main attraction is its Erzberg ironworks, which can be seen up close on underground *Schaubergwerk* tours of the mine, abandoned in 1986, or alternatively on overground tours in a 'Hauly' truck along roads cut into the mountain. Both tours are usually in German, with English-language notes available. Each Thursday at 9am you can also ride up in a Hauly and watch rock being blown up. The departure point is a 10-minute walk from the centre, following the river's course.

Dress warmly for the 90-minute *Schaubergwerk* tours. There are fine views along the way of the 60-minute *Hauly Abenteuerfahrt* tours.

Wehrkirche St Oswald CHURCH
(Kirchenstiege 4; ⏲9am-7pm Apr-Oct) More a fortress than a Gothic church, this soaring bastion gained its heavy walls in 1532 as protection against the Turks.

Activities

Eisenerz is surrounded by lots of trails. The tourist office (p200) has a free town map with trails marked, including to the idyllic **Leopoldsteiner See**, only 3km north on the road towards Admont. This small lake has a wall of granite rising to 1649m as a backdrop; you can hire boats in summer – it's a very chilly swim, though.

Sleeping & Eating

JUFA Hotel Eisenerz-Almerlebnis HOSTEL €
(☎05-7083 340; www.jufa.eu/hotel/eisenerz; Ramsau 1; s/d €48/72; P @ 📶) This lovely HI hostel is 5km southwest of Eisenerz. It's situated at an altitude of 1000m, and has a sauna and indoor and outdoor climbing walls, as well as hiking trails going off into the mountains. There's also a restaurant on-site. Bus 925 (€2.40, 30 minutes) runs to within a 15-minute walk from here a few times a day. A taxi costs about €15.

Eisenerzer Hof HOTEL €
(☎03848-255 10; www.eisenerzerhof.at; Hieflauerstrasse 17; s/d/tr €48/76/105; P 🚭 📶) Unlike many other places in Eisenerz, this centrally located hotel has a relatively large number of rooms – 25 in all, which are clean and functional. Book well in advance, though, as it fills up.

Gästehaus Tegelhofer GUESTHOUSE €
(☎03848-20 86; www.gaestehaus-tegelhofer.at; Lindmoserstrasse 8; s/d €42.50/75; P 🚭 📶) This modern guesthouse offers great value, with spacious and clean rooms, and a free

sauna and fitness room. There's also an inexpensive family apartment for two to six people.

Barbarastub'n CAFE €
(☎0676 5415 606; www.barbarastubn.sta.io; Bergmannplatz 2; apple strudel or cake €3.30; ⏲8am-7pm Mon-Fri, from 9am Sat, 2-7pm Sun) Drop by for delicious apple strudel or apple crumble, or to relax on the comfy chairs out back over a tea or coffee. Often has brochures and maps of the town, which are useful when the tourist office is closed.

Information

Tourist Office (☎03848-37 00; www.eisenerz.at; Dr Theodor Körner Platz 1; ⏲10am-noon & 3-5pm Mon-Fri) Helpful staff in the centre of the town. Good maps for hiking. There's a hotel screen outside.

Getting There & Away

Direct buses run hourly from Leoben to Eisenerz (€8.60, one hour), less frequently on Sundays. A couple connect Eisenerz and Admont on weekdays (€8.60, one hour). Another weekday option is to take the bus to Hieflau (€4.50, 20 minutes) and wait for a nonconnecting bus from Hieflau to Admont (€4.50, 30 minutes) or on to Liezen. If travelling west to the Salzkammergut or Schladming, it can make sense to backtrack to Leoben and use rail connections to Liezen and beyond.

Trains no longer operate to Eisenerz, except for the historic mini-rail **Nostalgie** (Nostalgic Train; ☎0664 5081 500; www.erzbergbahn.at; adult/child €16/8; ⏲Sun Jul-Sep) train, which takes you on a 70-minute return journey from Vordernberg to Erzberg Bahnhof and back. See the website for details.

For a taxi, call 03848-4636.

Nationalpark Gesäuse

Established in 2003, Gesäuse is Austria's newest national park, set in a pristine region of jagged mountain ridges, rock towers, deep valleys, alpine pastures and dense spruce forests. It is washed by the Enns River, which is a favourite of rafting connoisseurs, and a number of companies offer rafting trips during the summer months. Hiking and mountain climbing, and to a lesser extent mountain biking, also feature among the park's outdoor activities.

Among the six peaks over 2000m within the park, Hocktor (2369m) is the highest and is popular among hikers.

The park has been given *Genussregion* status, meaning it is known for a particular speciality, in this case game. A great majority of the food served in the huts, guesthouses and park cafes is local and organic. Apart from a few mountain huts, you'll need to sleep in Admont or Johnsbach.

The staffed **national park pavilion** (☎03611-211 01 20; Gstatterboden 25; ⏲10am-6pm May-Oct) is a useful source of information; the tourist office in Admont also has information on accommodation and activities in the park.

The park is easily reached by the daily afternoon train to Gstatterboden from May to early September (€4.50, 15 minutes) and Johnsbach im Nationalpark (€4.50, 10 minutes). Buses connect the park with Admont (bus 912; €4.50, 17 minutes, three to eight daily), via Bachbrücke/Weidendom (€4.50, 12 minutes). The Rufbus (p202) operates daily from Admont Bahnhof to Johnsbach between 8am and 8pm from May to October. This can drop you off close to Gstatterboden im Nationalpark. Cycling out here is also an option. **Pörl Sportshop** (☎03613-215 21; www.poerl-sport-shop.at; Hauptstrasse 18; per day mountain bike €25, e-mountain bike €35; ⏲9am-noon & 2-6pm Mon-Fri, 9am-noon Sat) in Admont rents out bikes.

Admont

☎03613 / POP 5010

Admont, nestled in a broad section of the Enns Valley, is a low-key town that revs up during the day when groups arrive in buses to see its spectacular abbey. Each night it sinks back into pleasant oblivion. The town makes a good base for kicking off deeper into the region.

Sights

★**Benedictine Abbey** ABBEY
(☎03613-231 20; www.stiftadmont.at; Admont 1; adult/child/family €11.50/6.50/26; ⏲10am-5pm late Mar-early Nov) Admont's Benedictine abbey is arguably Austria's most elegant and exciting baroque abbey. It brings together museums, religion, and modern art and architecture into an award-winning cultural ensemble.

The centrepiece of the abbey is its **Stiftsbibliothek**, the largest abbey library in the world. Survivor of a fire in 1865 that severely damaged the rest of the abbey, it displays about 70,000 volumes of the abbey's 200,000-strong collection, and is decorated with heavenly ceiling frescoes by Bartolomeo Altomonte (1694–1783) and statues (in wood, but painted to look like bronze) by Josef Stammel (1695–1765).

The abbey is also home to the **Kunsthistorisches Museum** (Art History Museum), featuring rare pieces such as its tiny portable altar from 1375, made from amethyst quartz and edged with gilt-silver plates; some Gerhard Mercator globes from 1541 and 1551; and monstrances from the 15th and 16th centuries. Each year innovative temporary exhibitions complement the permanent ones.

Another museum, the **Museum für Gegenwartkunst** (Museum for Contemporary Art), contains works by about 100 mainly Austrian artists, and has pieces you can explore with your hands. The **Naturhistorisches Museum** (Natural History Museum) began in 1674 with a small collection and today includes rooms devoted to flying insects (one of the largest collections in the world), butterflies, stuffed animals, wax fruit and reptiles. From the glass stairway and herb garden there are views to Gesäuse National Park.

Sleeping & Eating

★JUFA Hotel Schloss Röthelstein HOSTEL, HOTEL €€

(☎057 083 320; www.jufa.eu/hotel/roethelstein; Aigen 32; s/d/tr/q from €62.50/104/135/166; P ⊝ ᯤ) The monks from the abbey once used to spend the summer in this baroque castle from the 17th century, about 5km southwest of the centre off Aignerstrasse. The renovated palace is flanked by carefully manicured lawns, and has an elegant glass-roofed, arcaded inner courtyard and tastefully decorated rooms with wooden floors. Some of its 41 rooms are located in towers.

Hotel Spirodom Admont HOTEL €€

(☎03613-366 00; www.spirodom.at; Eichenweg 616; s/d €108/157; P @ ᯤ ≋) Admont's four-star hotel is located about 600m north of the abbey and lures guests with a pool, wellness facilities and views to either the abbey or parkland in tastefully appointed rooms. It also has city bike hire for guests (€2.50 per hour or €12 per day) and the excellent **Restaurant Pano Visum** (☎03613-366 00; www.spirodom.at; Eichenweg 616; mains €16.50-29.90; ⏲6-9pm; ✍) restaurant on the 3rd floor.

Hotel Gasthof Traube HOTEL €€

(☎03613-244 00; www.hotel-die-traube.at; Hauptstrasse 3; s €49-59, d €98-118; P ᯤ) One of the best places to stay in the centre of town, with friendly staff and modern rooms (some with great views to the mountains) that are a notch above the others on Hauptstrasse. It's a stone's throw from the tourist office and national park centre.

Gasthaus Kamper AUSTRIAN €

(☎03613-36 88; www.gh-kamper.at; Hauptstrasse 19; mains €8.50-16.90; ⏲9.30am-11pm Mon-Sat, to 3pm Sun, closed Mon Sep-Apr; ✍) Centrally located and serving earthy Styrian classics, including the local beef.

Information

Tourist Office (☎03613-211 60 10; www.gesaeuse.at; Hauptstrasse 35; ⏲9am-5pm Mon-Fri, 10am-4pm Sat, closed Sat Nov–mid-May) Opposite the *Rathaus* near the abbey church. It doubles as a national park office.

Getting There & Away

Admont is 15km to the east of Selzthal, but has very limited train services. Buses departing from Hieflau (€4.50, 30 minutes, three to eight daily) and Liezen (€4.50, 30 minutes, five to 12 daily) are the two main approaches to Admont. A couple of buses go to Eisenerz (€8.60, one hour) on weekdays only. Buses connect Admont with the national park office in Gstatterboden (€4.50, 17 minutes, three to eight daily), via Bachbrücke/Weidendom (€4.50, 12 minutes).

From April to October Pörl Sportshop rents mountain bikes (per day €25) and electric mountain bikes (per day €35). It's a 15km ride from Admont to Gstatterboden in the national park along the Enns River cycling route.

Johnsbach

☎03611 / POP 150

Situated 17km southeast of Admont, the tiny settlement of Johnsbach is the focal point for hiking, climbing and water sports in the region and for excursions in and around the Gesäuse National Park. It is wedged on a bucolic stream, with rugged mountains rising up on virtually all sides. In seasons of heavy snow, the settlement is sometimes cut off from visitors due to the danger of avalanches.

This is one of Austria's earliest mountain-climbing centres, and testimony to this is in the poignant Bergsteiger-Friedhof, where buried alongside local citizens are mountain climbers who have come to grief in the Gesäuse over the centuries. With its pretty whitewashed church, this is a beautiful and strangely touching place.

Sights & Activities

Bergsteiger-Friedhof CEMETERY
(Mountain Climber Cemetery; www.johnsbach.at; Friedhofweg; dawn-dusk) FREE A pretty and extremely touching place, this mountain cemetery is beautiful in itself, but also contains the graves of some of Austria's greatest mountaineers from 1810 onwards.

AOS Adventures KAYAKING, RAFTING
(03612-253 43; www.rafting.at; Gstatterboden 103, Gstatterboden; 3-4hr Enns 14km rafting tours €60; 8.30am-5pm Mon-Fri, tours 9am & 1.30pm, Gesäuse camp closed mid-Oct–Apr) Offers rafting, canyoning and kayaking on the Enns and Salza Rivers.

Haindlkarhütte Hike HIKING
(03611-221 15; www.alpenverein.at/haindlkarhuette; Johnsbach 100; May–mid-Oct) This alpine hut at 1121m is one of the more popular hiking destinations in the region. The tourist office (p201) in Admont can help with planning and details.

Sleeping

Campingplatz Forstgarten CAMPGROUND €
(0664 825 23 23; www.landesforste.at; Gstatterboden 105; adult/child/car/tent €6/4.50/2.50/5; May-Oct;) This camping ground is a perfect base for exploring the national park. It's located alongside the Gesäuse base camp for AOS Adventures rafting tours and has a common room with refrigerator and cooking facilities. There's wi-fi but it's a little unreliable.

★**Gasthof Kölblwirt** PENSION €
(03611-216; www.koelblwirt.at; Johnsbach 65; s €50, d €78-84;) Gasthof Kölblwirt has it all: a pension, a restaurant specialising in Styrian beef, and lots of suggestions for activities. Pine-clad rooms are sweetly simple and the welcome is warm. The organic beef served in the restaurant is from cattle that graze in summer around the family's own alpine meadow hut, the **Kölblalm**.

As well as enjoying a meal in the restaurant, consider working up an appetite on a hike or bike ride around the **Johnsbacher Almrunde** (7am-6pm May, Jun & Sep, to 8pm Jul & Aug) FREE, an 11km walking and cycling trail along forestry tracks. The Kölblalm is one of the stops along the way.

Gasthof zum Donner PENSION €
(03611-218; www.donnerwirt.at; Johnsbach 5; s/d/tr €46/76/114;) This traditional alpine hotel has bright, comfortable rooms, a bustling restaurant with nice terrace seating, and a sauna for posthike steams.

Getting There & Away

With your own wheels, take the B146 then follow the signposted turn-off to Johnsbach. Regular Postbus services run from Admont to the turn-off at Bachbrücke/Weidendom (€4.50, 12 minutes), from where it's a 5km walk. Call ahead for a **Rufbus** (Taxi bus; 03613-41 70, 03613-24 06; May-Oct), which operates daily from Admont Bahnhof to Johnsbach (€9.50) between 8am and 8pm from May to October.

Cycling out here is also an option. Pörl Sportshop (p200) in Admont rents out mountain bikes for €25 per day (e-mountain bikes €35).

WESTERN STYRIA

Like northern Styria, western Styria is a mountainous region divided by jagged ranges and alpine streams. Murau is a picturesque town well placed for hikes and cycle trips into the surrounding forests. If you're heading this way from Graz, consider a detour to Seckau or Oberzeiring. The former is famous for its **Benedictine Abbey** (03514-52340; www.abtei-seckau.at; Seckau 1, Oberzeiring; tours adult/child €7/4; 8am-8pm daily, tours 11am & 2pm Wed-Sun May-late Oct, daily Jul-Aug), a stunning Romanesque basilica and the mausoleum of Karl II, while the latter is known for its old **silver mine** (www.silbergruben.at; Marktplatz 3, Oberzeiring; adult/child/family €11.50/5/24; tours 10.30am, 1.30pm & 3pm daily May-Oct, 3pm Wed Nov-Apr), now resurrected as an exhibition mine and small health resort for sufferers of respiratory diseases.

Schladming

03687 / POP 6660

Situated deep in the Ennstal (Enns Valley) in western Styria at the foot of the glacial Dachsteingebirge (Dachstein mountains), Schladming is an easygoing ski resort that in summer also offers glacier skiing and snowboarding, easy access to hiking trails, white-water rafting on the Enns River and excellent mountain biking. On Hoher Dachstein (2995m), don't miss the opportunity to walk through a glacier crevice in the *Eispalast* (ice palace) or to admire views over the Ennstal from the Skywalk high-altitude panorama platform.

Sights

★Dachstein Eispalast GLACIER
(www.dachsteingletscher.at; Ramsau am Dachstein; Eispalast adult/child €10/5.50, gondola return plus all sights adult/child early Dec–mid-May €39/19.50, mid-May–early Dec €47.50/24.50; 8.30am-4.30pm, gondola every 20min 7.50am-5.30pm) Situated in a crevice of the Dachstein Glacier along a sheer cliff face, the *Eispalast* creates the strange effect of walking through an enormous, hollow ice cube. A gondola, one of the world's most spectacular, whisks you up and terminates with a vertical thrust at the Skywalk viewing platform. About 10 buses daily leave Planet Planai in Schladming for the base station near Ramsau. A 24-hour return bus ticket costs €9 (45 minutes).

During the summer months you can also buy the gondola ticket (€39.50/19.50) and individual admission tickets separately, but this generally works out to be more expensive unless you just want to see the glacier and stroll around a bit.

Activities

The area around Schladming has more than 900km of mountain-bike trails, divided among 20 routes shown on the excellent, free mountain-bike map from the tourist office (p205). Hiking trails begin almost from the centre of town – the tourist office's town map has trails marked.

Schladming Ski Fields SNOW SPORTS
(www.schladming-dachstein.at; day pass adult/child from €53.30/27) From December to March the area's 223km of downhill ski pistes and 86 ski lifts rev into action. Skiing and snowboarding on the Dachstein Glacier can be done year-round but not all lifts are open in summer.

Most of the cross-country skiing is done across the valley in Ramsau (about €18 for ski hire). A medium-quality snowboard for the pistes costs €34 with boots and snow-hiking shoes around €20. Prices on the glacier are similar.

Riesachfälle Waterfalls HIKING
You can begin this popular walk from Talbachgasse in Schladming. Follow the stream south out of town for about 40 minutes. From there it's about another 3½ hours' walk southeast along the stream to the waterfalls.

An alternative is to take the bus to the popular valley restaurant **Gasthof zu Riesachfall** (03687-616 78; www.gasthaus-riesachfall.at; Untertalstrasse 66, Untertal; mains €11-18; 10am-9pm mid-May–late Oct) and walk the forest trail (1½ hours, good shoes and head for heights required) or the gravel forestry road (two hours) to the falls and beyond to the Riesachsee (Lake Riesach). In summer at least five buses daily leave from Rathausplatz and Lendplatz to Riesachfall Wilde Wasser (€6.60, 35 minutes), the access point for the Riesachfälle waterfalls and the lake.

> **SOMMERCARD**
>
> From late May to late October, a Sommercard gives you various discounts and also free transport on the buses (not Postbus services, and not admission to the *Eispalast*). Most cable cars are also free, but only to the Dachstein if you stay two nights. You can't buy it, but when booking a place ask if one is included in your stay.

[pi:tu] Bikecenter CYCLING
(0680 320 78 62; www.bikeparkplanai.at; Coburgstrasse 52; per day €29-90) This pro mountain-bike rental place is located at the Planai Stadium. It offers some discounts with the Sommercard.

Trittscher BICYCLE, SKI RENTAL
(03687-22 64 70; www.tritscher.at; Salzburgerstrasse 24; during ski season 8.30am-7pm Mon-Sat, 8.30am-12.30pm & 3-6pm Sun, outside ski season 8.30am-6pm Mon-Fri, to 5pm Sat) In summer Trittscher rents mountain bikes and in winter it hires out ski equipment; see website for full price list as rates vary depending on equipment level.

Festivals & Events

Musikanten Ski-WM MUSIC
(03687-2277 722; www.musikanen-ski-wm.at; main tent per day €32; Wed-Sun early Apr) Young and old descend on Schladming *Dirndl-ed* and *Lederhosed* in early April for this ragey folk music festival; it takes place each year in a tent in town and several other spots around town that have extra admission prices.

Sleeping

In summer the considerable number of hotels means you can often get a good deal. But book well ahead during the ski season and be prepared for high prices. The tourist office can help you in finding smaller B&Bs and private rooms.

★Stadthotel Brunner SPA HOTEL €€
(☎03687-225 130; www.stadthotel-brunner.at; Hauptplatz 14; d €168-192; P⊜☎) This hotel on the Hauptplatz is a delight. Petra Brunner and Thomas Radzik, a chef and musician respectively, have worked some fresh ideas at this super-stylish but friendly and relaxed place. Spacious, sexy rooms are complemented with a beautiful rooftop sauna and tea lounge; the brimming breakfast buffet has Ayurvedic elements as well as top-quality traditional dishes.

JUFA Hotel Schladming HOSTEL €€
(☎05 708 33 30; www.jufa.at/schladming; Coburgstrasse 253; s €57, d €80-117; ⊙closed Apr-May & Oct-Nov; P⊜☎) Situated in the pedestrian zone close to the Planai base station, this excellent hostel has dorms with bunks, twins with beds you can shift together, as well as singles and family rooms, all neat, bright and mostly with wooden floorboards. It's got a drying room for your ski gear. Sommercard issued.

Post Hotel HOTEL €€
(☎03687-225 71; www.posthotel-schladming.at; Hauptplatz 10; s €89, d €168-188r, max 4-person apt per person €104; P⊜☎) The four-star Post Hotel has spacious, modern rooms decorated in tasteful tones. Some of its doubles have connecting doors for families, and its family apartment has a separate living room. It also has a sauna and a good half-board deal is available. It issues the Sommercard.

Eating

Stadtbräu AUSTRIAN €
(☎0664 517 96 20; www.tennestadl-schladming.com/stadtbraeu; Siedergasse 89; mains €12.90-17.90; ⊙10am-11.30pm Tue-Sun) A totally traditional vaulted dining room with Austrian classics, including the fleshtastic mixed grill of pork, chicken and steak, though it only does a pork schnitzel, not a true Vienna schnitzel from veal.

Bio Chi HEALTH FOOD €
(www.biochi.at; Martin Luther-Strasse 32; mains €10.50, salads €5.50-6.90; ⊙8am-6pm Mon-Fri, to 2pm Sat; ✎) This welcoming and well-stocked health-food shop is a local institution and whips up leafy salads, vegetarian mains and tempting sweets using organic ingredients, which you can wash down with freshly squeezed juices. It also does fresh, healthy breakfasts. The gluten-free cakes are excellent.

Julius ITALIAN €€
(☎0664 251 33 99; www.julius-kitchen.com; Martin-Luther-Strasse 31; mains €15-40; ⊙11.30am-11pm, shorter winter hours; ✎) This smart wine bar is a local favourite, not least because of its delicious, contemporary Italian food and outdoor seating in summer. It serves well-prepared pastas, red meat and above all fish (its speciality). There are a number of good meat-free pastas, and the kitchen is happy to do vegan dishes on request too.

Johann AUSTRIAN €€
(☎03687-225 71; www.posthotel-schladming.at; Hauptplatz 10; mains €16.50-33.90; ⊙11.30am-1.30pm & 5.30-9.30pm) The Post Hotel's Johann restaurant mixes cosy pine and fresh green-and-white textiles in a sweetly upmarket dining room. There's an excellent selection of rather pricey wines to go with its carefully cooked Styrian and Austrian dishes.

Die Tischlerei INTERNATIONAL €€€
(☎03687-221 92; www.dietischlerei.co.at; Rosegerstrasse 676; menus €39-50, mains €16-24; ⊙4pm-midnight Tue-Sat) On a corner just a short walk beyond the centre, this big, modern restaurant serves up a number of set menus and dishes à la carte that span Mediterranean and Austrian flavours, whether it be *Wiener Schnitzel* (in the true Viennese designation from veal) and a filet of dry-aged veal, or risotto and seafood inspired by Italian cuisine.

Drinking & Nightlife

Hohenhaus Tenne BAR
(www.tenne.com/schladming; Coburgstrasse 512; ⊙11am-8pm & 9.30pm-3.30am Nov-Mar) Finding après-ski in Schladming in the ski season is as easy as falling down an icy hill. The Hohenhaus Tenne is a reliable place to tumble.

Shopping

★Heimatgold FOOD & DRINKS
(☎03687-2250 5350; www.heimatgold.at; Coburgstrasse 49; ⊙9am-6pm Mon-Fri, to 3pm Sat) A wonderful place to stock up on picnic supplies, self-catering needs or take-home gourmet gifts, Heimatgold champions the products of local farmers, from chocolate to pickles to raw milk and freshly prepared Styrian stews in jars.

Information

Tourismusverband Schladming-Rohrmoos (03687-227 77 22; www.schladming.com; Rohrmoosstrasse 234; 9am-6pm Mon-Sat, closed Sat May & Nov;) Stocks mountain-bike and hiking trail maps, has lots of tips on the region and will organise accommodation if you call ahead. A useful accommodation board and free telephone are situated in a 24-hour lobby.

Getting There & Away

Every two hours trains pass through on their way to Graz (€29.90, 2¾ hours) and at least five times daily to Salzburg (€19.60, 1½ hours). The Dachsteinstrasse toll road to the gondola costs €14 for a passenger car (up to nine people). It's free if you punch the ticket when you purchase a gondola ticket. Bus passengers pay per adult/child €3/1.40 (punch these too).

Getting Around

[pi:tu] Bikecenter (p203) offers discounts on e-mountain bikes with the Sommercard. In summer Trittscher (p203) rents mountain bikes for €17 per day and e-bikes for €29 per day.

For a taxi, call 03687-212 10.

Murau

03532 / POP 3630

Murau, in the western reaches of the Murtal (Mur Valley) on the banks of the river, is an attractive town filled with pastel-coloured houses. It's also surrounded by forested hills and alpine meadows. Its close proximity to Stolzalpe to the north and the Metnitzer mountains to the south makes it an excellent base for hiking and cycling in summer

Sights

Schloss Murau CASTLE

(03532-23 02 58; www.murau-kreischberg.at; Schlossberg 1; tours adult/child €8/4; tours 2pm Wed & Sat mid-Jun–mid-Oct) Built in 1250 by the Liechtenstein family, who once ruled the region, Schloss Murau was transformed into its present late-Renaissance form in the 17th century. Tours take you through seven rooms, including the chapel and the Rittersaal (Knight's Room), where concerts are often held. The altar in the chapel dates from 1655 and was created by masters from the town of Judenberg. See the website for dates of special summertime children's tours (under 'Ausflugsziele/Schloss Murau').

Stadtpfarrkirche St Matthäus CHURCH

(Schlossberg 8; dawn-dusk) Situated just below the castle, this restored church has Gothic and baroque elements that work surprisingly well together, especially in the combination of the Gothic crucifixion group (1500) and the baroque high altar (1655). The beautiful frescoes date from the 14th to the 16th centuries.

Brewery Museum MUSEUM

(03532-32 66 500; www.murauerbier.at; Raffaltplatz 19-23; tours €16.50; 4pm Tue-Sat) Murau is famous in Austria for its Brauerei Murau, which has been brewing its amber fluid for over 500 years. These days it is a cooperative brewery with climate-neutral production and beers range from ale (pale) to *Zwickl* (yeasty). Two-hour tours take you through a display brewery and include a glass of the local brew or a soft drink. You can also buy beer shampoo and various other beer-based products here.

Sleeping & Eating

JUFA Hotel Murau HOSTEL €

(05 7083 280; www.jufa.eu/hotel/murau; St Leonhard Platz 4; s/d/tr/q/apt €66/82/110/138/158; closed Nov; P) This HI hostel is situated in four buildings

CYCLING & HIKING AROUND MURAU

Almost a dozen cycling tracks and mountain-bike trails can be accessed from Murau. The granddaddy of them all is the 450km-long **Murradweg**, which follows the course of the Mur River. Trails are numbered and routes marked on the Murau tourist office's useful *Rad & Mountainbike* booklet, also in English.

Hiking trails also branch out into the region from here, some beginning from the train station and others from the *Bundesstrasse* around Billa supermarket. A strenuous five-hour return hike to the Stolzalpe peak (1817m) begins at Billa. The tourist office has a useful *Wandern* booklet on hikes.

Intersport Pintar (03532-23 97; www.sportpintar.at; Bundesstrasse 7a; per day bike €18, e-bike €29; 8.30am-6pm Mon-Fri, to 12.30pm Sat), about 500m past the Billa supermarket, rents trekking and e-bikes.

near the train station, and has sleek, modern and spacious rooms, a sauna and a peaceful inner courtyard. Call ahead around November, when it closes for at least one month.

★**Hotel Gasthof Lercher** HOTEL, PENSION €€
(☎03532-24 31; www.hotel-restaurant-lercher.at; Schwarzenbergstrasse 10; s €48-81, d €96-172; P⊖@≋) Hotel Lercher is two places in one: a three-star *Gasthof* (inn) with inexpensive rooms and – still excellent value – a four-star hotel. Many of the rooms have views to the Stolzalpe, and even the cheapest are comfortably furnished. There's a sauna and steam bath. The restaurant serves delicious seasonal Styrian and Austrian classics (mains €12.60 to €18.60).

Hotel Rosenhof Murau HOTEL €€
(☎03532-23 18; www.rosenhof-murau.at; Roseggerstrasse 9; s €75-90, d €130-180; P⊖@≋) With pared-back, light-wood rooms, a sauna and herbal steam bath, and an attractive restaurant terrace (mains €14 to €28), Hotel Rosenhof has style and rustic cosiness. The more expensive larger rooms have balconies, and some have connecting doors for families.

Drinking & Nightlife

Bier Apotheke BREWERY
(☎0664 884 358 87; www.murauerbier.at/bierapotheke; Anna-Neumann-strasse 34; ⊙4-10pm Tue-Sat) Housed in a historic pharmacy, this small beer bar serves the range of beers produced by the local Murau brewery, which is located just down the road, but also sells various products made with beer.

Information

Tourist Office (☎03532-27 20-0; www.murau-kreischberg.at; Liechtensteinstrasse 3-5; ⊙9am-5pm Mon-Fri, to noon Sat, closed Sat Apr-Nov) Has loads of brochures on the town and its surrounds, including hiking and bicycle trails.

Getting There & Away

If you're coming from Salzburgerland, the most pleasant mode of transport is the **Murtalbahn** (☎03532-22 33; www.stlb.at; one way/return €17.60/25), a steam train that chugs its way between Tamsweg and Murau once every Tuesday and Thursday from mid-June to mid-September on a narrow-gauge line.

Every two to four hours direct ÖBB trains connect Murau with Tamsweg (€8.60, one hour). Trains to Leoben (€20.60, 1½ hours, every two hours) require a change in Unzmarkt, also the junction for trains from Murau to Klagenfurt (€22.90, 2¼ hours, every two hours).

The Salzkammergut

Includes ➡

Best Places to Eat

➡ Balthazar im Rudolfsturm (p212)

➡ Das gute Leben (p215)

➡ Restaurant zum Salzbaron (p212)

➡ Gjaid Alm (p213)

➡ Mostschenke im Heustadl (p220)

Best Places to Stay

➡ Heritage Hotel Hallstatt (p212)

➡ Erzherzog Johann (p215)

➡ Im Weissen Rössl (p223)

➡ Hallstatt Hideaway (p212)

Why Go?

The Salzkammergut is a dramatic region of alpine and subalpine lakes, deeply carved valleys, rolling hills and rugged, steep mountain ranges rising to almost 3000m. Much of the region is remote wilderness, and even in the heavily visited parts, such as the Wolfgangsee and Mondsee, you'll always find isolated areas where still, glassy waters provide limitless opportunities for boating, swimming, fishing or just sitting on the shore and skimming stones. The popular Hallstätter See, flanked by soaring mountains that offer great hiking, is arguably the most spectacular of the lakes.

Salt was once the 'white gold' of the Salzkammergut, and the mines that made it famous now provide an interesting journey back in time to the settlers of the Iron Age Hallstatt culture, and to the Celts and Romans.

When to Go

➡ July to early September is the perfect time to visit the Salzkammergut for outdoor activities like hiking and lake swimming. All the summer sights are open.

➡ The number of visitors is lower either side of the summer high season – except around Easter – but in April and September you can still visit most of the main sights.

➡ The ski resorts open in December, and from then until March you will find the best of the snow in the Dachstein mountains.

The Salzkammergut Highlights

❶ **5 Fingers Viewing Platform** (p213) Reeling from views high up in the Dachstein mountains.

❷ **Hallstätter See** (p211) Hiking the lake's edge from Obertraun to Hallstatt and cooling off in the crystal waters between trails.

❸ **St Wolfgang** (p223) Discovering Wolfgangsee's remarkable pilgrimage church, filled with priceless artworks.

❹ **Kaiservilla** (p209) Strolling through Franz Joseph's summer residence in Bad Ischl.

❺ **Dachstein Caves** (p213) Plunging into the chilling depths to marvel at masterfully illuminated towers of ice.

❻ **Gmunden** (p216) Hunting for vintage ceramics in the backstreets and market squares of this charming town.

❼ **Krippenstein** (p213) Skiing on the 11km alpine piste in the Dachstein mountains.

Getting There & Away

CAR & MOTORCYCLE

To get to the Salzkammergut from Salzburg by car or motorcycle, take the A1 to reach the north of the region, or Hwy 158 to Bad Ischl. Travelling north–south, the main road is Hwy 145 (the Salzkammergut Bundesstrasse), which follows the train line for most of its length.

TRAIN

By rail, the main routes into the province are from Salzburg or Linz, with a change at Attnang-Puchheim onto the regional north–south railway line. From Styria, change at Stainach-Irdning.

Getting Around

BOAT

Numerous operators ply the waters between towns on the Attersee, Traunsee, Mondsee, Hallstätter See and Wolfgangsee.

BUS

Regular bus services connect all towns and villages in the area; services on weekends are less frequent or not at all. Hourly buses depart Salzburg for various towns in the region, including Bad Ischl, Mondsee (every 30 minutes) and St Wolfgang; for services from Styria, see www.busbahnbim.at.

TRAIN

The Salzkammergut is crossed by regional trains on a north–south route, passing through Attnang-Puchheim on the Salzburg–Linz line and Stainach-Irdning on the Bischofshofen–Graz line. Hourly trains take 2½ hours to complete the journey. Attersee is also accessible by rail.

Small stations are not staffed; at an *unbesetzter Bahnhof* (unattended train station), use a platform ticket machine.

BAD ISCHL

06132 / POP 14,135

This spa town's reputation snowballed after the Habsburg Princess Sophie took a treatment here to cure her infertility in 1828. Within two years she had given birth to Emperor Franz Joseph I; two other sons followed and were nicknamed the Salzprinzen (Salt Princes). Rather in the manner of a salmon returning to its place of birth, Franz Joseph made an annual pilgrimage to Bad Ischl, making it his summer home for the next 60 years and hauling much of the European aristocracy in his wake. The fateful letter he signed declaring war on Serbia and sparking off WWI bore a Bad Ischl postmark.

Today's Bad Ischl is a handsome, if occasionally overrun, town that makes a handy base for visiting the region's five main lakes.

Sights

Kaiservilla PALACE

(06132-232 41; www.kaiservilla.at; Jainzen 38; adult/child €15/7.50, grounds only €5.10/4.10; 9.30am-5pm May-Sep, 10am-4pm Apr & Oct, 10am-4pm Sat & Sun Dec, 10am-4pm Wed Jan-Mar, closed Nov) Franz Joseph's sprawling summer residence, the Italianate-style Kaiservilla, was an engagement present for him and his princess-to-be, Elisabeth of Bavaria, from his mother Princess Sophie. Elisabeth, who loathed the villa and her mother-in-law in equal measure, spent little time here, but the emperor came to love it and it became his permanent summer residence for more than 60 years. His mistress, Katharina Schratt, lived nearby in a house chosen for her by the empress.

Stadtmuseum MUSEUM

(06132-254 76; www.stadtmuseum.at; Esplanade 10; adult/child €5.50/2.70; 2-7pm Wed, 10am-5pm Thu-Sun Apr-Oct & Dec, 10am-5pm Fri-Sun Jan-Mar, closed Nov) The City Museum showcases the long history of Bad Ischl and stages changing exhibitions. This also happens to be the building where Franz Joseph and Elisabeth were engaged, the day after they were formally introduced at a ball. You can also organise a tour of the historic **Lehàr Villa** (06132-254 76; Lehárkai 8; adult/child €5.80/2.70; 10am-5pm Wed-Sun May-Sep, plus Mon Jul & Aug) here (combined entrance adult/child €9.50/€5.40).

Activities

Salzkammergut Therme SPA

(06132-204 27 00; www.eurothermen.at; Voglhuberstrasse 10; 4hr ticket therme adult/child €19.50/14.50, day ticket therme adult/child €22/16.50, combi day ticket therme & saunas €27; 9am-midnight) If you'd like to follow in Princess Sophie's footsteps, check out treatments at this historic spa. Today it's a thoroughly modern operation, with the usual range of salt and spring thermal pools and European spa treatments, as well as the rather lame 'lazy river' slipstream and unimpressive salt 'grotto'. The saunas are only accessible with a combined day ticket.

Festivals & Events

Lehár Festival MUSIC
(www.leharfestival.at; tickets €26-83; ⌚Jul & Aug) The home of operetta composer Franz Lehár, Bad Ischl hosts the Lehár Festival, which stages musical works by Lehár and other composers.

Sleeping & Eating

Jugendgästehaus HOSTEL €
(☎06132-265 77; www.jugendherbergsverband.at; Am Rechensteg 5; dm/s/d €28/39/66; P ⊖ @ ☎) It might be a little short on character from the outside, but this hostel is well run, breakfast is decent and it has a great location in the town centre behind Kreuzplatz.

★**Goldenes Schiff** HOTEL €€
(☎06132-242 41; www.goldenes-schiff.at; Adalbert-Stifter-Kai 3; s €103-127, d €160-218, f ste €215-312; P ⊖ @ ☎) Most doubles in this four-star hotel have bathtubs, and the best rooms (superior doubles and suites) have a touch of glamour, with large windows that overlook the river. Some rooms can be very plain but there's also a **wellness centre** with solarium and sauna. Entrance is from Auböckplatz. The restaurant (mains €11.50 to €30) serves proficient Austrian classics, with some excellent wines.

Hotel Garni Sonnhof HOTEL €€
(☎06132-230 78; http://sonnhof.at; Bahnhofstrasse 4; s €70-95, d €90-150; ⌚Easter-Oct; P ⊖ ☎) Nestled in a leafy glade of maple trees next to the station, this lovely hotel has cosy, traditional decor, a beautiful garden complete with a pond, and a sunny conservatory. Large bedrooms mix interesting old furniture, rag rugs and wooden floors but are far from fussy. Use of the sauna and steam bath is included. Book well ahead, and note it's generally easier via third-party booking websites.

Cafe Zauner CAFE €
(www.zauner.at; Pfarrgasse 7; pastries €3.80-6; ⌚8.30am-6pm) Little has changed in grand Cafe Zauner since it opened in 1882. Its elegant interior with antique furnishings makes it the perfect place to relax over a luscious traditional pastry and black coffee.

Restaurant Esplanade AUSTRIAN €€
(www.zauner.at; Hasner Allee 2; mains €16.50-22.50; ⌚10am-9pm Jun-Oct, to 7pm Wed-Sun Nov-Dec & Mar-May) This offshoot of the famous pastry shop Cafe Zauner serves Austrian favourites, including trout and a real *Wiener Schnitzel* (breaded cutlet) from veal or the cheaper pork variety, in a fabulously pleasant location beside the river. Given Zauner's pedigree, desserts are a big draw, too. It's closed in January, and sometimes February too.

Drinking & Nightlife

K.u.K. Hofbeisl PUB
(☎06132-272 71; www.kukhofbeisl.com; Wirerstrasse 4; ⌚8am-2am Mon-Sat, 5pm-2am Sun) This rambling place has a *Beisl* (bistro pub; mains €11 to €22) open for lunch and dinner in one building, connected with a bar in the other, which is the liveliest late-night party place in town – DJs do their thing most Saturday nights. The cocktail list, though far from hipster-pleasing, is impressively ambitious, with about 150 cocktails in all.

Information

Salzkammergut Touristik (☎06132-2400 051; www.salzkammergut.co.at; Götzstrasse 12; ⌚9am-6pm Mon-Fri, to 2pm Sat & Sun, closed Sun Sep-Jun) A helpful private regional agency with trekking bikes (€15 for 24 hours), trekking e-bikes (€28) and a few e-mountain bikes (€35). Internet access in the office costs €1 per 15 minutes.

Tourist Office (☎06132-27 75 70; www.badischl.at; Auböckplatz 5; ⌚9am-6pm Mon-Sat, 10am-2pm Sun May-late Oct, 9am-5pm Mon-Sat, 10am-2pm Sun late Oct-Apr) Has helpful staff and lots of information on Bad Ischl and the region.

Getting There & Away

BUS

Postbus (☎05 17 17; www.postbus.at) services depart from outside the **train station** (Bahnhofstrasse 8), with hourly buses to Salzburg (€10.80, 1½ hours) via St Gilgen (€5.80, 36 minutes). Buses to St Wolfgang (€4.50, 32 minutes) go via Strobl.

CAR & MOTORCYCLE

Most major roads in the Salzkammergut go to or near Bad Ischl. Hwy 158 from Salzburg and the north–south Hwy 145 intersect just north of the town centre.

TRAIN

Hourly trains to Hallstatt Bahnhof (€5.50, 27 minutes) go via Steeg/Gosau and continue on to Obertraun (€5.50, 30 minutes). There are also hourly trains to Gmunden (€7.40, 45 minutes), as well as to Salzburg (€25.70, two hours) with various changes.

SOUTHERN SALZKAMMERGUT

Hallstätter See

The Hallstätter See, set among sharply rising mountains at an altitude of 508m in the Southern Salzkammergut, is one of the prettiest and most accessible lakes in the region. It offers some of the best hiking and swimming in summer, good skiing in winter, and a fascinating insight into the cultural history of the region any time of year. Just 5km around the lake lies Obertraun, the closest resort to the Dachstein ice caves.

The whole Hallstatt-Dachstein region became a Unesco World Heritage site in 1997.

Hallstatt

☎06134 / POP 780

With pastel-coloured houses casting shimmering reflections onto the looking-glass lake and with lofty mountains rearing up on all sides, Hallstatt's beauty borders on the surreal and the sublime. Boats glide tranquilly across the lake from the train station to the village, situated precariously on a narrow stretch of land between mountain and shore. (So small is the patch of land occupied by the village that its annual Corpus Christi procession takes place largely in small boats on the lake.) The sheer volume of visitors here can be nerve-fraying, especially in summer, with a sea of cars, buses and tour groups descending.

The centre of Hallstatt is at Hallstatt Markt, and Hallstatt Lahn is on the edge of town near the funicular to the *Salzbergwerk*. The train station is across the lake from Hallstatt; to get into town from there you have to take the ferry.

Sights

Salzwelten MINE

(☎06132-200 24 00; www.salzwelten.at; Salzbergstrasse 21; funicular return & tour adult/child/family €34/17/71; ⏲9.30am-2.30pm early Mar-late Mar & late Sep–mid-Dec, to 4.30pm late Mar-late Sep) The fascinating *Salzbergwerk* (salt mine) is situated high above Hallstatt on Salzberg (Salt Mountain) and is the lake's major cultural attraction. The bilingual German–English tour details how salt is formed and the history of mining, and takes visitors down into the depths on miners' slides – the largest is 60m (on which you can get your photo taken).

> **SALZKAMMERGUT ERLEBNIS CARD**
>
> The nontransferable Salzkammergut Erlebnis Card, available from tourist offices and hotels in the region, costs €4.90 and offers significant discounts for 21 days between 1 May and 31 October.

The **Hallstätter Hochtal** (Hallstatt High Valley) near the mine was also an Iron Age burial ground. An audio guide (€5), available from the base station of the funicular, takes you through the numbered stations and explains the site and rituals of burial.

The **funicular** (www.salzwelten.at; single/return adult €10/18, child €5/9; ⏲9am-6pm Apr-Sep, to 4.30pm Oct-early Jan & early Feb-late Mar, closed early Jan-early Feb) is the easiest way up to the mountain station, from where the mine is 15 minutes' walk; a switchback trail takes about 40 minutes to walk. Another option is to take the steps behind the Beinhaus and follow the trail until it joins the picturesque **Soleleitungsweg**; go left and follow the very steep trail past the waterfall and up the steps. It's a tough climb, and not really for children.

Beinhaus CHURCH

(Bone House; Kirchenweg 40; adult/child €1.50/0.50; ⏲10am-5pm May-Oct, 11.30am-3.30pm Wed-Sun Nov-Apr) This small ossuary contains rows of neatly stacked skulls, painted with decorative designs and the names of their former owners. Bones have been exhumed from the overcrowded graveyard since 1600, and although the practice waned in the 20th century, the last joined the collection in 1995. It stands in the grounds of the 15th-century Catholic **Pfarrkirche** (parish church), which has some attractive Gothic frescoes and three winged altars inside.

Weltkulturerbe Museum MUSEUM

(☎06134-8280 15; www.museum-hallstatt.at; Seestrasse 56; adult/child/family €10/8/20; ⏲10am-6pm May-Sep, closed Mon & Tue Nov-Mar, shorter hours Oct-Apr) This multimedia museum has a strong focus on the region's history of Iron Age/Celtic settlement and salt mining, taking you through 26 stations of Hallstatt's history. All explanations are in German and English. Its Celtic and Roman excavations can be seen beneath sports shop **Dachsteinsport Janu** (Seestrasse 50; ⏲9am-6pm) FREE, around the corner.

WORTH A TRIP

GOSAUSEE

This small lake is flanked by the impressively precipitous peaks of the Gosaukamm range (2459m). The view is good from the shoreline, and it takes a little over an hour to walk around the entire lake. The **Gosaukammbahn cable car** (www.dachstein.at; return adult/child €16/9.10; 8.15am-5.20pm early May-Oct) goes up to 1475m, where there are spectacular views and walking trails. One- to two-hourly Postbus (p210) services run to the lake from Bad Ischl (€6.50, 45 minutes) via Steeg.

Before reaching the lake you pass through the village of Gosau, which has its own **tourist office** (06136 8295; www.dachstein-salzkammergut.at; Gosauseestrasse 5, Gosau; 8.30am-6pm Mon-Fri, to 3pm Sat & Sun May-Oct, closed Sun Oct, closed Sat & Sun Nov-Dec, 8.30am-5pm Mon-Fri, 9am-3pm Sat & Sun Jan-Apr) with an accommodation board outside. Gosau is at the junction of the only road to the lake and can be reached by Hwy 166 from Hallstätter See.

Activities

Hallstätter See BOATING
(boat hire per hour from €13; May-Sep) You can hire boats and kayaks to get out on the lake.

Sleeping

Campingplatz Klausner-Höll CAMPGROUND €
(06134-83 22; www.camping.hallstatt.net; Lahnstrasse 7; camp sites per adult/child/tent/car €11.20/6.50/6/5; mid-Apr–mid-Oct; P) Located on a grassy meadow in Hallstatt Lahn, conveniently close to the centre and almost right on the lake, this camping ground has a small kiosk, a common room for camping guests and an on-site laundry.

Bräugasthof am Hallstätter See GUESTHOUSE €€
(06134-82 21; www.brauhaus-lobisser.com; Seestrasse 120; s/d/tr €65/105/156;) A central, friendly guesthouse with comfortable rooms decked out in light wood.

★ **Hallstatt Hideaway** BOUTIQUE HOTEL €€€
(0677 617 105 18; www.hallstatt-hideaway.com; Dr Friedrich-Morton-Weg 24; ste €270-480;) Six splendidly modern, beautifully textured private suites make up what is the region's most stylish accommodation choice. While prices reflect the varying sizes and facilities of each of the suites, they all have their own particular appeal – be that alpine charm, a stuccoed ceiling or contemporary design pieces and killer terraces with hot tub in the penthouse.

Heritage Hotel Hallstatt HOTEL €€€
(06134-200 36; www.hotel-hallstatt.com; Landungsplatz 102; d €199-342, ste €401;) Rooms in this luxury hotel are spread across three buildings. The main building may claim the town's prime position at the landing stage on the lake, but 500-year-old Stocker House, a grey-stone beauty up the hill, is by far the most atmospheric. Rooms across all three buildings offer stunning views and have modern, understated decor.

Eating

★ **Restaurant zum Salzbaron** EUROPEAN €€
(06134-82 63-0; www.gruenerbaum.cc; Marktplatz 104; mains €21.90-32.90; noon-10pm;) One of the best gourmet acts in town, the Salzbaron is perched alongside the lake inside the **Seehotel Grüner Baum** (s €150, d €250-380, ste €450;) and serves a seasonal pan-European menu – the wonderful local trout features strongly in summer.

Balthazar im Rudolfsturm AUSTRIAN €€
(06136-881 10; Rudolfsturm; mains €9.80-19.20; 11am-4.30pm Apr-Oct) Balthazar sits 855m above Hallstatt and has the most spectacular terrace in the region. The menu is Austrian comfort food and the service is charming, but you're here for the gobsmacking views. It's best accessed by the funicular (p211).

Information

Tourist Office (05950-95 30; www.dachstein-salzkammergut.at; Seestrasse 99; 8.30am-6pm Mon-Fri, 9am-2pm Sat & Sun May-Oct, 8.30am-5pm Mon-Fri, 9am-3pm Sat & Sun Nov-Apr) Turn left from the Hallstatt Markt ferry and walk along Seestrasse for about 10 minutes to the boat houses. It stocks a free leisure map of lakeside towns that shows hiking and cycling trails.

Getting There & Away

BOAT

Hemetsberger Hallstättersee Schifffahrt (06134-82 28; www.hallstattschifffahrt.at) does the excursion circuit to Hallstatt Lahn via Hallstatt Markt, Obersee, Untersee and Steeg (€15, 90 minutes, three daily) from mid-July to August, and other shorter ones.

BUS

At least nine daily buses connect Hallstatt (Lahn) town with the cable car at Obertraun-Dachstein-seilbahn (€2.20, eight to 15 minutes).

CAR

Access into the village is restricted: electronic gates are activated during the day. Parking costs €9.50 for 12 hours for day parking. Hotel shuttle buses run from the P1 parking area. Press 'Hotel Ticket' (€14 per day) if you're an overnight guest. See www.hallstatt.net/parken-in-hallstatt for more.

TRAIN

Trains connect Hallstatt and Bad Ischl (€5.50, 20 minutes, hourly), and Hallstatt with Bad Aussee (€3.30, 15 minutes) every two hours. Hallstatt's *Bahnhof* (train station) is across the lake from the village, and boat services (€3, 10 minutes, last ferry to Hallstatt Markt 6.50pm) coincide with train arrivals.

Obertraun

☎06131 / POP 726

More easygoing than Hallstatt, Obertraun is a sprawling, rather workaday village that offers great access to the Dachstein caves. It's also a good starting point for hikes around the lake, or more strenuous treks up to the caves themselves and beyond through alpine meadows.

Sights

★Dachstein Caves CAVE

(www.dachstein-salzkammergut.com; all cable car sections plus caves adult/child €48.20/26.60, one section plus caves €42.60/23.40; ⏲9.20am-3.30pm late Apr–mid-Jun & mid-Sep–Oct, to 4pm mid-late Jun, to 5pm late Jun–mid-Sep) Climb to the Dachstein caves (Dachsteinhöhlen) and you'll find yourself in a strange world of ice and subterranean hollows, extending 80km in some places. The two caves, the **Dachstein Rieseneishöhle** and the **Mammuthöhle**, take about 15 minutes to reach by foot, each in different directions from the Schönbergalm cable-car station at 1350m. Tours of each cave last an hour.

The ice in the Dachstein Rieseneishöhle is no more than 500 years old, and forms an 'ice mountain' up to 8m high – twice as high now as it was when the caves were first explored in 1910. The formations here are illuminated with coloured light and the shapes they take are eerie and surreal. This cave can only be seen on a guided tour; if you ask the tour guides they will offer the tour with English commentary as well as German.

The ice-free Mammuthöhle is among the 30 or so deepest and longest caves in the world. Tours offer insight into the formation of the cave, which also has installations and artworks based on light and shadow to heighten the experience.

Krippenstein VIEWPOINT

(www.dachstein-salzkammergut.com; cable car return adult/child €32/17.60; ⏲mid-Jun–Oct) From Obertraun you can catch a cable car to Krippenstein (2109m), where you'll find the **5 Fingers viewing platform**, which protrudes over a sheer cliff face in five differently shaped platforms (one is reminiscent of a diving board). On a clear day the views from here down across the lake are little short of magnificent; a glass floor allows you to peer directly down beyond your feet into a gaping void. It will either cure your vertigo or turn you into a blathering mess.

Activities

In winter Krippenstein is a ski and snowboard freeriding area (day pass €40.60). The cable car begins service in December, depending on completion of maintenance and snow conditions; it usually ends around Easter. Advanced cross-country ski hiking is also possible on the mountain.

For downhill skiers, the best piste is an 11km downhill run beginning at Krippenstein and going via Gjaid Alm station to the valley station. Hold onto your hat!

Cable Car CABLE CAR

(www.dachstein-salzkammergut.com; adult/child return €32/17.60; ⏲May-Oct & Dec-Easter) A highlight in itself, the cable car departs about every 15 minutes from the valley station and has several stages, becoming more remote the further you go. After the middle station, Schönbergalm – where you alight for the Dachstein caves – it continues to the highest point (2109m) of Krippenstein, where the eerie 5 Fingers viewing platform dangles over the precipice.

The final stretch is to Gjaid Alm, taking you away from the crowds to an area where walking trails wind across the rocky meadows or lead higher into the mountains. Some of these trails begin at the simple and sought-after **Gjaid Alm** (☎0680 325 31 38; www.gjaid.at; Winkl 31; dm/s/d incl half board €45/105/124; ⏲closed May & Nov;) guesthouse (also a working organic farm), which is situated 10 minutes by foot from the cable-car station.

Sleeping & Eating

Campingplatz Hinterer CAMPGROUND €
(☎06131-265; www.camping-am-see.at; Winkl 77; camp sites per adult/child/tent/car €10.30/9/12/3; ⊙May-Sep; P 🛜 ≋) This eco-sensitive, pleasantly leafy campground is by the lake (with its own beach) south of the river and has a bar. There are a few 'gypsy-style' caravans (€165 to €190 per night for two people) for hire, too.

Hotel Haus am See HOTEL €€
(☎0676 9300 007; Obertraun 169; s €70-80, d €100-200; P 🛜) Situated conveniently alongside the boat station and swimming area, this no-frills hotel has lots of comfortable rooms with balconies and views over the lake. Also rents e-mountain bikes for €30 per day.

★**Pizzeria-Kegelbahn** ITALIAN €
(☎06131-335; Seestrasse 178; mains €12.90-24.50, pizza €9.90-12.90; ⊙10am-midnight Wed-Sun) Easily the most atmospheric of all the budget restaurants in the region, this Italo-Austrian place with friendly Turkish owners has cosy indoor seating and outdoor tables alongside a gurgling brook. The pizza is great, and there's ten-pin bowling out the back.

Information

The very helpful **tourist office** (☎06131-351; www.dachstein-salzkammergut.at; Obertraun 180; ⊙8.30am-5pm Mon-Fri all year, plus 9am-1pm Sat Jun, 10am-2pm Sat Jul) has a free lake and hiking trail map. It's on the way to the Dachstein cable car from the train station.

Getting There & Away

A ferry (p212) in the summer months runs from Hallstatt Markt via Hallstatt Lahn to Obertraun (€8, 25 minutes, five daily).

At least nine daily buses connect Hallstatt (Lahn) town with the cable car (p213) at Obertraun-Dachsteinseilbahn (€2.20, eight to 15 minutes).

Obertraun-Dachsteinhöhlen is the train station for Obertraun settlement. There are trains to Bad Ischl (€5.50, 30 minutes, hourly) via Hallstatt (€2.20, three minutes).

Getting Around

City bikes can be hired from **Seecafe Obertraun** (☎0650 617 71 65; Strandbad Obertraun; city bike rental per day €12; ⊙May-Sep) and mountain bikes from **Dormio Resort Obertraun** (☎06131-2223-330; Obertraun 302; per day trekking and crossbikes €16, mountain bikes €25, e-mountain bikes €35).

A **taxi** (☎0064 4433 674, 0699 1175 4852) to the cable-car valley station or between Hallstatt and Obertraun costs about €15.

Bad Aussee

☎03622 / POP 4835

Quiet, staid Bad Aussee is the largest Styrian town in the southern Salzkammergut. It is close to two lakes, and convenient by rail and a walking and bike trail to a third, the Hallstätter See.

Although the actual sights in the town are very limited, activities are its strength; it has a couple of good places where you can rent mountain bikes and e-bikes, making it a useful base for heading off into the surrounding hills and lakes.

Sights

Salzwelten Altaussee MUSEUM
(☎06132-2002 400; www.salzwelten.at; Lichtersberg 25, Altaussee; adult/child/family €19/9.50/40; ⊙tours hourly 9am-4pm late Apr-early Sep, 9am, 11am, 1pm & 3pm early Sep-late Oct, 9am & 7pm Wed year-round; P 👪) Situated near the Altaussee about 6km north of Bad Aussee, this working salt mine was the secret hiding place for art treasures stolen by the Nazis during WWII. All tours are bilingual (in German and English). See the website for further opening times. Bus 955 (€2.40, 15 minutes) runs a few times each day from the Bad Aussee post office to the stop 'Altaussee Scheiben', 2.5km from the mine (though bike is a better option as the bus is infrequent).

Kammerhof Museum MUSEUM
(☎03622-537 25 11; www.badaussee.at/kammerhofmuseum; Chlumeckyplatz 1; adult/child/family €5/3/8; ⊙mid-Apr–early Sep) Kammerhof Museum, housed in a beautiful 17th-century building, covers local history and salt production. It also has some portraits of Anna Plöchl, the local postmaster's daughter who scandalously married a Habsburg prince. All explanations are in German but there's an English sheet available. See the website for opening times.

Activities

Loser Panoramastrasse SCENIC DRIVE
(toll per car €16) This usually fog-free road climbs most of the way up **Loser** (1838m), the main peak overlooking the Altausseer See. It's a stunningly scenic destination and a delightfully rustic journey. Snow chains are required in winter.

OUT & ABOUT AROUND BAD AUSSEE

Boat Trips

Five kilometres northeast of Bad Aussee, **Grundlsee** is a longer, thinner lake, with a good viewpoint at its western end, as well as water sports (including a sailing school) and walking trails. Extending from the eastern tip of the lake are two smaller lakes, **Toplitzsee** and **Kammersee**. Between Easter and October, three-hour **boat tours** (☎03622-860 443 33; www.schifffahrt-grundlsee.at; Mosern 22; adult/child €24/14; ⊙Easter-Oct) take you through all three.

Bus 956 departs almost hourly from the post office to Grundlsee Seeklause (€2.40, 10 minutes) weekdays, or every two hours at weekends.

Hiking

The **Koppentalweg** is a picturesque 10km hiking and cycling trail that runs west through the lush Traun River valley; it connects via the Koppenbrüllerhöhlen (caves) with the Ostuferwanderweg running along the Hallstätter See. The trail begins at the Bad Aussee train station.

Pick up a map of the region's hiking trails from the Bad Aussee tourist office.

Mountain Biking

Bike trails lead off from Bad Aussee to all the major lakes, including the Hallstätter See, and where there aren't trails the roads are generally suitable for riding. **Zweirad Friedl** (☎03622-529 18; www.zweiradfriedl.at; Meranplatz 38; mountain bike/e-bike rental per day €12/20; ⊙9am-noon & 3-6pm Mon-Fri, 9am-noon Sat) hires out mountain bikes, and **Sport Käfmüller** (☎03622-549 11; www.sport-kaefmueller.at; Ischlerstrasse 121; mountain bike/e-mountain bike rental per day €18/30; ⊙8.30am-12.30pm & 3-6pm Mon-Fri, 8.30am-12.30pm Sat, bicycle rental Apr-Oct) does the same; both also have e-bikes.

Sleeping

Pension Stocker PENSION €€
(☎03622-524 84; www.zimmer-ausseerland.at/stocker; Altausseerstrasse 245; s/d €48/90; P 🛜) Located 500m northwest of Kurhausplatz, this is a very pretty pension with wooden balconies, flower-filled window boxes and a large garden.

HI Jugendgästehaus HOSTEL €€
(☎05 7083 520; www.jufa.eu/hotel/badaussee; Jugend-herbergsstrasse 148; s/d €79/107; P ⊖ @ 🛜) This hostel has a wellness area with sauna and fitness facilities, as well as a playground for kids and a terrace for soaking up the mountain sunshine. It's located 15 minutes' walk from the post office by road, or less by quicker (but unlit) footpaths.

★**Erzherzog Johann** HOTEL €€€
(☎03622-52 50 70; www.erzherzogjohann.at; Kurhausplatz 62; s/d €149/298; P ⊖ @ 🛜 🏊) Bad Aussee's four-star hotel has rooms with comforts, but the facilities are what really catapult you into relaxation heaven: a wonderfully large sauna and wellness area, a 10m private swimming pool, and excellent bikes that are free for guests (or e-bikes for €20 per day). The hotel also caters to kids with a program of special activities.

Eating

★**Das gute Leben** CAFE
(☎03622-524 19; www.dasguteleben-aussee.at; Meranplatz 36; ⊙10am-10pm Tue-Sat) Das gute Leben is many different things at once. Between 10am and 2pm it serves breakfast as well as its excellent open sandwiches (€5.20 to €9.80), and anything except breakfast is also available between 5pm and 8pm. Aside from all this, it's a cosy and chic cafe and wine bar, and also sells ceramic from its back-room shop.

Information

Tourist Office (☎03622-523 23; www.ausseerland.at; Ischlerstrasse 94; ⊙9am-noon & 1-5pm Mon-Fri, 9am-noon Sat Sep-Jun, 9am-6pm Mon-Fri, 9am-noon Sat Jul & Aug) Excellent resource with helpful staff, located in the post office building. Pick up the town map, which has hiking trails marked for the region.

Getting There & Away

Buses arrive and depart from the tourist office/post office.

Bad Aussee is on the rail route between Bad Ischl (€7.40, 35 minutes) and Stainach-Irdning (€6.60, 35 minutes); trains run in both directions every two hours. Direct trains run to Hallstatt via the caves in Obertraun every two hours (€3.30, 15 minutes). The train station is 1.5km south of the town centre – after getting off the train, make a beeline to the bus stop out front for the connecting bus.

Getting Around

Bad Aussee has two very good bicycle rental places. Both Sport Käfmüller (p215) and Zweirad Friedl (p215) are centrally located and can help with maps and suggestions.

A **taxi** (03622-526 71, 0664 2000 902) from the train station to the centre costs about €7.50.

NORTHERN SALZKAMMERGUT

Traunsee

Traunsee is the deepest lake in Austria, going down to a cool 192m. The eastern flank is dominated by rocky crags, the tallest of which is the imposing Traunstein (1691m).

Traunsee Schiffahrt (07612-667 00; www.traunseeschiffahrt.at; Rathausplatz) offers round-trip cruises of the lake from late April to early October (adult/child €24/16, two hours five minutes, four daily). If you want to explore the lake under your own steam, you can rent pedal boats and electric boats from Schifffahrt Loidl (p219) in Traunkirchen.

Getting There & Away

The Traunsee resorts are strung along the western shore and are connected by rail to each other and then to Bad Ischl.

Getting Around

BOAT

Traunsee Schiffahrt vessels tour the shoreline between late April and early October. There are connections from Gmunden's Rathausplatz to Landhotel Grünberg am See (adult/child €3/2, seven minutes, at least three daily), Traunkirchen (adult/child €9/6, 45 minutes, four daily) and Ebensee (adult/child €12/8, one hour, four daily). **Water taxis** (050-42 24 22; www.traunseetaxi.at; adult/child €4/2; May-Sep) ply the southern region of the lake at regular intervals from May to September (adult/child €4/2), with Traunkirchen the main hub.

BUS

The touristy **Bummelzug** (0676-501 69 18; www.bummelzug-gmunden.at; adult/child/family return €6/3/14; 10am-5pm Fri, Sat & Sun May, daily Jun–mid-Sep) runs to Seeschloss Ort (in Gmunden) on the western shore.

CAR & MOTORCYCLE

The B145 runs along the entire western shore. The eastern shore is more isolated and the road peters out to cliffs about halfway along the length.

TRAIN

The Traunsee resorts are strung along the western shore and are connected by rail. Trains run between Gmunden and Traunkirchen (€3.30, 10 minutes, hourly) and Ebensee (€4.50, 20 minutes, hourly), continuing on to Bad Ischl (€7.40, 40 minutes).

Gmunden

07612 / POP 13,190

With its yacht marina, lakeside square and promenades, pretty, historic Gmunden exudes a breezy, riviera feel. It was known primarily for its large ceramics works and as a centre for the salt trade. While ceramics are still produced here, today it's mainly a weekend escape for fashionable Salzburgers.

Sights

★**Seeschloss Ort** CASTLE

(07612-7944 00; www.schloss-ort.at; Orth 1; adult/child €5/free; 9.30am-4.30pm Easter-Oct) This castle, set just beyond the lake's edge and reached by a walkway, is believed to have been built on the ruins of a Roman fortress. It dates from 909 or earlier (although it was rebuilt in the 17th century after a fire) and has a picturesque courtyard, a late-Gothic external staircase and sgraffito from 1578. Flanking the lake on the eastern side and forming a backdrop for the castle is a pretty nature reserve known as **Toscana Park**.

★**K-Hof** MUSEUM

(07612-79 44 20; https://museum.gmunden.at; Kammerhofgasse 8; adult/child/family €6/2/12; 10am-4pm Tue-Sun Jun-Sep, 10am-4pm Wed-Sun Oct-May) A double act that combines with one of Austria's most unusual and refreshing museums, the **Museum for Sanitary Objects** (Klo & So), the K-Hof museum complex gives a fascinating insight into the history of the region. Exhibits cover ceramics manufacture (for which Gmunden

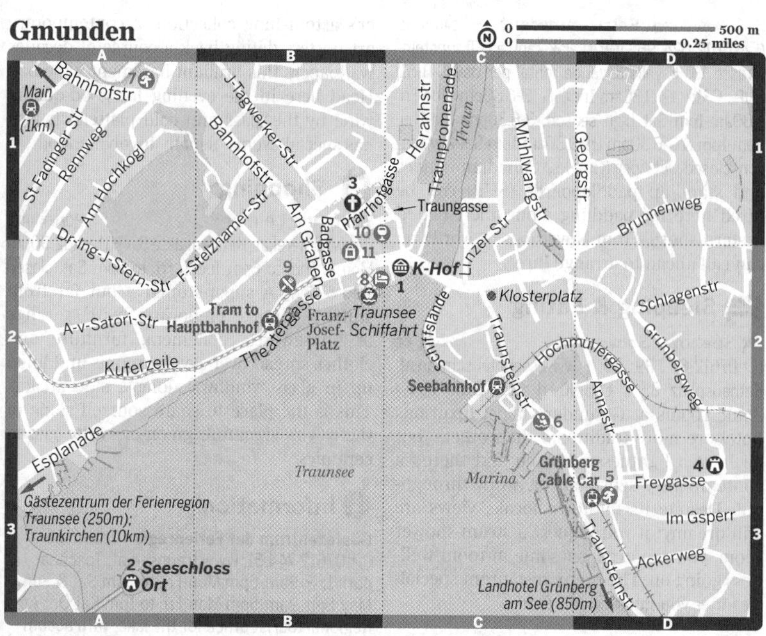

Gmunden

Top Sights

1	K-Hof	C2
2	Seeschloss Ort	A3

Sights

3	Pfarrkirche	B1
4	Schloss Weyer	D3

Activities, Courses & Tours

5	Grünberg Seilbahn	D3
6	Kajak & Kanu Salzkammergut	C2
7	Sport 2000	A1

Sleeping

8	Seehotel Schwan	B2

Eating

9	Konditorei Grellinger	B2

Drinking & Nightlife

10	Brot & Wein	B1

Shopping

11	Wolfgang Leimer	B2

Information

Tourist Office	(see 1)

is still famous), salt, fossils and the life of the 15th-century astronomer Johannes von Gmunden, whose theories influenced Copernicus.

Pfarrkirche CHURCH

(Kirchplatz; dawn-dusk) FREE North of the Rathausplatz lies the 12th-century Pfarrkirche, a Gothic church later remodelled in baroque style. The altar, by the sculptor Thomas Schwanthaler (1634–1707), dates from 1678.

Schloss Weyer PALACE

(07612-6501 813; Freygasse 27; adult/child €12/free; 10am-noon & 2-5.30pm Tue-Fri, to 1pm Sat Jul & Aug) This palace contains a good collection of Meissen porcelain, silver and jewellery, and has specialised temporary exhibitions dedicated to the same.

Activities

Grünberg Seilbahn CABLE CAR

(07612-501 40; www.gruenberg.info; return adult/child €18.20/10; 9am-7.30pm May-Sep, to 6.30pm Oct & Apr, to 5.30pm Nov) Leaving every 30 minutes, this modern cable car whisks visitors 984m up to the local mountain, Grünberg, where you'll find a lookout and numerous hiking and mountain bike trails, including a particularly pretty one down to the **Laudachsee**.

Kajak & Kanu Salzkammergut CANOEING
(☎07612-624 96; www.kajak-kanu.at; Traunsteinstrasse 13; kayaks & canoe rental per day €41-51, SUP €31; ⊙9.30am-1pm & 3-6.30pm Tue-Fri, 9.30am-1pm Sat high season, 3-6.30pm Tue-Thu, 9am-1pm & 3-6.30pm Fri, 9.30am-1pm Sat low season, closed Oct-Apr) Kayaks, Canadian canoes and stand-up paddleboards (SUP) can be hired here for paddling along the isolated eastern shore. From November to April you can call ahead to arrange hire.

Sleeping & Eating

★Seehotel Schwan HOTEL €€
(☎07612-63 39 10; www.seehotel-schwan.at; Rathausplatz 8; s €85-90, d €130-170; P 🛜) Some rooms at Gmunden's most luxurious hotel are more traditional than others, but all have a lightness of touch and there's a contemporary sensibility at work throughout. Despite its midtown locale, views are still dreamy; if you request a steam-shower room, you can even get some in-room wellness going on. The pretty restaurant specialises in – you guessed it – fish.

★Landhotel Grünberg am See GUESTHOUSE €€
(☎07612-777 00; www.gruenberg.at; Traunsteinstrasse 109; s €83-95, d €140-190; P ⊖ 🛜) Situated right on the lakeshore, a 10-minute drive from the town centre, this sweet, family-run hotel offers bright, spacious (if rather predictably furnished) rooms. It's worth opting for those with lake views and balconies. Lake fish is served in the dining room (€11.90 to €19.50), which also shares the views, while the book-lined breakfast room is a cosy treat. Half-board accommodation is available.

Konditorei Grellinger BAKERY €
(www.konditorei-grellinger.at; Franz-Josef-Platz 6; cakes & pastries €1.80-3.40, apple strudel €2.50; ⊙8.30am-6pm Thu-Tue) While the lakeside places overflow with visitors, this historic *Konditorei* (bakery) attracts a decidedly more local crowd. The beautifully evocative interior of original fittings brightened via a clever contemporary eye would be worth the price of a (very good) coffee alone, but the pastries here are also praise-worthy, from the simple nut or poppy-seed-stuffed *Kipferl* to elaborate tortes, and an excellent apple strudel.

Drinking & Nightlife

★Brot & Wein WINE BAR
(☎07612-703 56; www.brot-und-wein.at; Marktplatz 20; ⊙5-10pm Tue-Fri, from 12.30pm Sat) The owner's astonishing collection of contemporary art posters dating back a couple of decades wallpapers this brilliant basement wine bar. Head here in the evening for good-quality wine by the glass and cold platters. It also has special events, usually involving food.

Shopping

Wolfgang Leimer HOMEWARES
(www.leimerei.at; Kirchengasse 5; ⊙11am-12.30pm Mon & Thu, to 6pm Tue & Fri, to 5pm Sat, closed Wed & Sun) A super-stuffed – but far from stuffy – vintage emporium, with a range of housewares, ephemera, furniture and clothes spread over several rooms and lined up in glass windows along a side arcade. This is the place to snare yourself some of the town's signature green-on-white glazed ceramics.

Information

Gästezentrum der Ferienregion Traunsee (☎07612-744 51; www.traunsee.at; Toscanapark 1; ⊙9am-6pm Mon-Fri, to 3pm Sat & Sun May-Sep, 9am-5pm Mon-Fri, to 1pm Sat Oct-Apr) Regional tourist office for the lake, with accommodation booking service. Also handles tourist service for the town during the low season.

Tourist Office (☎07612-65 75 20; www.traunsee.at/gmunden; Kammerhofgasse 8; ⊙10am-4pm Tue-Sun) Has information and maps of the town and the lake. Helps with accommodation bookings.

Getting There & Away

BOAT

Boats operated by Traunsee Schiffahrt (p216) tour the shoreline from Gmunden to Ebensee between late April and early October. The one-way trip between Gmunden and Ebensee (adult/child €12/8) takes 55 minutes. The paddle steamer *Gisela* takes to the waves on Sunday in July and August (a €4 surcharge applies).

TRAIN

The **Gmunden Hauptbahnhof** is the main train station for the town; the rail service is on the Salzkammergut line from Attnang-Puchheim to Stainach-Irdning. Regular trains run to Bad Ischl (€7.40, 45 minutes, every one to 1½ hours); those to Salzburg require a change in Attnang-Puchheim (€18.70, 1½ hours). The Seebahnhof, near the marina, services the slow, private train line from Vorchdorf-Eggenburg.

The station is 2km northwest of the town centre, and is also where you can catch Austria's shortest (and its longest-running) tram service. Tram G (€2.20) runs to Franz-Josef-Platz and Rathausplatz after every train arrival.

Getting Around

Bus and tram tickets for city services cost €2.20. **Sport 2000** (07612-648 65; www.sport2000-gmunden.at; Bahnhofstrasse 22; per day e-mountain bikes/city bikes €35/30, conventional cross bikes €20; 9am-1pm & 2-6pm Mon-Fri, 9am-5pm Sat) rents out e-bikes and conventional bikes, but the stock is not large so reserve ahead.

Traunkirchen

07617 / POP 1625

The attractive hamlet of Traunkirchen sits on a spit of land about halfway along the western shore of the Traunsee. It's chiefly famous for the wooden Fischerkanzel in the Pfarrkirche.

Sights

Fischerkanzel SCULPTURE

(Fisherman's Pulpit; 07617-22 14; Klosterplatz 1; 8am-5pm) Carved in 1753 as part of the **Pfarrkirche**, this pulpit depicts the miracle of the fishes from the New Testament. It's a rather glam and glowing baroque take on this Bible story that is chiefly about the notion of spiritual plenty but obviously appealed to 18th-century fishermen in a more literal manner. Depicting the Apostles standing in a tub-shaped boat and hauling in fish-laden nets, the composition, colours (mostly silver and gold) and detail (even down to wriggling, bug-eyed fish) create a vivid impression.

Activities

Schifffahrt Loidl BOATING

(0664 371 56 46; www.schifffahrt-traunsee.at; Ortsplatz; pedal/electric boat rental per hour €10/15; 10am-6pm May-Sep) This operator rents out both pedal and electric boats, perfect for bobbing about on the Traunsee on your own.

Sleeping & Eating

Hotel Post HOTEL €€

(07617-230 70; www.hotel-post-traunkirchen.at; Ortsplatz 5; s €103, d €140-180; P) Most of the 55 spacious, contemporary and supremely comfortable rooms at this chalet-style hotel have balconies – with window boxes ablaze with geraniums in summer. Rooms at the front have dress-circle views of the mountain-framed lake. In-room amenities include minibars; downstairs, the restaurant (mains €13.90 to €19.90) serves hearty traditional Austrian fare.

The kitchen is open from noon to 9pm.

★ **Seehotel Das Traunsee** HOTEL €€€

(07617-221 60; www.dastraunsee.at; Klosterplatz 4; s €147, d €246-280, rooftop ste €316; P) Seehotel Das Traunsee is the prime address in Traunkirchen. It's contemporary, bright and with a stunning location on the lake, where you can relax on deckchairs in warm weather and listen to the lapping waves.

Restaurant Bootshaus AUSTRIAN €€€

(07617-22 16; www.dastraunsee.at; Klosterplatz 4; mains €48, 4-/6-/7-course menu €89/109/119; 6-9pm Thu, Fri & Mon, noon-2pm & 6-9pm Sat & Sun) A stunningly converted *Bootshaus* (boat house) at the lake's edge with panoramic views is the setting for locally sourced ingredients given the gourmet treatment by chefs Lukas Nagl and Michael Kaufmann: Traunsee freshwater crayfish along with lake fish or, moving away from the lake, organic lamb prepared in various styles are the order of the day in this very highly acclaimed restaurant.

Getting There & Away

Trains run hourly to Traunkirchen Bahnhof from Gmunden (€3.30, 15 minutes) and Ebensee (€2.50, 10 minutes), from where it's a 20-minute walk to town. Traunkirchen Ort is directly above town, but not all trains stop there. Check ahead.

Ebensee

06133 / POP 7715

Ebensee lies on the southern shore of the turquoise waters of Traunsee and is a charming, if unassuming, market town. It's surrounded by spectacular peaks and offers access to the low-key skiing of Feuerkogel.

Ebensee was the site of a WWII concentration camp, part of the Mauthausen (p169) network. It was considered one of the worst of the SS's forced labour camps, but there is little commemoration of this horrific past.

Activities

A **cable car** (return adult/child €22.50/11.20; hourly) runs up to **Feuerkogel** (1592m), where you'll find walking trails leading across a flattish plateau. Within an hour's walk is **Alberfeldkogel** (1708m), a nature reserve popular for hiking in summer and for cross-country skiing in winter; it has an excellent view over the two Langbath lakes. Feuerkogel also provides access to winter **skiing** (www.feuerkogel.net; day pass adult/child €38.70/16.40;), with easy-to-medium slopes.

Festivals & Events

Glöcklerlauf CULTURAL

(5 Jan) On Epiphany eve each year, the men of Ebensee don giant illuminated headdresses crafted from tissue paper for this pagan-inflected but now Christianised ritual. The 'Glöckler' – some 300 of them – roam through the streets when it gets dark, hoping to drive out evil spirits and win the favour of benevolent ones.

Sleeping & Eating

Landhotel Post HOTEL €€

(06133-5208; www.hotel-post-ebensee.at; Hauptstrasse 19; s €71-81, d €122-142, breakfast €13;) Landhotel Post is centrally located, while being just 300m from the lake. Rooms are clean and modern, and there's access to a steam bath that also converts to a sauna.

Hochsteg-Gütl HOTEL €€€

(06133 909 18; www.hochsteg.at; Almhausstrasse 28; r €208-238;) Hochsteg-Gütl is a modern four-star hotel that caters for tourists and seminar guests alike. Rooms are well sized, modern and bright, but it's the almost rural location on the edge of town and facilities such as a swimming pool, sauna and steam bath that make it so popular.

There's a two-night minimum stay on Friday and Saturday, and a three-night minimum in July and August. Right opposite is the **Mostschenke im Heustadl** (0650 386 99 25; www.moststadl.com; mains €9.80-14.60, mixed platter €9.80; 3pm-midnight Wed-Sat, from noon Sun), with delicious Austrian food and its own apple-pear *Most* (cider).

Information

Tourist Office (06133-80 16; www.ebensee.com; Hauptstrasse 34; 9am-noon & 1-5pm Mon-Fri, plus 9am-noon Sat early Jul-late Jul) Helpful for details on accommodation, and especially for activities such as hiking and mountain biking (bike hire and trails). Located by the Landungsplatz train station.

Getting There & Away

Trains from Salzburg stop at Ebensee-Landungsplatz before continuing to Ebensee Bahnhof (€22.10, 90 minutes, hourly to half-hourly).

Attersee

07666 / POP 1585

The largest lake in the Salzkammergut is flanked by hills that gradually turn into mountains the further south you go. Also known as Kammersee, from its main town's lakeside neighbourhood, it's one of the less scenic and also less visited of the Salzkammergut's lakes. That said, its winds and clear waters attract local sailors and, in high summer, lake swimmers. Its waters are also home to many fish, which you'll be able to sample in area restaurants.

Sights

Gustav Klimt Zentrum MUSEUM

(0664 8283 990; www.klimt-am-attersee.at; Hauptstrasse 30, Kammer; adult/child €7/4; 10am-4pm Wed-Sun May–mid-Jun & early Sep-late Oct, daily mid-Jun–early Sep) High-tech multimedia exhibits provide an overview of symbolist painter Gustav Klimt's life and works on the Attersee, which for Klimt fans is comparable to Claude Monet's Giverny. There's also a cinema screening informative films with English subtitles.

Gustav Klimt-Themenweg PUBLIC ART

(Gustav Klimt Artist Trail; Kammer) FREE This 2km-long lakeside trail has information boards with prints of works by Gustav Klimt. The Vienna Secessionist painter spent regular spells on the Attersee's shores at the turn of the 20th century, painting many of his renowned landscapes here; the trail passes his summer residences. The Gustav Klimt Zentrum rents audio guides for the trail (€4).

Activities

SUP Attersee WATER SPORTS

(699 8113 83 17; www.sup-attersee.at; Strandbad Litzlberg, Litzlberg; equipment rental per hour/day €12/50; 11am-7pm Jul-Aug) SUP Attersee rents stand-up paddleboards so you can get out on the lake's 26°C waters.

Attersee-Schifffahrt BOATING

(07666-78 06; www.atterseeschifffahrt.at; early Apr-Oct) Runs a four-stop northern tour of the lake (adult/child €13/6.50, 1¼ hours), a five-stop southern lake tour (adult/child €13/6.50, 1¼ hours), an 11-stop southern lake tour (€19/9.50, 2½ hours) and an 18-stop full lake tour (€22/11, 3¾ hours). Times vary considerably, so check the website, but generally trips are every day from July to early September.

Sleeping & Eating

Hotel Aichinger BOUTIQUE HOTEL €€

(07666-80 07; www.hotel-aichinger.at; Am Anger 1, Nussdorf am Attersee; r €85-159;) Rooms are modern and bright in Aichinger, which has wellness trimmings such as a spa area and outdoor pool (April to October). It's located about 750m from the lake and also has its own beach with jetty and loungers. The difference between room categories is their spaciousness, and some of the rooms are studios with kitchenettes.

The hotel very much forms its own cosmos in Nussdorf, with its American Bar across the road (from 9pm Wednesday to Sunday from late June to early September), a wine bar, and its own hotel restaurant, **Das Bräu** (07666-8007; www.hotel-aichinger.at; Am Anger 1, Nussdorf am Attersee; mains €17.50-29.50; noon-2pm & 6-9.30pm, closed some days Sep-Jun).

★ **Restaurant Langostinos** SEAFOOD

(07662-290 50; www.langostinos.at; Bahnhofstrasse 4, Kammer-Schörfling; mains €19-29; 11.30am-2pm & 6-11pm Fri-Tue) Langostinos in Kammer is the first place to head to if you would like to try the lake's delicious seafood. This is seasonal and depends on what the local fishing families have caught. But it also does a selection of meat dishes, all prepared with a Mediterranean angle. There's outdoor seating in summer, with marina and *Schloss* (castle) views.

Drinking & Nightlife

Die Bar Axxl BAR

(www.lexenhof.at; Am Anger 4, Nussdorf am Attersee; from 9pm Tue-Sat May-Sep, daily Jul & Aug) Part of the Hotel Lexenhof, Axxl is a popular Attersee hotspot after sunset, with DJs, occasional live music, and events.

Information

Tourist Office (07666-77 19; www.attersee.at; Nussdorferstrasse 15, Attersee am Attersee; 9am-noon & 2-5pm Mon-Fri, 9am-noon Sat & Sun, closed weekends Sep-Jun) Can help with hotel bookings, along with info for aquatic sports equipment hire.

Getting There & Away

The two lakeside towns of Attersee and Schörfling are each connected to the rail network by a line branching from the main Linz–Salzburg route (only regional trains stop); for Kammer-Schörfling change at Vöcklabruck, and for Attersee change at Vöcklamarkt.

Getting Around

Two-hourly direct buses connect Unterach with Nussdorf (€3.30, 17 minutes), continuing on to Litzlberg (€5.50, 36 minutes) and Kammer-Schörfling (45 minutes, €5.50) via Attersee (€4.50, 30 minutes). In the other direction around the lake buses run to Kammer-Schörfling every two hours (€5.50, 30 minutes) from Unterrach.

Wolfgangsee

Named after a local saint, this lake has two very popular resorts, St Wolfgang and St Gilgen (of which St Wolfgang is the most appealing). The third town on the lake, Strobl, is a less remarkable but pleasant place at the start of a scenic toll road to Postalm (1400m).

The Wolfgangsee is dominated by the 1783m **Schafberg** mountain on its northern shore. At the summit you'll find Austria's oldest mountain inn, a restaurant and phenomenal views over mountains and Mondsee, Attersee and, of course, Wolfgangsee. A cute historic steam train plies its way to the summit in summer, over lush fields and through dark forests.

St Gilgen

06227 / POP 3915

The ease of access to St Gilgen, 29km from Salzburg, makes this town very popular for day trippers, but it has also become popular in recent years because of its very scenic setting. Along with quieter Strobl, it's a good base for water sports on the lake, and is not quite as crowded as St Wolfgang.

Sights

Mozarthaus MUSEUM

(06227-202 42; www.mozarthaus.info; Ischlerstrasse 15; adult/child €4/2; 10am-4pm Tue-Sun Jun-Sep) There are numerous houses worldwide dedicated to Mozart, but this one takes the interesting approach of focusing mostly on the family, especially his sister 'Nannerl' (Maria Anna), an accomplished composer and musician in her own right. Multilingual films tell the story, and there's a small exhibition.

Musikinstumenten Museum der Völker MUSEUM

(Folk Music Instrument Museum; www.hoerart.at; Aberseestrasse 11; adult/child €4/2.50; 9-11am & 3-6pm Mon-Thu, 9-11am Fri, 3-6pm Sun early

Jan-May, 9-11am & 3-7pm Tue-Sun Jun–mid-Oct, 9-11am & 2-5pm Dec-early Jan, closed mid-Oct–Nov) This cosy little museum is home to 1500 musical instruments from all over the world, all of them collected by one family of music teachers. The son of the family, Askold zum Eck, can play them all and will happily demonstrate for hours. Visitors are sometimes allowed to play, too.

Heimatkundliches Museum MUSEUM
(☎06227-79 59; www.heimatkundliches-museum-sankt-gilgen.at; Pichlerplatz 6; adult/child €4/2.50; ⌚10am-noon & 3-6pm Tue-Sun Jun-Sep) The town museum has an eclectic collection ranging from embroidery – originally manufactured in the building – to religious objects and thousands of animal specimens.

Activities

Water sports such as windsurfing, water-skiing and sailing are popular activities in St Gilgen. There's a town swimming pool and a small beach (free) with a grassy area beyond the yacht marina.

The mountain rising over the resort is 1520m **Zwölferhorn** (www.12erhorn.at; cable car adult/child return €24.50/15; ⌚9am-4pm Oct-Mar, to 5pm Apr & Sep, to 6pm May-Aug), from where there are good views and **hiking trails** (two to 2½ hours) leading back to St Gilgen. In winter there's downhill **skiing**.

Sleeping & Eating

★Jugendgästehaus Schafbergblick HOSTEL €
(☎06227-23 65; www.jugendherbergsverband.at; Mondseer Strasse 7; dm/s/d €32.50/42.50/73; P ⊜ @ ᯤ) A pretty hostel with neat, bright rooms, grassy grounds and a fabulous lakeside location. It does, however, get a lot of school groups during term time.

Pension Falkensteiner PENSION €€
(☎06227-23 95; www.pension-falkensteiner.at; Salzburgerstrasse 13; s €72, d €108-124; P ⊜ ᯤ) A no-frills but spotless pension that has helpful management. All of the rooms are large, and all have balconies. It has its own lake access and some city bikes guests can use.

★Hotel Gasthof Zur Post HOTEL €€€
(☎06227-21 57; www.gasthofzurpost.at; Mozartplatz 8; s €156-164, d €212-228; P ⊜ ᯤ) This old inn's rooms are beautifully designed – some of the most stylish in the region. Some combine antique pieces set against a simple contemporary base, while others have a cosily modern-rustic style with bright felts and pale wood. The restaurant (mains €14.80 to €26.80) serves regional specialities in a low-ceilinged, whitewashed dining room, or outside on the elegant terrace.

★M. STEAK €€
(☎06227-270 67; www.mwolfgangsee.at; Ischlerstrasse 18; steaks €22.90-32.90, pasta €11.20-19.90, pizza €7.90-14.50; ⌚11.30am-2pm & 4.30-10pm Tue-Sat, 11.30am-9pm Sun) This relaxed 'Mediterranean' restaurant by the lake has a modern dining room and tables out in the garden. You can also order pizza to take away – they're nicely authentic – and there's a small, well-done (if somewhat predictable) menu of pastas, risottos and salads.

Drinking & Nightlife

12Alm Bar BAR
(www.facebook.com/12erAlmBar; Ischlerstrasse 18; ⌚9pm-4am Thu-Sun) An archetypal resort bar, the 12Alm Bar is a loud, colourful basement party zone that goes from drinking spot to disco after 9pm. Check the Facebook page for events and parties.

Information

Tourist Office (☎06227-23 48; https://wolfgangsee.salzkammergut.at; Mondsee Bundesstrasse 1a; ⌚9am-7pm Mon-Fri, to 5pm Sat, 10am-5pm Sun May-Sep, closed Sat & Sun Oct-Apr; ᯤ) Can help with finding accommodation. Brochures are also available inside the *Rathaus* (town hall) on Mozartplatz.

Getting There & Away

A **ferry service** (www.wolfgangseeschifffahrt.at; ⌚Apr-late Oct) operates roughly every 30 to 90 minutes daily from mid-April to late October between St Gilgen and Strobl (adult/child €10.60/5.30, 70 minutes), stopping at points en-route including St Wolfgang (adult/child €8/4, 45 minutes). Services are most frequent from late June to early September, and there are a couple of weekend services in early April as well. Between early June and early September some of these are paddle-wheel steamers (surcharge €1).

St Gilgen is 50 minutes from Salzburg by Postbus (p210), with at least hourly departures (€6.90) until late evening; buses from Salzburg continue on to Stobl and Bad Ischl (€5.80, 40 minutes). The bus station is near the base station of the cable car.

Hwy 154 provides a scenic route north to Mondsee.

St Wolfgang

06138 / POP 2770

St Wolfgang is a charming town situated on the steep banks of the Wolfgangsee. Although its streets can get clogged with visitors during the day, things usually settle down by early evening, which is the best time for a tranquil stroll along the forested lakeshore, past the gently creaking wooden boathouses.

The village's main fame arose as a place of pilgrimage, and today's visitors still come to see the same 14th-century church, packed with art treasures.

Sights

Wallfahrtskirche CHURCH

(Pilgrimage Church; 06138-23 21; www.pfarre-sankt-wolfgang.at; Markt; €1; 8am-7pm May-Sep, to 5pm Oct-Apr) St Wolfgang's impressive Wallfahrtskirche is a spectacular gallery of religious art, with glittering altars (from Gothic to baroque), an extravagant pulpit, a fine organ, and countless statues and paintings. The most impressive piece is the winged **high altar**, created by celebrated religious artist Michael Pacher between 1471 and 1481 – it's a perfect example of the German Gothic style, enhanced with the technical achievements of Renaissance Italy.

Activities

★ **Schafbergbahn** RAIL

(www.wolfgangseeschifffahrt.at; Schafbergbahnstrasse; adult/child one way €28.10/14.10, return €39.60/19.80; May-Oct) If you don't fancy the four-hour walk from St Wolfgang to the 1783m summit of Schafberg, ride this historic steam train, the steepest cogwheel railway in Austria. Featured in *The Sound of Music*, it's a cute, local icon, but also passes through some beautiful alpine scenery.

During the season there are at least hourly departures daily, starting either just before or just after 9am, depending on the month. Journey time is 40 minutes one way. The trip is so popular that you probably won't be able to get on the next train. Queue early, purchase a ticket for a specific service and then go for a wander along the lake or around St Wolfgang until your departure time.

★ **Wolfgangsee** SWIMMING

A number of hotels have jetties for swimming, and a tourist office booklet details the many water sports on offer here. You can spend a lovely afternoon with a walk or cycle to Strobl, 6km away (around 1½ hours on foot), ending the excursion with a swim.

Sleeping & Eating

★ **Hotel Cortisen am See** BOUTIQUE HOTEL €€

(06138-237 60; www.cortisen.at; Pilgerstrasse 15; d €164-238, ste €270-350; P) Hotelier Roland Ballner goes all out to make guests feel at home at this lakeside retreat, which may seem all Austrian tradition on the outside but is a riot of colour and individual style within. Apart from the charming interior spaces there are beautiful lakeside lounging areas and a pretty restaurant. Note: no children under 12 years.

Hotel Peter HOTEL €€

(06138-230 40; www.hotelpeter.at; Markt 54; d/ste from €140/182; P) The generous-sized rooms at this four-star hotel have balconies looking onto the lake, as well as large bathrooms and traditional decor. The restaurant (mains €15 to €36), which has a terrace overlooking the lake, serves truffle pasta, and the kitchen will whip up fish variations if you like; there's always a local fish dish on the menu.

★ **Im Weissen Rössl** LUXURY HOTEL €€€

(06138-23 06; www.weissesroessl.at; Markt 74; s €200, d €290-350; P@) St Wolfgang's most famous hotel was the setting for Ralph Benatzky's operetta *The White Horse*. Rooms are somewhat idiosyncratic, and a little tired for the price, but the more expensive ones have a balcony and view over the lake. In any case, everyone's here for the wellness area and the impeccable haute-European service.

See Eck AUSTRIAN €€

(0699 109 164 81; www.see-eck.at; Markt 92; mains €12.50-24.90; 3.30pm-midnight Tue-Sun) This smart and friendly wine bar does a small and very interesting dinner menu each night. The current offering is always posted on the website, generally with a very well prepared Austria-meets-Italy range of dishes. The extensive wine list is predominantly Austrian, there's champagne, and some of the wines are organic.

Information

Tourist Office (06138-80 03; https://wolfgangsee.salzkammergut.at; Au 140; 9am-7pm Mon-Fri, to 5pm Sat & Sun, closed Sun mid-May–mid-Sep, shorter hours Sep-Jun;) Helpful staff, and a wi-fi hotspot. Located at the eastern tunnel entrance.

Getting There & Away

The only road to St Wolfgang approaches from Strobl in the east.

A ferry service (p222) operates roughly every 30 to 90 minutes daily from mid-April to late October, stopping at St Wolfgang Markt on the route between St Gilgen (adult/child €8/4, 45 minutes) and Strobl (adult/child €6.10/3.10, 25 minutes). Wolfgangsee ferries stop at the village centre (Markt stop) and at the Schafberg railway (p223).

A Postbus (p210) service runs between St Wolfgang and St Gilgen (€4.70, 45 minutes) with a connecting transfer in Strobl (€2.60, 10 minutes). For buses to Salzburg (€9.10, 1¾ hours) you need to connect in St Gilgen or Strobl.

Getting Around

Pro Travel (06138-25 25; www.protravel.at; Markt 152; per day mountain-bike rental €25, e-bike rental €27, e-mountain bike €35-45; 9am-6pm, bike hire Apr-Oct) has a large range of bikes for hire, including e-bikes. They're happy to suggest walking and cycling itineraries; you can prebook the night before for their Schwarzensee shuttle service.

Strobl

06137 / POP 3645

While high-profile Wolfgangsee towns such as St Wolfgang and St Gilgen justifiably attract large numbers of visitors, the lesser-known and more low-key Strobl, at the eastern end of the lake, is well worth a visit for its friendly, low-key ambience and access to good hiking and cycling trails.

Schwarzensee HIKING

Situated 9km from Strobl at an altitude of 715m, Schwarzensee makes for a perfect day outing – either hiking or with conventional or e-bikes, which can be rented from **Sport Girbl** (06137-74 84; www.sport-girbl.at; Bahnstrasse 300; 8am-noon & 2.30-6pm). This picturesque and isolated swimming lake has a few small restaurants, including **Alm-Stadl Schwarzensee** (0664 266 44 98; www.almstadl-schwarzensee.at; Schwarzensee; mains €6.50-11.90; 10am-10pm Apr-Oct), which serves delicious smoked lake trout.

★ **Hotel Stroblerhof** HOTEL €€

(06137-73 08; www.stroblerhof.at; Ischlerstrasse 16; s/d €85/170; P@) This stylish hotel is the best place to stay and eat in Strobl. Combining a cosy chalet style with clean contemporary lines, and a very relaxing pool area, it's something of a surprise in this region.

An inexpensive Tex-Mex restaurant and a formal Austrian restaurant are set in the grounds; you can also opt for half board. Reserve ahead for an outside table in summer.

Getting There & Away

A ferry service (p222) operates roughly every 30 to 90 minutes daily from mid-April to late October between St Gilgen and Strobl (adult/child €10.60/5.30, 70 minutes), stopping at points en-route including St Wolfgang (adult/child €8/4, 45 minutes). Strobl to St Wolfgang takes 25 minutes and costs €6.10.

Postbus (p210) line 150 runs to St Gilgen and continues on to Salzburg (€8.90, 75 minutes, hourly). Bus 546 runs to/from St Wolfgang (€2.60, 10 minutes, about hourly).

Strobl is at the start of a scenic toll road (per car €10 to €12) to Postalm.

Getting Around

Sport Girbl rents city bikes, mountain bikes and e-bikes (city and mountain bikes) for €10 to €38 per day.

Mondsee

06232 / POP 3735

The town of Mondsee extends along the northern tip of the crescent-shaped lake, noted for its warm water. Coupled with its closeness to Salzburg (30km away), this makes it a highly popular lake for weekending Salzburgers, with the accompanying urban comforts and crowds.

Sights

Basilica Minor St Michael CHURCH

(www.pfarre-mondsee.com; Kirchengasse 1; by donation; 9am-7pm) If you're allergic to the film *The Sound of Music*, there's just one piece of advice: get out of town. Even the lemon-yellow baroque facade (added in 1740, incidentally) of the 15th-century parish church achieved notoriety by featuring in those highly emotional von Trapp wedding scenes in the film.

Museum Mondseeland und Pfahlbaumuseum MUSEUM

(www.museum-mondsee.at; Marschal-Wrede-Platz; adult/child €4/2; 10am-6pm Tue-Sun Jul & Aug, to 5pm Tue-Sun May, Jun & Sep, 10am-5pm Sat & Sun Oct) Next door to the parish church, this museum has displays on Stone Age finds and the monastic culture of the region (Mondsee is a very old monastery site).

Activities

Segelschule Mondsee WATER SPORTS
(☎06232-354 82 00; www.segelschule-mondsee.at; Robert Baum Promenade 3; rental per half-day windsurfing €50, kayaking €35, SUP €50, sailboat per hour/half-day from €10/35; ⌚9am-6pm May-Sep) This large outfit offers sailing, kayaking, windsurfing and SUP courses, as well as equipment hire.

Sleeping & Eating

Jugendgästehaus HOSTEL €
(☎06232-24 18; www.jugendherbergsverband.at; Krankenhausstrasse 9; dm/s/d €28.50/39/66; P⊗⑤) This modern HI hostel is a few minutes' walk up the hill from the centre of town. Its usual range of rooms are simple and streamlined.

Hotel Krone HOTEL €€
(☎06232-22 36; www.hotel-krone-mondsee.at; Rainerstrasse 1; s €98-112, d €140-185; P⊗⑤) This attractive, comfortable, centrally located three-star has neat if unremarkable rooms, some with balconies. There are doubles with connecting doors that families will find useful. The restaurant (mains €10.20 to €21.90) is open for lunch and dinner from Wednesday to Monday.

★**Seegasthof-Hotel Lackner** HOTEL €€€
(☎06232-23 59; www.seehotel-lackner.at; Mondseestrasse 1; d €280, junior ste €380-400, ste €440-460; P⊗⑤) Set on the shore of the Mondsee, the Lackner offers elegant, contemporary rooms with balconies and lovely lake views. A private beach is set among the reeds, and the excellent terrace restaurant (closed Wednesday; mains €29 to €35, six-course menu €80) serves venison and lamb dishes as well as fish, complemented by a *Vinothek* (wine bar).

★**Holzingerbauer** AUSTRIAN €
(☎06232-38 41; Oberburgau 12, Eisenaueralm; mixed platter €9.50; ⌚3-11pm Mon, Tue, Thu & Fri) This farm table a short drive from Mondsee proper serves *Jause* (snack platters) in a fabulously bucolic setting. As hearty and homemade as the spread is, the appeal for Austrian holidaymakers is Holzingerbauer's own *Most*, the famous local cider.

★**Schlossbräu Mondsee** AUSTRIAN €€
(☎06232-50 01; www.schlossbraeu-mondsee.at; Schlosshof 1a; mains €12.90-15.20; ⌚10am-2pm & 5pm-midnight Mon & Thu, 10am-midnight Fri, 9am-midnight Sat & Sun, closed Tue & Wed) This sprawling tavern somehow manages to be so much more than a hotel restaurant. It overlooks the main square and the Basilica of St Michael, and has a summer terrace outside and miles of woody tables under vaulted ceilings inside. Grab a bratwurst or grilled lake-fresh fish; young staff are friendly and happy to find you a beer you'll like.

Information

Tourist Office (☎06232-22 70; www.mondsee.at; Dr Franz Müller Strasse 3; ⌚8am-7pm Mon-Fri, from 9am Sat & Sun, closed from 5pm and Sat & Sun Oct-Apr; ⑤) Can help with accommodation and hiking maps. A digital board outside is also useful for room bookings and information.

Getting There & Away

Hourly Postbus (p210) services connect Mondsee with Salzburg (€6.90, 45 minutes); three to five direct buses run daily from May to mid-September to St Gilgen (€3.70, 20 minutes), but there's one direct late-morning or early-afternoon bus from Monday to Saturday year-round.

Expect to pay up to €30 for a ride to St Gilgen by **taxi** (☎0664 220 00 22).

Getting Around

Alpen-Bike.com (☎06232-365 11; www.alpen-bike.com; Steinerbachstrasse 20a; standard trekking/mountain bike per day €20/30, e-trekking/mountain bike €30/40; ⌚9am-1pm & 2-6pm Mon, Tue, Thu & Fri, 1-6pm Wed, 9am-noon Sat) rents trekking and mountain bikes if you want to explore the lakes on two wheels.

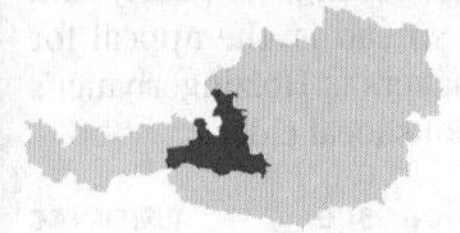

Salzburg & Salzburgerland

Best Places to Eat

➡ Esszimmer (p246)

➡ Obauer (p253)

➡ Steinerwirt (p259)

➡ Hammerwirt (p252)

➡ Fiakerwirt (p254)

➡ Blonde Beans (p265)

Best Places to Stay

➡ Haus Ballwein (p239)

➡ Hotel am Dom (p241)

➡ Hammerhof (p254)

➡ Steinerwirt (p259)

➡ Chalet-Hotel Senger (p267)

Why Go?

One of Austria's smallest provinces, Salzburgerland is proof that size really doesn't matter. Well, not when you have Mozart, Maria von Trapp and the 600-year legacy of the prince-archbishops behind you. This is the land that grabbed the world spotlight and shouted 'visit Austria!' with Julie Andrews skipping joyously down the mountainsides. This is indeed the land of crisp apple strudel, dancing marionettes and high-on-a-hilltop castles. This is the Austria of your wildest childhood dreams.

Salzburg is every bit as grand as you imagine it: a baroque masterpiece, a classical-music legend and Austria's spiritual heartland. But it is just the prelude to the region's sensational natural beauty. Just outside the city, the landscape is etched with deep ravines, glinting ice caves, karst plateaux and mountains of myth – in short, the kind of alpine gorgeousness that no well-orchestrated symphony or yodelling nun could ever quite capture.

When to Go

➡ Prices peak in family-friendly alpine resorts during winter, from December to early April. Salzburg twinkles at its Christmas markets. In January orchestras strike up at Mozartwoche, while hot-air balloons glide above Filzmoos' summits.

➡ Summer sees room prices soar in Salzburg and nosedive in alpine resorts (from June to September). Book months ahead for the colossal feast of opera, classical music and drama that is the Salzburg Festival, held from late July through August. Head for high-altitude hiking in the limestone Tennengebirge and Dachstein ranges and the glacier-capped Hohe Tauern National Park, or chill lakeside in Zell am See.

➡ Shoulder-season months April, May, October and November bring few crowds and low room rates. Salzburg hosts Easter classical-music festivals.

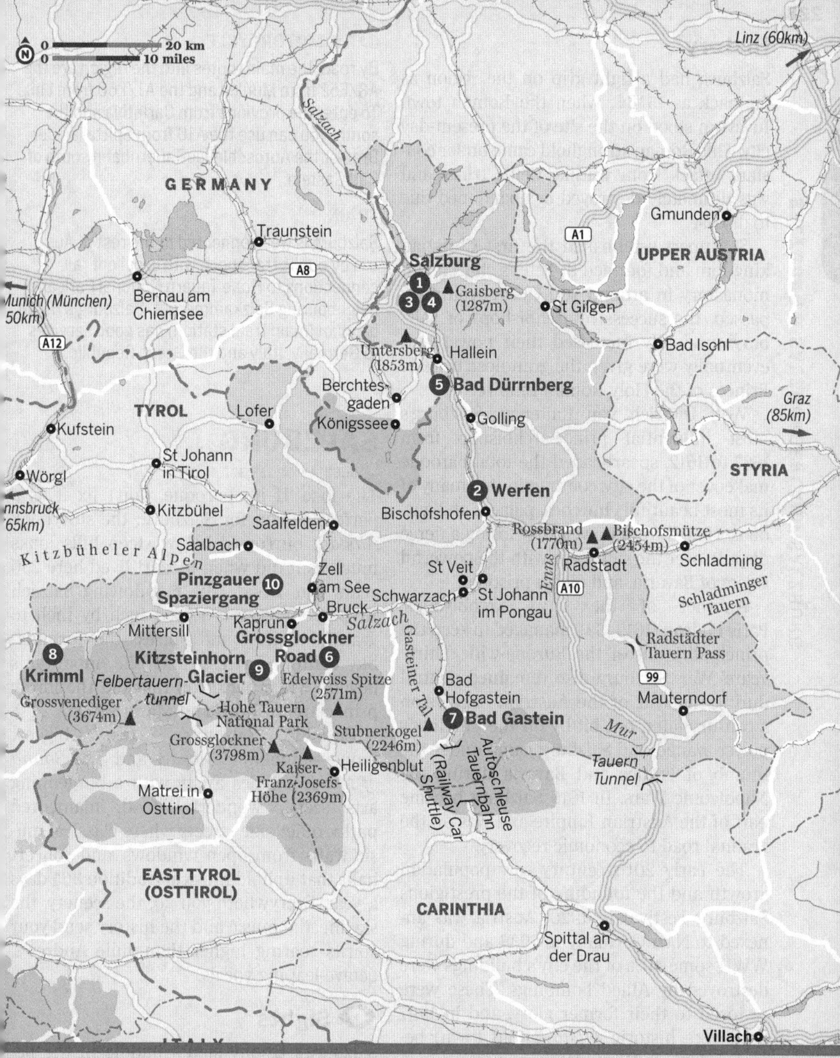

Salzburg & Salzburgerland Highlights

1 Festung Hohensalzburg (p228) Surveying Salzburg from its clifftop fortress.

2 Eisriesenwelt (p252) Going subzero in the world's largest ice cave in Werfen.

3 Schloss Hellbrunn (p229) Getting drenched by trick fountains at this summer palace just outside Salzburg.

4 Schloss Mirabell (p234) Singing 'Do-Re-Mi' in these exquisitely landscaped gardens.

5 Salzwelten (p250) Delving into Bad Dürrnberg's salt mine.

6 Grossglockner Road (p265) Driving helter-skelter on this phenomenal alpine road.

7 Felsentherme Gastein (p263) Bathing in healing waters in Bad Gastein.

8 Krimmler Wasserfälle (p268) Hearing the thunder of Europe's highest waterfall.

9 Kitzsteinhorn Glacier (p257) Hiking the trail and having a snowball fight on this 3029m glacier.

10 Pinzgauer Spaziergang (p260) Marvelling at alpine giants on this high-level hike.

History

Salzburg had a tight grip on the region as far back as 15 BC, when the Roman town Iuvavum stood on the site of the present-day city. This Roman stronghold came under constant attack from warlike Celtic tribes and was ultimately destroyed or abandoned due to disease.

St Rupert established the first Christian kingdom and founded St Peter's church and monastery in around 700 CE. As centuries passed, the successive archbishops of Salzburg gradually increased their power and eventually were given the grandiose titles of Princes of the Holy Roman Empire.

Wolf Dietrich von Raitenau, Salzburg's most influential prince-archbishop from 1587 to 1612, spearheaded the total baroque makeover of the city, commissioning many of its most beautiful churches, palaces and gardens. He fell from power after losing a fierce dispute over the salt trade with the powerful rulers of Bavaria, and died a prisoner.

Another of the city's archbishops, Paris Lodron (1619–53), managed to keep the principality out of the Europe-wide Thirty Years' War. Salzburg also remained neutral during the War of the Austrian Succession a century later, but bit by bit the province's power waned and Salzburg came under the thumb of France and Bavaria during the Napoleonic Wars. In 1816 Salzburg became part of the Austrian Empire and was on the gradual road to economic recovery.

The early 20th century saw population growth and the founding of the prestigious Salzburg Festival in 1920. Austria was annexed to Nazi Germany in 1938 and during WWII some 40% of the city's buildings were destroyed by Allied bombings. These were restored to their former glory, and in 1997 Salzburg's historic *Altstadt* (old town) became a Unesco World Heritage site.

Getting There & Away

AIR

Both scheduled and no-frills flights from Europe and the USA serve **Salzburg Airport** (☎0662-858 00; www.salzburg-airport.com; Innsbrucker Bundesstrasse 95; 📶), a 20-minute bus ride from the city centre.

BUS

Salzburg's efficient bus network, run by **Salzburger Verkehrsverbund** (SVV; www.salzburg-verkehr.at), makes it easy to reach the province's smaller villages.

CAR & MOTORCYCLE

By road, the main routes into the region are the A8/E52 from Munich and the A1/E60 from Linz. To enter the province from Carinthia and the south, you can use the A10 from Spittal an der Drau or the Autoschleuse Tauernbahn south of Bad Gastein.

TRAIN

Salzburg is well connected to the rest of Austria by public transport, with excellent rail connections to Hohe Tauern National Park and neighbouring Salzkammergut. Salzburg's *Hauptbahnhof* (main train station) has good services to Germany, Italy and the Czech Republic.

SALZBURG

☎0662 / POP 153,377

The joke 'If it's baroque, don't fix it' is a perfect maxim for Salzburg: the storybook *Altstadt* burrowed below steep hills looks much as it did when Mozart lived here 250 years ago. Beside the fast-flowing Salzach River, your gaze is raised inch by inch to graceful domes and spires, the formidable clifftop fortress and the mountains beyond. It's a backdrop that did the lordly prince-archbishops and Maria proud.

Beyond Salzburg's two biggest money-spinners – Mozart and *The Sound of Music* – hides a city with a burgeoning arts scene, wonderful food, manicured parks, quiet side streets where classical music wafts from open windows, and concert halls that uphold musical tradition 365 days a year. Everywhere you go, the scenery, the skyline, the music and the history send your spirits soaring higher than Julie Andrews' octave-leaping vocals.

Sights

Salzburg's trophy sights huddle in the pedestrianised **Altstadt**, which straddles both banks of the Salzach River but centres largely on the left bank. Here, the tangled lanes make for a serendipitous wander, leading to hidden courtyards and medieval squares framed by burgher houses and baroque fountains.

Many places close slightly earlier in winter and open longer – usually an hour or two – during the Salzburg Festival.

★**Festung Hohensalzburg** FORT
(www.salzburg-burgen.at; Mönchsberg 34; adult/child/family €10/5.70/22.20, incl funicular €12.90/7.40/28.60; ⏲9.30am-5pm Oct-Apr,

9am-7pm May-Sep) Salzburg's most visible icon is this mighty, 900-year-old clifftop fortress, one of the biggest and best preserved in Europe. It's easy to spend half a day up here, roaming the ramparts for far-reaching views over the city's spires, the Salzach River and the mountains. The fortress is a steep 15-minute walk from the centre or a speedy ride up in the glass **Festungsbahn funicular** (Festungsgasse 4; one way/return adult €6.90/8.60, child €3.70/4.70; ⏲9am-8.30pm May-Sep, to 5pm Oct-Apr).

The fortress began life as a humble bailey, built in 1077 by Gebhard von Helffenstein at a time when the Holy Roman Empire was at loggerheads with the papacy. The present structure, however, owes its grandeur to spendthrift Leonard von Keutschach, prince-archbishop of Salzburg from 1495 to 1519 and the city's last feudal ruler.

Highlights of a visit include the **Golden Hall** – where lavish banquets were once held – with a gold-studded ceiling imitating a starry night sky. Your ticket also gets you into the **Marionette Museum**, where skeleton-in-a-box Prince-Archbishop Wolf Dietrich steals the (puppet) show, and the **Fortress Museum**, which showcases a 1612 model of Salzburg, as well as medieval instruments, armour and some pretty gruesome torture devices.

The Golden Hall is the backdrop for year-round **Festungskonzerte** (fortress concerts), which often focus on Mozart's works. See www.salzburghighlights.at for times and prices.

Residenzplatz SQUARE

With its horse-drawn carriages, palace and street entertainers, this stately baroque square is the Salzburg of a thousand postcards. Its centrepiece is the **Residenzbrunnen**, an enormous marble fountain. The plaza is the late 16th-century vision of Prince-Archbishop Wolf Dietrich, who, inspired by Rome, enlisted Italian architect Vincenzo Scamozzi to design it.

★**Residenz** PALACE

(www.domquartier.at; Residenzplatz 1; DomQuartier ticket adult/child €13/5; ⏲10am-5pm Wed-Mon Sep-Jun, to 6pm daily Jul & Aug) The crowning glory of Salzburg's DomQuartier, the Residenz is where the prince-archbishops held court until Salzburg became part of the Habsburg empire in the 19th century. An audio-guide tour takes in the exuberant **state rooms**, lavishly adorned with tapestries, stucco and frescos by Johann Michael Rottmayr. The 3rd floor is given over to the **Residenzgalerie**, where the focus is on Flemish and Dutch masters. Must-sees include Rubens' *Allegory on Emperor Charles V* and Rembrandt's chiaroscuro *Old Woman Praying*.

Dom CATHEDRAL

(Cathedral; ☎0662-804 77 950; www.salzburger-dom.at; Domplatz; guided tours €5; ⏲8am-7pm Mon-Sat, from 1pm Sun May-Sep, shorter hours Oct-Apr) Gracefully crowned by a bulbous copper dome and twin spires, the *Dom* stands out as a masterpiece of baroque art. Bronze portals symbolising faith, hope and charity lead into the cathedral. In the nave, both the intricate stucco and Arsenio Mascagni's ceiling frescos recounting the Passion of Christ guide the eye to the polychrome dome.

Dommuseum MUSEUM

(www.domquartier.at; Domplatz; DomQuartier ticket adult/child €13/5; ⏲10am-5pm Wed-Mon Sep-Jun, 10am-6pm daily Jul & Aug) The Dommuseum is a treasure trove of sacred art. A visit whisks you past a cabinet of Renaissance curiosities crammed with crystals, coral and oddities such as armadillos and pufferfish, through rooms showcasing gem-encrusted monstrances, stained glass and altarpieces, and into the **Long Gallery**, which is graced with 17th- and 18th-century paintings, including Paul Troger's chiaroscuro *Christ and Nicodemus* (1739).

From the **Organ Gallery**, you get close-ups of the organ Mozart played and a bird's-eye view of the *Dom*'s nave.

Domgrabungsmuseum MUSEUM

(Cathedral Excavations Museum; ☎0662-62 08 08 131; www.salzburgmuseum.at; Residenzplatz; adult/child €3.50/1; ⏲9am-5pm Jul & Aug, by request Sep-Jun) Map out the city's past with a look at the rocks in this subterranean archaeology museum beside the Dom. Particularly of interest are fragments of Roman mosaics, a milestone hewn from Untersberg marble and the brickwork of the former Romanesque cathedral.

★**Schloss Hellbrunn** PALACE

(www.hellbrunn.at; Fürstenweg 37; adult/child/family €12.50/5.50/26.50, gardens free; ⏲9am-9pm Jul & Aug, to 5.30pm May, Jun & Sep, to 4.30pm Apr & Oct; 👪) A prince-archbishop with a wicked sense of humour, Markus Sittikus, built Schloss Hellbrunn in the early 17th century as a

Salzburg

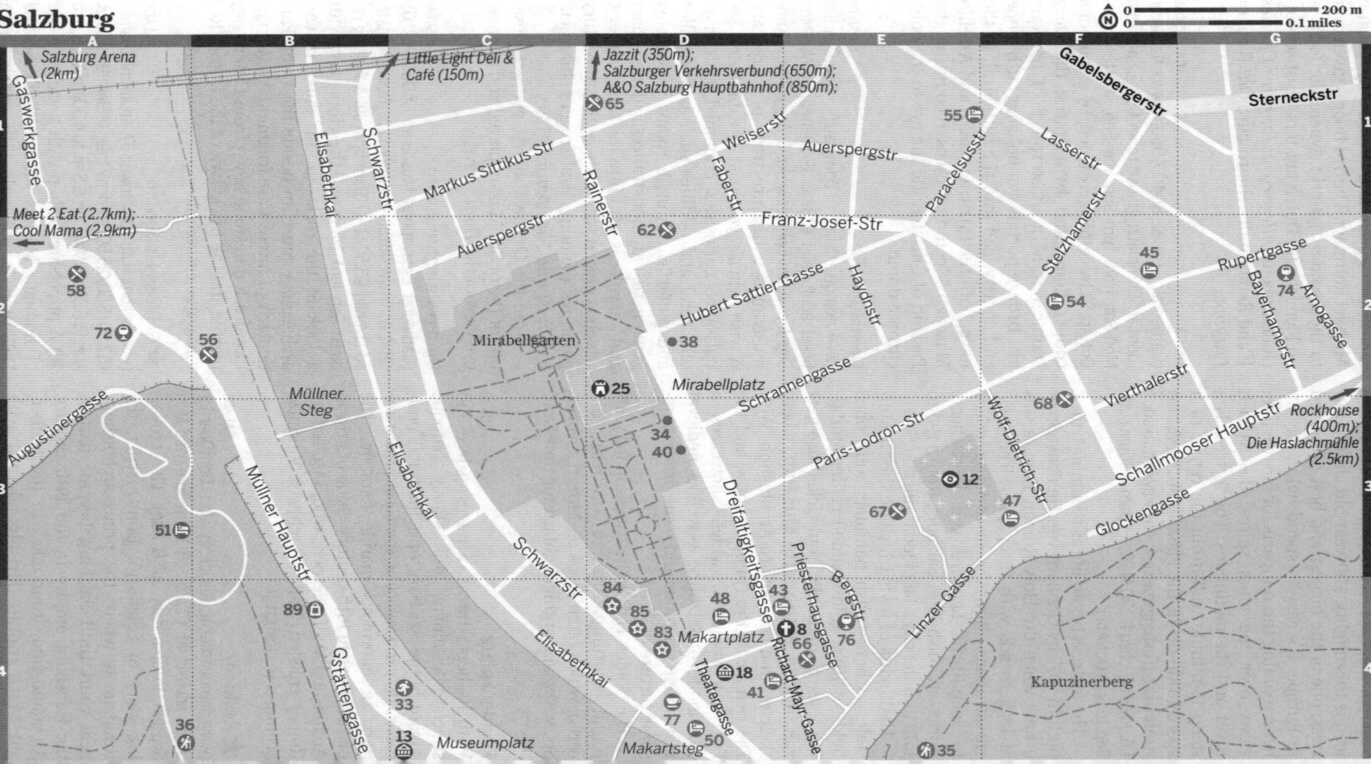
0 200 m
0 0.1 miles
Salzburg Arena (2km)
Little Light Deli & Café (150m)
Jazzit (350m); Salzburger Verkehrsverbund (650m); A&O Salzburg Hauptbahnhof (850m);
Meet 2 Eat (2.7km); Cool Mama (2.9km)
Rockhouse (400m); Die Haslachmühle (2.5km)
Gaswerkgasse
Gabelsbergerstr
Sterneckstr
Lasserstr
Paracelsusstr
Auerspergstr
Weiserstr
Faberstr
Markus Sittikus Str
Rainerstr
Schwarzstr
Elisabethkai
Franz-Josef-Str
Stelzhamerstr
Rupertgasse
Bayerhamerstr
Arnogasse
Hubert Sattler Gasse
Haydnstr
Mirabellgarten
Mirabellplatz
Schrannengasse
Viertahlerstr
Wolf-Dietrich-Str
Schallmooser Hauptstr
Paris-Lodron-Str
Glockengasse
Müllner Steg
Augustinergasse
Müllner Hauptstr
Gstättengasse
Dreifaltigkeitsgasse
Priesterhausgasse
Bergstr
Linzer Gasse
Makartplatz
Richard-Mayr-Gasse
Theatergasse
Museumplatz
Makartsteg
Kapuzinerberg
1
2
3
4
A
B
C
D
E
F
G
65
55
62
45
74
54
58
72
56
38
25
68
34
40
12
67
47
51
84
85
83
48
43
8
66
76
89
18
41
33
77
50
36
13
35

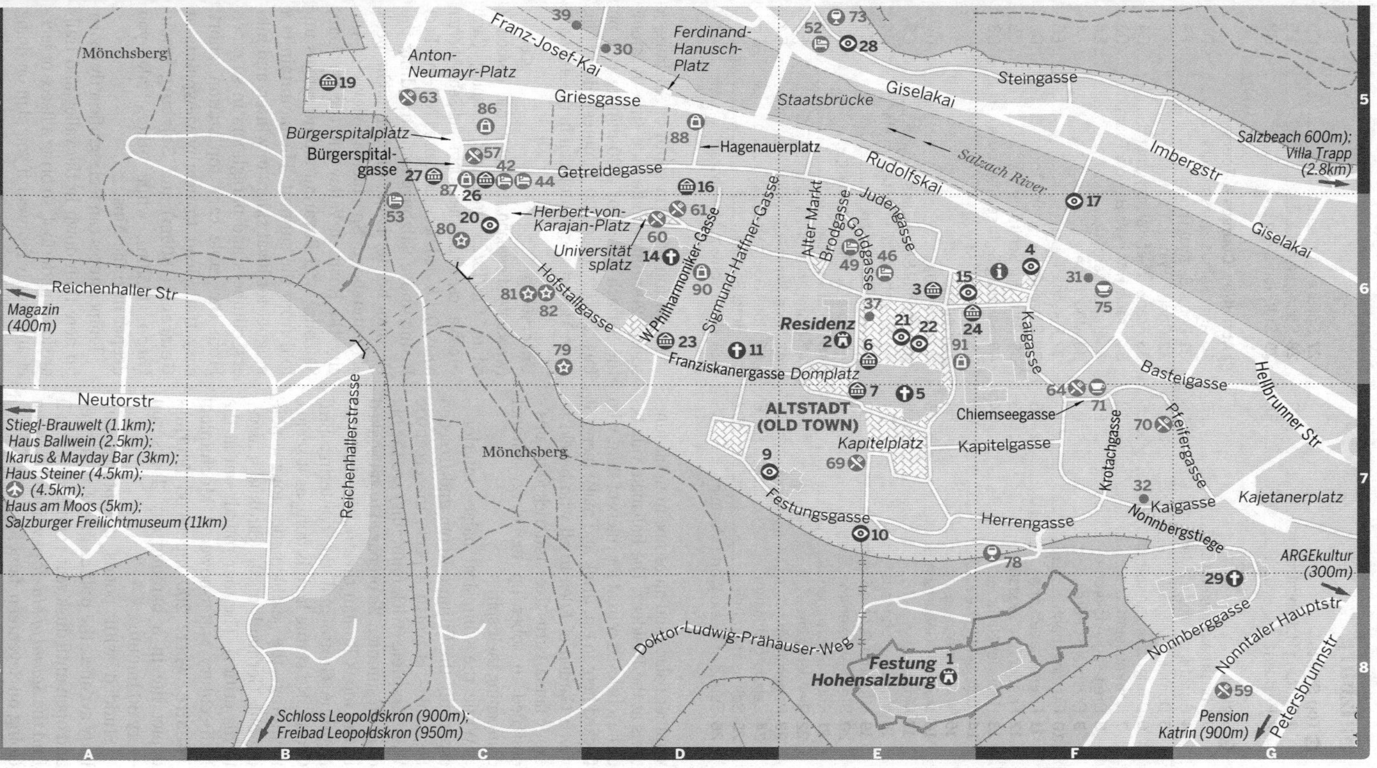

Mönchsberg
Anton-Neumayr-Platz
Franz-Josef-Kai
Ferdinand-Hanusch-Platz
Griesgasse
Staatsbrücke
Giselakai
Steingasse
Salzbeach 600m); Villa Trapp (2.8km)
Imbergstr
Bürgerspitalplatz
Bürgerspital-gasse
Hagenauerplatz
Getreidegasse
Rudolfskai
Salzach River
Herbert-von-Karajan-Platz
Universitätsplatz
Hofstallgasse
W Philharmoniker-Gasse
Sigmund-Haffner-Gasse
Alter Markt
Brodgasse
Goldgasse
Judengasse
Reichenhaller Str
Magazin (400m)
Residenz
Franziskanergasse
Domplatz
Kaigasse
Basteigasse
Hellbrunner Str
Neutorstr
Stiegl-Brauwelt (1.1km); Haus Ballwein (2.5km); Ikarus & Mayday Bar (3km); Haus Steiner (4.5km); (4.5km); Haus am Moos (5km); Salzburger Freilichtmuseum (11km)
Reichenhallerstrasse
ALTSTADT (OLD TOWN)
Chiemseegasse
Kapitelplatz
Kapitelgasse
Krotachgasse
Pfeifergasse
Mönchsberg
Kajetanerplatz
Festungsgasse
Herrengasse
Kaigasse
Nonnbergstiege
ARGEkultur (300m)
Nonnberggasse
Nonntaler Hauptstr
Doktor-Ludwig-Prähauser-Weg
Festung Hohensalzburg
Petersbrunnstr
Pension Katrin (900m)
Schloss Leopoldskron (900m); Freibad Leopoldskron (950m)

Salzburg

Top Sights
1 Festung Hohensalzburg E8
2 Residenz E6

Sights
3 Christmas Museum E6
4 Constanze Mozart Memorial F6
5 Dom E7
6 Domgrabungsmuseum E6
7 Dommuseum E7
8 Dreifältigkeitskirche E4
9 Erzabtei St Peter D7
10 Festungsbahn E7
11 Franziskanerkirche D6
12 Friedhof St Sebastian E3
13 Haus der Natur C4
14 Kollegienkirche D6
15 Mozartplatz E6
16 Mozart's Geburtshaus D5
17 Mozartsteg F6
18 Mozart-Wohnhaus D4
19 Museum der Moderne B5
20 Pferdeschwemme C6
21 Residenzbrunnen E6
22 Residenzplatz E6
23 Rupertinum D6
24 Salzburg Museum E6
25 Schloss Mirabell D2
26 Sound of Music World Museum C5
27 Spielzeugmuseum C5
28 Steingasse E5
29 Stift Nonnberg G8

Activities, Courses & Tours
30 Amphibious Splash Tours D5
31 Bob's Special Tours F6
32 Cook & Wine F7
33 Franz-Josef-Kai Playground C4
34 Fräulein Maria's Bicycle Tours D3
35 Kapuzinerberg E4
36 Mönchsberg A4
37 Rikscha Tours E6
38 Salzburg Panorama Tours D2
39 Salzburg Schifffahrt C5
40 Salzburg Sightseeing Tours D3

Sleeping
41 Arte Vida D4
42 Arthotel Blaue Gans C5
43 Gästehaus im Priesterseminar D4
44 Goldener Hirsch C5
45 Hotel & Villa Auersperg F2
46 Hotel am Dom E6
47 Hotel Amadeus F3
48 Hotel Bristol D4
49 Hotel Goldgasse E6
50 Hotel Sacher D4
51 Hotel Schloss Mönchstein A3

summer palace and an escape from his functions at the Residenz. The Italianate villa became a beloved retreat for rulers of state, who flocked here to eat, drink and make merry. It was a Garden of Eden to all who beheld its exotic fauna, citrus trees and trick fountains – designed to sober up the clergy without dampening their spirits.

While the whimsical palace interior – especially the Chinese Room and frescoed Festsaal – is worth a peek, the eccentric **Wasserspiele** (trick fountains) are the big draw in summer. Be prepared to get soaked in the mock Roman theatre, the shell-clad Neptune Grotto and the twittering Bird Grotto. No statue here is quite as it seems, including the emblematic tongue-poking-out Germaul mask (Sittikus' answer to his critics). The tour rounds out at the 18th-century water-powered **Mechanical Theatre**, where 200 limewood figurines depict life in a baroque city. Tours run every 30 minutes.

Studded with ponds, sculptures and leafy avenues, the **palace gardens** are free and open until dusk year-round. Here you'll find the *Sound of Music* pavilion of 'Sixteen Going on Seventeen' fame.

Hellbrunn is 4.5km south of Salzburg, a scenic 20-minute bike ride (mostly along the Salzach River) or a 20-minute ride on Bus 25 (€2, every 20 minutes), departing from Mozartsteg/Rudolfskai in the *Altstadt*.

Untersberg MOUNTAIN

(www.untersbergbahn.at; cable car up/down/return €16/15/25, free with Salzburg Card; cable car 8.30am-5.30pm Jul-Sep, shorter hours Oct & mid-Dec–Jun, closed Nov–mid-Dec) Rising above Salzburg and straddling the German border is the rugged 1853m peak of Untersberg. Spectacular views of the city, the Rositten Valley and the Tyrolean, Salzburg and Bavarian alpine ranges unfold from the summit. The mountain is a magnet for local skiers in winter, and hikers, climbers and paragliders in summer. From the cable car's top station, short, easy trails lead to nearby viewpoints at **Geiereck** (1805m) and **Salzburg Hochthron** (1853m), while others take you deeper into the Alps.

Temperatures can feel significantly cooler up here than down in the valley and trails are loose underfoot, so bring a fleece or jacket and sturdy footwear if you plan on doing some walking.

A cable car runs every half-hour to the peak. To reach the cable-car valley station, take bus 25 from Salzburg's *Hauptbahnhof* or Mirabellplatz to St Leonhard and the valley station.

Stift Nonnberg CONVENT
(Nonnberg Convent; Nonnberggasse 2; ⌚6.45am-dusk) FREE A short climb up the Nonnbergstiege staircase from Kaigasse or along Festungsgasse brings you to this Benedictine convent, founded 1300 years ago and made famous as the nunnery in *The Sound of Music*. You can visit the beautiful rib-vaulted **church**, but the rest of the convent is off limits. Take €0.50 to switch on the light that illuminates the beautiful **Romanesque frescos**.

If you're an early riser, time your visit to hear the nuns singing Gregorian chorales at 6.45am daily.

Museum der Moderne GALLERY
(www.museumdermoderne.at; Mönchsberg 32; adult/child €8/6, combined ticket with Rupertinum €12/8; ⌚10am-6pm Tue & Thu-Sun, to 8pm Wed; 👪) Straddling Mönchsberg's cliffs, this contemporary glass-and-marble oblong of a gallery stands in stark contrast to the fortress, and shows first-rate temporary exhibitions of 20th- and 21st-century art. The works of German expressionist Ernst Ludwig Kirchner and Austrian painter Oskar Kokoschka have previously been featured. There's a free **guided tour** of the gallery at 6.30pm every Wednesday. The Mönchsberg Lift (p237) whizzes up to the gallery year-round.

Mozartplatz SQUARE
(Mozart Place) On this stately baroque square, Mozart is literally and metaphorically put on a pedestal. The square hums with street entertainers and the clip-clop of horse-drawn carriages.

Salzburg Museum MUSEUM
(www.salzburgmuseum.at; Mozartplatz 1; adult/child €9/3; ⌚9am-5pm Tue-Sun; 👪) Housed in the baroque Neue Residenz palace, this flagship museum takes you on a fascinating romp through Salzburg past and present. Ornate rooms showcase everything from Roman excavations to royal portraits. There are free **guided tours** at 6pm every Thursday.

A visit starts beneath the courtyard in the strikingly illuminated **Kunsthalle**, presenting rotating exhibitions of art. Upstairs, prince-archbishops glower down from the walls at **Mythos Salzburg**,

SALZBURG CARD

If you're planning on doing lots of sightseeing, save by buying the **Salzburg Card** (1-/2-/3-day card €29/38/44). The card gets you entry to all of the major sights and attractions, unlimited use of public transport (including cable cars), and numerous discounts on tours and events. The card is half-price for children and €3 cheaper in the low season.

The card can be purchased at the airport, the tourist office and most hotels, or online at www.salzburg.info.

which celebrates the city as a source of artistic and poetic inspiration. Showstoppers include Carl Spitzweg's renowned painting *Sonntagsspaziergang* (Sunday Stroll; 1841), the portrait-lined **prince-archbishop's room** and the **Ständesaal** (Sovereign Chamber), an opulent vision of polychrome stucco curling around frescos depicting the history of Rome according to Titus Livius. The early-16th-century Milleflori tapestry, Prince-Archbishop Wolf Dietrich's gold-embroidered pontifical shoe, and Flemish tapestries are among the other attention-grabbers.

The **Panorama Passage** also provides some insight into Salzburg's past, with its Roman walls, potter's kiln and models of the city at different points in history.

Salzburg's famous 35-bell **carillon**, which chimes daily at 7am, 11am and 6pm, is on the western flank of the Neue Residenz.

Schloss Mirabell PALACE

(Mirabellplatz 4; Schloss Mirabell 8am-6pm, Marble Hall 8am-4pm Mon, Wed & Thu, 1-4pm Tue & Fri, gardens 6am-dusk) FREE Prince-Archbishop Wolf Dietrich built this splendid palace in 1606 to impress his beloved mistress, Salome Alt. It must have done the trick because she went on to bear the archbishop some 15 children (sources disagree on the exact number – poor Wolf was presumably too distracted by spiritual matters to keep count). Johann Lukas von Hildebrandt, of Schloss Belvedere fame, remodelled the palace in baroque style in 1721. The lavish interior, replete with stucco, marble and frescos, is free to visit.

Erzabtei St Peter MONASTERY

(St Peter's Abbey; www.stift-stpeter.at; Sankt-Peter-Bezirk 1-2; catacombs adult/child €2/1.50; church 8am-noon & 2.30-6.30pm, cemetery 6.30am-7pm, catacombs 10am-12.30pm & 1-6pm) A Frankish missionary named Rupert founded this abbey-church and monastery in around 700, making it the oldest in the German-speaking world. Though a vaulted Romanesque portal remains, today's church is overwhelmingly baroque, with rococo stucco, statues – including one of archangel Michael shoving a crucifix through the throat of a goaty demon – and striking altar paintings by Martin Johann Schmidt.

Mozart's Geburtshaus MUSEUM

(Mozart's Birthplace; www.mozarteum.at; Getreidegasse 9; adult/child €11/3.50; 9am-5.30pm Sep-Jun, 8.30am-7pm Jul & Aug) Wolfgang Amadeus Mozart, Salzburg's most famous son, was born in this bright-yellow town house in 1756, and spent the first 17 years of his life here. Today's museum harbours a collection of instruments, documents and portraits. Highlights include the mini-violin he played as a toddler, plus a lock of his hair and buttons from his jacket.

Mozart-Wohnhaus MUSEUM

(Mozart's Residence; www.mozarteum.at; Makartplatz 8; adult/child €11/3.50; 9am-5.30pm Sep-Jun, 8.30am-7pm Jul & Aug) Tired of the cramped living conditions on Getreidegasse, the Mozart family moved in 1773 to this roomier abode, where the prolific Wolfgang composed works such as the *Shepherd King* (K208) and *Idomeneo* (K366). Emanuel Schikaneder, a close friend of Mozart and the librettist of *The Magic Flute*, was a regular guest here. An audio guide accompanies your visit, serenading you with opera excerpts. Alongside family portraits and documents, you'll find Mozart's original fortepiano.

Sound of Music World Museum MUSEUM

(www.soundofmusicworld.com; Getreidegasse 47; €8; 10am-6pm) If you're mad about *The Sound of Music*, this museum will appeal. It spills the beans on different aspects of the making of the movie, as well as providing an insight into the real Trapp Family Singers, so you can contrast the film with the reality. Memorabilia, photos, costumes and furnishings bring the story to life.

Schloss Leopoldskron NOTABLE BUILDING

(www.schloss-leopoldskron.com; Leopoldskronstrasse 56-58) The grand rococo palace of

Schloss Leopoldskron is where the lake scene was filmed in *The Sound of Music*. Its Venetian Room was the blueprint for the Trapps' lavish ballroom, where the children bid their farewells. It's now a plush hotel, but you can admire it from the outside. It's a 15-minute walk from Festung Hohensalzburg (p228).

Christmas Museum MUSEUM

(☎0662-84 35 23; Mozartplatz 2; adult/child €6/3; ⏲10am-6pm Wed-Sun) If you wish it could be Christmas every day, swing on over to this museum. The private collection brings festive sparkle in the form of advent calendars, hand-carved cribs, baubles and nutcrackers.

Steingasse HISTORIC SITE

On the right bank of the Salzach River, this narrow, cobbled lane was, incredibly, the main trade route to Italy in medieval times. Look out for the 13th-century **Steintor** gate and the house of **Joseph Mohr**, who wrote the lyrics to the all-time classic Christmas carol 'Silent Night', composed by Franz Xaver Gruber in 1818. The street is at its most photogenic in the late morning, when sunlight illuminates its pastel-coloured town houses.

Friedhof St Sebastian CEMETERY

(Linzer Gasse 41; ⏲9am-6.30pm) Tucked behind the baroque Sebastianskirche (St Sebastian's Church), this peaceful cemetery and its cloisters were designed by Andrea Berteleto in Italianate style in 1600. Mozart family members and well-known 16th-century physician Paracelsus are buried here, but out-pomping them all is Prince-Archbishop Wolf Dietrich von Raitenau's mosaic-tiled mausoleum, an elaborate memorial to himself.

Dreifältigkeitskirche CHURCH

(Church of the Holy Trinity; Dreifaltigkeitsgasse 14; ⏲6.30am-6.30pm) Baroque master Johann Bernhard Fischer von Erlach designed this graceful church on the city's right bank. It's famous for Johann Michael Rottmayr's dome **fresco of the Holy Trinity**.

Pferdeschwemme FOUNTAIN

(Horse Trough; Herbert-von-Karajan-Platz) Designed by von Erlach in 1693, this is a horse-lover's delight, with rearing equine pin-ups surrounding Michael Bernhard Mandl's statue of a horse tamer.

Rupertinum GALLERY

(www.museumdermoderne.at; Wiener-Philharmoniker-Gasse 9; adult/child/family €6/4/8, combined ticket with Museum der Moderne €12/8/16; ⏲10am-6pm Tue & Thu-Sun, to 8pm Wed) In the heart of the *Altstadt*, the Rupertinum is the sister gallery of the Museum der Moderne (p233) and is devoted to rotating exhibitions of modern

SALZBURG IN...

Two Days

Get up early to see Mozart's Geburtshaus (p234) and boutique-dotted Getreidegasse before the crowds. Take in the baroque grandeur of Residenzplatz (p229) and the stately Residenz (p229) palace. Coffee at hip 220 Grad (p247) fuels an afternoon absorbing history at the hands-on Salzburg Museum (p233) or monastic heritage at Erzabtei St Peter (p234). Toast your first day with homebrews in the beer garden at Augustiner Bräustübl (p246).

Begin the second day with postcard views from the ramparts of Festung Hohensalzburg (p228), or absorbing cutting-edge art at Museum der Moderne (p233). Go for lunch at festival-inspired Triangel (p246) or hit the Grünmarkt (p242) before a picnic in the gardens of Schloss Mirabell. Chamber music in the palace's Marble Hall or enchanting puppetry at Salzburger Marionettentheater (p247) rounds out the day nicely.

Four Days

On day three, you can join a Mozart or *Sound of Music* **tour**. Hire a bike to pedal along the Salzach's villa-studded banks to summer palace Schloss Hellbrunn (p229). Dine in old-world Austrian style at Bärenwirt (p243) before testing the **right-bank nightlife**.

The fun-packed salt mines of **Hallein** and the Goliath of ice caves, Eisriesenwelt (p252) in Werfen, both make terrific day trips for the fourth day. Alternatively, grab your walking boots or skis and head up to Salzburg's twin peaks: Untersberg (p232) and Gaisberg (p237).

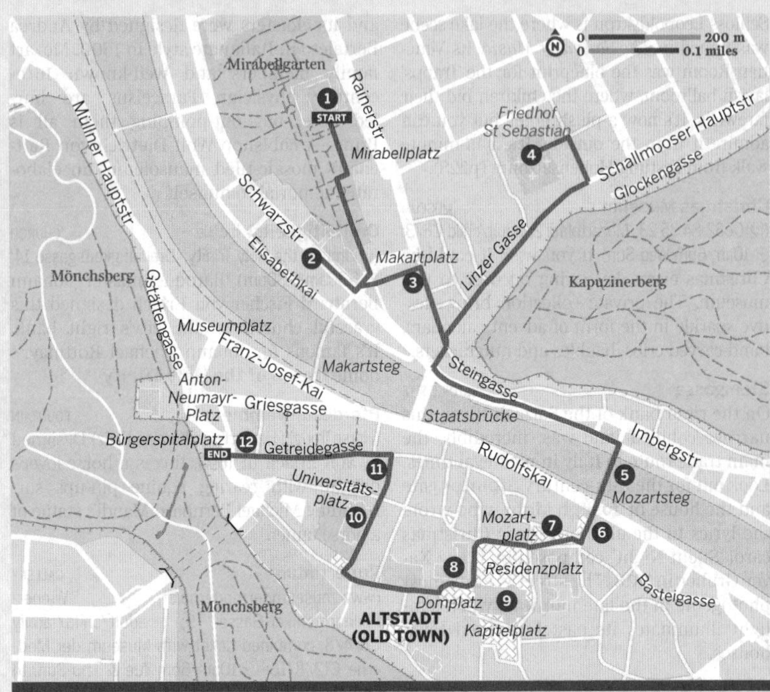

City Walk
In Mozart's Footsteps

START SCHLOSS MIRABELL
END FÜRST
LENGTH 3KM; 1½ HOURS

Mozart was the ultimate prodigy: he identified a pig's squeal as G-sharp when he was two, began to compose when he was five and first performed for Empress Maria-Theresia at six. Follow in his footsteps on this walking tour.

Begin at ❶ **Schloss Mirabell** (p234), where the Marmorsaal (Marble Hall) is often the backdrop for chamber concerts of Mozart's music. Stroll south through the fountain-dotted gardens, passing the strikingly angular ❷ **Mozarteum** (p249), a foundation honouring Mozart's life and works, and the host of the renowned Mozartwoche festival in January/February. Around the corner on Makartplatz is the 17th-century ❸ **Mozart-Wohnhaus** (p234), where you can see how the Mozart family lived and listen to rare recordings of Mozart's symphonies. Amble north along Linzer Gasse to ❹ **Friedhof St Sebastian** (p235), the Italianate arcaded cemetery where Wolfgang's father is buried. Retrace your steps towards the Salzach River, turning left onto Steingasse, then cutting through to Giselakai to cross the art-nouveau ❺ **Mozartsteg** (Mozart Bridge). Look out for the ❻ **memorial plaque** at No 8, the house where Mozart's beloved Constanze died, as you approach ❼ **Mozartplatz** (p233). On this square, a pensive Mozart is literally and metaphorically put on a pedestal in bronze. The statue was unveiled in 1842 in the presence of Mozart's sons. Across the way is the ❽ **Residenz** (p229) palace where Mozart gave his first court concert at the ripe old age of six. Beside it rests the ❾ **Dom** (p229), where Mozart's parents were married in 1747 and little Wolfgang was baptised in 1756; Mozart later composed sacred music here and was cathedral organist. Follow Franziskanergasse to reach the ❿ **Kollegienkirche** on Universitätsplatz, where Mozart's D Minor Mass (K65) premiered in 1769. On Getreidegasse, stop to contemplate the birthplace of a genius at ⓫ **Mozart's Geburtshaus** (p234) and buy some famous chocolate *Mozartkugeln* (Mozart balls) at ⓬ **Fürst** (p249).

art. There is a strong emphasis on graphic works and photography.

Franziskanerkirche CHURCH

(Franziskanergasse 5; ⌚6.30am-7.30pm) A real architectural hotchpotch, Salzburg's Franciscan church has a Romanesque nave, a Gothic choir with rib vaulting and a baroque marble altar (one of architect Fischer von Erlach's creations).

Kollegienkirche CHURCH

(Universitätsplatz; ⌚8am-6pm) Fischer von Erlach's grandest baroque design is this late-17th-century university church, with a striking bowed facade. The high altar's columns symbolise the Seven Pillars of Wisdom.

Activities

Salzburg's rival mountains are 540m Mönchsberg and 640m Kapuzinerberg – locals used to bigger things call them 'hills'. Both are thickly wooded and criss-crossed by **walking trails**, with photogenic views of the *Altstadt*.

There's also an extensive network of **cycling routes**, from a gentle 6km trundle along the Salzach River to Hellbrunn, to the 450km **Mozart Radweg** through Salzburgerland and Bavaria.

Salzbeach BEACH

(Volksgarten; ⌚9am-10pm May-Sep) Salzburg's urban beach – complete with sand, potted palms and *Strandkörbe* (wicker-basket chairs) – sprouts up in the Volksgarten each summer. Besides lounging, there's a volleyball court plus open-air events over the course of the summer, from free musical gigs to cinema nights.

Mönchsberg WALKING

(👪) Rising sheer and rugged above the city, 540m Mönchsberg commands photogenic views over the domes and spires of the *Altstadt* on one side, and of the fortress perched high on the hill on the other. Trails head out in all directions.

Arguably the most scenic trail is the 4km panoramic walking track from Stift Nonnberg (p233) to Augustiner Bräustübl (p246), taking in Festung Hohensalzburg (p228) and Museum der Moderne (p233) en route and affording views deep into the Austrian and Bavarian Alps. This trail is gentle enough to appeal to families, with ample shade in summer.

To get to the top, take the **Mönchsberg Lift** (Gstättengasse 13; one way/return €2.50/3.80, incl Museum der Moderne entry €9.10/9.70; ⌚8am-11pm Jul & Aug, to 7pm Mon, to 9pm Tue-Sun Sep-Jun).

Gaisberg HIKING

(www.gaisberg.at) A road snakes up to 1287m Gaisberg, where stellar views of the Salzburg Valley, the Salzkammergut lakes, the limestone Tennengebirge range and neighbouring Bavaria await. The best way to appreciate all this is on the 5km round-the-mountain circuit trail. Salzburgers also head up here for outdoor pursuits, from mountain biking to cross-country skiing.

Bus 151 (€3.70, 27 minutes) runs at least every two hours in summer from Mirabellplatz to Gaisberg. From November to March the bus only goes as far as Zistelalpe, 1.5km short of the summit.

Fly Salzburg PARAGLIDING

(☎0650 826 33 61; www.flytandem.at) The Alps beckon right on Salzburg's doorstep, and Fly Salzburg gives you an aerial view of those enticing peaks with tandem paragliding flights at nearby Gaisberg (€149) and Werfenweng (€139). Meeting points are arranged when you book.

Waldbad Anif SWIMMING

(www.waldbadanif.at; Waldbadstrasse 1; adult/child €6.50/4.50; ⌚9am-sunset May-Sep) A sylvan beauty of a turquoise, forest-rimmed lake. Go for a quiet dip or opt for activities such as canoeing, climbing, volleyball or table tennis. Take bus 170 to Maximarkt, a 1km walk from the lake.

Freibad Leopoldskron SWIMMING

(Leopoldskronstrasse 50; adult/child €5/2.80; ⌚9am-7pm May–mid-Sep; 👪) Salzburg's biggest outdoor pool, with laps for swimmers, kids' splash pools, diving boards and water slides, plus table tennis, minigolf and volleyball. Bus 22 to Wartbergweg stops close by.

Kapuzinerberg WALKING

Presiding over the city, the serene, thickly wooded 640m peak of Kapuzinerberg is criss-crossed by walking trails up to a **viewpoint** that gazes across the river to the castle-topped *Altstadt*. Note the six baroque Way of the Cross chapels as you make the short trek uphill.

The trails can be accessed from Linzer Gasse.

Tours

Rikscha Tours TOURS

(☎0662-634 02 40; www.rikschatours.at; Residenzplatz; ⏰mid-Apr–Oct) Whizzing around Salzburg by rickshaw is the latest thing – the clued-up guides will fill you in on anecdotes as they pedal. Tours range from a 40-minute spin around the historic centre (€36) to the 75-minute 'Round of Music' tour (€65), taking in the film locations of…you guessed it.

Stiegl-Brauwelt BREWERY

(☎050 14 92 14 92; www.brauwelt.at; Bräuhausstrasse 9; adult/child €13/8; ⏰10am-7pm Jul & Aug, to 5pm Sep-Jun) Brewing and bottling since 1492, Stiegl is Austria's largest private brewery. A tour takes in the different stages of the brewing process and (woo-hoo!) the world's tallest beer tower. A Stiegl beer and small gift are thrown in for the price of a ticket. The brewery is 1.5km southwest of the *Altstadt;* take bus 1 or 10 to Bräuhausstrasse.

Fräulein Maria's Bicycle Tours CYCLING

(www.mariasbicycletours.com; Mirabellplatz 4; adult/child €35/15; ⏰9.30am Apr-Oct, plus 4.30pm Jun-Aug) Belt out *The Sound of Music* faves as you pedal along on one of these jolly 3½-hour bike tours, taking in locations from the film, including Schloss Mirabell (p234), Stift Nonnberg (p233), Schloss Leopoldskron (p234) and Hellbrunn (p229). Advance bookings (tickets are available online) are highly recommended.

Amphibious Splash Tours CRUISE

(☎0662-82 57 69 12; www.amphibious-splash-tours.at; Makartsteg; adult/child €30/20; ⏰late Mar-Oct) Is it a boat? Is it a bus? No, it's an amphibious splash tour – a novel combination of the two and a cool new way to boat along the Salzach River. Tours last roughly 1½ hours, with several departures daily (see the website for times).

Salzburg Schifffahrt CRUISE

(☎0662-82 57 69 12; Makartsteg; adult/child €15/7.50; ⏰late Mar-Oct) A boat ride along the Salzach River is a leisurely way to pick out Salzburg's sights. Hour-long cruises depart from Makartsteg bridge, with some of them chugging on to Schloss Hellbrunn (adult/child €18/10, not including entry to the palace).

Bob's Special Tours BUS

(☎0662-84 95 11; www.bobstours.com; Rudolfskai 38; ⏰office 8.30am-5pm Mon-Fri, 1-2pm Sat & Sun) Minibus tours to *The Sound of Music* locations (€55), the Bavarian Alps (€55) and Grossglockner (€110). Prices include a free hotel pick-up for morning tours starting at 9am. Reservations are essential.

Salzburg Panorama Tours BUS

(☎0662-883 21 10; www.panoramatours.com; Mirabellplatz; ⏰office 8am-6pm) Boasts the 'original *Sound of Music* Tour' (€45) as well as a huge range of others, including one-hour hop-on, hop-off tours (€19), Mozart tours (€55) and Bavarian Alps excursions (€45).

Salzburg Sightseeing Tours BUS

(☎0662-88 16 16; www.salzburg-sightseeingtours.at; Mirabellplatz 2; ⏰office 8am-6pm) Sells a 24-hour ticket (adult/child €19/9) for a multilingual hop-on, hop-off bus tour of the city's key sights and *Sound of Music* locations.

Festivals & Events

Mozartwoche MUSIC

(Mozart Week; www.mozarteum.at; ⏰late Jan-early Feb) World-renowned orchestras, conductors and soloists celebrate Mozart's birthday with an 11-day feast of his music in January/February.

Osterfestspiele MUSIC

(Easter Festival; www.osterfestspiele-salzburg.at; ⏰Mar or Apr) Held in the week running up to Easter, this springtime shindig brings orchestral highlights, under Christian Thielemann's sprightly baton, to the Grosses Festspielhaus, as well as choral concerts and opera.

SommerSzene CULTURAL

(www.sommerszene.net; Anton-Neumayr-Platz 2, SzeneSalzburg; ⏰mid-late Jun) Boundary-crossing performing arts – including cutting-edge dance, plays, film, visual arts, poetry readings and DJ sets – are the focus of this event staged for 13 days in June.

Salzburg Festival CULTURAL

(Salzburger Festspiele; www.salzburgerfestspiele.at; ⏰late Jul-Aug) The absolute highlight of the city's events calendar is the Salzburg Festival. It's a grand affair, with some 200 productions – including theatre, classical music and opera – staged in the impressive surrounds of the Grosses Festspielhaus, **Haus für Mozart** (House for Mozart; ☎0662-804 50; www.salzburgerfestspiele.at; Hofstallgasse 1) and the baroque **Felsenreitschule** (Summer Riding School; Hofstallgasse 1). Tickets vary in price between €15 and €430; you'll need to book months in advance.

FESTIVAL TIME

In 1920 dream trio Hugo von Hofmannsthal, Max Reinhardt and Richard Strauss combined their creative forces, and the Salzburg Festival was born. Now, as then, one of the highlights is the staging of Hofmannsthal's morality play *Jedermann* (Everyman) on Domplatz. A trilogy of opera, drama and classical concerts of the highest calibre have propelled the five-week summer festival to international renown, attracting some of the world's best conductors, directors, orchestras and singers.

Come festival time, Salzburg crackles with excitement, as a quarter of a million visitors descend on the city for some 200 productions. Theatre premieres, avant-garde works and the summer-resident Vienna Philharmonic performing works by Mozart are all in the mix. The Festival District on Hofstallgasse has a spectacular backdrop, framed by Mönchsberg's cliffs. Most performances are held in the cavernous **Grosses Festspielhaus** (☎0662-804 50; Hofstallgasse 1), which accommodates 2179 theatregoers; the Haus für Mozart in the former royal stables; and the baroque Felsenreitschule.

If you're planning to visit during the festival, don't leave *anything* to chance – book your flights, hotel and tickets months in advance. Sometimes last-minute tickets are available at the **Festspiele Ticket Office** (☎0662-804 55 00; info@salzburgfestival.at; Herbert-von-Karajan-Platz 11; ⏱10am-6pm mid-Jul–Aug, 10am-12.30pm & 1-4.30pm Mon-Fri Sep–mid-Jul), but they're like gold dust. Ticket prices range from €15 to €430.

Jazz & the City MUSIC
(www.salzburgjazz.com; ⏱mid-Oct) Salzburg gets its groove on at some 70 free jazz, world-music and electro concerts over the course of five days, held at cafes, bars and hotels across the *Altstadt*. See the website for venue details.

Christkindlmarkt CHRISTMAS MARKET
(www.christkindlmarkt.co.at; ⏱late Nov-26 Dec) Salzburg is at its storybook best during Advent, when Christmas markets bring festive sparkle and choirs to Domplatz and Residenzplatz, starting in late November.

Sleeping

Salzburg is pricey, but you can find deals if you're willing to go the extra mile; ask the tourist office (p249) for a list of private rooms and pensions. Medieval guesthouses, avant-garde design hotels and chilled-out hostels all huddle in the *Altstadt*.

Note that high-season prices jack up another 10% to 20% during the Salzburg Festival. If Salzburg is booked solid, consider staying in Hallein or across the border in Bavaria.

★**Haus Ballwein** GUESTHOUSE €
(☎0662-82 40 29; www.haus-ballwein.at; Moosstrasse 69a; s €55-65, d €72-88, tr €85-90, q €90-100; P wi-fi) With its bright, pine-filled rooms, mountain views and garden, this place is big on charm. The largest, quietest rooms face the back and have balconies and kitchenettes. It's a 10-minute trundle from the *Altstadt*; take bus 21 to Gsengerweg. Breakfast is a whole-some spread of fresh rolls, eggs, fruit, muesli and cold cuts. Bring cash as credit cards are not accepted.

Haus am Moos GUESTHOUSE €
(☎0662-82 49 21; www.ammoos.at; Moosstrasse 186a; s/d €33/66; P wi-fi pool) This alpine-style chalet offers a slice of rural calm just a 15-minute ride from town on bus 21. Many rooms have balconies with gorgeous mountain views, and some come with canopy beds. The breakfast of muesli, cold cuts, eggs and fresh bread gears you up for the day, and there's an outdoor pool for an afternoon dip.

Haus Steiner GUESTHOUSE €
(☎0662-83 00 31; www.haussteiner.com; Moosstrasse 156; s/d €35/58, apt €73-83; P wi-fi) Good-natured Rosemarie runs a tight ship at this sunny yellow chalet-style guesthouse that's ablaze with flowers in summer. The pick of the petite rooms, furnished in natural wood, come with fridges, balconies and mood-lifting mountain views; the family-sized apartments have kitchenettes. It's just a 15-minute ride away from the *Altstadt* on bus 21 (get off at Hammerauerstrasse).

Yoho Salzburg HOSTEL €
(☎0662-87 96 49; www.yoho.at; Paracelsusstrasse 9; dm €23-34, d €70-88; @ wi-fi) Free wi-fi, secure lockers, comfy bunks, plenty of cheap beer and good-value schnitzels – what more could a backpacker ask for? Except, perhaps, a merry singalong with *The Sound of Music* screened daily (yes, *every* day). The

DIY SOUND OF MUSIC TOUR

Do a Julie Andrews and sing as you stroll on a self-guided tour of *The Sound of Music* film locations. Let's start at the very beginning:

The Hills Are Alive Cut! Make that *proper* mountains. The opening scenes were filmed around the jewel-coloured Salzkammergut lakes. Maria makes her twirling entrance on alpine pastures just across the border in Bavaria.

A Problem Like Maria Nuns waltzing on their way to mass at Benedictine Stift Nonnberg (p233) is fiction, but it's fact that the real Maria von Trapp intended to become a nun here before romance struck.

Have Confidence Residenzplatz (p229) is where Maria belts out 'I Have Confidence' and playfully splashes the spouting horses of the Residenzbrunnen fountain.

So Long, Farewell The magnificent rococo palace of Schloss Leopoldskron (p234), a 15-minute walk from Festung Hohensalzburg, is where the lake scene was filmed. Its Venetian Room was the blueprint for the Trapps' lavish ballroom, where the children bid their farewells.

Do-Re-Mi The Pegasus fountain, the steps with fortress views, the gnomes…the Mirabellgarten at Schloss Mirabell (p234) might inspire a rendition of 'Do-Re-Mi' – especially if there's a drop of golden sun.

Sixteen Going on Seventeen The loved-up pavilion of the century hides out in Hellbrunn Park (p232), where you can act out those 'Oh, Liesl'/'Oh, Rolf' fantasies.

Edelweiss & Adieu The Felsenreitschule (p238) is the dramatic backdrop for the Salzburg Festival in the movie, where the Trapp Family Singers win the audience over with 'Edelweiss' and give the Nazis the slip with 'So Long, Farewell'.

Climb Every Mountain To Switzerland, that is. Or content yourself with alpine views from Untersberg (p232), which appears briefly at the end of the movie when the family flees the country.

friendly crew can arrange tours, adventure sports such as rafting and canyoning, and bike hire (€10 per day).

A&O Salzburg Hauptbahnhof HOSTEL €
(☎0662-234 2000; www.aohostels.com; Fanny-von Lehnert-Strasse 4; dm €19-31, d €72-99; 📶) In a revamped bread factory just a couple of minutes' walk from Salzburg's *Hauptbahnhof*, this slickly modern hostel has airy, light-filled, wood-floored dorms and rooms that are among the city's cheapest. It makes a functional base for exploring and there's a children's corner to keep little ones amused.

Stadtalm HOSTEL €
(☎0662-84 17 29; www.stadtalm.at; Mönchsberg 19c; dm/d €23/50) This turreted hostel plopped on top of Mönchsberg takes in the entire Salzburg panorama, from the city's spires and fortress to Kapuzinerberg. Digs are simple but you won't find them cheaper elsewhere. There's a good-value restaurant on-site.

Die Haslachmühle GUESTHOUSE €€
(☎0664-179 90 60; www.haslachmuehle.at; Mühlstrasse 18, Gnigl; d €109-168; P📶) Sitting below Gaisberg and surrounded by attractive gardens and countryside, this charismatic B&B is lodged in a 17th-century flour mill. The family go out of their way to please, and the incredibly spacious, sunny, parquet-floored rooms feature touches such as ceramic ovens, mountain views and Nespresso machines. It's a 15-minute ride from the *Hauptbahnhof* on bus 155 (Salzburg Kühberg stop).

There's a minimum two-night stay in high season.

Gästehaus im Priesterseminar GUESTHOUSE €€
(☎0662-877 495 10; www.gaestehaus-priesterseminar-salzburg.at; Dreifaltigkeitsgasse 14; s €67-87, d €120-134) Ah, the peace is heavenly at this one-time seminary tucked behind the Dreifältigkeitskirche. Its bright, parquet-floored rooms have received a total makeover, but the place still brims with old-world charm thanks to its marble staircase, antique furnishings and fountain-dotted courtyard.

It's still something of a secret, though, so whisper about it quietly…

Arte Vida GUESTHOUSE €€

(☎0662-87 31 85; www.artevida.at; Dreifaltigkeitsgasse 9; d €110-145, apt €170-220; 📶) Arte Vida has the boho-chic feel of a Moroccan *riad* (house), with its lantern-lit salon, communal kitchen and serene garden. Asia and Africa have provided the inspiration for the rich colours and fabrics that dress the individually designed rooms. Affable hosts Herbert and Karoline happily give tips on Salzburg and its surrounds, and can arrange massages and private yoga sessions.

The generously sized apartments are big enough to accommodate families. There's a three-night minimum stay in July and August.

Pension Katrin PENSION €€

(☎0662-83 08 60; www.pensionkatrin.at; Nonntaler Hauptstrasse 49b; s €69-86, d €99-117, ste €121-139; P📶) With its flowery garden, bright, cheerful rooms and excellent breakfasts, this pension is incredibly homely. The Terler family keeps everything spick and span, and nothing is too much trouble for them. Take bus 5 from the *Hauptbahnhof* to Wäschergasse. There's a three-night minimum stay in July and August.

Hotel am Dom BOUTIQUE HOTEL €€

(☎0662-84 27 65; www.hotelamdom.at; Goldgasse 17; s €99-229, d €119-379; ❄📶) Antique meets boutique at this *Altstadt* hotel, where the original vaults and beams of the 800-year-old building contrast with razor-sharp design features. Artworks inspired by the musical legends of the Salzburg Festival grace the rooms, which sport caramel-champagne colour schemes, cool lighting, velvet throws and ultra-glam bathrooms.

Mozart BOUTIQUE HOTEL €€

(☎0662-87 22 74; www.themozarthotel.com; Franz-Josef-Strasse 27; s €90-115, d €140-190, tr €170-220; P📶) This old-timer has been given a super-chic boutique makeover, now cleverly contrasting original features with pared-back, modernist-style interiors. The parquet-floored rooms are painted in dove greys, with plush fabrics, tasteful artworks and green-tiled walk-in showers. Suites have the edge with free-standing tubs. Breakfast is a good spread, with fresh fruit, eggs, cold cuts and pastries.

Hotel Amadeus HISTORIC HOTEL €€

(☎0662-87 14 01; www.hotelamadeus.at; Linzer Gasse 43-45; s €85-191, d €155-335, q €233-454; 📶) Centrally situated on the right bank, this 500-year-old hotel has a boutique feel, with bespoke touches such as chandeliers and four-poster beds in the light, spacious, softly coloured rooms. Guests are treated to free tea, coffee and cakes in the lounge in the afternoon.

★Villa Trapp HOTEL €€

(☎0662-63 08 60; www.villa-trapp.com; Traunstrasse 34; s €76-135, d €90-280, ste €165-563; P📶) Marianne and Christopher have transformed the original von Trapp family home into a beautiful guesthouse (for guests only, we might add). The 19th-century villa is elegant, if not *quite* as palatial as in the movie, with tasteful wood-floored rooms and a balustrade for sweeping down à la Baroness Schräder.

Hotel Stein BOUTIQUE HOTEL €€€

(☎0662-874 34 60; www.hotelstein.at; Giselakai 3; d €229-491, ste €256-948) Hotel Stein looks the business following a two-year makeover. In the rooms, a clean aesthetic combines with pops of bright colour, wall murals, contemporary furnishings and Saint Charles Apothecary cosmetics. With its stucco-bedecked ceiling, Venetian glass and claw-foot bathtub, the honeymoon suite is quite something. Breakfast is an additional €28.

Hotel Goldgasse HISTORIC HOTEL €€€

(☎0662-84 56 22; www.hotelgoldgasse.at; Goldgasse 10; s €136-186, d €150-342, ste €202-485, q €450-580; ❄@📶) Bang in the heart of the *Altstadt*, this 700-year-old town house has much charm. All of the wood-floored rooms are individually and flamboyantly designed, with large-scale blown-up prints of Salzburg Festival performances. Espresso makers and free minibars are a bonus. The terrace overlooks the old-town rooftops, and the remarkable breakfast is extraordinarily served like high tea on a multi-tiered platter.

Hotel Schloss Mönchstein HERITAGE HOTEL €€€

(☎0662-848 55 50; www.monchstein.at; Mönchsberg Park 26; d €360-990, ste €695-1350; P❄📶) On a fairy-tale perch atop Mönchsberg and set in hectares of wooded grounds, this 16th-century castle is honeymoon (and second mortgage) material. Persian rugs, oil paintings and Calcutta marble finish the rooms to beautiful effect. A massage in the spa, a candlelit tower dinner for two with Salzburg views, a helicopter ride – just say the word.

Hotel & Villa Auersperg BOUTIQUE HOTEL €€€
(☎0662-88 94 40; www.auersperg.at; Auersperg-strasse 61; s €145-195, d €175-305, ste €240-355; P @) This charismatic villa and hotel duo fuses late-19th-century flair with contemporary design in rooms featuring wood floors, muted colours and Nespresso machines. Guests can relax by the lily pond in the vine-strewn garden or in the rooftop wellness area with its sauna, tea bar and mountain views. Local organic, vegan and gluten-free produce features at breakfast.

Hotel Sacher HERITAGE HOTEL €€€
(☎0662-88 97 70; www.sacher.com; Schwarzstrasse 5-7; s €226-336, d €298-1018, ste €502-1725; P ❄ @) Tom Hanks, the Dalai Lama and Julie Andrews have all stayed at this 19th-century pile on the banks of the Salzach. Scattered with oil paintings and antiques, the rooms have gleaming marble bathrooms, and fortress or river views. Compensate for indulging on chocolate *Sacher Torte* by hitting the health club.

Arthotel Blaue Gans BOUTIQUE HOTEL €€€
(☎0662-84 24 91; www.blaue-gans.com; Getreide-gasse 41-43; s €198-328, d €200-370, ste €449-579; ❄) At this marvellously atmospheric hotel, providing hospitality since 1350, contemporary design blends harmoniously with the original vaulting, beams and stone floors polished by centuries of shoes. Rooms are sleek and chic, with clean lines, lots of white and streamlined furnishings. The **restaurant** (☎0662-842 491 50; Getreidegasse 43; lunch specials €9.90-12.90, mains €21-28, 4-course menus €58-65; ⊙noon-10pm Mon-Sat) is highly regarded, too.

Goldener Hirsch LUXURY HOTEL €€€
(☎0662-808 40; www.marriott.com; Getreidegasse 37; r €195-813; P ❄ @) A skylight illuminates the arcaded inner courtyard of this 600-year-old *Altstadt* pile, where famous past guests include Queen Elizabeth II and Pavarotti. Countess Harriet Walderdorff tastefully scattered the opulent rooms with objets d'art and hand-printed fabrics.

Hotel Bristol LUXURY HOTEL €€€
(☎0662-87 35 57; www.bristol-salzburg.at; Makartplatz 4; s €200-300, d €285-480, ste €430-1010; P ❄) The Bristol transports you back to a more decadent era. Chandelier-lit salons, champagne at breakfast, exquisitely crafted furniture, service as polished as the marble – this is pure class. Even Emperor Franz Joseph and Sigmund Freud felt at home here.

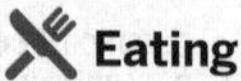

Eating

Stiftsbäckerei St Peter BAKERY €
(www.stiftsbaeckerei.at; Kapitelplatz 8; ⊙7am-5pm Mon, Tue, Thu & Fri, 7am-1pm Sat) Next to the monastery, where the watermill turns, this 700-year-old bakery turns out Salzburg's best sourdough loaves from a wood-fired oven.

Ludwig BURGERS €
(☎0662-87 25 00; www.ludwig-burger.at; Linzer Gasse 39; burgers €7.60-13.80; ⊙11am-10pm Tue-Fri, 9am-10pm Sat & Sun;) Gourmet burger joints are all the rage in Austria and this hip restaurant fits the bill nicely, with its burgers made from organic, regional ingredients, which go well with hand-cut fries and homemade lemonade and shakes. It also rustles up superfood salads and vegan nut-mushroom-herb burgers. An open kitchen is the centrepiece of the slick, monochrome interior.

Grünmarkt MARKET €
(Green Market; Universitätsplatz; ⊙7am-7pm Mon-Fri, 6am-3pm Sat) A one-stop picnic shop on one of Salzburg's grandest squares, for regional cheese, ham, fruit, bread and gigantic pretzels.

Organic Pizza Salzburg PIZZA €
(☎0664 597 44 70; www.organicpizza-salzburg.com; Franz-Josef-Strasse 24a; pizza €8.50-13.20; ⊙4-10pm Tue & Wed, noon-10pm Thu-Sat) Good-natured staff, cool music and awesome pizzas whipped up with super-fresh, organic ingredients make this a terrific choice. It's a tiny place so be prepared to wait at busy times – it's worth it.

Heart of Joy CAFE €
(☎0662-89 07 73; Franz-Josef-Strasse 3; lunch €8.30-10.40, snacks & mains €5.50-6.50; ⊙8am-7pm Mon-Thu, to 8.30pm Fri-Sun;) This Ayurveda-inspired cafe has an all-vegetarian, part-vegan and mostly organic menu. It does great bagels, salads, homemade cakes and juices, creative breakfasts, and day specials such as homemade pumpkin risotto with parmesan and quinoa-filled aubergines with cashew-coriander dip. Gluten-free options are available.

Little Light Deli & Café CAFE €
(☎0650 693 15 55; www.facebook.com/Lichthaus Salzburg; Elisabethkai 62; breakfast dishes & snacks €4-8; ⊙8.30am-6pm Mon-Fri) This chilled cafe by the river has attracted a loyal local following. Mellow music, low seating

and fresh flowers give the place a homely feel. Stop by for a healthy breakfast, or light bites such as quiches and homemade cakes, with good strong coffee.

IceZeit ICE CREAM €

(Chiemseegasse 1; scoop €1.50; noon-7pm;) Grab a cone at Salzburg's best ice-cream parlour, where flavours include salted peanut, caramel and passion fruit. There are also vegan options.

Magazin GASTRONOMY €€

(0662-84 15 84; www.magazin.co.at; Augustinergasse 13a; 2-course lunch €18, mains €18-29; noon-2pm & 6-10pm Tue-Sat) In a courtyard below Mönchsberg's sheer rock wall, Magazin shelters a deli, wine store and restaurant. The menus fizz with seasonal flavours – dishes such as scallops with white wine and coriander, and veal cheeks with wild broccoli, are matched with wines from the 850-bottle cellar, and served al fresco or in the industrial-chic, cave-like interior.

Humboldt AUSTRIAN €€

(www.humboldtstubn.at; Gstättengasse 4; lunch €9-11, mains €11.50-24; 11.30am-midnight Sun-Thu, to 2am Fri & Sat) Like a blast of nouveau alpine chic from the mountains, Humboldt keeps the vibe cool yet cosy, with exposed beams, a modern wall-of-glass fireplace, retro pendant lights and bistro seating. There's a good buzz, with locals flocking here for Austrian wines and all-organic, season-driven dishes such as cream of wild garlic soup and *Tafelspitz* (boiled beef with apple-horseradish and chives).

Imlauer Sky AUSTRIAN €€

(0662-88 978 666; www.imlauer.com; Rainerstrasse 6, Imlauer Hotel Pitter; mains €20-33.50; 11.30am-1.30am) From the lofty vantage point of this slickly modern, glass-fronted rooftop restaurant, Salzburg spreads out before you in all its glory – it's particularly spectacular after dark when the fortress lights up. Service is attentive and the menu swings from steaks and surf 'n' turf to well-executed classics such as *Wiener Schnitzel* (breaded veal cutlet) and *Tafelspitz*.

Johanneskeller im Priesterhaus AUSTRIAN €€

(0662-26 55 36; www.johanneskeller.at; Richard-Mayr-Gasse 1; mains €10-20; 5pm-midnight Tue-Sat) Full of cosy nooks and crannies, this brick-vaulted cellar is reached via a steep flight of stairs. The menu is succinct but well thought out, with mains swinging from classic Austrian – like Styrian pork roast with dumplings and sauerkraut – to Mediterranean numbers such as gyros (rotisserie meat) with tzatziki. It's cash only.

Cook&Wine INTERNATIONAL €€

(0662-23 16 06; www.cookandwine.at; Kaigasse 43; mains €19-26.50; 10am-midnight Tue-Sat) Highly regarded chef and food and wine connoisseur Günther Grahammer is the brains behind this slick operation. It combines a wine bar, a **cookery school** and a smart, bistro-style restaurant serving imaginative worldly dishes, such as steak tartare with wasabi cream, Asian-style bouillabaisse with lemongrass and chilli, and scallops with avocado-papaya salad.

Zum Zirkelwirt AUSTRIAN €€

(0662-84 27 96; www.zumzirkelwirt.at; Pfeifergasse 14; mains €11-20; 11am-midnight) A jovial inn serving good old-fashioned Austrian grub is what you get at Zum Zirkelwirt, which has a cracking beer garden on a tucked-away square and a cosy, wood-panelled interior for winter imbibing. Go straight for classics including *Kaspressknödelsuppe* (cheese dumpling soup) and *Schweinsbraten im Weissbier-Kümmelsafterl* (pork roast in wheat beer and cumin sauce).

Green Garden VEGETARIAN €€

(0662-84 12 01; www.thegreengarden.at; Nonntaler Hauptstrasse 16; mains €10.90-15.50; noon-3pm & 5.30-10pm Tue-Fri, 9am-2pm & 5.30-10pm Sat, 9am-2pm Sun;) The Green Garden is a breath of fresh air for vegetarians and vegans. Locavore is the word at this bright, modern cottage-style restaurant, pairing dishes such as summer rolls, truffle tortellini and vegan burgers with organic wines in a totally relaxed setting. It also rustles up tasty Buddha bowls, and weekend brunches (€25) are invariably popular.

Bärenwirt AUSTRIAN €€

(0662-42 24 04; www.baerenwirt-salzburg.at; Müllner Hauptstrasse 8; mains €12-20; 11am-11pm) Sizzling and stirring since 1663, Bärenwirt is Austrian through and through. Go for hearty *Bierbraten* (beer roast) with dumplings, locally caught trout or organic wild-boar bratwurst. A tiled oven warms the woody, hunting-lodge-style interior in winter, while the river-facing terrace is a summer crowd-puller. The restaurant is 500m north of Museumplatz.

SUPERPON/SHUTTERSTOCK ©

1. Eisriesenwelt (p252)
The world's largest accessible ice cave.

2. Hallstatt (p211)
Take the funicular to the Hallstatt Salzwelten, where you can learn the history of salt mining.

3. Grossglockner Road (p266)
Drive the ultra-scenic alpine road named after Austria's highest peak, the Grossglockner.

4. Salzburg (p228)
The fortress of Festung Hohensalzburg dominates the Salzburg skyline.

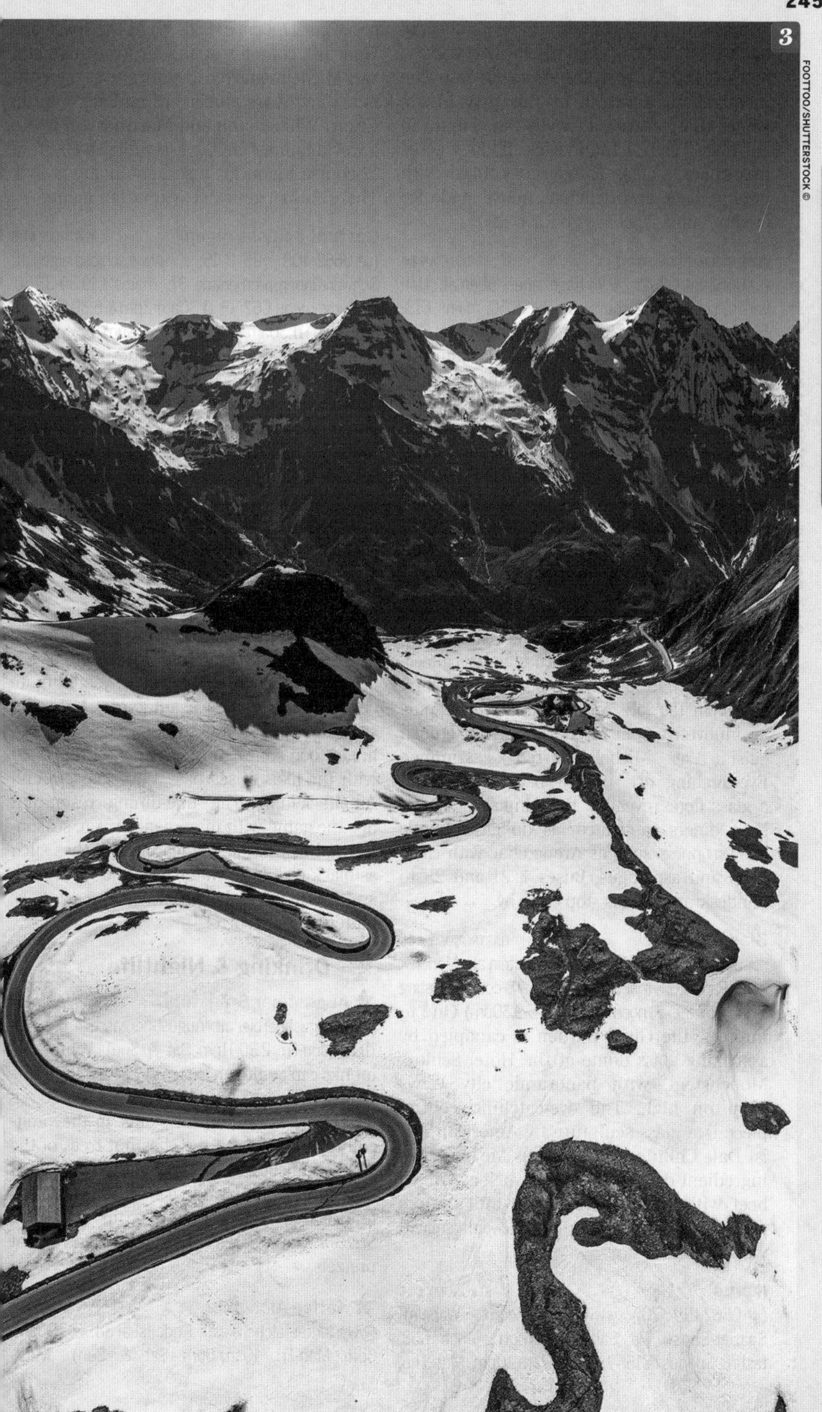

FOOTTOO/SHUTTERSTOCK ©

Triangel AUSTRIAN €€
(☎0662-84 22 29; Wiener-Philharmoniker-Gasse 7; mains €14.50-33; ⏰11.30am-10pm Tue-Sat) The menu is market-fresh at this arty bistro, where the picture-clad walls pay tribute to Salzburg Festival luminaries. It does gourmet salads, a mean Hungarian goulash with organic beef, and delicious house-made ice cream. Lunch specials go for €9.90.

Hagenauerstuben AUSTRIAN €€
(☎0662-84 08 45; www.hagenauerstuben.at; Universitätsplatz 14; 2-course lunch €8.50, mains €13-16.50; ⏰10am-10pm Sun-Tue, to midnight Wed-Sat) You'd be forgiven for thinking a restaurant tucked behind Mozart's Geburtshaus would have 'tourist trap' written all over it. Not so. The baroque-contemporary Hagenauerstuben combines a stylishly converted vaulted interior with a terrace overlooking the Kollegienkirche. Pull up a chair for good old-fashioned Austrian home cooking – spinach *Knödel* (dumplings), suckling pig with wild mushrooms, goulash and the like.

★**Esszimmer** FRENCH €€€
(☎0676 65 20 567; www.esszimmer.com; Müllner Hauptstrasse 33; 3-course lunch €45, tasting menus €79-128; ⏰6.30-10pm Tue & Wed, noon-2pm & 6.30-10pm Thu-Sat) Andreas Kaiblinger puts an innovative spin on market-driven French cuisine at Michelin-starred Esszimmer. Eye-catching art, playful backlighting and a glass floor revealing the Almkanal stream keep diners captivated, as do gastronomic showstoppers such as Arctic char with calf's head and asparagus. Buses 7, 21 and 28 to Landeskrankenhaus stop close by.

Glass Garden GASTRONOMY €€€
(☎0662-84 85 55 0; www.monchstein.at; Mönchsberg Park 26; mains €29-39, 5-/8-course tasting menu €57-89; ⏰noon-1.30pm & 6-9.30pm) One to impress, the Glass Garden is canopied by a striking glass dome at the Hotel Schloss Mönchstein, with panoramic city views from on high. The eye-catching centrepiece is a glass sculpture by American artist Dale Chihuly. Chef Markus Meyr creates ingredient-driven sensations such as Wagyu beef with truffle, and turbot and oysters with fennel, algae and lemon – all served with finesse.

Ikarus GASTRONOMY €€€
(☎0662-219 70; www.hangar-7.com; Wilhelm-Spazier-Strasse 7a, Salzburg Airport; lunch €58, tasting menus €155-190; ⏰7am-10pm Mon-Thu, noon-2pm & 7-10pm Fri-Sun; 🅥) At the space-age Hangar-7 complex at the airport, this glam two-Michelin-starred restaurant is the epitome of culinary globetrotting. Each month, Eckart Witzigmann and Martin Klein invite a world-famous chef to assemble an eight- to 12-course menu for a serious foodie crowd. There's also a gourmet vegetarian menu.

Gasthof Schloss Aigen AUSTRIAN €€€
(☎0662-408 15 15; www.schloss-aigen.at; Schwarzenbergpromenade 37; mains €19.30-33.50, 4-course menu €62; ⏰11.30am-2pm & 5.30-9.30pm Thu & Fri, 11.30am-9.30pm Sat & Sun) A country manor with an elegantly rustic interior and a chestnut-shaded courtyard, Gasthof Schloss Aigen excels in Austrian home cooking. The Forstner family's house speciality is 'Wiener Melange', four different cuts of Pinzgauer beef, served with apple horseradish, chive sauce and roast potatoes, best matched with robust Austrian wines. Bus 7 stops at Bahnhof Aigen, a 10-minute stroll away.

Carpe Diem FUSION €€€
(☎0662-84 88 00; www.carpediemfinestfingerfood.com; Getreidegasse 50; cones €6.50-20, tasting menus €85-118; ⏰cafe & bar 8.30am-midnight, restaurant noon-2pm & 6.30-10pm) A food-literate crowd flocks to this avant-garde, Michelin-starred lounge-restaurant for cocktails and finger-food cones, mini taste sensations filled with the likes of sea bass, olive gnocchi and Amalfi lemon. The fine-dining restaurant ups the game with ingredient-driven, season-focused tasting menus featuring dishes such as black cod, leek, watercress and grapefruit, and breast of veal with crayfish, asparagus, buttermilk and sorrel.

Drinking & Nightlife

★**Augustiner Bräustübl** BREWERY
(www.augustinerbier.at; Augustinergasse 4-6; ⏰3-11pm Mon-Fri, 2.30-11pm Sat & Sun) Who says monks can't enjoy themselves? Since 1621, this cheery, monastery-run brewery has served potent home brews in beer steins, in the vaulted hall and beneath the chestnut trees of the 1000-seat beer garden. Get your tankard filled at the foyer pump and visit the snack stands for hearty, beer-swigging grub including *Stelzen* (ham hock), pork belly and giant pretzels.

★**Kaffee Alchemie** CAFE
(www.kaffee-alchemie.at; Rudolfskai 38; ⏰7.30am-6pm Mon-Fri, 10am-6pm Sat & Sun) Mak-

ing coffee really is rocket science at this vintage-cool cafe by the river, which spotlights high-quality, fair-trade, single-origin beans. Talented baristas make spot-on espressos (on a Marzocco GB5, in case you're wondering), cappuccinos and speciality coffees, which go nicely with the selection of cakes and brownies. Not a coffee fan? Try the supersmooth coffee-leaf tea.

Apollo Bar COCKTAIL BAR

(www.monchstein.at; Mönchsberg Park 26; ⌚noon-11pm) Even if you can't afford to stay at Hotel Schloss Mönchstein, you can get a taste of the high life at this glass-domed, gold-kissed bar, a stylish haunt for rounding out the day over a gin garnished with fresh berries or a 'rosato' (hibiscus, Prosecco and orange).

Sacher CAFE

(www.sacher.com; Schwarzstrasse 5-7; ⌚7.30am-10.30pm) Nowhere is the chocolate richer, the apricot jam tangier and the cream lighter than at the home of the *Sacher Torte*. The cafe is pure old-world grandeur, with picture-lined walls and ruby-red banquettes. Sit on the terrace by the Salzach for fortress views.

Darwin's COCKTAIL BAR

(www.darwins-salzburg.at; Steingasse 1; ⌚9am-midnight Sun-Thu, to 2am Fri & Sat) Darwin might well have been partial to an expertly mixed cocktail or two at this glam vaulted bar, while dreaming up his theory of evolution or pondering the origin of the species. The great man himself is portrayed as an ape-man alongside other doodles of globes and quotes. The bar makes a mean espresso martini.

Natural Wine Dealers @ Enoteca Settemila a.C. WINE BAR

(www.naturalwinedealers.com; Bergstrasse 9; ⌚5-11pm Wed-Sat) This bijou wine shop and bar brims with the enthusiasm and passion of Rafael Peil and Nina Corti. Go to sample their well-curated selection of wines, including Austrian, organic and biodynamic offerings, with *taglieri* – sharing plates of cheese and *salumi* (salami, ham, prosciutto and the like) – from small Italian producers.

220 Grad CAFE

(www.220grad.com; Chiemseegasse 5; ⌚9am-7pm Tue-Fri, to 6pm Sat; 📶) In a tucked-away corner of the *Altstadt*, this retro-cool cafe is up there with the best for its freshly roasted coffee, breakfasts and decked terrace (always rammed in summer). Its name alludes to the perfect temperature for roasting beans, and the skilled baristas make a terrific single-origin espresso and house blends, which pair with cakes including sweet potato with lime cream.

Die Weisse PUB

(www.dieweisse.at; Rupertgasse 10; ⌚pub 10am-2am Mon-Sat, bar from 5pm) The cavernous brewpub of the Salzburger Weissbierbrauerei, this is the place to guzzle cloudy wheat beers, in the wood-floored pub or the shady beer garden out back. DJs work the decks in the Sudwerk bar, especially at the monthly Almrausch, when locals party in skimpy *Dirndls* and strapping *Lederhosen*.

StieglKeller BEER HALL

(www.restaurant-stieglkeller.at; Festungsgasse 10; ⌚11.30am-10pm Mon-Fri, 11am-10pm Sat & Sun) For a 365-day taste of Oktoberfest, try this cavernous, Munich-style beer hall, which shares the same architect as Munich's Hofbräuhaus. It has an enormous garden above the city's rooftops and a menu of meaty mains (€13 to €25) such as fat pork knuckles and schnitzel. Beer is cheapest from the self-service taps outside.

Mayday Bar COCKTAIL BAR

(www.hangar-7.com; Wilhelm-Spazier-Strasse 7a, Salzburg Airport; ⌚noon-midnight Sun-Thu, to 1am Fri & Sat) Peer down at the Flying Bulls aviation enthusiasts' rare historical aircraft through the glass walls at this crystalline bar, part of the airport's futuristic Hangar-7 complex. Strikingly illuminated by night, it's a unique place for cocktails such as Hendrick's heaven (Red Bull, gin, cucumber and lime).

☆ Entertainment

★Salzburger Marionettentheater PUPPET THEATRE

(☎0662-87 24 06; www.marionetten.at; Schwarzstrasse 24; tickets €28-152; 👪) The red curtain goes up on a miniature stage at this marionette theatre, a lavish stucco, cherub and chandelier-lit affair founded in 1913. The repertoire star is *The Sound of Music*, with a life-sized Mother Superior and a marionette-packed finale. Other enchanting productions include Mozart's *The Magic Flute* and Tchaikovsky's *The Nutcracker*. All have multilingual surtitles.

SALZBURG FOR CHILDREN

With dancing marionettes, chocolate galore and a giant fairy-tale fortress, Salzburg is kid nirvana. If the crowds prove unbearable with tots in tow, take them to the city's **adventure playgrounds** (there are 80 to pick from); the one on Franz-Josef-Kai is centrally located.

Salzburg's sights are usually half-price for children, and most are free for kids under six years of age. Many galleries, museums and theatres also have dedicated programs for kids and families. These include the Museum der Moderne (p233), which has workshops for kids and teens, and the matinee performances at the enchanting Salzburger Marionettentheater (p247). The Salzburg Museum (p233) has lots of hands-on displays, from harp playing to old-fashioned writing with quills. Pick up 'Wolf' Dietrich's cartoon guide at the entrance.

Other sure-fire kid-pleasers around Salzburg:

Haus der Natur (www.hausdernatur.at; Museumsplatz 5; adult/child/family €8.50/6/21.50; ⏲9am-5pm; 👪) Children will have a blast with natural history here, with fun facts on alpine crystals, dinosaurs, science and the human body. The highlight is the aquarium, with its clownfish and sharks.

Spielzeugmuseum (Toy Museum; www.spielzeugmuseum.at; Bürgerspitalgasse 2; adult/child/family €5/2/10; ⏲9am-5pm Tue-Sun; 👪) Salzburg's very own toy story, this museum is a rambling attic of toys old and new. There are even 'adult parking areas' where grown-ups can hang out while tots play.

Freilichtmuseum (www.freilichtmuseum.com; Hasenweg 1, Grossgmain; adult/child/family €11/5.50/22; ⏲9am-6pm Tue-Sun mid-Mar–early Nov, daily Jul & Aug; 👪) Take a whizz through Austrian farming life through the ages at this huge open-air museum, with animals to pet, crafts to explore and a big adventure playground to romp around in.

Salzburg Zoo (www.salzburg-zoo.at; Hellbrunnerstrasse 60, Anif; adult/child/family €11.50/5/26; ⏲9am-6.30pm Jun-Aug, shorter hours Sep-May; 👪) For more animal-themed fun, near Schloss Hellbrunn.

The theatre is a Unesco World Heritage site, proclaimed in 2017.

Schlosskonzerte CLASSICAL MUSIC
(www.schlosskonzerte-salzburg.at; tickets adult €34-40, child €15; ⏲concerts 8pm) With coloured marble, stucco and frescos, the baroque Marmorsaal (Marble Hall) at Schloss Mirabell (p234) is the exquisite setting for these chamber-music concerts. Internationally renowned soloists and ensembles perform Mozart and other well-known composers such as Haydn and Chopin. Tickets are available on the 1st floor of the palace from 3pm to 8pm.

ARGEkultur LIVE MUSIC
(www.argekultur.at; Ulrike-Gschwandtner-Strasse 5) This alternative cultural venue was born out of protests against the Salzburg Festival in the 1980s. Today it's a bar and performance hybrid. Traversing the entire arts spectrum, the line-up features concerts, cabaret, DJ nights, dance, poetry slams and world music. It's at the Unipark Nonntal campus, a five-minute walk east of the *Altstadt*.

Landestheater THEATRE
(☎0662-87 15 12; www.salzburger-landestheater.at; Schwarzstrasse 22; tickets €18-70; ⏲box office 9am-5pm Mon-Fri, to 1pm Sat; 👪) Opera, operetta, ballet and musicals dominate the stage at this elegant 18th-century playhouse. There's a strong emphasis on Mozart's music, with the Mozarteum Salzburg Orchestra often in the pit. There are dedicated performances for kids, and *The Sound of Music* musical is a winner with all ages.

Rockhouse LIVE MUSIC
(www.rockhouse.at; Schallmooser Hauptstrasse 46) Salzburg's hottest live-music venue, Rockhouse presents first-rate rock, pop, jazz, folk, metal and reggae concerts – see the website for details. There's also a tunnel-shaped bar with DJs (usually free) and bands. Rockhouse is 1km northeast of the *Altstadt*; take bus 4 to Canavalstrasse.

Salzburg Arena CONCERT VENUE
(☎0662-240 40; www.salzburgarena.at; Am Messezentrum 1) Under a domed wooden roof, this is Salzburg's premier stage for sporting events,

musicals and big-name concerts. The arena is 3km north of town; take bus 1 to Messe.

Jazzit JAZZ
(☎0662-88 32 64; www.jazzit.at; Elisabethstrasse 11; ⊙bar 6pm-midnight Tue-Sat) Hosts regular concerts, with performances ranging from tango to electro, as well as workshops and club nights. Don't miss the free Tuesday-night jam sessions in the adjacent Jazzit bar. It's 600m north of the Mirabellgarten along Elisabethstrasse.

Mozarteum CLASSICAL MUSIC
(☎0662-87 31 54; www.mozarteum.at; Schwarzstrasse 26; ⊙box office 10am-3pm Mon-Fri) Opened in 1880 and revered for its acoustics, the Mozarteum highlights the life and works of Mozart through chamber music (October to June), concerts and opera. The annual highlight is Mozart Week (p238) in January.

Shopping

★Fürst CHOCOLATE
(www.original-mozartkugel.com; Getreidegasse 47; ⊙10am-6.30pm Mon-Sat, noon-5pm Sun) Pistachio, nougat and dark-chocolate dreams, the *Mozartkugeln* (Mozart balls) here are still handmade to Paul Fürst's original 1890 recipe. Other specialities include cube-shaped *Bach Würfel* – coffee, nut and marzipan truffles dedicated to yet another great composer.

Ploom CLOTHING
(www.ploom.at; Ursulinenplatz 5; ⊙11am-6pm Thu & Fri, to 5pm Sat) Embracing the *Tracht* (traditional costume) trend is Ploom, where designer Tanja Pflaum has playfully and successfully reinvented the *Dirndl*. Her boutique is a wonderland of floaty femininity: a sky-blue bodice or a frothy cotton blouse here, a wisp of a turquoise *Schürze* (apron) or a silk evening gown there.

Salzburger Heimatwerk GIFTS & SOUVENIRS
(www.salzburgerheimatwerk.at; Residenzplatz 9; ⊙10am-6pm Mon-Fri, to 5pm Sat) As well as knocking fabrics into *Dirndls* and other dapper traditional costumes, Salzburger Heimatwerk does a fine line in local handicrafts, schnapps, preserves and honeys.

Spirituosen Sporer WINE
(Getreidegasse 39; ⊙9.30am-7pm Mon-Fri, 8.30am-5pm Sat) In Getreidegasse's narrowest house, family-run Sporer has been intoxicating local folk with Austrian wines, herbal liqueurs and famous *Vogelbeer* (rowan berry) schnapps since 1903.

Salzburg Salz GIFTS & SOUVENIRS
(Wiener-Philharmoniker-Gasse 6; ⊙10am-6pm Mon-Sat) Pure salt from Salzburgerland and the Himalayas, herbal salts and rock-salt tea lights are among the high-sodium wonders here.

Kaslöchl CHEESE
(Hagenauerplatz 2; ⊙9am-6pm Mon-Fri, 8am-3pm Sat; 📶) A mouse-sized Austrian cheese shop, crammed with creamy alpine varieties, holey Emmental and fresh cheese with herbs.

Drechslerei Lackner GIFTS & SOUVENIRS
(Badergasse 2; ⊙10am-6pm Mon-Fri, to 5pm Sat) The hand-carved nutcrackers, nativity figurines and filigree Christmas stars are the real deal at this traditional craft shop.

Information

Landeskrankenhaus Salzburg (☎05-725 50; Müllner Hauptstrasse 48) Hospital just north of Mönchsberg.

Main Tourist Office (☎0662-88 98 73 30; www.salzburg.info; Mozartplatz 5; ⊙9am-6pm Apr-Sep, closed Sun Oct-Mar) Helpful office with stacks of information about the city and its immediate surrounds. There's a ticket-booking agency (www.salzburgticket.com) in the same building.

Salzburgerland Tourismus (☎0662-66 88 44; www.salzburgerland.com; Wiener Bundesstrasse 23, Hallwang bei Salzburg; ⊙8am-5.30pm Mon-Thu, to 5pm Fri) Has information on the rest of the province outside Salzburg.

Getting There & Away

AIR

Salzburg Airport (p228), a 20-minute bus ride from the centre, has regular flights to destinations all over Austria and Europe. Low-cost flights from the UK are provided by **Ryanair** (www.ryanair.com) and **easyJet** (www.easyjet.com). Other airlines include **British Airways** (www.britishairways.com) and **Jet2** (www.jet2.com).

BUS

Salzburger Verkehrsverbund (☎24hr hotline 0662-63 29 00; www.svv-info.at) makes it easy to reach the province's smaller villages. Buses depart from just outside the *Hauptbahnhof* on Südtiroler Platz, where timetables are displayed. Bus information and tickets are available from the information points on the main station concourse.

For more information on buses in and around Salzburg and an online timetable, see www.postbus.at.

Buses leaving hourly for the Salzkammergut:
Bad Ischl €10.80, 1½ hours
Mondsee €6.90, 37 minutes
St Gilgen €6.90, 43 minutes
St Wolfgang €9.90, 1¾ hours

CAR & MOTORCYCLE

Three motorways converge on Salzburg to form a loop around the city: the A1/E60 from Linz, Vienna and the east; the A8 from Munich (Germany) and the west; and the A10 from Villach and the south. The quickest way to Tyrol is to take the road to Bad Reichenhall in Germany and continue to Lofer (B178) and St Johann in Tirol.

TRAIN

Salzburg has excellent rail connections with the rest of Austria from its recently revamped **Hauptbahnhof**.

Trains leave frequently for Vienna (€55.60, 2½ to three hours) and Linz (€28.60, 1¼ hours). There is a two-hourly express service to Klagenfurt (€42.20, three hours).

Direct trains run hourly to Innsbruck (€48.30, two hours) and Munich (€33.10, 1½ to two hours).

There are also several trains daily to Berlin (€160.40, 6½ to 8½ hours), Budapest (€94.60, 5¼ to 6½ hours), Prague (€78.60, 5½ to 7½ hours) and Venice (€60 to €105, six to eight hours).

For timetables, see www.svv-info.at.

Getting Around

TO/FROM THE AIRPORT

Salzburg airport is around 5.5km west of the centre along Innsbrucker Bundesstrasse. Buses 2, 10 and 27 (€2, 19 minutes) depart from outside the terminal roughly every 10 to 15 minutes and make several central stops near the *Altstadt*; buses 2 and 27 terminate at the *Hauptbahnhof*. Services operate roughly from 5.30am to 11pm. A taxi between the airport and the city centre costs €15 to €20.

BICYCLE

Salzburg is one of Austria's most bike-friendly cities. It has an extensive network of scenic cycling trails heading off in all directions, including along the banks of the Salzach River. See www.movelo.com for a list of places renting out e-bikes.

A'Velo (☎0676-435 59 50; Willibald-Hauthaler-Strasse 10; bicycle rental half-day/full day/week €14/20/75, e-bike €20/33/144; ⏲9.30am-6pm Mon-Fri, 9am-12.30pm Sat) provides bike and e-bike rental.

BUS

Bus drivers sell single (€2.70), 24-hour (€6) and weekly tickets (€16.40). Single tickets bought in advance from machines are slightly cheaper. Kids under six travel for free, while all other children pay half-price.

Bus routes are shown at bus stops and on some city maps; buses 1 and 4 start from the *Hauptbahnhof* and skirt the pedestrian-only *Altstadt*.

Information and timetables are available at www.salzburg-verkehr.at.

CAR & MOTORCYCLE

Parking places are limited and much of the *Altstadt* is only accessible on foot, so it's easier to leave your car at one of three park-and-ride points to the west, north and south of the city. The largest car park in the centre is the *Altstadt* Garage under Mönchsberg (€22 per day); some restaurants in the centre will stamp your ticket for a reduction. Rates are lower on streets with automatic ticket machines (blue zones); a three-hour maximum applies (€4.50, or €0.70 for 28 minutes) from 9am to 7pm on weekdays.

For car rental, try **Avis** (www.avis.com; Ferdinand-Porsche-Strasse 7; ⏲7.30am-5pm Mon-Fri), **Europcar** (www.europcar.com; Gniglerstrasse 12; ⏲7.30am-6pm Mon-Fri) or **Hertz** (www.hertz.com; Ferdinand-Porsche-Strasse 7; ⏲8am-6pm Mon-Fri, 8am-1pm Sat).

AROUND SALZBURG

Hallein & Around

☎06245 / POP 21,150 / ELEV 460M

Beyond its industrial outskirts, Hallein is a pristine late-medieval town, where lanes are punctuated by courtyards, galleries and boho cafes. Too few people visit, however, in their dash to Bavaria or Salzburg, but those who do are pleasantly surprised. Hallein's family attraction, the Salzwelten salt mine, is actually located in Bad Dürrnberg, 6km southwest of town.

Sights

★**Salzwelten** MINE

(www.salzwelten.at; Ramsaustrasse 3, Bad Dürrnberg; adult/child/family €23/11.50/48.50; ⏲9am-5pm; 👪) During Salzburg's princely heyday, the sale of salt filled its coffers. Today, at Austria's biggest show mine, you can slip into a boiler suit and descend to the bowels of the earth. The tour aboard a rickety train passes through a maze of claustrophobic passageways, over the border to Germany and down a 27m slide – don't brake, lift your legs and ask the guide to wax the slide for extra speed!

After crossing a salt lake on a wooden raft, a 42m slide brings you to the lowest point (210m underground) and back to Austria. Guided 70-minute tours depart every half-hour. Bus 41 runs from Hallein train station hourly on weekdays, less often at weekends.

Keltenmuseum MUSEUM
(Celtic Museum; www.keltenmuseum.at; Pflegerplatz 5; adult/child €7.50/2.50; 9am-5pm;) Overlooking the Salzach, the glass-fronted Keltenmuseum runs chronologically through the region's heritage in a series of vaulted rooms. It begins with Celtic artefacts, including Asterix-style helmets, an impressively reconstructed chariot and a selection of bronze brooches, pendants and buckles.

Stille Nacht Museum MUSEUM
(www.keltenmuseum.at; Gruberplatz 1; adult/child €4.50/2; 9am-5pm) Hallein's festive claim to fame is as the one-time home of Franz Xaver Gruber (1787–1863), who composed the carol *Stille Nacht* (Silent Night). Joseph Mohr penned the poem and Gruber, a schoolteacher at the time, came up with the melody on his guitar in 1818. The fabled guitar takes pride of place in Gruber's former residence, now the Stille Nacht Museum, next to Hallein's parish church. The museum tells the story of the carol through documents and personal belongings.

Activities

Keltenblitz ADVENTURE SPORTS
(06245-851 05; Bad Dürrnberg; adult/child incl chairlift €11.80/8.20; 11am-5pm Mon-Fri, 10.30am-5pm Sat & Sun May-early Oct;) In summer, families pick up speed on this toboggan run close to Salzwelten. A chairlift carries passengers to the top of Zinken mountain, where they board little wheeled bobsleds to race 2.2km down hairpin bends. The ride is over in a flash and affords fleeting views of the Salzach Valley.

Sleeping

Pension Hochdürrnberg GUESTHOUSE €
(06245-751 83; www.hochduerrnberg.at; Rumpelgasse 14, Bad Dürrnberg; s/d/tr/q €50/60/70/90; P) Surrounded by meadows, this farmhouse in Bad Dürrnberg has countrified rooms with warm pine furnishings and downy bedding. The animal residents (rabbits, sheep and cows) keep children amused.

FAST TRACK TO THE SALT MINES

All train stations in the region sell the money-saving **Salzwelten Hallein** ticket (adult/child €28.20/14.10), which covers a bus transfer to Bad Dürrnberg plus entry to Salzwelten and the Keltenmuseum.

Kranzbichlhof HOTEL €€
(06245-737 720; www.kranzbichlhof.net; Hofgasse 12, Bad Dürrnberg; s €89-92, d €124-154, f €180-195; P) In a serene location backing onto woods, this glorious rambling chalet has spacious, light, pine-clad rooms done out in contemporary style (many featuring balconies). There's also a lovely garden, a natural outdoor pool, and a spa offering everything from Ayurvedic treatments to yoga and even craniosacral therapy.

Hotel Auwirt HOTEL €€
(06245-804 17; www.auwirt.com; Salzburgerstrasse 42; camp sites per adult/child/tent €10/7/6.50, s €60-95, d €90-165, q €149-255; P) Auwirt's light-filled, wood-floored, alpine-trimmed rooms are spacious and comfy; some superior rooms come with balconies. The hotel is a good family base, with a tree-shaded garden and playground. You can also pitch a tent here.

Pension Sommerauer GUESTHOUSE €€
(06245-800 30; www.pension-hallein.at; Tschusistrasse 71; s €49-76, d €79-123, tr €102-158, q €125-200; P) Housed in a 300-year-old farmhouse, the rustic rooms at this guesthouse are a bargain. There's a heated pool and conservatory as well as kiddie entertainment including a playroom, sandpit and swings.

Eating

Pan Café CAFE €
(www.pancafe.at; Metzgergasse 9; breakfast €3-10, lunch special €7.20; 8.30am-6pm Sun, Mon & Fri, to 5pm Tue, to 3pm Sat;) If you're seeking freshly roasted Austrian speciality coffees, this wonderfully chilled cafe comes up trumps. The bright, minimalist, vaulted interior has a

SALZBURGERLAND CARD

Available online and at tourist offices in the province, the **Salzburgerland Card** (www.salzburgerlandcard.com) provides discounts on 190 attractions throughout the province. A six-day card costs €76/38 for an adult/child.

relaxed vibe, and the cafe does a fine line in creative breakfasts, cakes, muffins and homemade lemonade. Healthy vegan lunch specials swing from Thai curry to sweet potato and lentil stew.

Hammerwirt AUSTRIAN €€
(✆06245-216 59; www.hammerwirt-salzburg.at; Messinghammerweg 1, Oberalm; mains €13-23; ⌚5-10pm Wed & Thu, 11.30am-10pm Fri-Sun) Banquette seating, wood tables and brass lanterns keep the mood traditional and cosy at Hammerwirt, situated 3km north of Hallein. The real delight is the walled, chestnut-tree-canopied garden, however, which hums with happy diners in summer. Artfully presented Austro-Italian dishes range from the likes of *Backhendl* (crispy breaded chicken) with potato salad to fennel salami-chilli ravioli with rosemary-honey butter.

Information

The **tourist office** (✆06245-853 94; www.hallein.com; Mauttorpromenade 6; ⌚8.30am-5pm Mon-Fri) is on the narrow islet adjoining the Stadtbrücke bridge. You can download the free app from the website onto your mobile device.

Getting There & Away

Hallein is close to the German border, 18km south of Salzburg via the B150 and A10/E55 in the direction of Graz/Villach. It's a 25-minute train journey from Salzburg, with departures roughly every 30 minutes (€4.70, 15 to 24 minutes).

Werfen

✆06468 / POP 3027 / ELEV 525M

The world's largest accessible ice caves, the soaring limestone turrets of the Tennengebirge range and a formidable medieval fortress are but the tip of the superlative iceberg in Werfen. Such natural beauty hasn't escaped Hollywood movie producers – Werfen stars in WWII action film *Where Eagles Dare* (1968) and makes a cameo appearance in the picnic scene of *The Sound of Music* (1965).

Both the fortress and the ice caves can be squeezed into a day trip from Salzburg; start early, visit the caves first and be at the fortress for the last falconry show.

Sights

★Eisriesenwelt CAVE
(www.eisriesenwelt.at; Eishohlenstrasse 30; adult/child €12/7, incl cable car €24/14; ⌚8am-4pm Jul & Aug, to 3pm May, Jun, Sep & Oct) Billed as the world's largest accessible ice caves, Eisriesenwelt is a glittering ice empire spanning 30,000 sq metres and 42km of narrow passages burrowing deep into the heart of the mountains. A tour through these Narnia-esque chambers of blue ice is a unique experience. As you climb up wooden steps and down pitch-black passages, otherworldly ice sculptures shaped like polar bears and elephants, frozen columns and lakes emerge from the shadows.

A highlight is the cavernous **Eispalast** (ice palace), where the frost crystals twinkle when a magnesium flare is held up to them. A womb-like tunnel leads to a flight of 700 steps, which descends back to the entrance. Even if it's hot outside, entering the caves in any season is like stepping into a deep freeze – bring warm clothing and sturdy footwear.

In summer, minibuses (return adult/child €7/5) run at 8.18am, 10.18am, 12.18pm and 2.18pm from Werfen train station to Eisriesenwelt car park, which is a 20-minute walk from the bottom station of the cable car. The last return bus departs at 4.32pm. Allow roughly three hours for the return trip (including the tour). You can walk the whole route, but it's a challenging four-hour ascent, rising 1100m above the village.

Burg Hohenwerfen CASTLE
(Hohenwerfen Fortress; www.salzburg-burgen.at; adult/child/family €12.50/7/30, incl lift €16.50/9.50/39.50; ⌚9am-5pm May-Sep, shorter hours Mar, Apr & Oct) High on a wooded clifftop beneath the majestic peaks of the Tennengebirge range, Burg Hohenwerfen is visible from afar. For 900 years this fortress has kept watch over the Salzach Valley; its current appearance dates to 1570. The big draw is the far-reaching view over Werfen from the 16th-century belfry, though the **dungeons** (displaying the usual nasties such as the iron maiden and thumb screw) are also worth a look.

The entry fee also covers a **falconry show** in the grounds (11.15am and 3.15pm daily), where falconers in medieval costume release eagles, owls, falcons and vultures to wheel in front of the ramparts. There's commentary in English and German.

The brisk walk up from the village takes 20 minutes. If the uphill climb is not for you, a lift whisks you up there in a matter of seconds.

Activities

The Sound of Music Trail WALKING

Werfen looks like something Hollywood dreamed up, with its soaring mountains and whopping castle, and indeed it was the backdrop for some scenes in *The Sound of Music*. Launch yourself out into wild-flower-freckled meadows and hills on this 1.4km, hour-long trail following in the footsteps of the Trapp family, from the town centre to Gschwandtanger viewpoint. Begin at the tourist office.

Sleeping

Landgasthof Reitsamerhof GUESTHOUSE €

(☎06468-53 79; www.reitsamerhof.at; Reitsam 22, Werfen-Imlau; s €62-68, d €76-82, tr €104-110, f €122-125; P) Bedecked with geraniums in summer, this sunny yellow chalet sits just south of Werfen and commands rousing views of the limestone spires of the Tennengebirge. Decorated in modern rustic style, most of the parquet-floored, pine-clad rooms open onto balconies, and the restaurant (mains €10 to €17) plays up Austrian classics such as schnitzel and *Zwiebelrostbraten* (onion roast).

Weisses Rössl PENSION €

(☎06468-52 68; www.weisses-roessl-werfen.at; Markt 39; s/d/tr/q €46/82/101/122; P) In the village centre, this good-value pension has great views of the fortress and the Tennengebirge from its rooftop terrace. Rooms are a blast from the 1970s, but all are large and cosy, with sofas and cable TV.

Camping Vierthaler CAMPGROUND €

(☎06468-565 70; www.camping-vierthaler.at; Reitsam 8; camp sites per adult/child/tent €6/3/6.50, bungalows d/tr/q €29/38/47; ⊙mid-Apr–Sep) This lovely campground on the banks of the Salzach River has a back-to-nature feel. Facilities include a snack bar and playground. Bungalows with kitchenettes, patios and barbecue areas are also available.

Eating

Stiege No 1 AUSTRIAN €€

(☎06468-201 15; www.stiege-01.com; Markt 10; 2-course lunch €8.50, mains €11-27; ⊙11am-10pm Wed-Sun) Bang in the heart of the village, Stiege No 1 has a stripped-back, wood-ceilinged interior in modern alpine style. In summer, the pretty lantern-lit garden is the place to gaze up to the fortress over seasonal dishes such as chestnut soup with truffle.

Oedlhaus AUSTRIAN €€

(www.oedlhaus.at; Eishöhlenstrasse 30; snacks €5-9, mains €9-12.50; ⊙9am-3.45pm May, Jun, Sep & Oct, to 4.45pm Jul & Aug) Next to the Eisriesenwelt cable-car top station, this woodsy hut at 1574m fortifies walkers with mountain grub such as *Gröstl* (pan-fried potatoes, pork and onions topped with a fried egg). The terrace has views to rave about: you can see across the Salzach Valley to the chiselled limestone peaks of the Hochkönig range.

★Obauer EUROPEAN €€€

(☎06468-52 12; www.obauer.com; Markt 46; 3-course lunch €42.50, dinner menus €50-135; ⊙noon-2pm & 6.30-9pm Wed-Sun) The Obauers run the show at this highly regarded, ingredient-focused restaurant. Sit in the rustic-chic restaurant or out in the garden, where most of the fruit and herbs are grown. Dishes with a distinctly regional flavour are complemented by fine Austrian wines.

Information

Tourist Office (☎06468-53 88; www.werfen.at; Markt 24; ⊙9am-noon & 2-6pm Mon-Fri) Hands out information and maps, and makes hotel bookings free of charge.

Getting There & Away

Werfen is 45km south of Salzburg on the A10/E55 motorway. Trains run frequently to Salzburg (€8.90, 41 minutes).

SOUTHERN SALZBURG PROVINCE

Filzmoos

☎06453 / POP 1484 / ELEV 1055M

Theatrically set amid the jagged limestone spires of the Dachstein massif, rolling pastures and the aptly named Bischofsmütze (Bishop's Mitre) peaks, Filzmoos is quite the alpine idyll. Despite some wonderful hiking and skiing, the resort's out-of-the-way location deters the masses and the village has kept its rural charm and family-friendly atmosphere.

Activities

Ski Amadé SKIING

(☎06452-20 20 20; www.skiamade.com; full-region 6-day pass €275.50) Salzburgerland's Ski Amadé is Austria's biggest ski area, covering a whopping 760km of pistes in 25 resorts divided into five snow-sure regions. Among them are low-key Radstadt and family-friendly Filzmoos. Such a vast area means that truly every level is catered for: from gentle cruising on tree-lined runs to off-piste touring.

Gosaukamm Circuit WALKING

This spectacular two-day, 23km circuit gets you up close and personal with the ragged Gosaukamm range, sometimes dubbed 'Salzburg's Dolomites' because they are similar in size and scale. The highlight in every sense of the word is the 2012m **Steigl Pass**, an exposed, fixed-cable route involving some scrambling. Pick up the Freytag & Berndt map *WK 281: Dachstein* (1:50,000).

Filzmoos Aktiv ADVENTURE SPORTS

(☎0664 171 84 83; www.filzmoos-aktiv.at; Filzmoos 233; ⊙8am-6pm) A one-stop shop for outdoor activities, Filzmoos Aktiv arranges everything from themed mountain and glacier hikes and photography workshops to more challenging summit ascents, multiday hut-to-hut treks taking you deeper into the Alps of Salzburgerland, and climbing courses. Get in touch for dates, times and prices.

Dachsteinrunde CYCLING

(Dachstein Tour; http://dachstein.salzkammergut.at) For keen cyclists, the challenging 182km to 269km Dachsteinrunde, taking in Salzburgerland, Upper Austria and Styria and passing through some classic alpine terrain, is a must. Maps can be ordered online for €7, or you can pick one up at the Filzmoos tourist office for €2.90.

Dachstein Circuit WALKING

Heading up to an elevation of 2995m, the eight-day, 126km Dachstein Circuit is a phenomenal introduction to the jagged limestone Dachstein range. It takes in the entire spectrum of alpine landscapes: glaciers and high mountains, forests, karst, raging rivers and flower-dotted meadows.

Festivals & Events

Hanneshof Hot Air Balloon Week AIR SHOW

(www.ballonfahren-filzmoos.com; ⊙mid-Jan) In mid-January Filzmoos hosts the spectacular Hanneshof Hot Air Balloon Week. The highlight is the magical Night of Balloons, when 40 balloons illuminate the night sky.

Sleeping

Haus Obermoos GUESTHOUSE €€

(☎0664 1261 403; Neuberg 190; s/d €90/100, apt €150-260; P 📶) You'll receive the warmest of welcomes at Haus Obermoos. The bright, immaculate rooms and apartments are tastefully done out in wood furnishings and earthy hues, with pretty views of the surrounding forested mountains. A heated ski room and a spa area are welcome touches. Haus Obermoos is near the ski lifts, a 20-minute walk west of the centre.

Hammerhof HOTEL €€

(☎06453-82 45; www.hammerhof.at; Filzmoos 6; d €150-180; P 📶) Set in a beautifully converted 400-year-old farmhouse, this eco-friendly hotel is a find. Bathed in soft light, the rooms are decorated with natural wood and country touches; some have balconies and tiled ovens. The restaurant serves home-grown organic produce. Unwind in a herbal bath or saddle a horse to canter off into the hills. The owner, Matthias, arranges riding tours.

Landhaus Ena PENSION €€

(☎06453-83 56; www.ena-filzmoos.at; Neuberg 123; d €96-126, incl half board €110-144; P 📶) Handy for the slopes, this sweet, rustic pension has a fire blazing downstairs in winter and spotless rooms with mountain-facing balconies. There's table tennis and a games room.

Eating

Pilzstube AUSTRIAN

(☎0664 501 51 32; www.pilzstube.at; Filzmoos 8; mains €10-26; ⊙11am-2pm & 5-9pm Wed-Mon; 🌿 👪) As warm, woody and endearingly rustic as they come, this old-school Austrian restaurant on a hillside is at its most enchanting when the flakes fall in winter. But it's always an appealing choice for regional classics like gooey fondues, sizeable schnitzels, and venison ragout with *Spätzle* (eggy noodles) and red cabbage. Kids and vegetarians are also catered for.

Fiakerwirt AUSTRIAN €

(☎06453-82 09; www.fiakerwirt.co.at; Filzmoos 23; mains €9-15.50; ⊙10am-11pm Tue-Sun; 👪) This rambling, rustically timber-beamed farmhouse and beer garden serves meaty snacks and mains like schnitzel, goulash and pork roast. Kids will love the pet goats, ducks and ponies. In winter, horse-drawn sleighs depart from here (€22 per person), passing through the village and snowy forest en route to one of the surrounding *Almen* (alpine meadows).

Information

The centrally located **tourist office** (☎06453-82 35; www.filzmoos.at; Filzmoos 50; ⏲8.30am-12.30pm & 2-6pm Mon-Fri, 8.30am-12.30pm & 3-6pm Sat, 10am-noon Sun) provides stacks of information on activities in the region and will also help book accommodation.

Getting There & Away

Filzmoos is a 10km detour from the A10/E55 Tauern-Autobahn motorway. Several train–bus connections operate daily between Salzburg and Filzmoos (€14.60, 1½ to 1¾ hours); most require a change at Bischofshofen.

Radstadt

Low-key Radstadt has an attractively walled town centre, with round turrets and a Stadtpfarrkirche (town parish church) that's a potpourri of Gothic and Romanesque elements. Most people, however, come here for the mountains. The Alps that rear above the town are a vast playground for all manner of outdoor activities.

The majority of visitors come to Radstadt for the varied skiing and snowboarding. The resort is part of the vast Ski Amadé area, which is covered by a single ski pass and interconnected by ultramodern lifts and free ski buses.

The same mountains attract active types in summer, too, with more than 1000km of walking trails and opportunities for canyoning, climbing, white-water rafting and mountain biking.

Radstadt is 13km southwest of Filzmoos, and is connected by four daily buses (€5.80, 30 minutes). From Radstadt, the B99 climbs to the dramatic Radstädter Tauern Pass (1739m), then over to Carinthia. To the west is the A10/E55, which avoids the high parts via a 6km tunnel.

WORTH A TRIP

BURG MAUTERNDORF

Looking every inch the fairy-tale castle with its setting atop a rocky outcrop and sturdy towers, medieval **Burg Mauterndorf** (adult/child €9.50/5.50; ⏲10am-6pm May-Oct) is its village's pride and joy. It was built in the 13th century by the archbishops of Salzburg on the site of a Roman fort. The castle now houses a regional **museum** and provides the backdrop for various cultural events. Mauterndorf is on Hwy 99; buses run here several times daily from Radstadt (€9, 48 minutes).

HOHE TAUERN NATIONAL PARK

If you thought Mother Nature pulled out all the stops in the Austrian Alps, think again: Hohe Tauern National Park was her magnum opus. Welcome to Austria's outdoor wonderland and one of Europe's largest nature reserves (1786 sq km), which straddles Tyrol, Carinthia and Salzburgerland, and is overshadowed by the 3798m hump of Grossglockner, the country's highest peak.

Activities

Ranger Walks WALKING
(www.nationalparkerlebnis.at; ⏲Mon-Fri Jul-Sep) To get the most out of Hohe Tauern National Park, consider signing up for one of the guided walks led by well-informed rangers. On weekdays from July to September they offer 30 hikes – several of which are free with a guest card – covering everything from herb-discovery trails to high-altitude hikes, around-the-glacier tours, gorge climbing and wildlife spotting.

Innergschlöss Glacier Trail WALKING
One of the most spectacular half-day hikes in these parts, this walk kicks off at the Matreier Tauernhaus. From here, it's a 90-minute trudge to the dramatically crevassed Innergschlöss Glacier. Involving 500m of ascent, the challenging four- to five-hour circuit heads through a beautiful alpine valley, stippled with cotton grass and passing shimmering glacial lakes. Keep an eye out for bearded vultures.

Bergführer Kals CLIMBING
(☎0664 416 12 89; www.bergfuehrer-kals.at; Ködnitz 18, Kals am Grossglockner; Grossglockner normal route from €230, Grossvenediger from €125; ⏲office 3-7pm) If you're considering a two-day ascent to Austria's highest of the high, Grossglockner (3798m) or Grossvenediger (3666m), this team of mountain

guides, going strong for the past 150 years, provides expert assistance. Experience is essential. It also arranges other alpine climbs (the Lienzer Dolomites, for instance) as well as ski touring, freeriding, ice climbing and snowshoeing expeditions (call ahead). The website has details.

Sleeping & Eating

Erzherzog-Johann-Hütte HUT €
(☎0664 125 10 41; www.erzherzog-johann-huette.at; dm/r €33.80/42.80, incl half board €54/63; ⊙mid-Jun–Sep) Perched like an eyrie at 3454m, this is the highest of Austria's alpine huts and a mere two-hour climb from the summit of mighty Grossglockner. As you might expect at this giddy elevation, the wooden bunk room is bare bones and there are no wash rooms. The kitchen rolls out hearty grub, such as goulash, schnitzel and wood-oven strudel.

Hotel Tauernstern CHALET €€
(☎04822-248; www.tauernstern.at; Winklern 24, Winklern im Mölltal; s €57-77, d €104-124, ste €134-144, half board €15; P) Sweeping valley views extend from the timber balconies of this mountain-set gem. Four-poster pine-and-stone beds, in-room fridges, a sauna and spa built from local wood and slate, and an exceptional gourmet restaurant using ingredients from local farms all make Tauernstern a fabulous pit stop before tackling the Grossglockner High Alpine Road.

Matreier Tauernhaus GUESTHOUSE €€
(☎04875-88 11; www.matreier-tauernhaus.at; Tauer 22, Matrei in Osttirol; s €65-83, d €90-126, q €152;) Cowering in the shadow of some of Austria's highest peaks, Matreier Tauernhaus is a fine example of an alpine chalet, with recently revamped rooms sporting rustic wood furnishings and mountain prints. Run by the Brugger family for the past five generations, it was originally built for the Archbishop of Salzburg in 1207. It's a great base for an ascent of Grossvenediger.

Information

National Park Worlds (www.nationalparkzentrum.at; Gerlosstrasse 18, Mittersill; museum adult/child €10/5; ⊙9am-6pm;) Pick up information on the park and guided tours and maps at this visitor centre in Mittersill.

Getting There & Away

CAR & MOTORCYCLE

To limit traffic through the park, many of the roads have toll sections and some are closed in winter. The main north–south road routes are the year-round Felber-Tauern-Strasse (B108) between Mittersill and Lienz, and the spectacular Grossglockner Road (open May to October).

The 5.5km-long Felbertauerntunnel is on the East Tyrol–Salzburgerland border; the toll is €11 for cars and €10 for motorbikes. Buses on the Lienz–Kitzbühel route operate along this road.

HIKING & CLIMBING IN HOHE TAUERN NATIONAL PARK

Hohe Tauern's deep valleys, towering peaks and plateaux are a mecca to hikers and climbers. The reserve has treks to suit every level of ability, from gentle day walks to extreme expeditions to inaccessible peaks and ridges. **Freytag & Berndt** (www.freytagberndt.com) produce detailed 1:50,000 walking maps covering the national park and surrounding areas, available online, at the visitor centre National Park Worlds or in bookshops in larger towns. When planning a major trek, it's worth booking overnight stops in advance, as accommodation can be sparse the higher you go; local tourist offices can advise.

Popular hikes include the ascent of the eternally ice-capped **Grossvenediger** (3666m), flanked by glaciers. The closest you can get by road is the 1512m-high alpine chalet Matreier Tauernhaus, at the southern entrance to the Felbertauerntunnel. You can park here and within an hour's walk gain fine views of the mountain.

Anyone with climbing experience and a reasonable level of fitness can climb the mighty **Grossglockner** (3798m) via the 'normal' route, though a guide is recommended. The main trail begins at the Erzherzog-Johann-Hütte, a four- to five-hour hike from Heiligenblut. From here, the roughly two-hour route crosses ice and rocks, following a steel cable over a narrow snow ridge, to the cross at the summit. It's essential to have the proper equipment (maps, ropes, crampons etc) and to check weather conditions before setting out. For guides, contact the tourist office in Heiligenblut or check out the options with Bergführer Kals (p255).

TRAIN

The main hubs for train services are Zell am See (for services to Salzburg and points north via St Johann im Pongau) and Lienz (for trains east and west into Tyrol and Carinthia).

Getting Around

Train–bus combinations run four times daily from Zell am See to Matrei in Osttirol (€15.80, two hours), involving a change at Mittersill.

There are also regular bus services to Heiligenblut, one of the most central bases for exploring the park.

Zell am See

☎06542 / POP 9852 / ELEV 757M

Zell am See is an instant heart-stealer, with its bluer-than-blue lake (Zeller See), pocket-sized centre studded with brightly painted chalets, and the snowcapped peaks of the Hohe Tauern that lift your gaze to postcard heaven. Partake in its pleasures, diving into the lake and cycling its leafy shores, hiking and skiing in the mountains and driving high on the Grossglockner Road. Every year, more than one million visitors from all around the world – from families to playboys in sports cars – do just that, in search of the Austrian dream.

Activities

★Kitzsteinhorn Glacier SKIING, HIKING

(www.kitzsteinhorn.at; return cable car ticket adult/child €42/21, day ski pass €53/26) Winter or summer, the Kitzsteinhorn Glacier is one of Zell am See's must-do attractions, with enough snow for skiing 10 months of the year. A cable car whizzes up to top-station **Gipfelwelt 3000**, where two viewpoint platforms at 3029m command phenomenal alpine views into the Hohe Tauern National Park – look out for Grossglockner. From mid-May to mid-September there are free **guided tours** (10.30am and 1pm).

Adventure Service ADVENTURE SPORTS

(☎0664 5059 920; www.adventureservice.at; Salzachtal Bundesstrasse 22; ⏲9am-noon & 4-6pm Mon-Fri, 9am-noon Sat & Sun; 👪) A one-stop daredevil shop, this outfit offers a long list of adrenaline-charged activities, from tandem paragliding (€120) and white-water rafting (€55) to canyoning (€65 to €89) and guided half-day mountain-bike tours (€30). Less physically exerting are the 90-minute Segway tours (€45), taking in the lake and mountain scenery.

> **ZELL AM SEE–KAPRUN CARD**
>
> If you're in town in summer, ask at your accommodation for the free Zell am See–Kaprun Card. This gets you free entry to all major sights and activities in the region, including the swimming pools around the lake, Wildpark Ferleiten (p265) and the Krimmler Wasserfälle (Krimml Falls; p268). It also gives you a boat trip on the lake and one free ride per day on the cable cars that ascend to Schmittenhöhe and Kitzsteinhorn.

Zell am See Lido SWIMMING

(adult/child €7.90/4.30; ⏲9am-7pm Jul-Sep, 10am-7pm May & Jun; 👪) For a little vertical sightseeing and stellar views of Grossglockner as you swim laps, you can't beat this lido. It has sunbathing lawns, solar-heated pools and kids' splash areas. Free entry with the Zell am See–Kaprun Card.

Windsurfcenter Zell Am See WINDSURFING

(☎0664 644 36 95; www.windsurfcenter.info; Seespitzstrasse 13; 2hr beginner course €40; ⏲dawn-dusk May-Sep) Mountain breezes create ideal conditions for windsurfing and stand-up paddleboarding on Zeller See. This reputable windsurfing centre is 2km south of town; call for more information on its wide range of courses. You can also rent windsurfers/wetsuits/funboards per day for €60/20/86.

Tours

Rundfahrt Schmittenhöhe CRUISE

(www.schmitten.at; adult/child €15.50/7.50; ⏲10am-5pm Jun-Sep, 11am-4pm May & Oct) For a scenic spin on the lake – with cracking views of the Hohe Tauern mountains to boot (on cloudless days) – hop aboard one of these 45-minute panoramic boat tours.

Festivals & Events

Zell Summer Night PERFORMING ARTS

(⏲Wed Jul & Aug) The free Zell Summer Night festival draws bands, street entertainers and improvised theatre to streets and squares every Wednesday night in July and August.

Sleeping

Haus Haffner GUESTHOUSE €

(☎06542-72 39 60; www.haffner.at; Schmittenstrasse 29; s €24-37, d €46-99, apt €94-145; 🅿📶)

Zell am See

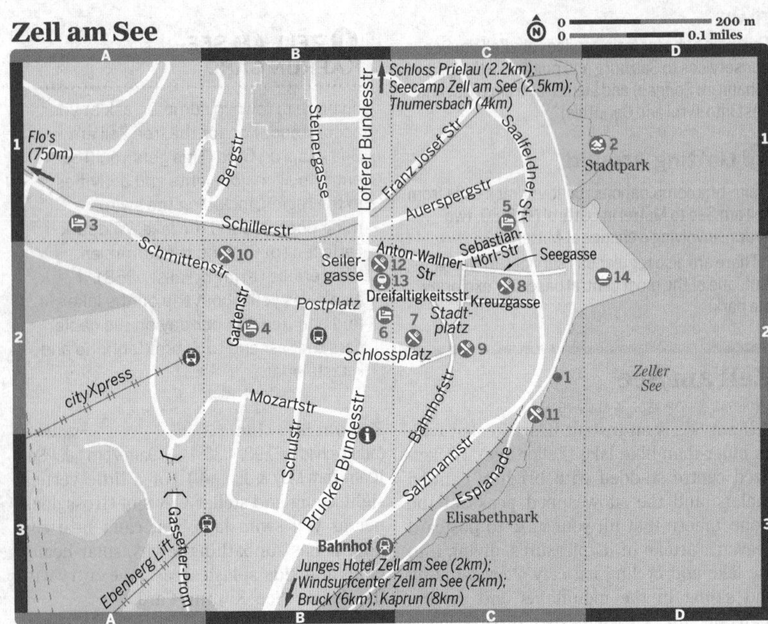

Tucked down a quiet backstreet near the ski lift, this cheery alpine-style chalet, ablaze with geraniums in summer, has spacious rooms and family apartments with rag rugs, kettles and lots of chunky wood furniture (the owner is a cabinet maker).

Junges Hotel Zell am See HOSTEL €
(☎06542-571 85; https://seespitz.hostel-zellamsee.at; Seespitzstrasse 13; dm €30-33, s €43.50, d €74; P 📶) Right at the lake and beach, a 15-minute walk south of town, these family-friendly digs are a great budget deal. Rooms are simple but well kept, the mountain views dreamy and there's always plenty going on, from volleyball matches to weekly barbecues.

Seecamp Zell Am See CAMPGROUND €
(☎06542-721 15; www.seecamp.at; Thumersbacherstrasse 34; camp sites per adult/child/tent €10.40/6.80/7.80; P 📶) If waking up to views of the snowcapped Kitzsteinhorn mountains appeals, camp out at this tree-shaded campground on the lakeshore. Facilities include a shop, restaurant and kids' club. Guided mountain-bike and hiking tours are available.

Pension Hubertus PENSION €€
(☎06542-724 27; www.hubertus-pension.at; Gartenstrasse 4; s €80-100, d €130-170; P) 🍃
Beate and Bernd extend a warm welcome at their eco-savvy chalet. Situated opposite the ski lifts, the pension uses 100% renewable energy (solar and wind power), and organic produce and fair-trade coffee are served at breakfast. The bright, airy rooms are decked out country-style, with lots of pine, floral drapes and downy bedding.

Zell am See

Activities, Courses & Tours
1 Rundfahrt Schmittenhöhe C2
2 Zell am See Lido D1

Sleeping
3 Haus Haffner A1
4 Pension Hubertus B2
5 Romantik Hotel Zell am See C1
6 Steinerwirt B2

Eating
7 Deins & Meins C2
8 Feinkost Lumpi C2
9 Heimatgold C2
10 Kraftwerk B2
Steinerwirt .... (see 6)
11 The Burger Factory C2
12 Zum Hirschen B2

Drinking & Nightlife
13 Ginhouse B2
14 Grand Café D2

Steinerwirt BOUTIQUE HOTEL €€
(☎06542-725 02; www.steinerwirt.com; Dreifaltigkeitsgasse 2; s €79, d €158-208; @📶) A 500-year-old chalet turned boutique hotel, Steinerwirt has light-filled rooms tastefully done out in muted tones and untreated pinewood, with flat-screen TVs and DVD players. The rooftop whirlpool, mountain-facing sauna, library and art gallery invite relaxation, as does the highly recommended restaurant. There are incredible views of Kitzsteinhorn glacier and Schmittenhöhe from the roof terrace.

Schloss Prielau HISTORIC HOTEL €€€
(☎06542-72 91 10; www.schloss-prielau.at; Hofmannsthalstrasse 10; s €165-185, d €210-290, ste €560-800; P@📶) A once-upon-a-dream fairy tale of a hotel, this 16th-century castle was once the haunt of Bavarian prince-bishops. Wood panelling and antiques add a touch of romance to the rustic-chic rooms; many feature lake and mountain views. With its private beach, spa and two-Michelin-star restaurant Mayer's (p261), this is luxury all the way. It's 2.5km northeast of the centre along the lakefront promenade.

Romantik Hotel Zell am See HOTEL €€€
(☎06542-725 20; www.romantik-hotel.at; Sebastian-Hörl-Strasse 11; d €190-230, ste €206-260; P@📶🏊) This dark-wood chalet, decorated with geraniums in summer, looks back on a 500-year history. Antique wood furnishings in the cosy rooms, a solar-heated pool with mountain views and a small spa with pampering treatments such as chocolate baths create an ambience of discreet luxury.

Eating

Burger Factory BURGERS €
(☎06542-474 65; Salzmannstrasse 2; burgers €9-13; ⏰noon-4.30pm & 6-9pm Tue-Sat, noon-7pm Sun; 🖉) This is a burger joint but not as you know it. Slick, contemporary and streamlined, it has fabulous lake views and does a brisk trade in organic burgers with a gourmet touch – everything from the fries down to the ketchup and mayo is homemade – and there are veggie options, too. Organic wine and beer make the perfect match.

Heimatgold CAFE €
(Bahnhofstrasse 1; snacks €5.50-12; ⏰9am-6pm Mon-Sat) This cracking deli-cafe is a fine place to stock up on regional products – sample some on the terrace while you're at it. Besides wholesome breakfasts, it does tasting plates of Salzburgerland cured hams and cheeses and Styrian fruit juices.

Feinkost Lumpi DELI €
(Seegasse 6; ⏰8.30am-6.30pm Mon-Fri, to 5pm Sat) This deli is picnic-central. Stop by for dense rye bread, Pinzgauer ham and cheese, homemade *Knödel* (dumplings) and local honey, herbs and liqueurs. The farm-fresh ice cream is superb, too.

★ **Steinerwirt** AUSTRIAN €€
(☎06542-725 02; www.steinerwirt.com; Dreifaltigkeitsgasse 2; lunch €14, mains €10-31.50; ⏰7am-midnight) Whether you dine in the modern bistro or the dark-wood-panelled Salzburger Stube, Steinerwirt is a winner. The menu plays up locally sourced ingredients in flavour-packed starters such as venison carpaccio with nut pesto and rocket, and traditional mains like *Zwiebelrostbraten* (grilled sirloin of beef in onion sauce) with baby dumplings. These are accompanied by wines drawn from the 600-year-old cellar.

Flo's AUSTRIAN €€
(☎06542-72 123; www.landhotel-martha.at; Schmittenstrasse 79; mains €17-29.50, 3-/4-/5-course menu €39/49/59; ⏰6-11pm Mon-Sat; 🖉👪) Worth the short hop out of town, this nicely chilled restaurant prides itself on season-driven modern Austrian cuisine with an experimental twist – and it delivers. The quality of ingredients is second to none in palate-awakening dishes such as celery and apple with buckwheat and parmesan, and wild sole with pak choi, paprika and gnocchi. Children and vegetarians are well catered for.

Kraftwerk AUSTRIAN €€
(☎0664 3888 016; www.kraftwerk-restaurant.at; Schmittenstrasse 12a; mains €17-24; ⏰2pm-midnight) Housed in a converted 1930s power station, this stylish postindustrial, brick-walled newcomer to Zell am See's dining scene puts an imaginative spin on excellent regional products in dishes such as goat's cheese crème brûlée with grapes and nuts, and corn-fed chicken with polenta, rhubarb and broccoli. Try homemade bread, smoked ham and schnapps from their own organic farm.

Deins & Meins FUSION €€
(☎06542-472 44; www.deins-meins.at; Schlossplatz 5; mains €14-35; ⏰5-10.30pm Mon-Sat; 📶🖉👪) Floor-to-ceiling glass, red velvet chairs and rotating exhibitions of modern

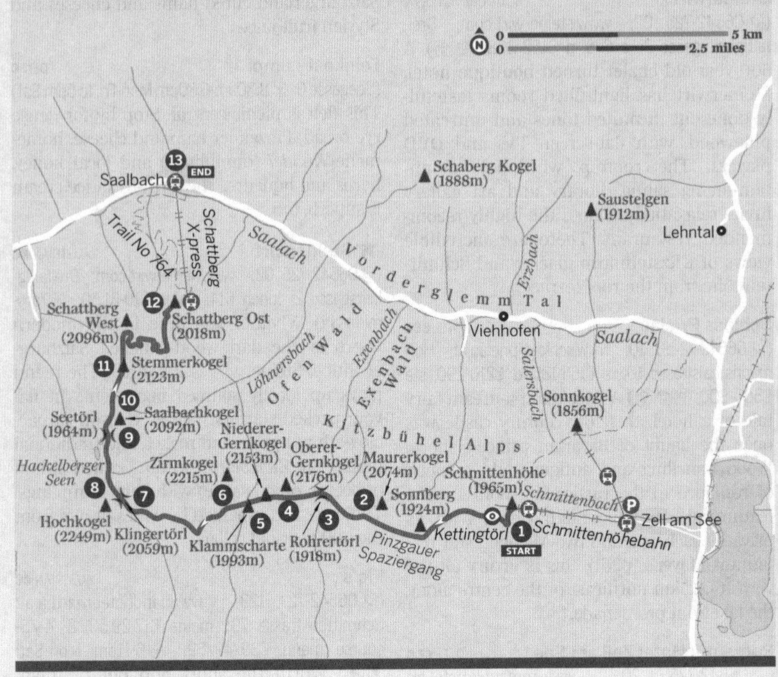

Walking Trail
Pinzgauer Spaziergang

START ZELL AM SEE
END SAALBACH
LENGTH 17KM; FIVE TO SIX HOURS

This moderately challenging day hike affords magnificent views of the Kitzbühel Alps and Hohe Tauern range. Bring supplies and consider buying Kompass 1:35,000 map No 30 *Zell am See–Kaprun*.

At **1 Schmittenhöhebahn** top station, begin a gradual descent from Saalbach/Pinzgauer Spaziergang, enjoying views of Zeller See and the glaciated Hohe Tauern range. The ever-narrowing path continues up an incline and passes through tarn-studded forest, occasionally drawing your gaze to shimmering Grossglockner and the Kitzsteinhorn Glacier to the south.

The landscape soon opens up as you wend through wildflower-streaked meadows and, after roughly an hour, contour the rounded summit of **2 Maurerkogel**. Make a short, painless ascent to **3 Rohrertörl** saddle, where you can contrast the limestone Kaisergebirge to the north with the icy Hohe Tauern peaks to the south.

Passing two junctions, follow a balcony trail that contours the base of **4 Oberer-Gernkogel** and gently mounts **5 Niederer-Gernkogel**. You'll soon reach the foot of **6 Zirmkogel**, which, with will and expertise, can be climbed in little over an hour.

The rocky trail runs through high meadows and mottled mountains, passing a small hut near a stream. Around four hours from the trailhead, the path ascends a steepish incline to the **7 Klingertörl** saddle, where a sign shows the way to Saalbach. Traverse the base of cliffs that sweep down from **8 Hochkogel** and make a short descent to the grassy col of **9 Seetörl**.

Walk north from here, either climbing over the **10 Saalbachkogel** or skirting its western slopes. The same option is repeated for **11 Stemmerkogel**. Descend the ridge and continue towards Schattberg, making a final ascent to the **12 Schattberg X-press** gondola and then down to **13 Saalbach**.

art define this slinky lounge-restaurant. Local chef and confectioner David Fischböck has put his stamp on the Slow Food menu: herby Mediterranean-inspired mains and spot-on steaks are followed by his delectable homemade desserts. A kids' menu is available.

Zum Hirschen AUSTRIAN €€
(☎06542-77 40; www.hotel-zum-hirschen.at; Dreifaltigkeitsstrasse 1; mains €11.50-32; ⏰11.30am-10pm) Warm pine panelling, flickering candles and friendly yet discreet service create an intimate feel in this smart restaurant. The chef makes the most of local ingredients, so expect dishes such as organic Pinzgauer beef *Tafelspitz*, local trout with dill potatoes and Tyrolean mountain lamb.

Mayer's GASTRONOMY €€€
(☎06542-72 91 10; www.mayers-restaurant.at; Hofmannsthalstrasse 10; tasting menus €95-175; ⏰7pm-midnight Wed-Sun) Andreas Mayer heads the stove at hotel Schloss Prielau's refined restaurant, holder of two Michelin stars. Freshness is key, with home-grown vegetables and organic produce shining through in ingredient-driven mains such as crépinette of pigeon with passionfruit and kohlrabi, and Pinzgau venison with sweet pepper, pesto and aubergine lasagne – all served with imagination and flair. One for special occasions.

Drinking & Nightlife

Ginhouse BAR
(www.ginhouse.at; Dreifaltigkeitsgasse 1; ⏰7pm-3.30am Fri & Sat) Move over Europop and shots – 'après chilling' is what the Ginhouse offers. It delivers, with 450 different varieties of gin, expertly mixed cocktails and mellow après-ski tunes, all in a kind of modern alpine pub.

Grand Café CAFE
(Esplanade 4; ⏰noon-6pm) You don't have to stay in the belle-époque finery of Grand Hotel Zell am See to appreciate the dreamy lake and mountain views from its tree-shaded cafe terrace. Watch ducks and boats glide by as you savour coffee with home-made cake and live piano music.

Information

Tourist Office (☎06542-770; www.zellam see-kaprun.com; Brucker Bundesstrasse 1a; ⏰8am-6pm Mon-Fri, 9am-noon Sat) The staff here will help you find rooms; there's also an accommodation board in the foyer with a free 24-hour telephone.

Getting There & Away

BUS

Buses leave from outside the *Hauptbahnhof* and from the **bus station** (Postplatz) behind the post office. They run to Kaprun (€3.70, 20 minutes, twice hourly) and Krimml (€10.80, 1½ hours, every two hours).

CAR & MOTORCYCLE

Zell am See is on the B311 running north to Lofer, where it joins the B178, which connects St Johann in Tirol with Salzburg (passing through Germany). It's also just a few kilometres north of the east-west highway linking St Johann im Pongau with Tyrol (via the Gerlos Alpine Road).

TRAIN

Hourly trains run from Zell am See to destinations including Salzburg (€15.90, 1½ to two hours), Kitzbühel (€12.90, 50 minutes) and Innsbruck (€31, 2½ hours).

Getting Around

You can hire bikes to pedal around the lake at any of the sports shops in town, such as Adventure Service (p257) and **Carve In** (www.sommer.carve-in.at; Postplatz 4; bike rental per day city/mountain/e-bike/children's €15/25/25/10; ⏰9am-noon & 3-6pm).

Bad Gastein

☎06434 / POP 3980 / ELEV 1000M

With belle-époque villas clinging to forest-cloaked cliffs that rise above thunderous falls, and views deep into the Gastein Valley, Bad Gastein is a stunner. The town runs both hot and cold, with first-class skiing, high-level hiking and hot springs still hailed for their miraculous healing properties. Though the damp is rising in places, the higgledy-piggledy resort has kept some of the grandeur of its 19th-century heyday, when Empress Elisabeth (Sisi) came to bathe and pen poetry here.

Sights

★**Gasteiner Wasserfall** WATERFALL
Bad Gastein's star attraction is this 341m waterfall, which rages over rugged cliff faces and through thick forest to tumble into three turquoise pools. The waterfall's wispy, ethereal beauty captured the imagination of Klimt, Max Liebermann, Schubert and Empress

Bad Gastein

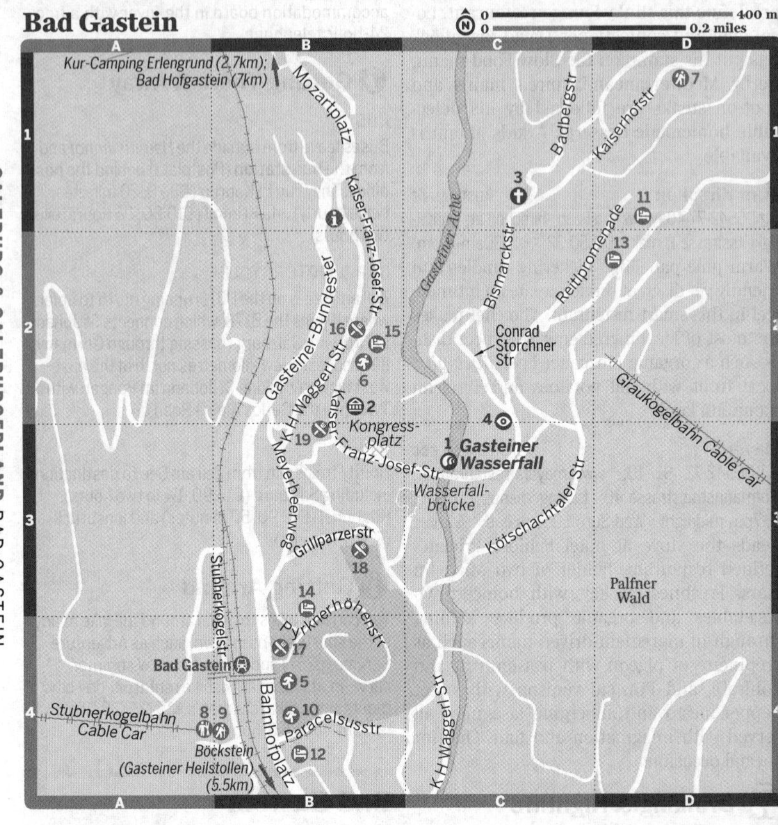

Bad Gastein

Top Sights

1 Gasteiner Wasserfall C3

Sights

2 Gasteiner Museum B2
3 Nikolauskirche C1
4 Thermalwasser Trinkbrunnen C2

Activities, Courses & Tours

5 Felsentherme Gastein B4
6 Flying Waters B2
7 Kaiser-Wilhem-Promenade D1
8 Ski Amadé A4
9 Stubnerkogel B4
10 Therapiezentrum B4

Sleeping

11 Alpenblick D1
12 Euro Youth Hotel Krone B4
13 Hotel Miramonte D2
14 Pension St Leonhard B3
15 Villa Solitude B2

Eating

16 Betty's Bar B2
17 Blonde Beans B4
18 Hofkeller B3
19 Jägerhäusl B3
Lutter & Wegner .... (see 15)

Elisabeth. The stone **Wasserfallbrücke** (waterfall bridge) is the best vantage point, and the trailhead for the **Wasserfallweg** (waterfall path) shadows the magnificent cataract and provides some great photo ops.

Gasteiner Museum MUSEUM
(www.gasteinermuseum.com; Kaiser-Franz-Josef Strasse 14, Grand Hotel de l'Europe; adult/child €5/free; ⌚2.30-6pm Wed-Sun) Tap into the source of Bad Gastein at this museum, which spells out the town's history and the wonders of it

thermal waters, from the bath-loving Romans to the Romantic painters inspired by its waterfall. The collection spans everything from *Krampus* (devil) costumes to vintage tourist posters and 19th-century oil paintings of Bad Gastein. English audio guides are available.

Nikolauskirche CHURCH
(Bismarckstrasse; ⏲7.30am-3.30pm Mon-Fri, 8am-7.30pm Sat & Sun) The late-Gothic Nikolauskirche is a little gem of a church, tiled with wood shingles and built around a central pillar. Its interior is simple yet beautiful, with an uneven flagstone floor, baroque altar and rudimentary frescoes that are fading with age. Look out for the statue of the 16th-century physician Paracelsus outside.

Thermalwasser Trinkbrunnen FOUNTAIN
To feel the benefits of Bad Gastein's thermal waters without tapping into your euros, fill your bottle at this drinking fountain for free. Two to six glasses per day are recommended for glowing health.

Activities

Ski Amadé SKIING
(www.skiamade.com; day pass adult/child €53.50/27) In winter the Gasteinertal's slopes and spas are a match made in heaven, with 208km of varied pistes to challenge confident beginner and intermediate skiers, including attractive wooded runs and some great carving opportunities. Mountain transport has been given a major boost recently with the opening of the state-of-the-art Schlossalmbahn.

The expansive Ski Amadé area comprises 760km of slopes, with skiing and snowboarding centred on **Stubnerkogel** (2246m) and **Graukogel** (2492m). Cross-country skiing is also big in Bad Gastein, with 90km of prepared *Loipe* (tracks), including a floodlit trail at **Böckstein** (3km south of Bad Gastein).

Stubnerkogel HIKING
(ascent & descent adult/child €26.50/13.50, day ski pass adult/child €57/28; ⏲8.30am-4pm) Stubnerkogel is excellent for summertime walking, with high-altitude trails traversing alpine pastures and craggy peaks. Stubnerkogel also has an impressive 140m-long suspension bridge (Europe's highest), with big-top views of the Hohe Tauern range. In winter there's fine skiing on slopes that vary from 860m to 2300m. The two-section **Stubnerkogelbahn cable car** is near Bad Gastein's train station.

Gasteiner Heilstollen SPA
(Gastein Healing Gallery; ☎06434-375 30; www.gasteiner-heilstollen.com; Heilstollenstrasse 19, Böckstein; trial session €32.40; ⏲8am-5pm Mon-Fri, to noon Sat) Böckstein's medieval gold mine has been reinvented as a much-celebrated health centre. Here you'll get a brief health check and board a small train that chugs 2km into the humid 38°C depths of Radhausberg mountain, where you'll absorb the healing radon vapours, said to cure everything from arthritis to fibromyalgia.

Alpentherme SPA
(☎06432-82 93; www.alpentherme.com; Senator-Wilhelm-Wilfling-Platz 1, Bad Hofgastein; 4hr ticket adult/child €29.50/17.50; ⏲9am-9pm Sun-Wed, to 10pm Thu-Sat) This architecturally innovative spa is split into four different 'worlds', where experiences stretch from relaxing in radon-rich thermal baths to racing down white-knuckle flumes. The sauna village comprises brine grottoes, loft saunas, red-hot Finnish saunas and an ice-cold plunge pool. For some pampering, pop over to the beauty centre, which offers treatments such as goat-milk wraps and silky smooth hot-chocolate massages.

It's 7km north of Bad Gastein. Frequent services on bus 550 run from the train station to the spa (€2.60, 15 minutes).

Felsentherme Gastein SPA
(☎06434-222 30; www.felsentherme.com; Bahnhofplatz 5; 3hr/day ticket adult €24.50/29, child €14/18; ⏲9am-9pm; 👪) A glass elevator zooms from street level up to Felsentherme Gastein, where you can take to the rejuvenating waters. The spa shelters grottoes, an adventure pool for kids and an outdoor thermal bath with pummelling massage jets and stellar views of the mountains. For those prepared to bare all, there are panoramic saunas and salty steam baths to test out.

Flying Waters ADVENTURE SPORTS
(☎0670 400 2350; Villa Solitude, Kaiser-Franz-Josef-Strasse 16; adult/child €20/15; ⏲11am-2pm & 3-6pm Wed & Fri-Sun mid-May–early Nov) The waterfall is a blur on this exhilarating zipline that threads 300m over the Gastein Valley, from Villa Solitude to the parkland below.

Kaiser-Wilhem-Promenade WALKING
There's no need to exert yourself for a view in Bad Gastein. Simply follow this balcony trail along Kaiserhofstrasse for deep views into the forest-cloaked, mountain-rimmed, villa-studded Gastein Valley. It's an easy

GASTEIN CARD

Pick up the free Gastein Card from your accommodation for some great freebies, including guided hikes and bike tours, spa concerts and history walks; the tourist office has full details. The card also yields substantial discounts on cable cars, buses, spas and activities. The winter card offers similar reductions plus free use of all buses, the ice-skating rink, toboggan rental and guided ski safaris.

45-minute walk, with prime photo ops at the **statue of Kaiser Wilhelm**, who gave Bad Gastein's curative waters the royal seal of approval by visiting 20 times in the late 19th century.

Therapiezentrum SPA
(☎06434-27 11; www.therapiezentrum-badgastein.at; Bahnhofplatz 7; radon bath €19; ⌚8am-12.30pm & 1.30-5pm Mon-Fri, 8am-noon Sat) Curative massages, radon baths, *fango* mud packs, acupuncture, cryotherapy and electrotherapy are available at the Therapiezentrum.

Festivals & Events

Gasteiner Krampuslauf CULTURAL
(⌚5 Dec) Horned, hairy and for kids pretty scary, *Krampus* rocks up at nightfall in the Gasteinertal on the eve of St Nicholas Day. Wearing a shaggy goat skin, ghoulish mask and goat horns, the *Krampus* is the antithesis of good ol' St Nick, there to punish misbehaving children. Seeing 80 to 100 of these monster-like characters rampage through the town centre is quite something.

FIS Snowboard World Cup Gastein SPORTS
(Buchebenwiese, Stubnerkogel; ⌚early Jan) See the world's best boarders battle it out on the slopes of Bad Gastein, the only Austrian stop on the World Cup tour.

Sleeping

Pension St Leonhard PENSION €
(☎06434 231 20; www.pension-leonhard.at; Pyrkershöhenstrasse 9; s €40-60, d €74-112; P 📶) Bedecked with flowers in summer and affording pretty mountain views, this sweet and simple family-run guesthouse near the train station is a find. Warm-hued rooms have traditional alpine wooden furniture, there's a spa area with a sauna for a post-ski or post-hike steam, and breakfast is a decent spread of cold cuts, eggs, cereals and fresh breads.

Euro Youth Hotel Krone HOSTEL €
(☎06434-23 30; www.euro-youth-hotel.at; Bahnhofsplatz 8; dm €30-50, s €38-58, d €66-102, per person half board €12; P 📶) With its well-kept, high-ceilinged rooms, this century-old manor has more charm than your average hostel. Backpackers praise the facilities, which include a restaurant, TV lounge and barbecue area. Staff can arrange adventure sports such as rafting, canyoning, paragliding, mountain biking and snowshoeing.

Kur-Camping Erlengrund CAMPGROUND €
(☎06434-302 05; www.kurcamping-gastein.at; Erlengrundstrasse 6; camp sites per adult/child/tent €9/5.30/14; P 📶 🏊) Close to a natural lake, this campground has shady pitches and, in summer, a heated pool is available. It's an hour's walk following the waterfall north of Bad Gastein to Kötschachdorf; bus 555 runs from the train station (€2.10, 15 minutes).

★ **Alpenblick** HOTEL €€
(☎06434-20 62; www.alpenblick-gastein.at; Kötschachtaler Strasse 17; s €71-85, d €126-170, apt €226-277; P 📶 🏊) The name says it all: the view of the Alps and deep into the Gastein Valley is phenomenal from this panoramically perched hotel at the foot of the Graukogel ski slope. The parquet-floored rooms are slickly traditional and the facilities are terrific, with a spa area, outdoor pool and gardens, plus a games room and playground for kids. Half board included.

Hotel Miramonte DESIGN HOTEL €€
(☎06434-25 77; www.hotelmiramonte.com; Reitlpromenade 3; s €105-200, d €140-220; P 📶) This hilltop hotel has a retro-chic design and a phenomenal mountain backdrop. A terrace overlooking forested peaks, a thermal spa with pampering Aveda treatments and yoga classes draw a style-conscious crowd here. The studio-style rooms are all about pared-down glamour, with bare-wood floors and cowskin rugs.

Villa Solitude HISTORIC HOTEL €€
(☎06434-51 01; www.villasolitude.com; Kaiser-Franz-Josef-Strasse 16; d €80-160, half board per person €30; P 📶) Once home to an Austrian countess, this belle-époque villa shelters six elegant suites with oil paintings and antiques. The intimate piano room downstairs is the place to slip into your role as lord or lady of the manor. Breakfast costs €15 extra. **Lutter & Wegner** restaurant, with its fusion menu and cracking terrace, is next door.

Eating

★Blonde Beans CAFE €

(☎0660 1385 366; www.facebook.com/theblondebeans; Bahnhofsplatz 4; snacks €4.50-6.50; ⊙9am-5pm Tue-Sat, 10am-4pm Sun) As hip as Bad Gastein gets, this Scandi-flavoured, retro-cool cafe does the best coffee in town, as well as a tasty array of snacks – from homemade cinnamon buns and cakes to wraps, sandwiches, paninis and wholesome soups. The vibe is chilled and they are on the ball when it comes to gluten- and lactose-free options.

Betty's Bar CAFE €

(☎0664 3646 655; Kaiser-Franz-Josef-Strasse 17; light bites €6-12; ⊙3-10pm Mon-Sat) Betty's has an easygoing boho feel, with mosaic tiles gracing white walls and a cute pavement terrace for drinks and nibbles. Come for the great coffee, smoothies, and snacks from baguettes to tapas plates and perfectly crisp tarte flambée.

Hofkeller AUSTRIAN €€

(☎06434-203 72 45; Grillparzerstrasse 1; mains €21.50-32; ⊙6-11pm Sun-Fri Dec-Apr;) In winter, there's no place like this stone cellar beneath the Salzburger Hof hotel for warming up over fondue, a raclette cheese fest or hot-stone specialities. Kids' menus are available.

Jägerhäusl AUSTRIAN €€

(☎06434-20254; www.jaegerhaeusl.com; Kaiser-Franz-Josef-Strasse 9; mains €15-30; ⊙noon-midnight) Besides wood-fired pizza, the menu at this galleried villa is packed with Austrian faves such as schnitzel and venison goulash with dumplings, plus local options like fillet of Gasteiner trout. Pull up a chair on the maple-tree-shaded terrace when the sun's out. There's often live Tyrolean music on summer evenings (see the website for details).

Information

Tourist Office (☎06434-339 35 60; www.gastein.com; Kaiser-Franz-Josef-Strasse 27; ⊙8am-6pm Mon-Thu) To get here, go left from the train-station exit and walk down the hill. Staff will find you accommodation free of charge. There's information on the national park in the foyer.

Getting There & Away

CAR & MOTORCYCLE

Driving south, you'll need to use the *Autoschleuse Tauernbahn* (railway car-shuttle service) through the tunnel that starts at Böckstein (one way €17). On the A10 Tauern-Autobahn from the north (Salzburg), take the Gasteinertal exit near Bischofshofen, then the B167.

TRAIN

Trains trundle through Bad Gastein's station every two hours, connecting the town to points north and south, including Spittal-Millstättersee (€11.60, 35 minutes), Salzburg (€15.90, 1½ hours) and Innsbruck (€58.20, 3½ hours).

When travelling north from Bad Gastein to Bad Hofgastein, sit on the right-hand side of the train for the best views.

Grossglockner Road

Austria's best road trip (p266) bar none, the **Grossglockner Road** (www.grossglockner.at; car €37.50; ⊙May-Nov) is phenomenally beautiful – provided, that is, the weather is fine enough for you to enjoy the views of the glacier-capped peaks, waterfalls and lakes you'll be driving past as you crunch gears on the hairpin bends. This marvel of 1930s engineering provides total immersion in Austria's highest Alps.

At the time of research the Grossglockner Road was on the Tentative List of Unesco World Heritage sites – watch this space.

Wildpark Ferleiten WILDLIFE RESERVE

(www.wildpark-ferleiten.at; adult/child €8/4; ⊙8am-dusk May-early Nov;) Wildpark Ferleiten is a 15-hectare reserve that's home to 200 alpine animals such as chamois, marmots, ibex, fallow deer, wild boar and brown bears. Kids can let off steam in the playgrounds or on the mini roller coasters.

Getting There & Away

You can travel the Grossglockner Road by bus, but it's not as fast or as easy as having your own wheels. Bus 5002 runs frequently between Lienz and Heiligenblut on weekdays (€11.10, 1¼ to 2¼ hours); less frequently at weekends. From late June to late September, four buses run from Monday to Friday and three at weekends between Heiligenblut and Kaiser-Franz-Josefs-Höhe (€6.10, 32 minutes).

Heiligenblut

☎04824 / POP 1020 / ELEV 1301M

One of the single-most striking images on the Grossglockner Road is of Heiligenblut, the needle-thin spire of its pilgrimage church framed by the glaciated summit of Grossglockner. The village's iconic scenery and easily accessible mountains lure skiers, hikers and camera-toting tourists. The compact centre is stacked with wooden chalets and, despite an overload of yodelling-kitsch souvenirs, retains some traditional charm.

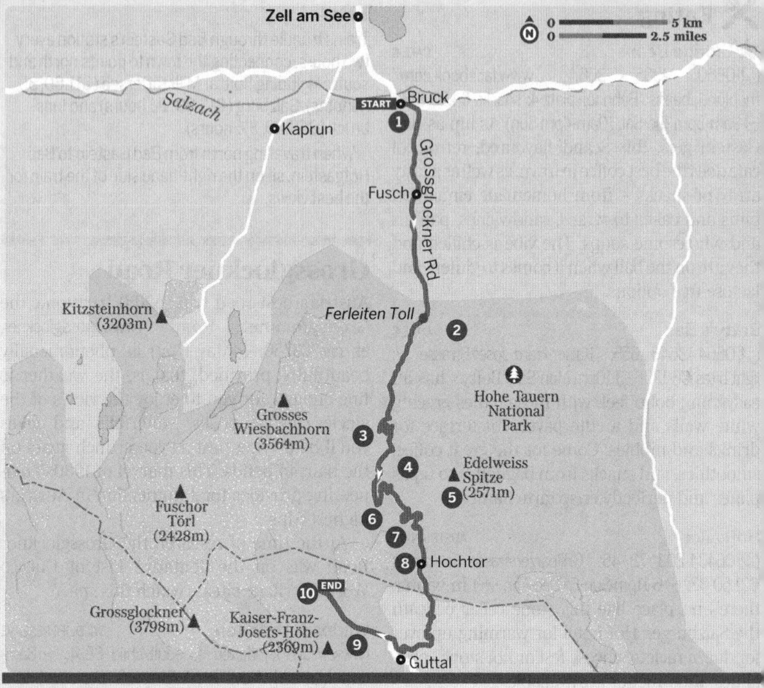

Zell am See
0 5 km
0 2.5 miles
Salzach
START
Bruck
Kaprun
Grossglockner Rd
Fusch
Ferleiten Toll
Kitzsteinhorn (3203m)
Hohe Tauern National Park
Grosses Wiesbachhorn (3564m)
Edelweiss Spitze (2571m)
Fuschor Törl (2428m)
Hochtor
END
Grossglockner (3798m)
Kaiser-Franz-Josefs-Höhe (2369m)
Guttal

Driving Tour Grossglockner Road

START BRUCK
END BRUCK
LENGTH 96KM; FOUR TO SIX HOURS

Buckle up for a great alpine drive. The Grossglockner Road consists of 48 glacier-gawping, wow-what-a-mountain kilometres.

Leaving ❶ **Bruck**, enter wild Fuschertal (Fuscher Valley), passing Fusch and ❷ **Wildpark Ferleiten** (p265). Once through the tollgate, the road climbs to ❸ **Hochmais** (1850m), where glaciated peaks including Grosses Wiesbachhorn (3564m) crowd the horizon. The road zigzags up to ❹ **Haus Alpine Naturschau** (2260m), which spotlights local flora and fauna. A little further, a 2km side road (no coaches allowed) corkscrews up to ❺ **Edelweiss Spitze** (2571m), the road's highest viewpoint. Climb the tower for staggering 360-degree views of more than 30 peaks of 3000m. Refuel with coffee and strudel on the terrace.

Get your camera handy for ❻ **Fuscher Törl** (2428m), with super views on both sides of the ridge, and gems of a lake ❼ **Fuscher Lacke** (2262m) nearby. Here a small exhibition documents the road's construction built by 3000 men over five years during the Depression.

The road wriggles on through meadows to ❽ **Hochtor** (2504m), the top of the pass, after which there's a descent to ❾ **Schöneck**. Branch off west onto the 9km Gletscherstrasse, passing waterfalls and *Achtung Murmeltiere* (Beware of Marmots) signs – you may well spot one of the burrowing rodents.

The Grossglockner massif slides into view on the approach to flag-dotted ❿ **Kaiser-Franz-Josefs-Höhe** (2369m), with views of the bell-shaped Grossglockner (3798m) and the retreating Pasterze Glacier. The 8km swirl of fissured ice is best appreciated on the short and easy Gamsgrubenweg and Gletscherweg trails. Allow time to see the glacier-themed exhibition at the visitor centre and the crystalline Wilhelm-Swarovski observatory before driving back to Bruck.

In summer, serious mountaineers head here to bag peaks in the Hohe Tauern National Park. Enquire at the tourist office for details on mountain-bike trails in the park.

Sights

Wallfahrtskirche St Vinzenz CHURCH

(Hof 2; dawn-dusk) As though cupped in celestial hands and held up to the mighty Alps, this 15th-century pilgrimage church lifts gazes, and spirits. Inside is a tabernacle, which purportedly contains a tiny phial of Christ's blood, hence the village name (*Heiligenblut* means 'holy blood'). Legend has it that the phial was discovered by a saint named Briccius, who was buried in an avalanche on this spot more than a thousand years ago.

Activities

Schareck SKIING

(www.skisport.com/Grossglockner; Kaiser-Franz-Josefs-Höhe; day pass €46;) Skiers can play on 55km of snow-sure slopes in the shadow of Grossglockner in Heiligenblut. This is perfect cruising terrain for beginners and easygoing intermediates, and families often choose the resort for its Snowland Kids' Club and gentle slopes. Most of the skiing takes place on the Schareck (2604m) peak.

Sleeping & Eating

Jugendherberge HOSTEL €

(04824-22 59; www.oejhv.or.at; Hof 36; dm/s/d €24/37.50/59;) Near the church, this chalet-style HI hostel has light, spacious dorms and handy extras, including ski storage and a common room. It's right next to the public swimming pool, sauna and climbing wall, too. Lunch and dinner are available (both cost €7.90).

Camping Grossglockner CAMPGROUND €

(04824-20 48; Hadergasse 11; camp sites per adult/child/car €9/3.50/3) Open year-round, this green and pleasant site on the outskirts of the village features a restaurant, and affords prime vistas of Grossglockner.

★**Chalet-Hotel Senger** HOTEL €€

(04824-22 15; www.romantic.at; Hof 23; s €52-86, d €115-200;) Colourful prayer flags flutter at this farmhouse, a tribute to the Tibetan monks who once stayed here. All cosy nooks, warm wood and open fireplaces, this is just the spot for a little mountain hibernation and soul searching. Most of the snug rooms have balconies; room 24 offers Grossglockner views instead. There's an intimate spa with a sauna and plunge pool.

Nationalpark Lodge Grossglockner BOUTIQUE HOTEL €€

(04824-22 440; www.nationalparklodge.at; Hof 6; s €98-111, d €170-212, ste €196-294;) Receiving high praise, this lodge-style hotel is at once distinctly alpine and thoroughly contemporary. Rooms are done out in soft colours and light pine furnishings, with the pick of them offering uplifting mountain views. There's an excellent spa with indoor pool and panoramic sauna, and a restaurant zooming in on regional ingredients such as Hohe Tauern venison in its modern alpine dishes.

The hotel arranges all kinds of outdoor activities with expert guides, from snowshoeing hikes to observe wildlife to ski touring, ice climbing and glacier trekking.

Kirchenwirt AUSTRIAN €€

(04824-246 10; www.kirchenwirt.restaurant; Hof 9; mains €10-24; 10.30am-9.30pm;) As cosy as they come in Heiligenblut, Kirchenwirt has a warm, woody interior for winter days and a cracking terrace gazing up to the high peaks of Hohe Tauern in summer. The mood is relaxed, the service friendly, and the menu is a hearty romp through Austrian classics like goulash soup, schnitzel and strudel, plus a handful of international and vegan faves.

Information

Tourist Office (04824-27 00 20; www.heiligenblut.at; Hof 4; 9am-6pm Mon-Fri, 2-6pm Sat & Sun) On the main street, close to the Hotel Post bus stop. Books mountain guides.

Getting There & Away

Bus 5002 runs between Lienz and Heiligenblut frequently on weekdays (€11.10, 1¼ to 2¼ hours), less frequently at weekends. From late June to late September, four buses run from Monday to Friday, three at weekends, between Heiligenblut and Kaiser-Franz-Josefs-Höhe (€6.10, 32 minutes).

Krimml

06564 / POP 844 / ELEV 1076M

A real crash-bang spectacle, the 380m-high, three-tier Krimmler Wasserfälle, Europe's highest waterfall, is the thunderous centrepiece of this tiny village. Those who look beyond the falls find even more to like about Krimml – gorgeous alpine scenery, fine mountain walks and farmstays that are great for tiptoeing back to nature for a few days.

Sights

★Krimmler Wasserfälle WATERFALL

(Krimml Falls; ☎06564-72 12; www.wasserfaelle-krimml.at; adult/child €4/1; ⏰9am-5pm mid-Apr–Oct) Enshrouded in mist, arched by a rainbow, frozen solid – this waterfall always looks extraordinary, no matter what time of year. The **Wasserfallweg** (Waterfall Trail), which starts at the ticket office and weaves gently uphill through mixed forest, has numerous viewpoints with photogenic close-ups of the falls.

It's about a two-hour round-trip walk, or double that if you want to continue along the glacial **Achental valley**, which shadows a burbling brook to Hölzlahneralm. Up here, you'll have fantastic views of boulder-strewn pastures and 3000m-high peaks – you can even stay the night if you're too tired to head back down to Krimml.

Activities

Tauernradweg CYCLING, WALKING

(www.tauernradweg.at) Well-marked cycling and hiking trails fan out from Krimml into the surrounding Alps. The Tauernradweg is a 310km bike route through the mind-blowing scenery of the Hohe Tauern National Park to Salzburg and then to Passau; it covers some high-altitude stretches and demands a good level of fitness. The Krimmler Wasserfälle Wasserfallweg walking trail begins near the Tauernradweg's starting point.

Zillertal Arena SKIING

(www.zillertalarena.at; 1-/3-/6-day pass €55.50/153.50/266.50; 👪) Krimml is part of the Zillertal Arena, which covers 143km of pistes that are mostly geared towards intermediate skiers. Krimml also appeals to families and nonskiers in winter, with low-key activities such as tobogganing, snowshoeing and horse-drawn-sleigh rides.

WasserWelten Krimml AMUSEMENT PARK

(www.wasserwelten-krimml.at; adult/child incl waterfall €10/5; ⏰9am-5pm May-Oct; 👪) This water-related theme park has loads of hands-on activities for kids, from physics experiments to art installations and outdoor games – the aim is to get completely soaked.

Sleeping & Eating

Burgeck Panorama Hotel GUESTHOUSE €€

(☎06564-72 49; www.burgeck.com; Oberkrimml 79; d €70-98; P 📶) Scenically perched above the village and next to forest, this guesthouse is run by the kindly Bachmaier family and has terrific waterfall views. The recently renovated rooms are modern, while others are done out in rustic alpine style. The restaurant makes the most of local, organic ingredients and home-grown herbs.

Hotel Klockerhaus HOTEL €€

(☎06564-72 08; www.klockerhaus.com; Oberkrimml 10; d €150-176, apt €173-200; P 📶 🏊) Plenty of pine keeps things cosy here, both in the spacious rooms with waterfall views and in the lounge with an open fire. There's a small spa with a sauna, saline steam bath and treatments such as Tibetan massage, as well as an untreated outdoor pool.

Hölzlahneralm AUSTRIAN €

(☎0664 507 83 48; www.hoelzlahner.at; Oberkrimml 66; light meals €8-15; ⏰8am-7pm May-Oct) This wood-shingled farmhouse is a cracking choice for a bite to eat. You'll need to do the legwork – it's a two-hour hike from Krimml via the Krimmler Wasserfälle – but that makes the *Kaspressknödel* (dumpling in gooey Pinzgauer cheese) all the more welcome.

Information

The **tourist office** (☎06564-72 39; www.krimml.at; Oberkrimml 37; ⏰8am-noon & 2-5pm Mon-Fri, 8.30-11.30am Sat) is in the village centre next to the white church.

Getting There & Away

The village is about 500m north of the Krimmler Wasserfälle, on a side turning from the B165. There are parking spaces near the path to the falls, which branches to the right just before the toll booths for the Gerlos Alpine Rd to Mayrhofen.

Buses run year-round from Krimml to Zell am See (€10.80, 1½ hours, every two hours).

Carinthia

Includes ➡

Best Places to Eat

- ➡ Restaurant Maria Loretto (p273)
- ➡ Princs (p274)
- ➡ Dolomitenhütte (p289)
- ➡ La Torre (p281)
- ➡ Bar Leon (p282)

Best Places to Stay

- ➡ Camping Klagenfurt am Wörthersee (p273)
- ➡ Hotel Mosser (p277)
- ➡ Hotel Schloss Leonstain (p282)
- ➡ Villa Verdin (p284)

Why Go?

Few regions in Europe match the rugged beauty of Carinthia, and you'll find that travelling here is often a serpentine journey. Carinthia can also, at times, seem larger than life, with its high peaks, gouged valleys and glistening lakes; the flamboyant show of opulence in the capital, Klagenfurt; and the resorts around the more famous of the region's 1270 pristine mountain lakes. The most popular of these lakes, such as the large Wörthersee, have waters warmed to a comfortable swimming temperature by thermal springs.

Carinthia's deep medieval heritage is another attraction – celebrated in picturesque walled villages such as Friesach and Gmünd, and impressive castles such as the hilltop fortress of Hochosterwitz. Many of the towns and villages nestled in Carinthia's rolling hills hold an annual summer festival, with roving performers coming from neighbouring Italy and Slovenia to take part alongside the locals.

When to Go

- ➡ Midsummer is the best time to make the most of Carinthia's lakes and excellent mountain hiking. The region gets more sunshine than elsewhere in Austria, so the lake temperatures are warmer here.
- ➡ In winter the province morphs into one of Austria's best ski regions, despite having a shorter ski season than elsewhere due to the warmer temps.
- ➡ The shoulder-season periods are less interesting here except for the valley hiking or cycling – the winter or summer outdoor action seasons are the best times to visit.

Carinthia Highlights

1. **Weissensee** (p285) Cycling and hiking the forest trails.
2. **Strandbad Klagenfurt** (p273) Swimming the shores of the Wörthersee at Europe's largest lake baths.
3. **Bar Leon** (p282) Lazing away the afternoon as swans glide by in Pörtschach.
4. **Heinrich Harrer Museum** (p281) Transporting yourself to the tranquil ambience of Tibet in Hüttenberg.
5. **Burg Hochosterwitz** (p281) Admiring the views from atop a spectacular medieval castle.
6. **Millennium-Express Cable Car** (p279) Skiing Nassfeld from the top of this 6km-long cable car, leaving from Tröpolach.
7. **Benediktinermarkt** (p275) Browsing the stalls and sampling local delicacies at the region's most famous market in Klagenfurt.

Getting There & Away

Klagenfurt's **airport** (www.klagenfurt-airport.com; Flughafenstrasse 60-66) has cheap connections to the UK with easyJet and to a few regional airports in Germany with Eurowings.

Klagenfurt and Villach are the main hubs for trains from elsewhere in Europe, especially Italy.

Getting Around

Carinthia is divided into regional zones for public transport, with either single tickets or passes that are valid for one day or longer. Ask what's cheapest when buying a ticket. Boat services operate on many of the lakes in summer.

The **Kärnten Card** (www.kaerntencard.at; 1-/2-week card €47/59) gives free or cheaper access to the province's major sights and a 50% discount on buses and trains. It's sold at hotels and tourist offices from April to late October.

KLAGENFURT

0463 / POP 99,800

Klagenfurt is an enjoyable, vibrant and sunny city with a compact Innere Stadt (inner city). While it may not be up there with Vienna or Graz in terms of urban lifestyle, it offers easy access to lakeside villages on and around the beautiful Wörthersee.

At the city's western limit is the wide green space of Europapark, along with Austria's largest bathing complex. It's a surprisingly lively place, both as a playground for partiers in summer and as a university town the rest of the year. Transport links also make it the best base for exploring the whole of Carinthia.

Sights & Activities

★Europapark — PARK

(Map p274;) The green expanse and its *Strandbad* (beach) on the shores of the Wörthersee are centres for aquatic fun and are especially great for kids. The park's biggest draw is **Minimundus** (Map p274; www.minimundus.at; Villacher Strasse 241; adult/child €19/10; 9am-6pm Apr, Oct & Nov, to 7pm May, Jun & Sep, to 10pm Jul & Aug; P), a 'miniature world' with around 140 replicas of the world's architectural icons, downsized to a scale of 1:25. To get here, take bus 10, 11, 12 or 22 from Heiligengeistplatz.

Eboard Museum — MUSEUM

(0699 1914 4180; www.eboardmuseum.com; Florian Gröger Strasse 20; adult/family €10/20; 2-7pm Sun-Fri, call ahead Sat; P) With the largest collection of keyboard instruments in Europe (more than 1300), this quirky museum is literally a 'fingers-on' experience: you are able to play most of the organs, including rare items such as a Model A Hammond from 1934. Live bands perform on Friday nights (except in July and August) at 8pm (cover charge €5 to €10).

Dragon Fountain — MONUMENT

(Map p272; Neuer Platz) Neuer Platz, Klagenfurt's central square, is dominated by the 16th-century Dragon Fountain, the emblem of the city and one of Central Europe's oddest urban sculptures. The blank-eyed, wriggling statue is modelled on the *Lindwurm* (dragon) of legend, which is said to have resided in a swamp here long ago, devouring cattle and virgins.

It has a curly, pig-like tail and spews water instead of fire.

Dom — CATHEDRAL

(Map p272; Domplatz 1; dawn-dusk) Klagenfurt's single-nave cathedral doesn't look like much from the outside, but inside it has an ornate marble pulpit and sugary pink-and-white stucco covering every other surface. The artistic highlight is an altar painting in the chapel by Paul Troger dedicated to St Ignatius. It's on the right as you look towards the altar.

Stadtgalerie — GALLERY

(Map p272; www.stadtgalerie.net; Theatergasse 4; adult/child €6/1; 10am-6pm Tue-Sun) A thoughtfully curated program of modern and contemporary international and Austrian artists is shown at the Carinthian state gallery, which has its main venue here on Theaterstrasse, plus a second location nearby in the **Alpen-Adria-Galerie im Stadthaus** (Map p272; Theaterplatz 3; adult/child €2.50/0.50).

MMKK — GALLERY

(Museum für Moderne Kunst Kärnten; Map p272; www.mmkk.at; Burggasse 8; adult/child €5/free; 10am-6pm Tue, Wed, Fri-Sun, to 8pm Thu) This gallery for modern and contemporary art stages three or four excellent temporary exhibitions a year based on its collection of Carinthian and mostly Austrian artists, including the likes of Arnulf Rainer and Hans Staudacher.

Stadthauptpfarrkirche St Egid — CHURCH

(Map p272; Pfarrplatz; church free, tower adult/child €4/2; tower 11am-2pm & 3-6pm Tue-Fri, 10am-2pm Sat Easter–mid-Sep) Climb the 225 steps of this baroque church's 90m-high tower for a bird's-eye view of town and the surrounding mountains. Down in the church there are some impressive trompe l'oeil frescoes.

Klagenfurt

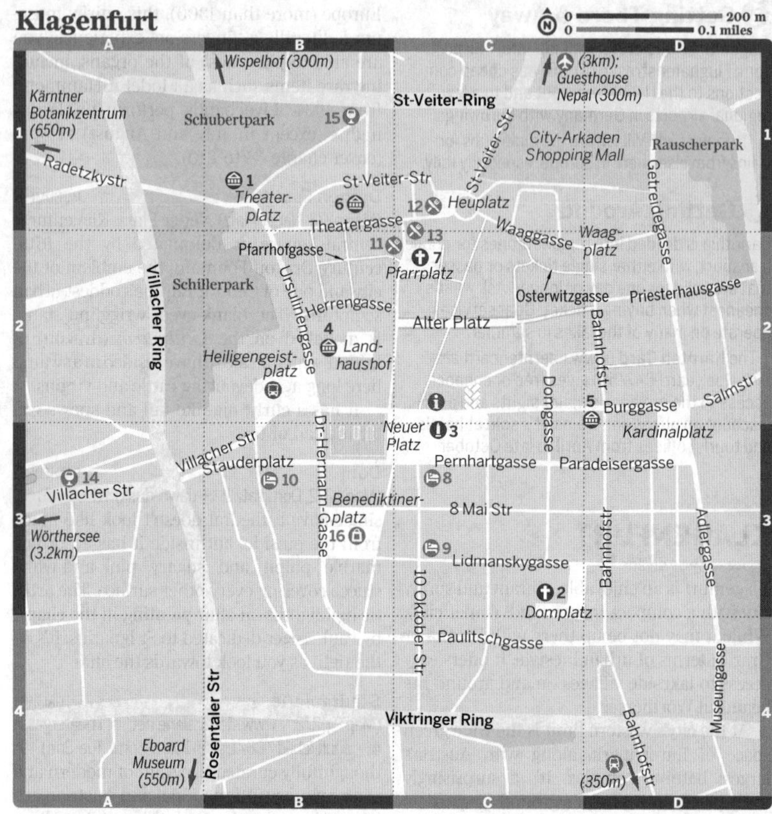

Klagenfurt

Sights
1 Alpen-Adria-Galerie im Stadthaus B1
2 Dom C3
3 Dragon Fountain C3
4 Landhaus B2
5 MMKK D2
6 Stadtgalerie B1
7 Stadthauptpfarrkirche St Egid C2

Sleeping
8 Hotel Palais Porcia C3
9 Lemon 7 .... C3
10 Sandwirth B3

Eating
11 Bierhaus zum Augustin B2
12 Dolce Vita C1
13 Princs C2

Drinking & Nightlife
14 Lendhafencafe A3
15 Park Haus Cafe B1

Shopping
16 Benediktinermarkt B3

Kärntner Botanikzentrum GARDENS
(www.landesmuseum.ktn.gv.at; Prof-Dr-Kahler-Platz 1; 10am-6pm daily May-Sep, to 4pm Mon-Thu Oct-Apr) FREE This small botanical garden is especially popular for its evocative landscape of small cliffs with alpine plants, and for another section with a waterfall and ponds. Adjoining it is the **Kreuzberglkirche**, perched on a hillock with pretty mosaics of the Stations of the Cross on the path leading up to it. Take bus 60 or 61 from Heiligengeistplatz to Kreuzbergl.

Landhaus HISTORIC BUILDING
(Map p272; www.landesmuseum.ktn.gv.at; Landhaushof 1; adult/child €4/2; 9am-4pm Mon-Fri, to 2pm Sat Apr-Oct, closed Mon Nov-Mar) The Renaissance *Landhaus* (state parliament) dates from the late 16th century and is still the

centre of political power today. The stairs on the right (facing the portico) lead up to the **Grosser Wappensaal** (Heraldic Hall), with its magnificent trompe l'oeil gallery painted by Carinthian artist Josef Ferdinand Fromiller (1693–1760).

Pilgrimage Church CHURCH
(Domplatz 1, Maria Saal; ⏲dawn-dusk) Maria Saal, a small town perched on a fortified hill 10km north of Klagenfurt, is worth the 10-minute bus journey to see its early-15th-century pilgrimage church. It was built from volcanic stone, some of it filched from a nearby Roman ruin. Although originally Gothic, it has Romanesque and baroque modifications.

★**Strandbad Klagenfurt** SWIMMING
(Map p274; www.stw.at; Metnitzstrand 2; adult/child €5/2; ⏲8am-8pm Jun-Aug, to 7pm May & Sep; 👪) Klagenfurt's wonderful lakeside beach is the largest complex of its kind in Europe and has cabins, restaurants and piers for basking like a seal. *Kästchen* (lockers large enough for day packs) cost €2, plus €20 deposit. There's good swimming outside the buoys further south, past the relaxed Maria Loretto beach. You can also indulge in paddle or electric boat escapades. Admission drops to €3.50 after 3pm.

Festivals & Events

Wörthersee Classics Festival MUSIC
(www.woertherseeclassics.com; ⏲mid-Jun) Five world-famous composers, each of whom grew up during the latter years of the Austrian empire, also lived and worked at some point on Wörthersee: Gustav Mahler, Alban Berg and Anton von Webern from Vienna, the adopted Viennese Johannes Brahms from Hamburg, and Hugo Wolf. All are celebrated in this annual four-day festival.

Sleeping

★**Camping Klagenfurt am Wörthersee** CAMPGROUND €
(Map p274; ☎0463-28 78 10; www.camping-woerthersee.at; Metnitzstrand 5; campsite per adult/child/tent €10.90/5.90/11.90; ⏲Apr-Sep; P 📶 🏊) This attractive, shady and well-organised camping ground offers free use of the *Strandbad* (a really good deal) and has bike rental. Rates drop considerably in April, May and September. Book ahead in July and August.

Guesthouse Nepal GUESTHOUSE €
(☎680-213 4518; Krassniggstrasse 29; s/d €40/80; P 📶) As close as Klagenfurt gets to a backpacker hostel, this three-room guesthouse occupying a large apartment is a clean, cheap and comfortable place to stay. There's a fully equipped kitchen and a guest lounge with a large terrace providing sunset views of the Alps. It's a short walk north of the city centre.

Jugendgästehaus Klagenfurt HOSTEL €
(Map p274; ☎0463-23 00 20; www.oejhv.or.at; Neckheimgasse 6; dm/s/d €24/32/52; P @ 📶) The modern HI hostel is near Europapark, a great location in summer. To get here from the centre, take bus 81 from the train station or 10 from Heiligengeistplatz and get off at Jugendgästehaus or Neckheimgasse.

Lemon 7 HOTEL €
(Map p272; ☎0463-577 93; 10 Oktober Strasse 11; dm/s/d €27/55/80; 📶) Arranged around a plant-filled vaulted atrium in a 400-year-old building, the freshly renovated rooms are simple and modern, and their wooden, almost ecclesiastical furnishings add warmth and character. A good budget find.

Sandwirth HOTEL €€
(Map p272; ☎0463-562 09; www.sandwirth.at; Pernhartgasse 9; s/d/apt from €79/95/190; P ❄ 📶) Sitting comfortably in Klagenfurt's *Altstadt* (old town) since 1735, this butter-yellow hotel extends a warm welcome. The parquet-floored rooms are crisp, bright and modern, with more spacious apartments ideal for families. Breakfast costs an extra €16 and is worth it, with the likes of smoked salmon, pastries and even Prosecco. There's also a rooftop gym and spa area with infrared heat chairs.

Hotel Palais Porcia HOTEL €€
(Map p272; ☎0463-511 59 00; www.palais-porcia.at; Neuer Platz 13; s/d €125/150; P ❄ 📶) This ridiculously ornate and old-fashioned hotel takes it to town with gilt, mirrors and red-velvet couches, and then a bit further with pink marble and gold taps in the bathrooms. It also has a private beach that guests can use, close to its other hotel in Pörtschach.

Eating

★**Restaurant Maria Loretto** AUSTRIAN €€
(Map p274; ☎0463-244 65; www.restaurant-maria-loretto.at; Lorettoweg 54; mains €18-28; ⏲10am-midnight Wed-Mon; 📶) Situated on a headland above Wörthersee, this restaurant near the *Strandbad* has bags of lakeside character and is generally regarded by locals as one of the town's best. It does good trout and fish grills, though don't expect Mediterranean lightness of touch, as dishes come with a solid Austrian richness. Reserve for an outside table.

Europapark Vicinity

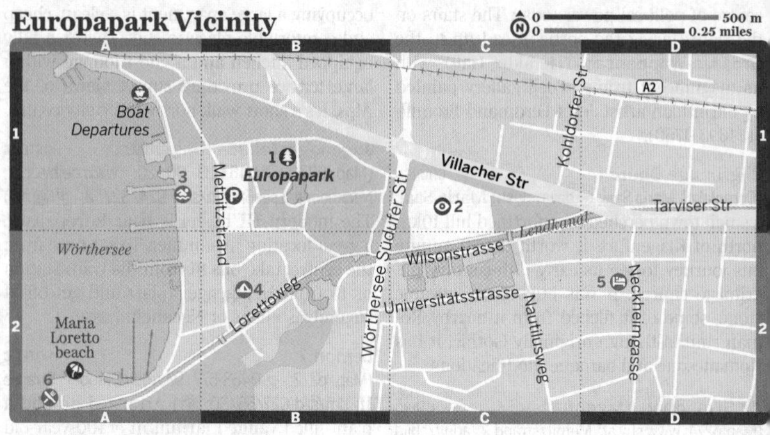

Europapark Vicinity

Top Sights
1 Europapark B1

Sights
2 Minimundus C1

Activities, Courses & Tours
3 Strandbad Klagenfurt A1

Sleeping
4 Camping Klagenfurt am Wörthersee B2
5 Jugendgästehaus Klagenfurt D2

Eating
6 Restaurant Maria Loretto A2

★Princs INTERNATIONAL €€
(Map p272; ☎0676 470 06 76; www.princs.com; Heuplatz 1; mains €8-25, pizza €7-12; ⊙8.30am-midnight Mon-Thu, to 1am Fri & Sat; 📶) The always lively kitchen here sends out endless pizzas, plates of pasta and a large menu of 'street food'. The bar is also one of Klagenfurt's most popular and DJs play on weekends. You can take away pizza or pasta from €8.

Wispelhof AUSTRIAN €€
(☎0463-553 98; www.wispelhof.at; Feldkirchnerstrasse 29; mains €16-34; ⊙11am-11pm Tue-Sat; 📶) This pared-back rustic dining room is beautifully stylish and is the perfect backdrop for a menu of Carinthian favourites – confit venison, fried liver and baked calf's head – along with Austrian standards and some nice Italian plates. The produce is usually from local farmers, and it has the best beef tartare in town.

Bierhaus zum Augustin PUB FOOD €€
(Map p272; www.gut-essen-trinken.at; Pfarrhofgasse 2; mains €9-17.50; ⊙11am-midnight Mon-Sat; 📶) This beer hall, part of a local chain, is one of Klagenfurt's liveliest haunts for imbibers, with a particularly warm traditional-pub atmosphere. There's a cobbled courtyard at the back for alfresco eating. The menu is as Carinthian as can be, with bar snacks of rye spread with a spicy meat paste, the delightful 'beer sandwich' and a trio of beef, brawn and aspic.

Dolce Vita ITALIAN €€
(Map p272; ☎0664 554 99; www.dolce-vita.at; Heuplatz 2; lunch dishes €14-28, mains €21-28, 4-/6-course menu €59-79; ⊙11.30am-3pm & 6pm-midnight Mon-Fri; 📶) In a region strongly influenced by northern Italian cuisine, this restaurant-*bistretto* is something of a local flagship. It offers an authentic seasonal menu revolving around fresh local produce and game; in summer lighter seafood specials like Venetian *sarde in saor* (sardines in a marinade) and *brodetto* (fish soup) are also served.

Drinking & Nightlife

★Lendhafencafe BAR
(Map p272; Villacher Strasse 18; ⊙9am-1pm & 6pm-midnight Tue-Sat; 📶) The best in a row of cafes and nightspots, this wonderfully rambling bar-cafe has a lovely outlook over the Lend Canal, along with a delightful ivy-clad internal courtyard. You can occasionally chance upon concerts, and things spill out to the pavilion downstairs where there's a range of studenty cultural events and parties.

Park Haus Cafe BAR

(Map p272; www.park-haus.at; St-Veiter-Ring 10; ⌚7.30am-midnight Mon, Tue & Thu, to 2am Fri, 6pm-2am Sat) An all-day hang-out for Klagenfurt's young and interesting, with sofas inside and a sunny terrace overlooking the park outside. While its by-day persona is very relaxed, at night it's party time, with DJs and other events.

Shopping

★ **Benediktinermarkt** MARKET

(Fruit & Vegetable Market; Map p272; Benediktinerplatz; ⌚6.30am-1pm Thu & Sat) On Thursday and Saturday mornings head here for a feast of local cheeses, salamis, fruit and veg at this superb market. Around the edges are other stalls selling baskets, secondhand knick-knacks, flowers and seedlings. During the rest of the week there are permanent restaurant stalls – some of Klagenfurt's best quick lunch spots.

Information

Tourist Office (☎0463-28 74 63; www.visitklagenfurt.at; Neuer Platz 5; ⌚9am-6pm Mon-Fri, to 5pm Sat, 10am-3pm Sun Jul, Aug & Dec, 9am-5pm Mon-Fri, 10am-4pm Sat rest of the year) Sells Kärnten cards and can book accommodation.

Getting There & Away

AIR

Klagenfurt's Kärnten Airport (p271) is 3km north of town. Eurowings flies from here to a number of destinations including Heathrow in the UK and Cologne Bonn in Germany, while easyJet flies to London Gatwick.

BOAT

The departure point for boat cruises on the lake is a few hundred metres north of the *Strandbad*.

BUS

Bus services depart from outside the *Hauptbahnhof* (main train station), and there's a timetable board outside. Direct buses connect Klagenfurt with Graz (€30, two hours).

CAR & MOTORCYCLE

The A2/E66 between Villach and Graz skirts the north of Klagenfurt. **Avis** (☎0463-559 38; www.avis.at; Kärnten Airport; ⌚8am-6.30pm & 8.30-9.30pm Mon-Thu, 8am-9.30pm Fri, 9am-3pm & 5.30-9.30pm Sat, 10am-noon & 5.30-9.30pm Sun) and **Megadrive** (Denzeldrive; ☎050105 4120; www.megadrive.at; Kärnten Airport; ⌚7.30am-6pm Mon-Fri, to noon Sat) are among the car-rental companies at Klagenfurt's airport.

TRAIN

Two direct trains an hour run from Klagenfurt to Vienna (€45, four hours). There are also services to Salzburg (€30, three hours, every two hours) and Graz (€40, 2¾ hours, every two to three hours), with a change at Leoben or Bruck an der Mur. Trains to western Austria, Italy, Slovenia and Germany go via Villach (€7.90, 30 to 40 minutes, two to four per hour).

Getting Around

TO/FROM THE AIRPORT

The airport is a 10-minute walk from the train station Klagenfurt Annabichl, which is served by InnerCity (IC) and S-Bahn trains (€2.80, five minutes). A better option is to take bus 40 or 42 to the *Hauptbahnhof*; these run every 30 minutes to one hour (every two hours on Sunday; €2.20, 30 minutes). A taxi from the airport costs about €13 to the centre of town.

BUS

City buses converge at a special **station** (Heiligengeistplatz) in the city centre. Single bus tickets (which you buy from the driver) cost €1.50 for two or three stops or €2.20 for one hour. Drivers also sell 24-hour passes for €5. You can also buy tickets at the train station and from some hotels. Validate your advance tickets after boarding.

TAXI

Call 311 11, 23 222 or 499 799 for a taxi. A taxi between the Wörthersee and Klagenfurt costs about €10 to €12.

CENTRAL CARINTHIA

Carinthia's central region is wedged between the Saualpe in the east and the Nock Mountains in the northwest. Small, historic villages dot lakelands and alpine slopes: beyond the relatively lively city of Villach, this is a profoundly rural and often very conservative place. Come here to get a taste of the Austrian scenery away from the crowds: the diverse landscape means a base in Villach can have you hiking snowcapped mountains in the morning and stand-up paddleboarding come afternoon.

Villach

☎04242 / POP 59,000

Low-key Villach is a lively and liveable city, long a historically important junction between the Alps and southern Austria. There may be more picturesque cities in the

Central Carinthia

region, however, with the town itself having little in the way of sights.

Like its close neighbour Klagenfurt, half an hour away on the motorway, the Italian influence here is strong. Consider using it as a base for activities and for exploring the region.

Sights

Stadtpfarrkirche St Jakob CHURCH
(Oberer Kirchenplatz 8; dawn-dusk) The Stadtpfarrkirche St Jakob dominates the old town and has frescoes, a stuccoed ceiling and a vast rococo altar in gold leaf, bedecked with fresh flowers. Some of the walls are studded with the ornate memorial plaques of the region's noble families. Climb the adjoining **Stadtpfarrturm** (adult/child €3.50/2.50; 10am-6pm Jul & Aug, to 4.30pm May, Jun, Sep & Oct) for far-reaching view of the town and beyond.

Museum der Stadt Villach MUSEUM
(04242-205 35 00; www.villach.at/museum; Widmanngasse 38; adult/child €4/free; 10am-4.30pm Tue-Sun) This museum covers local history, archaeology and medieval art; it also hosts occasionally interesting special exhibitions.

Relief Von Kärnten MUSEUM
(Peraustrasse 14; adult/child €3.50/2.50; 10am-4.30pm Mon-Sat May-Oct) Relief Von Kärnten is a huge relief model of Carinthia housed in Schillerpark, south of the old town. It covers 182 sq metres and depicts the province at a scale of 1:10,000 (1:5000 vertically, to exaggerate the mountains). New multimedia effects heighten the experience.

St Nikolai-Kirche CHURCH
(www.kath-kirche-kaernten.at; Nikolaigasse 1) The neo-Gothic church of St Nikolai might not have any real medieval cred, but what it lacks in age it makes up for in charm with its rustic Tyrolean interiors and frescoes.

Adler Arena CASTLE
(04242-428 88; www.adlerarena.com; Schlossbergweg, Burgruine Landskron; adult/child €13/6.50; falconry show 11am & 2.30pm May, Jun, Sep & Oct, 11am, 1pm, 3pm & 5.30pm Jul & Aug) Situated between Villach and the Ossiacher See, the castle ruins of Burg Landskron are home to the impressive Adler Arena, where a 40-minute spectacle features falcons. Affenberg, a monkey reserve, is also here. Five to 11 buses (€2.20, nine minutes) leave daily from alongside Villach's train-station stop in St Andrä.

Festivals & Events

Kirchtag MUSIC
(04242-205 66 00; www.villacherkirchtag.at; Aug) On the first Saturday in August, the pedestrian centre is taken over by the Kirchtag, a folk-music festival featuring national and local musicians. Many events begin during the preceding week, culminating on the Saturday.

Sleeping

Jugendherberge HOSTEL €
(04242-563 68; www.hiyou.at; St Martiner Strasse 13a; dm/s/d €24/32/56; P @) Located 1km west of the town centre, off St-Martiner-Weg, Jugendherberge also has sauna facilities and a children's playground.

WORTH A TRIP

DREILÄNDERECK

Walkers and mountain bikers will find much to do in the **Dobratsch** area, in the Villacher Alpen about 12km west of Villach. Just south of here, hiking trails go from the small town of Arnoldstein to the Dreiländereck – literally 'three country corner' – the point where Austria, Italy and Slovenia meet. At 1500m there's an **alpine garden** (☎0664-914 29 53; www.alpengarten-villach.at; adult/child €3/1; ⊙9am-6pm Jun-Aug) with flora from the southern Alps. In winter, Dobratsch is also popular with cross-country skiers.

Hotels and apartment rentals can be found in nearby Arnoldstein or Seltschach, or back in Villach. Staying over the border in Slovenia can add an interesting Slavic aspect to a holiday in the region, and rates here tend to be lower than in Austria.

Buses run to Villacher Alpe Rosstratte in the Naturpark Dobratsch, via the Alpenstrasse and the alpine garden. Frequent trains connect Villach and Arnoldstein (€5, 22 minutes). Check the Alpenstrasse website (www.villacher-alpenstrasse.at) for road closures in bad weather.

★Hotel Mosser HOTEL €€
(☎04242-241 15; www.hotelmosser.at; Bahnhofstrasse 9; s €66-99, d €95-165; P @ ☎) Some rooms in this friendly and efficient historic hotel have angled mirrors above the headboards, others have whirlpools for romantic interludes. Cheaper singles, in contrast, are functional and unremarkable. Obviously not one for the brokenhearted.

Palais 26 HOTEL €€
(☎04242-261 01; www.palais26.at; Hauptplatz 26; s €85-150, d €105-180; P ☎) The corridors of this smart, central and stylishly revamped hotel offer a foretaste of its charms, which include chandeliers and Asian rugs. The wooden furnishings have a light and breezy feel, and the lift and some of the joined doubles make this place ideal for families.

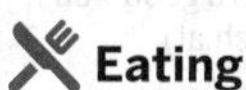

Eating

Villacher Brauhof AUSTRIAN €€
(☎04242-24222; www.villacherbrauhof.at; Bahnhofstrasse 8; mains €6-20; ⊙11am-midnight Mon-Sat, 10am-11pm Sun; ☎) This large brewery pub just across the bridge spanning the Drau is the place to go when you need a fix of Central European beer and meat. With its giant schnitzel, *Speckknödel* (bacon dumplings) and *Schweinebraten* (roast pork), the menu is *echt* Austrian, and there are eight types of draught Villacher beer to choose from.

ℹ Information

Tourismusinformation Villach-Stadt
(☎04242-205 29 10; www.visitvillach.at; Bahnhofstrasse 3; ⊙9am-6pm Mon-Fri, to 1pm Sat; ☎) The city tourist office helps with accommodation, and has a free city map and excellent free city environs map. Pick up a copy of the free walking booklet for a full overview of the town's attractions.

ℹ Getting There & Away

BOAT

Wernberg Bad Boat (www.drau-schiffahrt.at; adult/child €13.50/6.80; ⊙daily departures 11.45am & 2pm) This pleasure boat takes two hours to float from the Congress Center to Wernberg Bad and back again.

BUS

The bus station is in front of the train station.

TRAIN

Villach is situated on three Austrian IC and EuroCity (EC) rail routes, which serve Salzburg (€33, 2½ hours, every two hours), Lienz (€22, 1¾ hours, hourly) and Klagenfurt (€7.90, 30 to 40 minutes, two to four per hour).

Direct services run to many places, including Munich (€80, 4½ hours, four daily) in Germany; Ljubljana (€25, 1¾ hours, four daily) in Slovenia; Zagreb (€45, four hours, four daily) in Croatia; and Belgrade (€85, 11 hours, one daily) in Serbia.

Faaker See & Ossiacher See

One of the biggest attractions when staying in Villach is getting out to two major lakes nearby, both with low-key summer resorts. The Faaker See, situated 6km east of Villach and close to the Karawanken Range, and the Ossiacher See, 4km to the northeast, provide plenty of camping, boating and

Villach

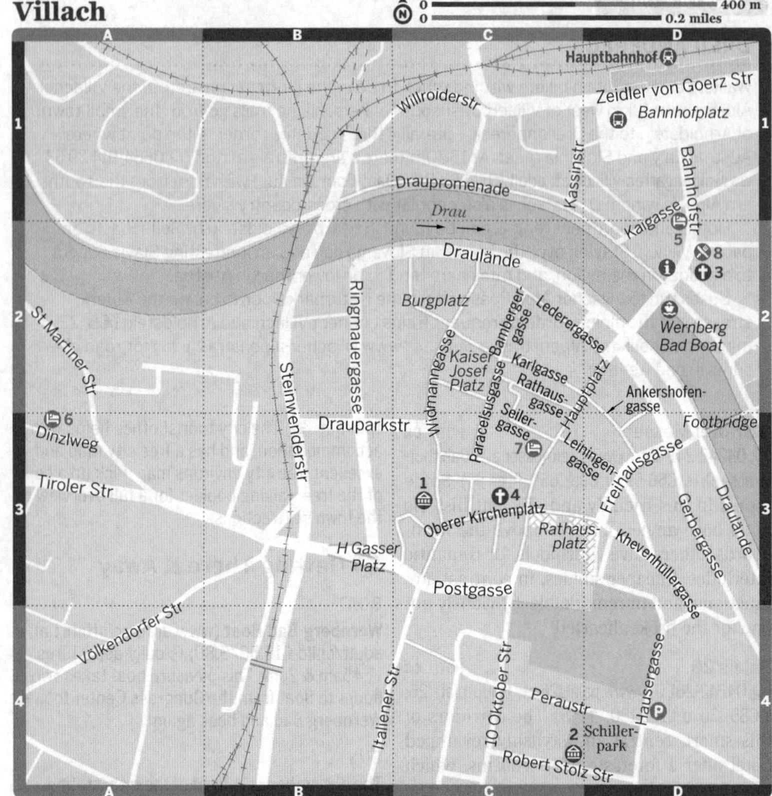

Villach

Sights
1 Museum der Stadt Villach C3
2 Relief Von Kärnten C4
3 St Nikolai-Kirche D2
4 Stadtpfarrkirche St Jakob C3
Stadtpfarrturm .... (see 4)

Sleeping
5 Hotel Mosser D2
6 Jugendherberge A3
7 Palais 26 .... C3

Eating
8 Villacher Brauhof D2

swimming opportunities. Above Annenheim and providing a backdrop to the Ossiacher See is **Gerlitzen** (1909m), a popular ski area. Expect to pay about €40 for a ski pass here.

Information

The regional tourist authority has a good website on the region (www.visitvillach.at).

Getting There & Away

Regular train and Postbus services leave weekdays from the Villach bus station and train station, running along the northern shore of Ossiacher See via Annenheim (€2.20, 12 minutes) and Bodensdorf (€4, 20 minutes). Regular trains run to Faak am See (€3.70, 30 minutes), and regular buses run to Drobollach (€2.20, 20 minutes), both on the Faaker See.

Getting Around

BICYCLE

You can explore the region by bicycle; these can be hired from train stations in Villach, Bodensdorf (Ossiacher See) and Faak (Faaker See). Hotels and campgrounds in the region hire them out, too.

BOAT

On the Ossiacher See, **Ossiachersee Schifffahrt boats** (☎ 0699-15 077 077; www.ossiachersee-schiffahrt.at; day ticket adult/child €14.90/7.50; ⏲ up to 8 services daily Apr-Oct) run by Drau Fluss Schiffahrt complete a 2½-hour criss-cross circuit between St Andrä and Steindorf. Boats run by the same company also navigate the Drau River from Villach Congress Center to Wernberg Bad (one way adult/child €10/4, 45 minutes) via St Niklas an der Drau (about 2km northeast of the Faaker See) up to four times a day between early May and mid-October.

Hermagor

☎ 04282 / POP 7000

Situated around 50km to the west of Villach, little Hermagor is popular as a base for skiing in the nearby **Nassfeld** ski slopes, where you can slither down over 100km of pistes and explore cross-country skiing trails and snowboarding runs. In summer it morphs into a quiet spot for hikers and mountain bikers. Hermagor is also the starting point for hiking the dramatic **Garnitzenklamm**, a narrow gorge some 2.5km west of town. Ask at the tourist office for advice.

Mountain bikers should pick up a copy of *The Best Bicycle & Bike Tours* from the tourist office in Hermagor, which gives an overview of trails, including an 11.7km downhill trail from the top of the Millennium-Express cable car to the Gmanberg station. Bikes are carried free of charge but can also be hired at the valley station.

Millennium-Express Cable Car CABLE CAR
(www.nassfeld.at; adult/child return €18/9) The Millennium-Express cable car climbs 6km up to Nassfeld, making it Austria's longest. The valley station is in Tröpolach, 8km west of Hermagor along the B111 and then B90; it can also be reached by train.

Villa Blumegg PENSION €€
(☎ 04282-20 92; www.villa-blumegg.at; Neupriessenegg 2; s €57-66, d €94-114, apt €141-224; P 📶) Filling a typical alpine property about 10 minutes' walk north of town along Radniger Strasse, this pension offers well-priced, comfortable rooms with and without balconies. There are also holiday apartments accommodating one to seven people.

ℹ Information

The **tourist office** (☎ 04285-82 41; www.nassfeld.at; Göseringlände 7; ⏲ 8am-5pm Mon-Fri, 9am-1pm Sat) is about 400m west of the train station on the B111. It has well-informed staff with information on skiing, guided and unguided hiking, alpine huts and mountain biking in the area.

ℹ Getting There & Away

Trains run to Hermagor from Villach (€10, 70 minutes) every one to two hours.

EASTERN CARINTHIA

Eastern Carinthia's prettiest medieval towns and most impressive castles lie north of Klagenfurt, on or close to Road 83 and the rail route between Klagenfurt and Bruck an der Mur. There are mountain ranges on either side: the Seetaler Alpen and Saualpe to the east and the Gurktaler Alpen to the west.

Friesach

☎ 04268 / POP 5000

Once a key staging post on the Vienna–Venice trade route, Friesach is Carinthia's oldest town. The hills on either side of town bristle with ruined fortifications, and the centre is surrounded by a moat (it's the only town in Austria that still has one) and a set of imposing, grey-stone walls. Once a year Friesach's gates are locked, everyone in town dresses up in medieval costumes and Friesach re-enacts its history.

Friesach has four medieval fortress ruins set along the hills rising above Hauptplatz to the west, all offering excellent views (and all free). The northernmost is **Burg Geyersberg**; the furthest south are the **Virgilienberg** ruins. The middle two (**Rotturm** and **Petersberg**) are the most easily visited from the centre and there are lovely views from Peterskirche.

All the fortresses are connected by the Burgwanderweg (walking trail) that winds through the bucolic landscape with views over town.

St Bartholomew Church CHURCH
(Sankt Bartholomäuskirche, Stadtpfarrkirche; Kirchgasse; ⏲ dawn-dusk) St Bartholomew's is a

towering 10th-century Gothic church that boasts some striking Romanesque elements, most notably the two almost-symmetrical towers.

Peterskirche CHURCH
(⌚11am-5pm Tue-Sun May-Sep) Parts of this pretty village church date back to the 13th century. It has unusually modest interiors that mix Gothic and later elements. The Peterskirche is accessible by paths ascending from the front of the Gothic St Bartholomew Church.

Spectaculum CULTURAL
(www.spectaculum-friesach.at; ⌚late Jul) On the last Saturday in July, electric lights are extinguished and the town is closed off and lit by torches and flares as jesters, princesses and knights stroll around juggling, fire-eating and staging jousting tournaments and duels. Friesach reverts to the currency that made it famous, with medieval meals from street stalls being paid for with Friesach pennies.

Petersberg Fortress Open-Air Theatre THEATRE
(www.burghofspiele.com; ⌚late Jun–mid-Aug) Petersberg Fortress is the site for open-air theatre in summer, where performances range from Shakespeare to Brecht. Obtain details and tickets from the Friesach tourist office.

Metnitztalerhof HOTEL €€
(☎04268-251 00; www.metnitztalerhof.at; Hauptplatz 11; d from €120; P 📶) This pastel-pink edifice at one end of the town's main square is the only four-star hotel in Friesach. The rooms are up to date, comfortable and have small balconies. There's a sauna, Jacuzzi and steam room on-site, plus a restaurant that serves Austrian and Carinthian specialities.

Cafe Konditorei Craigher CAFE €
(☎04268-2295; www.craigher.at; Hauptplatz 3; snacks from €2.50; ⌚7am-6.30pm Mon-Sat, 10am-6pm Sun; 📶) Connoisseurs of chocolate will love dipping into this place – all of their chocolate is made on the premises. Or come for some coffee and cake in the 100-year-old *Kaffeehaus* (coffee house).

ℹ Information

Tourist Office (☎04268-22 13 40; www.kaernten-mitte.at; Fürstenhofplatz 1; ⌚8am-4pm Mon-Fri, 10am-3pm Sat & Sun Jun-Sep, closed weekends Oct-May) Located a couple of minutes' walk north of Hauptplatz.

ℹ Getting There & Away

Friesach has direct train connections with Vienna Meidling (€50, 3¼ hours, three daily), Villach (€15.80, 1½ hours, hourly), St Veit (€8.10, 30 minutes, hourly) and Klagenfurt (€11.30, 50 minutes, hourly).

Gurk

☎04266 / POP 1220

This small town (Krka in Slovenian), some 18km west of the Friesach–Klagenfurt road, is famous for its former Dom (cathedral), built in the 12th century. The frescoes in the Bischofskapelle (dating from around 1200) are all the more beautiful for the use of raw colours. The church is a popular day-trip destination for history buffs.

Dom zu Gurk CATHEDRAL
(www.dom-zu-gurk.at; Domplatz 11; tours €5.50-9, crypt entry €2; ⌚9am-6pm, Sun service 10-10.45am, 90min tours 11am & 2.30pm) With its harmonious pillared crypt, the Dom (built between 1140 and 1200) is Austria's foremost church from the Romanesque epoch. Inside you will also find Gothic, baroque and rococo elements. The early-baroque high altar has 72 statues and 82 angel heads. The 90-minute tours of the whole building, including the crypt and the **Bischofskapelle** (Episcopal Chapel; ⌚9am-6pm), run twice a day.

ℹ Getting There & Away

Visit on a weekday if using public transport – take the hourly train from Klagenfurt to Treibach-Althofen, which connects with a bus (€12.70, 1¾ hours). Returning to Klagenfurt, the last bus from Gurk leaves at 5.47pm. With your own transport, take federal road 93.

Hüttenberg

☎04263 / POP 1400

Step off the bus in the tiny former mining village of Hüttenberg and you might be forgiven for thinking you've stumbled into Tibet, for here you'll see fluttering prayer flags rising up the cliff. Hüttenberg is the birthplace of Heinrich Harrer, who famously spent seven years in Tibet and was immortalised by Brad Pitt on screen.

The village's big attractions are the Heinrich Harrer Museum and the Lingkor walkway opposite, but stroll into the centre to see more of this typical alpine community, with its pretty square, church, cafes and guesthouses.

Heinrich Harrer Museum MUSEUM
(☎04263-81 08 20; Bahnhofstrasse 12; adult/child €12/8; ⏱10am-5pm May-Oct; 🅿) One of Carinthia's most fascinating attractions is the Heinrich Harrer Museum, a former school now packed with items shipped back from Harrer's expeditions to various corners of the world. For anyone inspired to take to the road by the book and Brad Pitt film *Seven Years in Tibet* it's an unmissable place, with an entire section devoted to Harrer himself.

Lingkor BUDDHIST MONUMENT
(Bahnhofstrasse; €2; ⏱24hr May-Oct) Insert a €2 coin into the turnstile set in a stupa to access this Buddhist walkway that climbs high above serene Hüttenberg. The metal staircases cling to the side of a sheer cliff (it's not for vertigo sufferers!) and pass prayer wheels, rock paintings and fluttering prayer flags.

Getting There & Away

To reach Hüttenberg from Klagenfurt, take the 9.04am train to Treibach-Althofen then change to a bus at 10am (€12.70, 80 minutes). To return, there are two afternoon buses to Görtschitztal Vierlinden, from where buses run to Klagenfurt (€11.30, one hour).

St Veit an der Glan

☎04212 / POP 12,600

St Veit was historically important as the seat of the dukes of Carinthia from 1170 until 1518. These days it's a mildly interesting, mid-sized town with a lovely baroque square.

The highlight on the town square is the Gothic *Rathaus* (town hall) from the 15th century, with its magnificent courtyard featuring sgraffito. St Veit's other main attraction is the hotel Kunsthotel Fuchspalast. This surrealist structure was designed by mystical artist Ernst Fuchs, and has blue and red glass tiles in fantastical and astrological designs – a theme that you'll find throughout St Veit's best place to sleep.

Sleeping

Kunsthotel Fuchspalast HOTEL €€
(☎04212-466 00; www.hotel-fuchspalast.at; Prof-Ernst-Fuchs-Platz 1; r per person from €58; 🅿📶) Blue and red glass tiles in amazing, surreal designs decorate this hotel's exterior. Inside, surrealism gives way to fluted columns and jewel-like mosaics, while rooms have a simplicity that hints at art-deco design. There's a sauna and restaurant on-site.

Hotel Taggenbrunn DESIGN HOTEL €€
(☎04212-307 00; www.taggenbrunn.at; Taggenbrunn 9; d from €120; 🅿📶) Some 3km east of St Veit, this design hotel at the new Weingut Taggenbrunn offers 31 wood-rich, grape-themed 21st-century rooms with pretty vineyard views. Rates include breakfast and impromptu wine-tasting sessions at the nearby winery. Welcoming guests to the complex is a huge, quite unusual statue by Austrian artist André Heller.

Eating

★**Taggenbrunn Heuriger** AUSTRIAN €€
(☎04212-30 200; www.taggenbrunn.at; Taggenbrunn 9; mains €6-20; ⏱3-10pm Wed-Fri, 11.30am-10pm Sat & Sun; 📶) The large restaurant at the Weingut Taggenbrunn, around 3km east of town, enjoys a fine setting amid the vineyards that almost brush the outdoor tables. The smart, casual dining room inside the ancient building is a relaxing place to enjoy locally sourced fare such as venison and boar, and of course the winery's own whites and reds.

★**La Torre** ITALIAN €€
(☎04212-392 50; www.latorre.at; Grabenstrasse 39; mains €16-30, 6-course menu €77; ⏱noon-2.30pm & 6-10pm Tue-Sat; 📶) This fantastic Italian restaurant is set in one of the towers of the 14th-century town wall. As well as the smart, romantic interior, there's a beautiful walled garden and terrace, and an Italian owner who exudes bonhomie. The seafood is particularly good here – how it comes so fresh on your plate this far from the sea is a family secret.

Getting There & Away

Trains run to Klagenfurt (€6.10, hourly, 18 minutes), 20km to the south.

Burg Hochosterwitz

This fairy-tale fortress of **Burg Hochosterwitz** (☎04213-2010; www.burg-hochosterwitz.com; Hochosterwitz 1; adult/child incl tour €15/8; ⏱9am-6pm May–mid-Sep, 10am-5pm mid-Sep–Oct) claims to be the inspiration for the castle in *Sleeping Beauty* and drapes itself around the slopes of a hill, with 14 gate towers on the path up to the final bastion. These were built between 1570 and 1586 by its former owner, Georg Khevenhüller, to ward off invading Turks.

A *Burgführer* information booklet (in English; €4) outlines the different challenges presented to attackers by each gate – some have spikes embedded in them, which could be dropped straight through unwary invaders passing underneath. The castle also has a museum featuring the suit of armour of one Burghauptmann Schenk, who measured 225cm at the tender age of 16.

There's a small cafe serving sausages, soup, rolls and coffee at the top. Regional trains on the St Veit–Friesach route stop at Launsdorf Hochosterwitz station, a 3km walk from the car park and the first gate, where a pricey lift (€9) ascends to the castle.

Wörthersee

The beautiful alpine Wörthersee stretches from west to east between Velden and Klagenfurt, and can easily be explored by bicycle on a 50km circuit. The southern shore is the most picturesque, but the northern shore has the best public transport access and is the busiest section.

A trip around the lake takes you past the genteel resort of Pörtschach, the nightlife hub of Velden and the small town of Maria Wörth. Five kilometres south of Velden is Rosegg, with its **Schloss** (☎04274-30 09; www.rosegg.at; Schloss Rosegg 1, Rosegg; adult/child €9/5.50; ⏲10am-6pm Apr-Sep, closed Mon Oct-Apr), and 8km southwest of Maria Wörth is the Aussichtsturm Pyramidenkogel, a hill topped by a 71m tower.

Sights & Activities

Aussichtsturm Pyramidenkogel TOWER

(☎04273-24 43; www.pyramidenkogel.info; Linden 62, Keutschach am See; adult/child €14/6.50, slide ride €4; ⏲9am-9pm Jul & Aug, 9am-8pm Jun, 10am-7pm May & Sep, 10am-6pm Oct, Mar & Apr, 10am-5pm Nov-Feb) On the hill southwest of Maria Wörth is the Pyramidenkogel, a hill topped by a 71m tower made of steel, with wooden beams spiralling up its exterior. This vertiginous tower has three viewing platforms, two of which are open to the elements, with the lowest, called the Sky Box, glass-encased. Climb the 400 steps, or take the glass panorama lift and return to earth via Europe's longest slide.

The relatively easy St Anna-Weg trail (90 minutes one way) leads here through forest from the street St-Anna-Weg, near the turn-off to the peninsula in Maria Wörth. The Maria Wörth tourist office can help with directions and maps. If driving, the turn-off is at Reifnitz.

Strand Club WATER SPORTS

(☎04274-511 01; www.strandclub.com; Seepromenade 15, Velden; ⏲activities dawn-dusk Apr-Oct, bar 7am-midnight Apr-Oct) Paragliding, waterskiing, wakeboarding and electric boat rental are all offered by the lakeside Strand Club; prices include wetsuit hire and are detailed on the website. You can relax afterwards at the bar and adjoining cafe.

Sleeping & Eating

★**Hotel Schloss Leonstain** RESORT €€€

(☎04272-28 16; www.leonstain.at; Leonstainerstrasse 1, Pörtschach; s €79-89, d €180-245) This is Austrian lakeside life at its most delightful, where hugely atmospheric rooms mix modern comfort with rustic antiques. It's totally traditional but has a breezy, holiday feel. The hotel's restaurant uses organic, local produce and the dreamy Bar Leon across the road gives you all-day lake access and more dining options.

★**Bar Leon** MEDITERRANEAN €€

(Leon Beach; ☎04272-28 16; www.leonstain.at; cnr Kärntnerstrasse & Hauptstrasse, Pörtschach; mains €15-26; ⏲8.30am-10pm Apr-Sep; 📶) The private 'beach' club of the grand Hotel Schloss Leonstain is open to nonguests and affords a rare glimpse into the genteel summer pleasures of the Austrian well-to-do. Come for breakfast or lunch in the garden, dinner upstairs in the lantern-lit summer house or loll with a Lillet spritz on the lake deck as swans glide by.

Fish on the menu come from the hotel's own pond. Book ahead for lunch or dinner in high summer.

Information

Tourist offices in **Pörtschach** (☎04272-23 54; www.poertschach.gv.at; Werzerpromenade 1; ⏲9am-6pm Mon-Fri, 10am-6pm Sat, 10am-4pm Sun Jul & Aug, shorter hours rest of year), **Velden** (☎04274-382 88; www.woerthersee.com; Villacher Strasse 19, Velden; ⏲8am-6pm Mon-Sat, 9am-5pm Sun, closed Sun late Oct–mid-Apr) and **Maria Wörth** (☎04273-224 00; www.maria-woerth.info; Seepromenade 5; ⏲8am-5pm Mon-Fri, 10am-2pm Sat & Sun) can help with accommodation, or you can book through the www.woerthersee.com website.

Getting There & Away

Klagenfurt's excellent bus network extends to the Wörthersee resorts. The tourism offices in Klagenfurt or around the lake can help with timetables.

WESTERN CARINTHIA

The main attractions of western Carinthia are Millstatt, with its serene lake, abbey and famous music festival; Spittal an der Drau, with its stately Renaissance palace and floral park; and the remote and beautiful Weissensee.

Gmünd

04732 / POP 2550

Gmünd is an attractive 11th-century village with a delightful walled centre and a 13th-century hilltop castle, Alte Burg. From 1480, Hungarians conducted a seven-year siege of the city, breaking through and partially destroying the castle. Today it's the setting for plays and musical events, as well as two unusual museums.

★ Porsche Museum Helmut Pfeifhofer MUSEUM
(www.auto-museum.at; Riesertratte 4a; adult/child €8/3.50; 9am-6pm mid-May–mid-Oct, 10am-4pm mid-Oct–mid-May) A slightly unexpected story in Gmünd is told by the Porsche Museum Helmut Pfeifhofer. A Porsche factory operated here from 1944 to 1950 and the first car to bear the famous name (a 356) was handmade here. One of these models is on display (only 52 were built), together with about 15 other models and a couple of the wooden frames used in their construction. There's a 15-minute film (in German and English) on Dr Porsche's life and work.

Pankratium MUSEUM
(04732-311 44; www.pankratium.at; Hintere Gasse 60; 1hr tour adult/child €9.90/6.50; 10am-5pm May-Oct; P) Gmünd's most atypical attraction is the Pankratium, an extraordinary space bringing together water, light and sound in hands-on pieces designed for the senses. You can bring sound gadgets and all manner of instruments to life on a tour that culminates in bubble-blowing in the yard. It's a sure-fire winner with kids.

Gasthof Kohlmayr GUESTHOUSE €€
(04732-214 90; www.gasthof-kohlmayr.at; Hauptplatz 7; s/d from €52/84; closed Nov; P) The comfortingly old-fashioned Kohlmayr has cosy and affordable rooms in a 400-year-old building right in the heart of Gmünd. The restaurant serves filling local fare and half board is also available.

Information

Tourist Office (04732-22 22; www.familiental.com; Hauptplatz 20; 8am-5pm Mon-Fri, 9am-3pm Sat Jul & Aug, closed Sat Sep-Jun) Has an excellent sheet map of town in English, German and Italian, with sights and galleries numbered and briefly explained.

Getting There & Away

Hourly buses connect Gmünd with Spittal an der Drau (€5, 30 minutes) from Monday to Friday.

Millstatt

04766 / POP 3460

The genteel lakeside village of Millstatt lies 10km east of Spittal an der Drau on the northern shore of the Millstätter See, a lake stretching 12km long and 1.5km wide. It's the second-largest lake in Carinthia. It was gouged out during the ice age about 30,000 years ago, with its warm waters (about 22°C to 26°C in summer) lending themselves to sailing, kayaking and swimming. Millstatt is said to have got its name from a duke named Domitian, an early Christian convert who tossed *mille statuae* – a thousand heathen statues – into the lake from here.

Sights & Activities

Stift Millstatt CHRISTIAN SITE
(www.stiftsmuseum.at; Stiftsgasse 1; adult/child €3.90/2.50; 10am-4pm mid-Jun–Sep) Apart from Lake Millstatt, the town's main attraction is its Romanesque Benedictine abbey, founded in 1070. This pretty complex consists of a moderately interesting **Stiftsmuseum** (Abbey Museum; 0676 360 06 92; tours €6; 10am-4pm May-Oct), the attractive 11th-century **abbey church**, a **graveyard**, and **abbey buildings** south of the church with lovely yards and arcades. If you walk downhill along Stiftsgasse from the church, you'll see on the left a **1000-year-old lime tree**. The abbey grounds and magnificent arcades and cloisters are free.

Surf und Segelschule Millstatt WATER SPORTS
(0676 751 19 39; www.surf-segelschulemillstatt.at; Seestrasse; hire per hour windsurfing board & rig €17-23, kayak €12, sailing boats €12, e-boats €14; 10am-7pm Mon-Fri, noon-7pm Sat & Sun Jul & Aug) This professional outfit alongside Villa Verdin rents equipment and holds individual and group windsurfing, sailing and kayak courses.

Festivals & Events

Musikwochen Millstatt MUSIC
(Millstatt Music Weeks; www.musikwochen.com; May-Sep) Brings performances of classical and jazz music every year from May to September; most performances take place in Millstatt's abbey church.

Sleeping & Eating

Pension Strobl PENSION €
(04766-22 63; www.pensionstrobl.at; Seemühlgasse 56a; d €75;) This budget hotel on the lake has watery views from its basic rooms. There's a useful guest kitchen and the owners can point you in the right direction when it comes to messing around on the lake.

★**Hotel See-Villa** HOTEL €€
(04766-2102; www.see-villa-tacoli.com; Seestrasse 68; s/d from €80/160; P) Comfy and welcoming, this turn-of-the-20th-century hotel sports lots of authentic historical charm. It's located right on the shore (perfect for sleeping with windows open), with a huge terrace restaurant (open daily for lunch and dinner), a private sauna and a swimming jetty.

★**Villa Verdin** HOTEL €€
(0699 1202 9862; www.villaverdin.at; Seestrasse 69; s/d from €55/110; P) This converted 19th-century villa-hotel mixes contemporary design style with antiques and interesting junk to create a comfortable, informal, yet stylish atmosphere. It's gay-friendly and has a retro beach cafe.

Die Forelle HOTEL €€€
(04766-205 00; www.hotel-forelle.at; Fischergasse 65; s €80-115, d €190-220, 2-6-person apt per person €70; P @) Some guests like its lakeside bar, others gravitate towards this large hotel for its wellness facilities, including the whirlpool and baths. Rooms are well sized, and the more expensive doubles have a balcony overlooking the lake. Its midpriced restaurant opens for lunch and dinner, and offers a reduced menu between meal times, and half board (€25 extra).

★**Fisch-Häusl Stark** SEAFOOD €€
(Kaiser-Franz-Josef-Strasse 134; mains €17-22; 11am-midnight Jun-Sep) This small place serves delicious fish straight from the Millstätter See and the Weissensee, including smoked trout, which the owners will pack for a picnic. Grab a bread roll from the bakery across the street.

Drinking & Nightlife

★**Kap 4613** BAR
(www.kap4613.at; Kaiser-Franz-Josef-Strasse 330; 8.30am-9pm Tue-Sun Mar-Dec;) Combining an atrium with a deck area and a beach bar extending over the water for summer sipping, this lakeside spot is easily Millstatt's best drinking venue.

Information

Millstatt Tourist Office (04766-370 0338; www.millstaettersee.com; Kaiser-Franz-Josef-Strasse 49; 9am-6pm Mon-Fri, 10am-noon & 4-6pm Sat & Sun) Located inside Millstatt's *Rathaus*; has useful information on the town.

Getting There & Away

Postbus services to Millstatt depart from outside Spittal train station (€4, 20 minutes, two hourly), with some continuing to Bad Kleinkirchheim (from Spittal €8, one hour).

Getting Around

Mountainbike Station Thomas Graf (0650 356 31 81; www.mountainbike-station.at; Kaiser-Franz-Josef-Strasse 59; mountain/e-bikes per 24hr €22.50/21; 9am-6pm Mon-Fri, to 3pm Sat May–mid-Oct) is the best place to rent bikes.

Spittal an der Drau

04762 / POP 15,900

Spittal is an important economic and administrative centre in upper Carinthia; its name comes from a 12th-century hospital and refuge that once provided succour to weary travellers.

Today it's a town with an impressive Italianate palace at its centre and a small but attractive park with splashing fountains and bright flower beds. Most travellers stop here for a couple of hours on the way elsewhere.

Sights

Schloss Porcia & Museum für Volkskultur PALACE
(Local Heritage Museum; 04762-28 90; www.museum-spittal.com; Burgplatz 1; adult/child €8/4; 9am-6pm mid-Apr–Oct, 1-4pm Mon-Thu Nov–mid-Apr) Boasting an eye-catching Renaissance edifice, Schloss Porcia was built between 1533 and 1597 by the fabulously named Graf von Salamanca-Ortenburg. Inside, Italianate arcades run around a

central courtyard used for summer theatre performances. The top floors contain the enormous Local Heritage Museum, which has lots of displays about Carinthia and 3D projections, such as a virtual navigation through the Hohe Tauern National Park.

Goldeck MOUNTAIN
(cable car one way/return €13/18, lift pass adult/child €36/18) In the summer months this peak (2142m) can be accessed either by cable car or the Goldeckstrasse toll road (€13; free with the Kärnten Card). The road stops 260m short of the summit. In winter, Goldeck is popular for skiing. The cable car doesn't operate from mid-April to mid-June or from mid-September to mid-December.

Sleeping

Draufluss Camping CAMPGROUND €
(04762-24 66; www.drauwirt.com; Schwaig 10; campsite per adult/child/tent/car €8/3/4/4; Jun-Sep; P) Spittal's small, cosy campground is about 3.5km from the town centre on the southern bank of the Drau River.

★ **Hotel Erlebnis Post** HOTEL €€
(04762-22 17; www.erlebnis-post.at; Hauptplatz 13; s/d from €77/128; P) This rather odd hotel has some vaguely themed rooms, unusual for Carinthia. There's the Patchwork room, the Pillow Fight room, or you might like to spend the night in the Jailhouse, which features beds from the local juvenile prison and an original cell door. Bonuses are the ski-storage room and transfers to the pistes.

Eating

★ **Restaurant Zellot** AUSTRIAN €€
(04762-21 13; Hauptplatz 12; mains €11-19; 11.30am-2pm & 5.30-9pm Mon-Sat;) This slightly eccentric restaurant does a decent steak and Austrian staples. Later in the evening it turns into a club and live venue, with part of the place decked out like a garage – its features become even more intriguing after your second drink.

Information

Tourist Office (04762-5650 223; www.spittal-drau.at; Burgplatz 1; 9am-6pm Mon-Fri, to noon Sat Jul-Sep, shorter hours & closed Sat rest of the year) On one side of Schloss Porcia, with maps and lots of useful information.

AUTOSCHLEUSE TAUERNBAHN

If you're driving to Bad Gastein from Spittal an der Drau, you'll need to use the **Autoschleuse Tauernbahn** (Railway Car Shuttle Service; www.gasteinertal.com/autoschleuse) through the tunnel from Mallnitz to Böckstein. The fare for cars is €17 one way or €30 return (valid for two months). For information, call 05 717. Departures are every 60 minutes, with the last train departing at 11.20pm heading south, and 10.50pm going north. The journey takes 11 minutes.

Getting There & Away

BUS

Postbus services run to Gmünd (€5, 24 minutes, hourly) and Millstatt (€3.90, 20 minutes, hourly).

TRAIN

Spittal-Millstättersee is an important rail junction: two-hourly IC/EC services run north to Bad Gastein (€11.60, 36 minutes); at least hourly regional services run west to Lienz (€12.70, one hour) and to Villach (€8.10, 25 minutes), 37km to the southeast. The railway line north via Mallnitz-Obervellach clings spectacularly to the valley walls.

Getting Around

More (04762-255 50; www.more-der-spezialist.at; Bahnhofstrasse 11; 8am-12.30pm & 2-6pm Mon-Fri, from 8.45am Sat) rents city and mountain bikes. Pick up the tourist office's free city/regional map, which has paths marked.

Weissensee

Wedged within a glacial cleft in the Gailtal Alps with mountain ridges flanking its northern and southern shores, Weissensee is Austria's highest swimmable glacial lake, the least developed of Carinthia's large lakes, and a spectacular and peaceful nature reserve. It stretches as a turquoise-and-deep-blue slither for almost 12km and in most parts is about 1km wide. Because it's at an altitude of 930m, the water is cooler than the Wörthersee, but in July and August you can expect temperatures of above 20°C in most parts.

Bergbahn Weissensee CHAIRLIFT
(04713-22 69; Techendorf; one way adult/child €10.50/6.40; 9am-5pm, closed Mon May, Jun & Sep, closed early Mar–mid-May & early Oct-Nov)

You'll either love the 12-minute ride on this open chairlift or see it as a necessary shortcut to reach the top of Naggler Alm – a 10-minute walk from the top – and the start of good walking trails above Techendorf. In winter it services the ski fields.

Hermagorer Bodenalm FARMSTAY €
(☎0650 400 24 88; www.hermagorer-bodenalm.at; Techendorf 68; per person half board €39; ⊙May-Sep; 📶) Sitting very prettily in an alpine meadow among picturesque mountains on the south side of the Weissensee, this 'hut' has basic rooms with shared bathrooms – bring warm pyjamas. The place makes its own cheese and cured meats to sustain hikers and mountain bikers during the day. This is the Austria you came to see.

It's a walk of about 1½ hours from Paterzipf boat station along Trail 27, also designated for mountain bikes.

Kohlröslhütte FARMSTAY €
(☎0664 8850 1860; www.kohlroesl.at; Jadersdorf 38; per person full board €41; ⊙mid-May–mid-Oct; 📶) Few alpine meadow huts have views like this one: deep into the Gitsch Valley to Sankt Lorenz and the Alps in three countries from an altitude of 1534m. The only way up here, above Techendorf in the Gail Valley Alps, is by foot (two hours from the chairlift mountain station) or mountain bike. Rooms with a shared bathroom are rustic and cosy.

ℹ Information

Tourist Office (☎04713-222 00; www.weissensee.com; Techendorf 78; ⊙8am-6.30pm Mon-Fri, 9am-12.30pm & 4-6pm Sat, 10am-12.30pm & 4-6pm Sun Jul & Aug, shorter hours Jun, Sep & Oct) Can help with options for diving, sailing, canoeing and kayaking, as well as finding accommodation on the lake.

ℹ Getting There & Away

The nearest train station is Greifenburg-Weissensee, 11km from the lake on the Villach–Spittal an der Drau–Lienz line. From here **Mobil Büro Hermagor** (☎reservations 04282-25 225; www.mobilbuero.com; one way €8; ⊙mid-May–late Sep & mid-Dec–Feb) runs a bus service to/from your place of stay on Weissensee. It's for overnight guests only. Book by telephone or online by 4pm the day before. Day guests can buy a day pass (€7.50) but only to Hotel Kreuzwirt, 4km from Techendorf. You can pick up the free but often infrequent Naturpark bus from there.

To reach the lake by car, take Bundestrasse 87 from Greifenburg or Hermagor. From Spittal an der Drau a road (L32) runs to the eastern end of the lake, ending there.

ℹ OSTTIROL CARD

Lienz' best summer deal is the three- or seven-day **Osttirol Card** (adult/child from €55/27.50), which is sold at the tourist office. The card is available from June to mid-September and covers all of Lienz' major sights, including Schloss Bruck and Aguntum, as well as the Galitzenklamm walkway, local swimming pools and cable cars.

ℹ Getting Around

Weissensee Schifffahrt (www.schifffahrt-mueller.at; 1-8 stops €2.50-8.50, day ticket €13.50; ⊙up to 10 services daily mid-May–mid-Oct) runs boats to all stops between Techendorf and Dolomitenblick three to 11 times daily, peaking in July and August.

Lienz

☎04852 / POP 11,900 / ELEV 673M

The Dolomites rise like an amphitheatre around Lienz, which straddles the Isel and Drau Rivers just 40km north of Italy. Those same arresting river and mountain views welcomed the Romans, who settled here some 2000 years ago and whose legacy is explored at medieval castle Schloss Bruck and archaeological site Aguntum. Looking up to the blushing Dolomites at sunset, it's easy to see why they were so taken with this region, which is an exclave of Tyrol.

👁 Sights

Schloss Bruck CASTLE
(www.museum-schlossbruck.at; Schlossberg 1; adult/child €8.50/2.50; ⊙10am-6pm Jul & Aug, to 4pm Tue-Sun Sep & Oct, to 5pm Tue-Sun Jun) Lienz' famous medieval fortress has a museum chronicling the region's history, as well as Roman artefacts, Gothic winged altars and local costumes. The **castle tower** is used for changing exhibitions; a highlight for art enthusiasts is the **Egger-Lienz-Galerie** devoted to the emotive works of Albin Egger-Lienz.

Aguntum MUSEUM, RUINS
(www.aguntum.info; Stribach 97; adult/child €7/4, combined entry with Schloss Bruck €11.50/9.50; ⊙9.30am-4pm Jun-Sep, closed Sun May & Oct; 👪) Excavations are still under way at the Aguntum archaeological site in nearby Dölsach to piece together the jigsaw puzzle of this

Lienz

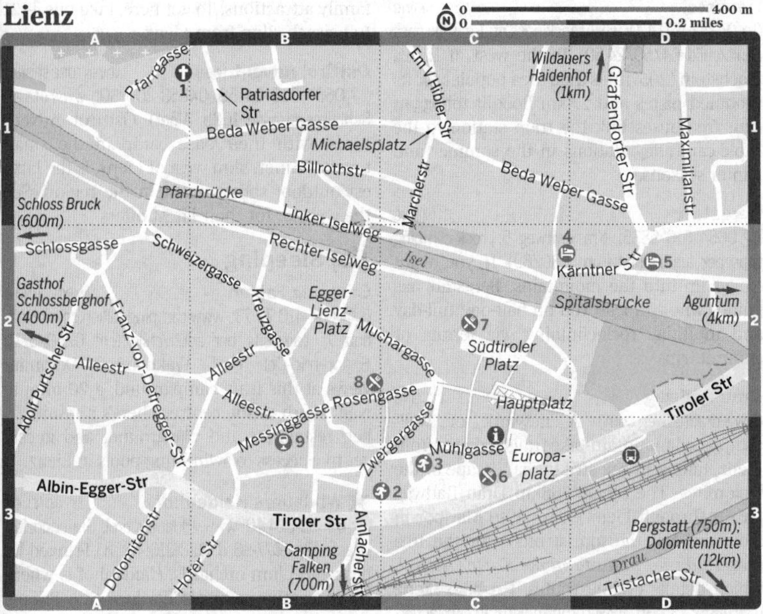

2000-year-old *municipium*, which flourished as a centre of trade and commerce under Emperor Claudius. Take a stroll around the excavations then visit the glass-walled museum to explore Lienz' Roman roots. Bus 4406 runs out here from Monday to Saturday.

Stadtpfarrkirche St Andrä CHURCH

(Pfarrgasse 4; dawn-dusk) The town's main church has an attractive Gothic rib-vaulted ceiling, a startling baroque altar, 14th-century frescoes and a pair of unusual tombstones sculpted in red Salzburg marble. Alongside is the solemn **Kriegergedächtniskapelle** (war memorial chapel) sheltering Albin Egger-Lienz' controversial frescoes, one depicting an emaciated Jesus postresurrection, which in 1925 so scandalised the Vatican that religious activity was banned here for the next 60-odd years. Pick up the keys hanging on the door at Pfarrgasse 13 (across the bridge behind the Kirchenwirt restaurant).

Activities

Zimml ADVENTURE SPORTS

(04852-611 99; www.zimml.at; Mühlgasse 15) The team at Zimml can organise everything from canyoning, kayaking and climbing in summer to ski touring, snowshoeing and ice-climbing in winter. Call for times and prices.

Lienz

Sights

1 Stadtpfarrkirche St Andrä A1

Activities, Courses & Tours

2 Probike Lienz C3
3 Zimml C3

Sleeping

4 Goldener Fisch C2
5 Grand Hotel Lienz D2

Eating

6 Da Leonardo C3
7 Garage C2
8 Gösser Bräu im Alten Rathaus B2

Drinking & Nightlife

9 Weinphilo B3

Zettersfeld SKIING

(www.topskipass.at; 1-day ski pass adult/child €47.50/24.50) Beginner and intermediate skiers should find enough of a challenge on Lienz' 40km of pistes, which afford seductive views of the rugged Dolomites. Most of the action takes place around Zettersfeld, located northeast of Lienz. A cable car and six lifts take skiers up to slopes reaching between 1660m and 2278m. Free buses link the Lienz train station to the cable-car valley stations.

Hochstein SKIING
(☎04242-570 470; www.topskipass.at; 1-day ski pass adult/child €47.50/24.50) To the west of Lienz, Hochstein (2057m) is a ski area popular for its groomed pistes and 2.5km floodlit toboggan run; free buses link the train station to the cable-car valley stations in the summer and winter seasons.

Bergstatt CLIMBING
(☎0664 516 5835; Kranewitweg 5; rock-climbing trips per adult/child from €80/60) If you want to get up into the mountains, Bergstatt has guides who can lead you on half-day, full-day and multiday rock-climbing, via ferrata or summit trips.

Drau Radweg CYCLING
(www.drauradweg.com) A network of well-signposted mountain-bike trails radiates from Lienz, taking in the striking landscape of the Dolomites. The scenic 366km Drau Radweg passes through Lienz en route to Maribor in Slovenia. Ask the tourist office for the free map *Rad und Mountainbike Karte Osttirol,* which details cycling routes. **Probike Lienz** (☎04852-735 36; www.probike-lienz.at; Amlacherstrasse 1a; per day mountain bike €22, city bike €18, e-bike €40; ⏲9am-noon & 2-6pm Mon-Fri, 9am-12.30pm Sat) is the most central place to hire your own bike.

Galitzenklamm ADVENTURE SPORTS
(www.galitzenklamm.info; adult/child €5/4; ⏲9am-6pm mid-Jun–mid-Sep, 10am-5pm mid-Sep–late Sep; 👪) This vertiginous walkway clings to the sheer cliffs of a gorge that rises above the swirling waters of the Drau River. There's also a water playground for kids and other family attractions. To get here, take bus 4421 to Leisach, 3km from Lienz.

Osttirol Adventures ADVENTURE SPORTS
(☎0664 356 04 50, 04853-200 30; www.ota.at; Schlaitnerstrasse 108b, Ainet) Osttirol Adventures, with their base camp in the small town of Ainet, 8km west of Lienz, is the largest outdoor-sports outfit in the region. See the website for their latest offers.

CABLE CARS & SUMMER PRICES

Cable cars to **Zettersfeld** and **Hochstein** stop from November to 8 December, and pause again after Easter. The Hochstein cable car starts running to the first station, Hochstein 1 (return adult/child €12/9), from Thursday to Sunday from May to mid-June, after which all summer cable cars are back in full swing daily. Hochstein 2 is winter only. The return cost to Zettersfeld per adult/child is €13/7 (or €21/10 including the chairlift to 2214m). If you're planning on making several trips, it's worth investing in the Osttirol Card (adult/child €55/27.50).

Sleeping

Camping Falken CAMPGROUND €
(☎0664 410 79 73; www.camping-falken.com; Eichholz 7; campsite per adult/child/tent €7.50/5/11; ⏲Apr–mid-Oct; P📶) Wake up to Dolomite views at this leafy campground, a 20-minute walk south of the centre. There's a minimarket, restaurant and playground, and guests get free access to swimming pools in Lienz.

★**Wildauers Haidenhof** HOTEL €€
(☎04852-624 40; www.wildauers.tirol; Grafendorferstrasse 12; s €77-96, d €128-216; P📶) Fringed by pear and plum orchards, Haidenhof is where rustic farmhouse meets Tyrolean chic. Rooms have plenty of natural light and stylishly done pine, and there's a sauna and roof terrace with vistas of the Dolomites. Almost everything in the restaurant is grown and produced here. In winter there's a candlelit basement; in summer there's a sunny Dolomites-facing terrace.

Gasthof Schlossberghof HOTEL €€
(☎04852-632 33; www.schlossberghof.at; Iseltaler Strasse 21; s/d €65/100; P) With rooms revamped in a contemporary style, this rustic, chalet-style guesthouse is a 10-minute stroll from the centre and is watched over by the Dolomites.

Goldener Fisch HOTEL €€
(☎04852-621 32; www.goldener-fisch.at; Kärntner Strasse 9; d from €116; P📶) The chestnut-tree-shaded beer garden is a big draw at this family-friendly hotel. The rooms are light and modern, though nothing fancy and sometimes on the small side. After a day on the slopes you can wind down in the sauna and herbal steam baths. Breakfast is a filling set-up for a day of physical activity.

★**Grand Hotel Lienz** HOTEL €€€
(☎04852-640 70; www.grandhotel-lienz.com; Fanny-Wibmer-Peditstrasse 2; s €150-200, d €220-470; P📶🏊) This faux fin-de-siècle hotel is Lienz' most upmarket choice. What it lacks in cool or historical texture, the Grand makes up for in luxury: impeccable service, a first-rate

spa and pool, fine dining on a terrace overlooking the Isel River and Dolomites, nightly turndown and in-room espresso machines.

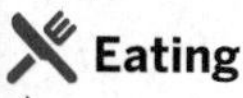

Eating

★Dolomitenhütte AUSTRIAN €€
(☎0664 225 37 82; www.dolomitenhuette.at; Amlach 39; mains €6-18) Clinging to a 1600m clifftop like an eagle's nest and watched over by jagged peaks, the Dolomitenhütte is extraordinary. With the Dolomites and larch woods as a mesmerising backdrop, it's like something out of a fairy tale. In summer, walkers and cyclists make the 12km jaunt south of Lienz for the enticing views from the terrace and the home cooking.

Garage EUROPEAN €€
(☎04852-645 54; www.garage-lienz.at; Südtiroler Platz 2; mains €9-23.50; ⊙11am-3pm & 6-11pm Tue-Sat) At this garage-style restaurant in the heart of Lienz, the decor is a new-old combination of dark beams, monochrome tones, marble-topped tables and vintage picture frames. Alongside faves like organic *Wiener Schnitzel* (breaded veal cutlet) you'll find bright flavours in dishes like basil falafel with rocket, five-spice sirloin with rosemary dumplings, and coconut-lemongrass chicken curry.

Da Leonardo PIZZA €€
(☎04852-699 44; www.daleonardo.at; Tiroler Strasse 30; pizza €8-16; ⊙11am-11pm;) World-champion pizza maker Leonardo Granata rests his dough for 24 to 48 hours, turning out authentic pizzas and running a 100% Italian operation with friendly, solicitous staff. Fabulous if you're missing *il bel paese*.

Gösser Bräu im Alten Rathaus AUSTRIAN €€
(☎04852-721 74; www.goesserbraeu-lienz.at; Johannesplatz 10; mains €8-17.50; ⊙9am-1am Mon-Thu, to 2am Fri & Sat, 9.30am-midnight Sun;) Gather around a horseshoe-shaped bar at this vaulted brewpub, whose draught Gösser Brau beers go well with the limited menu of traditional favourites. In summer move to the vine-clad terrace for well-presented Italian daily specials and Austrian standards.

Drinking & Nightlife

Weinphilo WINE BAR
(☎04852-612 53; www.weinphilo.com; Messinggasse 11; ⊙10am-7.30pm Mon-Fri, to 3pm Sat) A proper Italian wine shop and bar, where you can join locals for a glass of a beautiful small-producer wine from the Veneto, Friuli, Südtirol or even further south. There are meat and cheese platters and you can also pop in here in the morning for a coffee expertly made from Tuscany's Cafe Baratto beans.

RAFTING & CANYONING

The fast-flowing rivers, narrow gorges and forests of the Dolomites around Lienz are perfect for adrenaline-pumping sports, including rafting and canyoning. Expect to pay between €35 and €90 for rafting tours, and between €75 and €180 for canyoning.

Information

Tourist Office (Lienzer Dolimiten; ☎050 212 212; www.osttirol.com; Mühlgasse 11; ⊙8am-7pm Mon-Fri, 9am-noon & 1-6pm Sat, 9.30am-noon Sun Jul & Aug, slightly shorter hours rest of the year) The staff here will help you find accommodation (even private rooms) free of charge. The website also has information about the wider East Tyrol area.

Getting There & Away

Regional transport in Tyrol comes under the wing of the **Verkehrsverbund Tirol** (VVT; www.vvt.at). Check its website for information on VVT transport tickets, valid for travel between Tyrol and East Tyrol.

BUS

Bus departures are from in front of the train station. There are bus connections to regional ski resorts and northwards to the Hohe Tauern National Park. Buses to Kitzbühel (€15.80, 1¾ hours) are quicker and more direct than the train, but less frequent.

CAR & MOTORCYCLE

To head south, you must first divert west or east along Hwy 100, as the Dolomites are an impregnable barrier. The main north–south road routes are the year-round Felber-Tauern-Strasse (B108) between Mittersill and Lienz, the spectacular Grossglockner Road (open May to October) and the 5.5km-long Felbertauerntunnel (cars and motorcycles €11).

Hauptplatz has lots of parking in its Kurzparkzone, or park for free in front of Stadtpfarrkirche St Andrä.

TRAIN

Most trains to the rest of Austria, including Salzburg (€40.70, 3½ to 4½ hours, hourly), go east via Spittal-Millstättersee, where you usually have to change. The quickest and easiest route to Innsbruck (€23.50, 3½ to four hours) is to go west via Sillian and Italy, with a change in San Candido/Innichen and again in Fortezza/Franzensfeste.

Tyrol & Vorarlberg

Includes ➡

Best Places to Eat

- ➡ Die Wilderin (p299)
- ➡ Schulhaus (p306)
- ➡ Museum Restaurant (p328)
- ➡ Auracher Löchl (p314)
- ➡ Olive (p299)
- ➡ Paznaunerstube (p324)

Best Places to Stay

- ➡ Villa Licht (p312)
- ➡ Hotel Weisses Kreuz (p297)
- ➡ Gasthof Hirschen (p339)
- ➡ Hotel Gotthard (p330)
- ➡ Himmlhof (p328)
- ➡ Träumerei #8 (p314)

Why Go?

There's no place like Tyrol for the 'wow, I'm in Austria' feeling. Nowhere else in the country is the downhill skiing as exhilarating, the après-ski as pumping, the wooden chalets as chocolate box, the food as hearty. Whether you're schussing down the legendary slopes of Kitzbühel, cycling the Zillertal or hiking in the Alps with a big, blue sky overhead, the scenery here makes you glad to be alive. Welcome to a place where snowboarders brag under the low beams of a medieval tavern about awesome descents; where *Dirndls* and *Lederhosen* have street cred; and where *Volksmusik* (folk music) features on club playlists.

The Arlberg Alps give way to rolling dairy country in pleasingly low-key Vorarlberg. Spilling east to the glittering expanse of Bodensee (Lake Constance), this eastern pocket of the country swings happily between ecofriendly architecture on the cutting edge of design and deeply traditional hamlets with more cows than people.

When to Go

➡ In winter (December to early April), skiers flock to the Tyrolean Alps for snow and après-ski fun and prices soar, making advance booking essential. At Christmas, markets bring festive sparkle to towns and cities.

➡ In summer (June to September) room rates are lower in alpine resorts and this is prime time for high-altitude and hut-to-hut hikes, lake swimming and adventure sports such as rafting, paragliding and mountain biking. Zillertal rocks to summer folk music; the Bregenz Festival in mid-July lures opera fans to Bodensee.

➡ Crowds are few and room rates low in the shoulder seasons of April/May and October/November, though many places close in alpine resorts. Seasonal colour is at its best, with wildflowers in spring and foliage in autumn.

TYROL

Tyrol is as pure alpine as Austria gets, with mountains that make you want to yodel out loud and patchwork pastures chiming with cowbells. After the first proper dump of snow in winter, it's a Christmas-card scene, with snow-frosted forests and skiers whizzing down some of the finest slopes in Europe. Summer is lower key: hiking trails thread to peaks and mountain huts, while folk music gets steins swinging down in the valleys.

History

Despite its difficult alpine terrain, Tyrol has been settled since the Neolithic age, verified by the discovery of a 5400-year-old body of a man preserved in ice in the Ötztal Alps in 1991. The Brenner Pass (1374m), crossing into Italy, allowed the region to develop as a north–south trade route.

Tyrol fell to the Habsburgs in 1363, but it wasn't until the rule of Emperor Maximilian I (1490–1519) that the province truly forged ahead. He boosted the region's status by transforming Innsbruck into the administrative capital and a cultural centre. In 1511 the emperor drew up the Landibell legislation, allowing Tyroleans to defend their own borders, thus creating the *Schützen* (marksmen militia), which still exists today. When the last Tyrolean Habsburg, Archduke Sigmund Franz, died in 1665 the duchy of Tyrol was directly ruled from Vienna.

In 1703 the Bavarians attempted to capture Tyrol in the War of the Spanish Succession. In alliance with the French, they reached the Brenner Pass before being beaten back by the *Schützen*. In 1805 Tyrol passed into Bavarian hands under Napoleon, a rule that was short-lived and troublesome. In 1809 South Tyrolean innkeeper Andreas Hofer led a successful fight for independence, winning a famous victory at Bergisel. The Habsburg monarchy did not support his heroic stance and Tyrol was returned to Bavaria later that year.

The Treaty of St Germain (1919) dealt a further blow to Tyrolean identity: prosperous South Tyrol was ceded to Italy and East Tyrol was isolated from the rest of the province.

A staunch ally of Mussolini, Hitler did not claim back South Tyrol when his troops invaded Austria in 1938. In the aftermath of WWII, Tyrol was divided into zones occupied by Allied forces until Austria proclaimed its neutrality in 1955. Since then Tyrol has enjoyed peace and prosperity, and tourism, particularly the ski industry, has flourished.

Getting There & Away

AIR

Lying 4km west of Innsbruck's city centre, **Innsbruck Airport** (INN; ☎0512-22 52 50; www.innsbruck-airport.com; Fürstenweg 180) caters to a handful of national (Vienna) and international flights (London, Amsterdam, Frankfurt, Hamburg, Palma and Tel Aviv), handled mostly by Austrian Airlines, British Airways, easyJet, Eurowings, KLM and Lufthansa.

CAR & MOTORCYCLE

The main road and rail route in and out of Tyrol follows the Inntal (Inn River), with the east–west A12 cutting the province into almost equal halves, entering from Germany near Kufstein and exiting west of St Anton in Vorarlberg. The A13 connects Tyrol with Italy, crossing the Brenner Pass directly south of Innsbruck.

Getting Around

Regional transport, covering buses, trams and ÖBB (Österreiche Bundesbahn, Austrian Federal Railway) trains, is run by the Verkehrsverbund Tirol (www.vvt.at). Ticket prices depend on the number of zones you travel through; a single ticket costs €1.30, a day pass €5.80. Additionally, Tyrol is divided into overlapping transport zones. A regional pass costs €25/77.50 per week/month.

Innsbruck

☎0512 / POP 132,493 / ELEV 574M

Tyrol's capital is a sight to behold. The jagged rock spires of the Nordkette range are so close that within minutes it's possible to travel from the city's heart to more than 2000m above sea level and alpine pastures where cowbells chime. Summer and winter activities abound, and it's understandable why some visitors only take a peek at Innsbruck proper before heading for the hills. But to do so is a shame, for Innsbruck is in many ways Austria in microcosm: its late-medieval *Altstadt* (old town) is picture-book stuff, presided over by a grand Habsburg palace and baroque cathedral, while its Olympic ski jump with big mountain views makes a spectacular leap between the urban and the outdoors.

History

Innsbruck dates from 1180, when the little market settlement on the north bank of the Inn River spread to the south bank via an eponymous new bridge – Ynsprugg.

Tyrol & Vorarlberg Highlights

❶ **Kitzbühel** (p310) Saving your best schuss (and snowsuit) for this top-tier ski resort's legendary slopes.

❷ **Goldenes Dachl** (p295) Admiring Innsbruck's late-Gothic oriel, built for Holy Roman Emperor Maximilian I.

❸ **The Zillertal** (p303) Mountain biking and swinging to folk-music melodies in Tyrol's alpine heartland.

❹ **Aqua Dome** (p319) Peak-gazing and bathing in otherworldy pools at this spa in Längenfeld.

❺ **St Anton am Arlberg** (p324) Partying in the après-ski bars.

❻ **Hall in Tirol** (p301) Slipping back 500 years in this pristine medieval old town.

❼ **Bodensee** (p333) Splashing and cycling over borders this lake.

❽ **Bregenzerwald** (p336) Enjoying pure mountain loveliness and dairy-hopping in this off-the-radar region.

❾ **Feldkirch** (p339) Tiptoeing back to medieval times at the castles and towers in riverside Feldkirch.

❿ **Bludenz** (p341) Going to purple-cow heaven gorging on Milka chocolate in Bludenz.

Innsbruck

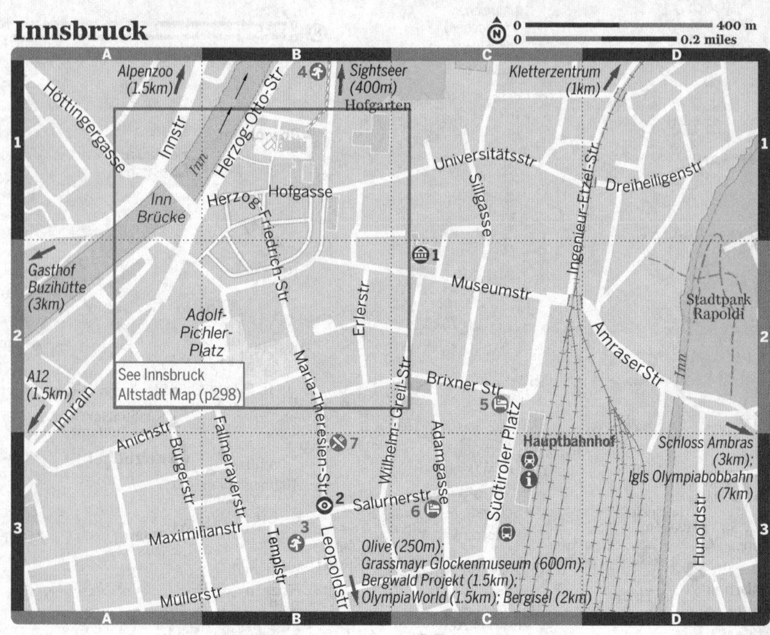

Innsbruck

Sights

1 Tiroler Landesmuseum Ferdinandeum C2
2 Triumphpforte B3

Activities, Courses & Tours

Die Börse .... (see 3)
3 Inntour B3
4 Nordkettenbahnen B1

Sleeping

5 Grand Hotel Europa C2
6 Pension Stoi C3

Eating

7 Oniriq B3

In 1420 Innsbruck became the ducal seat of the Tyrolean Habsburgs, but it was under the reign of Emperor Maximilian I that the city reached its pinnacle in power and prestige; many of the emperor's monuments, including the shimmering Goldenes Dachl, are still visible today. Maximilian was not the only Habsburg to influence the city's skyline: Archduke Ferdinand II reconstructed the Schloss Ambras, and Empress Maria Theresia the Hofburg.

Two world wars aside, Innsbruck has enjoyed a fairly peaceful existence over the centuries. More recently, the city held the Winter Olympics in 1964 and 1976, and the Winter Youth Olympic Games in 2012.

Sights

★Schloss Ambras PALACE

(www.schlossambras-innsbruck.at; Schlosstrasse 20; palace adult/child €12/free, gardens free; palace 10am-5pm, gardens 6am-dusk, closed Nov;) Picturesquely perched on a hill and set among beautiful gardens, this Renaissance pile was acquired in 1564 by Archduke Ferdinand II, then ruler of Tyrol, who transformed it from a fortress into a palace. Don't miss the centrepiece **Spanische Saal** (Spanish Hall), the dazzling **Armour Collection** and the gallery's Velázquez and Van Dyck originals.

The Spanische Saal is a 43m-long banquet hall with a wooden inlaid ceiling and Tyrolean nobles gazing from the walls. Also note the grisaille (grey relief) around the courtyard and the sunken bathtub where Ferdinand's beloved Philippine used to bathe.

Ferdinand instigated the magnificent Ambras Collection, encompassing three elements. Highlights of the Rüstkammer (Armour Collection) include the archduke's wedding armour – specially shaped to fit his bulging midriff! – and the 2.6m suit created for giant Bartlmä Bon. The **Kunst und Wunderkammer** (Art and Curiosity Cabinet) is crammed with fantastical objects, including a petrified shark, gravity-defying stilt shoes and the *Fangstuhl* – a chair designed to trap drunken guests at Ferdinand's raucous parties.

The **Portraitgalerie** features room upon room of Habsburg portraits, with paintings by Titian, Velázquez and Van Dyck. *Maria Anna of Spain* (No 126, Room 22) wins the prize for the most ludicrous hairstyle. When Habsburg portraits begin to pall, you can stroll or picnic in the extensive gardens, home to strutting peacocks.

Schloss Ambras is 4.5km southeast of the centre. The **Sightseer** (www.sightseer.at; adult/child day pass €16/10) bus runs every half-hour between the castle and central stops including the *Hauptbahnhof* (main train station) and Hofburg.

★Hofkirche
CHURCH

(Map p298; www.tiroler-landesmuseum.at; Universitätsstrasse 2; adult/child €7/free; 9am-5pm Mon-Sat, 12.30-5pm Sun) Innsbruck's pride and joy is the Gothic Hofkirche, one of Europe's finest royal court churches. It was commissioned in 1553 by Ferdinand I, who enlisted top artists of the age such as Albrecht Dürer, Alexander Colin and Peter Vischer the Elder. Top billing goes to the empty **sarcophagus of Emperor Maximilian I**, a masterpiece of German Renaissance sculpture, elaborately carved from black marble.

★Hofburg
PALACE

(Imperial Palace; Map p298; www.hofburg-innsbruck.at; Rennweg 1; adult/child €9.50/free; 9am-5pm) Grabbing attention with its pearly white facade and cupolas, the Hofburg was built as a castle for Archduke Sigmund the Rich in the 15th century, expanded by Emperor Maximilian I in the 16th century and given a baroque makeover by Empress Maria Theresia in the 18th century. The centrepiece of the lavish rococo state apartments is the 31m-long **Riesensaal** (Giant's Hall).

★Goldenes Dachl
MUSEUM

(Golden Roof; Map p298; Herzog-Friedrich-Strasse 15; museum adult/child €4.80/2.40; 10am-5pm May-Sep, Tue-Sun Oct & Dec-Apr) Innsbruck's golden wonder and most distinctive landmark is this Gothic oriel, built for Holy Roman Emperor Maximilian I, lavishly festooned with murals and glittering with 2657 fire-gilt copper tiles. It is most impressive from the exterior, but the museum is worth a look – especially if you have the Innsbruck Card (p296) – with an audio guide whisking you through the history. Keep an eye out for the grotesque tournament helmets designed to resemble the Turks of the rival Ottoman Empire.

Volkskunst Museum
MUSEUM

(Folk Art Museum; Map p298; www.tiroler-landesmuseum.at; Universitätstrasse 2; adult/child €11/free; 9am-5pm) The Volkskunst Museum presents a fascinating romp through Tyrolean folk art from hand-carved sleighs and Christmas cribs to carnival masks and cowbells. On the 1st floor is a beautifully restored Gothic *Stube* (parlour) complete with low ceiling, wood panelling and an antique tiled oven.

Bergisel
VIEWPOINT

(www.bergisel.info; adult/child €9.50/4.50; 9am-6pm Jun-Oct, 10am-5pm Wed-Mon Nov-May) Rising above Innsbruck like a celestial staircase, this glass-and-steel ski jump was designed by much-lauded Iraqi architect Zaha Hadid. It's 455 steps or a two-minute funicular ride to the 50m-high **viewing platform**, with a breathtaking panorama of the Nordkette range, Inntal and Innsbruck. Tram 1 trundles here from central Innsbruck.

From May to July, fans pile in to see athletes train, while preparations step up a gear in early January for the World Cup Four Hills Tournament.

Tiroler Landesmuseum Ferdinandeum
MUSEUM

(Map p294; 0512-594 89; www.tiroler-landesmuseum.at; Museumstrasse 15; adult/child €11/free; 9am-5pm Tue-Sun) This treasure trove of Tyrolean history and art moves from Bronze Age artefacts to the original reliefs used to design the Goldenes Dachl. Alongside brooding Dutch masterpieces of the Rembrandt ilk, the gallery displays an astounding collection of Austrian art including Gothic altarpieces, a handful of Klimt and Kokoschka paintings, and some shocking Viennese Actionist works.

Dom St Jakob
CATHEDRAL

(St James' Cathedral; Map p298; Domplatz; 10.30am-6.30pm Mon-Sat, from 12.30pm Sun) FREE Innsbruck's 18th-century cathedral is a feast of over-the-top baroque. The Asam brothers from Munich completed much of the sumptuous art and stuccowork, though the Madonna above the high altar is by German painter Lukas Cranach the Elder. You'll have to fork out €1 for photography permission.

Alpenzoo ZOO
(www.alpenzoo.at; Weiherburggasse 37; adult/child €11/5.50; ⏲9am-6pm Apr-Oct, to 5pm Nov-Mar) Billing itself as a conservation-oriented zoo, this is where you can get close to alpine wildlife such as golden eagles, chamois and ibex. It's a 10-minute uphill walk from Innstrasse, or you can take Bus W from the Marktplatz or the Hungerburgbahn to the Alpenzoo stop.

Grassmayr Glockenmuseum MUSEUM
(www.grassmayr.at; Leopoldstrasse 53; adult/child €8/5; ⏲10am-4pm Mon-Fri year-round, plus 10am-4pm Sat May-Sep) Showcases the Grassmayr family's 400 years of bell-making tradition. In addition to exhibits including some formidable Romanesque and Gothic bells, you can watch the casting process and have a go at ringing the bells to achieve different notes.

Stadtturm TOWER
(Map p298; Herzog-Friedrich-Strasse 21; adult/child €3.50/1.50; ⏲10am-8pm Jun-Sep, to 5pm Oct-May) Guards once kept watch over the city from this onion-domed tower, which was completed in 1450. Puff up 148 steps for 360-degree views of Innsbruck's rooftops, spires and the surrounding mountains.

Activities

Nordkettenbahnen CABLE CAR
(Map p294; www.nordkette.com; single/return to Hungerburg €5.40/9, to Seegrube €18.60/31.10, to Hafelekar €20.70/34.50; ⏲Hungerburg 7.15am-7.15pm Mon-Fri, 8am-7.15pm Sat & Sun, Seegrube 8.30am-5.30pm daily, Hafelekar 9am-5pm daily) Zaha Hadid's space-age funicular runs every 15 minutes, whizzing you from the Congress Centre to the slopes in no time. Walking trails head off in all directions from **Hungerburg** and **Seegrube**. For more of a challenge, there is a **downhill track** (⏲late May-early Nov) for mountain bikers and two **fixed-rope routes** (adult/child incl cable car €36.50/21.90; ⏲Jun-Sep) for climbers.

INNSBRUCK DISCOUNT CARDS

The money-saving **Innsbruck Card** allows one visit to Innsbruck's main sights and attractions, a return journey with any cable car or funicular, three hours' bike rental, a guided city walk and unlimited use of public transport including the Sightseer and Kristallwelten shuttle bus. The card also yields numerous discounts on tours and activities. It's available at the tourist office and costs €43/50/59 for 24/48/72 hours (half-price for children).

Stay overnight in Innsbruck and you'll receive a **Welcome Card**, giving discounts on transport and activities, entry to a number of pools and lidos, and allowing you to join the tourist office's free guided hikes in summer.

Olympia SkiWorld SKIING
(3-/6-day ski pass €140/235) Innsbruck is the gateway to a formidable ski arena, the Olympia SkiWorld Innsbruck, covering nine surrounding resorts and 300km of slopes to test all abilities. The OlympiaWorld Ski Pass covers all areas; ski buses are free to anyone with an Innsbruck Card.

Olympiabobbahn ADVENTURE SPORTS
(☎0512-338 382 21; www.olympiaworld.at; Heilwasserweg, Igls; €35; ⏲5-8pm Dec-Mar, 4-6pm Wed-Fri Jul & Aug) For a minute in the life of an Olympic bobsleigh racer, you can't beat the Olympiabobbahn, built for the 1976 Winter Olympics. Zipping around 10 curves and picking up speeds of up to 100km/h, the bob run is 800m of pure hair-raising action. You can join a professional bobsled driver in winter or summer; call ahead for the exact times. To reach it, take Bus J from the Landesmuseum to Igls Olympiaexpress.

Kletterzentrum CLIMBING
(☎0512-39 73 40; www.kletterzentrum-innsbruck.at; Matthias-Schmid-Strasse 12c; day ticket adult/child €13.50/7, complete set rental €8; ⏲9am-11pm Mon-Fri, to 10pm Sat & Sun; 👪) If you want to hone your climbing skills before heading up to the Alps, the Kletterzentrum is the go-to place. Spread across a whopping 6000 sq metres, this is one of the largest climbing centres in the world, with indoor and outdoor walls, speed walls and a boulder area. Courses can be arranged.

Nordpark SKIING
The most central place to pound powder is the Nordpark. Snowboarders are in their element at the **Nordkette Skylinepark** (www.nordkette.com; ⏲9am-5pm), with its quarter-pipe, kickers and boxes, while daring skiers ride the **Hafelekar-Rinne**, one of Europe's steepest runs with a 70% gradient.

Inntour ADVENTURE SPORTS
(Map p294; www.inntour.com; Leopoldstrasse 4; ⌚9am-6pm Mon-Sat) Inntour arranges guided cycling and mountain-biking trips, including routes along the Inn River.

Die Börse ADVENTURE SPORTS
(Map p294; www.dieboerse.at; Leopoldstrasse 4; ⌚9am-6pm Mon-Sat) Rents skis and snowboards (€20 to €40 per day) and city, electro, mountain, free-ride and downhill bikes (€20 to €50 per day).

Festivals & Events

Christkindlmarkt CHRISTMAS MARKET
(www.christkindlmarkt.cc; ⌚mid-Nov–6 Jan;) Innsbruck twinkles festively at Christmas markets in the *Altstadt,* Marktplatz and Maria-Theresien-Strasse from the middle of November to Epiphany. Kids love the fairy-tale-themed Kiebachgasse and Köhleplatzl.

Vierschanzentournee SPORTS
(Four Hills Tournament; www.vierschanzentournee.com; ⌚Dec-Jan) Innsbruck sees in the New Year by hosting one of four World Cup ski-jumping events at Bergisel.

Promenadenkonzerte MUSIC
(www.promenadenkonzerte.at; ⌚Jul) Every July Innsbruck hosts a series of free classical concerts set against the sublime backdrop of the Hofburg's inner courtyard. The full line-up is available online.

Festwochen der Alten Musik MUSIC
(Festival of Early Music; www.altemusik.at; ⌚Aug) This festival brings baroque concerts to venues such as Schloss Ambras, the Landestheater, Goldenes Dachl and Hofburg.

Sleeping

Nepomuk's HOSTEL €
(Map p298; ☎0512-58 41 18; www.nepomuks.at; Kiebachgasse 16; dm/d from €24/58;) Could this be backpacker heaven? Nepomuk's sure comes close, with its *Altstadt* location, well-stocked kitchen and high-ceilinged dorms with nice touches such as CD players. The delicious breakfast in attached Cafe Munding, with homemade pastries, jam and fresh-roasted coffee, gets your day off to a grand start.

Pension Stoi PENSION €
(Map p294; ☎0512-58 54 34; www.pensionstoi.at; Salurnerstrasse 7; s €48-62, d €75-92; P) This sweet, home-style, pink-fronted guesthouse extends a friendly welcome and keeps things low-key and simple in unfussy yet comfortable rooms, with pine and floral trappings. It's handily located for the main train station.

CITY WALKS & GUIDED HIKES

Innsbruck Information (p300) organises guided city walks, which meander through the historical centre. One-and-a-half-hour tours leave at 2pm daily (plus 11am in July and August) and are free with an Innsbruck Card (otherwise cost €12).

From late May to October, it also arranges daily guided hikes from Monday to Friday, including sunrise walks, lantern-lit strolls and half-day mountain jaunts, which are, incredibly, free to anyone with an Innsbruck Welcome Card. Pop into the tourist office to register and browse the program.

★**Hotel Weisses Kreuz** HISTORIC HOTEL €€
(Map p298; ☎0512-594 79; www.weisseskreuz.at; Herzog-Friedrich-Strasse 31; s €66-105, d €100-180; P@) Beneath the arcades, this atmospheric *Altstadt* hotel has played host to guests for 500 years, including a 13-year-old Mozart. With its wood-panelled parlours, antiques and twisting staircase, the hotel oozes history with every creaking beam. Rooms are supremely comfortable, staff are charming and breakfast is a lavish spread.

Stage 12 BOUTIQUE HOTEL €€
(Map p298; ☎0512-31 23 12; www.stage12.at; Maria-Theresien-Strasse 12; d €130-190; P) Minimalist cool, design-driven and cleverly tucked away in *Altstadt*, this 16th-century townhouse-turned-boutique hotel has slick, oak-floored rooms (opt for a mountain view with balcony for beguiling views of the Alps), a 6th-floor spa and an urban-chic cocktail bar with a good buzz. Breakfast is bang on the money, with bircher muesli, Austrian cheeses, smoked salmon and proper coffee.

Grand Hotel Europa LUXURY HOTEL €€
(Map p294; ☎0512-59 31; www.grandhoteleuropa.at; Südtiroler Platz 2; s €114-154, d €142-219; P❄@) This luxurious pile opposite the station has been given a facelift. Pared-down chic now defines the rooms, though old-world grandeur lingers in the opulent Baroque Hall and wood-panelled restaurant. Mick Jagger and Queen Elizabeth II are famous past guests.

Innsbruck Altstadt

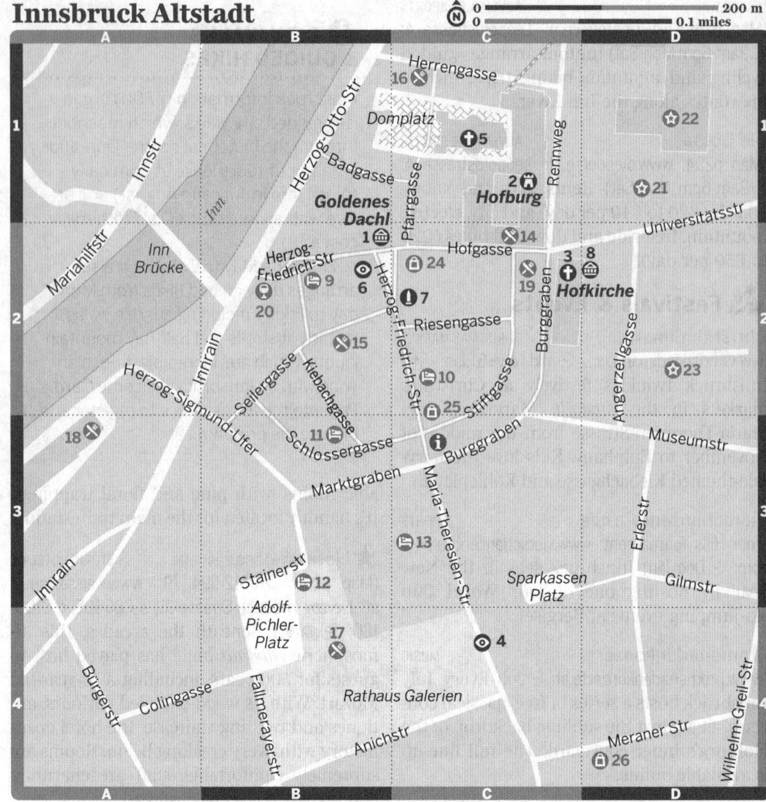

Innsbruck Altstadt

Top Sights
1 Goldenes Dachl B2
2 Hofburg C1
3 Hofkirche C2

Sights
4 Annasäule C4
5 Dom St Jakob C1
6 Hölblinghaus B2
7 Stadtturm C2
8 Volkskunst Museum D2

Sleeping
9 Goldener Adler B2
10 Hotel Weisses Kreuz C2
11 Nepomuk's B3
12 Penz Hotel B3
13 Stage 12 .... C3

Eating
14 Cafe Sacher C2
15 Die Wilderin B2
16 Fischerhäusl C1
17 Lichtblick B4
18 Markthalle A3
19 Stiftskeller C2

Drinking & Nightlife
360° .... (see 17)
20 In Vinum B2

Entertainment
21 Haus der Musik D1
22 Tiroler Landestheater D1
23 Treibhaus D2

Shopping
24 Acqua Alpes C2
25 Swarovski Crystal Gallery C2
26 Tiroler Heimatwerk D4

Goldener Adler HISTORIC HOTEL €€

(Map p298; ☎0512-571 111; www.goldeneradler.com; Herzog-Friedrich-Strasse 6; s €147, d €167-220; P ❄ 📶) Since opening in 1390, the grand Goldener Adler has welcomed kings, queens and Salzburg's two biggest exports: Mozart and Mrs Von Trapp. Rooms are elegant with gold drapes and squeaky-clean marble bathrooms. Downstairs there is a cracking traditional restaurant tucked under the arcades and spilling out on the cobbles.

Penz Hotel HOTEL €€€

(Map p298; ☎0512-575 657; www.the-penz.com; Adolf-Pichler-Platz 3; s €145-265, d €185-295; P ❄ 📶) Behind a sheer wall of glass, the Penz is a contemporary design hotel next to the Rathaus Galerien. The minimalist rooms in muted hues are spruced up with flat-screen TVs and shiny chrome fittings. At breakfast, a whole table is piled high with exotic fruits.

Eating

Olive VEGETARIAN €

(☎0512-35 90 75; Leopoldstrasse 36, Wiltener Platz'l; mains €10.50-14, 2-course lunch €9.50; ⏰11.30am-2pm & 6-11pm Mon-Fri; ✍ 👪) Vegetarians and vegans are in their element at this cute retro-flavoured bistro, with wood floors, a mishmash of vintage furniture and the warmest of welcomes. Wholesome veggies are knocked up into deliciously simple, season-driven dishes, be it sweet potato soup with ginger and pomegranate or coconut risotto with peaches, cashews and lime-coriander salsa. Book – it gets busy.

Markthalle MARKET €

(Map p298 www.markthalle-innsbruck.at; Herzog-Siegmund-Ufer 1-3; ⏰7am-6.30pm Mon-Fri, to 1pm Sat) Freshly baked bread, Tyrolean cheese, organic fruit, smoked ham and salami – it's all under one roof at this riverside covered market.

★ **Die Wilderin** AUSTRIAN €€

(Map p298; ☎0512-56 27 28; www.diewilderin.at; Seilergasse 5; mains €12.50-20; ⏰5pm-midnight Tue-Sun) Take a gastronomic walk on the wild side at this modern-day hunter-gatherer of a restaurant, where chefs take pride in local sourcing and using top-notch farm-fresh and foraged ingredients. The menu sings of the seasons, be it asparagus, game, strawberries or winter veg. The vibe is urbane and relaxed.

Buzihütte AUSTRIAN €€

(☎0512-28 33 33; www.buzihuette.at; Berchtoldshofweg 14; mains €10-22; ⏰6pm-midnight Wed-Fri, 11am-midnight Sat & Sun) With cracking views of Innsbruck from on high, the Buzihütte is a 3km hike northwest of town or a five-minute taxi ride. It's a deliciously alpine-style hut, with a peak-gazing terrace for summer dining and a dark, woodsy interior for hibernating on snowy days. On the menu are hearty faves such as schnitzel, *Spinatknödel* (spinach dumplings) and *Käsespätzle* (cheese noodles). Cash only.

Cafe Sacher CAFE €€

(Map p298; ☎0512-56 56 26; www.sacher.com; Rennweg 1; mains €19.50-22.50; ⏰8.30am-10pm Sun-Wed, to midnight Thu-Sat) Sidling up to the Hofburg, this grand chandelier-lit cafe is the place to linger over chocolate *Sacher Torte* with whipped cream (€7.50), salads or lunch. There are free classical concerts in the courtyard in summer.

Stiftskeller AUSTRIAN €€

(Map p298; www.stiftskeller.eu; Hofgasse 6; lunch menus €9.70-14.80, mains €10-25; ⏰10am-midnight; 👪) A vaulted restaurant with a large beer garden for Augustiner Bräu beers and hearty fare such as pork roast with lashings of beer sauce, dumplings and sauerkraut. Kids' menus are available.

Fischerhäusl AUSTRIAN €€

(Map p298; ☎0512-583 535; www.fischerhaeusl.com; Herrengasse 8; mains €11-17, 2-course lunch €8.30; ⏰10am-1am Mon-Sat) The lemon-fronted Fischerhäusl has stood in this hidden spot between Domplatz and the Hofburg since 1758. On the menu is Tyrolean grub such as *Kaspressknödelsuppe,* cheesy dumplings swimming in broth, and *Gröstl,* a potato, bacon and onion fry-up. The terrace fills quickly on warm days.

Oniriq GASTRONOMY €€€

(Map p294; ☎0650 451 06 24; www.oniriq.at; Maria-Theresien-Strasse 49; 7-course menu €74-98; ⏰6pm-midnight Mon-Thu & Sat, 11.30am-1.30pm & 6pm-midnight Fri; ✍) A welcome addition to Innsbruck's gastro scene, Oniriq is a standout for innovative tasting menus in stripped-back, industro-cool surrounds. Tucked just off Maria-Theresien-Strasse, the restaurant plays up seasonal flavours in menus (vegetarian and non) presented in the newfangled ingredient-driven way, say goat's cheese with Jerusalem artichoke, blueberry and dandelion, or rhubarb with pine wood, carrot and strawberry-seed oil.

Lichtblick INTERNATIONAL €€€
(Map p298; ☎0512-566 550; www.restaurant-lichtblick.at; Maria-Theresien-Strasse 18, Rathaus Galerien; lunch €9.90-13.90, set menus €46-52; ⏰10am-1am Mon-Sat) On the 7th floor of the Rathaus Galerien, this chic glass-walled restaurant has sweeping views over Innsbruck to the Alps beyond. Backlighting and minimalist design create a sleek backdrop for Mediterranean-inspired cuisine such as grilled octopus with pepper purée, basil and lemon mayonnaise, and homemade ravioli with aged pecorino and herbs.

Drinking & Nightlife

In Vinum WINE BAR
(Map p298; www.invinum.com; Innrain 1; ⏰11am-midnight Mon-Sat, 4-9pm Sun) This snug *Altstadt* wine bar is a relaxed choice to sample Austria's finest wines, which start at €2.80 a glass; see the website for details of the regular tastings. If you get peckish, you can snack on local cheese and ham.

360° BAR
(Map p298; www.360-grad.at; Rathaus Galerien; ⏰10am-1am Mon-Sat) Grab a cushion and drink in 360-degree views of the city and Alps from the balcony that skirts this spherical, glass-walled bar. It's a nicely chilled spot for a coffee or sundowner.

☆ Entertainment

Haus der Musik ARTS CENTRE
(Map p298; ☎0512-52 07 40; www.haus-der-musik-innsbruck.at; Universitätsstrasse 1; ⏰ticket office 10am-7pm Mon-Fri, to 6.30pm Sat) The Haus der Musik is one of Innsbruck's most striking contemporary architectural icons. Clad in ceramic tiles that shimmer from bronze to black depending on the light, the cuboid is an ultramodern venue for performing arts, with a line-up featuring plays, concerts and workshops.

Treibhaus ARTS CENTRE
(Map p298; www.treibhaus.at; Angerzellgasse 8; ⏰10am-1am Mon-Sat, 4pm-midnight Sun) This cultural complex draws a boho crowd with its big terrace, regular DJs and live music. In August, it hosts an open-air cinema.

Tiroler Landestheater THEATRE
(Map p298; ☎0512-520 744; www.landestheater.at; Rennweg 2; ⏰ticket office 10am-7pm Mon-Fri, to 6.30pm Sat) Innsbruck's imposing neoclassical theatre stages year-round performances of opera, dance, drama and comedy. Tickets cost between €4 and €70.

Shopping

Acqua Alpes PERFUME
(Map p298; Hofgasse 2; ⏰10am-6pm) If you've ever wished to bottle the pure, fresh scent of the Alps, someone has already done it – fragrances inspired by those meadows, crisp air and wildflowers are sold at this vaulted, blue-and-white perfumery. Each of the four perfumes corresponds to the elevation of one of the peaks close by.

Tiroler Heimatwerk ARTS & CRAFTS
(Map p298; Meraner Strasse 2; ⏰9am-6pm Mon-Fri, to noon Sat) Great for traditional gifts, this place sells everything from *Dirndls* to hand-carved nativity figurines, stained glass and Tyrolean puppets.

Swarovski Crystal Gallery GIFTS & SOUVENIRS
(Map p298; Herzog-Friedrich-Strasse 39; ⏰8am-7.30pm) Swarovski's flagship store in Innsbruck is this gallery-style boutique, crammed with sparkling crystal trinkets, ornaments and jewellery.

ℹ Information

Landeskrankenhaus (☎50 40; Anichstrasse 35) The *Universitätklinik* (University Clinic) at the city's main hospital has emergency services.

Innsbruck Information (☎0512-598 50, 0512-535 60; www.innsbruck.info; Burggraben 3; ⏰9am-6pm Mon-Sat, 10am-4.30pm Sun) Main tourist office with truckloads of info on the city and surrounds, including skiing and walking. It sells ski passes, public-transport tickets and city maps (€1); will book accommodation; and has an attached ticketing service (open 9am to 6pm Monday to Friday, and 9am to 12.30pm Saturday).

There is also a branch at the **Hauptbahnhof** (☎0512-58 37 66; www.innsbruck.info; Südtiroler Platz 1; ⏰10am-6pm Mon-Sat).

ℹ Getting There & Away

BUS

The bus station is at the southern end of the *Hauptbahnhof*; its ticket office is located within the station.

WORTH A TRIP

SWAROVSKI CRYSTAL WORLDS

The quaint village of Wattens has but one claim to fame (albeit an impressive one): it's the glittering heart of the Swarovski crystal empire. Call them kitsch or classy, but there is no doubting the pulling power of these crystals at the fantastical **Swarovski Kristallwelten** (Swarovski Crystal Worlds; www.kristallwelten.swarovski.com; Kristallweltenstrasse 1; adult/child €19/7.50; 8.30am-7.30pm Sep-Jun, to 10pm Jul & Aug;), one of Austria's most-visited attractions.

Top attractions include a giant's head that spouts water in the garden, where there are contemporary art and sound installations to explore. There's more sparkle about the Crystal Cloud, which floats above a mirrorlike pool and is bejewelled with 800,000 crystals that glitter like stars in the night sky.

Artists and designers from all over the world have pooled their creativity into the Chambers of Wonder, which showcases the likes of Alexander McQueen's wintry *Silent Light*, the *Eden* crystal forest where a waterfall flows and South Korean artist Lee Bul's perspective-bending *Into Lattice Sun*, a kind of crystal utopia.

Trains run every 15 minutes from Innsbruck to Fritzens-Wattens (€2.50, six minutes), 2km north of Swarovski Kristallwelten and on the opposite side of the river. It's perhaps more convenient to take the bus (€2.50, 11 minutes) from Hall's train station to Wattens Hauptplatz, a 10-minute walk west of Swarovski Kristallwelten.

CAR & MOTORCYCLE

The A12 and the parallel Hwy 171 are the main roads heading west and east. The B177, to the west of Innsbruck, continues north to Germany and Munich. The A13 is a toll road (€9.50) running south through the Brenner Pass to Italy and crossing the 192m Europabrücke, spanning the Sill River. Toll-free Hwy 182 follows the same route, passing under the bridge.

TRAIN

Fast trains depart daily every two hours for Bregenz (€39.80, 2½ hours) and Salzburg (€53.70, 1¾ hours). From Innsbruck to the Arlberg, the best views are on the right-hand side of the train. Two-hourly express trains serve Munich (€44.60, 1¾ hours) and Verona (€43.80, 3½ hours). Direct services to Kitzbühel also run every two hours (€17.50, 1¼ hours). There are roughly hourly connections to Lienz (€17.50, three to four hours); some pass through Italy while others take the long way round via Salzburgerland.

Getting Around

TO/FROM THE AIRPORT

The airport (p291) is 4km west of the centre and served by bus F. Buses depart every 15 or 20 minutes from Maria-Theresien-Strasse (€2.30, 16 minutes); taxis charge about €10 for the same trip.

PUBLIC TRANSPORT

Single tickets on buses and trams cost €3.10 from the driver, €2.50 if purchased in advance. If you plan to use the city's public transport frequently you're better off buying a 24-hour ticket (€5.80). Weekly and monthly tickets are also available (€22.20 and €56, respectively). Tickets bought in advance, which are available from ticket machines, *Tabak* (tobacconist) shops and Innsbruck Information, must be stamped in the machines at the start of the journey.

Hall in Tirol

05223 / POP 13,897 / ELEV 574M

Nestled beneath the Alps, just 9km east of Innsbruck, Hall is a beautiful medieval town that grew fat on the riches of salt in the 13th century. The winding lanes, punctuated by pastel-coloured town houses and lantern-lit after dark, are made for aimless ambling.

Sights

Burg Hasegg CASTLE

(www.muenz-hall.at; Burg Hasegg 6; adult/child tower €5.50/4.50, mint €8/5.50, combined ticket €11.50/8; 10am-5pm Tue-Sun;) Stepping south of the medieval centre is the Burg Hasegg, where a spiral staircase coils up to the 5th floor for far-reaching views over Hall. The castle had a 300-year career as a mint for silver *Thalers* (coins, the root of the modern word 'dollar'), and this history is unravelled in the **Münze Hall**, displaying water-driven and hammer-striking techniques. Audio guides are included in the price and kids can mint their own coin.

WORTH A TRIP

STUBAI GLACIER

One of Austria's biggest glacier skiing areas, the **Stubai Glacier** (www.stubaier-gletscher.com) is just 40km south of Innsbruck. Thanks to its elevation, topping out at around 3300m, there's some form of skiing and boarding available year-round. Other activities include hiking, paragliding, tobogganing and cross-country skiing. Villages sprinkle the valley that unfurls below it.

Guesthouses, holiday apartments and chalet hotels are strung along the Stubaital, with the highest concentration in Neustift, a fine base if you want a head-start to the glacier in the morning before the crowds descend. Visit www.stubai.at for listings.

Buses from Innsbruck journey to Neustift im Stubaital Mutterbergalm at the foot of the glacier (€11.30, 1¼ hours) twice hourly. From December to April a ski bus (free with a guest card) runs daily between Innsbruck and the Stubai Glacier.

Pfarrkirche St Nikolaus CHURCH
(St Nicholas Parish Church; ⌚dawn-dusk) This graceful 13th-century church is best known for its **Waldaufkapelle**, home to Florian Waldauf's grisly collection of 45 skulls and 12 bones, picked from the remains of minor saints. Each rests on embroidered cushions, capped with veils and elaborate headdresses, reminiscent of spiked haloes; the whole effect is both repulsive and enthralling.

Bergbau Museum MUSEUM
(www.hall-wattens.at; Fürstengasse; adult/child €5/3; ⌚tours 11.30am Mon, Thu & Sat) This reconstructed salt mine, complete with galleries, tools and shafts, can only be visited by 40-minute guided tour. Salt was mined in the valley for 800 years.

Tours

The tourist office organises hour-long guided tours of the town (adult/child €6/3.50) at 10am on Mondays, Thursdays and Saturdays.

Festivals & Events

Haller Weinherbst FOOD & DRINK
(⌚late Aug) If you're in town for the Weinherbst festival in late August, watch as the water in the Wilden Mannes fountain miraculously turns to wine.

Sleeping

Kontor BOUTIQUE HOTEL €€
(☎05223-238 01; www.hotel-kontor.at; Unterer Stadtplatz 7a; s/d/ste €105/160/205) Lodged in a grand old townhouse dating to 1450, Kontor is a characterful addition to Hall's hotel scene. No two rooms are alike, but all have tons of personality, with bay windows, lovingly restored wooden floors, and themes from Gothic (if you like beams) to nostalgic. A good breakfast with eggs cooked to your liking is served in the baroque hall.

Gasthof Badl GUESTHOUSE €€
(☎05223-567 84; www.badl.at; Innbrücke 4; s €55-69, d €78-150; P 📶) A short dash across the Inn River from the *Altstadt*, this gem of a guesthouse is housed in a converted 17th-century bathhouse. It makes a charming, friendly base, with immaculate rooms (most with river view) and a tavern that knocks up great strudel. Children will love the playground. Rent a bike to pedal along the banks to Innsbruck.

Eating

Morgenbrot CAFE €
(www.morgenbrot.at; Krippgasse 10; breakfast & light bites €5-12; ⌚8.30am-2pm Mon & Thu-Sat, to noon Sun; 🌶) With an atmosphere that's as warm as a hug, this prettily retro cafe in light pastels brims with vintage furniture. It's a very chilled spot for breakfasts that make the most of delicious regional produce (vegetarian and vegan options are available), waffles, or a slice of homemade cake with a freshly roasted coffee.

Goldener Löwe AUSTRIAN €€
(☎05223-415 50; www.goldenerloewe-hall.at; Obere Stadtplatz; mains €9.50-26; ⌚11am-2.30pm & 5.30pm-midnight Tue-Sat) The ambience is wonderfully cosy in this historic tavern on the main square. Join locals in a warren of dark-wood-panelled rooms for Austrian comfort food such as *Tafelspitz* (boiled beef with horseradish) and sweet dumplings, paired with local wines.

Information

Staff at the **tourist office** (☎05223-455 44; www.hall-wattens.at; Unterer Stadtplatz 19;

⌚ 9am-6pm Mon-Fri, to 1pm Sat) can help you sort out accommodation and organise guided tours.

Getting There & Away

The B171 goes almost through the town centre, unlike the A12, which is over the Inn River to the south. The train station is about 1km southwest of the centre; it is on the main Innsbruck–Wörgl train line. Trains run frequently to/from Innsbruck (€3.80, eight minutes).

Schwaz

☎ 05242 / POP 13,728 / ELEV 545M

What is today a sleepy little town with pastel-washed houses and winding streets was once, believe it or not, Austria's second-largest city after Vienna. Schwaz wielded clout in the Middle Ages when its eyes shone brightly with silver, past glory that you can relive by going underground to the show silver mine.

Sights

★ Silberbergwerk MINE

(Silver Mine; www.silberbergwerk.at; Alte Landstrasse 3a; adult/child/family €17/10/40; ⌚ 9am-5pm May-Sep, 10am-4pm Oct-Apr) You almost feel like breaking out into a rendition of 'Heigh-Ho' at Silberbergwerk Schwaz, as you board a mini train and venture deep into the bowels of the silver mine for a 90-minute trundle through Schwaz' illustrious past. The mine is about 1.5km east of the centre.

Altstadt HISTORIC SITE

Schwaz hides a remarkably well-preserved *Altstadt*, built high on the riches of medieval silver. Taking pride of place on pedestrianised Franz-Josef-Strasse, the Gothic **Pfarrkirche** (Parish Church; Franz-Josef-Strasse; ⌚ dawn-dusk) immediately catches your eye with its step-gabled roof bearing 14,000 copper tiles. Not far south is the Gothic-meets-baroque **Franziskanerkirche** (Gilmstrasse; ⌚ dawn-dusk).

Sleeping & Eating

Gasthof Einhorn Schaller GUESTHOUSE €€

(☎ 05242-740 47; www.gasthof-schaller.at; Innsbruckerstrasse 31; s €51-66, d €84-114; P ⓦ) This super-central, family-friendly *Gasthöfe*(inn) combines modern rooms, done out in light pine wood and splashes of bright colour, with a traditional restaurant dishing up regional fare (mains €11 to €20) such as *Tiroler Käsespätzle*, eggy noodles topped with cheese and onions.

Information

The helpful **tourist office** (☎ 05242-632 40; www.silberregionkarwendel.at; Münchnerstrasse 11; ⌚ 8am-6pm Mon-Fri, to noon Sat) provides information on sights and accommodation in Schwaz.

Getting There & Away

Schwaz is 30km east of Innsbruck and 10km west of the Zillertal on the A12 Inntal-Autobahn. There are frequent trains between Innsbruck and Schwaz (€7.50, 26 minutes).

The Zillertal

Sandwiched between the Tuxer Voralpen and the Kitzbüheler Alpen, the Zillertal (Ziller Valley) is storybook Tyrol. A steam train chugs through the broad valley, passing fertile farmland and wooded mountains, and affording snatched glimpses of snowy peaks and the fast-flowing Ziller River.

Activities

Adrenaline-based activities include rafting, rock climbing, paragliding and cycling. The Ziller and its tributaries are also good for fishing, but permits are only valid for certain stretches.

Skiing

While Mayrhofen is the prime spot for serious skiing, there is plenty of downhill and cross-country skiing elsewhere. The Zillertaler Superskipass (two/four/six days €109.50/191.50/266.50) covers all 530km of slopes in the valley, including the snow-sure pistes at the Hintertux Glacier. Ski buses connect the resorts.

Summer Activities

In summer, the alpine valley morphs into excellent walking territory, with high-altitude trekking in the Tuxer Voralpen and myriad trails fanning out from the resorts of Ried, Kaltenbach, Aschau, Zell am Ziller and Ramsau. Mountain huts at elevations of around 1800m beckon weary hikers; visit www.alpenverein.at for details of huts in the valley. A detailed walking map covering the entire region is the Kompass *Zillertaler Alpen-Tuxer Alpen* (scale 1:50,000).

Cycling

The Zillertal is cycling nirvana, particularly for serious mountain bikers, many of whom limber up here before heading high into the Alps. The wide, sunny valley and surrounding

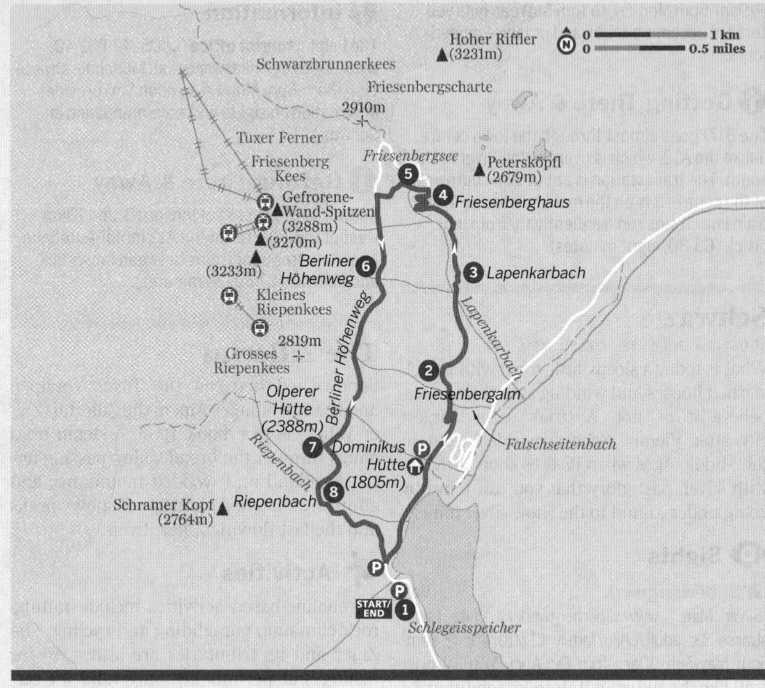

Walking Trail Zillertal Circuit

START SCHLEGEISSPEICHER
END SCHLEGEISSPEICHER
LENGTH 11KM; FIVE TO SIX HOURS

This high-level circuit provides tremendous views to the startlingly turquoise Schlegeisspeicher and snowcapped Zillertal Alps. Though the trek involves 850m of incline, the path is well graded and mostly gentle; however, use care in bad weather. Kompass 1:50,000 map No 37 *Zillertaler Alpen-Tuxer Alpen* covers the walk in detail.

Begin at the 1 **Schlegeisspeicher**, ringed by rugged 3000m-high peaks. From the northeast end of the car park follow signs towards the Dominikus Hütte, bearing right towards Friesenberghaus alpine hut. The path emerges at the tree line near the alpine pasture of 2 **Friesenbergalm** after about 45 minutes. It flattens to cross tarn-dotted pastures. Sidle around a shoulder and enter a valley overshadowed by Hoher Riffler.

Boulder-strewn meadows give way to scree patches and the 3 **Lapenkarbach** stream. The trail winds uphill via long bends, then tight switchbacks, to the 4 **Friesenberghaus** at the head of the valley around 1½ hours from Friesenbergalm. This is a scenic spot for a break.

Retrace your steps for 50m, following the signs right towards the Olperer Hütte and the Berliner Höhenweg. The trail descends slightly, crossing the outlet stream of 5 **Friesenbergsee**, then makes a short, steep ascent up the rocky slope on the other side. Turn left when you reach a junction and contour the mountainside ahead. The next 1½ hours follow an easygoing balcony trail, part of the multiday 6 **Berliner Höhenweg** route. It leads under the glacier-capped peaks of the Gefrorene-Wand-Spitzen.

About two hours from Friesenberghaus, cross a stream to reach 7 **Olperer Hütte**, a great place for a drink. Then it's a steady descent to the reservoir, winding gently over grassy hummocks before zigzagging down beside the 8 **Riepenbach** stream to the road (1½ hours from the Olperer Hütte). Turn left and head 1km to the parking area.

3000m peaks are laced with 800km of well-marked routes that reach from easygoing two-hour jaunts along the valley floor to panoramic mountain passes, such as the notoriously tough 56km trail from Fügen to Kellerjoch, a test of stamina and condition.

You can access many of the high-altitude and downhill routes using the cable cars in the valley, and local trains will transport your bike for free. Bikes are available for hire at major stations throughout the Zillertal, including Zell am Ziller and Mayrhofen, for €10/14 per half-/full day; e-bikes cost €18/26 respectively. For free maps, detailed route descriptions and downloadable GPS bike tours, visit www.zillertal.at or www.best-of-zillertal.at.

Festivals & Events

Almabtriebe HERITAGE

(late Sep-early Oct) The Zillertaler celebrate the coming home of the cows, which are adorned with elaborate floral headdresses and bells. The event is a valley-wide party with feasting, *Volksmusik* and schnapps before another harsh winter shovelling cow dung.

Information

Practically every resort has its own tourist office, but the main **tourist office** (05288-871 87; www.zillertal.at; Bundesstrasse 27d, Schlitters; 8.30am-noon & 1-5.30pm Mon-Thu, 8.30am-noon Fri) covering the whole valley is in Schlitters, 6km from Jenbach. It stocks plenty of information on outdoor activities, along with the *Zillertaler Gästezeitung* (partially in English) magazine.

Getting There & Away

The Zillertal is serviced by a private train line, the Zillertalbahn (www.zillertalbahn.at), which travels the 32km from Jenbach to Mayrhofen. Those with a thirst for nostalgia can take a *Dampfzug* (steam train) along the valley. It runs at 10.42am from Jenbach to Mayrhofen and at 2.33pm from Mayrhofen to Jenbach. A one-way/return ticket for the 1¾-hour journey costs €15/22. If you just want to get from A to B, it's better to take the ordinary train (€8.80, 54 minutes), which runs twice hourly.

Zell am Ziller

05282 / POP 1758 / ELEV 575M

Scenically located at the foot of knife-edge Reichenspitze (3303m), Zell am Ziller is a former gold-mining centre. There's now less sparkle and more swoosh about this rural and deeply traditional little village, with its fine skiing and thrilling 7.5km floodlit toboggan run. In summer, active types come to hike in the mountains or pedal up the Gerlos Alpine Rd to Krimml in the Hohe Tauern National Park.

Activities

Gerlos Alpine Road SCENIC DRIVE

(www.gerlosstrasse.at; toll car/motorcycle €9.50/6.50) Open year-round, the highly scenic Gerlos Alpine Rd links the Zillertal in Tyrol to Krimml in Salzburgerland, winding 12km through high moor and spruce forest, and reaching a maximum elevation of 1630m. The lookout above the turquoise *Stausee* (reservoir) is a great picnic stop, with a tremendous vista of the Alps. On the approach to Krimml near Schönmoosalm, there are bird's-eye views of the Krimml Falls.

Jodel Wanderweg WALKING

(Yodel Hiking Trail; www.jodelweg.at; Wald-Königsleiten) If you've ever felt the urge to burst into song Julie Andrews–style as you skip through meadows ablaze with wildflowers, you'll love the Jodel Wanderweg in Königsleiten, on the Gerlos Alpine Rd between Zell am Ziller and Krimml. You can practise your high notes at huts with giant cowbells, alpine horns and listen-repeat audio clippings.

Aktivzentrum Zillertal ADVENTURE SPORTS

(0664 5059594; www.aktivzentrum-zillertal.at; Freizeitpark Zell;) Craving a little adventure? This specialist takes you paragliding (€70 to €170), rafting on the Ziller (€40 to €65), canyoning (€30 to €85) and via ferrata climbing (€25 to €70) in summer. Winter activities include snowshoe hikes (€50), ski touring (€90) and ski triking (€30).

Arena Coaster ADVENTURE SPORTS

(www.zillertalarena.com; Zillertal Arena; adult/child coaster only €5.40/3.60, incl cable car €24.90/12.50; 9.30am-6pm late Jun-early Sep, shorter hours rest of year;) Feel your stomach do backflips with a whizzy, loop-the-loop ride on Zell's 1.5km roller-coaster bob. Kids love it.

Tours

Goldschaubergwerk TOURS

(www.goldschaubergwerk.com; Hainzenberg 73; adult/child €14/7; 9am-6pm) Goldschaubergwerk is a two-hour tour of a gold mine, 2km east of Zell on the Gerlos road. The entry price covers a cheese tasting in the show dairy and a visit to the animal enclosure with deer, emus and llamas.

Festivals & Events

Gauderfest BEER

(www.gauderfest.at; ⏲early May) Over-strenuous activities are not recommended after a bellyful of super-strong Gauderbier (reputedly over 10% alcohol), brewed specially for this shindig. As well as eating, dancing and excessive drinking, there's a historical parade and alpine wrestling.

Sleeping

Enzianhof FARMSTAY €

(☎05282-22 37; www.enzianhof.eu; Gerlosberg 23; s/d €41/70, half board per person extra €11; P 📶) High on a hilltop at 1272m, this rustic farmhouse is perfectly located for hiking and skiing, and has warm, spacious rooms. The farmer makes his own gentian schnapps and smokes his own ham, and you can fill up on Zillertaler specialities such as *Pressknödelsuppe* (Tyrolean dumpling soup) and goulash in the wood-beamed restaurant.

Camping Hofer CAMPGROUND €

(☎05282-22 48; www.campingdorf.at; Gerlosstrasse 33; campsite per adult/child/tent €8/5.70/9.50, d €58; P @ 📶 🏊) This tree-shaded site's first-rate facilities include a playground, a barbecue area and a heated pool. If you don't fancy pitching a tent, check out the well-kept, pine-panelled rooms in the guesthouse.

Gasthof Schulhaus GUESTHOUSE €€

(☎05282-33 76; www.schulhaus.tirol; Zellberg 162; d €70-90; P) Once a schoolhouse, Gasthof Schulhaus is now top of the hospitality class. You'll receive a warm welcome from the Geissler family at their hilltop abode in Zellberg, with stirring valley and mountain views, and a restaurant championing Slow Food. The spacious rooms and apartments are done Tyrolean-style, and local farm-fresh goodies appear at breakfast, which costs an extra €12.

ZILLERTAL ACTIVECARD

If you're planning on spending a week or more in the valley between late May and early October, the value-for-money Zillertal Activecard (six/nine/12 days €61.50/87.50/149.50) covers public transport, one journey per day on any of the Zillertal cable cars and entry to swimming pools.

Hotel Englhof BOUTIQUE HOTEL €€

(☎05282-31 34; www.englhof.at; Zellbergeben 28; s/d €74/118; 📶) Beautiful blond-wood-panelled, white-linen-dressed rooms (many with balconies) and amenities including free DVD rental make Englhof a superb place to stay. But what really seals the deal is its in-house gourmet restaurant and world-class cocktail bar with Austria's second-largest collection of spirits (over 1400 varieties), mixing incredible cocktails like a Bloody Mary with frozen cherry tomatoes and barbecued black-pepper seasoning.

Eating

★**Schulhaus** AUSTRIAN €€

(☎05282-33 76; www.schulhaus.tirol; Zellberg 162; mains €18-34; ⏲5-10pm Wed-Sat, from noon Sun) On its panoramic perch above Zell am Ziller, this old schoolhouse turned restaurant is Tyrolean through and through. The larch-wood interior is drenched in honeyed light, the terrace plays up the views deep into the valley and to the mountains beyond, while the succinct menu speaks of a family that believes in local sourcing and farm-fresh products.

Gasthof Bräu AUSTRIAN €€

(☎05282-231 30; www.hotel-braeu.at; Dorfplatz 1; mains €14-30; ⏲8am-11.30pm) With parlours as warm, woody and old-school rustic as they come, Gasthof Bräu rolls out traditional and hearty Austrian grub along the lines of *Graukäse Schlutzkrapferl* (ravioli-like pasta filled with Tyrolean grey cheese), organic pork cheeks cooked in Zillertal dark beer, and local venison. Pair with excellent home brews.

Information

The **tourist office** (☎05282-22 81; www.zell.at; Dorfplatz 3a; ⏲8am-noon & 1-6pm Mon-Fri, 8.30-12.30pm Sat) near the train tracks is a mine of information on walking, skiing and adventure activities in the area.

Getting There & Away

Normal trains to Mayrhofen (€2.50, 11 minutes) and Jenbach (€7.50, 40 minutes) are cheaper than the steam train. Twice-hourly trains to and from Innsbruck (€15, 1½ hours) require a change at Jenbach.

Zell am Ziller is the start of the Gerlos Alpine Rd (p305). By car between Zell am Ziller and Krimml, you can avoid the Gerlos Alpine Rd toll by following the (easy-to-miss) signs to Wald im Pinzgau, 6km north of Krimml.

Mayrhofen

☎05285 / POP 3858 / ELEV 630M

Mayrhofen is ever so traditional in summer, with its alpine dairies, trails twisting high into the mountains and stein-swinging *Volksmusik* pouring out of every *Gasthöfe*. But it dances to a different tune in winter. The skiing at Ahorn and Penken is some of the country's finest, a double whammy of cruising and kamikaze in the shadow of the glaciated Zillertal range, and the après-ski is the hottest this side of the Tyrolean Alps.

Sights & Activities

Penken MOUNTAIN
(www.mayrhofner-bergbahnen.com; action day ticket adult/child €30.40/15.20) Mayrhofen's 'action mountain', the Penken is where it is at in both winter and summer. Opened in 2015, the slick cable car affords panoramic views as it glides up to 1790m. Downhill mountain bikers are in heaven here, with numerous tours from easy-peasy to demanding. The website www.mayrhofen.at has a virtual bike map. It's also a magnet for hikers, paragliders and climbers, and skiers and freeriders in winter, with the Harakiri and Vans Penken Park.

Zillertal 3000 SNOW SPORTS
(www.zillertal.at; 2-/6-day Zillertal Superskipass €109.50/266.50) Mayrhofen is the showpiece of the Zillertal 3000, which covers 199km of slopes and 66 lifts (some pretty high-tech) in the highly scenic Zillertal. Ski buses connect the resorts. As well as being intermediate heaven, Mayrhofen has Austria's steepest black run, the kamikaze-like Harakiri, and appeals to freestylers for its fantastic terrain park. Even if snow lies thin in the valley, it's guaranteed at the nearby **Hintertuxer Gletscher** (Hintertux Glacier; www.hintertuxergletscher.at; day ski pass summer/winter €46/55.50).

Erlebnis Sennerei Zillertal FOOD
(www.erlebnissennerei-zillertal.at; Hollenzen 116; with/without tasting €18.90/12; ⏲9am-5pm) For a fly-on-the-wall tour of a working dairy, head to the Sennerei Zillertal, where a 30-minute tour guides you through the cheese-making processes, from culturing in copper vats to mould ripening. The final products are huge wheels of *Tilsiter*, *Bergkäse* and *Graukäse*, a grey cheese that is virtually fat-free. A tasting lets you try seven different cheeses. In summer, this is accompanied by live Tyrolean music at 3pm every Friday.

Action Club Zillertal ADVENTURE SPORTS
(☎05285-629 77, 0664 4413074; www.action club-zillertal.at; Hauptstrasse 458; ⏲9am-6pm) Action Club Zillertal is the place to go for adventure sports from rafting the raging waters of the Ziller River (€40) to canyoning (€45 to €120), tubing (€50), climbing (€60 to €100), guided mountain biking (€50 to €90) and tandem paragliding (€65 to €160).

Run & Walk Park RUNNING
The Run & Walk Park challenges Nordic walkers and joggers. The eight different routes, colour coded according to difficulty – blue is easy, red moderate, black difficult – include the Harakiri, only slightly easier to run than it is to ski! The tourist office has a route map.

Skischule Habeler SKIING
(☎05285-628 29; www.skimayrhofen.com; Hauptstrasse 458; ⏲8am-noon & 3.30-6pm Sun-Fri, 9am-noon & 1-7pm Sat) Chris Habeler, son of famous mountaineer Peter Habeler, runs this small, highly personal ski school with a passion. It offers both group and private lessons; prices are given on the website.

Stocky Air PARAGLIDING
(☎0664 3407976; www.stockyair.com; Hauptstrasse 456; ⏲9am-1pm & 3-6pm) This paragliding specialist will help you spread your wings in the surrounding Zillertaler Alps, with tandem flights costing between €85 and €320.

Vans Penken Park SNOW SPORTS
(www.vans-penken-park.com; Penken) Snowboarders are in their freestyle element in six areas with 11 kickers, 34 boxes and rails and a half-pipe at the Vans Penken Park in the Penken area, ranked one of Europe's best terrain parks.

Salewa Mountain Shop CLIMBING
(☎05285-632 58; www.salewa.com; Hauptstrasse 412; ⏲8.30am-6pm Mon-Sat, from 10am Sun) Runs climbing, via ferrata, glacier and ice-climbing tours, and rents out climbing equipment (€12).

Festivals & Events

Snowbombing SPORTS
(www.snowbombing.com; ⏲early Apr) The self-proclaimed greatest show on snow, Snowbombing in early April is Mayrhofen's biggest shindig. Some of the world's top boarders compete on the slopes, but most

people are just here for the party – six solid days of drinking and dancing to a cracking line-up of bands and DJs (Fatboy Slim headlined in 2019), plus fun from igloo raves to fancy-dress street parties in the mix.

Sleeping

Gästehaus Birkenhof GUESTHOUSE €
(05285-634 03; www.birkenhof.cc; Schwendaustrasse 184; d €78-94; P) This sweet, simple chalet run lovingly by the Moigg family is a bargain. Central yet still peaceful, the Birkenhof offers large, light rooms fitted out in pine-wood furnishings, which open onto balconies. There's a pretty garden for lingering in summer, a small fitness area, plus a playground and table tennis for kids.

Alpin Hotel Garni Eder HOTEL €€
(0664 506 03 69; www.eder-mayrhofen.at; Zillergrundweg 572; s/d/tr €47.50/95/134) Huddled away in a serene part of town yet close to the ski lifts, this alpine chalet gets the hotel-as-home concept spot on and the location is unbeatable. You're made to feel like one of the family: the pine-trimmed rooms are spacious and beautifully kept, the owners go out of their way to help, and breakfasts are copious.

Hotel Garni Glockenstuhl HOTEL €€
(05285-631 28; www.glockenstuhl.com; Einfahrt Mitte 431; s €77-80, d €128-134; P) Good old-fashioned Austrian hospitality, dreamy alpine views, free bike rental and a relaxing spa make this chalet stand head and shoulders above most in town. If you can drag yourself out of the comfiest of beds, you'll find a delicious breakfast with fresh eggs on the table.

Alpenhotel Kramerwirt HOTEL €€
(05285-67 00; www.kramerwirt.at; Am Marienbrunnen 346; incl half board s €86-101, d €138-200, ste €184-214; P) Ablaze with geraniums in summer, this rambling 500-year-old chalet has corridors full of family heirlooms, spacious, warm-hued rooms and a rooftop spa area with saunas and hot tubs affording surround views of the mountains. Get your tongue in a twist at the restaurant (mains €8 to €21) asking for the tasty *Zillertaler Bauernschmaus* (farmers' platter with meat, dumplings and sauerkraut).

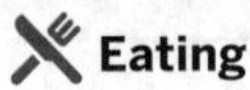

Eating

Gasser BURGERS €
(www.gasserspeck.at; Hauptstrasse 475; snacks €3-7; 7am-6pm Mon-Sat) This award-winning butcher is the perfect spot to grab a snack on the way down from the slopes. It does a mighty fine bratwurst, as well as burgers, sandwiches and smoked hams. Vegetarian options are also available.

Cafe-Konditorei Kostner CAFE €
(Hauptstrasse 414; snacks & mains €4-12; 6.30am-6pm) This candyfloss-pink villa has a popular terrace when the sun shines. The bakery side of it rolls out great spelt and rye bread, while the cafe rustles up tasty breakfasts, ice cream, speciality coffees and homemade cakes, alongside salads, toasties and heart-warming dishes such as goulash.

Metzgerei Kröll DELI €
(Scheulingstrasse 382; snacks €3-8; 7.30am-1pm & 3-6pm Mon-Fri, 7am-noon Sat) This family-run butchery is famed for its unique *Schlegeis-Speck* ham, cured in a hut at 1800m for three months to achieve its aroma. There are a handful of tables where you can sample this speciality and the delicious home-made sausages.

Gasthof Perauer AUSTRIAN €€
(05285-625 66; www.perauer.at; Ahornstrasse 854; mains €12-32; 11am-10pm;) With its tiled oven and all-wood interior, this *Gasthöfe* is as gorgeously Tyrolean as they come. On the meaty menu are home-cooked dishes prepared with top-quality regional ingredients and hearty specials from the family butchery, including game goulash with dumplings, crispy knuckle of pork in black beer jus and bang-on-the-money steaks. There are plenty of veggie options, too.

Wirtshaus Zum Griena AUSTRIAN €€
(0664 99327196; Dorfhaus 768; mains €8-16; 11am-11pm Wed-Mon;) Set in high pastures, this woodsy 400-year-old chalet is the kind of place where you pray for a snow blizzard, so you can huddle around the fire and tuck into the likes of *Schlutzkrapfen* (fresh pasta filled with cheese) and *Speckknödel* (bacon dumplings).

Drinking & Nightlife

White Lounge BAR
(www.white-lounge.at; Ahorn; 10am-4pm) Kick your skis off and chill over cocktails at this

2000m ice bar, with a big sunny terrace for catching rays. Things heat up with DJs and night sledding at Tuesday's igloo party (begins 8pm).

Ice Bar BAR
(Hauptstrasse 470, Hotel Strass; 3-10pm Dec-Apr) A loud, lary, anything-goes après-ski haunt brimming with boot-stomping revellers, Europop beats and, occasionally, go-go polar bears (we kid you not!). Arena nightclub is under the same roof.

Butcher Bar BAR
(www.perauer.at; Ahornstrasse 854; 4pm-1am) Taking its name from the family butchery that's part of Gasthof Perauer, this vaulted, incredibly cosy, nouveau-rustic bar is a fine choice for a home-brewed beer, gin or cocktail with antipasti.

Entertainment

Brück'n Stadl LIVE MUSIC
(Ahornstrasse 850, Gasthof Brücke; 3pm-4am) For year-round *Spass* (fun), you can't beat this lively barn and marquee combi. *Lederhosen*-clad folk stars get beer glasses swingin' in summer, while plentiful schnapps and DJ Mütze fuel the après-ski party in winter.

Information

The ultramodern **tourist office** (05285-67 60; www.mayrhofen.at; Dursterstrasse 225; 9am-6pm Mon-Sat, to 1pm Sun;) stocks loads of information and maps on the town. Look for the comprehensive *Info von A-Z*; it's free and written in English. There is a handy topographic model of the surrounding Alps, a 24-hour accommodation board and free wi-fi.

Getting There & Away

By the normal train that runs twice hourly, it's €8.80 each way to Jenbach (52 minutes). For the Zillertal Circuit, buses run between Mayrhofen and the Schlegeisspeicher reservoir (one way €7.50, 50 minutes, seven daily).

Ginzling

05286 / POP 400 / ELEV 999M

For a taste of what the Austrian Alps looked like before the dawn of tourism, head to Ginzling, an adorable little village 8km south of Mayrhofen.

Naturpark Zillertaler Alpen NATURE RESERVE
(www.naturpark-zillertal.at) The main draw for hikers in Ginzling is the Naturpark Zillertaler Alpen, a 379-sq-km nature park and pristine alpine wilderness of deep valleys and glaciated peaks. The Naturparkhaus Zillertaler Alpen runs 200 excellent themed guided hikes, most costing between €5 and €10, from May to October. The extensive program includes everything from llama trekking to sunrise photo excursions, herb walks and alpine hikes.

Be sure to reserve your place by 5pm on the day before your planned hike.

Gasthaus Alt-Ginzling GUESTHOUSE €€
(05286-202 96; www.ferienwohnungen-ginzling.at; Ginzling 240; d €94-108, apt €100-150; P) The most charming place to stay is Gasthaus Alt-Ginzling, once a wayside inn for smugglers travelling to Italy. The 18th-century farmhouse oozes history from every creaking beam, and the low-ceilinged, pine-panelled rooms are supremely cosy. The restaurant serves local rainbow trout.

Information

For details on activities in the park, including guided hikes, stop by the **Naturparkhaus Zillertaler Alpen** (05286-521 81; www.naturpark-zillertal.at; Ginzling 239; 8.30am-noon & 1-5pm Mon-Thu, 8.30am-noon Fri).

Getting There & Away

In winter, free ski buses run frequently to Mayrhofen; otherwise there is an hourly service (€3.80, 20 minutes). A road (toll car/motorcycle €12.50/8.50) snakes on from Ginzling up the valley to the Schlegeisspeicher reservoir, the trailhead for the stunning Zillertal Circuit.

Achensee

The fjord-like Achensee is Tyrol's largest lake and one of its loveliest, flanked by thickly wooded mountains. Days here unfold with boat tours of the lake or jaunts up to **Erfurter**, which opens up an alpine playground, with hiking, paragliding, ziplining and a via ferrata.

Rofanseilbahn CABLE CAR
(www.rofanseilbahn.at; adult/child return €21.50/13, Airrofan Skyglider €11.50/8; 8.30am-5pm Apr-Oct) Sweeping views over Achensee and the surrounding peaks can be had from Erfurter (1831m), which is easily reached by the Rofanseilbahn cable car from Maurach. To up the thrill factor, test out the Airrofan Skyglider, a kind of giant, multiperson zip line. Other adventure pursuits include paragliding

and flirting with climbing on the five-peak, six- to eight-hour via ferrata.

Achensee Boat Tours BOATING
(www.tirol-schiffahrt.at; adult/child €21/10.50; May-Oct) These two-hour spins of the fjord-like Achensee are a soothing way to take in the scenery.

Getting There & Away

The **Achenseebahn** (www.achenseebahn.at; one way/return €24/31), a private cogwheel steam train, trundles to the lake from Jenbach between May and October. Buses run regularly between Jenbach and Maurach/Achensee Seespitz (€3.80, 24 minutes).

Kitzbühel

05356 / POP 8272 / ELEV 762M

Ask an Austrian to rattle off the top ski resorts in the country, and Kitzbühel will invariably make the grade. Ever since Franz Reisch slipped on skis and whizzed down the slopes of Kitzbüheler Horn way back in 1893, so christening the first alpine ski run in Austria, Kitzbühel has carved out its reputation as one of Europe's foremost ski resorts. Legends have been made and born on these pistes, not least three-time Olympic medallist Toni Sailer.

Kitzbühel began life in the 16th century as a silver and copper mining town, and today continues to preserve a charming medieval centre despite its other persona as a fashionable and prosperous winter resort. It's renowned for the white-knuckled Hahnenkamm-Rennen downhill ski race in January and the excellence of its slopes.

Sights

Alpine Flower Garden GARDENS
(8.30am-5pm May-Sep) FREE Arnica, edelweiss and purple bellflowers are among the 400 alpine blooms flourishing at this quiet garden atop Kitzbüheler Horn. It's a four-hour (14km) hike one way, or a speedy cable-car ride. A highly scenic road also twists up to the mountain (toll per car/motorcycle €10/5, plus €3 per person).

Museum Kitzbühel MUSEUM
(www.museum-kitzbuehel.at; Hinterstadt 32; adult/child €7/free; 10am-5pm Fri-Wed, to 8pm Thu Apr-late Sep, reduced hours late Sep-Mar) This museum traces Kitzbühel's heritage from its Bronze Age mining beginnings to the present day. The big emphasis is on winter sports, and the permanent collection pays tribute to home-grown legends including ski racing champ Toni Sailer and winter landscape painter Alfons Walde. Head up to the roof terrace for far-reaching views over the *Altstadt* to the peaks beyond.

Activities

Streif SKIING
The mind-bogglingly sheer, breathtakingly fast Streif downhill course lures hard-core skiers to Kitzbühel – even experts feel their hearts do somersaults on the Mausefalle, a notoriously steep section with an 85% gradient. Jumps reach up to 80m and speeds can top 145km/h, which is sheer insanity on skis. One of the most terrifying World Cup courses, it's the stuff of legend.

Hahnenkammbahn CABLE CAR
(Hahnenkamm Cable Car; adult/child return €26.50/9.30, day ski pass adult/child €57/28) This cable car whisks you up to the summit of 1712m Hahnenkamm, a magnet for hikers and downhill bikers in summer and hard-core skiers – many attempting the legendary Streif race – in winter.

Element 3 ADVENTURE SPORTS
(05356-723 01; www.element3.at; Klostergasse 8; 9am-12.30pm & 2.30-5pm Mon-Fri) A ski school in winter, in summer this is a one-stop shop for adventure sports, including canyoning (€70), paragliding (€125) and via ferrate (€115).

Ski Safari SKIING
Confident intermediates up for a challenge can tackle the incredibly scenic 35km Ski Safari, linking the Hahnenkamm to Resterhöhe/Pass Thurn. The alpine tour is marked by elephant signs and is a good introduction to the entire ski area.

Schwarzsee SWIMMING
(adult/child €5/2.70; 8am-6pm Jun-Aug) For a cool summer swim, venture 3km northwest of the centre to Kitzbühel's natural swimming hole, the tree-flanked Schwarzsee. This lakeside lido has open-air pools and pedalo rental.

Kitzbüheler Hornbahn CABLE CAR
(Kitzbüheler Horn Cable Car; adult/child return €26.50/9.30) Hitching a ride on this cable car brings you to the Alpine Flower Garden. Hiking and mountain-biking trails fan out from the summit. A panoramic pick is the 2.4km Karstweg circuit, which affords

Kitzbühel

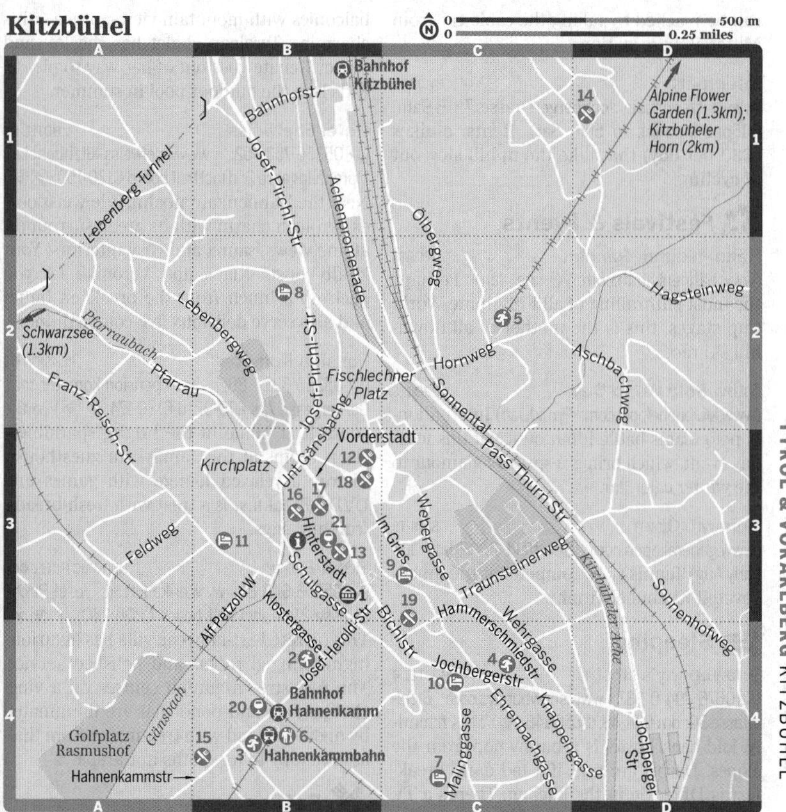

Kitzbühel

Sights
1 Museum Kitzbühel B3

Activities, Courses & Tours
2 Element 3 .... B4
3 Hahnenkammbahn B4
4 Intersport C4
5 Kitzbüheler Hornbahn C2
6 Streif B4

Sleeping
7 Hotel Edelweiss C4
8 Hotel Erika B2
9 Pension Kometer C3
10 Snowbunny's Hostel C4
11 Villa Licht B3

Eating
12 First Lobster B3
13 Huberbräu Stüberl B3
14 Kupferstube D1
15 Mocking B4
16 Pano B3
17 Restaurant Zur Tenne B3
18 Simple Food B3
19 s'Kitz C3

Drinking & Nightlife
20 Hahnenkamm Pavillon B4
21 Leo Hillinger B3

impressive glimpses of the surrounding karst landscape. In winter, Kitzbüheler Horn attracts novice skiers, with gentle cruising on sunny slopes.

Snowpark Kitzbühel SKIING
(www.snowpark-kitzbuehel.at; Hanglalm) Snowpark Kitzbühel is boarder and freeskier heaven with its rails, kickers, boxes, tubes and 35 obstacles. The snowpark at Hanglalm

can be reached by taking the cable car from Mittersill base station.

Intersport CYCLING
(www.kitzsport.at; Jochbergerstrasse 7; ⏲9am-6.15pm Mon-Fri, to 5pm Sat) Rents e-bikes (€30 per day) that take the uphill slog out of cycling.

Festivals & Events

Hahnenkamm-Rennen SPORTS
(www.hahnenkamm.com; ⏲late Jan) Perhaps the most enthralling of all FIS Alpine World Cup stages, this is the mother of all downhill ski races.

Snow Polo World Cup SPORTS
(www.kitzbuehelpolo.com; ⏲mid-Jan) International polo teams battle it out on ice at this four-day event, which brings a spritz of glamour to the winter calendar.

Generali Open SPORTS
(www.generaliopen.com; Sportfeld 2; ⏲late Jul-early Aug) Tennis stars compete for the much-coveted Kitzbühel Trophy.

Sleeping

Snowbunny's Hostel HOSTEL €
(☎0676 794 02 33; www.snowbunnys.com; Bichlstrasse 30; dm €24-48, d €66-146; 📶) This friendly, laid-back hostel is a bunny-hop from the slopes. Dorms are fine, if a tad dark; breakfast is DIY-style in the kitchen. There's a TV lounge, a ski storage room and cats to stroke.

★ **Villa Licht** HOTEL €€
(☎05356-622 93; www.villa-licht.at; Franz-Reisch-Strasse 8; d apt €130-580; P @ 📶 🏊) Pretty gardens, spruce modern apartments with pine trappings, living rooms with kitchenettes, balconies with mountain views, peace – this charming Tyrolean chalet has the lot, and owner Renate goes out of her way to please. Kids love the outdoor pool in summer.

Hotel Edelweiss HOTEL €€
(☎05356-752 52; www.edelweiss-kitzbuehel.at; Marchfeldgasse 2; d incl half board €120-150; P 📶) Near the Hahnenkammbahn, Edelweiss oozes Tyrolean charm with its green surrounds, alpine views, sauna and cosy interiors. Your kindly hosts Klaus and Veronika let you pack up a lunch from the breakfast buffet and also serve delicious five-course dinners.

Pension Kometer PENSION €€
(☎05356-622 89; www.pension-kometer.com; Gerbergasse 7; s €70-92, d €130-174; P 📶) Make yourself at home in the bright, sparklingly clean rooms at this family-run guesthouse. There's a relaxed lounge with games and DVDs. Breakfast is a treat with fresh breads, fruit and eggs.

Hotel Erika HISTORIC HOTEL €€€
(☎05356-648 85; www.erika-kitz.at; Josef-Pirchl-Strasse 21; d incl half board €206-280; P 📶 🏊) This turreted art-nouveau villa has luxurious high-ceilinged rooms and polished service. The rose-strewn garden centres on a vine-clad pagoda and pond that are illuminated by night. Unwind with treatments from thalassotherapy to hay baths in the spa.

Eating

Simple Food CAFE €
(☎0664 1652866; Im Gries 8; light bites €4.50-9; ⏲7am-7pm Mon-Fri) It's something of a godsend in pricey Kitzbühel to find a place like this: no fuss, no frills, just good honest grub from cooked breakfasts to healthy salads and smoothies, and burgers that deserve the credit they are given locally. The vibe is totally relaxed and friendly in the wood-lined interior.

Pano CAFE €
(☎05356-654 61; Hinterstadt 12; light bites €5-9; ⏲8am-6pm) Placing the emphasis on organic, wholesome ingredients, contemporary cafe Pano makes a relaxed postski or -hike pit stop for filling sandwiches, soup with wood-oven bread, salads such as lentil-feta with rocket, quiches, omelettes and homemade cakes.

★ **Restaurant Zur Tenne** AUSTRIAN €€
(☎05356-644 44-0; www.hotelzurtenne.com; Vorderstadt 8-10; mains €18-45; ⏲11am-11pm) Choose between the rustic, beamed interior

KITZBÜHEL AREA SKI PASSES

One-/three-/six-day passes cost €57/158/277 in the high winter season and €51.50/142/249.50 at all other times. Passes cover lifts, cable cars and ski buses as far south as Thurn Pass. If you plan to cover a lot of terrain, the **Super Ski Card** (1-/3-/6-day pass €59/166/283; www.superskicard.tirol) is your best bet; it spans the entire Kitzbühel Alps and covers some 2750km of pistes.

where an open fire crackles and the more summery conservatory at Hotel Tenne's highly regarded restaurant. Service is polished and the menu swings from classics such as beef goulash to seasonal meats (goose, venison) and fish dishes such as roasted trout with sweet potato mash and black garlic.

Mocking AUSTRIAN €€
(☎05356-665 44; www.mocking-kitzbuehel.at; Hahnenkammstrasse 8; mains €17.50-27; ⊙10am-9.30pm Wed-Sat, to 4pm Sun) At the bottom of the slopes, this rustic-chic restaurant keeps the mood delightfully cosy with its all-wood interior. Here the chef puts his own stamp on regional ingredients. Meals begin with homemade bread, butter, bacon and chives, moving on to dishes like eel with beetroot and mushroom powder, ravioli with nettle, curd and black pudding, and schnitzel with cranberries.

First Lobster SEAFOOD €€
(☎05356-666 98; www.firstlobster.com; Im Gries 6; mains €22.50-50; ⊙4-11.30pm Mon-Sat) Oyster shells mounted on brick walls are a quirky nod to what's on the menu at this slick, bistro-style restaurant, with banquette seating. The chef takes pride in sourcing the freshest fish and seafood for dishes such as Gillardeau oysters, warm octopus salad with fennel and tomato, or half a lobster sliding into chilli-spiced spaghetti. It's terrific.

Huberbräu Stüberl AUSTRIAN €€
(☎05356-656 77; Vorderstadt 18; mains €9-19; ⊙8am-11.30pm Mon-Sat, from 9am Sun; 👪) An old-world Tyrolean haunt with vaults and pine benches, this tavern favours substantial portions of Austrian classics, such as schnitzel, goulash and dumplings, cooked to perfection. Cash only.

s'Kitz AUSTRIAN €€
(☎05356-753 26; www.skitz.at; Bichlstrasse 7; mains €10.50-19; ⊙9.30am-midnight Mon-Sat) A real local's haunt, s'Kitz reels in a lively crowd with its beer garden terrace and laid-back vibe. The food is good honest Austrian home cooking: goulash, lentil stew, *Schlutzkrapfen* (Tyrolean-style ravioli filled with cheese and spinach) and lighter options such as roast beef salad with Styrian pumpkin oil. Lunch specials go for a reasonable €8.70.

Kupferstube GASTRONOMY €€€
(☎05356-631 81; www.tennerhof.com; Griesenauweg 26; 4-/7-course tasting menu €95/140; ⊙7-9pm Wed-Sun) Fine dining in Kitzbühel doesn't get better than at the Kupferstube in the five-star Hotel Tennerhof. Award-winning chef Stefan Lenz puts an imaginative spin on carefully sourced regional ingredients, which might, season depending, mean beautifully cooked organic pigeon with plum and hay milk or Viennese catfish and snails with beurre blanc and lovage – all served with panache in refined surrounds.

KITZBÜHEL DISCOUNT CARDS

Stay in Kitzbühel and you'll automatically receive the **Red Card**, which entitles you to a number of discounts on local attractions and activities, plus free guided hikes.

You can save in summer (May to October) by investing in the **Kitzbüheler Alpen Summer Card** (three-day pass with/without bus €63.40/55), which covers 36 lifts and cable cars. Children pay half-price.

Drinking & Nightlife

Leo Hillinger WINE BAR
(☎05356-202 51; Rathausplatz 5; ⊙noon-midnight) This ultra-chic wine bar and shop has a terrace that is great for people-watching over fine wines and small plates.

Hahnenkamm Pavillon BAR
(www.pavillon-kitz.at; Hahnenkammstrasse 2; ⊙2-10pm Dec-Apr) This slope-side pick opposite Hahnenkammbahn is a rollicking après-ski haunt in winter, with DJs, singing, schnapps-drinking and skiers jiggling to Austrian beats in their ski boots.

Information

The central **tourist office** (☎05356-666 60; www.kitzbuehel.com; Hinterstadt 18; ⊙8.30am-6pm Mon-Fri, 9am-6pm Sat, 10am-noon & 4-6pm Sun) has loads of info in English and a 24-hour accommodation board.

Getting There & Away

Kitzbühel is on the B170, 30km east of Wörgl and the A12 motorway.

The main train station is 1km north of central Vorderstadt. Trains run frequently from Kitzbühel to Innsbruck (€17.50, 1¼ hours) and Salzburg (€32.30 to €44.80, two to 2½ hours). For Kufstein (€12.50, 50 minutes), change at Wörgl.

Kufstein

05372 / POP 19,223 / ELEV 499M

In the 1970s, Karl Ganzer sang the praises of Kufstein in his hit yodelling melody 'Perle Tirols' (The Pearl of Tyrol) and rightly so. Resting at the foot of the mighty limestone Kaisergebirge and crowned by a fortress, Kufstein's backdrop is picture-book stuff. Control of the town was hotly contested by Tyrol and Bavaria through the ages until it finally became Austrian property in 1814.

Sights

★Festung Kufstein FORTRESS
(www.festung.kufstein.at; Oberer Stadtplatz 6; adult/child €12.50/7.50; 9am-6pm) Lifted high on a rocky crag like an offering to the alpine peaks that surround it, Kufstein's turreted castle provides a fascinating insight into the town's turbulent past. The fortress dates from 1205 (when Kufstein was part of Bavaria) and was a pivotal point of defence for both Bavaria and Tyrol during the struggles. The round Kaiserturm (Emperor's Tower) is a 1522 addition.

Römerhofgasse HISTORIC SITE
A classic saunter leads along gingerbready Römerhofgasse, a reconstructed medieval lane that looks fresh-minted for a Disney film set with its overhanging arches, lanterns and frescoed facades. Even the crowds and souvenir kitsch – marmot ointment, *Dirndls*, strapping *Lederhosen*, you name it – detract little from its appeal.

Activities

★Kaisergebirge OUTDOORS
Rising like a sheer curtain of limestone to the east, the Kaisergebirge range reaches up to 2300m and stretches as far as St Johann in Tirol. It attracts walkers, mountaineers and skiers alike. The Kaisergebirge is actually two ranges, split by the east–west Kaisertal valley. The northern range is the **Zahmer Kaiser** (Tame Emperor) and the southern the **Wilder Kaiser** (Wild Emperor) – no medals for guessing which has the smoother slopes! Pick up a free *Wanderkarte* (walking map) from the tourist office.

Hechtsee SWIMMING
(www.hechtsee.at; adult/child €4.50/2; 9am-7pm late May-early Sep) This crystal-blue, mountain-rimmed lake sits 3km to the northwest of Kufstein. As well as a beach for swimming, there are also other activities such as rowing boats, table tennis and volleyball. A free city bus goes to Hechtsee in summer during fine weather (ask at the tourist office).

Stimmersee SWIMMING
(adult/child €4.50/2; late May-early Sep) Stimmersee, 2.5km southwest of Kufstein, is hailed for having some of the cleanest waters in Austria. Rimmed by forest and ragged mountain peaks, the glassy green lake is fed by mountain streams. It has sunbathing lawns, cafes, hiking trails, beach volleyball and a playground for kids.

Sleeping

Camping Maier CAMPGROUND €
(05372-583 52; www.camping-maier.com; Egerbach 54, Schwoich; campsite per adult/child/tent €5.50/4/8;) Bordering woodland, this friendly campground 5km south of Kufstein has tree-shaded pitches, plus a playground and an outdoor pool.

Träumerei #8 BOUTIQUE HOTEL €€
(05372-621 38; www.auracher-loechl.at; Römerhofgasse 4; s €85, d €137.50-191, ste €348; @) No two rooms are alike at alpine-chic Träumerei #8, squeezed between Römerhofgasse and the Inn River. The 34 highly original rooms are themed on 'dream cities', from Amsterdam with its clogs and windmill sails to the crimson-kissed romance of Paris, with its quirky corset wallpaper. Breakfast is fantastic, with antipasti, regional cheeses, cold meats and yoghurts, and a muesli bar.

Hotel Kufsteinerhof HOTEL €€
(05372-714 12; www.kufsteinerhof.at; Franz-Josef-Platz 1; s €58-76, d €116-124, f €144-164; P) With its spacious, parquet-floored rooms in clean, contemporary style and substantial breakfasts, the Kufsteinerhof is one of the best central picks in Kufstein. It's just a three-minute walk from the fortress.

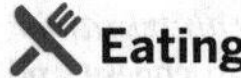

Eating

★Auracher Löchl AUSTRIAN €€
(05372-621 38; www.auracher-loechl.at; Römerhofgasse 4; mains €13-28; 11am-10pm) Creaking with the weight of its 600-year history this enticingly cosy, low-beamed restaurant is the one-time haunt of Tyrolean hero Andreas Hofer. The kitchen rolls out brilliant

WORTH A TRIP

THE INNTAL

Shadowing the turquoise, swiftly flowing Inn River, the Inntal (Inn Valley) has few major sights but the scenery is beautiful, particularly around **Pfunds** with its jagged peaks and thickly forested slopes. Many of the ornately frescoed houses here are similar in design to those found in the Engadine in Graubünden, Switzerland, further up the Inntal.

South of Pfunds, you have a choice of routes. If you continue along the Inn you'll end up in Switzerland (infrequent buses). Alternatively, if you bear south to castle-crowned **Nauders** you'll soon reach South Tyrol (Italy) by way of the Reschen Pass (open year-round).

Accommodation is plentiful in the form of alpine chalet-style hotels, B&Bs and holiday apartments in the pretty medieval villages of Pfunds or Nauders. Browse the Tirol Oberland website (www.tiroler-oberland.com) for suggestions.

Pfunds and Nauders are your best bets for a bite to eat. Here you'll find rural mountain inns where you can dig into Austrian classics and fondue, as well as a few cafes and bars.

Buses run roughly hourly from Landeck to Pfunds (€8.80, 42 minutes) and Nauders (€11.30, one hour), where it's possible to head on with public transport to Merano in Italy, but at least three changes are required.

incarnations of Austrian classics such as *Kaspressknödel* (cheesy dumplings), pork roast and goulash, plus hot-stone steaks. For a taste of everything, opt for a Tyrolean tapas sharing plate.

Bräustüberl AUSTRIAN €€
(05372-224 68; www.braeustueberl-kufstein.at; Oberer Stadtplatz 5a; day special €8.90, mains €9-18.50; 10am-2.30pm & 5pm-midnight Mon-Fri, 10am-11pm Sat) As traditionally Austrian as they come, this brewpub-restaurant dishes up satisfying Tyrolean and Bavarian grub, from schnitzel as big as a boot to goulash and bratwurst with lashings of sauerkraut – all of which go well with the freshly tapped brews. The atmosphere is laid-back and the terrace has castle views. Gluten-free, vegetarian and children's options are also available.

Purlepaus FUSION €€
(05372-636 33; www.purlepaus.at; Unterer Stadtplatz 18; lunch €6.90-8.20, mains €9-19.50; 11am-10pm) This is a perennially popular choice with a stylish vaulted interior and a big chestnut tree–shaded terrace. The worldly menu skips from pasta and tarte flambée to Thai curries and Tyrolean grub. Vegetarian picks are also available.

Drinking & Nightlife

Stollen 1930 COCKTAIL BAR
(www.auracher-loechl.at; Römerhofgasse 5; 6pm-2am) If you're seriously into gin, Stollen 1930 is unmissable. The atmosphere is incredible as it's set in a cave that was hacked out of the fortress mountain more than 600 years ago. Without losing a jot of original character, it has been done up in the style of a glam speakeasy, with cage chandeliers, velvet armchairs and soft backlighting.

Fritz Wein Cafe WINE BAR
(www.fritz-wein-cafe.com; Unterer Stadtplatz 18; 4pm-midnight Tue-Fri, from 11am Sat) Adding a dash of urban slickness to Kufstein's after-dark scene, this wood-floored wine bar, lit by globe lights, has a terrific assortment of Austrian wines, which pair nicely with the day specials, tapas and cheese tasting plates on offer.

Information

At the **tourist office** (05372-622 07; www.kufstein.com; Unterer Stadtplatz 8; 9am-6pm Mon-Fri, 9am-1pm Sat), staff will hunt down accommodation without charging commission. If you stay overnight, ask for the Gästekarte, which has different benefits in summer and winter.

Getting There & Away

The frequent trains to Kitzbühel (€12.50, 50 minutes) require a change at Wörgl. The easiest road route is also via Wörgl. Kufstein is on the main Innsbruck–Salzburg train route. Direct trains to Salzburg (€37.50, 1¼ hours) run at least every two hours; those to Innsbruck (€17.50, 40 minutes) are half-hourly. Buses leave from outside the train station.

Söll

05333 / POP 3631 / ELEV 703M

Söll is a well-known ski resort 10km south of Kufstein. A favourite of boozy, raucous visitors in the 1980s, the resort has successfully reinvented itself and is now a family-oriented place with myriad outdoor activities.

The highest skiing area overlooking the resort is Hohe Salve at 1828m.

Activities

Hohe Salve WALKING

(www.kitzbueheler-alpen.com; cable car one way/return €14.50/19; 9am-5pm;) Walkers and paragliders are drawn to the heights of Hohe Salve in summer. At the first stage of the cable car climbing the mountain is **Hexenwasser**, a walking trail dotted with fun family activities. Along the route are water obstacles, sundials, playgrounds, a working mill and bakery, and an apiary. Throughout the summer you can see (and sample) bread, schnapps and cheese made the traditional way.

The same slopes swish to the sound of skis in winter.

Skiwelt SKIING

(www.skiwelt.at) Straddling the ragged limestone mountains of the Wilder Kaiser Brixental, Skiwelt comprises 284km of pistes, most of which are easy or moderate. Passes are €48 for a day in the high season. Cross-country skiing is also a popular winter pastime, with trails running as far as St Johann in Tirol.

Festivals & Events

Almabtrieb CULTURAL

(late Sep) Locals wait quite literally for the cows to come home at this late-September festival, when the bell-swinging cows are paraded down from their summer pastures to the village, decorated in floral finery. Brass bands and market stands selling farm-fresh produce complement the parade.

Sleeping & Eating

Eggerwirt HERITAGE HOTEL €€

(05333-52 36; www.eggerwirt.cc; Dorf 14; s €57-59, d €96-100, tr €160-168;) The welcome is heartfelt at this family-run, chalet-style hotel, with fine mountain views and a lounge warmed by an open fire in winter. The warm-hued rooms come with pine trappings. In summer, the outdoor pool and sun terrace are big draws, while the sauna area is great for a postski steam in winter. Bike rental is available on request.

Auf da Mühle AUSTRIAN €€

(05333-205 90; www.aufdamuehle.at; Dorf 89; mains €12-40; 10am-2pm & 4pm-midnight Mon & Wed-Fri, 10am-11pm Sat & Sun;) Chipper staff bring sizzling, top-quality steaks, salads, wok dishes and pizza to the table at Auf da Mühle, bang in the centre of Söll. The look is contemporary, with sleek contours and smooth wood panelling, and a long list of cocktails fuels the buzzy vibe. Day specials go for €7.50 (vegetarian) to €8.50 (with fish or meat).

Information

The **tourist office** (050-509 210; www.wilderkaiser.info; Dorf 84; 8am-noon & 1-6pm Mon-Fri, 3-6pm Sat, 9am-noon Sun), in the centre of the village, provides information on activities and will help you find accommodation.

Getting There & Away

Söll is on the B178 between Wörgl and St Johann in Tirol. It's not on a train line, but there are plenty of buses from Kufstein (€5, 27 minutes).

Seefeld

05212 / POP 3440 / ELEV 1180M

Seefeld sits high on a south-facing plateau, ringed by the fearsome limestone peaks of the Wetterstein and Karwendel Alps. While most Tyrolean resorts are crazy about downhill, Seefeld's first love is *Langlauf* (cross-country skiing), and fans of the sport flock here to skate and glide along 279km of prepared trails in winter.

Seefeld was the proud cohost of the Winter Olympic Games in 1964 and the FIS Nordic World Ski Championships in 2019.

Sights

Pfarrkirche St Oswald CHURCH

(Dorfplatz; 8am-7pm) Seefeld's trophy sight is this late-Gothic parish church, the supposed location of a miracle. The story goes that Oswald Milser gobbled a wafer reserved for the clergy at Easter communion here in 1384. After almost being swallowed up by the floor, the greedy layman repented, but the wafer was streaked with blood – not from foolish Oswald but from Christ, naturally. You can view the **Blutskapelle** (Chapel of the Holy Blood), which held the original wafer, by climbing the stairway.

Activities

Seefeld's raison d'être is cross-country skiing. Some 256km of well-groomed *Loipen* (trails) criss-cross the sunny plateau to Mösern, 5km away, where there are fine views of the Inn River and the peaks beyond.

The 48km of downhill skiing here is best suited to beginners and intermediates. Your pass to the slopes is the multiday Happy Ski Card (three-day pass adult/child €127.50/76.50), covering all lifts in Seefeld. The two main areas are Gschwandtkopf (1500m) and Rosshütte (1800m); the latter connects to higher lifts and slopes on the Karwendel range.

For some challenging walks, cable cars ascend nearby Seefeld Spitze (2220m) and Reither Spitze (2374m); consult the tourist office for more information or join one of its regular guided walks.

Sleeping

★Hotel Helga HOTEL €€
(☎05121-23 26; www.hotel-helga.at; Haspingerstrasse 156; incl half board s €76-111, d €138-222; P 📶) The Kratzer-Pilotto family bend over backwards to please at this homely chalet, with sweet and simple rooms dressed in traditional Tyrolean style, with lots of wood and florals. Stay here for the mountain views, the terrific four-course dinners, the familiar atmosphere and the silence needed for a sound night's sleep. A sauna takes the chill out of winter.

Central HOTEL €€
(☎05212-32 88; www.central-seefeld.at; Münchnerstrasse 41; s €71-131, d €112-224, half board €19; P 📶) Friendly service, an attractive spa and kids' play areas make the Central a good choice. The well-lit rooms with balconies are contemporary Tyrolean in style, with light birch wood and earthy hues. The food makes the most of local products and there are organic options at breakfast.

Eating

Waldgasthaus Triendlsäge AUSTRIAN €€
(☎05121-25 80; www.triendlsaege.at; Triendlsäge 259; mains €10-22; ⏲11.30am-10pm Thu-Tue) A romantic slice of Tyrolean rusticity, this woody restaurant, named after its sawmill, hides in the forest, a 20-minute walk north of town. Or reach it on cross-country skis or by horse-drawn carriage in winter. Sit by the open fire or on the terrace for regional dishes that play up seasonal, farm-fresh ingredients, from trout to game and wild mushrooms.

Strandperle INTERNATIONAL €€
(☎05121-909 97; www.strandperle.at; Innsbrückerstrasse 500; mains €11-28; ⏲10am-10pm) Overlooking the calm waters of Wildsee, Strandperle is a funky glass-and-granite place. The menu delivers Med-inspired flavours such as rack of milk-fed lamb with kohlrabi salad, and herb-crusted tuna sashimi with herb risotto and balsamic tomatoes. The decked terrace has the finest views of the Alps anywhere in Seefeld.

Information

The **tourist office** (☎050-88 00; www.seefeld.com; Bahnhofplatz 115; ⏲8.30am-6pm Mon-Sat, 10am-12.30pm & 3-5pm Sun) at the main train station has stacks of info on accommodation and outdoor activities.

Getting There & Away

Seefeld is 25km northwest of Innsbruck, just off the Germany-bound B177. The track starts climbing soon after departing Innsbruck, providing spectacular views across the whole valley. Trains run to/from Innsbruck (€6.30, 37 minutes), Mittenwald (€7.20, 19 minutes) and Garmisch-Partenkirchen (€12.40, 43 minutes) in Germany.

Stams

☎05263 / POP 1495 / ELEV 672M

The pride and joy of tiny Stams is its striking Cistercian abbey, easily identified from afar by its twin cupolas. The abbey is by far the biggest draw, but should you wish to linger in this peaceful corner of the Inn Valley, there are some lovely walking trails heading up into the surrounding hills and oak woods.

Stift Stams ABBEY
(www.stiftstams.at; Stiftshof 3; tours adult/child €12.50/6; ⏲guided tours hourly 9-11am & 1-5pm Mon-Sat, 1-5pm Sun Jun-Sep, 4pm Thu Oct-May) One of Tyrol's true architectural highlights is the ochre-and-white Zisterzienstift in Stams, founded in 1273 by Elizabeth of Bavaria, the mother of Konradin, the last of the Hohenstaufens. Set in pristine grounds, the

monumental facade stretches 80m and is easily recognised by its pair of silver cupolas at the front, which were added as a final flourish when the abbey was revamped in baroque style in the 17th century.

Orangerie Stams AUSTRIAN €€

(☎05263-202 08; www.orangeriestams.at; Stiftshof 7; lunch €8.50, mains €13.50-22.50; ⏰10am-10pm Mon-Sat, to 6pm Sun; 👪) With its atmospheric stone vaults and cosy niches, this restaurant within the abbey complex is big on charm. The menu emphasises high-quality regional produce. Snag a table to dig into dishes such as South Tyrolean beef tartare, Styrian chicken salad with pumpkin oil or *Stamser Pfandl*, grilled pork with garlic butter, root vegetables and roast potatoes. Vegetarian options are available.

Kloster Shop FOOD & DRINKS

(⏰9am-noon & 1-5pm Mon-Sat, 1-5pm Sun Jun-Sep, 9am-noon & 2-5pm Mon-Sat Oct-May) Marmalade, juice, honey, liqueurs and schnapps made on the Stift Stams premises can be bought from the Kloster shop, plus bread that's freshly baked here on Monday, Wednesday and Friday.

Getting There & Away

Stams is on the train route between Innsbruck and Landeck (both €10, 40 minutes). Both the A12 and B171 pass near the abbey.

The Ötztal

POP 12,000

Over millennia, the Ötztal (Ötz Valley) has been shaped into rugged splendour. No matter whether you've come to ski its snow-capped mountains, raft its white waters or hike to its summits, this valley is all about big wilderness. Guarding the Italian border and dominated by Tyrol's highest peak, Wildspitze (3774m), this is one of three river valleys running north from the Ötztaler Alpen to drain into the Inn River.

Sights

Ötzi Dorf MUSEUM

(www.oetzi-dorf.at; Am Tauferberg 8, Umhausen; adult/child €8.10/4; ⏰9.30am-5.30pm May-Oct; 👪) This small open-air museum cleverly brings to life the Neolithic world of Ötzi, the ice man. A visit takes in traditional thatched huts, herb gardens, craft displays and enclosures where wild horses, Mangalitza pigs, rare-breed Soay sheep and oxen roam. Multilingual audio guides are available. See the website for times of kid-pleasing activities (most costing between €5.90 and €7.90), which range from shooting with a yew bow to making a flint knife.

Stuibenfall WATERFALL

(👪) From Ötzi Dorf, it's a beautiful 20-minute forest walk to Tyrol's longest waterfall, the wispy Stuibenfall, cascading 159m over slate cliffs and moss-covered boulders.

ICE MAN

In 1991 German hiker Helmut Simon came across the body of a man preserved within the Similaun Glacier in the Ötztaler Alpen, some 90m within Italy. Police and forensic scientists were summoned to the scene. Carbon dating revealed that the ice man, nicknamed 'Ötzi', was nearly 5400 years old, placing him in the late Stone Age and making him the oldest and best-preserved mummy in the world.

Ötzi became big news, more so because his state of preservation was remarkable; even the pores of his skin were visible. In addition, Ötzi had been found with 70 artefacts, including a copper axe, bow and arrows, charcoal and clothing. Physiologically he was found to be no different from modern humans. X-rays showed he had suffered from arthritis, frostbite and broken ribs.

Not everybody was worried about these finer points, however. Several Austrian and Italian women contacted Innsbruck University shortly after the discovery and asked to be impregnated with Ötzi's frozen sperm, but the all-important part of his body was missing.

Ötzi was relinquished to the Italians to become the centrepiece of a museum in Bolzano in 1998. In September 2010 the family of the late Helmut Simon were awarded €175,000 for his groundbreaking discovery. In 2017 Ötzi was in the news again as fresh research revealed he has 19 genetic relatives living in Tyrol.

You can continue for another 40 minutes up to the top viewing platform and hanging bridge. A thrilling 450m *Klettersteig* (via ferrata) takes you right over the waterfall; bring your own karabiner and helmet.

Activities

★Aqua Dome SPA

(☎05253-6400; www.aqua-dome.at; Oberlängenfeld 140, Längenfeld; 3hr card adult/child Mon-Fri €21.50/12, Sat & Sun €24.50/15, sauna world €15; ⊙9am-11pm, sauna world 10am-11pm) Framed by the Ötztaler Alps, this crystalline spa looks otherworldly after dark when its trio of flying saucer–shaped pools are strikingly illuminated. And there's certainly something surreal about gazing up to the peaks and stars while floating in a brine bath, drifting around a lazy river or being pummelled by water jets.

Area 47 ADVENTURE SPORTS

(☎05266-876 76; www.area47.at; Ötztaler Achstrasse 1, Ötztal Bahnhof; water park adult/child/family €25/15/62; ⊙10am-6pm May-early Oct; 👪) Billing itself as the ultimate outdoor playground, this huge sports and adventure park is the Ötztal's flagship attraction, dramatically set at the foot of the Alps and on the edge of a foaming river. The place heaves with families and flirty teenagers in summer.

Sölden SKIING

(www.soelden.com; 1-/6-day pass €52/302.50) An Alpine Ski World Cup venue, Sölden is a snowsure ski resort with a high-speed lift network and fun-loving après-ski scene. Spread between 1350m and 3340m, the resort's 144km of slopes attract confident intermediates and are complemented by glacier skiing at Rettenbach and Tiefenbach. For many, the highlight is the 50km **Big 3 Rally**, a four-hour downhill marathon which begins at Giggijoch gondola and takes in three 3000m peaks.

With snow from October to May, the resort has one of the longest seasons in the Tyrolean Alps.

Timmelsjoch Pass SCENIC DRIVE

(www.timmelsjoch.com; car/motorbike €16/14, with Ötztal Card free; ⊙Jun-Oct) Often nicknamed the 'secret pass to the south', this little-driven but nevertheless startlingly beautiful pass road wiggles from the Ötztal and the Passeier Valley in the Italian South Tyrol. Known since the Stone Age, the route attracted traders and smugglers in the Middle Ages. Negotiating 30 hairpin bends, it crests the highest point at 2509m, where a tavern awaits.

> **ÖTZTAL CARD**
>
> You can save in summer by investing in the Ötztal Card (three/seven/10 days €58/80/102, half-price for children). From June to early October the pass covers public transport and cable cars in the valley, attractions such as Ötzi Dorf, activities from outdoor swimming pools to bike rental, plus one free entry to Aqua Dome and Area 47.

Alpin Zeit CLIMBING

(☎0650 9003038; www.alpinzeit.tirol) If you want to brush up your climbing skills in the Ötztal – and frankly there's no better place in Tyrol to do just that – you can hook onto courses with the experts at this centre, ranging from one-and-a-half-hour intro sessions (€19) to guided via ferrata tours of the Stuibenfall (€60) and high mountain tours (from €350 per day).

Obergurgl & Hochgurgl SKIING

(www.obergurgl.com; day ski pass adult/child €49/30; 👪) Around 14km south of Sölden is family-friendly Obergurgl (1930m), Austria's highest parish, with skiing largely aimed at beginners and intermediates. Obergurgl is actually at the head of the valley, but the road doubles back on itself and rises to Hochgurgl (2150m), where the pistes are steeper and the views equally impressive.

Sleeping & Eating

★Hotel Rita SPA HOTEL €€

(☎05253-53 07; www.hotel-rita.com; Oberlängenfeld 44a, Längenfeld; incl full board s €112-125, d €194-228, ste €222-272; P 📶 🏊) The Lengler family extend a heartfelt welcome at this pretty chalet hotel, a five-minute walk from Aqua Dome. Set in gardens with mountain views, Hotel Rita has spacious, contemporary rooms and a terrific spa area with an indoor pool, a whirlpool, herb-scented saunas and a hammam. It's all about the details here: from lovingly prepared six-course dinners to free guided hikes and bicycle, map and walking-pole rental.

Natur & Aktiv Resort RESORT €€

(☎05252-603 50; www.nature-resort.at; Piburgerstrasse 6, Ötz; incl half board d €174-278; P @ 📶) 🍃 This riverside retreat has eco-chic chalet rooms, warmly decorated in sustainable pine. It's a solid family choice, with free activities such as guided mountain hikes and

IMST HOLIDAY PASS

The Imst Holiday Pass, which you automatically receive when you stay overnight in town, entitles you to free use of public transport, admission to sights such as the Haus der Fasnacht, plus numerous discounts on outdoor activities.

bike tours, plus deals on rafting and canyoning. That's if you can tear yourself away from the saunas and open fire in the spa.

Gampe Thaya AUSTRIAN €€
(0664 1972 544; www.gampethaya.riml.com; Gampealm 1; mains €11-25; 8.30am-5.30pm mid-Jun–Oct & Dec-Apr;) High above Sölden, this dream of a mountain hut has ringside views of the Ötztal Alps from its sun terrace – equally lovely whether snowbound in winter or with cows grazing the flowery pastures in summer. Come for hearty, cheese-driven treats such as *Ötztaler Kasknödelsuppe* (regional cheese dumpling soup) and sauerkraut with homemade sausage and bacon dumplings.

Information

The valley's main **tourist office** (057 2000; www.oetztal.com; Gemeindestrasse 4, Sölden; 8am-6pm Mon-Sat, 9am-noon & 3-6pm Sun) is in Sölden, though there are others in villages such as Ötz and Längenfeld. All can arrange accommodation and have brochures on activities in the area.

Getting There & Away

From Ötztal Bahnhof, buses head south roughly hourly to destinations including Umhausen (€5, 31 minutes) and Sölden (€10, one hour).

With your own wheels you should be able to get at least as far as Hochgurgl all year, but the road beyond into Italy via the high-alpine 2509m Timmelsjoch Pass (p319) is often blocked by snow in winter.

Trains arrive at Ötztal Bahnhof at the head of the valley and run frequently to Innsbruck (€12.50, 22 to 49 minutes), Imst-Pitztal (€3.80, nine minutes) and Landeck (€7.50, 26 minutes).

Imst

05412 / POP 10,504

Beautifully situated in the wide Gurgltal (Gurgl Valley) and spreading towards a range of thickly wooded mountains, Imst is famous for its many springs. While the town itself won't keep you long, its surrounding meadows, rugged peaks and gorges might. Imst makes a fine base for hiking and skiing in the nearby Ötztal.

Sights & Activities

★ **Rosengartenschlucht** GORGE
(Rose Garden Ravine; Rosengartlweg; May-Oct;) FREE An easygoing family hike is the 5km (approximately three-hour) loop through the dramatic 200m-high Rosengartenschlucht, where boarded walkways make for a gentle ascent and afford sterling views of a waterfall. At the top, the walk continues through forest and along a trail overlooking the Lechtaler Alps. You can't miss the **Blaue Grotte**, a cave pool that is a startling shade of blue.

The trail starts and ends at the Johanneskirche (St John's Church) opposite the tourist office, which stocks maps of the walk.

From May to October you can hook onto the tourist office's guided hike at 2pm on Monday (reserve your place by 10am). It's free with the Imst Holiday Pass, or otherwise €10 per person. Wear sturdy shoes.

Haus der Fasnacht MUSEUM
(www.fasnacht.at; Streleweg 6; adult/child €5/1; 4-7pm Fri) Every four years, Imst plays host to a Shrovetide festival, the Unesco-listed **Schemenlaufen** (ghost dance); the most recent was on 9 February 2020. The highlight is the vibrant parade of characters, from hunchback *Hexen* (witches) to *Spritzer* that squirt water at spectators. This museum homes in on this centuries-old tradition and exhibits many of the hand-carved ghost masks.

Starkenberger Biermythos BREWERY
(05412-662 01; www.starkenberger.at; Griesegg 1, Tarrenz; tour adult/child €7/free; 10am-5pm Tue-Sun May-Oct, 10am-noon & 1-4pm Tue-Fri Nov-Apr) Housed in a medieval castle, this 200-year-old brewery sits 3km north of Imst in Tarrenz. A visit dashes through the brewing process and includes a beer tasting. If you can't get enough of the stuff, you can even bathe in it by calling ahead – it does wonders for the complexion, apparently.

Alpine Coaster ADVENTURE SPORTS
(Hoch-Imst; adult/child €7.50/5.30; 10am-5pm May-Oct;) The Alpine Coaster is billed as the world's longest alpine roller coaster and offers a thrilling ride down the mountains. A gondola shuttles passengers uphill to the starting point, where they board self-controlled bobs

to catapult 3.5km downhill, negotiating tricky bumps and hairpin bends.

Sleeping

Romedihof HOSTEL €

(☎05412-222 12 10; www.romedihof.at; Brennbichl 41; dm €23-27, d €56;) Lodged in a 16th-century farmhouse, Romedihof is a terrific base for hiking, cycling and skiing. The interiors have been carefully restored, with beams, fireplaces and stucco adding a historic edge. Room rates include bread delivered fresh from a local baker for preparing your own breakfast in the shared kitchen. Take the train to Imst-Pitztal then walk 10 minutes: see the website for a detailed map.

Hotel Hirschen HOTEL €€

(☎05412-69 01; www.hirschen-imst.com; Thomas-Walch-Strasse 3; s €65-94, d €114-158;) This central guesthouse has bright, comfy, pine-clad rooms, an indoor pool and a modern spa area (check out the water beds in the relaxation room for a posthike snooze). A plate of venison ragout is never far away in the wood-panelled restaurant (mains €10 to €18), where stag heads stud the walls.

Information

The **tourist office** (☎05412-691 00; www.imst.at; Johannesplatz 4; 8am-5pm Mon, 9am-5pm Tue-Fri, 9am-noon Sat;) is highly informed on accommodation and activities in Imst and its surrounds; there's also free wi-fi.

Getting There & Away

The town is slightly to the north of the main east–west roads (the A12 and B171), and is served by frequent buses and trains (from Innsbruck €15, 40 minutes).

Getting Around

Adults may feel slightly silly boarding the Imster Bummelbär (adult/child €3/2, twice daily) tourist train, but it's handy for reaching nearby sights including Starkenberger Biermythos.

The tourist office has a list of outfits with bike and e-bike rental.

Ehrwald

☎05673 / POP 2593

Nudging the German border, this bijou town is dwarfed by colossal peaks, including the craggy limestone peaks of the Wetterstein range and Germany's highest of the high – 2962m Zugspitze. In summer, its hiking trails thread high to waterfall-laced mountains, while in winter it offers well-groomed slopes for beginner and intermediate skiers.

Zugspitze VIEWPOINT

(www.zugspitze.at; cable car one way/return €30/46.50) Ehrwald's crowning glory is the glaciated 2962m Zugspitze, Germany's highest peak, straddling the Austro-German border. From the crest there's a magnificent panorama of the main Tyrolean mountain ranges, as well as the Bavarian Alps and Mt Säntis in Switzerland. North of Zugspitze is Garmisch-Partenkirchen, Germany's most popular ski resort.

Information

For information on accommodation and activities, contact the **tourist office** (☎05673-20 00 02 08; www.ehrwald.com; Kirchplatz 1; 8.30am-5pm Mon-Fri) in the heart of the town. Staff will help find rooms free of charge.

Getting There & Away

Trains from Innsbruck (€17.50, 1¾ hours) to Ehrwald pass through Germany; you must change at Garmisch-Partenkirchen. Austrian train tickets are valid for the whole trip.

Landeck

☎05442 / POP 7725

Landeck is an ordinary town with an extraordinary backdrop: framed by an amphitheatre of forested peaks, presided over by a medieval castle, and bordered by the fast-flowing Inn and Sanna Rivers. The town makes a good-value base for outdoor activities and exploring the nearby Inntal and Patznauntal valleys.

Sights

Schloss Landeck CASTLE

(www.schlosslandeck.at; Schlossweg 2; adult/child €7.70/2; 10am-5pm mid-Apr–late Oct, 1-5pm mid-Dec–early Jan;) Standing sentinel above Landeck, this 13th-century hilltop castle is visible from afar. The 1st-floor **museum** showcases everything from Celtic figurines to hand-carved *Krampus* (devil) masks, as well as a wonderful mechanised nativity scene during Advent. Climb the dizzying staircase to the tower for sweeping views over Landeck and the Lechtaler Alps.

Stanz VILLAGE

(www.brennereidorf.at) If all the fresh air and activity of Landeck have worked up a thirst, pop over to Stanz, 3km away. Set on a sunny plateau dotted with apple and plum orchards, the village has 150 houses and a whopping 60 schnapps distilleries. There are a number of rustic huts where you can kick back and taste the local firewater before rolling back down to the valley.

Zammer Lochputz GORGE
(www.zammer-lochputz.at; adult/child €4.50/3.50; ⏲9.30am-5.30pm May-Sep, 10am-5pm Sat-Mon Oct) A roller coaster of water thrashes the limestone cliffs at Zammer Lochputz gorge just outside of Landeck. Leading up through pine forest, a trail passes viewpoints and some interesting rock formations – look out for the head of a bull and a nymph.

Activities

Landeck attracts the odd skier to its 22km of mostly intermediate slopes (a day ski pass costs €39), but is better known for its hiking trails. The magnificent **Adlerweg** (Eagle Trail) stops off in Landeck on its 280km journey through Tyrol. Many footpaths can be accessed by taking the Venet cable car up to Krahberg (2208m).

Sport Camp Tirol ADVENTURE SPORTS
(☎05442-626 11; www.sportcamptirol.at; Mühlkanal 1; 👪) This is a one-stop action shop for activities including paragliding (€125), canyoning (€58 to €95), white-water rafting (€38 to €62) and climbing (€60). You can also rent mountain bikes here (half-/full day €20/25) to head off on one of the tourist office's free GPS tours or tackle the downhill Inn Trail.

Festivals & Events

Stanz Brennt FOOD & DRINK
(Stanz bei Landeck; ⏲Sep) In early September, the village of Stanz hosts Stanz Brennt, a distillery festival with plenty of the local schnapps, live music, food stalls and a farmers market selling fruit-based goodies.

TIROLWESTCARD

If you're staying overnight in summer, pick up the TirolWestCard (www.tirolwest.at; available from your accommodation on arrival) for free access to the major sights, outdoor pools and the bus network. In summer, the tourist office arranges guided walks from herb strolls to mountain hikes (free with the TirolWestCard), and can advise on activities from llama trekking to vie ferrate.

Sleeping

Gasthof Greif GUESTHOUSE €
(☎05442-622 68; www.gasthof-greif.at; Marktplatz 6; s €50-58, d €76-88; P) Greif sits on a quiet square above the main street just down from the castle. Its 1970s-style rooms are large and tidy, and its restaurant (mains €9 to €16) serves solid Tyrolean cuisine.

Hotel Mozart HOTEL €€
(☎05442-642 22; www.mozarthotels.at; Adamhofgasse 7; s/d/f incl half board €88/156/230; P 🏊) It's amazing how far Amadeus travels in Austria. This particular Mozart pleases with big sunny rooms opening onto balconies and broad mountain views. The flowery gardens and indoor pool with a little spa area invite relaxation, and there's ample bike storage.

Eating

Cafe Haag CAFE €
(Maisengasse 19; snacks €3.50-6; ⏲8am-noon & 2-6pm Mon-Fri, 9am-noon Sat) Local plums, nuts and honey go into this cafe's divine chocolate, made with the milk of Tyrolean grey cattle, and the cakes are just the sugar kick needed for the uphill trudge to the castle.

Schrofenstein AUSTRIAN €€
(☎05442-623 95; www.schrofenstein.at; Malserstrasse 31; lunch €10.50, mains €14-20; ⏲11.30am-9pm; 👪) With a generous helping of Austrian heartiness and a dash of Mediterranean lightness, Schrofenstein's elegantly rustic restaurant moves with the seasons: from spring asparagus to summer berries and mushrooms and autumn game. Dishes such as steak tartare with quail egg and sourdough bread, and roasted pikeperch with purple potato mash, spinach and lemongrass hit the mark every time.

Information

The friendly staff at the **tourist office** (☎05442-656 00; www.tirolwest.at; Malserstrasse 10; ⏲8.30am-noon Mon-Fri; 📶) can help book accommodation and have a list of local pensions.

Getting There & Away

Trains run roughly hourly to Innsbruck (€17.50, 44 minutes to one hour) and at least every two hours to Bregenz (€26.10, 1¾ hours). Buses depart from outside the train station and/or from the bus station in the centre. The train station is 1.5km to the east; to get into town walk left on leaving the station and stay on the same side of the river.

The A12 into Vorarlberg passes by Landeck, burrowing into a tunnel as it approaches the town. The B171 passes through the centre of town.

Getting Around

In summer, the **Venet** (www.venet.at; adult/child one way €14.40/8.20, return €16.50/9.80; 8am-5pm) cable car zooms up to Krahberg (2208m), where there is a web of marked footpaths.

THE PAZNAUNTAL

POP 5950

Grazing the Swiss border and running west of the Inntal, the Paznauntal (Paznaun Valley) is a dramatic landscape overshadowed by the pearly white peaks of the Silvretta range. The villages are sleepy in summer, a lull that is broken in winter when skiers descend on party-hearty resorts such as Ischgl.

Ischgl

05444 / POP 1593 / ELEV 1377M

Ischgl becomes a quintessential powdersville in winter, with snow-sure slopes straddling the Swiss border, and a boisterous après-ski scene. The resort is a bizarre combination of rural meets raunchy; a place where table-dancing bars, folk music and techno happily coexist. Summer is decidedly more chilled and arguable more authentic, attracting hardcore hikers, mountain bikers and climbers to higher reaches.

Activities

Silvretta Arena SKIING

(full-region 1-/3-/6-day pass €56/166.50/307.50) Ischgl is the centrepiece of the vast Silvretta Arena, offering fabulous skiing on 239km of groomed slopes, ultramodern lifts (heated seats and all) and few queues. Suited to all except absolute beginners, the resort has great intermediate runs around Idalp, tough black descents at Greitspitz and Paznauer Taya, and plenty of off-piste powder to challenge experts.

Skiing to Samnaun in Switzerland for lunch adds the novelty factor. Boarders can play on the half-pipe, jumps, rails and boarder-cross at two snowparks.

Silvretta Mountain Bike Arena MOUNTAIN BIKING

Few Austrian resorts can match Ischgl for mountain biking. The mammoth Silvretta Mountain Bike Arena features 1000km of bikeable territory, ranging from downhill tracks to circular trails. Pick up a map of the area at the tourist office.

For bike rental, try Bründl Sports.

Skyfly ADVENTURE SPORTS

(adult/child €39/25; 10am-4.30pm Tue-Sun Nov–early May, 11am-6pm Tue-Sun late Jun–mid-Sep) The mountains are but a blur on this high-flying addition to Ischgl. The 50m-high, 2km-long zipwire whisks you above the valley and it's seriously fast and fun – picking up speeds of up to 85 km/h. Kids should be at least eight years old and 1.2m tall; under-10-year-olds need to be accompanied by an adult.

Silvretta Bike Academy MOUNTAIN BIKING

(www.silvretta-bikeacademy.at; Paznaunweg 15; 9am-6pm) The Silvretta Bike Academy offers fat-bike rental (€54 per day) and arranges technique training and freeride day tours costing €51 to €60.

Klettersteige WALKING

A step up from the alpine hikes heading out from Ischgl is the more ambitious scrambling on the *Klettersteige* (fixed-rope routes) at 2871m Greitspitz and 2929m Flimspitze.

Toboggan Track SNOW SPORTS

(adult/child €14/8.50) The 7km toboggan track offers a bumpy downhill dash through the snow from Idalp to Ischgl, which is particularly scenic when floodlit on Monday and Thursday nights from 7pm to 10pm. Toboggans can be hired at the mountain station for €9/4.50 for adults/children.

Bründl Sports CYCLING

(www.bruendl.at; Dorfstrasse 64; 9am-6pm) This central sport shop rents out mountain bikes (€28), e-bikes (€42) and downhill bikes (€57) in summer.

Festivals & Events

Top of the Mountain MUSIC

(late Nov & late Apr) This winter-season opening and closing concert has welcomed a host of stars, including Lenny Kravitz in 2019.

Ironbike SPORTS

(Silvrettaparkplatz, Partenen; Aug) Super-fit mountain bikers compete in this 75.8km obstacle course of a race, involving steep climbs and exhilarating descents in the Silvretta massif.

Sleeping

Hotel Alpenstern HOTEL €
(☎05444-512 01; www.alpenstern.at; Versahlweg 5; d €76; P 📶) Nice surprise: one of Ischgl's sweetest hotels is also among its cheapest. The friendly Walser family keeps the modern alpine-style rooms spotless and serves generous breakfasts. In winter, the spa is great for postski downtime.

Gletscherblick B&B €€
(☎05444-52 52; www.gletscherblick-ischgl.at; Kirchenweg 12; s €87-123, d €134-196, tr €186-279; P 📶) The slickly contemporary, wood-and-stone-built Gletscherblick bills itself as a B&B but is a cut above with its boutiquey flair and first-rate facilities. The welcoming owners have put a lot of detail into the wood-floored, modern-alpine rooms, with pops of purple and pink, and picture windows framing the view, plus there's an appealing spa for a post-ski steam.

AlpVita Piz Tasna HOTEL €€
(☎05444-52 77; www.piztasna.at; Stöckwaldweg 5; s €75, d €138-152, half board €17; P @ 📶) Picturesquely set on a slope, Piz Tasna gets rave reviews for its heartfelt welcome, big, comfy rooms with fine mountain views, and superb food that places the accent on regional, organic ingredients (half board is worth the extra). The spa has an indoor pool, saunas, herbal steam rooms and a relaxation zone with hay and water beds.

Eating

Kitzloch INTERNATIONAL €€
(☎05444-56 18; www.kitzloch.at; Galfeisweg 3; mains €14.50-31; ⏲après-ski 4-7pm, restaurant 8-11pm Dec-Apr) Wild après-ski shenanigans (DJs, fancy dress and all) should work up an appetite for dinner in the rustic, fire-warmed restaurant. Go for the famous sticky spare ribs, a pot of bubbling fondue or classics such as crispy pork belly with sauerkraut. Portions are very generous.

Paznaunerstube GASTRONOMY €€€
(☎05444-600; www.trofana-royal.at; Dorfstrasse 95, Hotel Trofana Royal; menus €60-120; ⏲7-10pm Mon-Sat) Much-lauded chef Martin Sieberer turns every meal into a gastronomic event at this restaurant. In a refined wood-panelled parlour lit by chandeliers, regional specialities such as milk-fed Galtür lamb are given an inventive twist, served with panache and paired with top wines.

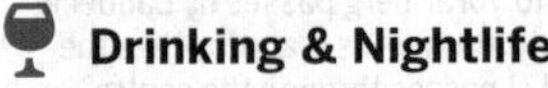

Drinking & Nightlife

Kuhstall BAR
(www.kuhstall.at; Dorfstrasse 74; ⏲11am-1am) This funky little shack is *the* place for slope-side socialising, with DJs, dancing and good vibes. Gear up for a big night out in Ischgl here.

Trofana Alm BAR
(www.trofana-alm.at; Dorfstrasse 91; ⏲3-8pm) A huge wooden barn with live Austrian bands and potent apple schnapps working the crowd into a singing, dancing frenzy.

Information

The **tourist office** (☎050-990 100; www.ischgl.com; Dorfstrasse 43; ⏲8am-noon & 1-5pm) stocks heaps of literature on hiking, biking and skiing in the area, plus accommodation brochures.

Getting There & Away

Buses operate hourly between Ischgl and Landeck (€8.80, 43 minutes).

Arlberg Region

The wild and harshly beautiful Arlberg region, shared by Vorarlberg and Tyrol, comprises several linked resorts and offers some of Austria's finest skiing. Heralded as the cradle of alpine skiing, St Anton am Arlberg is undoubtedly the best-known and most popular resort.

St Anton am Arlberg

☎05446 / POP 2372 / ELEV 1304M

Once upon a time St Anton was but a sleepy village, defined by the falling and melting of snow and the coming and going of cattle, until one day the locals beheld the virgin powder on their doorstep and discovered their happy-ever-after... In 1901 the resort founded the first ski club in the Alps and downhill skiing was born, so if ever the ski bug is going to bite you it will surely be here.

Nestled at the foot of 2811m-high Valluga and strung out along the northern bank of the Rosanna River, St Anton am Arlberg is a cross between a ski bum's Shangri La and Ibiza in fast-forward mode – the terrain fierce, the nightlife hedonistic.

Sights

St Anton Museum MUSEUM

(www.museum-stanton.com; Rudi-Matt-Weg 10; adult/child €5/3; ⏲noon-6pm Tue-Sun) Set in attractive gardens above St Anton and housed in a beautiful 1912 villa, this nostalgic museum traces St Anton's tracks back to the good old days when skis were little more than improvised wooden planks. Audio guides are available in English, German, Italian and French.

Activities

Winter Activities

St Anton is the zenith of Austria's alpine skiing, with the state-of-the-art cable cars connecting it to over-the-mountain Lech and Zürs. The terrain is vast, covering 306km of slopes, and the skiing challenging, with fantastic backcountry opportunities (200km of off-piste runs) and exhilarating descents including the **Kandahar** run on Galzig.

Cable cars ascend to **Valluga** (2811m), from where experts can go off-piste all the way to Lech (with a ski guide only). For fledglings, there are nursery slopes on **Gampen** (1850m) and **Kapall** (2330m). **Rendl** is snowboarding territory with jumps, rails and a half-pipe. A 10-minute stroll east of St Anton is **Nasserein**, where novices can test out the nursery slopes.

A single ski pass (one-/three-/six-day pass €56.50/164/300) covers the whole Arlberg region and is valid for all 88 lifts.

Ski Arlberg SNOW SPORTS

(www.skiarlberg.at; 1-/3-/6-day pass €56.50/164/300) Ski Arlberg is one of Austria's most famous skiing regions and deservedly so. Its centrepiece is St Anton am Arlberg, a mecca to expert skiers and boarders, with its great snow record, challenging terrain and terrific off-piste; not to mention the most happening après-ski in Austria, if not Europe. Its over-the-valley neighbours are the resorts of Lech and Zürs in Vorarlberg.

Arlrock ADVENTURE SPORTS

(www.arlrock.at; Bahnhofstrasse 1; adult/child climbing wall €9/5, boulder wall €6.50/5; ⏲9am-8pm) This striking leisure centre by the train station has climbing and boulder walls, kids' play areas, a bowling alley and tennis courts. It's also the home base of **H2O Adventure** (☎05472-66 99; www.h2o-adventure.at; Bahnhofstrasse 1, Arlrock; rafting €53-99, canyoning €65-150, mountain biking €39-59; ⏲9am-6pm May–mid-Oct), offering adrenaline-based activities from rafting on the Sanna River to canyoning, ziplining and downhill mountain biking.

Run of Fame SKIING

An epic run if ever there was one, St Anton's Run of Fame is an 85km marathon ski, covering an altitude difference of 18,000m. The run covers the entire Arlberg skiing area and takes the best part of a day, so brace yourself (and your legs) for one hell of a burner.

Rodelbahn SNOW SPORTS

(adult/child €13/6.50, sled rental €9; ⏲7.30-9.30pm Tue & Thu Dec-Apr) Fancy a twilight dash through the snow? Every Tuesday and Thursday evening in winter, the 4km-long Rodelbahn toboggan run from Gampen to Nasserein is floodlit. Simply grab your sled and away you go! Sleds can be rented at the Talstation base station.

Summer Activities

Walking in the mountains is the most popular summertime activity, and the meadows full of wildflowers and grazing cattle are pure Heidi. A handful of cable cars and lifts rise to the major peaks. If you're planning on going hiking, pick up a detailed booklet and map from the tourist office.

The tourist office also produces a small booklet with a number of suggested **cycling** trails in the area.

ST ANTON AM ARLBERG DISCOUNT CARDS

St Anton wings its way into summer with the fantastic **Summer Card**, free from your hotel or guesthouse when you stay overnight. It yields some excellent benefits, including one day of cable-car use, one entry to Arlberg Well.com (p327), one guided walk, one green fee, entry to the museum, one other activity (these range from yoga to e-bike tours), children's activities, plus free transport on buses between Landeck and St Christoph.

Upgrade to a **Premium Card** (three/five/seven days €55/66/77, children pay half-price) and you get daily use of the pool at Arlberg Well.com, cable cars and all activities for the duration of your stay. Activities can be prebooked at the tourist office or online at www.sommerkarte.at.

St Anton am Arlberg

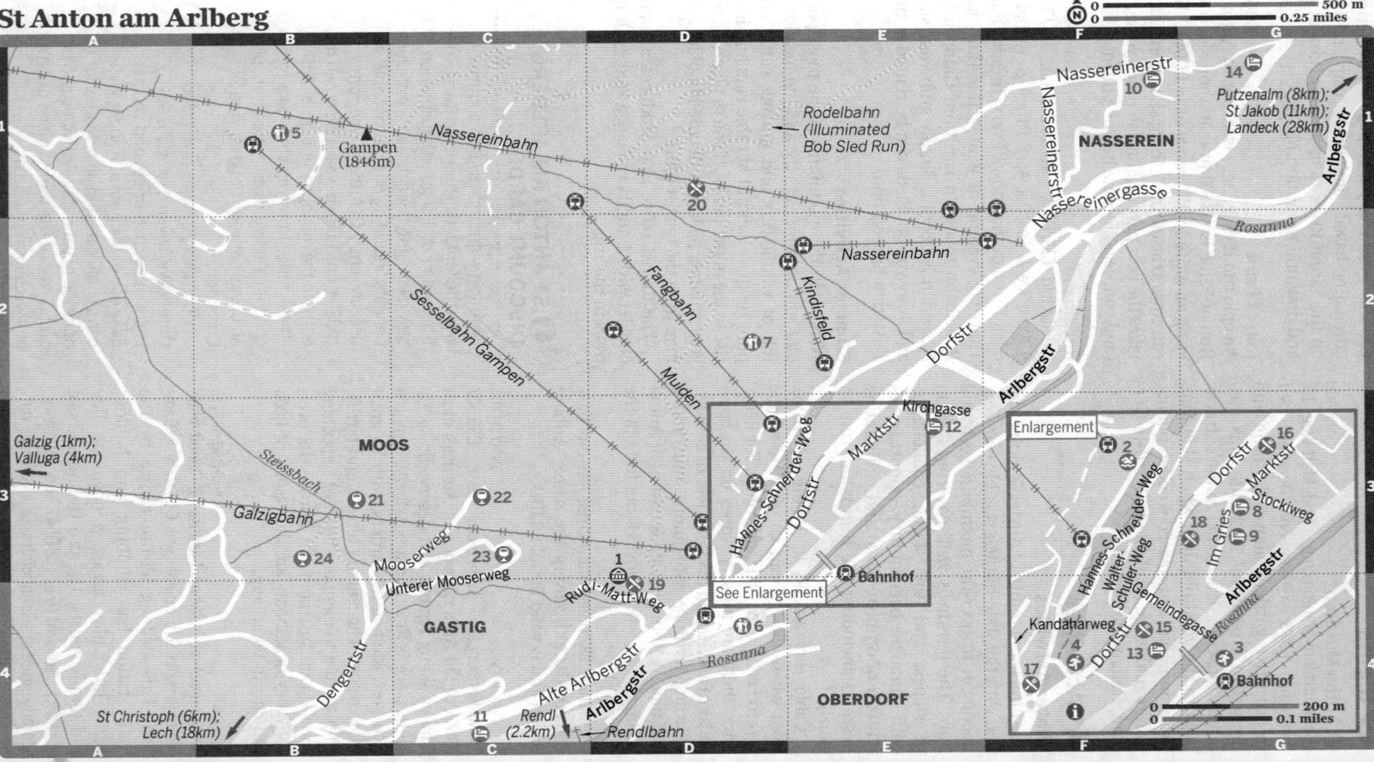

St Anton am Arlberg

Sights

1	St Anton Museum	D3

Activities, Courses & Tours

2	Arlberg Well.com	F3
3	Arlrock	G4
	H2O Adventure	(see 3)
4	Intersport Arlberg	F4
5	Rodelbahn	B1
6	Run of Fame	D4
7	Ski Arlberg	D2

Sleeping

8	Altes Thönihaus	G3
9	Himmlhof	G3
10	Hotel Garni Ernst Falch	F1
11	Lux Alpinae	C4
12	Piltriquitron Shelter	E3
13	Rundeck	F4
14	Sonnbichl	G1

Eating

15	Bodega	F4
16	Fuhrmann Stube	G3
17	Galzig Bistro	F4
18	m3 Restaurant	G3
19	Museum Restaurant	D4
20	Rodelalm	D1

Drinking & Nightlife

21	Heustadl	B3
22	Krazy Kanguruh	C3
23	Mooserwirt	C3
24	Sennhütte	B3
	Taps	(see 22)

Arlberg Well.com SWIMMING

(www.arlberg-wellcom.at; Hannes-Schneider-Weg 11; adult/child €8/4.50, incl sauna €16; ⌚9am-9pm) You can gaze up to the Alps from the indoor and outdoor pools or warm up in the sauna complex at this striking glass-and-wood leisure centre. There's also curling (summer) and ice skating (winter), plus a tennis court and fitness centre.

Intersport Arlberg CYCLING

(www.intersport-arlberg.com; Dorfstrasse 1; mountain bike/e-bike/ski rental per day €27/39/36; ⌚8.30am-1pm & 2-6pm) Bang in the centre of the village, Intersport is well stocked with sports equipment. In summer you can rent bikes, e-bikes and even walking boots; in winter, skis and cross-country skis. You can also enlist the services of a professional hiking, biking or skiing guide here.

Festivals & Events

Arlberg Adler SPORTS

(www.arlbergadler.eu) The Arlberg Adler triathlon kicks off with *der weisse Rausch* (the white thrill) ski race in April; then the Jakobilauf half-marathon in July, and the Bike Marathon in August.

Mountain Yoga Festival SPORTS

(www.mountainyogafestivalstanton.at; ⌚early Sep) Do you know your downward-facing dog from your tree pose? If the answer is yes, head on over to Mayrhofen's Mountain Yoga Festival. Held against the stunning backdrop of the Arlberg Alps, the four-day festival attracts yoga instructors from all over the world.

Almabtrieb CULTURAL

(Griesplatz; ⌚mid-Sep) The cows come home in their floral finery at September's Almabtrieb, a village-wide excuse for a party.

Sleeping

Piltriquitron Shelter GUESTHOUSE €

(☎0676 7400908; www.piltriquitron.com; Kirchgasse 10; s €44-64, d €58-81) One for serious outdoor-lovers, this Nordic-cool guesthouse is super central. Jacob, the Danish owner, is a terrific host and his incredible photography of the Alps and Patagonia adorns the communal lounge, where complimentary tea and coffee are available. A keen mountaineer and expeditioner, he can provide tips and help arrange hiking, trail running, climbing, fly fishing, kayaking and more.

Sonnbichl HOTEL €€

(☎05446-22 43; www.dassonnbichl.at; St Jakober Dorfstrasse 11; d €118-278) In a tranquil spot close to St Jakob, this family-run, adults-only chalet extends a friendly welcome. Decked out in pine furnishings and affording mountain views, the rooms are spacious, spotless and bright – the pick of which have balconies. There's a sauna for a postslope unwind and a highly regarded traditional restaurant (mains €17 to €24) serving the likes of venison ragout and schnitzel.

Hotel Garni Ernst Falch GUESTHOUSE €€

(☎05446-28 53; www.hotelfalch.at; Ing-Gomperz-Weg 26; d €82-114; P 📶) The Falch family are the heart and soul of this wonderful B&B, perched above St Anton, a five-minute stroll from the Nassereinbahn. The homely rooms are bright and pine-clad, with balconies for soaking up the alpine views. Nothing is too much trouble: whether you need a pick-up from the station or Nordic poles for a hike, just say the word.

Altes Thönihaus GUESTHOUSE €€

(05446-28 10; www.altes-thoenihaus.at; Im Gries 1; s €69-73, d €134-142; P) Dating to 1465, this listed wooden chalet oozes alpine charm from every last beam. Fleecy rugs and pine keep the mood cosy in rooms with mountain-facing balconies. Downstairs there's a superb little spa and restored *Stube*.

★**Himmlhof** GUESTHOUSE €€€

(05446-232 20; www.himmlhof.com; Im Gries 9; d €266-348, ste €312-998; P@) This *himmlisch* (heavenly) Tyrolean chalet has wood-clad rooms brimming with original features (tiled ovens, four-poster beds and the like). An open fire for afternoon tea and a cosy spa with a grotto-like plunge pool beckon after a day's skiing.

Rundeck HOTEL €€€

(05446-31 33; www.hotelrundeck.at; Arlbergstrasse 59; d €198-312; @) Clean lines, earthy tones and nutwood panelling define the streamlined rooms at design-focused Rundeck. There's a sleek spa and a backlit bar with an open fire for relaxing moments, plus a playroom for the kids. Summer rates are roughly half those quoted here.

Lux Alpinae DESIGN HOTEL €€€

(05446-301 08; www.luxalpinae.at; Arlbergstrasse 41; d incl half board €170-440; P) This design hotel wings you into the 21st century with glass-walled rooms that bring the mountains indoors and industrial-chic interiors blending concrete, wood and steel. Personalised service (including a driver to take you to the slopes), a first-rate restaurant and a spa add to its appeal. There's a minimum two- or three-night stay, depending on dates, in winter.

Eating

Putzenalm AUSTRIAN €

(Putzen Alpe; snacks €1.50-9; 8am-8pm mid-Jun–mid-Sep) A beautiful 8km uphill hike from St Anton, this mountain hut sits in a tranquil alpine meadow, where you can often spot marmots if you look carefully. It does a great *Brettljause* (tasting platter), featuring the cheese from its 50 cows, which you can, incidentally, see coming down from the pastures around 5pm, their clanging bells resonating through the valley.

★**Museum Restaurant** AUSTRIAN €€

(05446-24 75; www.museum-restaurant.at; Rudi-Matt-Weg 10; mains €18-37.50; noon-10pm) On the fringes of the village, this utterly charming restaurant is housed in the picture-perfect chalet of the St Anton Museum. Winter salad with caramelised nuts, pear and smoked goose breast, and the most succulent Tyrolean beef and trout fished fresh from the pond outside land on your plate at this intimate wood-panelled restaurant.

★**Rodelalm** AUSTRIAN €€

(0676 886486000; www.rodelalm.com; Nassereinerstrasse 106; mains €14.50-21.50; 10am-11pm, closed Wed;) With glowing faces and frosty fingers, most sledders heading down Rodelbahn stop at this hut located halfway, to warm up with schnapps and a big plate of *Schweinshaxe* (pork knuckles), *Gröstl* or cheese fondue. An open fire keeps things toasty in the pine-panelled interior.

Verwallstube GASTRONOMY €€

(05446-235 25 10; www.verwallstube.at; Galzigbahn top station; mains €23-40; 11.30am-3pm Dec-Apr) Wow, what a view! The mountain panorama that opens up at this 2085m-high location is uplifting – as is the food. Billing itself as one of the highest gourmet restaurants in Europe, Verwallstube is a wonderful pick for a pre- or postski lunch. Delicately presented, flavour-charged dishes range from bouillabaisse to veal cheeks braised in red wine until meltingly tender, served with truffle mash.

Galzig Bistro BISTRO €€

(05446-425 41; www.galzigbistrobar.at; Kandaharweg 2; mains €15-39; 8am-1am) Winningly fresh produce is the secret to the bistro-style dishes served at Galzig, which stretch from gourmet salads (wild herb and pine nut, for instance) to tagliatelle with king prawns, capers and endives, and roasted duck breast with black truffle. It's uniformly delicious. The slick, contemporary interior and terrace attract a style-conscious, cocktail-sipping crowd after dark.

m3 Restaurant INTERNATIONAL €€

(05446-29 68; www.m3hotel.at; Dorfstrasse 56; mains €18-33, pizza €14-29; 6.15pm-midnight Dec–mid-Apr) A prime people-watching terrace fronts this super-slick restaurant, with vaulted ceilings and art-slung walls. Austro-Italian specialities are presented with an eye for presentation, with flavours striking the right chord in dishes such as Tyrolean beef carpaccio with parmesan and rocket, homemade linguine with penny bun mushrooms, and crispy pork belly with thyme jus. The wood-oven pizza is great too.

Fuhrmann Stube AUSTRIAN €€
(☎05446-29 21; Dorfstrasse 74; mains €10-17; ⏲10am-10pm) When snow blankets the rooftops, this is a cosy hideaway for tucking into *Knödel* (dumplings), a carnivorous *Tiroler Bauernplatte* (Tyrolean farmers' platter) or a generous helping of strudel.

Bodega TAPAS €€
(☎05446-427 88; Dorfstrasse 40; tapas €4.50-12.50; ⏲4pm-1am Mon-Sat, to midnight Sun) Excellent tapas, vino and live music reel in the crowds to this buzzy Spanish haunt. You can't book, so be prepared to wait for a table.

Drinking & Nightlife

★**Mooserwirt** BAR
(www.mooserwirt.at; Unterer Mooserweg 2; ⏲11am-8pm) One word: *craaaazy*. Come teatime Mooserwirt heaves with skiers guzzling beer (the place sells around 5000L a day), dancing to Eurotrash and sweating in their salopettes. The first challenge is to locate your skis, the second to use them to get back to St Anton in one piece.

Sennhütte BAR
(www.sennsationell.at; Dengerstrasse 503; ⏲3-6pm) A sunny terrace, feisty schnapps, locals jiggling on the tables, live bands – what more après-ski could one ask for? In summer there's a wonderful herb garden, treehouse and cow-themed walking trail for kids.

Krazy Kanguruh BAR
(www.krazykanguruh.com; Mooserweg 19; ⏲10am-8pm) Owned by St Anton ski legend and two-time slalom world champion Mario Matt, this slopeside hotspot is loud, fun and jam-packed after 5pm. One too many tequilas will indeed send you bouncing (on skis) back to the valley.

Heustadl BAR
(www.heustadl.com; Dengerstrasse 625; ⏲10am-7pm) Just north of Sennhütte, this rollicking shack is always fit to bursting with beery throngs at its postski parties. There's live music from 3pm to 6pm daily.

Taps BAR
(www.taps-stanton.com; Mooserweg 15; ⏲11am-8pm) Taps is a pumping après-ski place with the cheapest beer on the mountain and DJs keeping the party in full swing. There's a huge sun terrace for chilling and often free homemade schnapps (mind-blowing stuff) doing the rounds.

Information

The centrally located **tourist office** (☎05446-226 90; www.stantonamarlberg.com; Dorfstrasse 8; ⏲8am-noon & 1-5pm Mon-Fri, 9am-noon Sat & Sun) has information on outdoor activities and places to stay as well as maps and free wi-fi. There's an accommodation board and free telephone outside

Getting There & Away

The ultramodern train station is on the route between Bregenz (€13.80, 1¼ hours) and Innsbruck (€17.50, 1¼ hours), with fast trains every one or two hours. St Anton and St Christoph are close to the eastern entrance of the Arlberg Tunnel (cars and minibuses €10), the toll road connecting Vorarlberg and Tyrol. You can avoid the toll by taking the B197, but no vehicles with trailers are allowed on this winding road.

Buses depart from stands southwest of the tourist office.

Getting Around

Bicycles can be rented for €27 per day from Intersport Arlberg (p327).

Free local buses go to outlying parts of the resort (such as St Jakob). Buses run to Lech (€5, 29 minutes) and Zürs (€4, 23 minutes) in Vorarlberg; they are hourly (until about 6pm) in winter, reducing to four a day in summer.

A minibus taxi can be shared between up to eight people; the trip from St Anton to Lech costs €37/55 in the day/night. Local **taxis** (☎0664 2302618) are also available.

Lech & Zürs

☎05583

Mountains huddle conspiratorially around the snow-sure slopes of the rugged Arlberg region, one of Austria's top ski destinations. The best-known villages are picture-postcard Lech (1450m) and its smaller twin Zürs (1716m), 6km south. Because of their relative isolation, fabulous skiing and five-star hotels, the resorts attract royalty (Princess Diana used to ski here), celebrities and anyone who pretends to be such from behind Gucci shades.

Activities

Remember Bridget Jones hurtling backwards down the mountain on skis in *The*

Edge of Reason? That was filmed on Lech's scenic, forest-streaked runs. The terrain is best suited to beginners and intermediates, with off-piste possibilities and the famous 22km Weisse Ring (White Ring) appealing to more advanced skiers.

These resorts in Western Arlberg are linked to St Anton over the mountain, opening up Austria's biggest integrated ski area, with a whopping 306km of slopes to carve – from easy-peasy to pitch black – and 88 ski lifts. A one-/three-/six-day pass will set you back €56.50/164/300.

Tours

From July to September the tourist office organises free themed walks such as sunrise hikes and botanical strolls every Monday and Thursday. You can also go it alone on 250km of signed hiking trails, ranging from high-alpine treks to gentle lake walks, as well as dedicated running and Nordic walking trails.

Sleeping & Eating

★Hotel Gotthard HOTEL €€
(☎05583-35 60; www.gotthard.at; Omesberg 119, Lech; s €87-91, d €170-180, ste €226-240; P 📶 🏊) It's the little touches that make all the difference at this chalet hotel, such as the oven-warm bread at breakfast (owner Clemens is a baker) and yoga room for Zen moments. Splashes of fuchsia and forest green jazz up the contemporary, pine-wood rooms, most of which have balconies, DVD players and iPod docks. There's a spa, an indoor pool and a children's playroom.

Hotel Garni Lavendel PENSION €€
(☎05583-26 57; www.lavendel.at; Dorf 447, Lech; s €60-75, d €110-140, apt €120-290; P 📶) The affable Mascher family make you feel at home at this cosy pension next to the ski lifts. Many of the spacious, immaculate rooms and apartments sport balconies, and there's a little spa for a posthike or après-ski unwind.

Hûs Nr 8 AUSTRIAN €€
(☎05583-332 20; www.hus8.at; Omesberg 8, Lech; mains €20-40; ⏲11am-1am) Raclette, fondue and crispy roast chicken are the stars of the menu at this rustic chalet, going strong since 1760. Snuggle up in an all-wood interior in winter or sit on the patio when the sun's out.

Information

The central **tourist office** (☎05583-216 10; www.lechzuers.com; Dorf 2, Lech; ⏲9am-noon & 1-6pm Mon-Sat, 10am-noon & 3-5pm Sun) has bags of info on skiing and walking possibilities, and an accommodation board.

Getting There & Away

Buses run between Lech and Zürs (€1.50, six minutes); both resorts have connections to St Anton am Arlberg (€5, 29 minutes).

One kilometre south of Zürs is the Flexen Pass (1773m), occasionally blocked off by snow in winter, after which the road splits: the western fork leads to Stuben (1407m), the eastern one to St Anton am Arlberg in Tyrol. In summer, Lech can also be approached from the north, via the turning at Warth (1494m).

VORARLBERG

In Austria's far west, the Vorarlberg nudges up against Germany, Switzerland and Liechtenstein. Parts of it remain gloriously off-the-radar, with narrow valleys carving up mighty peaks and forests. The snowcapped heights of the Silvretta-Montafon give way to the wavy hills and lush dairy country of the Bregenzerwald, which in turn fall to the Bodensee (Lake Constance). Though renowned Austria-wide for its innovative architecture, this remains a remarkably peaceful and deeply traditional corner of the country.

History

Vorarlberg has been inhabited since the early Stone Age but it wasn't until the Celts arrived in 400 BC, followed by the Romans in around 15 BC, that lasting settlements were maintained. Brigantium, the forerunner of Bregenz, was a Roman stronghold until around the 5th and 6th centuries, when the raiding Germanic Alemanni tribes increased their influence and effectively took over.

Peace reigned in the province until the early 15th century, when it suffered substantial damage during the Appenzell War with the Swiss Confederation. Relations with its neighbour later improved to such an extent that in 1918 Vorarlberg declared independence from Austria and sought union with Switzerland. The move was blocked by the Allied powers in the postwar reorganisation of Europe; fears that an even smaller Austria would be easily absorbed by a recovering Germany were certainly founded. Today, Vorarlberg still looks first towards its westerly neighbours, and then to Vienna, 600km to the east.

Getting There & Away

AIR

Friedrichshafen airport (07541-2840; www.bodensee-airport.eu; Am Flugplatz 64), in Germany, is the closest major airport serving domestic and European destinations.

CAR & MOTORCYCLE

The A14 connects the province to Germany in the north and the rest of Austria via the 14km Arlberg Tunnel, which runs under the Arlberg mountains. To the west, there are plenty of border crossings into Liechtenstein and Switzerland.

Getting Around

Vorarlberg is broken down into *Domino* (individual zones). A Maximo pass, costing €14.50/41.30 per day/week, covers the entire province. Single *Domino* tickets cost €1.50 and a day pass is €2.80 – these cover city transport in Bregenz, Dornbirn, Götzis, Feldkirch, Bludenz, Lech and Schruns/Tschagguns. Information and timetables are available from the Verkehrsverbund Vorarlberg (www.vmobil.at).

Bregenz

05574 / POP 29,806 / ELEV 427M

What a view! The locals proudly agree, Bregenz does indeed have the loveliest of views: before you the Bodensee, Europe's third-largest lake, spreads out like a liquid mirror; behind you the Pfänder (1064m) climbs to the Alps; to the right you see Germany, to the left the faint outline of Switzerland. Just wow.

Whether contemplating avant-garde art and architecture by the new harbour, sauntering along the promenade on a summer's evening or watching opera under the stars at the much-lauded *Festspiele* (festival), you can't help but think – clichéd though it sounds – that Vorarlberg's pocket-sized capital has got at least a taste of it all.

Sights

★Pfänder Cable Car — CABLE CAR

(www.pfaenderbahn.at; Steinbruchgasse 4; adult/child one way €7.70/3.80, return €13.20/6.60; 8am-7pm) A cable car whizzes to the 1064m peak of the Pfänder, a wooded mountain rearing above Bregenz and affording a breathtaking panorama of the Bodensee and the snowcapped summits of the not-so-distant Alps in Austria, Switzerland and Germany. At the top is the Alpine Game Park Pfänder.

★Kunsthaus — GALLERY

(www.kunsthaus-bregenz.at; Karl-Tizian-Platz; adult/child €11/free; 10am-6pm Tue, Wed & Fri-Sun, to 8pm Thu;) Designed by Swiss architect Peter Zumthor, this giant glass and steel cube is said to resemble a lamp, reflecting the changing light of the sky and lake. The stark, open-plan interior is perfect for rotating exhibitions of contemporary art – the work of British artist Ed Atkins and the haunting, semi-abstract paintings of Swiss artist Miriam Cahn have recently featured. Check the website for details on everything from guided tours to kids' workshops.

★Vorarlberg Museum — MUSEUM

(www.vorarlbergmuseum.at; Kornmarktplatz 1; adult/child €9/free; 10am-6pm Tue, Wed & Fri-Sun, to 8pm Thu) One of Bregenz' most striking landmarks is this white cuboid emblazoned with what appears to be 16,656 flowers (actually PET bottle bases imprinted in concrete). The gallery homes in on Vorarlberg's history, art and architecture in its permanent exhibitions, including one on the Roman archaeological finds of Brigantium. It also stages rotating exhibitions, such as recent ones spotlighting the Bregenzer Festspiele and mining in the Eastern Alps.

Rheindelta — NATURE RESERVE

(www.rheindelta.org; Hard) Easily explored on foot or by bike, this nature reserve sits 5km south of Bregenz, where the River Rhine flows into the Bodensee. The mossy marshes, reeds and mixed woodlands attract more than 300 bird species, including curlews, grey herons and rare black-tailed godwits.

Alpine Game Park Pfänder — NATURE RESERVE

(www.pfaender.at; Pfänder; sunrise-sunset) FREE At the top of the Pfänder, a 30-minute circular trail brings you close to deer, wild boar, ibex and whistling marmots at the year-round Alpine Game Park Pfänder.

Oberstadt — HISTORIC SITE

Slung high above the lake is the Oberstadt, Bregenz' tiny old town of winding streets, candy-coloured houses and flowery gardens. It's still enclosed by defensive walls and the sturdy **Martinstor** (St Martin's Gate).

Festspielhaus — LANDMARK

(05574-41 30; www.festspielhausbregenz.at; Platz der Wiener Symphoniker 1) Even if you can't bag tickets for the Bregenzer Festspiele (p333), the Festival Hall is a must-see. All tinted glass, smooth concrete and sharp angles, this is one

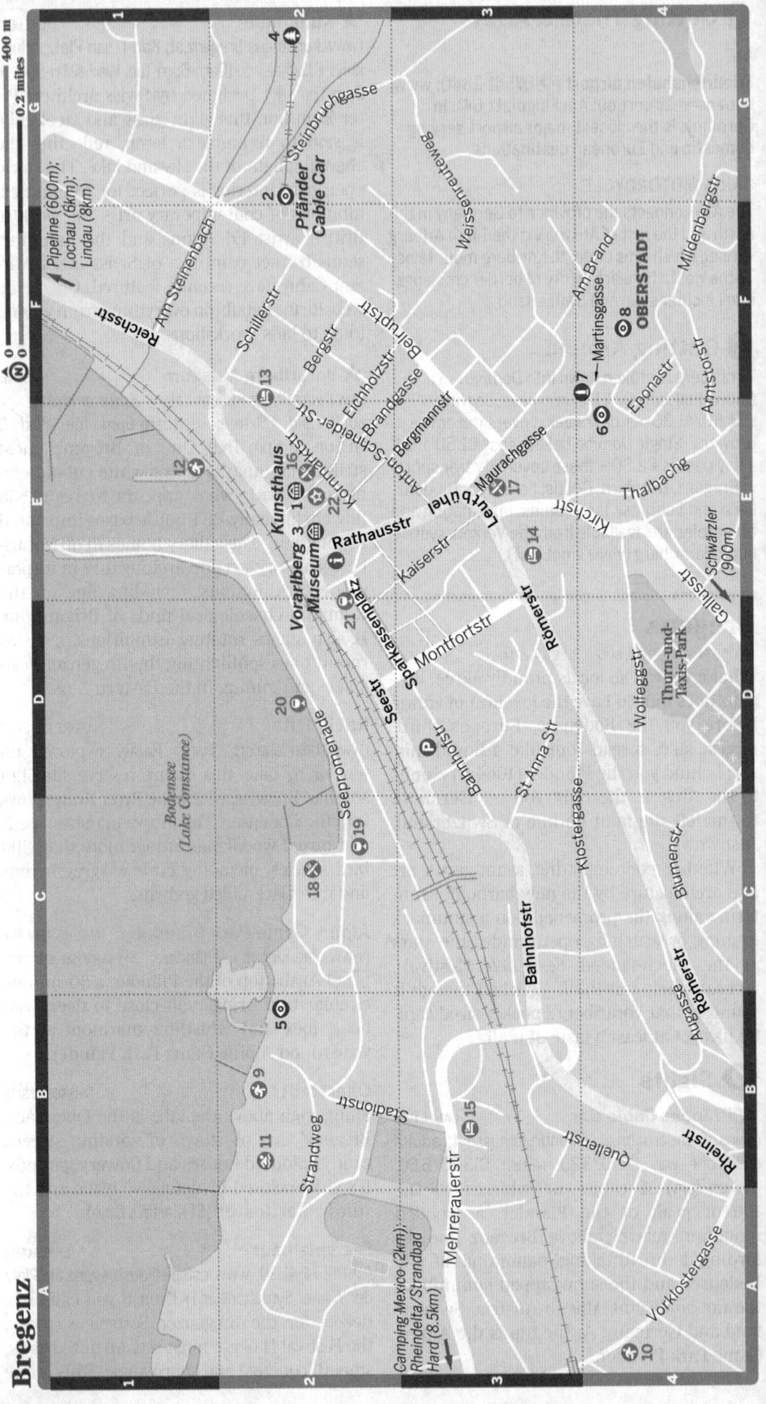

Bregenz

0 — 400 m
0 — 0.2 miles

Pipeline (600m); Lochau (6km); Lindau (8km)
Bodensee (Lake Constance)
Reichsstr
Am Steinenbach
Schillerstr
Steinbruchgasse
Pfänder Cable Car
Kunsthaus
Vorarlberg Museum
Kornmarktstr
Anton-Schneider-Str
Bergstr
Eichholzstr
Brandgasse
Bergmannstr
Belruptstr
Weissenreuteweg
Rathausstr
Seestr
Sparkassenplatz
Kaiserstr
Montfortstr
Leutbühel
Maurachgasse
Seepromenade
Strandweg
Stadionstr
Camping Mexico (2km); Rheindelta/Strandbad Hard (8.5km)
Mehrerauerstr
Bahnhofstr
St Anna Str
Römerstr
Klostergasse
Kirchstr
Am Brand
Martinsgasse
OBERSTADT
Eponastr
Thalbachg
Amtstorstr
Mildenbergstr
Wolfeggstr
Thurn-und-Taxis-Park
Gallusstr
Schwärzler (900m)
Blumenstr
Augasse
Rheinstr
Quellenstr
Vorklostergasse

1 2 3 4 5 6 7 8 9 10 11 12 13 14 15 16 17 18 19 20 21 22

A B C D E F G
1 2 3 4

Bregenz

of Bregenz' most visible icons. Many festival performances are held on the semicircular Seebühne stage jutting out onto the lake.

Martinsturm TOWER
(St Martin's Tower; www.martinsturm.at; Martinsgasse 3b; adult/child €3.50/1; ⊙10am-6pm May-Oct) Not far past Martinstor (p331) is this baroque tower, topped by the largest onion dome in Central Europe. It's worth seeing the 14th-century Gothic frescoes in the chapel before climbing up to the small military museum for fine views over Bregenz' rooftops.

Activities

Everybody who arrives in Bregenz is bewitched by the **Bodensee**, Europe's third-largest lake, straddling Austria, Switzerland and Germany. In summer, the lake shores becomes an autobahn for lycra-clad *Radfahrer* (cyclists); shoulder seasons are considerably more peaceful. Other activities on the lake include sailing and diving at Lochau, and swimming. Alternatively, there are numerous boat companies that ferry passengers across the lake from April to mid-October.

Bodensee Cycle Path CYCLING
(www.bodensee-radweg.com) When the sun's out, there's surely no better way to explore Bodensee than with your bum in a saddle. The well-marked Bodensee Cycle Path makes a 273km loop of the Bodensee, taking in vineyards, meadows, orchards, wetlands and historic towns. There are plenty of small beaches where you can stop for a refreshing dip in the lake. Visit the website for itineraries and maps.

Vorarlberg Lines BOATING
(www.vorarlberg-lines.at; Seestrasse; ⊙early Apr–mid-Oct) This is one of a number of companies taking you out onto the lake from April to mid-October. There are two-hour Bodensee panorama cruises (adult/child €19.90/9.90), one-hour Bregenz trips (€12.40/6.20) and regular boat transfers to lake destinations including Lindau (€6.40), Mainau (€19), Friedrichshafen (€15.80) and Konstanz (€19).

Pipeline SWIMMING
The most central place for a quick dip or a barbecue is the Pipeline, a stretch of pebbly beach north of Bregenz, so named for the large pipeline running parallel to the lake.

Strandbad Bregenz SWIMMING
(Strandweg; adult/child €5.20/2.60; ⊙9am-8pm early May-early Sep; 👪) Packed with bronzed bods, overexcited kids and flirty teens in summer, this central lido has a lakeside beach, several outdoor pools with waterslides, and activities including volleyball and table tennis.

Integra – Fahrradverleih Bregenz CYCLING
(www.integra.or.at/fahrradservice; Vorklostergasse 51; per day city bike/e-bike €15/27; ⊙8-11.30am & 1-4.30pm Mon, Tue & Thu, 8am-noon Wed & Fri) Rents quality city and e-bikes.

Festivals & Events

Bregenzer Festspiele CULTURAL
(Bregenz Festival; ☎05574-40 76; www.bregenzer festspiele.com; ⊙mid-Jul–mid-Aug) The Bregenzer Festspiele is the city's premier cultural festival. World-class operas, orchestral works and other highly imaginative productions are staged

on the open-air Seebühne, a floating stage on the lake, in the Festspielhaus (p331) and at the Vorarlberger Landestheater. Information and tickets (€40 to €358) are up for grabs about nine months before the festival.

Sleeping

JUFA Gästehaus Bregenz HOSTEL €
(05708-35 40; www.jufa.eu/hotel/bregenz; Mehrerauerstrasse 5; s/d €68/109, f €125-154; P) Housed in a former needle factory near the lake, this HI hostel now reels backpackers in with excellent facilities including a common room, cafe, and reasonably priced singles and doubles. It's welcoming to families, too, with a playroom, a playground and bike rental.

Camping Mexico CAMPGROUND €
(0660 7039430; www.camping-mexico.at; Hechtweg 4; campsite per adult/child/tent €10/5.50/8; late Apr-Sep;) This eco-labelled campground by the lake uses solar energy, recycles waste and serves organic food in its restaurant. The leafy pitches offer plenty of shade.

Schwärzler HOTEL €€
(05574-49 90; www.schwaerzler.s-hotels.com; Landstrasse 9; d €166-276; P) This turreted, ivy-clad place is a far cry from your average business hotel. Contemporary rooms are done out in earthy hues and blond wood, with comforts including bathrobes, flat-screen TVs and minibars. Regional produce from organic farms features on the breakfast buffet, and there's an indoor pool and sauna area.

Hotel Weisses Kreuz HOTEL €€
(05574-498 80; www.hotelweisseskreuz.at; Römerstrasse 5; s €98-125, d €125-275, ste €175-335; P) Right in the heart of Bregenz' *Altstadt*, this central pick has a cocktail bar and a vaulted **restaurant** (05574-428 15; Kirchstrasse 8; lunch €8.20, mains €9-22; 11am-10pm Wed-Mon) rustling up seasonal Austrian fare. The smart, spacious rooms sport cherry-wood furnishings, flat-screen TVs and organic bedding. Breakfast is a terrific spread of cold cuts, cereals and fresh breads.

Hotel Bodensee HOTEL €€
(05574-423 00; www.hotel-bodensee.at; Kornmarktstrasse 22; s €76-99, d €134-179; P) Right in the thick of things, this hotel's best rooms are spacious, tastefully decorated in muted tones and sport flat-screen TVs. Breakfast is a wholesome fresh fruit, muesli and regional produce affair.

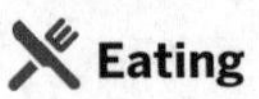

Eating

Bauernmarkt MARKET
(Kaiserstrasse; 8am-noon Fri) You can grab picnic fixings and stock up on farm-fresh produce at Bregenz' weekly *Bauernmarkt* (farmers market).

Lieblingscafe CAFE €
(www.lieblingscafe.at; Maurachgasse 6; light bites €5-9; 11.30am-5pm Tue, 9am-5pm Wed-Fri, 10am-4pm Sat & Sun;) Vegetarians and vegans will find a lot to love about this colourful, bijou cafe in Bregenz' *Altstadt*. Go for wholesome soups, wraps and salads, or a slice of homemade coffee and cake. There's a tiny pavement terrace for watching the world go by.

Kornmesser AUSTRIAN €€
(05574-548 54; www.kornmesser.at; Kornmarktstrasse 5; 2-course lunch €9.40, mains €19-35; 9am-midnight Tue-Sun) Dine on local favourites in the vaulted interior or chestnut-shaded beer garden of this 18th-century baroque *Gästehaus*. These include pork knuckle with bread dumplings and potato salad, roast local trout with parsley potatoes, boiled beef with horseradish, pasta with picked-the-same-day chanterelles, and an 'emperor's pancake' (with stewed plums).

Wirtshaus am See AUSTRIAN €€
(05574-422 10; www.wirtshausamsee.at; Seepromenade 2; mains €15-27; 9am-midnight;) Snag a table on the lakefront terrace at this mock half-timbered villa, dishing up local specialities such as buttery Bodensee whitefish and venison ragout. Vegetarian options abound. It's also a relaxed spot for quaffing a cold one. Service can be hit-and-miss.

Drinking & Nightlife

Fischersteg Sunset Bar BAR
(www.facebook.com/Fischersteg; Seepromenade; 2-10pm Mon-Fri, to 11pm Sat & Sun) The clue's in the name: there's no finer spot for a sundowner than this cute pavilion jutting out onto the lake. Come for a pastel sunset across the Bodensee or to see the lights twinkle after dark.

Beach Bar Bregenz BAR
(www.wirtshausamsee.at/de/beachbar; Seepromenade 2; 4pm-midnight Mon-Fri, from 2pm Sat, from 11am Sun late Apr-early Sep) Cool cocktails, palm trees, chilled DJ beats – it's the Costa del Bodensee every summer at this lakefront beach bar. Work your relaxed look in a *Strandkörbe* (wicker-basket chair). It also

stages occasional events, such as silent open-air cinema sessions.

Wunderbar BAR
(www.wunderbar.at; Bahnhofstrasse 4; 11am-3am Mon-Thu, to 4am Fri & Sat, noon-3am Sun;) Bordello meets neobaroque at the Wunderbar, where candles illuminate blood-red walls, cherubs and velvet sofas. Browse the papers, bag a swing on the terrace or sip cocktails as smooth funk plays.

Entertainment

Vorarlberger Landestheater THEATRE
(05574-428 70; www.landestheater.org; Seestrasse 2; ticket office 8am-12.30pm Mon-Thu, 8am-12.30pm & 1.30-5.30pm Fri) Also known as the Theater am Kornmarkt, this German-language theatre is Vorarlberg's main stage for opera, drama, comedy and musicals.

Information

Bodensee-Vorarlberg Tourism (05574-434 43; www.bodensee-vorarlberg.com) Free regional accommodation booking service.

Tourist Office (05574-49 59; www.bregenz.travel; Rathausstrasse 35a; 9am-6pm Mon-Fri, to noon Sat) Information on the city and the surrounding area, and help with accommodation.

Getting There & Away

BUS

Long-distance buses – among them are services operated by **FlixBus** (+49 30 300 137 300; https://global.flixbus.com/bus/austria) – depart in front of the *Hauptbahnhof*.

CAR & MOTORCYCLE

Bregenz has good motorway connections to neighbouring Germany and Switzerland. The A14 powers north, linking up to the A96 to Munich (just over a two-hour drive away), while just west of town you can pick up the A1 to Zürich (around 1¾ hours). The A14 south links up to towns including Feldkirch and Bludenz.

There's parking at 30 locations dotted around the centre, including at the main train station, costing €0.60 to €1 per hour.

TRAIN

Four direct trains daily head for Munich (€53.40, three hours) via Lindau (€3, 12 minutes), while trains for Konstanz (€27.20, two hours) go via the Swiss shore of the lake and may be frequent, but require up to four changes. There are frequent departures for Zürich (€36.80, two hours), all of which call in at St Gallen (€14.60, 47 minutes). There are roughly hourly trains to Innsbruck (€39.80, 2½ hours), calling en route at Dornbirn (€3, nine minutes), Feldkirch (€7, 46 minutes) and Bludenz (€10.90, 50 minutes).

Getting Around

Integra – Fahrradverleih Bregenz (p333) rents quality bikes and has free Bodensee cycling maps.

Dornbirn

05572 / POP 46,885 / ELEV 437M

Ragged, thickly wooded limestone pinnacles are the dramatic backdrop to Dornbirn, Vorarlberg's largest city. While nowhere near as appealing as Bregenz, it's worth a visit for its refreshing lack of tourists and remarkable museums.

Hohenems, 6km south of Dornbirn, sheltered a large Jewish community in the 17th century. Their numbers dwindled in the 1860s, when Jews were eligible to live anywhere under Habsburg rule.

Sights & Activities

Altstadt HISTORIC SITE
Dornbirn's compact old town centres on the Marktplatz, where your gaze is drawn to the crooked, 17th-century Rotes Haus (p336), which owes its intense red hue to an unappetising mix of oxblood and bile. Next door, the neoclassical columns and free-standing Gothic belfry of **Pfarrkirche St Martin** catch your eye.

Inatura MUSEUM
(www.inatura.at; Jahngasse 9, Dornbirn; adult/child €11.50/5.70; 10am-6pm;) Dornbirn's biggest draw is this hands-on museum. It's a wonderland for kids who can pet (stuffed) foxes and handle (real) spiders, whip up tornadoes, conduct light experiments and generally interact with science, nature and technology. There's also a climbing wall and 3D cinema.

Jüdisches Museum Hohenems MUSEUM
(www.jm-hohenems.at; Schweizer Strasse 5, Hohenems; adult/child €8/free; 10am-5pm Tue-Sun) Housed in the Rosenthal villa in Hohenems, 6km south of Dornbirn, this museum zooms in on Hohenems' long-defunct Jewish community with photos, documents and religious artefacts. The Rosenthals built up a considerable textile business in the town, and part of their wealth – especially gorgeous period furniture – is also on show.

Rolls-Royce Museum MUSEUM
(www.rolls-royce-museum.at; Gütle 11a; adult/child €6/3; ⏲10am-6pm Tue-Sun) Situated at the bottom of Rappenlochschlucht and ensconced in a 19th-century cotton mill, this museum harbours the world's largest collection of Rolls-Royces. Highlights include a reconstruction of Royce's Cooke St factory in Manchester and a hall of fame showcasing vintage Rollers that once belonged to the likes of Queen Elizabeth, Franco and George V. Stay for tea in the ever-so-British rosewood tearoom.

Rappenlochschlucht WALKING
(Rappenloch Gorge; www.rappenlochschlucht.at; 👪) Just 4km south of Dornbirn is the narrow Rappenlochschlucht, gouged out by the thundering Dornbirner Ache. A 10-minute walk leads up to a good viewpoint and a 30-minute trail to the **Staufensee**, a turquoise lake ringed by forest.

Sleeping & Eating

Hotel Hirschen HOTEL €€
(☎05572-263 63; Haselstauderstrasse 31; s €85, d €126-135; P 📶) Heading into its third generation with the same family, the Hirschen's contemporary, minimalist-style rooms come with appealing personal touches – starry ceilings or wood-burning stoves, wind chimes made by local creatives and DVD players. There's even a pillow menu (sheep's wool, pine and the like) and hot-water bottles to ensure a sound night's slumber.

Vienna House Martinspark DESIGN HOTEL €€
(☎05572-37 60; www.viennahouse.com; Mozartstrasse 2; s €103-115, d €130-198; P ❄ 📶) 🍃 Winging Dornbirn into the future, this architecturally innovative, ecofriendly hotel makes quite a design statement in central Dornbirn. The pared-back, parquet-floored rooms are contemporary in style, and the restaurant (mains €14 to €26) places the accent on regional produce in dishes from Bregenzerwald mountain cheese soup to pike-perch fillet in a basil-and-pine-nut crust.

Rotes Haus AUSTRIAN €€
(☎05572-315 55; www.roteshaus.at; Marktplatz 13; ⏲11.30am-2.30pm & 5.30pm-midnight Tue-Sun) For a meal with a generous slice of history, book a table at this Dornbirn institution, lodged in an oxblood-red house dating to 1639. A tiled oven warms the ever-so traditional, wood-clad interior, where classic and more creative dishes swing from goat's cheese terrine with wild garlic sorbet and confit tomatoes to fillet steak with shallot-port-wine sauce and riesling risotto.

Information

Dornbirn's centrally located **tourist office** (☎05572-22 18 80; https://en.dornbirn.info; Rathausplatz 1a; ⏲9am-6pm Mon-Fri, to noon Sat) is a handy first port of call.

Getting There & Away

Dornbirn has frequent connections to Bregenz (€3, nine minutes) and Hohenems (€2, eight minutes) on the Bregenz–Innsbruck railway line. Bus 47 departs from Dornbirn train station and passes by the Rappenlochschlucht (€2, 19 minutes, nine daily).

Bregenzerwald

The wooded limestone peaks, cow-nibbled pastures and bucolic villages of the Bregenzerwald unfold to the south of Bregenz. This rural region is great for getting back to nature for a few days, whether cheese-tasting in alpine dairies, testing out hay and herbal treatments in spa hotels, or curling up by the fireside in a cosy farmhouse. One lungful of that good clean air and you'll surely want to grab your boots, slip into your skis or get on your bike and head outdoors.

Sights

★ **Angelika Kauffmann Museum** MUSEUM
(www.angelika-kauffmann.com; Brand 34, Schwarzenberg; adult/child €7.50/5.50; ⏲10am-5pm Tue-Sun) This ultramodern museum houses rotating exhibitions in summer of Swiss-Austrian neoclassical painter Angelika Kauffmann's works. The artist had strong connections to the village where her father was born. A ticket covers entry to the neighbouring **Heimat Museum** (Heritage Museum), a pristine alpine chalet. Displays of traditional painted furniture, extraordinary headwear, hunting paraphernalia and filigree iron crosses focus on rural 19th-century life.

Werkraum ARCHITECTURE
(www.werkraum.at; Hof 800, Andelsbuch; adult/child €7.50/free; ⏲10am-6pm Tue-Sat) The brainchild of much-lauded Pritzker Prize–winning architect Peter Zumthor, the slickly minimalist Werkraum, with its low-rise, timber-and-concrete, glass-fronted facade mirroring the landscape, is worth a peek for its design alone. Inside, it represents a major showcase

for the one-of-a-kind heritage of craftsmanship and design in the Bregenzerwald, with rotating exhibitions of the members' work.

Käsekeller Lingenau FARM
(www.kaesekeller.at; Zeihenbühel 423, Lingenau; 10am-6pm Mon-Fri, 9am-5pm Sat, shorter hours in winter) Step into the foyer of this modern cheese-maturation cellar to glimpse robots attending to wagon wheel-sized cheeses through a glass wall. It's famous for its tangy *Bergkäse* (mountain cheese). A tasting of cheeses with wine and bread costs from €7.80 to €10.90.

Käse-Molke Metzler FARM
(05512-30 44; www.molkeprodukte.com; Bruggan 1025, Egg; 8am-noon & 1.30-6pm Mon-Fri, 8am-noon Sat) This architecturally innovative dairy churns out fresh *Wälderkäsle* ('forest cheese') among others, arranges farm tours and tastings (adult/child €19.50/10) and runs four-hour cheese-making workshops (€69). Kids will love the pen where goats and cows hang out. If you'd like to try milking them as well, the price is €25/12.50 per adult/child. See the website for exact dates and times; booking is essential.

Bergkäserei Schoppernau FARM
(www.bergkaeserei.at; Unterdorf 248, Schoppernau; 8.30-11.30am & 3-6pm Mon-Fri, 8.30-11.30am & 3-5pm Sat) Discover cheese-making secrets (including why Emmentaler is holey) at this show dairy, famous for its award-winning tangy *Bergkäse*, matured for up to 12 months.

Activities

The hills buzz with hikers, climbers and cyclists in summer. Local tourist offices also arrange **themed walks**, including some geared towards families. **Paragliders** can launch themselves off mountains in Andelsbuch, Bezau and Au-Schoppernau; tandem flights cost around €100.

Downhill Skiing

Though lesser known than other Austrian ski regions, the Bregenzerwald has fine downhill skiing on 247km of slopes, well suited to beginners, intermediates and ski tourers (three-valley three-/six-day pass adult €139/222, child €70/117. Lift queues are virtually nonexistent and free ski buses shuttle between resorts. Nonskiers can shuffle through snowy forests on cross-country or snowshoe trails, go winter hiking or bump downhill on toboggan runs in Au and Damüls.

Baumgarten CABLE CAR
(www.seilbahn-bezau.at; cable car one way/return €13/19; 9am-5pm late Mar-early Nov;) For some of the most compelling views in the Bregenzerwald, hop on the cable car from Bezau to Baumgarten, where a 360-degree panorama taking in three countries (Germany, Switzerland and Austria), the Alps and the not-so-distant Bodensee opens up. The summit is the trailhead for high-altitude hikes in summer and snowshoeing in winter.

Festivals & Events

Schubertiade MUSIC
(05576-720 91; www.schubertiade.at) The highly acclaimed Schubertiade festival brings the *Lieder* (songs) and chamber music of the great Austrian Romantic composer Franz Schubert to atmospheric venues in Schwarzenberg (mid-June to early September) and Hohenems (dates in May, July, August, September and October). Tickets are like gold dust and should be booked well in advance.

Sleeping & Eating

Kräuterbauernhof Erath FARMSTAY €
(05515-22 98; www.kuhforyou.at; Argenau 116, Au; d/tr/q €52/67/82) This 300-year-old farmhouse is a fantastic place to stay, with spacious apartments full of woody charm, a herb garden and plenty of dairy goodness at breakfast. Should you so wish, you can also adopt a cow (various packages are offered).

Bio-Pension Beer PENSION €
(05515-23 98; www.bio-pension.at; Gräsalp 357, Schoppernau; d €76-81;) The light, cheery rooms at this pension are done out in sustainable wood from the Beer family forest. You'll feel right at home at this ecofriendly country retreat, complete with pure spring water, clucking chickens and organic produce at breakfast.

Hotel Bären DESIGN HOTEL €€
(0 5518 2207; www.baerenmellau.at; Platz 66, Mellau; s €91-115, d €150-193; P) A modern-day take on an alpine chalet, architect-designed, family-run Hotel Bären goes for a pared-back aesthetic in wood-floored, light-filled interiors bearing the hallmark of regional craftsmen. Studios decorated in sustainable materials open into balconies with dreamy mountain views, and there's a chilled spa area with a Finnish sauna and relaxation room.

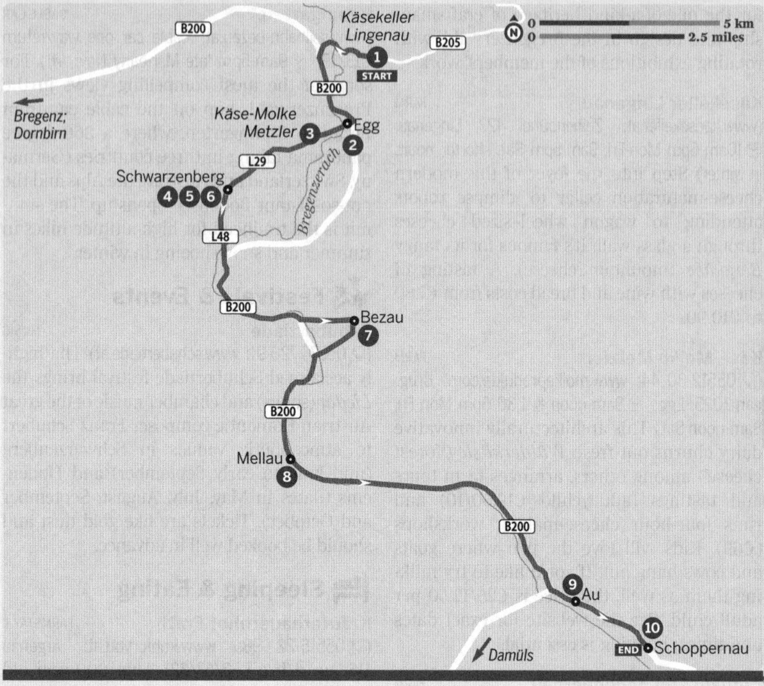

Driving Tour
Bregenzerwald Käsestrasse

START KÄSEKELLER LINGENAU
END SCHOPPERNAU
LENGTH 35KM; FOUR HOURS

The Bregenzerwald's dairy country is best explored on the Käsestrasse (Cheese Rd), which refers to the cheese-producing region rather than the route. This tour (40 minutes' without stops) takes in the highlights, threading through villages and stopping for silo-free milk and cheese at local *Sennereien* (dairy farms). Spring through autumn is the best time to visit. See www.kaesestrasse.at for details.

Take a peek inside the huge cellars of the ultramodern **1 Käsekeller Lingenau** (p337) to see how cheese is matured, and taste flavoursome *Bergkäse* ('mountain cheese') with a glass of wine. Hit the pretty, church-topped village of **2 Egg**, and, 2.5km west, **3 Käse-Molke Metzler** (p337), an avant-garde dairy and farmhouse duo. Here you can sample creamy *Wälderkäsle* ('forest cheese'), made from cow's and goat's milk, or call ahead to join a cheese-making workshop.

Veer southwest to the village of **4 Schwarzenberg**, where old farmhouses tiled with wood shingles and studded with scarlet geraniums crowd the narrow streets. Contemplate art in the **5 Angelika Kauffmann Museum** (p336) before lunching on cheese-rich *Kässpätzle* (egg noodles) in the wood-panelled parlour or garden at **6 Gasthof Hirschen**.

The narrow country lane now wends its way to **7 Bezau**, 7km southeast, where the Bregenzerach river flows past forest-cloaked slopes rising to jagged limestone crags. The village has a handful of shops where you can buy cheese, honey, herbs and schnapps. Continue southeast towards the Arlberg and mountainous **8 Mellau**, where the tourist office organises cheese walks in summer.

Driving southeast brings you to peaceful **9 Au**, affording deep views into a U-shaped valley, particularly beautiful on a golden autumn day. Round out your tour with total cheese immersion at the **10 Bergkäserei Schoppernau** (p337), where you can try the famous *Bergkäse*.

★Gasthof Hirschen HISTORIC HOTEL €€€

(☎05512-29 44; www.hotel-hirschen-bregenzerwald.at; Hof 14, Schwarzenberg; d €189-270, ste €261-310; P 📶) This is a 265-year-old dream of a *Gasthöfe*. The wood-shingle facade is festooned with geraniums, while inside low-ceilinged corridors lead to antique-filled nooks, individually designed rooms and an appealing spa area. *Dirndl*-wearing waitstaff serve up spot-on regional fare such as local game, fish and cheeses in the snug timber-clad restaurant (mains €15 to €34).

Hotel Gasthof Gams BOUTIQUE HOTEL €€€

(☎05514-22 20; www.hotel-gams.at; Platz 44, Bezau; d €206-246, ste €310-350; P 📶) A real glamour puss of a hotel, the Gams (chamois) whispers romance from every last gold-kissed, heart-strewn, candlelit corner. An open fire in the dreamlike Da Vinci spa, starry ceilings, a whirlpool with mountain views, a gourmet restaurant with a walk-in wine tower – this is definite honeymoon material.

Gasthaus Löwen AUSTRIAN €

(☎05515-259 64; www.gasthaus-loewen.at; Rehmen 87, Au; light bites €5-12.50; ⏲10am-6pm Wed-Sat, 9am-6pm Sun) Opening onto a terrace, this delightfully cosy, wood-panelled tavern does a fine line in traditional grub, from goulash with *Spätzle* to pork roast with horseradish. The family also runs it as a distillery, producing fiery schnapps and liqueurs with flavours ranging from mountain hay to gentian and summer mint.

ℹ Information

The **Bregenzerwald tourist office** (☎05512-23 65; www.bregenzerwald.at; Impulszentrum 1135, Egg; ⏲9am-5pm Mon-Fri) should be your first port of call for details on the region's sights, activities and accommodation. The shelves are well stocked with maps and brochures.

ℹ Getting There & Away

Buses run roughly twice hourly to Bezau (€6, 53 minutes) from Bregenz, but for most other destinations a change at Egg (€5, 35 minutes) is required. From Dornbirn, Schwarzenberg (€34, 29 minutes), Mellau (€6, 49 minutes), Au (€7.90, 70 minutes) and Schoppernau (€7.90, 80 minutes) can all be reached a couple of times daily (times vary from season to season). From Bregenz to Damüls (€10.90, 1½ to two hours), a change at Au is required. For timetables, visit www.vmobil.at.

Feldkirch

☎05522 / POP 33,420 / ELEV 458M

On the banks of the turquoise Ill River, Feldkirch sits prettily at the foot of wooded mountains, vineyards and a castle-crowned hill. It's a joy to stroll the well-preserved old town, which wings you back to late-medieval times with its cobbled, arcaded lanes, towers and pastel-coloured town houses. The town springs to life in summer with pavement cafes and open-air festivals.

Sights & Activities

★Schattenburg CASTLE

(www.schattenburg.at; Burggasse 1; adult/child €7/3.50; ⏲9am-5pm Mon-Fri, from 10am Sat & Sun) This 13th-century hilltop castle is storybook stuff with its red turrets and creeping vines. It's a steep climb up to the ramparts, which command far-reaching views over Feldkirch's rooftops. Once the seat of the counts of Montfort, the castle now houses a **museum** displaying religious art, costumes and weaponry.

★Domkirche St Nikolaus CATHEDRAL

(Domplatz; ⏲8am-6pm) Identified by a slender spire, Feldkirch's cathedral has a large, forbidding interior complemented by late-Gothic features and dazzling stained glass. The painting on the side altar is by local lad Wolf Huber (1480–1539), a leading member of the Danube School.

Wildpark WILDLIFE RESERVE

(www.wildpark-feldkirch.at; Ardetzenweg 20; ⏲dawn-dusk;) FREE Facing the castle across the town is Ardetzenberg (631m), a heavily forested hill. At its northern end is this wildlife park, with a woodland trail, an adventure playground, barbecue areas, and animal-friendly enclosures home to marmots, ibex and wild boar. From central Feldkirch, take the Himmelsstiege steps and Weinbergstiege. It's around a 20-minute walk.

Churertor TOWER

(Heiligkreuzbrücke; off Hirschgraben) The towers surviving from the old fortifications include the step-gabled Churertor, once the gateway to the bridge that was used to transport salt across the Ill River to Switzerland.

Dreiländerweg CYCLING

(Three Country Trail) The Feldkirch region is criss-crossed with cycling trails, including

Feldkirch

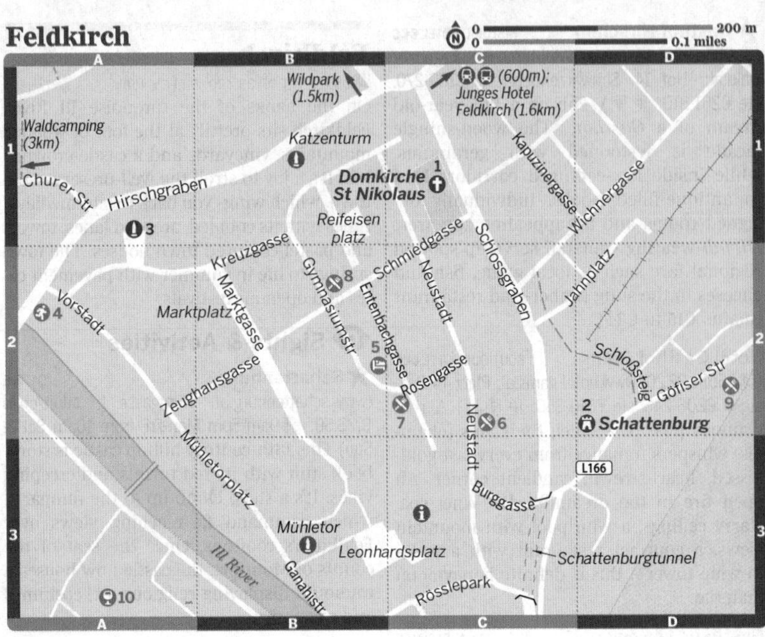

Feldkirch

Top Sights
1 Domkirche St Nikolaus C1
2 Schattenburg D2

Sights
3 Churertor A1

Activities, Courses & Tours
4 Dreiländerweg A2

Sleeping
5 Gutwinski Hotel B2

Eating
6 April C2
7 Gutwinski C2
8 Magma Köstliches B2
9 Wirtschaft Zum Schützenhaus D2

Drinking & Nightlife
10 Poolbar A3

the 30km Dreiländerweg, taking in beautiful scenery in Austria, Switzerland and Liechtenstein. Pick up the free *Feldkircher Radwegkarte* map from the tourist office.

Festivals & Events

Gauklerfestival STREET CARNIVAL
(late Jul) Jugglers and fire-eaters entertain the crowds at this enormous street party.

Lichtstadt LIGHT SHOW
(www.lichtstadt.at; early Oct) FREE This biennial event, occurring in even years, dramatically lights up Feldkirch with a series of light installations and laser shows happening in and around the *Altstadt*.

Sleeping

Junges Hotel Feldkirch HOSTEL €
(05522-731 81; www.oejhw.at; Reichsstrasse 111; dm/d €15.50/45; P) A 700-year-old infirmary has been converted into this HI hostel, which exudes charm with its creaking beams, vaulted lounge and ivy-clad courtyard. A spiral staircase twists up to light-filled dorms with pine bunks. Buses 59, 60 and 68 stop here.

Gutwinski Hotel BOUTIQUE HOTEL €€
(05522-721 75; www.gutwinski.cc; Rosengasse 4-6; s/d €122/192, ste €448; @) Hidden down a quiet backstreet, this 16th-century merchant's house has a touch of old-fashioned romance, with its lime-shaded garden and Biedermeier salon. The rooms blend contem-

porary and classic – think lots of polished wood, muted colours and decadent mirrors and fabrics. The suite ramps up the luxury with its own whirlpool. Modern riffs on Austrian classics feature on the restaurant menu.

Eating

★April CAFE €

(www.aprilcafe.at; Neustadt 39; breakfast €4.90-16.20, lunch €11; ⏲9am-6pm Thu-Mon;) Bright flowerpots and upside-down watering cans guide the way to this wholesomely hip and wonderfully laid-back cafe. Bag a spot on one of the sofas or on the pocket-sized terrace for a latte adorned with flowers or butterflies (Ingo is a 'coffee artist'). Lavish breakfasts, open sandwiches, Ayurvedic dhals, and dips and vegan cakes feature on the all-organic menu.

Magma Köstliches INTERNATIONAL €€

(☎05522-322 55; www.koestliches.at; Schmiedgasse 12; mains €12-17; ⏲9am-6.30pm Tue & Wed, to midnight Thu & Fri, to 3pm Sat;) A slick combination of deli and bistro, Magma places the accent on top-quality regional ingredients in a minimalist white-walled, art-slung, vaulted space. Besides creative breakfast, it rustles up healthy mains (including many vegetarian and vegan options) such as porcini risotto and tandoori chicken with watermelon and buffalo mozzarella salad.

Wirtschaft Zum Schützenhaus AUSTRIAN €€

(☎05522-852 90; www.schuetzenhaus.at; Göfiser Strasse 2; mains €11.50-17.50; ⏲5pm-midnight Mon, Thu & Fri, 10am-midnight Sat, 10am-10pm Sun;) *Schiessen und Geniessen* (shoot and enjoy!) is the motto at this half-timbered tavern, where *Lederhosen*-clad staff bring the likes of humungous schnitzels and *Kässpätzle* (cheese-topped pasta with fried onions) to the table. The appealing tree-shaded beer garden has prime views of the castle and the Alps beyond.

★Gutwinski AUSTRIAN €€€

(☎05522-721 75; www.gutwinski.cc; Rosengasse 4-6; mains €26-34, 4-course menu €59; ⏲noon-2pm & 6-10pm Tue-Sat) In fine weather, head to Gutwinski's tree-shaded terrace to dine on classics such as *Wiener Schnitzel* (breaded veal cutlet) with parsley potatoes and cranberry compote, or brighter, more inventive dishes such as Arctic char with ginger mousse and gin-laced cucumber, and crème brûlée with lavender ice cream. When it's chilly, the candlelit, champagne-kissed interior, with high-back velvet chairs and banquettes, makes an ideal refuge.

Drinking & Nightlife

Poolbar BAR

(www.poolbar.at; Reichenfeldgasse 9) Feldkirch's old public swimming pool in the Reichenfeld district has been born again as the ultrahip Poolbar, the venue of the summertime **Poolbar Festival** (www.poolbar.at; ⏲early Jul–mid-Aug).

Information

The helpful **tourist office** (☎05522-9009; www.feldkirch.travel; Montfortplatz 1; ⏲9am-6pm Mon-Fri, to noon Sat) has stacks of information and free town maps.

Getting There & Away

Trains head north to Bregenz (€7, 32 minutes) and Dornbirn (€5, 21 minutes), and southeast to Bludenz (€5, 15 minutes).

Feldkirch is on the A14 motorway that heads north to Bregenz, a 30-minute drive away, and southeast to Bludenz, a 15-minute drive away. The town sidles up to the border with Liechtenstein, accessed via the A13 heading southwest of town.

Bludenz

☎05552 / POP 14,577 / ELEV 588M

The Alps provide a spectacular backdrop to Bludenz, the only town in Austria – perhaps the world – that can lay claim to having purple cows; the Milka ones churned out from the Suchard factory. Gorging on chocolate aside, Bludenz' arcaded old town takes you back to its heyday as the seat of the Habsburg governors from 1418 to 1806. Bludenz also makes a good base for exploring the surrounding valleys.

Sights

St Laurentiuskirche CHURCH

(Schloss-Gayenhof-Platz 6; ⏲9am-5pm) Climb the covered staircase to this Gothic parish church, dominated by an octagonal onion-domed spire. There are stellar views over the town's rooftops to the Alps beyond from up here.

Activities

To explore Bludenz' attractions, join a free city tour organised by the tourist office, departing at 10.15am on Thursday from mid-May till October.

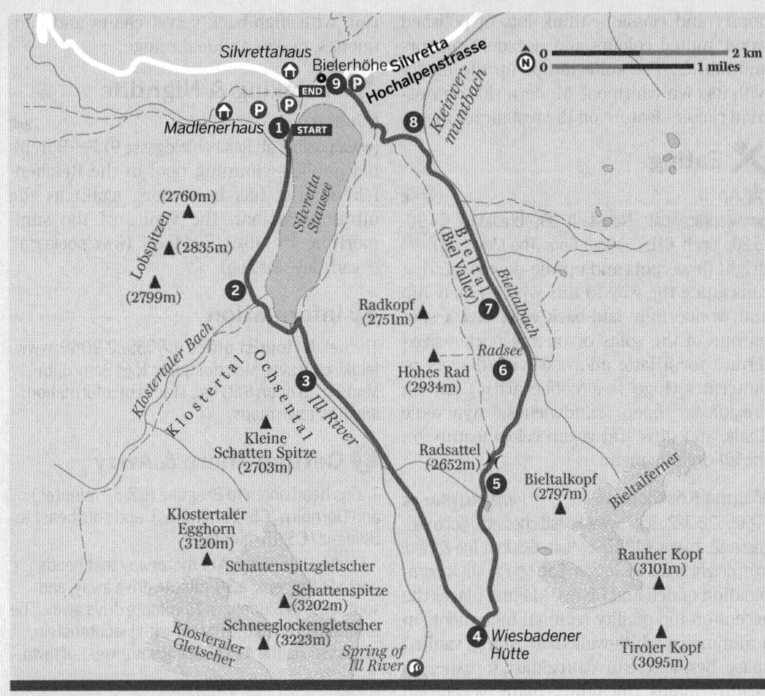

Walking Trail
Radsattel Circuit, Bielerhöhe

START SILVRETTA STAUSEE
END BIELERHÖHE
LENGTH 15KM; FIVE TO SIX HOURS

This is one of Vorarlberg's most spectacular hikes, exploring two valleys linked by a pass and taking you high into the realms of 3000m mountains and glaciers. Best tackled in July or August, the route demands a moderate level of fitness. The Alpenvereinskarte 1:25,000 map No 26 *Silvrettagruppe* covers the trail in detail.

From the 1 **Silvretta Stausee** (p344) car park, walk over the dam to join the well-worn path skirting the western shore of the turquoise reservoir. Stick to the shoreline around the southern end of the lake, crossing one bridge over the 2 **Klostertaler Bach**, then another over the fast-flowing 3 **Ill River**. At the junction, turn right up the trail signed to the Wiesbadener Hütte.

An amphitheatre of glistening blue, heavily crevassed glaciers appears as you gradually gain height. Continue your steady ascent, stopping for refreshment on the sunny terrace of the 4 **Wiesbadener Hütte** after two to 2¼ hours. At the back of the hut, veer left towards the Radsattel on a red-and-white-marked trail that becomes increasingly narrow and rough underfoot. The path zigzags steeply up the slope and over a small stream. Keep right and ascend a rise topped by a large cairn. Cross a shallow pool outlet before the final steep climb to the 2652m 5 **Radsattel**, where a sign marks the Vorarlberg–Tyrol border, one to 1½ hours from the hut.

Drop steeply down the boulder-strewn eastern side of the pass, keeping an eye out for ibex. You will pass several small lakes including the jewel-like 6 **Radsee** as you take the small path down to the remote meadows of the 7 **Bieltal** (Biel Valley). Follow the path along the west bank of the babbling 8 **Bieltalbach** stream and continue west to the Silvretta Stausee, turning right along the reservoir. Back at the main road, turn left and walk 300m to return to 9 **Bielerhöhe** (1½ to two hours from the Radsattel).

There are 15 skiing areas within a 30km radius and ski bus transport to/from Bludenz is sometimes included in the price of ski passes. Walking and cycling are other popular activities; the tourist office has thick booklets on summer and winter outdoor pursuits.

Muttersberg WALKING
(www.muttersberg.eu; Hinterplärsch; cable car adult/child one way €10/6, return €16/9; cable car 9am-5pm) About 1km north of the town centre, a cable car rises up to this 1401m peak, the starting point for numerous hiking, Nordic-walking and cycling trails. If you don't want to walk it, catch Bus 1 from in front of the train station to the cable-car station.

Kletterhalle Klimmerei CLIMBING
(www.klimmerei.at; Quadrella 10, Bürs; adult/child €11/7; hall 7am-10pm, ticket office 6-10pm Mon-Fri, 2-6pm Sat & Sun;) Practise clambering up boulders before tackling the real thing in the Alps at this excellent hall, which is run in association with the Austrian Alpine Club.

Festivals & Events

Milka Chocolate Festival FOOD & DRINK
(www.milkaschokofest.at; early Jul;) Bludenz' sweetest event is the Milka Chocolate Festival in July, when 1000kg of *Schokolade* is up for grabs in prizes. There's also a purple cow-themed parade, music and games, and plenty of kids full of sugar.

Sleeping

Das Tschofen BOUTIQUE HOTEL €€
(05552-208 77; www.dastschofen.at; Rathausgasse 2; s/d €115/180;) A terrific addition to Bludenz' sleeping scene, Das Tschofen manages the delicate act of combining contemporary design with the original features of a listed building. The 11 white-walled rooms sport hardwood floors, streamlined decor, pops of saffron and the occasional period flourish, such as stucco ceilings. A spa, a garden and a highly regarded restaurant are extra boons.

Schlosshotel Dörflinger HISTORIC HOTEL €€
(05552-630 16; www.schlosshotel.cc; Schloss-Gayenhof-Platz 5; s €85-125, d €137-178; P @) Clinging to the cliffs above Bludenz, this smart hotel shelters modern rooms, many with balconies. There's a mountain-facing terrace for warm evenings, free mountain-bike hire for guests and a smart restaurant (mains €16 to €30) dishing up Austrian fare.

Eating

Remise CAFE €
(www.cafe-remise.at; Am Raiffeisenplatz 1; lunch €7.40-11.60, snacks €4-8; 10am-midnight Mon-Sat;) This contemporary cafe attracts arty types and serves snacks from toasties to creative salads. The cultural centre next door regularly hosts exhibitions, film screenings and concerts. There's a kids' playground outside.

Wirtshaus Kohldampf AUSTRIAN €€
(05552-653 85; www.fohren-center.at; Werdenbergerstrasse 53; lunch €8.90, mains €13-20; 11am-10pm) A five-minute amble west of the centre lies this cavernous brewpub-cum-beer garden. Meaty grub such as schnitzel, pork roast and goulash is washed down with Fohrenburger beer from the brewery opposite.

Shopping

Milka Shop CHOCOLATE
(Fohrenburgstrasse 1; 9am-noon Mon & Sat, to 4.30pm Tue-Fri) You can stock up on the chocolate made by purple cows – and discover how it is made – at Milka's flagship shop.

Information

Bang in the heart of the historic centre, the **tourist office** (05552-302 27; www.vorarlberg-alpenregion.at; Rathausgasse 12; 8am-6pm Mon-Fri) is well stocked with information on Bludenz and the surrounding region.

Getting There & Away

Bludenz is on the east–west InterCity (IC) express rail route to Innsbruck (€29.60, 1¾, every two hours) and Bregenz (€10.90, 40 minutes, hourly).

The A14 motorway passes just south of the Ill River and the town centre. Buses run down all five valleys around Bludenz.

Montafon

POP 16,545

The Montafon's pristine wilderness and potent schnapps had Ernest Hemingway in raptures when he wintered here in 1925 and 1926, skiing in blissful solitude and penning *The Sun Also Rises*. Silhouetted by the glaciated Silvretta range and crowned by the 3312m arrow of Piz Buin, the valley remains one of the most serene and unspoilt in the Austrian Alps.

Partenen marks the start of the serpentine 23km Silvretta Hochalpenstrasse, which wends its way under peaks rising to well over 2500m before climbing over the 2036m Bielerhöhe Pass via a series of tight switchbacks.

Sights

Silvretta Stausee LAKE

Glittering at a giddy 2030m above sea level, this startlingly aquamarine reservoir mirrors the snowcapped diamond of 3312m Piz Buin on bright mornings. The lake is the start and end point of the fabulous but challenging Radsattel Circuit (p342), a five- to six-hour, 15km hike that traverses the Radsattel at 2652m, crossing from one valley to another.

Silvretta Hochalpenstrasse AREA

(www.silvretta-bielerhoehe.at; car/motorcycle €16.50/13.50; early Jun-late Oct) The 23km-long Silvretta High Alpine Rd twists and turns beneath peaks rising to well over 2500m before climbing over the 2036m Bielerhöhe Pass via 34 knuckle-whiteningly tight switchbacks. At the top of the pass is the Silvretta Stausee.

Activities

Mile upon glorious mile of alpine trails, including the Radsattel Circuit (p342), attract hikers in summer. Cable cars and lifts can be accessed with the regional Montafon-Brandnertal Card (three/seven days €51/84).

In winter, Montafon draws families who come to carve its 246km of uncrowded pistes and go cross-country skiing, snowshoeing, ski touring and sledding. The Skipass-Montafon (three-/six-day pass €150/269) covers public transport and 19 lifts in the valley.

Silvretta-Montafon SNOW SPORTS

(www.silvretta-montafon.at; Vorarlberg; 1-/2-day pass €54/104) The iconic arrow-shaped peak of Piz Buin (3312m) dominates the Silvretta-Montafon ski area. Tucked away in the southeast corner of Vorarlberg, this serene and beautiful valley's low-key resorts appeal to families, cruisers and ski tourers. Besides 140km of slopes and a snowpark to play on, there is off-piste fun from sledding to winter hiking.

Sleeping

Posthotel Rössle HISTORIC HOTEL €€

(05558-833 30; www.posthotel-roessle.at; Dorfstrasse 4, Gaschurn; d incl half board €156-314;) Hemingway once stayed in this 200-year-old chalet – whether with his mistress or wife remains a mystery. The friendly Kessler family will show you the guestbook he signed and the bed he slept in. Within easy reach of the Silvretta Nova ski arena, the hotel has well-kept rooms, a superb wood-panelled restaurant, indoor and outdoor pools, and a spa.

Silvrettahaus HUT €€

(05558-42 46; www.silvretta-bielerhoehe.at; s/d €73.50/121, incl half board €91/156; mid-Jun-early Oct & mid-Dec–Easter) For more creature comforts at 2000m, check into the architecturally innovative Silvrettahaus at Bielerhöhe, which has bright, contemporary rooms and spellbinding mountain views.

Information

Montafon Tourism (050-668 62 00; www.montafon.at; Silvrettastrasse 6, Schruns; 8am-6pm Mon-Fri, 9am-noon & 3-6pm Sat & Sun) has the lowdown on accommodation and activities in the valley.

Getting There & Away

Trains run frequently from Bludenz to Schruns (€3, 19 minutes), from where up to five buses daily continue onto Partenen (€4, 38 minutes) at the base of the Silvretta pass. From mid-July to mid-October, eight buses daily climb from Partenen to the Silvretta Stausee (€4, 31 minutes).

Understand Austria

The Marmorsaal (Marble Hall) in Schloss Mirabel (p234), Salzburg

History

Although Austria's territorial heartland has always been modest in size, the Habsburg monarchy ruled a mighty empire that spanned continents and was once at the very pinnacle of politics and high culture. Reverberations of this are still felt to this day in the country's grand palaces, monasteries and cathedrals. Austria's history is a story of conflated empires and powerful monarchs, war and revolution, cultural explosion, Austro-fascism, occupation by foreign powers and stable democracy.

Civilisations & Empires

The alpine regions of Austria were cold, inhospitable places during the last ice age 30,000 years ago and virtually impenetrable for human and beast. So it's not surprising that while mammoths were lumbering across a frozen landscape, the more accessible plains and Danube Valley in Lower Austria developed into early centres of civilisation. Several archaeological finds can be traced back to this period, including ancient Venus figurines that are today housed inside Vienna's Naturhistorisches Museum. The starlet among the collection is the Venus of Willendorf, discovered in 1908 in the Wachau region of the Danube Valley. The diminutive and plump 11cm figurine is made of limestone and estimated to be around 25,000 years old.

A proto-Celtic civilisation known as the Hallstatt culture – named after the town of Hallstatt in the Salzkammergut where there was a burial site – took root in the region around 800 BCE. These proto-Celts mined salt in the Salzkammergut and maintained trade ties with the Mediterranean. When other Celts settled in the late Iron Age (around 450 BCE) from Gaul (France) they chose the valley of the Danube River, but also the salt-rich regions around Salzburg, encountering Illyrians who had wandered there from the Balkan region as well as the Hallstatt proto-Celts. Gradually an Illyric-Celtic kingdom took shape, known as Noricum, that stretched from eastern Tyrol to the Danube and the eastern fringes of the Alps in Carinthia, also extending into parts of Bavaria (Germany) and Slovenia. Today the towns of Hallstatt and Hallein have exhibits and salt works focusing on the Hallstatt culture and these Celtic civilisations.

TIMELINE

30,000–25,000 BCE

The 30,000-year-old Venus of Galgenberg (aka Dancing Fanny) and the 25,000-year-old buxom beauty the Venus of Willendorf are crafted – both are now in Vienna's Naturhistorisches Museum.

3300 BCE

The Neolithic 'Ötzi' dies and is mummified in a glacier in the Ötztal. After discovery in 1991, several Austrian and Italian women ask to be impregnated with his frozen sperm.

800–400 BCE

The Iron Age Hallstatt-kultur (Hallstatt culture) develops in southern Salzkammergut, where settlers work salt mines. Around 450 BCE Celts arrive in the region and build on this flourishing culture.

Romans

The Romans, who crossed the Alps in force in 15 BCE and settled south of the Danube River, carved up regions of Austria into administrative areas and built *Limes* (fortresses) and towns such as Carnuntum, Vindobona (the forerunner of Vienna), Brigantium (Bregenz), Juvavum (Salzburg), Flavia Solva (Leibnitz in Styria), Aguntum and Virunum (north of Klagenfurt). However, the Western Empire created by the Romans collapsed in the 5th century, leaving a vacuum that was filled by newly arriving tribes: the Germanic Alemanni in Vorarlberg, Slavs who pushed into Carinthia and Styria, and Bavarians who settled south of the Danube in Upper and Lower Austria, Tyrol and around Salzburg. The Bavarians proved to be the most successful, and by the 7th century they had most regions of Austria in their grip, creating a large German-speaking territory.

The Carolingian Empire

Once the Roman Empire had collapsed in the 5th century, it was difficult to talk about fully fledged empires. This changed in Europe and in Austria itself with the growth of the Carolingian Empire in the 6th century. This was Europe's most powerful empire in its day. It originated in western France and Belgium, grew into a heavyweight under Charlemagne (747–814) and took its inspiration from the Romans. Significantly for future Austria, Charlemagne created a buffer region in the Danube Valley, later dubbed Ostmark (Eastern March), which shored up the eastern edge of his empire, and in 800 he was crowned kaiser by the pope.

The Babenberg Dynasty

Fate took a decisive turn in 976, when Ostmark landed in the hands of Leopold von Babenberg (940–94), a descendent of a noble Bavarian family. Leopold received territory as a gift from Otto II (955–83), a Holy Roman emperor whom Leopold had supported during an uprising in Bavaria. The Babenbergs were a skilful clan who in the 11th century expanded their small territory to include most of modern-day Lower Austria (with Vienna), and a century later Styria (1192) and much of Upper Austria. In 1156, under the Babenberg monarch Heinrich II 'Jasomirgott', the Ostmark (still a political fence until that time) was elevated to a duchy (ie with its own duke and special rights) and Vienna became its capital.

In 1246 the last Babenberg, Duke Friedrich II, died (leaving no heirs) following a battle with the Hungarians over the border between Hungary and his lands in Austria. This allowed the ambitious Bohemian king Ottokar II to move in and assert his control. He bolstered his claim to the Babenberg lands by marrying Friedrich's widow, but he refused to

The patron saint of Austria is St Leopold III of Babenberg (1073–1136), known as Leopold the Good. He is commemorated for fostering the development of his country and founding many monasteries.

15 BCE–600 CE

Romans establish relations with Celts and Nordic tribes. Roman occupation begins in the provinces of Rhaetia, Noricum and Pannonia. Slavic, Germanic and other tribes later overrun the territories.

8 CE

Vindobona, the forerunner of Vienna's Innere Stadt, becomes part of the Roman province of Pannonia.

795

Charlemagne creates a buffer region in the Danube Valley, later dubbed Ostmark (Eastern March) by the Nazis; this shores up the eastern edge of his empire.

976 & 996

The Babenbergs are entrusted with the Ostmark in 976 and administer it as margraves; in 996 this appears for the first time in a document as Ostarrîchi.

swear allegiance to Rudolf von Habsburg, who had been elected ruler of the Holy Roman Empire in 1273. This caused one of the most celebrated clashes in Austrian history when in 1278 the House of Habsburg and its Bohemian arch-rival Ottokar II (who now controlled Styria and Carinthia) went to battle on the Marchfeld, 30km northeast of Vienna. Ottokar, held up while trying to penetrate Drosendorf's fortress en route to the battle, was killed, allowing the Habsburg family to reign uncontested over Austria and marking the beginning of the Habsburg's grip over the nebulous Holy Roman Empire until it finally collapsed in 1806.

Early Habsburg Monarchy

The rise of the Habsburgs to rule was shaky at first. The period directly leading up to the election of Rudolf I was known as the Interregnum, a time when the Holy Roman Empire failed to produce an unchallenged and enduring monarch. After Rudolf died in 1291, the crown slipped out of Habsburg hands for a few years until the non-Habsburgian successor was slain by the Hungarians and Rudolf's eldest son, Albert I, was elected to head the empire in 1298.

The Habsburgs initially suffered some humiliating setbacks, including at the hands of the Swiss, who had begun forming political unions to help maintain peace following the death of Rudolf I. These unions subsequently fought the Habsburgs on numerous occasions and created the basis for greater autonomy and, much later, Swiss independence from the Habsburgs.

The distended lower jaw and lip, a family trait of the early Habsburgs, is discreetly downplayed in official portraits by artists wishing not to cause offence to the crown.

In Austria itself, however, the Habsburgs managed to consolidate their position: Carinthia (as well as Carniola in Slovenia) lost its independence and was annexed in 1335, followed by Tyrol in 1363. These foundations allowed Duke of Austria Rudolf IV (1339–65) to forge ahead with developing his lands: he founded the University of Vienna in 1365 and he created Vienna's most visible landmark today by ordering the building of Gothic Stephansdom in 1359, justifiably earning himself the moniker 'Rudolf the Founder'.

Keeping it Habsburg

Marriage, not muscle, was the historic key to Habsburg land gains. The Hungarian king Matthias Corvinus (1443–90) once adapted lines from Ovid when he wrote: 'Let others wage war but you, lucky Austria, marry! For the empires given to others by Mars are given to you by Venus.'

The age of the convenient wedding began in earnest with Maximilian I (1459–1519), whose moniker was the Last Knight because of his outdated predilection for medieval tournaments. His other loves were Renaissance art, his own grave (which he commissioned during his lifetime) and Albrecht Dürer (1471–1528), whom Maximilian commissioned

1137
Vienna is first documented as a city in the Treaty of Mautern between the Babenbergs and the Bishops of Passau.

1156
As consolation for relinquishing Bavaria, Austria becomes a duchy (Privilegium Minus) and the Babenberg ruler Heinrich Jasomirgott (1107–77) becomes Austria's first duke, residing in Vienna.

1192
Styria is given to Babenberg Leopold V (1157–94) on the condition that it stays part of Austria forever. Styria then includes chunks of Slovenia and Lower and Upper Austria.

1246–78
Last Babenberg dies in 1246. Habsburg Rudolf I is elected king of the Holy Roman Empire in 1273; he defeats Bohemian Ottokar II in the 1278 Battle of Marchfeld

to work on the very same grave before he stepped into it. It is now in Innsbruck's Hofkirche.

But it was Maximilian's affection for Maria of Burgundy (1457–82) that had the greatest influence on the fortunes of the Habsburgs. The two married, and when Maria fell from a horse and died as a result of a miscarriage in 1482, Burgundy, Lorraine and the Low Countries fell into Habsburg hands. In their day, these regions were the last word in culture, economic prosperity and the arts. However, this began a difficult relationship with France that stuck to the Habsburg shoe for centuries.

The 'Spanish Marriage' in 1496 was another clever piece of royal bedding. When Maximilian's son Philipp der Schöne (Philip the Handsome) married Juana la Loca (Johanna the Mad; 1479–55), Spain and its resource-rich overseas territories in Central and South America became Habsburgian. When their son Ferdinand I (1503–64) married Anna of Hungary and Bohemia (1503–47), fulfilling a deal his grandfather Maximilian I had negotiated with King Vladislav II (1456–1516), Bohemia was also in the Habsburg fold. In the same deal, Maria von Habsburg (1505–58) married into this Polish-Lithuanian Jagiellonen dynasty, which traditionally purveyed kings to Poland, Bohemia and Hungary at that time.

AUSTRIA & THE HOLY ROMAN EMPIRE

The Holy Roman Empire was Europe's oddest 'state'. Its foundations were laid when the Carolingian king, Pippin, rescued a beleaguered pope and became *Patricius Romanorum* (Protector of Rome), making him Caesar's successor. The title 'kaiser' is derived from 'Caesar'. Pippin, with Italian spoils on his hands (one being the present-day Vatican), gave these to the pope. Pippin's son, Charlemagne, continued this tradition as protector (which meant he had the title kaiser), and in 962, with the crowning of Otto I (912–73) as Holy Roman Emperor, the empire was officially born.

Kings in the empire were elected in political horse-trading by a handful of prince electors, but for a king to take the next step and become kaiser (and protector of the pope), he had to be crowned by the pope. Depending on how feisty the pope happened to be, this brought other troubles. In 1338 enough was enough and the electors threw the pope overboard, deciding they could elect their own kaiser.

In 972, just before Otto I died, borders of the empire included present-day Austria, Slovenia, Czech Republic, Germany, Holland, Belgium and much of the Italian peninsula. These borders ebbed and flowed with the times. When Rudolf I arrived in 1273, all – or what remained of it – belonged to the Habsburgs.

The empire was formally buried in 1806 when Napoleon Bonaparte tore through Europe, and by the time the Austro-Hungarian Empire (a dual monarchy of Austria and Hungary) took shape in 1867, it was little more than a dim and distant reminder of medieval times.

1335 & 1363

Bavarian Ludwig IV (1314–47) gives Carinthia to the Habsburgs in 1335; territories include Austria (Ostarrîchi), Styria and Carinthia. In 1363 Margarethe Maultasch (1318–63) dies and Tyrol is added.

1420–21

Under Duke Albrecht V, the first large-scale persecution of Jews (known as the *Wiener Geserah*) in Austria's capital takes place.

1496

Habsburg Philipp der Schöne (Philip the Handsome) marries Juana la Loca (Johanna the Mad) in the 'Spanish Marriage': Spain and its resource-rich Central and South American territories became Habsburg.

1517

Theology professor Martin Luther sparks the Reformation when he makes public his 95 theses that call into question corrupt practices of the church, and most of Austria becomes Lutheran (Protestant).

By 1526, when her husband Ludwig II (1506–26) drowned in a tributary of the Danube during the Battle of Mohács against the Turks, Silesia (in Poland), Bohemia (in the Czech Republic) and Hungary were all thoroughly Habsburg.

Under Karl V (1500–58), the era of the universal monarch arrived, and the Habsburgs had added the kingdom of Naples (southern Italy, including Sicily). That was about as good as it got.

Reformation & the Thirty Years' War

The 16th century was a crucial period in Austria during which the country came to terms with religious reformation brought about by Martin Luther, Counter-Reformation aimed at turning back the clock on Luther's Church reforms, and a disastrous Thirty Years' War that saw the Habsburgs' German territories splinter and slip further from their grasp.

Historic Palaces

Schloss Schönbrunn, Vienna

Schloss Belvedere, Vienna

Schloss Eggenberg, Graz

Festung Hohensalzburg, Salzburg

In the German town of Wittenberg in 1517, theology professor Martin Luther (1483–1546) made public his 95 theses that questioned the papal practice of selling indulgences to exonerate sins. Threatened with excommunication, Luther refused to recant, broke from the Catholic Church, was banned by the Reich, and whilst in hiding translated the New Testament into German. Except in Tyrol, almost the entire population of Austria had become Protestant. In 1555 Karl V signed the Peace of Augsburg, which gave the Catholic and Protestant churches equal standing and allowed each local prince to decide the religion of their principality. The more secular northern principalities of the German lands adopted Lutheran teachings, while the clerical lords in the south, southwest and Austria remained Catholic or adopted Catholicism. Not only does this explain the patchwork of Protestant and Catholic religions today in many regions that used to be part of the Holy Roman Empire, but it also made a mess of one Habsburg vision: Emperor Karl V had dedicated his life to creating a so-called universal Catholic monarchy. Seeing the writing clearly on the wall, he abdicated in 1556 and withdrew to a monastery in Spain to lick his wounds and die.

The spoils were divided up among the Habsburgs. The brother of Karl V, Ferdinand I, inherited Austria as well as Hungary and Bohemia, and Karl V's only legitimate son, Philip II (1527–98), got Spain, Naples and Sicily, the Low Countries, and the overseas colonies. To bolster Catholicism in Austria, Ferdinand I invited the Jesuits to Vienna in 1556; in contrast, his successor Maximilian II was extremely tolerant of Protestantism and the ideas of the Reformation. When the fanatically Catholic Ferdinand II took the throne in 1619 and put his weight behind a Counter-Reformation movement, the Protestant nobles in Bohemia finally rebelled in an armed conflict that quickly spread and developed into the pan-European Thirty Years' War; Sweden and France had joined

1529

The first Turkish siege of Vienna takes place, undertaken by Süleyman the Magnificent, but Süleyman's forces are not strong enough to take control of the city.

1556

Abandoning the idea of uniting an empire under Catholicism, Karl V abdicates – the Spanish part goes to his son Philip II, and Ferdinand I gets Austria, Bohemia and largely Turkish-occupied Hungary.

1618–48

Antireformer Ferdinand II challenges Bohemia's confessional freedom. Habsburg counsels are thrown out of a window (the Prague Defenestration), triggering the Thirty Years' War.

1670

Leopold I drives the Jews out of Unterer Werd in Vienna and the quarter is renamed Leopoldstadt, the name it bears today.

this by 1635. In 1645 a Protestant Swedish army marched to within sight of Vienna but did not attack.

Calm was restored with the Peace of Westphalia (1648) but it left the Habsburgs' Reich – embracing more than 300 states and about 1000 smaller territories – a nominal, impotent state. Switzerland and the Netherlands gained formal independence, and the Habsburgs lost territory to France.

Turks & the Siege of Vienna

The Ottoman Empire viewed Vienna as 'the city of the golden apple', but it wasn't *Apfelstrüdel* they were after in their great sieges. The first, in 1529 during the reign of Karl V, was begun by Süleyman the Magnificent, who advanced into Hungary and took Budapest before beginning an 18-day siege to capture Vienna. This was the meeting of two powers almost at their peaks, but – for reasons that are unclear today – the Ottomans suddenly withdrew back to Hungary. The Turkish sultan died at the siege of Szigetvár, yet his death was kept secret for several days in an attempt to preserve the morale of his army. The subterfuge worked for a while. Messengers were led into the presence of the embalmed body, which was placed in a seated position on the throne. They then relayed their news to the corpse.

At the head of the second Turkish siege in 1683 was the general and grand vizier Kara Mustapha. Amid the 25,000 tents of the Ottoman army that surrounded Vienna's medieval centre, he installed 1500 concubines, guarded by 700 Black eunuchs. Their luxurious quarters contained gushing fountains and regal baths, all set up in haste but with great effect.

Again, it was all to no avail, even though Vienna was only lightly defended by 10,000 men. Mustapha's overconfidence was his downfall; failing to put garrisons on Kahlenberg, he and his army were surprised by a swift attack from this famous hill. Mustapha was pursued from the battlefield and defeated once again, at Gran. At Belgrade he was met by the emissary of Sultan Mehmed IV. The price of failure was death, and Mustapha meekly accepted his fate. When the Austrian imperial army conquered Belgrade in 1718 the grand vizier's head was dug up and brought back to Vienna in triumph.

Austria's greatest military hero, Prince Eugene of Savoy, was in fact French. Refused entry to the French army by Louis XIV, Eugene went on to humiliate him on the battlefield.

Maria Theresia

Maria Theresia (1717–80), whose plump figure in stone fills a regal stool on Maria-Theresian-Platz in Vienna today, was something of the mother of the nation. Thrust into the limelight when her father died with no male heirs, she ruled for 40 years while also managing to give birth to 16 children – among them Marie Antoinette, future wife of Louis XVI. Maria Theresia's fourth child, Joseph II, weighed a daunting 7kg at birth.

1683

Turkish siege of Vienna. Christian Europe is mobilised and the threat persists until 1718, after which the Ottoman Empire gradually wanes.

1740–48

Maria Theresia inherits Habsburg possessions, Prussia seizes Silesia (in Poland today) and the Austrian War of Succession starts a power struggle between Prussia and Habsburg-controlled Austria-Hungary.

1751

Tiergarten Schönbrunn is established in Vienna, making it the world's oldest zoological garden.

1752

Maria Theresia introduces the short-lived Commission Against Immoral Conduct, which pillages homes and attempts to snatch men entertaining loose women.

Although Maria Theresia is famous for her many enlightened reforms, she was remarkably prudish for a family that had married and bred its way to power. One of her less popular measures was the introduction of the short-lived Commission Against Immoral Conduct in 1752, which raided private homes, trying to catch men entertaining loose women – the commission even tried to snare Casanova during his visit to Vienna, throwing him out of the city in 1767.

Historic Sights

Vienna's Hofburg

Stift Melk in the Wachau

Neolithic Ötzi Dorf

Maria Theresia's low take on fornication (and Casanova's womanising and proclivity for urinating in public) was no doubt coloured by the conduct of her husband, Francis I, who was apparently very adept and enthusiastic when it came to fornication. Yet despite her husband's philandering, Maria Theresia felt she should remain loyal to her spouse, and when he died suddenly in 1765 she stayed in mourning for the rest of her life. She retreated to Schloss Schönbrunn in Vienna, left the running of the state in the hands of Joseph II (of 7kg fame) as coregent, and adopted a low profile and chaste existence.

The period of the Enlightenment began under Maria Theresia and continued during the coreign of Joseph II in the late 18th century. Vienna was transformed from being a place in which the Habsburgs lived and ruled into an administrative capital. A functioning bureaucracy was established for the first time and this was directly responsible to the monarchy. Joseph was mostly of the same mettle as his mother. He ushered in a period of greater religious tolerance and in 1781 an edict ensured Protestants would enjoy equal rights with Catholics. While decrees gave Jews much more freedom, paving the way for a more active role in trade and education, paradoxically he promoted assimilation of Jews into the Austrian mainstream, banning whatever customs he thought hindered this.

Napoleon, Revolution & Empire

The French Revolution of 1789–99 was a political explosion that ushered in a new age of republicanism in Europe and challenged surviving feudalistic undertakings like the Holy Roman Empire. It also led to the rise of Napoleon Bonaparte (1769–1821), Europe's diminutive moderniser. His code of law, the Napoleonic Code, was the backbone of modern laws and was anathema to precisely those privileges of rank and birth that had allowed the Habsburgs to rule and govern for so long.

Austria played a role in virtually all the Napoleonic wars from 1803 to 1815, the year Napoleon was finally defeated at Waterloo. He occupied Vienna twice (in 1805 and 1809) and in April 1809, during occupation of Austrian regions, Tyrol – which had fallen into the hands of Bavaria – was the scene of discontent when innkeeper Andreas Hofer (1767–1810) led a rebellion for independence. For his troubles, Hofer was put on trial

1764

Reformer Kaiser Joseph II (1741–90) takes the throne and the Age of Enlightenment that began under Maria Theresia is in full swing. The power of the church is curbed.

1789–99

The French Revolution takes place, bringing a new age of republicanism to Europe and challenging feudalistic establishments such as the Holy Roman Empire.

1793

Following a marriage to French king Louis XVI (1754–93), Maria Theresia's 15th child, Marie Antoinette – whom the French call 'L'Autrichienne' (the Austrian) – is beheaded during the French Revolution.

1804–05

Napoleon (1769–1821) occupies Vienna in 1805. The Holy Roman Empire is abolished. Franz II reinvents himself as Austrian Kaiser Franz I. In 1809 the Frenchman returns to retake Vienna.

and executed at Napoleon's behest. His body is entombed in Innsbruck's Hofkirche.

Despite ultimately being defeated, Napoleon's ventures triggered the collapse of the Holy Roman Empire. Its ruler Franz II reinvented himself as Franz I of Austria, and the man he appointed to help draw up a post-Napoleon Europe, the chief minister Klemens von Metternich, rose to dominate Europe's biggest diplomatic party, the Congress of Vienna, held in 1814–15 to reshape the continent. The Habsburgs survived all this and in the post-Napoleon Vormärz (Pre-March) years, they dominated a loose Deutscher Bund (German Alliance) comprising hundreds of small 'states' cobbled together in an oppressive period of modest cultural flourish and reactionary politics called the Biedermeier period.

Revolutions of 1848

With citizens being kept on a short leash by their political masters in the first half of the 19th century, it's not surprising that they began to seek new freedoms. Klemens von Metternich, who had become court and state chancellor, believed in absolute monarchy and his police took a ferocious approach to liberals and Austrian nationalists who demanded their freedom. Meanwhile, nationalism – one of the best chances of liberalising Austrian society at that time – was threatening to chip away the delicate edges of the Habsburg empire. On top of this, atrocious industrial conditions added fuel to fires of discontent.

The sparks of the Paris revolution in February 1848 ignited Vienna in March 1848. Reflecting the city–country divide, however, the uprising failed to take hold elsewhere in Austria except in Styria. A similar revolution in Germany meant that some Austrian revolutionaries were now in favour of becoming part of a greater, unified and liberal Germany. This was the difficult Grossdeutsch-Kleindeutsch (Greater Germany–Lesser Germany) question – Germany with or without Austria – and reflects the unsettled relationship between the Austrian and German nations.

The rebels demanded a parliament, and in May and June 1848 Kaiser Ferdinand I issued manifestos that paved the way for a parliamentary assembly a month later. He packed his bags and his family and fled to Innsbruck. This should have been the end of the Habsburgs. It wasn't. Parliament passed a bill improving the lot of the peasants, and Ferdinand cleverly sanctioned this, overnight winning the support of rural folk in the regions. Meanwhile, the Habsburgs received a popular boost when General Radetzky (1766–1858) won back Lombardy (Italy) in successful military campaigns.

In October 1848, however, the revolution escalated and reached fever pitch in Vienna. Although this uprising could be quashed, the Habsburgs decided to dispense with Ferdinand I, replacing him with his nephew

When then-governor Arnold Schwarzenegger allowed an execution to go ahead in California in 2005, some Austrians wanted to revoke his Austrian citizenship. Austria first abolished capital punishment in 1787.

1809

In the midst of the Napoleonic occupation, Tyrol – which has fallen under Bavarian control – is the scene of another rebellion when innkeeper Andreas Hofer leads a bid for independence.

1813 & 1815

Napoleon is defeated in Leipzig in 1813 and, in his final battle, at Waterloo in 1815.

1815–48

The Metternich system, aimed at shoring up the monarchies of Austria, Russia and Prussia, ushers in the stifling Biedermeier period.

1818

The Austrian tailor Josef Madersperger invents the world's first sewing machine.

Franz Joseph I, who introduced his own monarchical constitution and dissolved parliament in early 1849. It would only be revived properly in 1867.

By September 1849 it was time to weigh up the damage, count the dead and, most importantly, look at what had been won. Austria was not a democracy, because the kaiser retained absolute powers that allowed him to veto legislation and govern by decree if he wished. The revolutions, however, had swept away the last vestiges of feudalism and, by giving them a taste of parliamentary rule, made state citizens out of royal subjects.

Austro-Hungarian Empire

In 1867 a dual monarchy was created in Austria and Hungary. This was an attempt by the Habsburgs to hold onto support for the monarchy among Hungarians by giving them a large degree of autonomy. The Austro-Hungarian Empire would grow to include core regions of Austria, Hungary, the Czech Republic, Slovakia, Slovenia, Croatia and Bosnia-Herzegovina, as well as regions like the Voivodina in Serbia, and small chunks in northern Italy, Romania, Poland and Ukraine.

Generally it is known as the 'KuK' (*König und Kaiser*; king and kaiser) monarchy – the kaiser of Austria was also king of Hungary. In practice, the two countries increasingly went separate ways, united only by the dual monarch and a couple of high-level ministries like 'war' and 'foreign affairs'. This so-called Danube Monarchy or Austro-Hungarian Empire was the last stage of development in the Habsburg empire and would endure until 1918, when it collapsed completely.

Fin-de-Siècle Austria

The roots of Austria's Österreichische Volkspartei (ÖVP; Austrian People's Party) go back to 1887; a forerunner of the Sozialdemokratische Partei Österreichs (SPÖ; Social Democratic Party of Austria) was founded a year later.

Austria in the late 19th century followed a similar pattern of industrialisation and growth of political parties based around workers' movements that occurred in other continental European countries. The country's oldest political party, the Sozialdemokratische Partei Österreichs (SPÖ; Social Democratic Party of Austria), was founded as the Social Democratic Workers' Party in 1889, based on German models. By the turn of the 20th century, Austria – and Vienna in particular – was experiencing one of its most culturally exciting periods. The capital's population had almost doubled between 1860 and 1890, growing to more than two million inhabitants.

This was the political and cultural hub of an empire that spanned Austria and Hungary, but also included 15 other countries, proving a magnet for artists, architects, the persecuted and plain hangers-on who wanted to try their luck in the capital of an empire. In this empire, however, Austrians and Hungarians enjoyed a higher status than Slavs, leading to exploitation and often tensions in the capital.

1848

Revolution topples Chancellor Klemens von Metternich, who flees disguised as a washerwoman. Franz Joseph I abolishes many reforms. Austria's first parliament is formed.

1850

Vienna's city limits are expanded, mostly to include the area within the Linienwall (today the Gürtel). Districts are numbered – the old city becoming the 1st, the *Vorstädte* (inner suburbs) the 2nd to 9th.

1857

Vienna's city walls are demolished to make way for the creation of the monumental architecture today found along the Ringstrasse.

1866

Austria and its allied principalities in Germany fight the Austro-Prussian War, which leads to victory for Prussia and creates the groundwork for a unified Germany that excludes Austria.

Architecturally, Austria's capital was transformed by a spate of building and infrastructure projects that, among other large projects, saw it receive a metro system. The Secession movement, the Austrian equivalent of art nouveau, sprang up and rejected historicism. Villas sprouted out of the ground in Vienna and across the country, and coffee houses, especially in the capital, became the centre of literary activity and music. In 1913 Arnold Schönberg began developing his 'atonal' style of musical composition when he conducted his famous Watschenkonzert ('clip-over-the-ear concert') in Vienna's Musikverein. For a public used to the primrose tones of Romanticism, it must have felt like an unmitigated aural assault.

Women in Austria gained the right to vote in national elections in 1919, hot on the heels of Britain and Germany (1918).

Meanwhile, Sigmund Freud (1856–1939) had set up his practice in Vienna's Bergstrasse and was challenging the sexual and psycho-social mores of the previous century. He used the term *psychoanalysis* and explained the role of sexuality in human life. This was, in fact, a highly sexualised period, with writers such as Arthur Schnitzler and expressionist artists like Egon Schiele, Gustav Klimt and Oskar Kokoschka taking sexuality as a major theme in their works. WWI brought all this to an end.

World War I

The assassination of Franz Ferdinand, the nephew of Franz Joseph, in Sarajevo on 28 June 1914 triggered the first of Europe's two cataclysmic wars in the 20th century. Overnight, the cultural explosion of fin-de-siècle Austria was replaced by the explosion of shells in the trenches. Austria responded to the assassination by declaring war on Serbia one month later, in what it believed would be a short, punitive campaign. Austria-Hungary was poorly equipped, however, and the war rapidly escalated into a pan-European affair in which Germany, Austria-Hungary and Turkey found themselves pitted against a European power coalition made up of Russia, Britain, France and Italy. Halfway through the war Franz Joseph died and was replaced by Karl I. Ultimately, military revolt by troops in Italy spread and caused the rest of the army to lay down its arms, bringing defeat and collapse of the empire. WWI resulted in about 1.4 million military casualties for Austria-Hungary, and another 3.5 million Austro-Hungarians were wounded. In the rest of Europe, it was perceived as unprecedented in the scale of destruction and suffering it caused, and so horrific that it was dubbed 'the war to end all wars'.

The First Republic

With defeat and the abdication of Karl I, Austria declared itself a republic on 12 November 1918, having been reduced to a small country of about 6.5 million inhabitants, most of whom spoke German. South Tyrol

1867
Weakened by loss against Prussia, Austria is now forced by Hungary to create a dual Austro-Hungarian monarchy (the Ausgleich). Austria establishes a democratic parliament.

1874
Viennese privatier Jakob Zelzer is buried in Vienna Zentralfriedhof (Central Cemetery) as its first deceased resident; today there are about 2.5 million.

1878
To prevent the Russians increasing their influence in the Balkans after they win the Russo-Turkish War of 1877–78, Austria-Hungary occupies Bosnia and Herzegovina.

1897
The giant Ferris wheel (Riesenrad) is built in Vienna's Prater recreational area, which until 1766 had been a royal hunting ground for Habsburgs.

Carl E Schorske magically interlinks seven essays on the intellectual history of Vienna in his seminal work *Fin-de-Siècle Vienna*. It's essential reading for a deep understanding of late-19th- and early-20th-century Vienna.

was carved off from the rest of Austria and given to Italy, and the perception at the time was that a country of Austria's size would have little chance of surviving. Austria was therefore caught between contrasting movements that either wanted to unite with Germany, return to a monarchical system, or simply break away and join another country, as was the case with Vorarlberg (which sought union with Switzerland). The loss of land caused severe economic difficulties. Whole industries collapsed and unemployment soared, fuelled by the return of ex-soldiers and the influx of refugees, but also by a huge number of bureaucrats who, with the collapse of the monarchy, now had no job to return to.

One of the most serious problems facing the new republic was the divide between the socialist-governed cities, especially 'Red Vienna', and the extremely conservative rural regions. The 30,000-strong army created to ensure the country's existence was an additional conservative force in the country. The weakness of this army was matched by a police force that was helpless in thwarting the creation of left- and right-wing paramilitary forces.

The Social Democratic Workers' Party created its Republican Defence League (Schutzbund), whereas on the other side of the political fence the Christlichsoziale Partei (Christian Social Party), a Catholic nationalist party that had emerged in the late 19th century and survived until 1934, fostered close ties with a number of ultraconservative paramilitary groups.

By the mid-1920s armed paramilitary groups from both sides were roaming the streets of Vienna and elsewhere engaging in bloody clashes. When in 1927 a court in Vienna acquitted members of the right-wing paramilitary Frontkämpfer (Front Fighters) on charges of killing two people during demonstrations, left-wing groups rose up and stormed the city's Justizpalast (Palace of Justice). The police moved in and regained control of the building, but about 90 people died in the revolt and over 1000 were injured. Troubled times had come.

Jewish History in Austria

As Austria entered the 1930s, the threat to its Jewish population intensified and would culminate in cultural, intellectual and above all human tragedy.

Austrian Jewry enjoys a long and rich history. The first mention of Jews in Vienna was in 1194, when a minter by the name of Schlom was appointed by the crown. The very same man was subsequently murdered along with 16 other Viennese Jews by zealous crusaders on their way to the Holy Land. Gradually, a ghetto grew around today's Judenplatz in Vienna, where a large synagogue stood in the 13th century.

1900

Vienna becomes the centre of the *Jugendstil* (art nouveau) movement through its association with Otto Wagner and related artists called Vienna's Secession.

1905

Austrian writer and pacifist activist Bertha von Suttner becomes the first woman to win the Nobel Peace Prize.

1908

Fatefully, Austria-Hungary is given a mandate to occupy and administer Bosnia and Herzegovina, with the expectation that it will later be annexed completely.

1910

Vienna's population breaks the two million barrier, the largest it has ever been. The rise is mainly due to exceptionally high immigration numbers – the majority of immigrants are Czechs.

Historically, Jews could only work in some professions. They were seldom allowed into tradesmen's guilds or to engage in agriculture, and therefore earned a living through trading goods and selling, or through money lending, which explains many of the clichés of the past and present. Two 'libels' in the Middle Ages made life difficult for Jews. One of these was the 'host desecration libel', which accused Jews of desecrating Christ by acts such as sticking pins into communion wafers and making them weep or bleed. The second was the 'blood libel', which accused Jews of drinking the blood of Christians during rituals. In 1420 these libels culminated in one of Vienna's worst pogroms, during which many Jews committed collective suicide. The synagogue on Vienna's Judenplatz was destroyed and the stones of the synagogue were used to build the old university.

Vienna's population peaked at more than two million between 1910 and 1914. After WWI, Vienna was one of the world's five largest cities.

Jews were officially banned from settling in Vienna until 1624, but this law was regularly relaxed. It did mean, however, that Vienna's Jews had a particularly rough time of it, and in 1670 when Leopold I (1640–1705) drove them out of Unterer Werd, the quarter was re-christened Leopoldstadt, the name it bears today. They returned, however, and this district remained Vienna's largest Jewish quarter until WWII.

When money was tight following the 1683 Turkish siege, Jews were encouraged to settle in town as money lenders. Interestingly, once the threat subsided from 1718, Sephardic Jews from Spain arrived and were allowed to establish their own religious community. An edict from Kaiser Joseph II (1741–90) improved conditions for Jews, and after Kaiser Franz I remodelled himself into Austria's kaiser and allowed Jews to establish schools, some of Vienna's Jewry rose into bourgeois and literary circles.

The revolution of 1848 brought the biggest changes, however. Vienna's Jews were at the forefront of the uprising, and it brought them freedom of religion, press and schooling. Indirectly, it also led to the founding of the Israelitische Kultusgemeinde (Jewish Religious Community), more than a century after the Sephardic Jews had founded their own. Today this is the largest body that represents religious Jews in Austria.

In 1878 Jewry in Austria was shaken up again by the arrival from Budapest of Theodor Herzl (1860–1904), who founded political Zionism, a concept that brought together the ideas of the workers movement with support for a Jewish state. His book *Der Judenstaat* (The Jewish State; 1896) would later be crucial to the creation of Israel.

Beginning with Adolf Fischhof (1816–93), whose political speech on press freedom in 1848 helped trigger revolution, and continuing with Herzl and with the founding father of Austrian social democracy, Viktor Adler (1852–1918), Jews drove reforms in Austria and played a key role during the 'Red Vienna' period of the 1920s and early 1930s.

1914

Austrian archduke Franz Ferdinand is assassinated in Sarajevo by a Serbian nationalist, triggering WWI, which sees Austria-Hungary in alliance with Germany and the Ottoman Empire.

1918

WWI ends and Karl I abdicates after the humiliating defeat; the First Republic is proclaimed in Vienna. The Habsburg empire is shaved of border nationalities; Austria keeps most German-speaking regions.

1920s

The Social Democratic Party of Austria controls 'Red Vienna', its heart set on Austro-Marxism, while the provinces are controlled by conservative forces.

1934

Austrian politics is polarised, paralysed by paramilitary groups. In 1934 parliament is gridlocked and Austria collapses into civil war – hundreds die in three-day fighting culminating in Social Democrat defeat.

Anschluss & WWII

Austria's role in WWII is one of the most controversial aspects of its modern history. Hitler was popular inside Austria, and Austria itself supplied a disproportionately large number of officers for the SS and the German army. What Hitler and the Nazis couldn't achieve through pressure, large numbers of Austrians themselves helped achieve through their active and passive support for Nazism and Hitler's war.

Hella Pick's *Guilty Victim: Austria from the Holocaust to Haider* is an excellent analysis of modern-day Austria, and gives a fascinating insight into the country's struggle to forget.

Austro-Marxism & Austro-Fascism

The worldwide economic depression triggered by the crash of stock exchanges in 1929 further fuelled the flames of discontent and division. About 25% of the working population was now unemployed. Austro-Marxism, which sought a third way between Russian Leninism and the revisionism cropping up in some European social democratic movements, enjoyed a strong following in the cities. Key figures behind it – today reading like a who's who of street names in Vienna – were Karl Renner (1870–1950), Otto Bauer (1881–1938), Friedrich Adler (1879–1960), Max Adler (1873–1937) and Rudolf Hilferding (1877–1941). In contrast to revolutionary Marxism, leaders were committed to 'winning over minds, not smashing in heads' as Otto Bauer so aptly put it.

The first government of the Austrian Republic was a coalition of left- and right-wing parties under Chancellor Karl Renner. A key figure of the right was Ignaz Seipl (1876–1932), who was chancellor twice during the 1920s and saw his calling in opposing the Marxists.

In 1930 right-wing conservatives forced through a constitutional change that gave more power to the president and weakened parliament. In a radicalisation of politics, paramilitary groups close to the right formally backed home-grown Austrian fascism, and when Engelbert Dollfuss (1892–1934) became chancellor in 1932, Austria moved a step closer to becoming a fascist state.

During the chaos, in a parliamentary session in 1933 following strikes by workers and a harsh response by the government, Dollfuss declared his intention to rule without parliament. This marked the beginning of a period when socialists and social democrats were gradually being outlawed and the workers' movements weakened. In 1933 police forced their way into the headquarters of the (left-wing) paramilitary Schutzbund triggering an uprising in Linz, Vienna and other industrial centres that virtually led to civil war. The army quashed the uprising. Leading social democrats were executed and the social democratic movement declared illegal, turning the fight against fascism into an underground movement.

In 1934 Dollfuss – a deeply religious man who was backed by the Italian dictator Benito Mussolini – was murdered in a failed putsch staged by Austrian Nazis, whom he had also banned.

1938

Nazi troops march into Vienna; Hitler visits his beloved Linz, and Vienna to address 200,000 ecstatic Viennese on Heldenplatz. After a rigged referendum, Austria becomes part of Hitler's Reich.

1938–39

In the Pogromnacht of November 1938, Jewish businesses and homes are plundered and destroyed across Austria; 120,000 Jews leave Vienna over the next six months.

1939–45

War and genocide in Austria. Over 100,000 of Vienna's 180,000 Jews escape, but 65,000 die. In 1945 the Red Army liberates Vienna. Austria and Vienna are divided among the Allied powers.

1948

Graham Greene flies to Vienna for inspiration for a film that becomes *The Third Man*, starring Orson Welles and featuring an iconic scene on the city's Riesenrad (Ferris wheel).

While Hitler was seizing power in Germany in 1933 and subsequently closing down all opposition, across the border in Austria, an Austrofascist government lifted the ban on local chapters of Hitler's Nationalsozialistische Deutsche Arbeiterpartei (National Socialist Democratic Workers' Party; NSDAP), which was neither democratic, sympathetic to workers nor socialist. This was done under pressure from Hitler, allowing Austrian Nazis to make a power grab at home. On 12 March 1938, Hitler's troops crossed the border and occupied Austria, in the so-called Anschluss (annexation), according to which Austria became part of a greater Germany. This ended a period of contradiction in which Austria's leaders had virtually set themselves up as dictators, but did not like the idea of becoming part of Hitler's Nazi Germany. A few days later, Hitler held his famous speech to a cheering crowd of tens of thousands on Vienna's Heldenplatz, declaring Austria part of the German nation.

The Holocaust

The events of the Nazi era, culminating in the Holocaust, are etched in the collective memory of Jews everywhere: the prohibitive Nuremberg Laws, the forced sale and theft of Jewish property, and Reichspogromnacht (also known as *Kristallnacht,* 'The Night of Broken Glass') on 9 and 10 November 1939 when synagogues and Jewish businesses were burnt and Jews were attacked openly on the streets.

The arrival of Hitler in Vienna in March 1938 raised the stakes among those Jews who had not yet managed to flee the country. Vienna's 'father' of modern psychoanalysis, Sigmund Freud, had not wanted to read the signs for a long time; in June that year, however, he fled to England. The 20th century's most innovative classical composer, Arnold Schönberg (1874–1951), lost his job as a lecturer in Berlin in 1933 and went to the US. They were just two of many prominent Austrian Jews forced into exile.

Others were not as fortunate. The Holocaust (or Schoa), Hitler's attempt to wipe out European Jewry, was a brutal and systematic act that saw some 65,000 Austrian Jews perish in concentration camps throughout Europe. It ruptured Jewish history in Austria dating back to the early Middle Ages, and even today it's not really possible to talk about a 'recovery' of Jewish culture in the country.

Because of atrocities perpetrated on the Jewish population by the Nazis, today the Jewish community is only a fraction of its former size. About 8000 religiously affiliated Jews live in Austria, and there are about another 3000 to 5000 who are not affiliated with a community. The number was boosted by the arrival of Jews from the former Soviet Union in the 1990s, and increasingly Jews from Hungary, where anti-Semitism is on the rise, are moving to Vienna.

Take a virtual tour through Jewish history in Austria from the Middle Ages to the present in the Jewish Virtual Library at www.jewishvirtuallibrary.org.

1955

Austrian *Staatsvertrag* (state treaty) is ratified. Austria declares sovereignty and neutral status, ending a decade of occupation. Post-WWII international bodies come to Vienna; the UN later sets up offices here.

1955–66

'Grand coalitions' of major parties govern Austria based on a system of *Proporz* (proportion), whereby ministerial posts are divided among the major parties. This becomes a hallmark of Austrian politics.

1972–78

Vienna's Donauinsel (Danube Island) is created to protect the city against flooding. Today it serves as one of the city's recreation areas, with parks, river beaches, trails and forest.

1979

A third UN headquarters is opened up in Austria's capital. It is the headquarters for the International Atomic Energy Agency, Drugs & Crime office, and other functions.

Resistance & Liberation

With the annexation of Austria in 1938, opposition turned to resistance. As elsewhere, whenever Hitler's troops crossed a border, resistance from within was extremely difficult. Interestingly, Tyrolean resistance leaders often rallied opposition to Nazism by recalling the revolt of Andreas Hofer in 1809 when Tyrol's innkeeper led his rebellion for independence. An Österreichische Freiheitsbataillon (Austrian Freedom Battalion) fought alongside the Yugoslav People's Liberation Army, and partisan groups in Styria and Carinthia maintained links with other partisans across the Yugoslavian border. Unlike other countries, Austria had no government in exile.

Resistance increased once the war looked lost for Hitler. The Austrian Robert Bernardis (1908–44) was involved in the assassination attempt on Hitler by high-ranking officers on 20 July 1944 and was then executed by the Nazis. Another involved in that plot, Carl Szokoll (1915–2004), survived undetected. The most famous resistance group, however, was called 05, whose members included Austria's president from 1957 to 1965, Adolf Schärf (1890–1965).

With the Red Army approaching Vienna in 1945, the resistance group 05 worked closely with Carl Szokoll and other military figures in Operation Radetzky to liberate Vienna in the last days of the war. Although they were able to establish contact with the Red Army as it rolled towards the city, they were betrayed at the last moment and several members were strung up from street lanterns. The Red Army, not Austrians, would liberate the capital.

Austria after 1945

Soon after liberation Austria declared its independence from Germany. A provisional federal government was established under socialist Karl Renner, and the country was occupied by the Allies – the Americans, Russians, British and French. Vienna was itself divided into four zones; this was a time of 'four men in a jeep', so aptly depicted in Graham Greene's book and film *The Third Man.*

Discover more about the history of Austria from the Babenbergs to the country's entry into the EU in *The Austrians: A Thousand Year Odyssey* by Gordon Brook-Shepard.

Delays caused by frosting relations between the superpowers ensured that the Allied occupation dragged on for 10 years. On 15 May 1955 the Austrian State Treaty was ratified, with Austria proclaiming its permanent neutrality. The Soviet Union insisted that Austria declare its neutrality as a condition for ending Soviet occupation in 1955. At the last minute, recognition of Austria's guilt for WWII was struck out of the state treaty.

The Allied forces withdrew, and in December 1955 Austria joined the United Nations (UN). The economy took a turn for the better through the assistance granted under the Marshall Plan, and the cessation of the

1981

Hohe Tauern National Park is established as the first of seven national parks in Austria.

1986

Presidential candidate Kurt Waldheim (1918–2007) is accused of war crimes. Waldheim wins a tough election but is stained. The Historians Commission finds Waldheim unhelpful, but no proof of crimes.

1986

Vienna ceases to be the capital of surrounding *Bundesland* of Niederösterreich (Lower Austria), replaced by Sankt Pölten.

1995

Austria joins the EU in 1995, but because of guarantees in 1955 to Moscow to remain neutral it forgoes NATO membership.

CUCKOO CLOCK STABILITY

In 1948 the British author Graham Greene flew to Vienna and roamed the bomb-damaged streets looking for inspiration for a film he had been commissioned to write about the occupation of post-WWII Vienna. As chance would have it, Greene penned the script for one of Europe's finest films about the era – *The Third Man*, starring Orson Welles as the penicillin racketeer Harry Lime. At one point in Vienna's Prater, Orson Welles as Lime waxes lyrical about how under the bloody reign of the Borgias Italy produced some of its finest art. 'In Switzerland they had brotherly love, 500 years of democracy and peace, and what did they produce? The cuckoo clock.' Never mind that the cuckoo clock comes from Germany's Black Forest – not exactly a model of stability over the centuries. But that's another matter.

removal of industrial property by the Soviets. As the capital of a neutral country on the edge of the Cold War front line, Vienna attracted spies and diplomats: Kennedy and Khrushchev met here in 1961, Carter and Brezhnev in 1979; the UN set up shop in 1979.

Kurt Waldheim Affair

Austria's international image suffered following the election in 1986 of President Kurt Waldheim who, it was revealed, had served in a German *Wehrmacht* (armed forces) unit implicated in WWII war crimes. Austria was forced to seriously confront its Nazi past. Accusations that Waldheim had committed these crimes while a lieutenant serving with the German army in the Balkans could never be proved, but Austria's elected president was unwilling to fully explain himself or express misgivings about his wartime role.

In 1993 Chancellor Franz Vranitzky finally admitted that Austrians were 'willing servants of Nazism'. Since then, however, Austria has attempted to make amends for its part in atrocities against the Jews. In 1998 the Austrian Historical Commission, set up to investigate and report on expropriations during the Nazi era, came into being, and in 2001 Vienna's mayor Dr Michael Häupl poignantly noted that after having portrayed itself as the first victim of National Socialism for many years, Austria now had to admit to its own active participation in the regime's crimes. This marked a more critical approach to Austria's role during the Nazi dictatorship.

'Westernisation' of Austria

According to the Hungarian political historian Anton Pelinka, Austria spent the first few decades of the Second Republic defining and asserting its own home-grown political and social path, but since the mid-1980s

1999
Austria introduces the euro and abolishes the Austrian schilling as its currency, having easily satisfied the criteria for the level of debt and the inflation rate.

2003
Styrian muscle man, actor and director Arnold 'Arnie' Schwarzenegger is elected governor of California after becoming a US citizen in 1983.

2007
A grand coalition government of Social Democrats (SPÖ) and the Austrian People's Party (ÖVP) is formed under Alfred Gusenbauer.

2008
Austria cohosts football's European Cup with Switzerland.

has followed a course of 'Westernisation'. Two features of this are its membership in the European Union (EU) since 1995 and adoption of the euro currency when it was introduced in 1999.

The political consensus that saw the two larger parties, the SPÖ and Österreichische Volkspartei (ÖVP), completely dominate politics has given way to a polarisation. In 1986 Die Grünen (The Greens) party was founded, with close links to a similar ecologically focused party in Germany. On the other side of the political spectrum is the Freiheitliche Partei Österreichs (FPÖ; Freedom Party of Austria), which was founded in 1955 and had a high proportion of former Nazis in its ranks. In 1986, however, its charismatic leader Jörg Haider reinvented the party as a populist right-wing party with a focus on immigration issues, asylum laws and integration – issues that today figure strongly in its policies.

In 2000 the FPÖ formed a federal coalition for the first time with the ÖVP, resulting in regular 'Thursday demonstrations' against the FPÖ within Austria to protest its participation in government, and in sanctions imposed on Austria by other EU members. Splintering has continued in recent years, best exemplified by the formation in 2012 of Team Stronach, founded by Austria's most powerful industrialist, Frank Stronach, with a political platform bearing many of the hallmarks of right-wing populism.

Recent History

Austrian politics have been a rollercoaster ride of late. ÖVP chairman Sebastian Kurz (b. 1986) was hailed as a political wunderkind when he became chancellor, and the EU's youngest head of government, at 2017's snap elections. He was ousted in May 2019 after footage emerged of his FPÖ coalition partner Heinz-Christian Stracher attempting to trade political favours for state contracts on the island of Ibiza, prompting snap elections. Brigitte Bierlein, head of the constitutional court, stepped in as Austria's first female chancellor.

Kurz returned to power after the 2019 legislative election in coalition with the environmentalist Greens (Die Grünen – Die Grüne Alternative, aka Grüne). Shortly after the cabinet's inauguration in January 2020, the COVID-19 pandemic eclipsed their political agenda. Pollical turmoil ensued again when, in October 2021, Kurz' office was searched over accusations that between 2016 and at least 2018, he had manipulated opinion polls in his favour using taxpayers' money. While he was replaced as chancellor by Alexander Schallenberg, Kurz remained party and parliamentary group leader, with immunity as an MP. In November 2021, however, MPs voted his immunity be lifted. The corruption investigation was ongoing at the time of writing; a guilty finding would hobble his chances of regaining the chancellorship.

2010

SPÖ preferred presidential candidate Heinz Fischer is re-elected as an independent; populist right-wing candidate Barbara Rosenkranz is resoundingly defeated.

2017

Pro-EU centrist Alexander Van der Bellen becomes president. ÖVP leader Sebastian Kurz claims victory at the 2017 elections; aged 31, he is Austria's youngest-ever chancellor.

2019–20

The ÖVP-FPÖ coalition government collapses following the 'Ibiza-gate' scandal. Kurz is re-elected, forming a coalition with the Greens (Grüne). The Covid-19 pandemic begins.

2021

Kurz resigns amid a corruption scandal. ÖVP foreign minister Alexander Schallenberg takes over as chancellor.

Architectural Splendour

Thanks to the Habsburgs and their obsession with creating grand works, Austria is packed with high-calibre architecture. The earliest 'architectural' signs are ancient grave mounds from the Iron Age Hallstatt culture, and the slightly more recent Roman ruins of Vienna and Carnuntum. In later centuries and millennia, Romanesque, Gothic, Renaissance and especially baroque buildings popped up all over.

Baroque Rocks

Everywhere you look in Austria you'll see that the country adheres to that old adage – if it's baroque, don't fix it. The height of the baroque era of building was in the late 17th and early 18th century in Austria. It only moved into full swing after the Ottoman Turks had been beaten back from the gates of Vienna during the Turkish siege of 1683. It took the graceful columns and symmetry of the Renaissance and added elements of the grotesque, the burlesque and the saccharine.

A stellar example of such architecture is the Karlskirche (Church of St Charles) in Vienna. Here you find towering, decorative columns rising up on Karlsplatz, a lavish cupola embellished with frescoes and an interior replete with golden sunrays and stucco cherubs. The church was the brainchild of Habsburg Karl VI following the plague of 1713, and it was dedicated to St Charles Borromeo, who succoured the victims of plague in Italy. It is arguably the most beautiful of the baroque masterpieces.

Bernhard Fischer von Erlach

The mastermind behind the Karlskirche was Johann Bernhard Fischer von Erlach (1656–1723). Fischer von Erlach was Austria's first, and possibly greatest, baroque architect. Born in Graz, he began working as a sculptor in his father's workshop before travelling to Rome in 1670 and spending well over a decade studying baroque styles in Italy. He returned to Austria in 1686 and in 1693 completed one of his earliest works in the capital, the magnificent Pestsäule: a swirling, golden, towering pillar commemorating the end of the plague.

Fischer von Erlach's greatest talent during these early years was his interior decorative work, and in Graz he was responsible for the baroque interior of the Mausoleum of Ferdinand II. In 1689 he began tutoring

c CE 40
Romans establish Carnuntum and build military outpost Vindobona, today's Vienna.

11th Century
Gurk's Romanesque *Dom* (cathedral) and Benedictine abbey Stift Millstatt are built (both in Carinthia).

12th Century
Early versions of Vienna's Stephansdom rise up.

12th–15th Centuries
Gothic Stephansdom in Vienna, the Hofkirche in Innsbruck and the Domkirche in Graz are built.

16th Century
The Renaissance in Austria produces Burg Hochosterwitz and Burg Landskron in Carinthia, Schallaburg in Lower Austria, Schloss Ambras in Innsbruck and the Schweizer Tor in Vienna's Hofburg.

17th–Mid-18th Centuries
The baroque era results in an overwhelming number of masterpieces throughout Austria, among them Vienna's Schloss Belvedere and Schloss Schönbrunn.

Mid-18th–Mid-19th Centuries
Neoclassicism takes root and the Burgtor is built in Vienna and Schloss Grafenegg in Lower Austria.

1815–48
A Biedermeier style casts off some of the strictness of classicism, focusing on housing with simple yet elegant exteriors and on light, curved furnishings and interior decoration.

Don't Miss...

Vienna: Hofburg, Museums Quartier, Karlskirche, Schloss Schönbrunn and Kunsthistorisches Museum

Graz: Kunsthaus and Schloss Eggenberg

Salzburg: Festung Hohensalzburg

Melk: Stift Melk

Innsbruck: Hofburg and Hofkirche

the future Kaiser Joseph I (1678–1711) in architecture, before being appointed court architect for Vienna in 1694. Despite his high standing and connections to the royal court, he found himself without commissions, however, and worked in Germany, Britain and Holland until his favourite student, Joseph I, elevated him in 1705 to head of imperial architecture in the Habsburg-ruled lands.

Although Fischer von Erlach's original plans for Schloss Schönbrunn in Vienna would be revised, it remains his pièce de résistance. It counts among the world's finest baroque palaces and its landscaped gardens include ornate fountains, mythological figures inspired from classical epochs, and an area used for hunting game that today is Vienna's zoo.

Johann Lukas von Hildebrandt

Alongside Schloss Schönbrunn, Vienna's other baroque palace masterpiece, Schloss Belvedere, was designed by Austria's second starchitect of the era, Johann Lukas von Hildebrandt (1668–1745).

In his day, Hildebrandt was eclipsed by dazzling Fischer von Erlach. Like his renowned fellow architect, Hildebrandt headed the Habsburgs' Hofbauamt (Imperial Construction Office). His great works were not churches – although he built several of these – or grand abodes for the royal court, but primarily palaces for the aristocracy. He became the architect of choice for the field marshal and statesman Prince Eugene of Savoy, and it was Prince Eugene who commissioned Hildebrandt to build for him a summer residence in Vienna. Today the magnificent ensemble of palaces and gardens comprising Schloss Belvedere is Hildebrandt's most outstanding legacy.

Baroque Across Austria

Vienna's palaces and churches were a high point in the art of the baroque, but the style swept right across Austria. In Salzburg, when fire reduced the Romanesque cathedral to smithereens, the new Salzburger Dom (Salzburg Cathedral) – a baroque stunner completed in 1628 – replaced it. Meanwhile, in Melk on the Danube River, Jakob Prandtauer (1660–1726) and his disciple Josef Munggenast (1660–1741) worked their magic on the monastery Stift Melk between 1702 and 1738. In Graz, Schloss Eggenberg was commissioned in 1625 to the Italian architect Giovanni Pietro de Pomis (1565–1633), giving Austria another fine baroque palace and gardens.

Baroque Conversions

It is said that the baroque was a leveller of styles, which is ironic considering that its grandeur was also an over-the-top display of power and wealth. Once the fad caught on, churches almost everywhere were pimped up and brought into line with the style.

'Prose is architecture, not interior decoration, and the baroque is over.' Ernest Hemingway, inadvertently revealing to us what he thought of baroque architecture (and also why he wrote about bullfights and not, say, Austrian churches).

The baroque era in Austria, as elsewhere, had begun in architecture before gradually spreading into the fine arts. The fresco paintings of Paul Troger (1698–1762) would become a feature of the late baroque. Troger is Austria's master of the baroque fresco and he worked together with Munggenast on such buildings as Stift Melk, where he created the library and marble hall frescoes, using light cleverly to deliver a sense of space.

The Austrian kaisers Leopold I (1640–1705), Joseph I and Karl VI (1685–1740) loved the dramatic flourishes and total works of art of the early baroque. During the late 17th century the influence of Italy and Italian masters such as Solari (of Salzburger Dom fame), de Pomis (Schloss Eggenberg) and other foreigners was typical of the movement. Vorarlberg, however, was an exception, as here Austrians, Germans and Swiss played the lead roles. While the zenith of baroque was reached during the era of Fischer von Erlach from the early 18th century, during the reign of Maria Theresia (1717–80) from the mid-18th century Austria experienced its largest wave of conversion of older buildings into a baroque style. This, however, brought little in the way of new or innovative buildings. A neoclassicist movement was gaining popularity, and in Austria as elsewhere the movement left behind the saccharine hype and adopted a new style of strict lines.

Back to the Future – Neoclassicism & Revivalism

Walk around the Ringstrasse of Vienna today, admire the Burgtor (Palace Gate) fronting the Hofburg on its southwest side and dating from the early 19th century, the Neue Burg (New Palace) from the late 19th century, or the parliament building designed by the Dane Theophil von Hansen (1813–91) and you may feel as though you have been cast into an idealised version of ancient Greece or Rome. In Innsbruck, the 1765 Triumphpforte (Triumphal Arch) is an early work of neoclassicism in Austria and creates a similar impression.

In Austria, the love of all things classical or revivalist moved into full swing from the mid-19th century. The catalyst locally was the tearing down of the old city walls that had run around the Innere Stadt (Inner City), offering the perfect opportunity to enrich the city's architecture with grand buildings.

Ancient Greek Inspiration

The age of neoclassicism took root during the second half of the 18th century, and over the next 100 years buildings inspired by ancient civilisations would spring up across Austria and elsewhere in Europe. By the mid-19th century, an architectural revivalist fad had taken root that offered a potpourri of styles: neo-Gothic, neo-Renaissance and even a 'neo' form of neoclassicism.

Since the early days of the Renaissance, architects had looked to the ancient Greeks for ideas. The architecture of Rome was well known, but from the 18th century, monarchs and their builders were attracted to the purer classicism of Greece, and some of these architects travelled there to experience this first-hand. One of the triggers for this newly found love of all things Greek was the discovery in 1740 of three Doric temples in southern Italy in a Greek-Roman settlement known as Paestum.

Mid-19th Century Onward

Lingering neoclassicism spills over into other revivalist styles, giving 'neo' prefixes to Gothic, baroque, Renaissance and other architecture on Vienna's Ringstrasse and across the country.

Late 19th–Early 20th Century

Backward-looking historicism is cast aside for lighter, modern styles such as Vienna's Secession building.

20th Century

While the Secession can still be felt, the Rotes Wien (Red Vienna) period produces large-scale workers' housing, and later postmodernist and contemporary buildings like Graz' Kunsthaus spring up.

21st Century

Austria reveals its innovative streak in futuristic glass-clad buildings, many with impeccable eco credentials. A raft of new buildings are popping up in cities across the country, such as the concertina-like, 250m-high DC Tower 1 topping Vienna's new urban district Donau City. Linz, Graz and the Bregenzerwald are other architectural trailblazers.

Ringstrasse

Vienna's medieval fortress had become an anachronism by the mid-19th century and the clearings just beyond the wall had been turned into Glacis (exercise grounds and parkland). In stepped Emperor Franz Joseph I. His idea was to replace the Glacis with grandiose public buildings that would reflect the power and the wealth of the Habsburg empire. The Ringstrasse was the result. It was laid out between 1858 and 1865, and in the decade afterwards most of the impressive edifices that now line this busy thoroughfare were already being built. It is something of a shopping list of grand buildings: the Staatsoper (National Opera; built

BOGGY22/GETTY IMAGES ©

Top Otto Wagner's Karlsplatz station, Vienna

Bottom KunstHausWien (p88), designed by Friedensreich Hundertwasser

OTTO WAGNER – AUSTRIA SHAPES UP FOR THE MODERN

No single architect personifies the dawning of Austria's modern age in architecture more than Vienna-born Otto Wagner. Wagner, who for many years headed the Hofbauamt, ushered in a new, functional direction around the turn of the 20th century. When he was finished with Austria's capital it had a subway transport system replete with attractive art-nouveau stations, he had given the flood-prone Wien River a stone 'sarcophagus' that allowed the surrounding area to be landscaped and part of it to be given over to the Naschmarkt food market, and he had given us the Postsparkasse building and a sprinkling of other interesting designs in Vienna and its suburbs.

Wagner's style was much in keeping with the contours of his epoch. He was strongly influenced in his early years by the architects of the Ringstrasse buildings and the revivalist style (which entailed resurrecting mostly the styles of ancient Rome and Greece), and he even (unsuccessfully) submitted his own plans for the new Justizpalast (Palace of Justice) in Vienna in a Ringstrasse revivalist style. Gradually, though, Wagner grew sceptical of revivalism and spoke harshly about his early works, characterising revivalism as a stylistic, masked ball. His buildings dispensed with 19th-century classical ornamentation and his trademark became a creative use of modern materials like glass, steel, aluminium and reinforced concrete. The 'studs' on the Postsparkasse building are the perfect example of this. Those who venture out to his 1907 Kirche am Steinhof will find another unusual masterpiece: a functional, domed art-nouveau church built in the grounds of a psychiatric institution.

One of Wagner's most functional pieces of design was the Vienna U-Bahn (subway) system. He developed the system between 1892 and 1901 during his long spell heading the construction office of Vienna and he was responsible for about 35 stations in all – stops like Josefstädter Strasse on the U6 and Karlsplatz on the U4 are superb examples. One interesting way to get a feel for Wagner's masterpieces is simply to get onto the U-Bahn and ride the U6 north from Westbahnhof. It's sometimes called Wagner's *Gesamtkunstwerk* (total work of art) – in this case, one you can literally sit on.

1861–69), the Museum für Angewandte Kunst (MAK; Museum of Applied Arts; 1868–71), the Naturhistorisches Museum (Museum of Natural History; 1872–81), the *Rathaus* (town hall; 1872–83), Kunsthistorisches Museum (Museum of Art History; 1872–91), the parliament building (1873–83), Burgtheater (1874–88) and the Heldenplatz section of the Hofburg's Neue Burg (1881–1908).

Hansen's parliament, with its large statue of Athena out front, possibly best symbolises the spirit of the age and its love of all things classical, but also ancient Greece as a symbol of democracy. One of the finest of the Ringstrasse buildings, the Kunsthistorisches Museum, is not only a neo-Renaissance masterpiece but also a taste of movements to come. This museum, purpose-built by the Habsburgs as a repository for their finest collection of paintings, is replete with colourful lunettes, a circular ceiling recess that allows a glimpse into the cupola when you enter, and paintings by Gustav Klimt (1862–1918). WWI intervened and the empire was lost before Franz Joseph's grand scheme for the Ringstrasse could be fully realised.

By then, however, Gustav Klimt and contemporaries of his generation were pushing Austria in new directions.

'People love everything that fulfils the desire for comfort. They hate everything that wishes to draw them out of the secure position they have earned. People therefore love houses and hate art.' Adolf Loos

Secession & Art Nouveau

They called it a 'temple for bullfrogs' or a temple for an anarchic art movement. Other unflattering names for the Secession building were 'the mausoleum', 'the crematorium' or, because of the golden filigree dome perched on top, 'the cabbage head'. Others still, according to today's Secession association, thought it looked like a cross between a greenhouse and an industrial blast furnace.

Friedensreich Hundertwasser (1928–2000) abhorred straight lines. He claimed in his *Mould Manifesto* to have counted 546 on a razor blade. He moved towards spiritual ecology, believing that cities should be in harmony with their natural environment, a philosophy that is represented metaphorically in his 'wobbly' KunstHausWien and Hundertwasserhaus in Vienna.

In 1897, 19 progressive artists broke away from the conservative artistic establishment of Vienna and formed the Vienna Secession *(Sezession)* movement. In Austria, the movement is synonymous with art nouveau, although its members had a habit of drawing upon a broad spectrum of styles. Its role models were taken from the contemporary scene in Berlin and Munich, and its proponents' aim had been to shake off historicism – the revivalist trend that led to the historic throwbacks built along Vienna's Ringstrasse. At the time, the Kunstlerhaus (Artists' House) of Vienna was the last word in the arts establishment, and Secessionists, including Gustav Klimt, Josef Hoffman, Kolo Moser and Joseph M Olbrich, distanced themselves from this in order to form their association.

Olbrich, a former student of Otto Wagner, was given the honour of designing an exhibition centre for the newly formed Secessionists. The 'temple for bullfrogs' was completed in 1898 and combined sparse functionality with stylistic motifs.

Initially, Klimt, Olbrich and their various colleagues had wanted to build on the Ringstrasse, but the city authorities baulked at the idea of watering down their revivalist thoroughfare with Olbrich's daring design. They agreed, however, to the building being situated just off it – a temporary building where for 10 years the Secessionists could hold their exhibitions.

Because art nouveau was essentially an urban movement, the scenes of its greatest acts were played out in the capitals or large cities: Paris, Brussels, New York, Glasgow, Chicago and Vienna. Like the Renaissance and baroque movements before it, Secession broke down the boundaries between painting and architecture. But it was also a response to the industrial age (although it used a lot of metaphors from nature), and the new movement sought to integrate traditional craftsmanship into its philosophy. The British were its role models for the crafts, and in 1903 Josef Hoffmann and Kolo Moser founded the Wiener Werkstätte (Vienna Workshop), which worked together with Vienna's School of the Applied Arts and the Secession movement to promote their ideas.

Another feature of Secession is its international tone. Vienna was a magnet for artists from the Habsburg-ruled lands. The movement was also greatly influenced by Otto Wagner. The Secession building, for instance, may have been domed by a floral 'cabbage', but its form had the hallmarks of Otto Wagner's strictness of lines.

ADOLF LOOS – 'EVERY CITY GETS THE ARCHITECTURE IT DESERVES'

In 1922 a competition was held to build 'the most beautiful and distinctive office building in the world' for the Chicago *Tribune* newspaper. The greats of the architectural world vied for the project, and one of them was Czech-born Adolf Loos (1870–1933). As fate would have it, a neo-Gothic design trumped Loos' entry, which resembled a Doric column on top of what might easily have passed for a car factory.

Loos studied in Bohemia and later Dresden, then broke out for the US, where he was employed as a mason and also did stints washing dishes. He was influenced strongly by Otto Wagner, but it is said that his time as a mason (less so as a dishwasher) heightened his sensitivity to materials. He detested ornamentation, and that's why he also locked horns with the art nouveau crew, whose flowers and ornamental flourishes (the golden cabbage-head dome of the Secession building, for instance) were anathema to his functional, sleek designs. Space, materials and even the labour used to produce a building ('Ornament is wasted labour and therefore a waste of good health') had to be used as fully as possible. Today, anyone who squeezes into Loos' minuscule American Bar in Vienna, with its mirrors, glistening onyx-stone surfaces and illusion of space, will get not only a decent cocktail but a good idea of what the architect was about.

Contemporary Icons

Austrian architecture is more than historic masterpieces. Up and down the country, a flurry of new-wave architects have revamped, constructed and envisaged some extraordinary contemporary designs in recent years to harbour museums, offices and events venues. Many of these slot neatly in between the grand old buildings – their architectural antithesis.

Schloss Grafenegg near the Danube Valley in the lush, rolling hills of Lower Austria is a fine instance of a postmodern concert location. Here a neoclassical palace on the shores of a lake – long a venue for classical-music events – was given a striking new addition: a 15m open-air stage called the Wolkenturm (Cloud Tower), designed by Viennese architects nextENTERprise. Set in a cleft in manicured parkland, this shiny, jagged, sculpture-like stage is a natural amphitheatre and takes on the hue of the surrounding parkland.

A similar reflection of surroundings is incorporated into the postmodern Loisium Weinwelt in Langenlois. This brings together a modern hotel complex and tours through historic cellars with an aluminium cube designed by New York architect Steven Holl. Meanwhile, further along the Danube River in Linz, the capital of Upper Austria, the Lentos Kunstmuseum is a cubic, postmodern construction with a glass facade that kaleidoscopically reflects its surroundings.

The remote forested hills and mountains of Vorarlberg might seem like an unlikely spot for architects to make their mark, but here you'll find Werkraum in Andelsbuch – a showcase for a cooperative of 90 regional craft companies. The slick, sustainable black-concrete-and-glass edifice, by Pritzker Prize–winning architect Peter Zumthor, was designed to merge with the surrounding landscape. In Bregenz, the Vorarlberg Museum, its facade blooming with 16,656 recycled PET bottles, sheds light on the region's one-of-a-kind contemporary architecture.

States of Flux

This idea of the modern building reflecting or absorbing the tones of its environment contrasts with another approach in modern Austrian architecture: a building that is in a state of flux. Also in Linz, the postmodern Ars Electronica Center received an addition alongside its original modern building. The added dimension of an LED facade encloses both buildings and lights up and changes colour at night. Another example of this style is the Kunsthaus in Graz, which quickly became a new trademark of Styria's capital. Sitting on the Mur River, this slug-like construction – the work of British architects Peter Cook and Colin Fournier – has an exterior that changes colour through illumination. The building's modernity seeks to create an 'aesthetic dialogue' with the historic side of Graz rising up on a bluff on the other side of the river. This dialogue is linked by the Murinsel (Mur Island), a swirl-shaped pontoon bridge situated in the middle of the river with a cafe, a children's playground and an amphitheatre for performance.

> 'Because ornamentation is no longer an organic part of our culture it no longer expresses our culture. An ornament created today has nothing to do with us, no connection to human beings and nothing to do with the world order. It's not capable of developing any further.'
> Adolf Loos

MuseumsQuartier

One of the most innovative architectural works of recent years has been the MuseumsQuartier in Vienna. The MuseumsQuartier has retained an attractive ensemble of 18th-century buildings that once served as the royal stables for the Habsburgs, added cafes and shops, and augmented these with new buildings, such as the dark-basalt Museum Moderner Kunst (MUMOK) and the Leopold Museum. These two museums are separated by the Kunsthalle and a bold public space that has grown to become a favourite gathering place in the inner city.

Visual Arts & Music

For a country of such diminutive proportions, Austria's impact on the arts has been phenomenal. The Habsburgs left a legacy of historic paintings, sculptures, concert halls and the Vienna Philharmonic – one of the world's finest orchestras. This is where child prodigy Mozart excelled and where Strauss taught the world to waltz; it is also the birthplace of golden wonder Klimt and expressionist Schiele. Today, art and music are still ingrained in the weft and warp of the Austrian psyche.

Visual Arts

The Great Fresco Artists

Austria's tradition of fresco painting dates back to the mid-Romanesque era of the 11th century, when frescoes appeared for the first time in churches, depicting religious scenes. In around 1200 original Romanesque frescoes were painted inside the former *Dom* (cathedral) in Gurk in eastern Carinthia, and in 1270 these were revamped with a 'zigzag' style, giving naturalistic figures long, flowing robes with folds; you can see some of these in Gurk today.

In the Gothic era that followed from about the 14th century (as for instance in Vienna's Stephansdom), fresco painting reached spatial limits due to vaulted ceilings and large windows (this encouraged glass painting). The height of magnificent fresco painting was therefore achieved in the baroque period of the 17th and early 18th centuries, when fresco painting is associated with three major figures: Johann Michael Rottmayr (1654–1730), Daniel Gran (1694–1757) and Paul Troger (1698–1762). Today the works of these three greats predominate in Vienna and especially in Lower Austria.

The Habsburgs were avid supporters of the arts, commissioning fresco painters to lend colourful texture and new dimensions to their buildings and using music as an expression of their own power and pomp.

Rottmayr and Gran were active during the high baroque, which spans the late 17th century and early 18th century. Paul Troger, however, produced most of his work during the late baroque or rococo period from the mid-18th century. Troger spent several years in Italy learning techniques there and worked in Salzburg before moving to Vienna, where Rottmayr had been setting the tone for fresco painting since 1696. Over time Troger became the painter of choice for churches and monasteries in Lower Austria, and fine examples of his work survive in Stift Melk, Stift Zwettl and Stift Altenburg, as well as in the *Dom* in Klagenfurt, where you can find a Troger altar painting. Schloss Schönbrunn in Vienna also has work by Troger.

Rottmayr was Austria's first and the country's foremost baroque painter. He spent his early years as a court painter to the Habsburgs in Salzburg before he moved to Vienna in 1696, dominating the scene there for the next three decades. He became the favoured fresco painter of the architect Johann Bernhard Fischer von Erlach and is often compared to the Flemish painter Peter Paul Rubens. His work brought together Italian and Flemish influences into a style that featured plenty of bouncy, joyous figures and bright colours. Fine frescoes from Rottmayr can be found in Vienna decorating the Karlskirche, where a glass lift ascends over 70m into the cupola for a close-up view. In Lower Austria his work adorns Stift Melk and Klosterneuburg.

Daniel Gran, the third in the triumvirate of baroque fresco greats, also studied in Italy, but unlike those of Troger and Rottmayr his style reined in the most extravagant features and offered a foretaste of neoclassicism – perhaps best illustrated by his ceiling fresco in the Nationalbibliothek (National Library) in Vienna.

Jugendstil & the Secession

Vienna's branch of the Europe-wide art nouveau movement, known as *Jugendstil* ('Youthful Style'), had its genesis from within the Akademie der Bildenden Künste (Academy of Fine Arts). The academy was a strong supporter of neoclassicism and wasn't interested in supporting any artists who wanted to branch out, so in 1897 a group of rebels, including Gustav Klimt (1862–1918), seceded. Architects, such as Otto Wagner, Joseph Maria Olbrich (1867–1908) and Josef Hoffman (1870–1956), followed.

By the second decade of the 20th century, Wagner and others were moving towards a uniquely Viennese style, called Secession, which stripped away some of the more decorative aspects of *Jugendstil*. Olbrich designed the Secession Hall, the showpiece of the Secession, which was used to display other graphic and design works produced by the movement. The building is a physical representation of the movement's ideals, functionality and modernism, though it retains some striking decorative touches, such as the giant 'golden cabbage' on the roof.

Hoffman, who was inspired by the British Arts and Crafts movement, led by William Morris, and also by the stunning art-nouveau work of Glaswegian designer Charles Rennie Mackintosh, ultimately abandoned the flowing forms and bright colours of *Jugendstil* in 1901, becoming one of the earliest exponents of the Secession style. His greatest artistic influence in Vienna was in setting up the Wiener Werkstätte design studio, which included Klimt and Kolo Moser (1868–1918), who set out to break down the high-art–low-art distinction, and brought *Jugendstil* into middle-class homes. In 1932 the WW closed, unable to compete with the cheap, mass-produced items being churned out by other companies.

No one embraced the sensualism of *Jugendstil* and Secessionism more than Gustav Klimt. Perhaps Vienna's most famous artist, Klimt was traditionally trained at the Akademie der Bildenden Künste but left in 1897 to pursue his own colourful and distinctive, non-naturalistic style. Klimt's fascination with women is a common thread in his paintings, and his works are as resonant and alluring today as they were when he sent ripples of scandal through fin-de-siècle Vienna, with his exotic, erotic style. The use of gold-leaf and mosaic-like detail is typical of Klimt's golden period, which was inspired by the Byzantine imagery he saw on his travels to Venice. Home to the world's largest Klimt collection, Vienna's Schloss Belvedere provides total immersion.

20 BCE Roman

With the building of the fortress of Carnuntum in Lower Austria, the Romans use decorative mosaics, some of which survive today in Carnuntum's open-air museum.

8th–12th Century Romanesque

Salzburg becomes the centre for frescoes, many of which have Byzantine influences.

13th Century Early Gothic

A transition from Romanesque to Gothic occurs, exemplified by frescoes today found in the former cathedral of Gurk.

14th Century High Gothic

Ribbed Gothic interiors and high windows leave little space for frescoes but create new opportunities for glass painting. Altar painting establishes itself in churches.

16th Century Danube School

In the transition from late Gothic to the Renaissance, a Danube School of landscape painting arises from the early 16th century, later absorbed into the Renaissance.

1680–1740 High & Late Baroque

Fresco painting reaches dizzying heights of achievement in the age of Johann Michael Rottmayr, Paul Troger and Daniel Gran.

Early 19th Century Biedermeier

Amid a wave of neoclassical and revivalist painting, the Biedermeier painter Ferdinand Georg Waldmüller becomes Austria's best-known painter of the era.

Schiele, Kokoschka & the Expressionists

Tulln is a sleepy town slaked by the waters of the Danube River, with one major claim to fame: it is the birthplace of Austria's most important expressionist painter, Egon Schiele (1890–1918), and a museum there tells the story of his life through a sizeable collection of his paintings and sketches. Other works are held in Austria's foremost museum for expressionist art, the Leopold in Vienna's MuseumsQuartier, where Schiele's art hangs alongside the expressionists Oskar Kokoschka, Klagenfurt-born Herbert Boeckl, as well as Gustav Klimt.

Egon Schiele

In his day, Schiele was one of the country's most controversial artists. He left Tulln in 1906 to attend the Vienna's Akademie der Bildenden Künste, one of Europe's oldest academies. It is now famous, incidentally, for having turned down Adolf Hitler in 1907. Schiele cofounded a group in Vienna known as the Neukunstgruppe (New Art Group) and around that time his work began to resonate with the public. Although he was very strongly influenced by one of the leading forces behind the Secession movement and art nouveau in Austria, Gustav Klimt, he is much more closely associated with expressionism than Klimt.

Vienna's famous psychologist, Sigmund Freud, apparently felt no affinity with expressionists like Schiele, preferring classical art and its neoclassical incarnations, but both Freud and Schiele were bedfellows in one way: the concept of the erotic. While Freud was collating his theories on Eros and the unconscious, Schiele was capturing the erotic on canvas, often taking death and lust as his explicit themes.

He had come a long way from the conservative, idyllic Tulln countryside – a little too far, some thought. In 1912 Schiele was held in custody for three weeks and later found guilty of corrupting minors by exposing them to pornography. His arrest and imprisonment were the culmination of a series of events that saw the painter and his 17-year-old lover and model 'Wally' Neuzil flee the Vienna scene and move to Bohemia (Česky Krumlov in the Czech Republic), from where the two soon fled again. Today the Tulln museum dedicated to Schiele has a reconstruction of the prison cell near St Pölton where he was imprisoned.

Oskar Kokoschka

Like Schiele, Oskar Kokoschka, the second of the great Austrian expressionists, was born on the Danube River. Kokoschka comes from Pöchlarn, near Melk. Like Klimt, he studied at the Kunstgewerbeschule (School of Applied Arts) in Vienna. Like Schiele, he was strongly influenced by Klimt, but another of his influences was Dutch post-impressionist Vincent van Gogh. From 1907 he worked in the Wiener Werkstätte. His earliest work had features of the Secession and art nouveau movements, but

WOULD IT HAVE CHANGED HISTORY?

Vienna's Academy of Fine Arts was famous not only for being a place Oskar Kokoschka unkindly described as 'a hotbed of conservatism and somewhere you went to become an artist in a velvet skirt and beret'. In 1907 an aspiring young Adolf Hitler sat the entry exam at the academy (the exam themes were Expulsion from Paradise, Hunting, Spring, Building Workers, Death – you get the idea). There were 128 applicants in Hitler's year and 28 were successful. Not Adolf. He desolately crawled back to Linz to lick his wounds and lived from his allowance as an orphan (his mother had died) before trying and failing a second time. Disillusioned, Hitler enlisted to fight on the Western Front in WWI. The rest is history.

later he moved into expressionism. The Österreichische Galerie in Schloss Belvedere (Oberes Belvedere) has a collection of about a dozen of his oil paintings; some of these portraits highlight Kokoschka's skill for depicting the subject's unsettled psyche without in any way resorting to bleak colours.

Kokoschka's long life was punctuated by exile and travel. He moved to Prague in 1934 to escape the extreme right-wing politics of the day; once the Nazis came to power and declared his works 'degenerate' in 1937, seizing over 400 of them in German museums, Kokoschka packed his bags for Britain and became a UK citizen.

If Kokoschka was 'degenerate' and shocked the Nazis, it was a good thing the 'brown' men and women of the Thousand Year Reich were not around to see what would come later. It was called Viennese Actionism – and now even the mainstream art establishment was being sent into a state of shock.

Actionism – Shocking the Republic

Art has always loved a juicy scandal. The expressionist Egon Schiele and the architect Adolf Loos were – rightly or wrongly – embroiled in moral charges that resulted in partial convictions. Kokoschka and Klimt explored themes of eroticism, homoeroticism, and adolescence and youth. One day in 1968, however, the stakes were raised significantly higher when a group of artists burst into a packed lecture hall of Vienna's university and began an action that became known as the Uni-Ferkelei (University Obscenity). According to reports, at least one member of the group began masturbating, smearing himself with excrement, flagellating and vomiting. Lovely, but was it art? One member was possibly singing the Austrian national anthem, another seemed to be rambling on about computers. Court cases followed, and so too did a couple of convictions and a few months in prison for two of those involved. It was all about breaking down social taboos.

If some of the art of the 1960s, like the Fluxus style of happenings (picked from a similar movement in the US), was theatrical and more like performance on an impromptu stage, Actionism took a more extreme form and covered a broad spectrum. Some of it was masochistic, self-abasing or employed blood rituals. At the hardcore end of the spectrum a picture might be produced in an orgy of dramatics with colour and materials being splashed and smeared collectively from various bodily cavities while the artists ascended into ever-higher states of frenzied ecstasy. At the more harmless end, a few people might get together and squirt some paint.

Actionism doesn't lend itself to the formal gallery environment. Some of it has been caught on video – salad-smeared bodies, close-ups of urinating penises, that sort of thing – and is often presented in Vienna's MUMOK (Museum Moderner Kunst). The Uni-Ferkelei action survives only in a few photographs and a couple of minutes of film footage. Günter Brus (b 1938), one of the participants, was convicted of 'denigrating an Austrian symbol of state'. His colleague of the day, Oswald

1900 Art Nouveau

Vienna becomes the world's art nouveau capital, with the likes of Gustav Klimt, Hans Makart and Kolo Moser working in the city.

1910–20 Expressionism

Seeking a new language of art, expressionists Egon Schiele and Oskar Kokoschka move to the forefront of Austrian painting.

1918–1939 New Objectivity

Post-expressionism takes root and international movements such as surrealism, futurism and cubism reach Austria, while from 1925 Neue Sachlichkeit (New Objectivity) moves away from the 'subjective' approach of expressionism.

1960s Viennese Actionism

After the Nazi era (when little of lasting significance was achieved), a period of post-WWII fantastic realism adopts esoteric themes; later Viennese Actionism brings 'happenings': pain, death, sex and abasement move to the fore.

21st Century Contemporary

A neo-expressionist Neue Wilde (New Wild Ones) movement in the 1980s gives way to 21st-century explorations using digital graphics to complement conventional forms of painting.

Wiener (b 1935), is now an author and respected academic who went on to win one of the country's most prestigious literary prizes. Meanwhile, Hermann Nisch (b 1938), who staged theatrical events in the early 1960s based on music and painting and leaned heavily on sacrificial or religious rituals, has advanced to become Austria's best-known contemporary Viennese Actionist. His work can be found in Vienna's MUMOK, the Lentos Museum in Linz and in St Pölten's Landesmuseum.

The innovative composer Arnold Schönberg (1874–1951) stretched tonal conventions to snapping point with his 12-tone style of composition. The most influential of his pupils were Alban Berg (1885–1935) and Anton von Webern (1883–1945); both were born in Vienna and continued the development of Schönberg's technique.

Music

Habsburg Musical Tradition

The Habsburgs began patronising court musicians as far back as the 13th century, and by the 18th and 19th centuries they had created a centre for music that was unrivalled in the world. Many of the Habsburgs themselves were gifted musicians: Leopold I (1640–1705) composed, Karl VI (1685–1740) played violin, his daughter Maria Theresia (1717–80) played a respectable double bass, while her son Joseph II was a deft hand at harpsichord and cello.

Vienna Classic

Wiener Klassik (Vienna Classic) dates back to the mid- and late 18th century and very much defines the way we perceive classical music today. Music moved away from the celestial baroque music of the royal court and the church, and brought forms of classical music such as opera and symphonies to the salons and theatres of the upper middle classes of Vienna and Austria.

The earliest of the great composers was Joseph Haydn (1732–1809), who in his long career would tutor a budding young German-born composer by the name of Ludwig van Beethoven (1770–1827). Other well-known figures of the epoch include Franz Schubert (1797–1828), followed by a wave of classical composers in the 19th century, such as Franz Liszt (1811–86), Johannes Brahms (1833–97) and Anton Bruckner (1824–96).

That Mozart Magic

Wolfgang Amadeus Mozart (1756–91) was born in Salzburg. The ultimate child prodigy, he tinkled out his first tunes on the piano at the age of four years, securing a dazzling reputation as Austria's Wunderkind. Aged just six, he performed for a rapturous Maria Theresia in 1762 at Schloss Schönbrunn. According to his father, Leopold, 'Wolferl leapt onto Her Majesty's lap, threw his arms around her neck and planted kisses on her face.'

In the years following Mozart's meteoric rise, Salieri, an Italian composer, was appointed by the Habsburgs to head Italian opera at the royal court. The stage was set for rivalries and intrigue, eventually culminating in rumours that Salieri had murdered Mozart. We will never know whether he did or not (it's extremely unlikely that he did), but this is a moot point. The interesting thing is how much art has been born of the rumours. One artistic masterpiece is the film *Amadeus* (1984), directed by Miloš Forman (1932–2018). It won eight Academy awards and is widely considered to be the best of its ilk.

Mozart was insanely prolific during his lifetime, writing some 626 pieces; among the greatest are *The Marriage of Figaro* (1786), *Don Giovanni* (1787), *Così fan tutte* (1790) and *The Magic Flute* (1791). The *Requiem Mass,* apocryphally written for his own death, remains one of the most powerful works of classical music. Have a listen to Piano Concerto Nos 20 and 21, which comprise some of the best elements of Mozart: drama, comedy, intimacy and a whole heap of ingenuity in one easy-to-appreciate package.

When not composing, Mozart enjoyed billiards, heavy drinking sessions and teaching his pet starling to sing operettas. It has been speculated that he had Tourette's syndrome, which would have accounted for his sudden outbursts of rage and compulsive utterance of obscenities. But his genius is undisputed. Indeed, when a boy once asked him how to write a symphony, Mozart recommended he begin with ballads. 'But you wrote symphonies when you were only 10 years old,' said the boy. 'But I didn't have to ask how,' retorted Mozart.

Vormärz & Revolutionary Ideas

The epoch of Wiener Klassik began losing momentum in 19th-century Vienna and, with Mozart, Salieri, Haydn, Beethoven and the other great proponents dead or dying off, Austrian society and Europe as a whole experienced a period of repressive conservatism that culminated in revolutions across the continent in 1848 aimed at liberal reform. The prerevolutionary period was known as the Vormärz ('Pre-March' – the revolutions began in March 1848); the Vormärz sounded the final death knell for Wiener Klassik and produced a creative lull in music. It was only once the noise of the revolutions had died down that a new wave of composers – the likes of Franz Liszt, Johannes Brahms and Anton Bruckner – arrived on the scene to seize the reins of the Wiener Klassik and transform it into new and exciting forms.

For more on what's happening in contemporary music (rock, jazz, pop, electronic, world music, classical and everything between and beyond), check out Music Austria: www.musicaustria.at.

Life after Mozart

Austria has some great musicians and contemporary acts. Although none so far has achieved the international fame of Falco (real name Hans Hölzel; 1957–98), whose 'Rock Me, Amadeus' topped the US charts in 1986, there are some great acts to check out.

Klagenfurt, the provincial capital of Carinthia, has brought forth some good musicians. While Penny McLean (born as Gertrude Wirschinger) gave the 1970s one of its iconic disco songs in the form of 'Lady Bump', the indisputable king is the crooner Udo Jürgens. He has been long seen as a *Schlager* singer (a broad genre of folksy soft pop with a sentimental edge), but he composed hits for US greats such as Shirley Bassey and Frank Sinatra, and his style is comparable with Sinatra's.

Naked Lunch (www.nakedlunch.de) is probably the best-known Austrian indie band. Going a bit deeper into the underground, the duo Attwenger (www.attwenger.at) has a large following for its music with flavours of folk, hip-hop and trance. Completing the triumvirate of relative old hands, Graz-based Rainer Binder-Krieglstein has gone from an eclectic blend of headz, hip-hop, groove and nujazz to concentrate on folk music today.

For pure hip-hop, Linz-based Texta (www.texta.at) is the most established in the art. The vocal groove project from Lower Austria Bauchklang (www.bauchklang.com) is remarkable for using a cappella – only voices, no instruments – for its reggae- and ethnic-influenced hip-hop and trance. Other names to watch out for are funky pop duo Bilderbuch, drum 'n' bass duo Camo & Krooked and Fatima Spar, whose worldly beats shift from Balkan to Swing.

Those into electric swing might be familiar with Parov Stelar, a musician, producer and DJ from Linz. His clubby tracks blend jazz, house, electro and breakbeat.

Kaffeehäuser – Austria's Living Rooms

Swing open the heavy wooden door of one of Vienna's *Kaffeehäuser* (coffee houses) and it's as though the clocks stopped in 1910. The waiters are just as aloof, the menu still baffles and newspapers outnumber smartphones. Outside life rushes ahead, but the coffee house is a world unto itself, immune to time and trends. The story of their evolution from the Turkish siege of Vienna to today is an interesting one sprinkled with not just a few grains of fiction.

Magic Beans

Like many a good fairy tale, Vienna's coffee-house culture began with some magic beans. Back in Vienna in 1683, the Ottoman Turks were conducting their second great onslaught to wrest control of the Occident, the Second Turkish Siege, which saw the Turkish general and grand vizier Kara Mustapha along with his eunuchs, concubines and 25,000 tents huddle on the fringe of fortified central Vienna in the *Vorstädte* (inner suburbs; places like Josefstadt and Alsergrund today).

According to legend, a certain Georg Franz Koltschitzky dressed himself up as a Turk and brought a message behind Turkish lines from the field marshal Karl I of Lothringen and was rewarded for his efforts with some war booty that included sacks of coffee beans. Legend also says that although some dismissed the beans as camel feed or dung, clever Koltschitzky sniffed the beans and knew he had struck gold. He saw his chance to establish Vienna's first *Kaffeehaus* and is said to have been the first person to mix milk and sugar into the exotic elixir.

Coffee-house etiquette? Wait to be seated in formal places, take your pick of the tables in casual coffee houses. You're welcome to linger over a single cup if you wish; the waiter shouldn't move you on until you ask for the *Rechnung* (bill).

The Habsburgs went mad for it. *Kaffeehäuser* soon flourished in Vienna, where coffee was served with a glass of water. *Kaffeehäuser* in the 17th century also had a billiard table, but playing cards in them wasn't allowed until the late 18th century.

Gradually, newspapers were introduced, and from the late 18th century the *Konzertcafe* (concert cafe) took hold – places where music was played. This cast the humble *Kaffeehaus* into a new role of being a place where the likes of Mozart, Beethoven and later Johann Strauss (the elder) could try out their works in the equivalent of open-stage or 'unplugged' performances.

When Austria adopted Napoleon's trade embargo against Britain in 1813 it lost almost its entire source of imported coffee beans. Although alternatives like chicory, rye and barley were tried, in the end the *Kaffeehäuser* started serving food and wine, which is why today you can still get a light meal or a drink in a traditional *Kaffeehaus*.

COFFEE CONUNDRUMS

Coffee really is rocket science here and you'll need to know your *Mokka* (black coffee) from your *Brauner* (black coffee with a tiny splash of milk) to order Viennese style. A quick glance at a menu will uncover a long list of choices, so brush up on the ones below. A good coffee house will serve the cup of java on a silver platter accompanied by a glass of water and a small sweet.

Brauner Black but served with a tiny splash of milk; comes in *Gross* (large) or *Klein* (small).

Einspänner With whipped cream, served in a glass.

Fiaker *Verlängerter* with rum and whipped cream.

Kapuziner With a splash of milk and perhaps a sprinkling of grated chocolate.

Maria Theresia With orange liqueur and whipped cream.

Masagran, Mazagran Cold coffee with ice and Maraschino liqueur.

Melange Viennese classic; served with milk, and maybe whipped cream too; similar to a cappuccino.

Mocca, Mokka, Schwarzer Black coffee.

Pharisäer Strong *Mocca* topped with whipped cream, served with a glass of rum.

Türkische Comes in a copper pot with coffee grounds and sugar.

Verlängerter *Brauner* weakened with hot water.

Wiener Eiskaffee Cold coffee with vanilla ice cream and whipped cream.

Literary Coffee Houses

Come the late 19th century, elegant *Kaffeehäuser* sprang up along Vienna's Ringstrasse and everywhere a new 'literary coffee house' developed where writers could work in the warm. Café Griensteidl (now closed) was the first, but Café Central, the favourite of writers Peter Altenberg and Alfred Polgar, and architect Adolf Loos, is the best-known literary *Kaffeehaus*.

The writer Stefan Zweig saw them as an inimitable 'democratic club' bearing no likeness to the real world, but your average *Kaffeehaus* did have a clear pecking order. At the bottom of the heap was the *piccolo* who set the tables and topped up the guests' water glasses, while flirting like a gigolo with the grand ladies whenever a spare moment presented itself. The cashier (in the ideal case of coffee-house tradition, buxom, blonde and with jewellery dripping from her ears) wrote the bills and kept a watchful eye on the sugar.

At the top of the heap was the *Oberkellner* (*Herr Ober*, for short, or head waiter), who until 1800 used to be a ponytailed fellow with a dinner jacket, white tie, laced shoes, striped stockings and often a green apron. No *Herr Ober* dresses like this today (there are hints of the old garb, but none of the kinky stuff), but they do still rule the tables and the spaces between them in their dark attire.

Today you find more of a *Konditorei* (cake shop) atmosphere, and most continue to be the living rooms of the Viennese. These are places where you can drink coffee or wine, eat a goulash or light meal, read the newspapers or even enjoy a lounge vibe.

For total immersion into the scene, hook onto one of Space and Place's English-language Coffeehouse Conversation evenings, where visitors get the chance to engage with locals over dinner, drinks and deeply probing questions at a local coffee house. See www.spaceandplace.at for details and dates.

The Austrian Alps

For many people, Austria is the Alps and no wonder. After all, these are the alpine pastures where Julie Andrews twirled in *The Sound of Music*; the mountains that inspired Mozart's symphonies; the slopes where Hannes Schneider revolutionised downhill skiing with his Arlberg technique. Olympic legends, Hollywood blockbusters and mountaineering marvels have been made and born on these peaks for decades.

Alpine Landscapes

The Alps engulf nearly two-thirds of the 83,858 sq km that is Austria. It's almost as though someone chalked a line straight down the middle and asked all the Alps to shuffle to the west and all the flats to slide to the east, so stark is the contrast in this land of highs and lows. Over millennia, elemental forces have dramatically shaped these mountain landscapes, etched with wondrous glaciers and forests, soaring peaks and gouged valleys.

The Austrian Alps divide neatly into three principal mountain ranges running in a west–east direction. The otherworldly karst landscapes of the Northern Limestone Alps, bordering Germany, reach nearly 3000m and extend almost as far east as the Wienerwald (Vienna Woods). The valley of the Inn River separates them from the granitic Central Alps, a chain that features the highest peaks in Austria dwarfed by the majestic summit of Grossglockner (3798m). The Southern Limestone Alps, which include the Karawanken Range, form a natural barrier with Italy and Slovenia.

From snow-melt streams to misty falls, water is a major feature of the Austrian Alps. Mineral-rich rivers, such as the Enns, Salzach and Inn, wend their way through broad valleys and provide a scenic backdrop for pursuits like rafting in summer. Lakes, too, come in all shapes and sizes, from glacially cold alpine tarns to the famously warm (around 28°C) waters of Wörthersee in Carinthia.

Best Places to (Maybe) See...

Marmots *Kaiser-Franz-Josefs-Höhe, Grossglockner Rd*

Golden eagles *Hohe Tauern National Park*

Lynx *Nationalpark Kalkalpen*

Falcons *Nationalpark Gesäuse*

Ibex *Northern Limestone Alps*

Wildlife in the Austrian Alps

Nature reigns on an impressive scale in the Austrian Alps. The further you tiptoe away from civilisation and the higher you climb, the more likely you are to find rare animals and plant life in summer. Besides a decent pair of binoculars, bring patience and a sense of adventure.

Alpine Flora

Below the tree line, much of the Austrian Alps is thickly forested. At low altitudes you can expect to find deciduous birch and beech forests, while coniferous trees such as pine, spruce and larch thrive at higher elevations. At around 2000m trees yield to *Almen* (alpine pastures) and dwarf pines; beyond 3000m only mosses and lichens cling to the stark crags.

A highlight of the Austrian Alps are its wildflowers, which bring a riot of scent and colour from May to September. The species here are hardy, with long roots to counter strong winds, bright colours to repel some insects, and petals that can resist frost and dehydration.

Spring brings crocuses, alpine snowbells and anemones; summer alpine roses and gentians; and autumn thistles, delphiniums and blue aconites. Tempting though it may be to pick them, these flowers really do look lovelier on the slopes and most are protected species.

Men once risked life and limb to pluck edelweiss from the highest crags of the Alps for their sweethearts. The woolly bloom is Austria's national flower, symbolising bravery, love and strength.

The Environment Agency Austria website, www.umweltbundesamt.at/naturschutz, is a one-stop shop for info on the country's landscape, flora and fauna.

Watching Wildlife

Dawn and dusk are the best times for a spot of wildlife-watching, though a lot boils down to luck. High on the must-see list is the ibex, a wild goat with curved horns, which was at one stage under threat but is fortunately now breeding again. It is the master of mountain climbing and migrates to 3000m or higher in the Austrian Alps come July. The chamois, a small antelope more common than the ibex, is equally at home scampering around on mountain sides. It can leap an astounding 4m vertically and its hooves have rubber-like soles and rigid outer rims – ideal for maintaining a good grip on loose rocks.

At heights of around 2000m, listen and look out for marmots, fluffy rodents related to the squirrel and native to the Alps. This sociable animal lives in colonies of about two dozen members. Like meerkats, marmots regularly post sentries, which stand around on their hind legs looking alert. They whistle once for a predator from the air (like an eagle) and twice when a predator from the ground (such as a fox) is approaching, and the whole tribe scurries to safety down a network of burrows.

Ornithologists flock to the Austrian Alps for a chance to see golden eagles, falcons and vultures – both bearded and griffin.

Endangered Species

Austria's most endangered species is the *Bayerische Kurzohrmaus* (Bavarian pine vole), which is endemic to Tyrol and found only in six localities. Following close behind is the *Kaiseradler* (imperial eagle), at one time extinct in Austria but fortunately staging a comeback through re-immigration. The *Europäische Hornotter* (long-nosed viper) may be a venomous snake at home in Carinthia, but humans are a far greater threat to its survival than its bite will ever be to ours.

A right pair of love birds, golden eagles stay together for life. See www.birdlife.at (in German) to find out more about these elusive raptors and other Austrian birdlife.

Teetering on the brink of extinction, the Austrian Alps' population of brown bears is very low (estimated at less than 10), boosted now and then by inquisitive souls arriving from Slovenia and Italy. They only really appear in the Karawanks (Karawanken), Karnisch Alps (Karnischen Alpen) and Gailtal Alps (Gailtaler Alpen) in Carinthia, as well as in Osttirol. The survival of local populations and safety of transitory bears very much depends on the efforts of organisations like Austria's Brown

SEASON'S GREETINGS

Spring When the snow melts, the springtime eruption of colourful wildflowers sets senses on high alert. Look out for bell-shaped purple gentian and startlingly pink alpine roses.

Summer Stay overnight in a mountain hut, bathe in pristine alpine lakes and bring your walking boots for some highly scenic hiking on passes above 2000m.

Autumn The larch trees turn a beautiful shade of gold in late autumn and you might spot rutting stags. Come in late September for the *Almabtrieb*, where cows adorned with flowers and bells are brought down from the pastures for the winter.

Winter Snow, snow and more glorious snow. Enjoy first-class skiing, crisp mountain air and cheese-loaded alpine food. Your snug wood chalet on the mountainside awaits.

MARTIN STEINTHALER/GETTY IMAGES ©

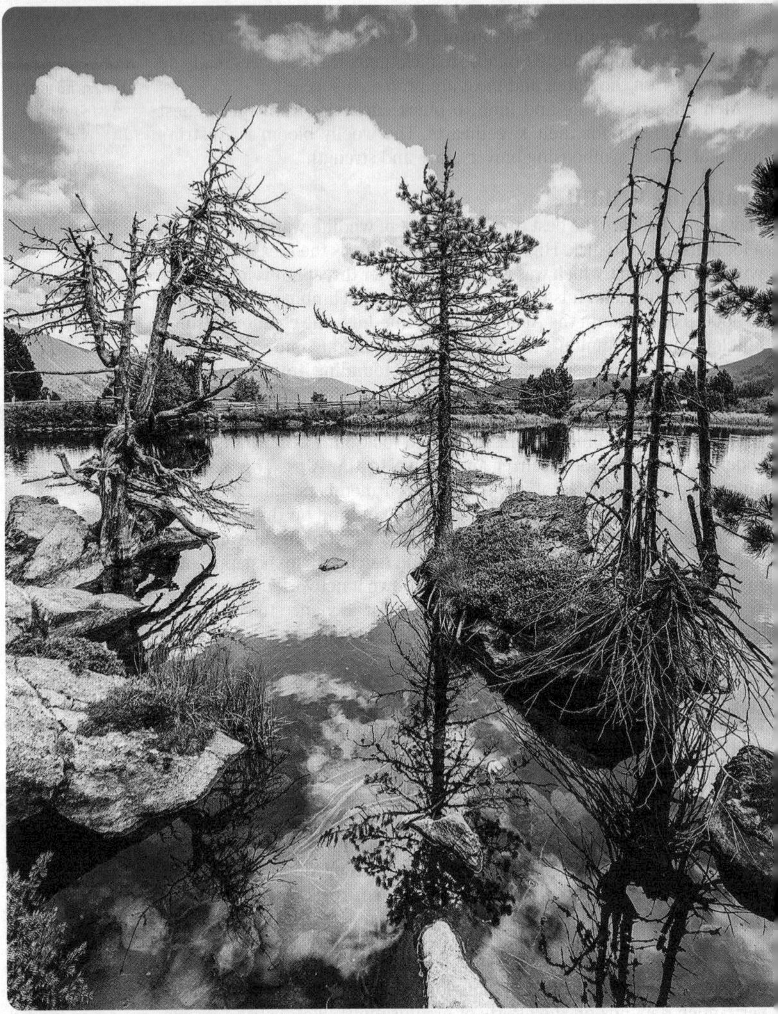

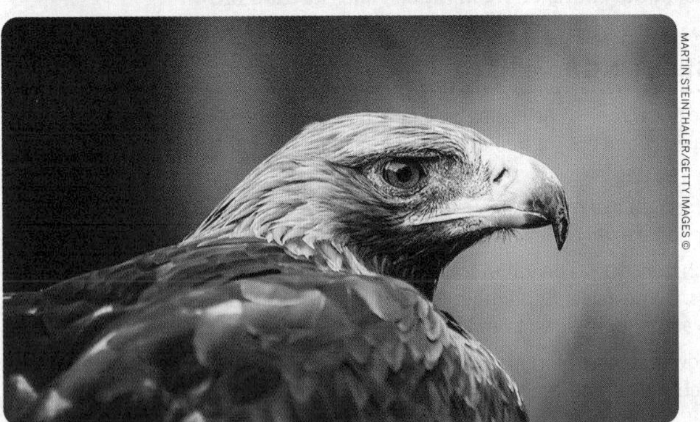

Top Nockberge Biosphere Reserve

Bottom A golden eagle in Hohe Tauern National Park (p255)

Bear Life Project and the WWF who have invested millions of euros into bringing the bear back to the Alps and fostering awareness.

For the lowdown on endangered species, consult the Rote Liste (www.umweltbundesamt.at, in German), collated by the Umweltbundesamt (Federal Environment Agency).

National Parks in the Austrian Alps

For an area of such mind-blowing natural beauty, it may come as a surprise to learn that there are just three national parks (Hohe Tauern, Kalkalpen and Gesäuse) as well as one major nature reserve (Nockberge) in the Austrian Alps. But statistics aren't everything, particularly when one of these national parks is the magnificent Hohe Tauern, the Alps' largest and Europe's second-largest national park, which is a tour de force of 3000m peaks, immense glaciers and waterfalls.

The national park authorities have managed to strike a good balance between preserving the wildlife and keeping local economic endeavours such as farming, hunting and tourism alive. The website www.nationalparksaustria.at has links to all national parks and a brochure in English to download.

Aside from national parks, protected areas and nature reserves are dotted all over the Austrian Alps, from the mesmerising mountainscapes of Naturpark Zillertaler Alpen in Tyrol to the lakes of the Salzkammergut. See www.naturparke.at for the lowdown on Austria's nature parks.

Austria's Alpine Environment

Given the fragile ecosystem of the Austrian Alps, conservation, renewable energy and sustainable tourism are red-hot topics. In the face of retreating glaciers, melting snow, dwindling animal numbers and erosion, the people of the Alps come face-to-face with global warming and human impact on the environment on a daily basis.

Measures have been in place for years to protect Austria's alpine regions, yet some forest degradation has taken place due to air and soil pollution caused by emissions from industrial plants, exhaust fumes and the use of agricultural chemicals.

ALPINE NATIONAL PARKS

PARK (AREA)	FEATURES	FAUNA	ACTIVITIES	BEST TIME	WEBSITE
Hohe Tauern (1786 sq km)	classic alpine scenery with 3000m mountains, glaciers, lakes, high alpine pastures	ibex, chamois, marmots, bearded vultures, golden eagles	hiking, rock climbing & mountaineering, skiing, canyoning, paragliding	year-round	https://hohetauern.at
Gesäuse (110 sq km)	rivers, meadows, gorges, thick forest, limestone peaks	owls, eagles, falcons, deer, bats, woodpeckers	hiking, rafting, caving, mountain biking, rock climbing	spring, summer, autumn	www.nationalpark.co.at
Kalkalpen (210 sq km)	high moors, mixed forest, rugged limestone mountains	lynx, brown bears, golden eagles, owls, woodpeckers, butterflies	hiking, cycling, rock climbing, cross-country skiing	year-round	www.kalkalpen.at
Nockberge (184 sq km)	gentle rounded peaks, alpine pastures, woodlands	marmots, snow eagles, alpine salamanders, butterflies	walking, climbing, cross-country & downhill skiing	year-round	www.biosphaerenparknockberge.at

The good news is that Austrians are, by and large, a green and nature-loving lot. Recently, everyone from top hoteliers in St Anton to farmers in Salzburgerland has been polishing their eco-credentials by promoting recycling and solar power, clean energy and public transport.

The government has moved to minimise pollutants, assist businesses in waste avoidance and encourage renewable energy, such as wind and solar power. Some buses are gas powered and environmentally friendly trams are a feature of many cities.

Superlatives

Europe's highest waterfall *The 380m-high Krimmler Wasserfälle*

The world's largest accessible ice caves *Eisriesenwelt, Werfen*

The largest national park in the Alps *Hohe Tauern (1786 sq km)*

The longest glacier in the Eastern Alps *The 8km Pasterze Glacier*

Austria's highest peak *3798m Grossglockner (literally 'Big Bell')*

Global Warming

With global warming a sad reality, 'snow-sure' is becoming more wishful thinking in resorts at lower elevations in the Austrian Alps. Every year, the snow line seems to edge slightly higher and snow-making machines are constantly on standby.

A United Nations Environment Programme (UNEP) report on climate change warned that rising temperatures could mean that 75% of alpine glaciers will disappear within the next 45 years, and that dozens of low-lying ski resorts such as Kitzbühel (762m) will be completely cut off from their slopes by 2030. Forecasts suggest that the snowline will shift from 1200m to 1800m by 2100. As well as the impact on Austria's tourist industry, the melting snow is sure to have other knock-on effects, including erosion, floods and an increased risk of avalanches.

Skiing

Austria's highly lucrative ski industry has its own environmental footprint to worry about. As their very survival has become threatened by warming temperatures, resorts find themselves pressured to develop higher up on the peaks to survive. For many years, ski resorts have not done the planet many favours: mechanically grading pistes disturbs wildlife and causes erosion, artificial snow affects native flora and fauna, and trucking in snow increases emissions.

However, many Austrian resorts now realise that they are walking a thin tightrope and are mitigating their environmental impact with renewable hydroelectric power, biological wastewater treatment and ecological buildings.

Eco Snow

In a bid to offset the impact of skiing, many Austrian resorts are taking the green run with ecofriendly policies.

- Lech in Vorarlberg scores top points for its biomass communal heating plant, the photovoltaic panels that operate its chairlifts and its strict recycling policies.
- Zell am See launched Austria's first ISO-certified cable car at the Kitzsteinhorn Glacier. It operates a free ski bus in winter and runs an ecological tree- and grass-planting scheme.
- Kitzbühel operates green building and climate policies, and is taking measures to reduce traffic and the use of nonrenewable energy sources.
- St Anton am Arlberg has created protected areas to reduce erosion and pumps out artificial snow without chemicals. Its excellent train connections mean fewer cars.
- Ischgl uses renewable energy; recycles in all hotels, lifts and restaurants; and has a night-time driving ban from 11pm to 6am.
- Mayrhofen operates its lifts on hydroelectricity, separates all waste and has free ski buses to reduce traffic in the village.

Survival Guide

A mountainbiker in Salzburgerland (p226)

Directory A–Z

PRACTICALITIES

Seasonal Prices In mountain resorts, high-season prices can be up to double the prices charged in the low season (May and November, which fall between the summer and winter seasons in mountains). In other towns, the difference may be 10% or less.

Concession Prices Many museums and sights have discounted concession prices for families and for children (generally for children under 16 years). Some places also have reduced admission prices for students and senior citizens, which are generally slightly higher than the child's price. Children under 12 years usually receive a substantial discount on rooms they share with parents; ask when booking. Children also travel at reduced rates on public transport.

Weights & Measures Austria uses the metric system.

Smoking Officially banned in public places since 2009; smoking in cafes, bars and restaurants was banned in November 2019.

Accessible Travel

Austria scores highly when it comes to accessible travel in Vienna, but outside the capital it's still by no means plain sailing. Ramps leading into buildings are common but not universal; most U-Bahn stations have wheelchair lifts but on buses and trams you'll often be negotiating gaps and one or more steps. Download Lonely Planet's free Accessible Travel Guide from https://shop.lonelyplanet.com/categories/accessible-travel.com.

For distance travel, **Österreiche Bundesbahn** (ÖBB; ☎05 1717; www.oebb.at) has a section for people with disabilities on its website. Change to the English-language option, then go to 'travel planning & services' and select 'barrier-free travelling'. Use the 05 171 75 number for mobility assistance (you can do this while booking your ticket by telephone). Staff at stations will help with boarding and alighting. Order this at least 24 hours ahead of travel (48 hours ahead for international services). No special service is available at unstaffed stations. Passengers with disabilities get a 50% discount off the usual ticket price.

The detailed pamphlet *Accessible Vienna* is available in German or English from **Tourist Info Wien** (☎01-245 55; www.wien.info; 01, Albertinaplatz; ⊙9am-7pm; 📶; 🚋D, 1, 2, 71 Kärntner Ring/Oper, Ⓤ Stephansplatz). A comprehensive list of places in Vienna catering to visitors with special needs can be downloaded from www.wien.info/en/travel-info/accessible-vienna. In other cities, contact the tourist office directly for more information.

Some of the more expensive hotels (four-star or above, usually) have facilities tailored to travellers with disabilities; cheaper hotels invariably don't.

There is no national organisation for the disabled in Austria, but the regional tourist offices or any of the following can be contacted for more information:

Behinderten Selbsthilfe Gruppe (☎03332-654 05; www.bsgh.at) Maintains a database at www.barrierefreier urlaub.at listing hotels and restaurants suitable for those with disabilities.

Bizeps (☎01-523 89 21; www.bizeps.at; 02, Schönngasse 15-17, Vienna; Ⓤ Messe-Prater) A centre providing support and self-help for people with disabilities. Located two blocks north of Messe-Prater U-Bahn station in Vienna.

Upper Austria Tourist Office (www.barrierefreies-oberoesterreich.at) Information and listings for people with disabilities travelling in Upper Austria.

WUK (☎01-401 21-0; www.wuk.at; 09, Währinger Strasse 59, Vienna) Offers information to young people with disabilities. Located just north of Vienna's Pilgramgasse U-Bahn station.

Accommodation

Booking Services

Local city and regional tourist office websites often have excellent accommodation booking functions.

Austrian National Tourist Office (www.austria.info) The Austrian National Tourist Office has a number of overseas offices. There is a comprehensive listing on the ANTO website.

Bergfex (www.bergfex.at) Hotels, guesthouses, hostels, B&Bs, farms and huts searchable by region.

Best Alpine Wellness Hotels (www.wellnesshotel.com) The pick of Austria's top family-run spa hotels.

Camping in Österreich (www.camping.info/österreich) Search for campgrounds by location, facilities or reviews.

Lonely Planet (www.lonelyplanet.com/austria/hotels) Recommendations.

Hotels & Pensions

The majority of travellers stay in either a hotel or a pension or *Gasthof* (inn or restaurant, usually with accommodation). All are rated by the same criteria (from one to five stars).

Hotels invariably offer more services, including bars, restaurants and garage parking, whereas pensions and *Gasthöfe* tend to be smaller than hotels and have fewer standardised fixtures and fittings but sometimes larger rooms.

TWO STARS

Budget hotels or pensions consist of functional rooms with cheap furnishings. Most cost under €40/80 per single/double; in many cases you're better off booking a good hostel room, although they are often more central than a hostel and near the train station. Breakfast is unlikely to thrill. The shower is in the room, but might be a booth.

THREE STARS

Most accommodation in Austria is in this midrange category. The majority of singles cost about €60 to €70, doubles €100 to €130 (from about €70/140 for a single/double in Vienna).

Expect good clean rooms and a decent buffet breakfast with cold cuts of meat, cheese, eggs and bread rolls. Usually there will be a minibar and maybe snacks too; often you'll have a place to sit or a desk to write on. Internet and either wi-fi or cable LAN is available, mostly free or inexpensively. Some specialise in catering to business travellers, with conference facilities and workstations. Rooms have showers and TVs (often flatscreens).

FOUR & FIVE STARS

Rooms in a four-star hotel or pension are generally larger than a three star and should have better sound insulation as well as contemporary or quality furnishings. Expect decent wellness facilities in a four-star option and premium facilities in five-star hotels.

ECO-HOTELS

So-called *Bio-* or *Öko-* ('eco') hotels are widespread in Austria. Most of them are located outside towns in picturesque settings. Quite a few of the hotels have wellness facilities such as saunas and steam baths, and because of their rural location they often have winter skiing and activities. Generally, you will need to have your own wheels – a car or a bicycle – to reach these. Tourist offices keep lists or have a special section in their accommodation listings and on their websites. The website www.biohotels.info also has a brief list.

Camping & Holiday Parks

Austria has some 500 camping grounds that offer a range of facilities, such as washing machines, electricity connections, on-site shops and, occasionally, cooking facilities. Camping gas canisters are widely available. Camp sites are often scenically situated in out-of-the-way places by rivers or lakes – fine if you're exploring the countryside but inconvenient if you want to sightsee in a town. For this reason, camping is more viable if you have your own transport. Prices can be as low as €5 per person or small tent and as high as €12.

The majority of camping grounds close in winter. If demand is low in spring and autumn, some may decide to shut then too, even though their booking information says they're open, so telephone ahead to check during these periods.

SLEEPING PRICE RANGES

The following price ranges refer to a double room with a bathroom for two people, including breakfast.

€ less than €80

€€ €80–200

€€€ more than €200

Free camping in camper vans is allowed in autobahn rest areas and alongside other roads, as long as you're not causing an obstruction. It's illegal to camp in tents in these areas.

While in the country, pick up camping guides in bookshops or from the Österreichischer Camping Club (www.campingclub.at) and the useful *Camping* brochure-map from the national tourism authority Österreich Werbung (www.austria.info), with international representatives.

Farmstays

If you have your own transport and want to get away from the towns, staying on a farm is a nice way to get away from it all. You will find lots of conventional *Bauernhöfe* (farmhouses) in rural areas. Most rent out apartments for a minimum of three nights, but some also have rooms accepting guests for one night. Depending on the region and type of accommodation, the cheapest cost from about €35 per person, going up to about €100 or more per night for a slick apartment with all mod cons.

In mountainous regions you will find *Almhütten* (alpine meadow huts), usually part of a farmstead. Some of these can be accessed by cable car and road, while the more isolated ones are accessible only by foot or mountain bike on forestry tracks. Most are closed from October to April or May. The huts serve snacks or meals to hikers and mountain bikers, and many offer simple, rustic rooms (usually with shared bathrooms). Full board is sometimes available.

The websites www.urlaubaufderalm.com and www.farmholidays.com are good places to look for farmstays, whereas tourist offices can also help with local mountain-top *Almhütten*.

Hostels

Austria is dotted with *Jugendgästehäuser* (youth hostels) and *Jugendherbergen* (youth guesthouses). Facilities are often excellent: four- to six-bed dorms with shower and toilet are the norm in hostels, while many guesthouses have double rooms or family rooms; internet facilities, free wi-fi and a restaurant or cafe are commonplace.

Austria has over 100 hostels affiliated with Hostelling International (www.hihostels.com), plus a smattering of privately owned hostels.

Membership cards are always required, except in a few private hostels, but nonmembers pay a surcharge of about €3.50 per night and after six nights the stamped Welcome Card counts as full membership. Most hostels accept reservations by telephone or email and are part of the worldwide computer reservations system through the HI website. Average dorm prices are about €22 per night.

HI hostels are run by two hostel organisations, the **Österreichischer Jugendherbergsverband** (ÖJHV; ☎01-533 53 53; www.oejhv.at; 01, Zelinkagasse 12, Vienna; ⏰9am-1pm Mon, Wed & Fri, to 4pm Tue & Thu; 🚋1, 31 Schottenring, Ⓤ Schottenring) and **JUFA** (☎reservations 05 70 83 800; www.jufa.eu). There are 40 JUFA guesthouses scattered around Austria, any of which can be booked by telephone on a local number, through the central booking service or online. They generally offer a higher standard of facilities than youth hostels and specialise in singles, doubles and family rooms. An average price is about €40 to €60 for a single room with bathroom and toilet, and €35 to €40 per person in a double or family room. No membership fees apply. Prices usually vary by demand.

Private Rooms

Rooms in private houses are cheap (often about €60 per double) and in most towns you will see *Privat Zimmer* (private room) or *Zimmer Frei* (room free) signs. Most hosts are friendly; the level of service, though, is lower than in hotels.

Rental Accommodation

Ferienwohnungen (self-catering holiday apartments) are very common in Austrian mountain resorts, though it is sometimes necessary to book these well in advance. The best idea is to contact a local tourist office for lists and prices or to book online using the tourist office website.

University Accommodation

Studentenheime (student residences) are available to tourists over university summer breaks (from the beginning of July to around the end of September). Some rooms have a private bathroom but often there's no access to the communal kitchen. The widest selection is in Vienna, but tourist offices in Graz, Salzburg, Krems an der Donau and Innsbruck can point you in the right direction. Prices per person are likely to range from €20 to €75 per night and sometimes include breakfast.

PLAN YOUR STAY ONLINE

For more accommodation reviews by Lonely Planet authors, check out www.lonelyplanet.com. You'll find independent reviews, as well as recommendations on the best places to stay.

Climate

Innsbruck

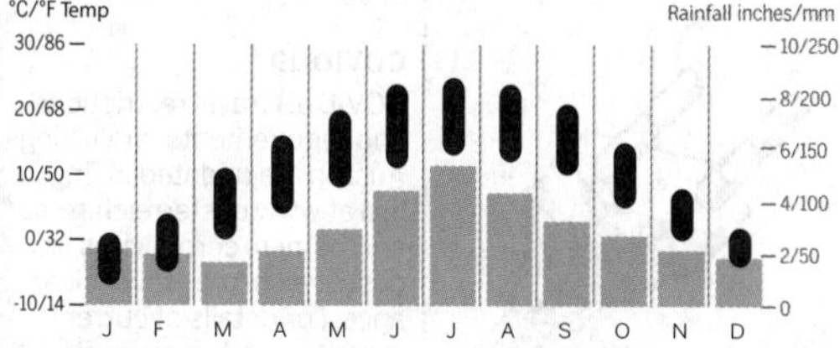

Salzburg

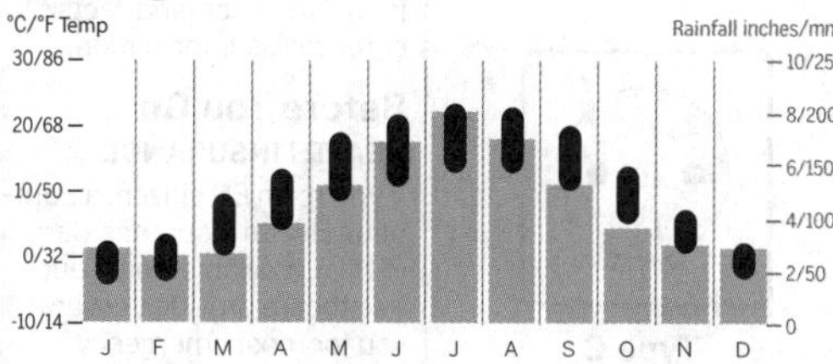

Vienna

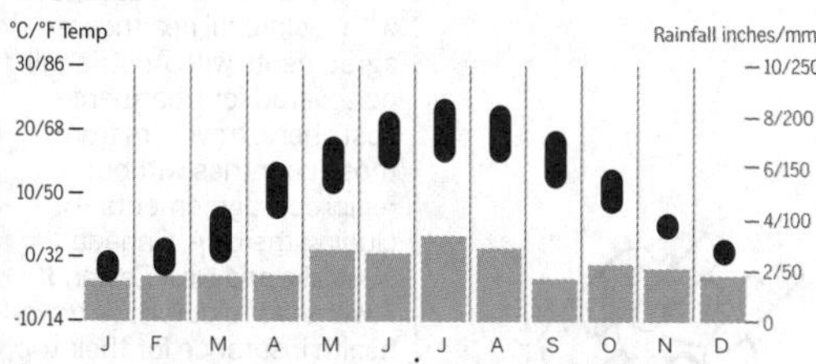

Children

With its parks, playgrounds and great outdoors, Austria has plenty to keep kids amused.

➡ Regional tourist offices often produce brochures aimed directly at families.

➡ Museums, parks and theatres often have programs for children over the summer holiday periods, and local councils occasionally put on special children's events and festivals.

➡ Many lakes have a supervised beach area, with children's splash areas, and slides and games for little ones.

➡ Family walks ranging from gentle to challenging abound, even in high alpine terrain.

➡ Many museums in Vienna are free for those under 18 or 19 years.

For helpful travelling tips, pick up a copy of Lonely Planet's *Travel with Children*.

Practicalities

Facilities Facilities for travellers with kids are good. Some museums (especially in Vienna) have a children's play area; restaurants have high chairs; and many hotels have rooms that are connected by a door, making them especially suitable for families. In most hotels and pensions, children under 12 years receive substantial discounts, depending on exact age. Midrange and better hotels have cots (but book ahead). Family- or child-friendly hotels are highlighted in our listings.

Restaurants Most midrange restaurants have a child's menu or will prepare smaller portions for children if you ask. A few have a play area.

Travelling with babies In bigger cities, breastfeeding in public won't cause eyelids to bat. Everything you need for babies, such as formula and disposable nappies (diapers), is widely available (in *Drogerien*, or drug stores). Nappy-changing facilities are commonly available in major restaurants, hotels and train stations.

Getting around with kids Rental car companies can arrange safety seats. Newer public transport, such as trams and buses in Vienna, are easily accessible for buggies and prams, but the older models can prove a nightmare. Children under six years usually travel free on public transport, or half-price until 15 years of age.

Resources Log on to www.kinderhotels.at for information on child-friendly hotels throughout the country.

Customs Regulations

Austrian customs regulations are in line with all other EU countries.

Items such as weapons, certain drugs (both legal and illegal), meat, some plant materials and animal products are subject to strict customs control. All goods must be for personal use.

The Ministry of Finance website (http://english.bmf.gv.at) has an overview of regulations.

Below are some key guidelines for anyone 17 years or older importing items from an EU or non-EU country. The amounts in brackets are for items imported from outside the EU; if tobacco products don't have health warnings in the German language, these too are limited to the amounts given in brackets.

Alcohol Beer 110L (16L); or spirits over 22% 10L (1L); or spirits under 22%, sparkling wine, wine liqueurs 20L (2L); or wine 90L (4L).

Cigarettes 800 (200); or cigarillos 400 (100); or cigars 200 (50); or tobacco 1kg (250g).

Money Amounts of over €10,000 in cash or in travellers cheques (or the equivalent in cash in a foreign currency) must be declared on entering or leaving the EU. There is no limit within the EU, but authorities are entitled to request accurate information on the amount you are carrying.

Discount Cards

Various discount cards are available, many covering a whole region or province. Some are free with an overnight stay (eg Neusiedler See Card in Burgenland and Zell am See–Kaprun Summer Card in Salzburgerland); others cost a few euros (eg Salzkammergut Erlebnis Card). Others, such as the Kärnten Card in Carinthia and the Innsbruck Card, must be purchased, but yield more substantial benefits such as free entry to museums and attractions as well as discounts on public transport.

Senior Cards In some cases senior travellers will be able to get discount admission to sights, but local proof is often required. (It can't hurt to ask and show proof of age, though.) The minimum qualifying age for Austrians is 60 or 65 for men and 60 for women.

Student & Youth Cards International Student Identity Cards (ISIC) and European Youth Card (check www.eyca.org for discounts) will get you discounts at most museums, galleries and theatres. Admission is generally a little higher than the price for children.

Electricity

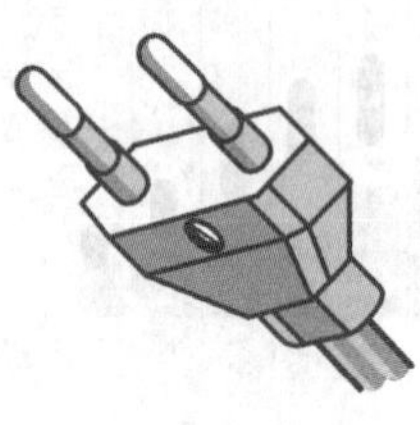

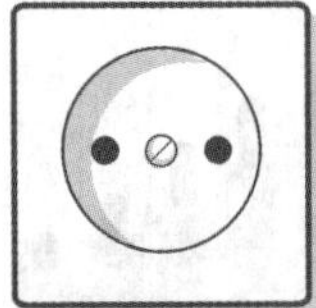

Type C
220V/50Hz

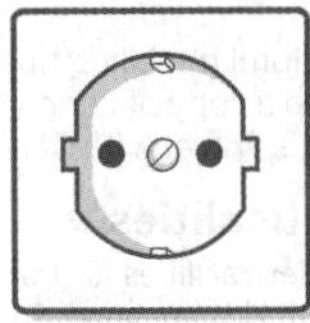

Type F
230V/50Hz

Health

Travelling in Austria presents very few health risks. The water everywhere can be safely drunk from the tap, while the water in lakes and streams is for the most part excellent and poses no risk of infection.

COVID-19

COVID-19 travel restrictions and requirements for visiting Austria are updated in English at www.oesterreich.gv.at/en/themen/coronavirus_in_oesterreich/pre-travel-clearance. For details of current measures in Austria during your visit check www.austria.info/en/service-and-facts/coronavirus-information.

Before You Go

HEALTH INSURANCE

If you're an EU citizen, a European Health Insurance Card (EHIC), available from your healthcare provider, covers you for most emergency medical care in Austria.

Travellers from countries with reciprocal healthcare agreements with Austria will be covered for treatment costs here; travellers from those countries without reciprocal agreements – including the USA, Canada, Australia and New Zealand – will need to purchase travel health insurance for their trip.

Make sure you get a policy that covers you for the worst possible scenario, such as an accident requiring an emergency flight home. Find out in advance if your insurance plan will make payments directly to providers or reimburse you later for overseas health expenditures, and whether it covers all activities (like skiing or climbing).

RECOMMENDED VACCINATIONS

The World Health Organization (WHO) recommends that, regardless of their destination, all travellers should be covered for diphtheria, tetanus, measles, mumps, rubella and polio, as well as hepatitis B. A vaccination for tick-borne encephalitis is also highly advisable.

In Austria

COST OF HEALTH CARE

An EHIC card will cover you for medical emergencies. Otherwise, expect to pay anything from €40 to €75 for a straightforward, nonurgent consultation with a doctor.

Health care in Austria isn't cheap, and treatment for a skiing injury, for instance, can quickly amount to thousands, so ensure that you have adequate travel health insurance before travelling.

ENVIRONMENTAL HAZARDS

Wasps can be a problem in the countryside in midsummer but are only dangerous for those with an allergy or if you get stung in the throat. Look before you take a sip outdoors from a sweet drink.

Mosquitoes can be a nuisance around lakes.

INFECTIOUS DISEASES

Ticks can carry Lyme disease and encephalitis (TBE), and pose a serious outdoor hazard to health in many parts of Europe. They are usually found at altitudes below 1200m, in undergrowth at the forest edge or beside walking tracks.

Wearing long trousers tucked into walking boots or socks and using a DEET-based insect repellent is the best prevention against tick bites. If a tick is found attached to the skin, press down around the tick's head with tweezers, grab the tick as close as possible to the head and rotate continuously in one direction, without pulling, until the tick releases itself. Pharmacies sell plastic or metal tweezers especially for this purpose (highly recommended for hikers). Avoid pulling the rear of the body or smearing chemicals on the tick.

Insurance

Components of insurance worth considering include repatriation for medical treatment; burial or repatriation in the event of death; search and rescue; the cost of returning home in case of illness or the death of a close relative; personal liability and legal expenses; the loss of your passport; luggage loss or delay; and expenses due to cancellations for a variety of reasons.

EATING PRICE RANGES

The following price ranges refer to the cost of a two-course meal, excluding drinks.

€ less than €15

€€ €15–30

€€€ more than €30

Internet Access

Wi-fi This is available in most hotels, numerous cafes and bars, and (increasingly) for free in public spaces. Many tourist offices also have WLAN ('vee-lan') as it's called in German. A wi-fi icon in our listings means a venue has wi-fi access either for free or for a moderate charge.

Internet terminals Some hotels have internet terminals that guests can use for free or for a small cost. Icons in our listings indicate these places.

Public access Small towns often won't have internet cafes but the local library will probably have a terminal.

Internet on smartphones GPS and navigation work fine in most areas.

Hotspot resources See www.freewave.at/en/hotspots for free hotspots in Vienna, and www.freewlan.at for Austria-wide hotspots.

Legal Matters

Carry your passport or a copy of your passport with you at all times, as police will occasionally do checks. If you're arrested, the police must inform you of your rights in a language that you understand.

In Austria, legal offences are divided into two categories: *Gerichtsdelikt* (criminal) and *Verwaltungsübertretung* (administrative). If you are suspected of having committed a criminal offence (such as assault or theft), you can be detained for a maximum of 48 hours before you are committed for trial. If you're arrested for a less serious, administrative offence, such as being drunk and disorderly or committing a breach of the peace, you will be released within 24 hours.

Driving while drunk is an administrative offence, even if you have an accident. However, if someone is hurt in the accident it becomes a criminal offence. Possession of a controlled drug is usually a criminal offence. Possession of a large amount of cannabis or selling it (especially to children) could result in a five-year prison term. Prostitution is legal provided prostitutes are registered and have a permit.

LGBTIQ+ Travellers

Vienna is reasonably tolerant towards LGBTIQ+ travellers, more so than the rest of the country.

Online information (in German) can be found at www.gayboy.at, www.rainbow.at and www.gaynet.at. The *Spartacus International Gay Guide*, published by Bruno Gmünder (Berlin), is a good international directory of LGBTIQ+ entertainment venues worldwide (mainly for men). Or check it out online at https://spartacus.gayguide.travel.

Since 2019, same-sex marriage has been legal in Austria.

Money

ATMs

Bankomaten are extremely common everywhere and accessible till midnight; some are 24 hours. Most accept at the very least Maestro debit cards and Visa and MasterCard credit cards. There are English instructions and daily withdrawal limits of €400 with credit and debit cards. Check with your home bank before travelling for charges for using a *Bankomat*; there's usually no commission to pay at the Austrian end.

Credit & Debit Cards

Visa and MasterCard (EuroCard) are accepted a little more widely than American Express (Amex) and Diners Club, although a surprising number of businesses refuse to accept any credit cards at all. Upmarket shops, hotels and restaurants will accept cards, though. Train tickets can be bought by credit card in main stations. Credit cards allow you to get cash advances on ATMs and over-the-counter at most banks.

Currency

Like other members of the European Monetary Union (EMU), Austria's currency is the euro, which is divided into 100 cents. There are coins for one, two, five, 10, 20 and 50 cents, and for €1 and €2. Notes come in denominations of €5, €10, €20, €50, €100, €200 and €500.

Tipping

Bars About 5% at the bar and 10% at a table.

Hotels One or two euros per suitcase for porters and for valet parking in top-end hotels. Leaving loose change for cleaners is appreciated.

Restaurants Tip about 10% (unless service is abominable). Round up the bill, state the amount as you hand the bill back or leave the tip in the bill folder when you leave.

Taxis About 10%.

Opening Hours

Banks 8am or 9am–3pm Monday to Friday (to 5.30pm Thursday)

Cafes 7am or 8am–11pm or midnight; traditional cafes close at 7pm or 8pm

Offices/government departments 8am–3.30pm, 4pm or 5pm Monday to Friday

Post offices 8am–noon and 2–6pm Monday to Friday; some open Saturday morning

Pubs and bars 5.30pm–between midnight and 4am

Restaurants Generally 11am–2.30pm or 3pm and 6–11pm or midnight

Shops 9am–6.30pm Monday to Friday (often to 9pm Thursday or Friday in cities), 9am–5pm Saturday

Seasonal Opening Hours

Opening hours can vary significantly between the high season (April to October) and winter – many sights and tourist offices are on reduced hours from November to March. Opening hours we provide are for the high season, so outside those months it can be useful to check ahead.

Post

➡ Austria's postal system (www.post.at) is reliable, inexpensive and reasonably quick.

➡ Stamps are available at post offices and authorised shops and tobacconists. Post boxes and vans are bright yellow.

➡ The cost of sending a letter depends on its weight – letters weighing up to 20g cost €0.74 in Austria, €1 to anywhere in the EU and €1.80 to the rest of the world.

Public Holidays

New Year's Day (Neujahr) 1 January

Epiphany (Heilige Drei Könige) 6 January

Easter Monday (Ostermontag) March/April

Labour Day (Tag der Arbeit) 1 May

Whit Monday (Pfingstmontag) 6th Monday after Easter

Ascension Day (Christi Himmelfahrt) 6th Thursday after Easter

Corpus Christi (Fronleichnam) 2nd Thursday after Whitsunday

Assumption (Maria Himmelfahrt) 15 August

National Day (Nationalfeiertag) 26 October

All Saints' Day (Allerheiligen) 1 November

Immaculate Conception (Mariä Empfängnis) 8 December

Christmas Day (Christfest) 25 December

St Stephen's Day (Stephanitag) 26 December

Safe Travel

Austria is a very safe country. Visitors will generally have no trouble walking around at night in cities.

Theft Take usual common-sense precautions: keep valuables out of sight (on your person and in parked cars). Pickpockets occasionally operate on public transport and at major tourist sights.

Natural Dangers Every year people die from landslides and avalanches in the Alps. Always check weather conditions before heading out; consider hiring a guide when skiing off-piste. Before going on challenging hikes, ensure you have the proper equipment and fitness. Inform someone at your hotel/guesthouse where you're going and when you intend to return.

Telephone

➡ Austria's international access code is 00; its country code is 43.

➡ Each town and region has its own area code beginning with '0' (eg '01' for Vienna). Drop this when calling from outside Austria; use it for all landline calls inside Austria except for local calls or special toll and toll-free numbers.

➡ Austrian mobile *(Handy)* phone numbers begin with 0650 or higher up to 0699 (eg 0664 plus the rest of the number). Numbers beginning with 0900 are expensive and best avoided. Some large organisations have '050' numbers, which do not need an area code (a local call from a landline, but more expensive from a mobile phone).

Emergency & Important Numbers

To dial from outside Austria, dial the international access code, country code, city code, then number.

Austria's country code	☎43
International access code	☎00
International operator & information	☎11 88 77 (inland, EU & neighbouring countries); ☎0900 11 88 77 (other countries)
Mountain rescue	☎140
Emergency (police, fire, ambulance)	☎112

Mobile Phones

Travellers from outside Europe will need a tri- or quad-band (world) mobile phone for roaming. Local SIM cards (about €15) are easily purchased for 'unlocked' phones. Visitors from the EU can roam freely at domestic prices.

ROAMING

The *Handy* network works on GSM 1800 and is compatible with GSM 900 phones; it is not compatible with systems from the US unless the mobile phone is at least a tri-band model that can receive one of these frequencies. Japanese mobile phones need to be quad-band (world phone) to work in Austria. Roaming can get very expensive if your provider is outside the EU.

PREPAID SIM CARDS

Phone shops sell prepaid SIM cards for phone calls and SIM cards capable of being used on smart phones for data as well as making calls. Typically, you pay about €15 for a SIM card and receive about €10 free credit. To use one, your mobile phone must not be locked to a specific carrier.

WI-FI & DATA

Make sure your data transfer capability is deactivated while roaming. Austria has lots of wi-fi hotspots that can be used for surfing or making internet calls using smart phones with wi-fi capability.

Time

In 2019, the European Parliament voted to scrap daylight saving time. The law had yet to be finalised at the time of research. Austria has summer and winter time. Daylight saving time *(Sommerzeit)* begins on the last Sunday in March; all clocks are put forward by one hour. On the last Sunday in October, normal Central European Time begins and clocks are put back one hour.

Note that in German *halb* (half) is used to indicate the half-hour **before** the hour, hence *halb acht* means 7.30, *not* 8.30.

Toilets

➡ Public toilets are generally widely available at major stations and tourist attractions, but you'll always need a €0.50 or €1 coin handy (it helps to have a stash of these – exact change is required).

➡ Bars and cafes don't take kindly to passers-by using their facilities without buying a drink at least, but they might let you if you ask nicely.

Tourist Information

Austria Info (www.austria.info) Official Austria tourism website.

Bodensee-Vorarlberg Tourism (☎05574-434 43; www.bodensee-vorarlberg.com) Based in Bregenz and giving the lowdown on the Vorarlberg region.

Burgenland Tourismus (www.burgenland.info) This website should be your first port of call for a visit to Burgenland, with information on everything from events and activities to transport and accommodation. Brochures and apps are available for download.

Graz Tourismus (☎0316-807 50; www.graztourismus.at; Herrengasse 16; ⏰10am-5pm Jan-Mar & Nov, to 6pm Apr-Oct & Dec; 📶; 🚊1, 3, 4, 5, 6, 7 Hauptplatz) For information on exploring Graz.

Innsbruck Information (☎0512-598 50, 0512-535 60; www.innsbruck.info; Burggraben 3; ⏰9am-6pm Mon-Sat, 10am-4.30pm Sun) Great planning information for Innsbruck and its surrounds.

Kärnten Information (www.visitcarinthia.at) The tourism portal for Carinthia. This multilingual website has some great travel information on Carinthia's attractions and activities, plus an online booking service.

Niederösterreich Werbung (www.niederoesterreich.at) Lower Austria's official tourism website, with a breakdown of regions and details on sights, activities, culture, food and drink, accommodation and more.

Oberösterreich Tourismus (www.oberoesterreich.at) Great first port of call for Upper Austria.

Salzburg Info (www.salzburg.info) Handy first port of call for Salzburg.

Salzburgerland Tourismus (☎0662-66 88 44; www.salzburgerland.com; Wiener Bundesstrasse 23, Hallwang bei Salzburg; ⊗8am-5.30pm Mon-Thu, to 5pm Fri) Information on the wider Salzburg region.

Salzkammergut Touristik (☎06132-2400 051; www.salzkammergut.co.at; Götzstrasse 12, Bad Ischl; ⊗9am-6pm Mon-Fri, to 2pm Sat & Sun, closed Sun Sep-Jun) Check out the website for the inside scoop on Salzkammergut.

Steirische Tourismus (www.steiermark.com) A comprehensive overview of Styria and all it has to offer, from its culinary scene and culture, to skiing and hiking holidays. You can search and book hotels online.

Tirol Info (www.tirol.at) Tyrol's official tourism website has loads of great information on the region, plus an interactive map, booking service, and downloadable brochures and apps.

Tourist Info Wien (☎0732-7070 2009; www.linztourismus.at; Hauptplatz 1; ⊗9am-7pm daily May-Sep, to 5pm Mon-Sat, 10am-5pm Sun Oct-Apr) Vienna's official tourism website

Tourist Information Linz (☎0732-7070 2009; www.linztourismus.at; Hauptplatz 1; ⊗9am-7pm daily May-Sep, to 5pm Mon-Sat, 10am-5pm Sun Oct-Apr) Upper Austria information, brochures and accommodation listings..

Visas

From late 2022, citizens of countries that don't require a visa for entry to the Schengen area (eg nationals of the UK, US, Australia, Canada etc) will need prior authorisation to enter under the European Travel Information and Authorisation System (ETIAS). Travellers will be able to apply online; the cost is €7 for a three-year, multi-entry authorisation. With ETIAS preauthorisation, visitors who require it can stay for 90 days out of 180 days.

Nationals of other countries generally require a Schengen visa. A visa for any Schengen country should be valid throughout the Schengen area, but it pays to double-check with the embassy or consulate of each country you intend to visit. Note that Ireland (although an EU country) and the UK (no longer part of the EU since Brexit) are not Schengen countries.

The Federal Ministry for Europe, Integration & Foreign Affairs (www.bmeia.gv.at) website has a list of Austrian embassies where you can apply. For more information, visit www.lonelyplanet.com/articles/visa-requirements-for-austria.

Volunteering

Volunteering is a good way to meet people and get involved with local life, with projects lasting anything from a week to 18 months or more. In Austria, maintaining hiking trails is popular, but other volunteer projects range from joining a performance group on social issues to repairing school fences outside Vienna. Hook up with the networks in your home country and/or, if you speak German, approach an Austrian organisation directly.

Bergwald Projekt (☎0512-595 47 47; www.alpenverein.at; Olympiastrasse 37, Innsbruck) Excellent volunteer work programs protecting and maintaining mountain forests in Austria, Germany and Switzerland. Generally, the Austrian programs last one week.

Freiwilligenweb (www.freiwilligenweb.at) Official Austrian government portal for volunteer work.

International Voluntary Service Great Britain (www.ivsgb.org) The UK organisation networked with the Service Civil International (SCI).

International Volunteers for Peace (www.ivp.org.au) An Australian organisation networked with the SCI.

Service Civil International (SCI; www.sciint.org) Worldwide organisation with local networks.

Work

➡ EU, EEA and Swiss nationals may work in Austria without a work permit or residency permit, though as intending residents they need to register with the police.

➡ Non-EU nationals need both a work permit and a residency permit, and will find it pretty hard to get either unless they qualify for a Red-White-Red Card, which is aimed at attracting highly skilled workers. Your employer in Austria must apply for your work permit. You must apply for your residency permit via the Austrian embassy in your home country.

➡ Teaching is a popular field for those seeking work in Austria; look under '*Sprachschulen*' in the *Gelbe Seiten* (yellow pages) for a list of schools. In professions outside of that and barkeeping, you'll struggle to find employment if you don't speak German.

Some useful job websites:

Arbeitsmarktservice Österreich (www.ams.or.at) Austria's Labour Office.

Monster (www.monster.at)

StepStone (www.stepstone.at) Directed towards professionals.

Virtual Vienna Net (www.virtualvienna.net) Aimed at expats, with a variety of jobs, including UN listings.

Transport

GETTING THERE & AWAY

Austria is well connected to the rest of the world. Vienna and several regional capitals are served by no-frills airlines (plus regular airline services). Europe's extensive bus and train networks criss-cross the country and there are major highways from Germany and Italy. It's also possible to enter Austria by boat from Hungary, Slovakia and Germany.

Entering the Country

Paperwork Citizens of the EU, EEA and Switzerland can enter Austria with an ID card. Other nationalities need a passport valid for at least six months; some require a Schengen visa. From late 2022, citizens of countries that don't require a Schengen visa need pre-authorisation through the ETIAS (www.etias.com) process.

Border procedures Formal border controls have been abolished for those entering from another EU country or Switzerland, but spot checks may be carried out at the border or inside Austria itself.

Air

Vienna is the main transport hub for Austria, but Graz, Linz, Klagenfurt, Salzburg and Innsbruck all receive international flights. Flights to these cities are often a cheaper option than those to the capital, as are flights to Airport Letisko (Bratislava Airport), which is only 60km east of Vienna, in Slovakia. Bregenz has no airport; there are limited flights to nearby Friedrichshafen in Germany and much better connections at Zürich in Switzerland.

Airports & Airlines

Austrian Airlines (www.austrian.com) The national carrier, based in Vienna; it's a member of **Star Alliance** (www.staralliance.com).

Blue Danube Airport Linz (BTS; ☎02-3303 3353; www.bts.aero; Ivanská cesta) Located 12km southwest of Linz, with flights to Vienna, Frankfurt and Düsseldorf, plus several other European cities in summer.

Bratislava Airport (BTS; ☎02-3303 3353; www.bts.aero; Ivanská cesta) Nine kilometres northeast of the centre. Connections to Italy, Germany, Spain, Greece, UK cities and more.

Graz Airport (GRZ; ☎0316-290 21 72; www.flughafen-graz.at) Located 10km south of the centre and is served by carriers including easyJet, Austrian Airlines, KLM, Eurowings and Lufthansa.

CLIMATE CHANGE & TRAVEL

Every form of transport that relies on carbon-based fuel generates CO_2, the main cause of human-induced climate change. Modern travel is dependent on aeroplanes, which might use less fuel per kilometre per person than most cars but travel much greater distances. The altitude at which aircraft emit gases (including CO_2) and particles also contributes to their climate change impact. Many websites offer 'carbon calculators' that allow people to estimate the carbon emissions generated by their journey and, for those who wish to do so, to offset the impact of the greenhouse gases emitted with contributions to portfolios of climate-friendly initiatives throughout the world. Lonely Planet offsets the carbon footprint of all staff and author travel.

DEPARTURE TAX

Departure tax is included in the price of a ticket.

Innsbruck Airport (INN; ☎0512-22 52 50; www.innsbruck-airport.com; Fürstenweg 180) EasyJet flies to Innsbruck Airport, 4km west of the city centre.

Kärnten Airport (www.klagenfurt-airport.com; Flughafenstrasse 60-66) Klagenfurt's airport, 3km north of town, is served by the airlines easyJet, Austrian, Transavia and Eurowings.

Salzburg Airport (☎0662-858 00; www.salzburg-airport.com; Innsbrucker Bundesstrasse 95; 📶) A 20-minute bus ride from the city centre, this airport has regular scheduled flights to destinations all over Austria and Europe.

Vienna International Airport (VIE; ☎01-700 722 233; www.viennaairport.com; 📶) Has good connections worldwide. The airport is in Schwechat, 18km southeast of Vienna.

Land

Border Crossings

There are numerous entry points by road from Germany, the Czech Republic, Slovakia, Hungary, Slovenia, Italy and Switzerland. Liechtenstein is so small that it has just one border-crossing point, near Feldkirch in Austria. The Alps limit the options for approaching Tyrol from the south (Switzerland and Italy). All border crossing points are open 24 hours.

Bus

Travelling by bus is a cheap but less comfortable way to reach Austria from other European countries. Options include Eurolines, Flixbus, Busabout and ÖBB Intercity Bus.

EUROLINES

Eurolines (☎+49 69 971 944 836; www.eurolines.com) buses serve Austrian cities including Vienna, Graz, Linz, Salzburg, Klagenfurt and Innsbruck. They also serve numerous cities in neighbouring Italy, Germany, the Czech Republic and Hungary.

Passes are priced according to season: a 15-day pass is €225 to €375 for adults; a 30-day pass is €340 to €490 (cheaper for those under 26 and over 60). A pass covers 49 cities across Europe (including Vienna).

London Buses connect London (Victoria coach station) and Vienna Erdberg (one way/return €83/146, 24 hours); anyone under 26 or over 60 gets a 10% discount on most fares and passes.

Prague Buses (one way/return €26/52, six hours) run twice daily.

Bratislava From Vienna 14 buses run daily (one way/return €9/18, one hour to 80 minutes).

FLIXBUS

Low-cost operator **FlixBus** (☎+49 30 300 137 300; https://global.flixbus.com/bus/austria) has become big in recent years, with coach services running between most Austrian cities and towns, and to/from some 28 European countries. See the website for a route map, timetables and pricing.

INTERNATIONAL RAIL CONNECTIONS

ROUTE	PRICE (€)	DURATION (HR)
Belgrade–Villach	82	11
Budapest–Graz	79	6
Dortmund–Linz	169	9 (departs Vienna, changes in Stuttgart or Würzburg for northern Germany)
Ljubljana–Graz	32	3¾ (some services continue to Zagreb & Belgrade)
Ljubljana–Villach	17	1¾
Munich–Graz	96	6 (via Salzburg)
Munich–Innsbruck	45	2
Munich–Salzburg	41	1¾
Munich–Villach	79	4½
Prague–Linz	51	5½
Verona–Innsbruck	44	3½
Zagreb–Villach	48	4
Zürich–Innsbruck	70	3½

VIENNA'S HAUPTBAHNHOF

With its diamond-shaped, translucent glass-and-steel roof, Vienna's *Hauptbahnhof* (main train station) is an architectural triumph. Opened in December 2015, it was designed and built by acclaimed Austrian firm Strabag. Up to 1000 trains per day carrying some 145,000 passengers now pass through the station, which also has 84 shops, bars and restaurants; parking for 600 cars; three bike garages; electric bike-charging points; and two Citybike Wien bike-share rental stations.

Located 3km south of Stephansdom, the *Hauptbahnhof* handles all international trains, as well as services to/from all of Austria's provincial capitals, and many local and regional trains.

S-Bahn S-Bahn lines S1, S2 and S3 connect *Hauptbahnhof* with Wien Meidling, Wien-Mitte and Praterstern.

U-Bahn U1 serves Karlsplatz and Stephansplatz.

Tram 0 to Praterstern, 18 to Westbahnhof and Burggasse/Stadthalle. Tram D connects *Hauptbahnhof-Ost* with the Ringstrasse.

Bus 13A runs through Vienna's *Vorstädte* (inner suburbs) Margareten, Mariahilf, Neubau and Josefstadt, all between the Ringstrasse and the Gürtel.

BUSABOUT

UK-based **Busabout** (☎+44 808 281 1114; www.busabout.com) provides hop-on/hop-off passes enabling travel to around 50 European cities from May to late October.

The stops are arranged into different 'loops', which can be combined. The **Northern Loop** features Vienna, Salzburg, Prague, Amsterdam, Paris and a number of German cities. The website has further details.

ÖBB INTERCITY BUS

An **ÖBB** (☎05 1717; www.oebb.at) Intercity bus connects Klagenfurt via Villach and Udine with Venice (€29, 4¼ hours, three times daily).

Car & Motorcycle

To enter Austria by car, you'll need proof of ownership and third-party insurance (p398), as well as a sticker on the rear of the vehicle clearly displaying the country of origin. You will also need a *Vignette* if you plan on using the autobahn (p398).

All border crossing points are open 24 hours, and petrol stations are usually handily located nearby.

Train

Austria benefits from its central location within Europe by having excellent rail connections to all important destinations. Passengers do not need to disembark at borders, but do need to ensure they have any necessary visas.

The website **The Man in Seat 61** (www.seat61.com) has helpful tips and details on booking trains across Europe.

TIMETABLES

European Rail Timetable (www.europeanrailtimetable.eu) Contains all train schedules, supplements and reservations information. The monthly edition can be ordered online. A digital edition and app is also available.

ÖBB (☎05 1717; www.oebb.at) With national and international connections, plus online national train booking. The website also shows Postbus services.

Deutsche Bahn (www.bahn.de) Useful for finding special deals to/from Germany or to check connections (but not prices and bookings) in Austria.

TICKETS

International Rail (☎+44 (0)871 231 0790; www.internationalrail.com) Handles bookings for a minimum UK£10 surcharge by telephone and also online; tickets from many different countries can be booked through the website. It's often cheapest to book the continental Europe leg, then find the best Eurostar deal.

Deutsche Bahn (www.bahn.com) Also useful, especially for taking advantage of savings through early booking.

SERVICES

Extra charges can apply on fast trains and international trains, and it's a good idea (and sometimes obligatory) to make seat reservations for peak times and on certain lines. Prices we give for national and international trains can vary slightly according to the route and type of train.

➡ Express trains can be identified by the symbols EC (EuroCity, serving international routes) or IC (InterCity, serving national routes). RailJet national and international train services are faster than IC/EC trains and cost the same but have perks like free wi-fi (in many) and power outlets alongside all seats. The French Train à Grande Vitesse (TGV) and the German InterCityExpress (ICE) trains are high-speed trains; surcharges are levied for these.

➡ Overnight trains usually offer a choice between a *Liegewagen* (couchette) or a more expensive *Schlafwagen* (sleeping car). Long-distance trains have a dining car or snacks available.

River

The Danube (Donau) is Austria's major waterway, and cruises head east from here. Ensure you have any necessary visas before entering Austria.

Danube Cruises

Avalon Waterways (www.avaloncruises.co.uk) is an international cruise operator with a branch in the UK, as well as Australia (www.avalonwaterways.com.au), Canada (www.avalonwaterways.ca) and the USA (www.avalonwaterways.com). It can also handle bookings from other regions.

Typical cruises include eight days from Budapest to Vienna (from US$1659), nine days from Vienna to Munich (from US$2209) and 15 days from Amsterdam to Budapest (from US$5949). All prices exclude air connections.

International Services

Twin City Liner (☎01-904 88 80; www.twincityliner.com; 01, Schiffstation, Schwedenplatz, Vienna; one way adult €30-35; 🚋1, 2 Schwedenplatz, Ⓤ Schwedenplatz) Runs a two-way service between Vienna and Bratislava (1¼ hours) three to five times daily from late March to early November. Ships dock at the Twin City Liner terminal on the Danube Canal.

LOD (☎in Slovakia 421 2 529 32 226; www.lod.sk; Vienna departure point 02, Schiffstation Reichsbrücke, Handelskai 265, Bratislava; one way/return €24/39; ⏱late Apr-early Oct; Ⓤ Vorgartenstrasse) Slovakian ferry company with hydrofoils between Bratislava and Vienna (1½ hours), running five to seven days per week from late April to late October. Best value is on weekends and for return trips. Booking is online, unless you call the office in Bratislava to reserve and then pay cash on the ship.

TRANSPORT GLOSSARY

Abfahrt Departure

Ankunft Arrival

Bahnhof (Bf) Station

Bahnsteig Track (the track number)

Einfache Fahrt ('hin') One way

Erste Klasse First class

Fahrkarte (Fahrausweis) Ticket

Gleis Platform

Hauptbahnhof (Hbf) Main station

Retour Return

Speisewagen Dining carriage

Täglich Daily

Umsteigen Change of trains

Wagen Carriage

Zweite Klasse Second class

GETTING AROUND

Air

Flying within a country the size of Austria is rarely necessary. The main exception is to/from Innsbruck (in the far west of Austria).

The national carrier **Austrian Airlines** (www.austrian.com) offers several flights daily between Vienna and Graz, Innsbruck, Klagenfurt, Linz and Salzburg.

Bicycle

Most regional tourist boards have brochures on cycling facilities and routes within their region. Separate bike tracks are common in cities, and long-distance tracks and routes also run along many of the major valleys such as the Danube, Enns and Mur. Others follow lakes, such as the tracks around the Neusiedler See in Burgenland and the Wörthersee in Carinthia. *Landstrassen* (L) roads are usually good for cyclists.

The **Danube cycling trail** is like a Holy Grail for cyclists, following the entire length of the river in Austria between the borders with Germany and Slovakia. The **Tauern Radweg** is a 310km trail through the mountain landscapes of Hohe Tauern National Park.

Hire

All large cities have at least one bike shop that doubles as a rental centre. In places where cycling is a popular pastime, such as the Wachau in Lower Austria and the Neusiedler See in Burgenland, almost all small towns have rental facilities. Rates vary from town to town, but expect to pay around €15 to €25 per day.

Some regions have summer bicycle-rental stations where you can rent and drop off a bicycle at different stations, often using a credit card. In Lower Austria and Burgenland the system is very well established. A similar network is also located around the Wörthersee in Carinthia. Vienna also has a pick-up and drop-off service using credit cards.

Electric Bikes

Touring electric bikes (e-bikes) are available in most regions. Pedal cleverly using energy-saving options and you can get well over 100km out of some models. A few places also rent e-mountain bikes (e-MBs) which cope with the hills and distances remarkably well. Taking advantage of energy options and the terrain on a good model, it's even possible to return an e-MB with almost as much juice as you set out with.

Bike Transport

It's possible to take bicycles on trains with a bicycle symbol at the top of its timetable. You can't take bicycles on bus services.

➡ You must purchase a ticket for your bicycle (10% the cost of your train ticket; a minimum fee of €2 applies).

➡ Weekly and monthly tickets are also available.

➡ It is not possible to reserve spaces on regional, regional express and S-Bahn train services – simply check if space is available.

➡ For long-distance trains (RailJet, InterCity, EuroCity and EuroNight trains), you can reserve a space for your bicycle in advance for €3.50 at ÖBB ticket counters or by calling +43 (0)5 1717.

➡ To make the journey run smoothly, ask train station staff where on the platform to wait so you'll be in front of the wagon with your reserved space when the train stops.

Mountain Biking

Austria's regions are well equipped for mountain biking of various levels of difficulty. Carinthia (around Hermagor) and northern Styria (the Gesäuse, Schladming and Mariazell) are excellent places. The **Dachstein Tour** can be done over three days, whereas the **Nordkette Single Trail** in Innsbruck is one of the toughest and most exhilarating downhill rides in the country.

Boat

The Danube serves as a thoroughfare between Vienna and Lower and Upper Austria. Services are generally slow, scenic excursions rather than functional means of transport. Some of the country's larger lakes, such as Bodensee and Wörthersee, have boat services.

Bus

Rail routes are complemented by Postbus services, which really come into their own in the more inaccessible mountainous regions. Buses are fairly reliable, and usually depart from outside train stations.

➡ In remote regions plan a day or two ahead and travel on a weekday; services are reduced or nonexistent on Saturdays, and often nonexistent on Sundays.

➡ Pay attention to timetables on school buses in remote regions. These are excellent during the term (if a little loud) but don't operate outside school term.

➡ For online information consult www.postbus.at or www.oebb.at. Local bus stations or tourist offices usually stock free timetable brochures for specific bus routes.

➡ Reservations are usually unnecessary. It's possible to buy tickets in advance on some routes, but on some you can only buy tickets from the drivers.

➡ Oddly, travel by Postbus can work out to be more expensive than train, especially if you have a *Vorteilscard* for train discounts (only family *Vorteilscards* are valid on buses). The ÖBB intercity bus between Graz and Klagenfurt (€30.60, two hours) is cheaper, more direct and slightly faster than the train. Generally, though, buses are slower.

Car & Motorcycle

➡ Autobahn are marked 'A'; some are pan-European 'E' roads. You can only drive on them with a *Vignette* (motorway tax). *Bundesstrassen* or 'B' roads are major roads, while *Landstrassen* (L) are places to enjoy the ride rather than get quickly from one place to another.

➡ Some minor passes are blocked by snow from November to May. Carrying snow chains in winter is highly recommended and is compulsory in some areas.

➡ Winter or all-weather tyres are compulsory from 1 November to 15 April.

➡ GPS navigation systems work well in Austria, but as elsewhere, use your eyes and don't rely on them 100%.

➡ Motorcyclists and passengers must wear a helmet. Dipped lights (low beams) must be used in daytime. You must carry a first-aid kit.

➡ The **National Austrian Tourist Office** (www.austria.info) has an *Austrian Classic Tour* brochure, which covers 3000km of the best roads for motorcyclists in the country.

➡ A number of train services allow you to transport a car with you.

Hire

It is much easier to hire cars in Austria in large cities. Small towns either have no hire companies or a very limited number of vehicles and can be expensive and booked out. If you've got time, shop around for small companies as they can be cheaper (but more restrictive conditions often apply).

Although companies accept any licence that is written in Roman letters, a translation or International Driving Permit (IDP) is required by the traffic police for any non-EU licence not in German.

MINIMUM AGE REQUIREMENTS

The minimum age for hiring small cars is 19 years; for prestige models, 25 years. A valid licence issued at least one year prior is necessary. If you plan to take the car across the border, especially into Eastern Europe, let the rental company know beforehand and double-check for any add-on fees and possible age requirements.

INSURANCE

Third-party insurance is a minimum requirement in Austria. All companies offer personal accident insurance (PAI) for occupants and collision damage waiver (CDW) for an additional charge. (PAI may not be necessary if you or your passengers hold personal travel insurance.)

HIRE COMPANIES

Auto Europe (☎in Germany +49 89 412 07 295; www.autoeurope.de) Books with other car-hire companies; prices can be at a lower rate than by going directly through a company.

Avis (☎0800 10 44 07; www.avis.at) Reputable car-rental company with outlets across Austria.

Europcar (☎01-866 16; www.europcar.at) Car hire at multiple locations across Austria.

Hertz (☎01-795 32; www.hertz.at) Major car-hire company with offices all over Austria.

Holiday Autos (☎in UK +44 20 3740 9859; www.holidayautos.com) Often offers very low rates and has offices or representatives in over 100 countries and regions. By booking early, you can find prices that are about 60% of those charged by the international companies.

Megadrive (☎05 01 05-4120; www.megadrive.at) Good network in major cities, with often cheaper rates.

Sixt (☎01-505 26 40 00; www.sixt.at) Has offices throughout Austria.

Bringing Your Own Vehicle

You'll need to have proof of ownership papers and third-party insurance. The car must also display a sticker on the rear indicating the country of origin.

DRIVING LICENCES

A driving licence and proof of ownership of a private vehicle should always be carried while driving. EU licences are accepted in Austria; all other nationalities require a German translation or an IDP. Translations can be obtained on the spot for a small fee from automobile associations.

INSURANCE

Third-party insurance is a minimum requirement in Europe and you'll need to carry proof of this in the form of a Green Card. If you're a member of an automobile association, ask about free reciprocal benefits offered by affiliated organisations in Europe.

AUTOMOBILE ASSOCIATIONS

Two automobile associations serve Austria. Both provide free 24-hour breakdown service to members and have reciprocal agreements with motoring clubs in other countries; check with your local club before leaving. Both have offices throughout Austria, and it is possible to become a member, but you must join for six months minimum; expect to pay around €45. For a small fee, the associations also translate non-German-language driving licences.

If you're not entitled to free assistance, you'll incur a fee for call-outs, which varies depending on the time of day.

ARBÖ (☎information 050 123 123, roadside assistance 123; www.arboe.at)

ÖAMTC (☎24hr emergency assistance 120, office 01-711 99 10200; www.oeamtc.at; Schubertring 1-3, Vienna; ⌚8am-6pm Mon-Fri, 9am-1pm Sat; 🚊2 Weihburggasse, Ⓤ Stadtpark)

AUTOBAHN TAX & TUNNEL TOLLS

A *Vignette* (motorway tax) is imposed on all autobahn; charges for cars below 3.5 tonnes are €9.20 for 10 days, €26.80 for two months and €89.20 for one year. For motorbikes expect to pay €5.30 for 10 days, €13.40 for two months and €35.50 for one year. *Vignette* can be purchased from motoring organisations, border crossings, petrol stations, post offices and *Tabak* (tobacconist) shops.

A toll (which is *not* covered by the motorway tax) is levied on some mountain roads and tunnels. For a full list of toll roads, consult one of the automobile associations.

Road Conditions, Hazards & Rules

Drive on the right-hand side of the road. The minimum driving age is 18.

Alcohol The penalty for driving while drunk – if you have over 0.05% BAC (blood-alcohol concentration) – is a hefty on-the-spot fine and confiscation of your driving licence.

Children Those under 14 who are shorter than 1.5m must have a special seat or restraint.

Fines Can be paid on the spot, but ask for a receipt.

Giving way Give way to the right at all times except when a prior-

ROAD DISTANCES (KM)

	Bad Ischl	Bregenz	Bruck an der Mur	Eisenstadt	Graz	Innsbruck	Kitzbühel	Klagenfurt	Krems	Kufstein	Landeck	Lienz	Linz	Salzburg	St Pölten	Vienna	Villach
Bregenz	432																
Bruck an der Mur	170	577															
Eisenstadt	297	704	127														
Graz	193	600	54	175													
Innsbruck	239	193	384	511	407												
Kitzbühel	191	300	275	469	400	113											
Klagenfurt	245	510	145	298	133	322	264										
Krems	222	626	175	132	229	433	372	320									
Kufstein	161	271	331	460	356	78	37	286	355								
Landeck	316	117	461	588	484	77	186	394	510	155							
Lienz	232	424	266	393	277	178	94	144	432	142	248						
Linz	103	507	190	246	237	314	247	253	145	236	391	359					
Salzburg	58	374	228	362	264	181	129	223	257	103	258	180	138				
St Pölten	206	610	140	123	194	417	356	285	32	339	494	416	129	241			
Vienna	266	670	145	50	191	477	420	316	79	399	554	411	189	301	66		
Villach	250	486	178	335	170	287	226	37	353	251	370	109	330	188	318	353	
Wiener Neustadt	268	675	98	31	146	482	441	267	137	431	559	364	237	339	114	53	316

ity road sign indicates otherwise, or when one street has a raised border running across it (the vehicle entering from such a street must give way). Note: the 'give way to the right' rule also applies at T-junctions.

Helmets Compulsory for motorcyclists and their passengers (as well as for children under 13 years on bicycles).

Parking Most town centres have a designated *Kurzparkzone* (short-term parking zone), where on-street parking is limited to a maximum of 1½ or three hours (depending upon the place) between certain specified times. *Parkschein* (parking vouchers) for such zones can be purchased from *Tabak* shops or pavement dispensers and then displayed on the windscreen. Outside the specified time, parking in the *Kurzparkzone* is free.

Safety Carrying a warning triangle and first-aid kit in your vehicle is compulsory in Austria.

Seat belts Compulsory.

Speed limits During the day, it's 50km/h in built-up areas, 130km/h on autobahn and 100km/h on other roads. In some places, the speed on country roads is restricted to 70km/h. From 10pm to 5am – except for the A1 between Vienna and Salzburg and the A2 between Vienna and Villach – the speed limit on autobahn is 110km/h.

Trams These always have priority. Vehicles should wait behind while trams slow down and stop for passengers to get on and off.

Local Transport

Austria's local transport infrastructure is excellent, inexpensive and safe.

Buses & Trams Bus services operate in most cities and are complemented by a few night-bus lines. Tram and bus services in most places run from about 5am to 11pm or midnight. You usually need to press the stop-request button, even on trams.

Metro In Vienna, the metro runs all night on Friday and Saturday nights. From Sunday night to Thursday night it stops around midnight or 12.30am. No other towns have metro systems.

Taxis Austrians mostly call ahead or use taxi ranks. Flagging down a taxi usually works, though. Drivers always expect a 10% tip.

Tickets

Ticketing systems and prices vary from region to region. Often they're sold from machines at stops. Universally, tickets are cheaper from any *Tabak* shop, also known as a *Trafik*. Passes for single trips, 24 hours and several days or a week are usually available. All tickets need to be validated by stamping them in the machines before you begin your journey.

Fines are stiff if you don't have a ticket – about €60 to €100 is common – and checks are frequent, especially in the provincial capitals.

Austrian Railways

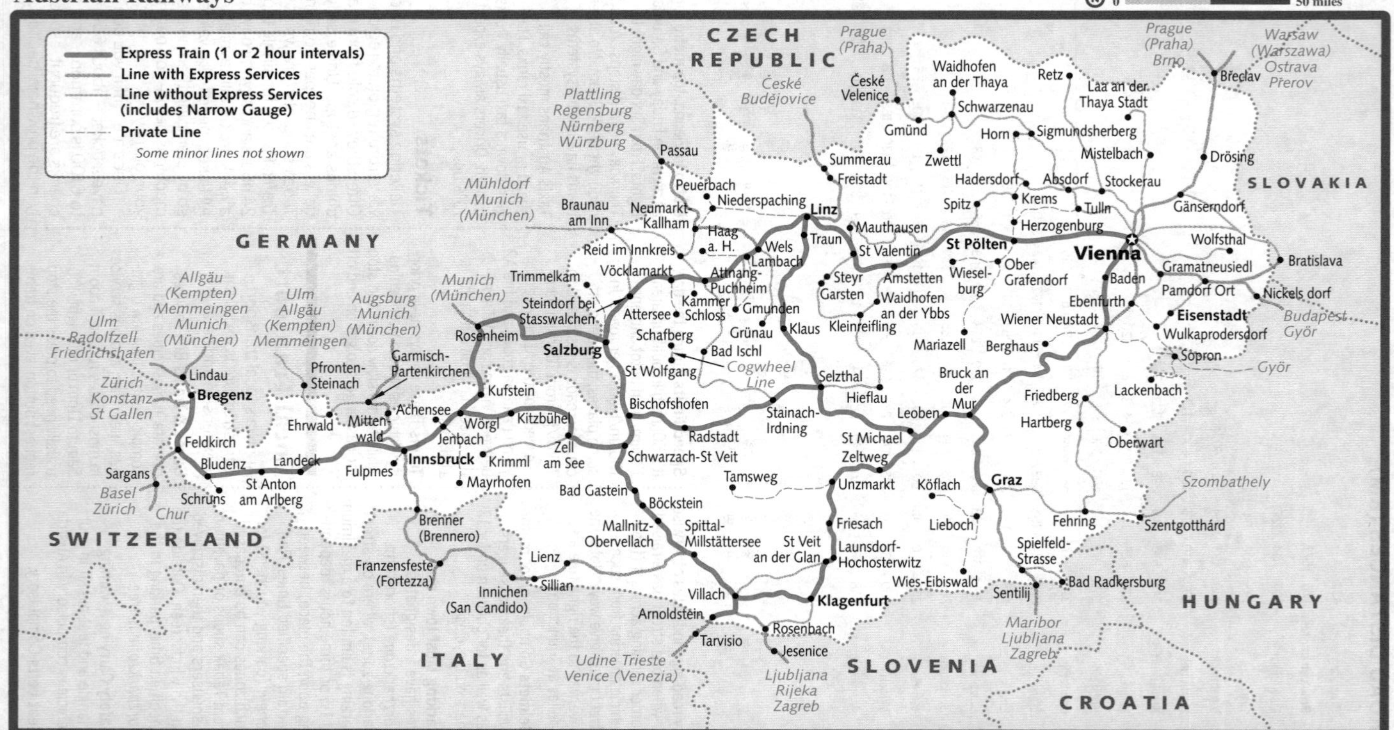

Train

While the country bemoans the state of its 'rundown' rail system, travellers praise it to the heavens. It's good by any standard, and if you use a discount card it's inexpensive.

The **ÖBB** (Österreichische Bundesbahnen; Austrian Federal Railways; 24-hour hotline 05 1717; www.oebb.at) is the main operator, supplemented by a handful of private lines. You can call to book a ticket or get information. Its website has national and international connections, and online national train booking. Only national connections have prices, unless they are special deals to and from neighbouring countries. The website also shows Postbus services.

Buying tickets Tickets can be purchased by telephone (you'll be given a 12-digit collection code for printing the ticket at a machine or at the service desk). Other methods include online (with registration and self-printing), from staffed counters at stations and from machines at stations.

Reservations Cost €3.50 for most 2nd-class express services within Austria. If you haven't reserved ahead, check before you sit whether your intended seat has been reserved by someone else. Reservations are recommended for weekend travel.

Passengers with disabilities Call 05 1717 for travel assistance (you can also do this while booking your ticket by telephone). Staff at stations will help with boarding and alighting. Order this at least 24 hours ahead of travel (48 hours ahead for international services).

Etiquette The ÖBB takes a strong stand on putting your feet on the seats. You can be fined for it.

Rail Costs

Depending on the exact route, a fare can vary slightly.

- Tickets can be bought online or by telephone with credit cards (Visa, Diners Club, MasterCard, Amex and JCB), and additionally with cash or a Maestro card at machines and service desks.
- EURegio tickets are discount return tickets between Austria and the Czech Republic, Hungary or Slovakia and can be great value for short visits.
- If you board and go immediately to the conductor to pay your fare, only a €3 surcharge will be applied to the normal price of the ticket. If you don't do this, a fee and fine totalling €95 will have to be paid (unless you board at an unstaffed station without a ticket machine or the ticket machine is out of order).
- Children aged six to 15 travel half-price; younger kids travel free if they don't take up a separate seat.
- Kept in suitable containers, small pets travel free; larger pets travel half-price.
- One-way tickets for journeys of 100km or less are valid for only one day, and the journey can't be broken. For trips of 101km or more, the ticket is valid for one month and you can alight en route. This is worth doing, as longer trips cost less per kilometre. Return tickets of up to 100km each way are valid for one day; tickets for longer journeys are valid for one month, though the initial outward journey must still be completed within six days. A return fare is usually the equivalent price of two one-way tickets.

Rail Passes

Depending on the amount of travelling you intend to do and your residency status, rail passes can be a good deal. They can be purchased from any major train station.

VORTEILSCARD

These **ÖBB** discount tickets can be purchased by anyone. They offer a 45% discount on inland trains for tickets purchased at the counter and 50% if you buy at a ticket machine. After purchasing one (bring a photo and your passport or other ID), you receive a temporary card and can begin using it right away. The plastic permanent card is posted to your home address. It's valid for one year, but not on buses. For more information visit the ÖBB website, and look under Tickets & Discounts.

Classic (€99) For those over 26.

Family (€19) Valid for up to two adults and any number of children. The children must be travelling with you. Children under 14 years travel free on this card. Also offers 50% discount on Postbus services for adults and up to two children.

Jugend <26 (€19) For those under 26.

Senior (€29) For women or men over 60 years.

EURAIL PASS

Available to non-European residents, Eurail passes are valid for unlimited 2nd-class travel on national railways and some private lines in 31 countries. You can also pay a supplement if you want to travel 1st-class. Those under 27 receive substantial discounts. See www.eurail.com for all options.

Global Pass Options for travelling 10/15 days within two months (€399/491), or continuous travel for a period from 15 days to one month (€441 to €667).

Eurail One-Country Pass Adult 2nd-class three/four/five/eight days within a month €146/172/196/257.

INTERRAIL

Passes are for European citizens or anyone who has lived in Europe for at least six months. Those under 26 receive substantial discounts. See www.interrail.eu for all options.

One-Country Pass Austria Adult 2nd-class three/four/five/eight days within a month €146/173/197/258.

InterRail Global Pass Valid for a certain number of days or continuously in up to 31 countries; five days' travel within a month costs €282, seven days' travel in one month costs €335 and one month of continuous travel costs €670.

Language

The national language of Austria is German, though there are a few regional dialects. For example, the dialect spoken in Vorarlberg is much closer to Swiss German (Schwyzertütsch) – a language all but incomprehensible to most non-Swiss – than it is to the standard High German (Hochdeutsch) dialect. Nevertheless, Austrians can easily switch from their dialect to High German.

There are many words and expressions in German that are used only by Austrians, some throughout the country and others only in particular regions, although they'll probably be understood elsewhere. Most of these would not automatically be understood by non-Austrian German speakers. On the other hand, the 'standard' German equivalents would be understood by all Austrians. The greetings and farewells included in this chapter are specific to Austria.

Pronunciation

It's easy to pronounce German because almost all sounds are also found in English. If you read our coloured pronunciation guides as if they were English, you'll be understood.

Note that the vowel ü sounds like the 'ee' in 'see' but with rounded lips. As for the consonants, the kh sound is pronounced like a hiss from the back of the throat (as in the Scottish *loch*). The r sound is pronounced at the back of the throat, almost like saying a g sound, but with some friction – a bit like gargling.

WANT MORE?

For in-depth language information and handy phrases, check out Lonely Planet's *German Phrasebook*. You'll find it at **shop.lonelyplanet.com**.

As a general rule, word stress in German falls mostly on the first syllable. In our pronunciation guides the stressed syllable is indicated with italics.

BASICS

German has polite and informal forms for 'you' (*Sie* and *du* respectively). When addressing people you don't know well, use the polite form (though younger people will be less inclined to expect it). In this language guide the polite form is used unless indicated with 'inf' (for 'informal') in brackets.

Hello.	*Servus.*	*zer*·vus
Goodbye.	*Auf Wiedersehen.*	owf vee·der·zay·en
Yes.	*Ja.*	yah
No.	*Nein.*	nain
Please.	*Bitte.*	*bi*·te
Thank you.	*Danke.*	*dang*·ke
You're welcome.	*Bitte sehr.*	*bi*·te zair
Excuse me.	*Entschuldigung.*	ent·*shul*·di·gung
Sorry.	*Entschuldigung.*	ent·*shul*·di·gung

How are you?
Wie geht es Ihnen/dir? — vee gayt es *ee*·nen/deer (pol/inf)

Fine, thanks. And you?
Danke, gut. — *dang*·ke goot
Und Ihnen/dir? — unt *ee*·nen/deer (pol/inf)

What's your name?
Wie ist Ihr Name? — vee ist eer *nah*·me (pol)
Wie heißt du? — vee haist doo (inf)

My name is ...
Mein Name ist ... — main *nah*·me ist ... (pol)
Ich heiße ... — ikh *hai*·se ... (inf)

Do you speak English?
Sprechen Sie Englisch? shpre·khen zee *eng*·lish

I don't understand.
Ich verstehe nicht. ikh fer·*shtay*·e nikht

ACCOMMODATION

Do you have a room?
Haben Sie ein Zimmer? *hah*·ben zee ain *tsi*·mer

How much is it per night/person?
Wie viel kostet es pro Nacht/Person? vee feel *kos*·tet es praw nakht/per·*zawn*

air-con	*Klimaanlage*	klee·ma·*an*·lah·ge
bathroom	*Badezimmer*	*bah*·de·tsi·mer
campsite	*Campingplatz*	*kem*·ping·plats
double room	*Doppelzimmer*	*do*·pel·tsi·mer
guesthouse	*Pension*	pahng·*zyawn*
hotel	*Hotel*	ho·*tel*
inn	*Gasthof*	*gast*·hawf
single room	*Einzelzimmer*	*ain*·tsel·tsi·mer
window	*Fenster*	*fens*·ter
youth hostel	*Jugendherberge*	*yoo*·gent·her·ber·ge

DIRECTIONS

Where's (a bank)?
Wo ist (eine Bank)? vaw ist (*ai*·ne bangk)

What's the address?
Wie ist die Adresse? vee ist dee a·*dre*·se

Can you please write it down?
Könnten Sie das bitte aufschreiben? *kern*·ten zee das *bi*·te *owf*·shrai·ben

Can you show me (on the map)?
Können Sie es mir (auf der Karte) zeigen? *ker*·nen zee es meer (owf dair *kar*·te) *tsai*·gen

at the corner	*an der Ecke*	an dair *e*·ke
at the traffic lights	*bei der Ampel*	bai dair *am*·pel
behind ...	*hinter ...*	*hin*·ter ...
far away	*weit weg*	vait vek
in front of ...	*vor ...*	fawr ...
left/right	*links/rechts*	lingks/rekhts
near	*nahe*	*nah*·e
next to ...	*neben ...*	*nay*·ben ...
opposite ...	*gegenüber ...*	gay·gen·*ü*·ber ...
straight ahead	*geradeaus*	ge·rah·de·*ows*

EATING & DRINKING

A table for (two) people, please.
Einen Tisch für (zwei) Personen, bitte. *ai*·nen tish für (tsvai) per·*zaw*·nen *bi*·te

What would you recommend?
Was empfehlen Sie? vas emp·*fay*·len zee

What's in that dish?
Was ist in diesem Gericht? vas ist in *dee*·zem ge·*rikht*

I don't eat ...
Ich esse kein ... ikh *e*·se kain ...

Cheers!
Prost! prawst

That was delicious.
Das war sehr lecker. das vahr zair *le*·ker

The bill, please.
Die Rechnung, bitte. dee *rekh*·nung *bi*·te

Key Words

appetisers	*Vorspeisen*	*fawr*·shpai·zen
ashtray	*Aschenbecher*	*a*·shen·be·kher
bar	*Kneipe*	*knai*·pe
bottle	*Flasche*	*fla*·she
bowl	*Schüssel*	*shü*·sel
breakfast	*Frühstück*	*frü*·shtük
cold	*kalt*	kalt
cup	*Tasse*	*ta*·se
dinner	*Abendessen*	*ah*·bent·e·sen
drink list	*Getränkekarte*	ge·*treng*·ke·kar·te
food	*Essen*	*e*·sen
fork	*Gabel*	*gah*·bel
glass	*Glas*	glahs
grocery store	*Lebensmittelladen*	*lay*·bens·mi·tel·lah·den
hot (warm)	*heiß*	hais
knife	*Messer*	*me*·ser
local speciality	*örtliche Spezialität*	*ert*·li·khe shpe·tsya·li·*tayt*
lunch	*Mittagessen*	*mi*·tahk·e·sen
main courses	*Hauptgerichte*	*howpt*·ge·rikh·te
menu	*Speisekarte*	*shpai*·ze·kar·te
market	*Markt*	markt
plate	*Teller*	*te*·ler
restaurant	*Restaurant*	res·to·*rang*
spicy	*würzig*	*vür*·tsikh
spoon	*Löffel*	*ler*·fel
vegetarian food	*vegetarisches Essen*	ve·ge·*tah*·ri·shes *e*·sen
with/without	*mit/ohne*	mit/*aw*·ne

Meat & Fish

bacon	*Speck*	shpek
beef	*Rindfleisch*	*rint*·flaish
brains	*Hirn*	heern

carp	*Karpfen*	*karp*·fen
chicken	*Huhn*	hoon
duck	*Ente*	*en*·te
eel	*Aal*	ahl
fish	*Fisch*	fish
goose	*Gans*	gans
ham	*Schinken*	*shing*·ken
hare	*Hase*	*hah*·ze
lamb	*Lamm*	lam
liver	*Leber*	*lay*·ber
minced meat	*Hackfleisch*	*hak*·flaish
plaice	*Scholle*	*sho*·le
pork	*Schweinfleisch*	*shvai*·n·flaish
salmon	*Lachs*	laks
tongue	*Zunge*	*tsung*·e
trout	*Forelle*	fo·*re*·le
tuna	*Thunfisch*	*toon*·fish

KEY PATTERNS

To get by in German, mix and match these simple patterns with words of your choice:

When's (the next flight)?
Wann ist (der nächste Flug)? — van ist (dair *naykhs*·te flook)

Where's (the station)?
Wo ist (der Bahnhof)? — vaw ist (dair *bahn*·hawf)

Where can I (buy a ticket)?
Wo kann ich (eine Fahrkarte kaufen)? — vaw kan ikh (*ai*·ne *fahr*·kar·te *kow*·fen)

Do you have (a map)?
Haben Sie (eine Karte)? — *hah*·ben zee (*ai*·ne *kar*·te)

Is there (a toilet)?
Gibt es (eine Toilette)? — gipt es (*ai*·ne to·a·*le*·te)

I'd like (a coffee).
Ich möchte (einen Kaffee). — ikh *merkh*·te (*ai*·nen *ka*·fay)

I'd like (to hire a car).
Ich möchte (ein Auto mieten). — ikh *merkh*·te (ain *ow*·to *mee*·ten)

Can I (enter)?
Darf ich (hereinkommen)? — darf ikh (her·*ein*·ko·men)

Could you please (help me)?
Könnten Sie (mir helfen)? — *kern*·ten zee (meer *hel*·fen)

Do I have to (book a seat)?
Muss ich (einen Platz reservieren lassen)? — mus ikh (*ai*·nen plats re·zer·*vee*·ren *la*·sen)

turkey	*Puter*	*poo*·ter
veal	*Kalbfleisch*	*kalp*·flaish
venison	*Hirsch*	hirsh

Fruit & Vegetables

apple	*Apfel*	*ap*·fel
apricot	*Aprikose*	a·pri·*ko*·ze
asparagus	*Spargel*	*shpar*·gel
banana	*Banane*	ba·*nah*·ne
beans	*Bohnen*	*baw*·nen
beetroot	*Rote Rübe*	*raw*·te *rü*·be
cabbage	*Kohl*	hawl
carrots	*Karotten*	ka·*ro*·ten
cherries	*Kirschen*	*kir*·shen
corn	*Mais*	mais
cucumber	*Gurke*	*gur*·ke
garlic	*Knoblauch*	*knawp*·lowkh
grapes	*Trauben*	*trow*·ben
green beans	*Fisolen*	fee·*zo*·len
mushrooms	*Pilze*	*pil*·tse
onions	*Zwiebeln*	*tsvee*·beln
pear	*Birne*	*bir*·ne
peas	*Erbsen*	*erp*·sen
peppers	*Paprika*	*pap*·ri·kah
pineapple	*Ananas*	a·na·*nas*
plums	*Zwetschgen*	*tsvech*·gen
potatoes	*Kartoffeln*	kar·*to*·feln
raspberries	*Himbeeren*	*him*·bee·ren
spinach	*Spinat*	shpi·*naht*
strawberries	*Erdbeeren*	*ert*·bee·ren
tomatoes	*Tomaten*	to·*mah*·ten

Other

bread	*Brot*	brawt
butter	*Butter*	*bu*·ter
cheese	*Käse*	*kay*·ze
chocolate	*Schokolade*	sho·ko·*lah*·de
cream	*Sahne*	*zah*·ne
dumplings	*Knödel*	*kner*·del
eggs	*Eier*	*ai*·er
honey	*Honig*	*haw*·nikh
jam	*Marmelade*	mar·me·*lah*·de
mustard	*Senf*	zenf
nut	*Nuss*	nus
oil	*Öl*	erl
pasta	*Nudeln*	*noo*·deln
pepper	*Pfeffer*	*pfe*·fer
rice	*Reis*	rais

salad	*Salat*	za·*laht*
salt	*Salz*	zalts
sugar	*Zucker*	*tsu*·ker

Drinks

beer	*Bier*	beer
coffee	*Kaffee*	ka·*fay*
(orange) juice	*(Orangen-) saft*	(o·*rahng*·zhen·) zaft
milk	*Milch*	milkh
red wine	*Rotwein*	*rawt*·vain
tea	*Tee*	tay
(mineral) water	*(Mineral-) wasser*	(mi·ne·*rahl*·) va·ser
white wine	*Weißwein*	*vais*·vain

EMERGENCIES

Help!
Hilfe! — *hil*·fe

Leave me alone!
Lassen Sie mich in Ruhe! — *la*·sen zee mikh in *roo*·e

I'm lost.
Ich habe mich verirrt. — ikh *hah*·be mikh fer·*irt*

Call the police!
Rufen Sie die Polizei! — *roo*·fen zee dee po·li·*tsai*

Call a doctor!
Rufen Sie einen Arzt! — *roo*·fen zee *ai*·nen artst

I'm sick.
Ich bin krank. — ikh bin krangk

It hurts here.
Es tut hier weh. — es toot heer *vay*

I'm allergic to (antibiotics).
Ich bin allergisch gegen (Antibiotika). — ikh bin a·*lair*·gish *gay*·gen (an·ti·bi·*aw*·ti·ka)

Where is the toilet?
Wo ist die Toilette? — vaw ist dee to·a·*le*·te

SHOPPING & SERVICES

I'd like to buy ...
Ich möchte ... kaufen. — ikh *merkh*·te ... *kow*·fen

I'm just looking.
Ich schaue mich nur um. — ikh *show*·e mikh noor um

Can I look at it?
Können Sie es mir zeigen? — *ker*·nen zee es meer *tsai*·gen

How much is this?
Wie viel kostet das? — vee feel *kos*·tet das

That's too expensive.
Das ist zu teuer. — das ist tsoo *toy*·er

Can you lower the price?
Können Sie mit dem Preis heruntergehen? — *ker*·nen zee mit dem prais he·*run*·ter·gay·en

SIGNS

Ausgang	Exit
Damen	Women
Eingang	Entrance
Geschlossen	Closed
Herren	Men
Offen	Open
Toiletten	Toilets
Verboten	Prohibited

There's a mistake in the bill.
Da ist ein Fehler in der Rechnung. — dah ist ain *fay*·ler in dair *rekh*·nung

ATM	*Geldautomat*	*gelt*·ow·to·maht
PIN	*Geheimnummer*	ge·*haim*·nu·mer
post office	*Postamt*	*post*·amt
tourist office	*Fremden-verkehrsbüro*	*frem*·den·fer·*kairs*·bü·raw

TIME & DATES

What time is it?
Wie spät ist es? — vee shpayt ist es

It's (one) o'clock.
Es ist (ein) Uhr. — es ist (ain) oor

Half past one.
Halb zwei. (lit: 'half two') — halp tsvai

morning	*Morgen*	*mor*·gen
afternoon	*Nachmittag*	*nahkh*·mi·tahk
evening	*Abend*	*ah*·bent
yesterday	*gestern*	*ges*·tern
today	*heute*	*hoy*·te
tomorrow	*morgen*	*mor*·gen

Monday	*Montag*	*mawn*·tahk
Tuesday	*Dienstag*	*deens*·tahk
Wednesday	*Mittwoch*	*mit*·vokh
Thursday	*Donnerstag*	*do*·ners·tahk
Friday	*Freitag*	*frai*·tahk
Saturday	*Samstag*	*zams*·tahk
Sunday	*Sonntag*	*zon*·tahk

January	*Januar*	*yan*·u·ahr
February	*Februar*	*fay*·bru·ahr
March	*März*	merts
April	*April*	a·*pril*
May	*Mai*	mai
June	*Juni*	*yoo*·ni
July	*Juli*	*yoo*·li

August	*August*	ow·gust
September	*September*	zep·*tem*·ber
October	*Oktober*	ok·*taw*·ber
November	*November*	no·*vem*·ber
December	*Dezember*	de·*tsem*·ber

TRANSPORT

Public Transport

boat	*Boot*	bawt
bus	*Bus*	bus
plane	*Flugzeug*	*flook*·tsoyk
train	*Zug*	tsook

At what time does it leave?
Wann fährt es ab? van fairt es ap

At what time does it arrive?
Wann kommt es an? van komt es an

I want to go to ...
Ich mochte nach ... fahren. ikh *merkh*·te nahkh ... *fah*·ren

Does it stop at ...?
Hält es in ...? helt es in ...

I want to get off here.
Ich mochte hier aussteigen. ikh *merkh*·te heer *ows*·shtai·gen

one-way ticket	*einfache Fahrkarte*	*ain*·fa·khe *fahr*·kar·te
return ticket	*Rückfahrkarte*	*rük*·fahr·kar·te
first	*erste*	*ers*·te
last	*letzte*	*lets*·te
next	*nächste*	*naykhs*·te
aisle seat	*Platz am Gang*	plats am gang
platform	*Bahnsteig*	*bahn*·shtaik
ticket office	*Fahrkartenverkauf*	*fahr*·kar·ten·fer·*kowf*
timetable	*Fahrplan*	*fahr*·plahn
train station	*Bahnhof*	*bahn*·hawf
window seat	*Fensterplatz*	*fens*·ter·plats

QUESTION WORDS

How?	*Wie?*	vee
What?	*Was?*	vas
When?	*Wann?*	van
Where?	*Wo?*	vaw
Who?	*Wer?*	vair
Why?	*Warum?*	va·rum

NUMBERS

1	*eins*	ains
2	*zwei*	tsvai
3	*drei*	drai
4	*vier*	feer
5	*fünf*	fünf
6	*sechs*	zeks
7	*sieben*	zee·ben
8	*acht*	akht
9	*neun*	noyn
10	*zehn*	tsayn
20	*zwanzig*	*tsvan*·tsikh
30	*dreißig*	*drai*·sikh
40	*vierzig*	*feer*·tsikh
50	*fünfzig*	*fünf*·tsikh
60	*sechzig*	*zekh*·tsikh
70	*siebzig*	*zeep*·tsikh
80	*achtzig*	*akht*·tsikh
90	*neunzig*	*noyn*·tsikh
100	*hundert*	*hun*·dert
1000	*tausend*	*tow*·sent

Driving & Cycling

I'd like to hire a ...	*Ich möchte ein ... mieten.*	ikh *merkh*·te ain ... *mee*·ten
bicycle	*Fahrrad*	*fahr*·raht
car	*Auto*	ain ow·to
motorcycle	*Motorrad*	*maw*·tor·raht

child seat	*Kindersitz*	*kin*·der·zits
helmet	*Helm*	helm
mechanic	*Mechaniker*	me·*khah*·ni·ker
petrol/gas	*Benzin*	ben·*tseen*
pump	*Luftpumpe*	*luft*·pum·pe
service station	*Tankstelle*	*tangk*·shte·le

Does this road go to ...?
Führt diese Strasse nach ...? fürt *dee*·ze *shtrah*·se nahkh ...

Can I park here?
Kann ich hier parken? kan ikh heer *par*·ken

The car has broken down (at ...).
Ich habe (in ...) eine Panne mit meinem Auto. ikh *hah*·be (in ...) *ai*·ne *pa*·ne mit *mai*·nem *ow*·to

I have a flat tyre.
Ich habe eine Reifenpanne. ikh *hah*·be *ai*·ne *rai*·fen·pa·ne

I've run out of petrol.
Ich habe kein Benzin mehr. ikh *hah*·be kain ben·*tseen* mair

Behind the Scenes

SEND US YOUR FEEDBACK

We love to hear from travellers – your comments keep us on our toes and help make our books better. Our well-travelled team reads every word on what you loved or loathed about this book. Although we cannot reply individually to your submissions, we always guarantee that your feedback goes straight to the appropriate authors, in time for the next edition. Each person who sends us information is thanked in the next edition – the most useful submissions are rewarded with a selection of digital PDF chapters.

Visit **lonelyplanet.com/contact** to submit your updates and suggestions or to ask for help. Our award-winning website also features inspirational travel stories, news and discussions.

Note: We may edit, reproduce and incorporate your comments in Lonely Planet products such as guidebooks, websites and digital products, so let us know if you don't want your comments reproduced or your name acknowledged. For a copy of our privacy policy visit lonelyplanet.com/privacy.

OUR READERS

Many thanks to the travellers who used the last edition and wrote to us with helpful hints, useful advice and interesting anecdotes:

Mark Reese, Veronica Bolognesi

WRITER THANKS

Catherine Le Nevez

Vielen Dank first and foremost to Julian, as well as all the locals and fellow travellers in Vienna and throughout Austria for insights, information and good times during this update and over the years. Huge thanks too to my Vienna co-author Kerry and the Austria team, and to Brana Vladisavljevic, Dan Fahey, and everyone at Lonely Planet. As ever, *merci encore* to my parents, brother, *belle-sœur*, *neveu* and *nièce*.

Marc Di Duca

Huge thanks go to Manuela of Weingut Burg Taggenbrunn and all the staff at various tourist offices, but in particular those in Klagenfurt, Krems and Eisenstadt. Finally, enormous thanks to my wife Tanya for holding the fort while I was away researching.

Anthony Haywood

Many thanks to those who gave valuable insights and tips on the road. Special thanks to Gert and Susie in Graz for sharing their knowledge of the region, to Markus and Sibylle, and to the many helpful people at the information offices and places along the way who answered my even more numerous questions.

Kerry Walker

A big thank you goes out to all the people who I met on my Austria travels, including tourism professionals Bettina Jamy-Stowasser and Helena Hartlauer in Vienna, Martina Trummer in Salzburg, and Peter Unsinn in Innsbruck. Special thanks, too, to Eugene Quinn at Space and Place in Vienna and Maggie Ritson in St Anton for ideas and inspiration.

ACKNOWLEDGEMENTS

Climate map data adapted from Peel MC, Finlayson BL & McMahon TA (2007) 'Updated World Map of the Köppen-Geiger Climate Classification', *Hydrology and Earth System Sciences*, 11, 1633–44.

Cover photograph: Salzburg in winter, canadastock/Shutterstock ©

THIS BOOK

This 10th edition of Lonely Planet's *Austria* guidebook was researched and written by Catherine Le Nevez, Marc Di Duca, Anthony Haywood and Kerry Walker. The previous edition was also written by Catherine, Marc, Anthony and Kerry. This guidebook was produced by the following:

Destination Editor Brana Vladisavljevic

Senior Product Editors Kate Chapman, Sandie Kestell, Kathryn Rowan

Regional Senior Cartographer Mark Griffiths

Assisting Cartographer Mick Garrett, Anthony Phelan

Product Editor James Appleton, Barbara Delissen

Book Designer Lauren Egan

Assisting Editors Ronan Abayawickrema, Janet Austin, Nigel Chin, Andrea Dobbin, Trent Holden, Jodie Martire, Amy Lynch, Rosie Nicholson, Lauren O'Connell, Kristin Odijk, Mani Ramaswamy, Claire Rourke, Fionnuala Twomey

Cover Researcher Gwen Cotter

Thanks to Daniel Bolger, Victoria Harrison, Clare Healy, Sonia Kapoor, Gabrielle Stefanos, Angela Tinson

Index

Map Pages **000**
Photo Pages **000**

Map Pages **000**
Photo Pages **000**

N

Map Pages **000**
Photo Pages **000**

Map Legend

Sights

- Beach
- Bird Sanctuary
- Buddhist
- Castle/Palace
- Christian
- Confucian
- Hindu
- Islamic
- Jain
- Jewish
- Monument
- Museum/Gallery/Historic Building
- Ruin
- Shinto
- Sikh
- Taoist
- Winery/Vineyard
- Zoo/Wildlife Sanctuary
- Other Sight

Activities, Courses & Tours

- Bodysurfing
- Diving
- Canoeing/Kayaking
- Course/Tour
- Sento Hot Baths/Onsen
- Skiing
- Snorkelling
- Surfing
- Swimming/Pool
- Walking
- Windsurfing
- Other Activity

Sleeping

- Sleeping
- Camping
- Hut/Shelter

Eating

- Eating

Drinking & Nightlife

- Drinking & Nightlife
- Cafe

Entertainment

- Entertainment

Shopping

- Shopping

Information

- Bank
- Embassy/Consulate
- Hospital/Medical
- Internet
- Police
- Post Office
- Telephone
- Toilet
- Tourist Information
- Other Information

Geographic

- Beach
- Gate
- Hut/Shelter
- Lighthouse
- Lookout
- Mountain/Volcano
- Oasis
- Park
- Pass
- Picnic Area
- Waterfall

Population

- Capital (National)
- Capital (State/Province)
- City/Large Town
- Town/Village

Transport

- Airport
- Border crossing
- Bus
- Cable car/Funicular
- Cycling
- Ferry
- Metro station
- Monorail
- Parking
- Petrol station
- S-Bahn/Subway station
- Taxi
- T-bane/Tunnelbana station
- Train station/Railway
- Tram
- U-Bahn/Underground station
- Other Transport

Routes

- Tollway
- Freeway
- Primary
- Secondary
- Tertiary
- Lane
- Unsealed road
- Road under construction
- Plaza/Mall
- Steps
- Tunnel
- Pedestrian overpass
- Walking Tour
- Walking Tour detour
- Path/Walking Trail

Boundaries

- International
- State/Province
- Disputed
- Regional/Suburb
- Marine Park
- Cliff
- Wall

Hydrography

- River, Creek
- Intermittent River
- Canal
- Water
- Dry/Salt/Intermittent Lake
- Reef

Areas

- Airport/Runway
- Beach/Desert
- Cemetery (Christian)
- Cemetery (Other)
- Glacier
- Mudflat
- Park/Forest
- Sight (Building)
- Sportsground
- Swamp/Mangrove

Note: Not all symbols displayed above appear on the maps in this book

OUR STORY

A beat-up old car, a few dollars in the pocket and a sense of adventure. In 1972 that's all Tony and Maureen Wheeler needed for the trip of a lifetime – across Europe and Asia overland to Australia. It took several months, and at the end – broke but inspired – they sat at their kitchen table writing and stapling together their first travel guide, *Across Asia on the Cheap*. Within a week they'd sold 1500 copies. Lonely Planet was born.

Today, Lonely Planet has offices in the US, Ireland and China, with a network of over 2000 contributors in every corner of the globe. We share Tony's belief that 'a great guidebook should do three things: inform, educate and amuse'.

OUR WRITERS

Catherine Le Nevez

Upper Austria, Vienna Catherine's wanderlust kicked in when she roadtripped across Europe from her Parisian base aged four, and she has been hitting the road at every opportunity since. She has travelled to some 60 countries, completing her doctorate of creative arts in writing, master's in professional writing, and postgrad qualifications in editing and publishing along the way. Over the past 15 years, she has written scores of Lonely Planet guides and articles covering Paris, France, Europe and far beyond. Her work has also appeared in numerous online and print publications. Topping Catherine's list of tips is to travel without any expectations.

Marc Di Duca

Lower Austria & Burgenland, Carinthia A travel author for over a decade, Marc has worked for Lonely Planet in Siberia, Slovakia, Bavaria, England, Ukraine, Austria, Poland, Croatia, Portugal, Madeira and on the Trans-Siberian Railway, as well as writing and updating dozens of guides for other publishers. When not on the road, Marc lives near Mariánské Lázně in the Czech Republic with his wife and two sons.

Anthony Haywood

Styria, The Salzkammergut Born in the port city of Fremantle, Western Australia, Anthony first pulled anchor in the late 1970s to travel Europe, North Africa and the US. Later he studied comparative literature and Russian language at university. Anthony works as a freelance journalist and writer based in Germany. Publications include Lonely Planet guidebooks, *Siberia – A Cultural History* (Signal Books/Oxford University Press), travel articles, short stories and translations.

Kerry Walker

Salzburg & Salzburgerland, Tyrol & Vorarlberg, Vienna Kerry is an award-winning travel writer, photographer and Lonely Planet author, specialising in Central and Southern Europe. Based in Wales, she has authored/co-authored more than a dozen Lonely Planet titles. An adventure addict, she loves mountains, cold places and true wilderness. She features her latest work at https://its-a-small-world.com and tweets @kerryawalker. Kerry's insatiable wanderlust has taken her to all seven continents and shows no sign of waning. Her writing appears regularly in publications like *Adventure Travel* magazine and she is a *Telegraph* travel expert for Austria and Wales. Kerry also wrote the Plan Your Trip, Understand and Survival Guide sections.

Published by Lonely Planet Global Limited
CRN 554153
10th edition – May 2022
ISBN 978 1 78868 766 9

10 9 8 7 6 5 4 3 2 1
Printed in Singapore